Aldo Leopold

Portrait of Leopold taken shortly after his appointment in 1925 as assistant director of the U.S. Forest Products Laboratory in Madison, Wisconsin (Leopold Collection, UW Archives)

Aldo Leopold

HIS LIFE AND WORK

Curt Meine

The University of Wisconsin Press

The University of Wisconsin Press
1930 Monroe Street, 3rd Floor
Madison, Wisconsin 53711-2059
uwpress.wisc.edu

3 Henrietta Street
London WC2E 8LU, England
eurospanbookstore.com

5   4   3   2   1

Printed in the United States of America

Library of Congress Cataloging-in-Publication Data
Meine, Curt
Aldo Leopold: his life and work
Bibliography: pp. 589–620
Includes index.
1. Leopold, Aldo, 1887–1948. 2. Naturalists—
Wisconsin—Biography. I. Title
QH31.L618M45   1987   508.32' 4 [B]   87-40367
ISBN 0-299-11490-2 (cloth)

ISBN 978-0-299-24904-5 (pbk.)
ISBN 978-0-299-24903-8 (e-book)

To my grandparents

Joseph and Helen DeVivo

Whither, midst falling dew
While glow the heavens with the last steps
            of day,
Far, through their rosy depths, dost thou pursue
            Thy solitary way?

William Cullen Bryant
"To a Waterfowl"

We shall not cease from exploration
And the end of all our exploring
Will be to arrive where we started
And know the place for the first time.

T. S. Eliot
"Little Gidding"

Contents

Contents

Aldo Leopold:
A Reader's Testimony

I FIRST read *A Sand County Almanac* by Aldo Leopold many years ago—as time is reckoned by us short-lived humans. By that reading I acquired an influence that would be permanently with me. Leopold's way of looking and his way of thinking have affected my looking and thinking as subtly and persistently as a familial landscape. Although I share Leopold's preoccupation with the land and its fate, I have not had the benefit of his scientific training and discipline, and so knowing I am on his side has given me a measure of assurance I would not otherwise have had. Many others could offer substantially the same testimony.

A Sand County Almanac is not a book to be accompanied by trumpets. It does not try to be overwhelming or sensational. It is a quiet book, and its quietness is that of a man unusually resolved and confident. In the personal essays the writer feels no need to persuade himself or his readers of the authenticity of his pleasures or his worries, and he knows that for involved observers such pleasures and such worries are not extraordinary. The more scholarly or polemical essays are quiet in a different way. They have the tone of responsible discourse, which is necessarily quiet. They are well studied and well argued. Leopold wrote sentence after sentence that goes straight to the core of some problem that is still waiting to be solved. The only significant limitation of those essays is that Leopold could not have imagined the magnitude to which some of the problems have grown after sixty years.

Nobody who has read them needs to be told that the essays in *A Sand County Almanac* are ably and even beautifully written. There is a level of distinction below which they never dip. But their unique excellence comes from a wholeness that originates in the writer. Their preparation clearly was begun in a responsible life. Even when writing on technical or scientific subjects, Leopold never writes with the assumed dispassion or jargon of the modern specialist. "Well-rounded" is a term often used as a (customarily frustrated) goal of education; it is often misused in description. Leopold, however, really was well-rounded. In his writing he does not discard any perspective in order to speak from a different one. His sense of humor, which everywhere seasons his thought and steadies his voice, owes much to his awareness of the multiplicity of points of view. It is a part of his sense of responsibility that he writes always as himself. Everything of his that I have read is conditioned by the full extent of his knowledge, his experience, and his concern. When this is not explicit in his words, it is implicit in the shaping and energy of his sentences. We feel his presence in what he says. As much as any writing I know, Leopold's essays require us to recognize character as a literary quality.

Because his writing has, to such an extent, the quality of his character, and because his character was so much that of a conservationist, it is particularly needful that we should know the story of his life. Curt Meine has supplied this need, and he helps us to see clearly how Leopold's writing originated in his life. It is sometimes easy to wonder why we need a biography of a writer. We have none of Homer, almost none of Shakespeare, and it would be a waste of time to wish otherwise. But Leopold was indistinguishably a man of words and a man of deeds, and we see this more clearly in Meine's biography than in Leopold's writings.

The sense of completeness in Leopold's life and work—his completeness in himself and his understanding of the original completeness of the natural world—shows us how we are failing. Our bumper-sticker slogans ("Think globally, act locally") and our T-shirt vocabulary ("sustainable," "green," and "environment") we seem to have caught from the failure of discourse in politics. I don't know that Leopold would have endorsed, by this time, my own total dislike of the word "environment"—maybe in some uses it is pardonable—but it is important to see that in his writing "the environment," which has become so witless an abstraction, is characteristically embodied as "the land" or as places specifically named. And whereas the word "environment" now seems to take for granted a fundamental difference between ourselves and the world that supposedly "environs" or "surrounds" us, Leopold understood carefully that we and the world, the land and its places, are ultimately gathered into a single membership. His understanding of this membership, which he worked out in his life, in his long study of actual places, and in the common cause he made in his life with one actual place, informs at every point the always-responsible discourse of his writing.

᠊᠊᠊᠊᠊

My reading of Leopold involves a couple of embarrassments. I did not find and read *A Sand County Almanac* until I was in my mid-thirties, after I had begun to write of the beauties and troubles of my own home country. If I had read the book earlier, it would have been a much-needed help. My copy is well-worn and cluttered with successive markings in ink and pencil, because I have kept returning to it, as later to other essays, in my continuing need for help. But those returns were intermittent. It was not until I was invited to write this essay that I began a course of reading Leopold, reading about him, and thinking about him and his work every day for several months. My embarrassment, as before, is that I wish I had not waited so long. My preparation for this writing has given me a renewed, and sometimes predictably a new, astonishment at the quality, breadth, and depth of his work. It has also renewed and sharpened my dismay that conservationists and environmentalists have parceled his thinking into halves, one of which they have largely ignored.

It is possible if you are so inclined—and if you don't mind being half right—to understand Leopold's concern for the welfare of the land as divisible into a concern, on the one hand, for the preservation of substantial tracts of wilderness in as many regions as possible, and a concern, on the other hand, for the maintenance of health ("the capacity of the land for self-renewal") in the much greater area of the economic landscapes.

Having thus falsely divided the principle and the work that Leopold espoused, it becomes possible to concentrate almost exclusively, as concerned individuals and organizations have often done, upon wilderness preservation (with occasional attention to popular emergencies) while neglecting erosion, pollution, loss of biotic diversity, economic ruin, and social devastation in the economic landscapes.

Leopold would have called this "lopsided conservation," and it has been a tragic mistake, a courtship with disaster. If we cannot preserve land health or wildness merely by preserving wilderness—as preservationists have confessed by their constant campaigning to enlarge the preserves— then we have no choice but to look to the possibility of preserving wildness and health in the economic landscapes. Like most conservationists, Leopold loved the "unspoiled" wilderness. He wished to preserve it, not just for its own sake, but also because he saw that it gives us the only viable model and standard for land *use*.

For him, the love of wilderness led logically and directly to concern for the health of farms and ranches, such woodlands and wetlands as they may include, and the working forests. There is no discontinuity between his interest in wilderness and his interest in "the back forty." He said, "You cannot build the forest and mine the farm. The land is one organism." He said, "Conservation is a state of harmony between men and land," and he understood that this harmony necessarily was practical and economic. What is most instructive and exciting in Leopold's story, as Mr. Meine tells it, is the growth of his insight into the difference between land use modeled on the standards, patterns, and demands of the industrial economy and "biotic" land use modeled on the structure of natural ecosystems. In his understanding of this difference he went *far* beyond conservation as it was in his time, and *far* beyond conservation or environmentalism as it is in ours.

The next logical step that Leopold took also isolates him far in the forefront of conservation as we know it now. If we understand that conservation of wildness and land health cannot be adequately performed in wilderness preserves alone, with government agencies as caretakers, but must be performed as well in the economic landscapes, then the only possible caretakers, such as they may be, will be the owners and users of those landscapes. Some owners and users have been abusive, no doubt about that, but some have not been. Some who have been abusive have changed or are changing to ways of good use. There *are* ways of land use that seem sustainable, and may prove more or less to be so. Such distinctions have eluded the comprehension of many conservationists and environmentalists. By countenancing the all-out industrialization and commodification of the economic landscapes, the mainstream conservationists and environmentalists have helped to deprive those landscapes of a population adequate to care properly for them, and moreover they have consented to a land economy in which the remnant population is insufficient, and can hardly afford, to care properly for the land.

By ignoring the economic landscapes as they have become more and more impoverished of life and health, the main thrust of conservation has pushed past the most urgent questions concerning industrialism. Leopold clearly came to doubt the possibility of harmony between industrialism, supported by a scientific establishment increasingly oriented to commercial and political power, and healthful land membership. His doubt has been aboundingly confirmed in the years since his death. It is possible to suppose that industrialization might have been acceptable on ecological terms, conferring a net benefit, *up to a point*. But the impetus of industrialization recognizes no such point. It foresees no time to stop and respects no limit. Though nobody, apparently, has tried to compute the net result of the industrial "progress" of the last two hundred years, by now the question of a possible net benefit has been overwhelmed by a machine-made alternative world entirely indifferent to the nature and needs of the actual world. The clear tendency of industrial agriculture, to look at the most obvious example, has been to destroy any living thing that cannot be sold—including, by now, almost all farmers and farm communities.

And so Leopold was correct in understanding the living world as a "membership" to which we humans inescapably belong. In the economic landscapes, we are under obligation to live and work as conscious, conscientious "functional members of the land." To make arbitrary divisions between (let us say) land health and farms, and then between farms and farmers, and then between farmers and food—to assume that we can have any one of these without the others—is not merely to risk destruction of the entire membership. It is to invite it.

૭

Of all the conservationists who have preceded us, Leopold was the most radical, the most complete, and therefore the most needed. He was the most radical, simply, because he got nearest to the root of our problem: the lack of an appropriate standard by which to measure and guide our economic life. I have been asking, as I have been reading and thinking about him, how he achieved so much. What formed him into the man he finally was? I don't think he can be accounted for simply by his exceptional intelligence or his command of ecological science or his gift for observation or his sense of country or his energy and curiosity. Two further things were absolutely critical to his making: he was a hunter and he was a working land steward.

Both hunters and land stewards enter into practical relationships with the land. In our present state of ignorance, some would question whether such practical relationships should exist. But membership and plain citizenship in an ecosystem call necessarily for local practice of some kind, and so the relevant question is about the quality of the practice. Humans, like other species, live from nature and so must make use of it. But how well do they use it? And what do they learn from their use of it? Those questions define Leopold's preoccupation and his work. His practices of hunting and land stewardship always involved what he was not embarrassed to call "husbandry"—a word that has disappeared by now from the sciences of land use—and from this husbandry he learned a great deal that he needed to know.

As a hunter, he knew as a matter of course that wildlife can be found outside designated wildernesses and nature preserves. It can be found on farms and ranches and in working woodlands. Moreover, and this is most important, he would have observed that the better the land is used, by the standard of ecological health, the greater abundance and diversity of native species it will support and the greater will be its capacity for resilience.

That land use can fail by that standard he knew from the most direct experience. He knew that land could be "farmed out" because in 1935 he and his family bought an exhausted Wisconsin "sand county" farm. On probably the best days of his life he painstakingly studied that place and its resident creatures, and, with his family's help, restored it by planting thousands of native trees and shrubs, prairie grasses and wildflowers. His work as a conservationist found its most necessary instruction and its truest expression not in thought only, and not even in writing, but rather in skilled handwork under the disciplines of local knowledge and local affection. Curt Meine has served us indispensably by telling us, among other stories, the story of Aldo Leopold, his family, their "Shack," and their land.

Wendell Berry

March 2010
Port Royal, Kentucky

Preface to the 2010 Edition

I N his influential essay "The Land Ethic," completed in the final year of his life, Aldo Leopold summarized the lessons he had learned across four decades as a conservation scientist, advocate, practitioner, and teacher. Leopold argued that the next phase of human ethical development must include the expansion of our sphere of moral concern to include the land. Only through such an expanded ethic, he held, could human and natural communities, in all their diversity, productivity, and beauty, function well and thrive together over the long run. "I do not imply that this philosophy of land was always clear to me," Leopold admitted. "It is rather the end-result of a life-journey, in the course of which I have felt sorrow, anger, puzzlement or confusion over the inability of conservation to halt the juggernaut of land abuse."[1]

My purpose in writing this biography was to explore that "life journey" in order to understand more fully Leopold's continuing (and changing) influence in conservation and American culture. This book first appeared in the spring of 1988, a year after the centennial of Leopold's birth. By the 1980s Leopold was well recognized as a central figure in the history of conservation and environmental thought. For most, however—including me—that reputation rested almost exclusively upon his authorship of the classic *A Sand County Almanac*. The centennial provided an opportunity to examine with fresh eyes the life behind the *Almanac*'s timeless prose.

One did not need special insight to see that there was much to learn about, and from, that life. All one needed was the opportunity (which happened to come my way) to learn something of his story and to read a bit into his other writings, published and unpublished. At the time much

---

1 Aldo Leopold, "Foreword" (unpublished foreword to *A Sand County Almanac*), in *Companion to A Sand County Almanac*, edited by J. Baird Callicott (Madison: University of Wisconsin Press, 1987), 282.

of Leopold's story was held in the memory of his aging contemporaries, and much of the documentary record was buried deep in archival vaults or lay dormant in library stacks. But even a small sampling of these sources was enough to excite the imagination.

One did not need to be prophetic in the 1980s to understand that Leopold's legacy would grow more important in the years to come. As I worked on this book, the headlines of the day told the tale, across the nation and around the world: increasingly polarized environmental politics in Washington and in the American hinterland; continuing struggles to curtail land, water, and air pollution; economic crisis and ecological degradation across the agricultural Midwest; decline in America's older industrial cities and the relentless march of suburban development across the countryside; loss of open space and the isolation and fragmentation of wildlands; relentless cutting of America's old-growth forests, followed by wrenching change in forest-dependent communities and the demonization of the northern spotted owl; recognition of the destructive impacts of acid rain; depletion of the Earth's protective ozone layer and the global response leading to the 1987 Montreal Protocol; rising demands upon the world's fresh water supply; degradation of the oceans and commercial fisheries; accelerated loss of the world's biological diversity, especially in the species-rich tropical forests; the systematic piecing together of scientific understanding of global climate change. Leopold's vision of conservation as "a state of harmony" between people and land seemed both painfully remote and utterly necessary.

Within months of this book's publication, extensive drought was searing much of the American landscape. Yellowstone burned. Media coverage of the fires fanned the political flames.[2] Dr. James Hansen testified before Congress about climate change and the risks associated with increased greenhouse gas emissions—and political reaction to the science began to mount. Meanwhile, the fatal flaws in the Soviet Bloc had surfaced and the Cold War would soon come to its astonishing end. Some suggested that history itself ended with it.[3] No environmental historian, however, could be content with such a thesis. With the collapse of the Iron Curtain a new reality of change, promise, and challenge emerged, one in which the intertwined fate of humanity and the rest of creation would continue to unfold—for ill or good, with increasing wisdom or with compounded ignorance.

Amid the turbulence, I found calm in my scholar's cocoon. Aldo Leo-

---

2 See Rocky Barker, *Scorched Earth: How the Fires of Yellowstone Changed America* (Washington, D.C.: Island Press, 2005).

3 Francis Fukuyama, "The End of History?" *National Interest* 16 (Summer 1989): 3–18.

pold's experience, ideas, science, politics, and character provided quiet refuge. Through him, I (and, I hoped, readers) could find critical appreciation of how land changes, how our relationship to it changes, how such change reveals our values and our priorities, and how we might yet come to a healthier place.

Leopold's passion for wild places, for vibrant human landscapes and communities, for sound economies rooted in ecological realities, and for adventure and exploration crossed the sensitive fault lines of modern environmentalism and political ideology. Leopold anticipated our attention to global-scale human impacts on what he called "the land"—the soil, water, atmosphere, oceans, plants, animals, and people—even while he focused on the local and particular. He had useful and incisive things to say about urgent specific concerns (such as the ecological function of fire, in fact), about great themes (such as the broad history of human-land interactions), and about the connections between them. Devoted to positive and progressive reform, he was also a pragmatist with deep understanding of human dilemmas and the impediments to change. In the heyday of an environmental movement and an emerging anti-environmental backlash that were often in the news but too frequently lacked historical perspective, I found Leopold's story to be powerfully *grounded* and *grounding*. It provided connections across generations and perspectives and landscapes. It exposed forgotten foundations and offered continuity amid complexity.

Now I find that grounding and continuity more important than ever. As I write, crude oil gushes out from the depths of the Gulf of Mexico, bringing devastation to the Gulf's waters and wildlife, the coastal wetlands, and the region's human communities and economies. In the oil's sheen we see mingled reflections of all our daunting contemporary issues and anxieties: climate disruption and ocean degradation, fossil fuel dependence and economic upheaval, biodiversity loss and food security, corporate irresponsibility and political corruption. It would be comforting if we could now read Leopold's story and find it dated and nostalgic. We cannot. We have not yet fulfilled what Leopold once called "the oldest task in human history: to live on a piece of land without spoiling it."[4]

⌒

4 Leopold's statement is from a lecture, "Engineering and Conservation," delivered on April 11, 1938, at the University of Wisconsin College of Engineering. See Susan L. Flader and J. Baird Callicott, eds., *The River of the Mother of God and Other Essays by Aldo Leopold* (Madison: University of Wisconsin Press, 1991), 254.

My original goals in writing this biography were to explore the full breadth of Leopold's experience, and to place that experience in the context of American history, the changing landscape, and the evolving relationship between people and nature. Ambitious aims, but I benefitted from fortunate timing. In the decades following Leopold's passing in 1948, a generation of writers—including such voices as Lewis Mumford, Joseph Wood Krutch, Rachel Carson, Wallace Stegner, Peter Matthiessen, Sigurd Olson, Wendell Berry, Gary Snyder, N. Scott Momaday, Edward Abbey, Annie Dillard—had risen up to speak for and from the American land. They gathered the "cultural harvest" from the land that Leopold anticipated.[5]

Even as I was researching and writing, whole new fields of study were emerging to inform the task. In the sciences, the boundaries of established disciplines and natural resource management specialties (forestry, fisheries and wildlife management, range management, etc.) dimmed as new and more integrated fields gained ground: conservation biology, restoration ecology, sustainable agriculture, landscape ecology, ecological economics.[6] Social scientists examined in new ways the intimate connections among culture, communities, economies, and the natural world. Environmental ethics, environmental history, and a burgeoning literature of *place* explored the vital spaces where traditional academic domains intersected.

Scientists, scholars, writers, and conservation practitioners in all these fields recognized a kinship with Aldo Leopold. Leopold was one who understood, on both practical and theoretical grounds, the hazards of rigid disciplinary thinking. "All the sciences and arts are taught as if they were separate," he once wrote. "They are separate only in the classroom. Step out on the campus and they are immediately fused. Land ecology is putting the sciences and arts together for the purpose of understanding our environment."[7] That boldness in fusing fields of knowledge was characteristic of Leopold. Increasingly we appreciate how necessary this is, not only in enriching our understanding, but in solving our problems,

---

5 Aldo Leopold, *A Sand County Almanac and Sketches Here and There* (New York: Oxford University Press, 1949), ix.

6 See Richard L. Knight and Sarah F. Bates, eds., *A New Century for Natural Resources Management* (Washington, D.C.: Island Press, 1995); Ben A. Minteer and Robert E. Manning, eds., *Reconstructing Conservation: Finding Common Ground* (Washington, D.C.: Island Press, 2003); Richard L. Knight and Courtney White, eds., *Conservation for a New Generation: Redefining Natural Resources Management* (Washington, D.C.: Island Press, 2009).

7 Aldo Leopold, "The Role of Wildlife in a Liberal Education," *Transactions of the Seventh North American Wildlife Conference* (Washington, D.C.: American Wildlife Institute, 1942); see also Flader and Callicott, 302–3.

sustaining our economies, fulfilling our responsibilities, expressing our hopes, and deepening our joys.

By striving, as he memorably put it, to "think like a mountain," Leopold altered the course of conservation history. Remarkably, his impact is evident in many of the trends that have reshaped conservation thought, science, policy, and practice since this book was first published:

Dynamic ecology and landscape change. Among ecologists the notion of a stable and static natural world tending toward a state of perpetual balance has faded, replaced by a view that emphasizes patterns of change, flux, and resilience in ecosystems. As early as the 1920s Leopold explicitly rejected simplistic notions of the "balance of nature," based especially on his growing understanding of landscape history and the dynamics of wildlife populations. Through the chaotic environmental conditions of the 1930s Leopold developed an ever-deeper appreciation of the intricate functioning of biotic communities and of what he began to call "land health." Change, at all scales of time and space, was basic to Leopold's emerging ecological worldview.[8]

Biodiversity and conservation biology. These terms had not yet been coined in Leopold's day. His work prepared the way for their emergence and adoption in the mid-1980s. A growing recognition of the value of biological diversity runs like a bright line across Leopold's career. It transformed his definition of conservation, from one based on the Progressive Era's quantitative standards of economic efficiency and sustained yield to one based on the quality of entire, healthy, functioning landscapes and communities, with special emphasis on the maintenance of biological diversity. As the field of conservation biology came together to help guide this new approach, Leopold has come to be recognized as one of its early exemplars.[9]

The critique of wilderness. Since the 1980s biologists, historians,

---

8 For a critical assessment of this theme in Leopold's work, see J. Baird Callicott, "Do Deconstructive Ecology and Sociobiology Undermine Leopold's Land Ethic?" *Environmental Ethics* 18, 4 (1996): 353–72; and J. Baird Callicott, "From the Balance of Nature to the Flux of Nature: The Land Ethic in a Time of Change," in *Aldo Leopold and the Ecological Conscience*, edited by Richard L. Knight and Susan Reidel, 90–105 (New York: Oxford University Press, 2002).

9 See Reed Noss, "Aldo Leopold Was a Conservation Biologist," in *Aldo Leopold and the Ecological Conscience*, edited by Richard L. Knight and Susan Reidel, 105–17 (New York: Oxford University Press, 2002); Curt Meine, *Correction Lines: Essays on Land, Leopold, and Conservation* (Washington, D.C.: Island Press, 2004), 117–31; Curt Meine, Michael Soulé, and Reed Noss, "'A Mission-Driven Discipline': The Growth of Conservation Biology," *Conservation Biology* 20, 3 (June 2006): 631–51.

philosophers, geographers, and others have strongly challenged, on various grounds, long-established ideas about the definition, nature, and value of wilderness. Lively debates have focused especially on the definition of wilderness as pristine space, separate (and *separable*) from historical, cultural, and ecological realities. Amid the smoke, there has been some cleansing flame. This postmodern critique has yielded more subtle understandings of many aspects of the relationship between people and land. It has clarified the social, cultural, environmental, and political context of wilderness and the evolving role of native peoples worldwide in shaping landscapes and ecosystems over the millennia. It has made more visible the varied values associated with wildlands at all scales. It has helped to redefine the role of protected areas in conservation planning. For some, the critique of wilderness called into question a core aspect of Leopold's life's work, for he has long been recognized as one of America's foremost champions of "wild things" and wild places. However, the critique also brought more careful scrutiny of Leopold's wilderness ideas and advocacy, demonstrating the evolution of his wilderness values and highlighting especially his integration of wilderness within a comprehensive conservation vision.[10]

Landscape-scale approaches. Natural resource managers—including foresters, fish and wildlife managers, range managers, soil and water conservationists, civil engineers, urban and land use planners—no longer have the luxury of thinking of themselves in isolation from one another. They work within the same landscapes, watersheds, and communities. Their lines of activity invariably intersect, and the state of the land testifies to their ability—or failure—to work together. Leopold strove to communicate this theme through his entire conservation career. In the last twenty years, this perspective has gained ground through the science of landscape ecology (among other interdisciplinary fields) and in the shift toward ecosystem management as a unifying approach within the various natural resource professions. It has also served to bind conservation efforts together across the landscape, from our wild and rural lands to our suburbs and cities, and including our shared oceans and atmosphere.[11]

10 Many of the core historical and contemporary commentaries on wilderness have been gathered in two collections: J. Baird Callicott and Michael P. Nelson, eds., *The Great New Wilderness Debate* (Athens: University of Georgia Press, 1998); and Michael P. Nelson and J. Baird Callicott, eds., *The Wilderness Debate Rages On: Continuing the Great New Wilderness Debate* (Athens: University of Georgia Press, 2008). See also Meine, *Correction Lines*, 89–116.

11 Landscape ecology and its conservation implications are explored in Richard L. Knight and Peter B. Landres, eds., *Stewardship Across Boundaries* (Washington, D.C.: Island Press, 1998); Monica G. Turner, Robert H. Gardner, and Robert V. O'Neill, *Landscape Ecology in Theory and Practice:*

Private land conservation. "The thing to be prevented," Leopold wrote in 1934, "is destructive private land-use of any and all kinds. The thing to be encouraged is the use of private land in such a way as to combine the public and private interest to the greatest possible degree."[12] Through the 1960s and 1970s the environmental movement focused strongly on issues involving public lands, and neglected the challenge of private land conservation. Over the last two decades that has changed. Around the country conservationists have fostered "smart growth" programs, a robust land trust movement, and other efforts to protect and restore "working" farms, rangelands, and forests. In 1996 the USDA's Soil Conservation Service was rechristened the Natural Resource Conservation Service, with a strengthened mandate to serve the nation's private landowners in becoming better land stewards.[13] The challenge of conserving private land is plainly monumental and sobering; nonetheless, the reclaiming of this aspect of conservation history has been one of the key achievements of the last several decades.

Food, agriculture, and conservation. Closely tied to the theme of private land conservation is the surge of interest in organic, sustainable, and local (including urban) food production. Many of the forces driving the dominant industrial agricultural model first gained traction in the years following World War II, as war-spawned technologies, demographic trends, economic incentives, and government programs changed the face of farming and ranching.[14] Leopold lived just long enough to see the impact of those gathering forces. He warned in 1945 that the "tremendous momentum of industrialization" on the farm, left unchecked, would "[generate] new insecurities, economic and ecological, in place of those it was meant to abolish. In its extreme form, it is humanly desolate and economically unstable."[15] The intimate connections between land, food, health, security, and community have now again come into focus. They

---

Pattern and Process (New York: Springer, 2001); and Kevin J. Gutzwiler, ed., *Applying Landscape Ecology in Biological Conservation* (New York: Springer-Verlag, 2002).

12 Aldo Leopold, "Conservation Economics," *Journal of Forestry* 32, 5 (1934): 542; see also Flader and Callicott, 200.

13 See *America's Private Land: A Geography of Hope* (Washington, D.C.: USDA Natural Resources Conservation Service, 1996).

14 A concise history of sustainable agriculture can be found in Randall S. Beeman and James A. Pritchard, *A Green and Permanent Land: Ecology and Agriculture in the Twentieth Century* (Lawrence: University Press of Kansas, 2001).

15 Aldo Leopold, "The Outlook for Farm Wildlife," *Transactions of the Tenth North American Wildlife Conference* (Washington, D.C.: American Wildlife Institute, 1945), 168; see also Flader and Callicott, 326.

will continue to reshape conservation and agriculture into the indefinite future.

Ecological restoration. In his introduction to *A Sand County Almanac* Leopold stated: "On this sand farm in Wisconsin, first worn out and then abandoned by our bigger-and-better society, we try to rebuild, with shovel and axe, what we are losing elsewhere."[16] It was the most personal of Leopold's career-long efforts to restore natural things: game and wildlife populations, watersheds, forests and rangelands, prairies and wetlands, diversity and beauty, ecosystem function and land health. Beginning in 1934, Leopold and his colleagues at the University of Wisconsin Arboretum in Madison pioneered a new dimension of conservation: ecological restoration. Especially since the 1970s, the science and practice of restoration have spread to institutions, agencies, and ecosystems worldwide, providing conservationists with a wider range of tools and an active complement to the preservation and sustainable use of land.

Ecosystem services. Even by his own standards, Leopold could be especially succinct on the theme of ecological economics: "We fancy that industry supports us, forgetting what supports industry."[17] Since the 1980s creative economists and conservationists have together explored new methods of assessing natural assets, emphasizing especially the value of such ecological "services" as carbon sequestration, pollination, freshwater filtering, flood protection, and pest control. Long ignored by traditional schools of economics, these values are now at least part of the discussion, and the idea has moved from the realm of abstract concept to real-world policy-making.

Community-based conservation. As a young ranger in the early U.S. Forest Service, Aldo Leopold personified the top-down approach of the Progressive conservation movement. Over his career, however, he wrestled with geographically extensive challenges: soil erosion, watershed rehabilitation, and wildlife restoration. As a result, he pioneered new ways of involving local landowners and other citizens in their home landscapes. Over the last several decades this same need to work from the bottom up has inspired work through a tremendously diverse array of local conservation organizations. This trend is evident not only in the United States but in conservation programs around the world.[18]

16 Leopold, *A Sand County Almanac*, viii.
17 Ibid., 178.
18 A rich literature of community-based conservation has developed over the last two decades. A sampling includes: David Western and Mary C. Pearl, eds., *Conservation for the Twenty-First Century* (New York: Oxford University Press, 1989); R. Michael Wright, David Western, and Shirley C. Strum, eds., *Natural Connections: Perspectives on Community-Based Conservation*

The greening of religion and philosophy. In "The Land Ethic" Leopold observed ruefully that "No important change in ethics was ever accomplished without an internal change in our intellectual emphasis, loyalties, affections, and convictions. The proof that conservation has not yet touched these foundations of conduct lies in the fact that philosophy and religion have not yet heard of it."[19] It is no longer unusual for philosophers, ethicists, and theologians to address the moral and ethical dimensions of our environmental challenges and human-nature relationships. The last two decades have been a time of vibrant scholarship and reflection, as students within a wide array of faith communities and philosophical schools have reexamined the ecological insights of their traditions. Philosophy and religion have now "heard of" conservation, while many conservationists have come to listen differently to the language of belief and philosophical inquiry.[20]

Environmental justice. The face of conservation in Leopold's day was largely white, male, and rural, with its strongest base of support among sportsmen, farmers, and foresters. The environmental movement was largely dominated by urban and suburban baby-boomers, and was especially attentive to outdoor recreation and environmental quality issues. Entire segments of American society and culture were underserved and underrepresented in the conservation arena until a new wave of advocates unfurled the banner of environmental justice beginning in the early 1990s.

(Washington, D.C.: Island Press, 1994); William Vitek and Wes Jackson, eds., *Rooted in the Land: Essays on Community and Place* (New Haven: Yale University Press, 1996); Ted Bernard and Jora Young, *The Ecology of Hope: Communities Collaborate for Sustainability* (Gabriola Island, British Columbia: New Society Publishers, 1997); G. K. Meffe, L. A. Nielsen, R. L. Knight, and D. A. Schenborn, *Ecosystem Management: Adaptive, Community-Based Conservation* (Washington, D.C.: Island Press, 2002); Minteer and Manning, *Reconstructing Conservation*; Knight and White, *Conservation for a New Generation*; Paul Hawken, *Blessed Unrest: How the Largest Movement in the World Came into Being and Why No One Saw It Coming* (New York: Viking Press, 2007).

19 Leopold, *A Sand County Almanac*, 209–10.

20 I am especially grateful to my friends and mentors Gretchen Schoff, Baird Callicott, Cal DeWitt, Strachan Donnelly, and Ron Engel for helping me to understand more fully the nature of these transformations. Particularly useful contributions in this work include the ten-volume World Religions and Ecology Series (published between 1997 and 2004 by Harvard University Press); the related work of the Forum on Religion and Ecology (FORE), led by Mary Evelyn Tucker and John Grim; and Bron Taylor and Jeffrey Kaplan, eds., *Encyclopedia of Religion and Nature* (London: Continuum International Publishing Group, 2005).

Aldo Leopold spoke or wrote on matters of race, class, gender, and ethnicity only infrequently (despite the fact that his wife Estella was Hispanic). Leopold's call for a durable ethic of "love and respect" for land as a community, however, resonates increasingly among those working to build a more inclusive conservation movement, as well as those seeking to understand the historical roots of environmental justice issues.[21]

Sustainability and resilience. Since the 1980s, *sustainability*—however awkward the term—has served to bind together the many intersecting social and environmental issues of our day, from climate change, energy, and biodiversity loss to population growth, global poverty, and public health. The term is, in a sense, a proxy. We needed a word to convey the idea of connection in the world and among multiple needs and concerns. It indicates that we are still striving, as did Leopold, to "[put] the sciences and arts together for the purpose of understanding our environment." And *resilience* has come to signify our commitment to making those connections healthier. It in fact adheres very closely to Leopold's definition of land health as "a state of vigorous self-renewal" within our comingled human and natural communities.[22]

These many trends have been converging in ways that are fundamentally reconfiguring traditional conservation and environmentalism. For some, this is a long-unfulfilled hope and a long-overdue need, especially in the face of mounting environmental woes. For others, these changes may be vaguely threatening—as they are to any simple notion of what conservation was, is, and is becoming. Aldo Leopold's story shows that many of these trends have deep historical roots, with shoots that are only now greening up. "Conservation," Leopold wrote in 1940, "viewed in its entirety, is the slow and laborious unfolding of a new relationship between people and land."[23] That new relationship is far from being fully developed. But it continues, vigorously, to unfold.

As conservation has changed, interest in Leopold's life and work has

21 See Wendell Berry, *The Hidden Wound* (Boston: Houghton Mifflin, 1970); Peter S. Wenz, *Environmental Justice* (New York: SUNY Press, 1988); Robert D. Bullard, ed., *Unequal Protection: Environmental Justice and Communities of Color* (San Francisco: Sierra Club Books, 1994); Alison H. Deming and Lauret E. Savoy, eds., *The Colors of Nature: Culture, Identity, and the Natural World* (Minneapolis: Milkweed Editions, 2002); Carolyn Merchant, "Shades of Darkness: Race and Environmental History," *Environmental History* 8, 3 (July 2003): 380–94; Sylvia Hood Washington, *Packing Them In: An Archeology of Environmental Racism in Chicago, 1865–1954* (Lanham, Md.: Lexington Books, 2005).

22 Meine, *Correction Lines*, 63–85. See p. 465 of this volume.

23 Leopold, "Wisconsin Wildlife Chronology," *Wisconsin Conservation Bulletin* 5, 11 (1940): 6.

continued to grow. It has, in fact, expanded well beyond the conservation and environmental arenas. Leopold was a keen observer, not only of the land, but of the course of American development. He became a fierce, if carefully measured, critic of his home culture. The increasing appreciation of this aspect of Leopold's record is due partly to the fact that scholars and readers can now explore his multifaceted life in ways that were not possible when I worked on this biography. Since 1988 many of Leopold's most significant non–*Sand County Almanac* writings have been published for the first time, or republished.[24] My colleagues in the scholarly community have published several additional book-length studies and commentaries on Leopold.[25] The Aldo Leopold Foundation and the University of Wisconsin–Madison Archives have also digitized and made available over the Internet the extraordinary collection of Leopold's papers.[26]

Leopold remains a unique link between Progressive Era conservation, modern environmentalism, and the still-emerging successor to these movements. One of the hopes I had for this biography was that it might stimulate interest in themes, topics, events, and people in Leopold's experience that deserved further attention. It is especially rewarding to see that hope realized. We have an ever-richer trove of historical studies, for example, of contemporaries of Leopold, including Charles Elton, Sigurd Olson, Benton MacKaye, and Charles Stoddard;[27] of conservation themes, including

24 *The River of the Mother of God and Other Essays by Aldo Leopold*, edited by Flader and Callicott; David E. Brown and Neil B. Carmony, eds., *Aldo Leopold's Southwest* (Albuquerque: University of New Mexico Press, 1995) [originally published as *Aldo Leopold's Wilderness: Selected Early Writings by the Author of A Sand County Almanac* (Harrisburg, Penn.: Stackpole Books, 1990)]; Aldo Leopold, *For the Health of the Land: Previously Unpublished Essays and Other Writings*, edited by J. Baird Callicott and Eric T. Freyfogle (Washington, D.C.: Island Press, 1999); Curt Meine and Richard L. Knight, eds., *The Essential Aldo Leopold: Quotations and Commentaries* (Madison: University of Wisconsin Press, 1999).

25 Marybeth Lorbiecki, *Aldo Leopold: A Fierce Green Fire* (Helena, Mont.: Falcon Press, 1996); Knight and Reidel, *Aldo Leopold and the Ecological Conscience*; Julianne Lutz Newton, *Aldo Leopold's Odyssey* (Washington, D.C.: Island Press, 2006); Michael J. Lannoo, *Leopold's Shack and Rickett's Lab: The Emergence of Environmentalism* (Berkeley: University of California Press, 2010).

26 The Aldo Leopold Papers can be viewed online at http://digicoll.library.wisc.edu/AldoLeopold.

27 Peter Crowcroft, *Elton's Ecologist: A History of the Bureau of Animal Population* (Chicago: University of Chicago Press, 1991); David Backes, *A Wilderness Within: The Life of Sigurd F. Olson* (Minneapolis: University

environmental ethics, wilderness, sustainable agriculture, ecological res-
toration, private property and land conservation;[28] and of key places in
Leopold's life, including the Colorado River delta, the Kaibab Plateau,
Mexico's Rio Gavilan, the upper Great Lakes forests, and Wisconsin.[29]
I pulled together my own "further thoughts" on Leopold and his legacy
in *Correction Lines: Essays on Land, Leopold, and Conservation*.[30]

The opportunities for fresh historical analysis are hardly exhausted.
There is still work to do on Leopold's relationship to Native Americans,
on the exceptional contributions of the Leopold children, and on the tra-
jectory of the land ethic in postwar America, to cite just a few topics. More
broadly, our placing of Leopold within the expansive narrative of conservation and environmental history is, and ought to be, subject to constant
reconsideration. As far-sighted as Leopold was in his day, and as timeless
as his legacy remains, he was of his time and subject to its limitations. The

of Minnesota Press, 1997); Ben A. Minteer, *The Landscape of Reform: Civic Pragmatism and Environmental Thought in America* (Cambridge, Mass.: MIT Press, 2006); Albert G. Way, "Burned to Be Wild: Herbert Stoddard and the Roots of Ecological Conservation in the Southern Longleaf Pine Forest," *Environmental History* 11, 3 (July 2006): 500–526.

28 Roderick F. Nash, *The Rights of Nature: A History of Environmental Ethics* (Madison: University of Wisconsin Press, 1989); Paul S. Sutter, *Driven Wild: How the Fight against Automobiles Launched the Modern Wilderness Movement* (Seattle: University of Washington Press, 2002); Beeman and Pritchard, *A Green and Permanent Land*; William R. Jordan III, *The Sunflower Forest: Ecological Restoration and the New Communion with Nature* (Berkeley: University of California Press, 2003); Eric T. Freyfogle, *The Land We Share: Private Property and the Common Good* (Washington, D.C.: Island Press, 2003).

29 Christian C. Young, *In the Absence of Predators: Conservation and Controversy on the Kaibab Plateau* (Lincoln: University of Nebraska Press, 2002); William deBuys and Joan Myers, *Salt Dreams: Land and Water in Low Down California* (Albuquerque: University of New Mexico Press, 1999); William Fleming and William Forbes, "Following in Leopold's Footsteps: Revisiting and Restoring the Rio Gavilan Watershed," *Ecological Restoration* 24, 1 (2006): 25–31; Robert Gough, *Farming the Cutover: A Social History of Northern Wisconsin, 1900–1940* (Lawrence: University Press of Kansas, 1997); James Kates, *Planning a Wilderness: Regenerating the Great Lakes Cutover Region* (Minneapolis: University of Minnesota Press, 2001); Lynne Heasley, *A Thousand Pieces of Paradise: Landscape and Property in the Kickapoo Valley* (Madison: University of Wisconsin Press, 2005); Donald M. Waller and Thomas P. Rooney, *The Vanishing Present: Wisconsin's Changing Lands, Waters, and Wildlife* (Chicago: University of Chicago Press, 2008).

30 See n. 9 above.

conservation movement that Leopold knew has morphed into a diverse and global environmental movement. The ecological science that Leopold knew has grown vastly in sophistication and complexity. The society in which Leopold lived has an even more tenuous hold on its roots in the land. We may honor Leopold's legacy most appropriately by bringing to our moment in history the same critical perspective that he brought to his.

༄

I made a pact with myself to reread this book once every ten years in order to gauge my own changing perspective on Leopold and his story. In reading it at the twenty-year mark, I was struck by several things. From a stylistic standpoint, I found myself wishing the biographer had departed more often from the strict chronological structure, and made more creative connections across time. (The younger biographer responds: "My main priority at the time was just to get the story straight!") The biographer also relied unusually heavily on extensive quotation of Leopold. (The biographer responds: "The fellow was *quotable*. And because much of Leopold's writing was not available at the time, I felt the need to include as much of his finer prose in the story as possible.") And I found the occasional thickets of "man," "mankind," and masculine pronouns awkward. (The biographer sheepishly responds: "Mea culpa.")

More broadly, I see themes that perhaps reflected the tenor of the 1980s. A strong wilderness thread weaves through the narrative, and with good cause. Leopold's defense of wildness in general and of wilderness lands in particular was a constant—though constantly changing—theme in his life and work. As noted above, the recent critique of wilderness alters our interpretation of Leopold's commitment, but I do not think it undermines the fundamental point: that Leopold did not perform triage with land, and wilderness was not his sole focus. All land deserved, and was worthy of, "love and respect" (as he phrased it in the introduction to *A Sand County Almanac*). And so the theme of conservation across the entire landscape—in cities and suburbs and small towns, on farms and ranches and managed forests, in the remaining wild places, in whole watersheds and flyways and regions—was also constant, and essential to the integrity of his conservation vision.

This suggests another theme that stands out even more vividly after twenty years: Leopold's lifelong search for common ground in conservation. In Leopold's time, as in ours, the forces of self-interest, parochialism, specialization, and crass materialism served to divvy up the land and its values, to pit one generation against the next, to distract us tragically from shared commitment to the common good. In a 1939 article, "The Farmer as a Conservationist," Leopold pithily skewered the attitude that had brought on the Depression and the Dust Bowl. Of his times Leopold wrote, "Everybody worried about getting his share; nobody worried about doing his bit."[31] History, it seems, has brought us around the circle once more.

The quest to build a more durable and self-renewing relationship between people and land is the paramount challenge for this generation, and for as many generations as we care to look into the future. That challenge contains within it the other, multiple challenges we face involving energy, climate, the oceans, biodiversity, water, food, human health, and the creation of a healthful economy. With his distinctive mix of pragmatism and idealism, Leopold recognized that "We shall never achieve harmony with land, any more than we shall achieve absolute justice or liberty for people. In these higher aspirations the important thing is not to achieve, but to strive."[32] Aldo Leopold's is a human story, of one who *strove*. By knowing his story, we can see deeper into conservation's story. By knowing conservation's story, we gird ourselves for the work ahead.

౮

In my own recent rereading, I also became much more strongly aware of the degree to which this biography was a community effort, involving fellow historians, conservationists, scientists, and Aldo Leopold's family, friends, associates, and students. I am pleased to thank once again all the people and organizations that first made this work possible. I am especially indebted to the members of the Leopold family, who have remained good friends and colleagues. Their example of dedication, leadership, good humor, and disinterested scholarship was, in retrospect, a biographer's dream; it remains a standard to aspire to.

I am honored and grateful to have Wendell Berry's appreciation included in this new edition. It is no exaggeration to say that Wendell's work helped put me on the path to Leopold. To have the path come around in this way is deeply fulfilling.

To my original list of acknowledgments I can add more than two decades' worth of gratitude to countless friends and colleagues who have continued to build the land ethic in their own ways and places. "Nothing so important as an ethic is ever written," Leopold paradoxically wrote in "The Land Ethic"; it "evolve[s] in the minds of a thinking community."[33]

---

31 Aldo Leopold, "The Farmer as a Conservationist," *American Forests* 45, 6 (1939): 323; see also Flader and Callicott, 265.

32 Luna B. Leopold, ed., *Round River: From the Journals of Aldo Leopold* (New York: Oxford University Press, 1953), 55.

33 Leopold, *A Sand County Almanac*, 225.

To be a part of that expanding community has been my good fortune. In the 1980s I felt like the young kid asking the community elders to tell me their stories. Now most of those same elders are gone, and the obligation of sharing stories with the next generation—and of creating new chapters—has been passed on. To that next generation, I dedicate this new edition.

⌣

In preparing this edition I felt it preferable to preserve the original text, with its flaws, than to rewrite it to any great extent. And so I have made only minimal changes, mostly minor corrections of stylistic lapses and particular inaccuracies. Fortunately, subsequent scholarship has exposed few large or debilitating blunders.

In at least one instance, however, new information has clarified a critical moment in Leopold's life—and in the history of twentieth-century conservation. Chapter 4 describes Leopold's early years as a forester in his first job on the Apache National Forest. It was there, I surmised in my original account, that the wolf-shooting incident that Leopold described so memorably in his essay "Thinking Like a Mountain" occurred in 1909 (see pp. 93–94). However, hard documentary evidence of the episode was lacking, and remained so for years. Then, in 2009, a new collection of Leopold family letters came to light. In one of these, a letter to his mother dated September 22, 1909, Leopold alluded directly to the shooting.

It was hardly a world-shaking moment at the time. In his letter Leopold mentioned it in his report home only in passing; he was plainly more concerned about having lost a new pipe. The "green fire" that he saw in the eyes of the dying mother wolf that day was only an initial spark. But with time and over a life, that moment would evoke in Leopold a new way of understanding complexity in the natural world, and our changing roles and responsibilities within it. In peering into the wolf's eyes Leopold began to see himself anew, and to reexamine the ever-evolving relationship between people and land. And in Leopold's story we may see different dimensions of, and new directions for, that relationship in our own experience.

June 9, 2010
Sauk Prairie, Wisconsin

Preface to the 1988 Edition

I FIRST learned of Aldo Leopold the same way so many others have: a friend told me that I ought to read *A Sand County Almanac.* I did not know at the time that the book was considered a classic in environmental literature, nor was I aware of Leopold's considerable fame and accomplishments within the conservation movement. I never did finish the book that first time around. I was impressed by Leopold's obvious skills as a naturalist, and I sympathized in a vague way with his outlook, but his writing was just not of the sort that appealed to me at the time.

I returned to the book in a roundabout fashion. My latent interest in the outdoors had led me into graduate studies in the history of conservation. When the time came for me to choose a thesis topic, I decided to investigate the development of Leopold's oft-quoted essay "The Land Ethic." That thesis led, in turn, to an opportunity to write a full biography of Leopold.

Although long revered as one of conservation's foremost figures, Leopold has not until now been the subject of a comprehensive biography. Because this is the first such attempt, I have tried to present a solid account of Leopold's life and work that will appeal to scholars and general readers alike. For forty years Leopold has been known to the public mainly as the poet of *Sand County* fame. This is appropriate enough, but relatively few ·realize that behind the poetry there was a man whose deeds were at least as noteworthy as his words. Accordingly, I have tried to present the whole Leopold: wordsmith, scientist, activist, thinker, outdoorsman, and family man. The range of Leopold's experience was immense, and I cannot claim to have explored every corner and covert of his life in ultimate detail, but I have tried to tell his story as fairly, accurately, and completely as possible.

A biography of Leopold must, as a matter of course, be more than just one man's story. It must also, by virtue of Leopold's deep involvement in so many phases of twentieth-century conservation, be a personal history of the conservation movement in America. At every juncture, it seems, we find Leopold at the cutting edge of conservation activity and environmental thought. His actions and ideas defined the basic issues that challenged conservation in his time—and continue to do so in ours. Still, I hope the reader will remember that there were many others at work in these fields, and that a biography can necessarily focus on only one. For those interested in further exploration, the bibliography may provide some starting points.

Every biographer faces the challenge of maintaining a critical view of one's subject. Fortunately, I have been able to turn to Leopold's own high standards of critical thought for assurance. He, of all people, would have protested a study that was either too hard or too soft on its subject. Leopold once defined an ecologist as one who is "skillful in seeing facts, ingenious in forming hypotheses, and ruthless in discarding them when they don't fit." Those criteria suffice, I think, to define successful scholarship in any field, in history as well as science.

I hope the reader will come away from this book with a greater understanding of a man whose work has enriched us all, and whose legacy grows only more important with time. I hope, too, that the reader will gain, through Leopold's experience, a deeper appreciation of the changes that have taken place, and continue to take place, on the face of the American land—across the breadth of the continent as well as in our own backyards. His was only one life, but it contained significant passages from the American drama, and exemplified that creative tension between the Old World and the wilderness which has played such a crucial role in the formation of our nation's character. The history and geography of this continent shaped Leopold's life unmistakably; his life, in turn, tells us much about how we have defined ourselves, and our land. As we continue that process of definition, perhaps Leopold's insights may add to our understanding, our appreciation, and our sense of wonder.

June 3, 1987
Madison, Wisconsin

Acknowledgments

O NLY at the end of a project like this does one begin to realize how many have lent a hand. At the risk of forgetting some of those who have helped along the way, I would like to express a few special thank-yous.

First things first. For help in arranging and providing the funding that kept my rent paid for the duration, thanks to the Aldo Leopold Shack Foundation, the Sand County Foundation, the National Wildlife Federation, the Vernon Taylor Foundation, Reed Coleman, and Ronald Mattox.

My work could not have been started, nor finished, without the support, encouragement, and understanding of the entire Leopold family. Without exception, they were open and cooperative, and urged me to take my own approach to this material. I am likewise grateful to all of Leopold's colleagues and students with whom I had the opportunity to work. I am particularly indebted to Robert McCabe, Joe Hickey, Frederick and Frances Hamerstrom, Arthur Hawkins, Douglas Wade, Albert Hochbaum, Lyle Sowls, and Bill Elder for their contributions.

I was guided in my work by an enthusiastic committee of academic advisors. John Ross always kept his office door open, while providing invaluable wise counsel and logistical support. Gretchen Schoff, Tom Vale, Allan Bogue, Robert McCabe, and Joseph Hickey read and reread my drafts and were always eager to sit down and talk it over. Their dedication and the interest of their respective families have been, to say the least, greatly appreciated.

Many other members of the University of Wisconsin staff and faculty assisted me at one time or another. Special thanks to Tim Allen, Grant Cottam, John Thomson, Hugh Iltis, Cal DeWitt, Arthur Hasler, Orrin Rongstad, Bill Jordan, Madeleine Doran, and Clarence Schoenfeld. The staff and students of the Institute for Environmental Studies were a steady source of support over the long haul, especially Arthur Sacks, Barbara Borns, Eileen Hanneman, Beverly Helms, Emily Earley, Steve Pomplun,

Acknowledgments

and Tom Sinclair. The Department of Agricultural Journalism also contributed immensely to this work; extra special thanks to Debbie Dunn, who spent untold hours at the word processor with this manuscript. The Department of Wildlife Ecology graciously adopted me as one of their own for the duration of my research and writing. My good friends in the dungeon were particularly helpful, offering their encouragement and enduring patiently my constant stream of questions. James Liebig of the University of Wisconsin Archives shared the many long hours of archival research that went into this book, keeping me going with his coffee, his cooperation, and his tales of life in Beaver Dam. Thanks also to Frank Cook and Bernie Schermetzler of the University Archives, to George Talbot of the State Historical Society of Wisconsin, to Jim Voegeli, and to Drs. Avery Harrington and Jeffrey Brown of the University of Wisconsin Hospital and Clinics, who helped me with some medical questions.

Anyone interested in Aldo Leopold's life owes a great deal to Dr. Susan Flader of the University of Missouri. This biography could not have gotten off the ground without her foundation of scholarship. In this regard, I would also like to thank J. Baird Callicott of the University of Wisconsin — Stevens Point for sharing of his expertise.

My friend Anne Ross generously donated her time and her sound legal advice to this effort. For his early encouragement, thanks to Bill Kurtis of Oxford University Press. The unflagging interest of everyone at the University of Wisconsin Press made this book possible. Alice Van Deburg took this project on as if it were her own, while Jack Kirshbaum edited the manuscript and shepherded it into production with patience and care.

My research took me far afield and gave me the opportunity to work with editors, librarians, historians, foresters, wildlifers, rangers, and administrators from Tucson to Seattle to New Haven. Among those who guided me through the unfamiliar territory of the American Southwest: Eddie Alford, Elliot Barker, Anne Bordenave, Jerry Davis, Bruce Donaldson, Leon Fisher, David Gillio, Bill Hurst, Bergere Kenney, Jack Kenney, Martin McAllister, Wayne Nicolls, Peter Pilles, John Ross, Bob Shiowitz, Dick Spray, Bill Snyder, Lowell Sumner, George Taylor, Norm Tessman, Jesse Williams, John Young, and Bill Zeedyk. Out east, I relied on Judy Stark, Ann Ramadei, and Joe Miller at Yale University; Francis Dykman of the Lawrenceville School; Richard McCabe of the Wildlife Management Institute; Tom Watkins of the Wilderness Society; and Dennis Roth of the history section of the U.S. Forest Service. Thanks also to Steven Brower, Jim and Jane Spring, and Mr. Frederic Leopold of Burlington, Iowa.

For contributions of friendship, I owe much to: Paul and Martha Rome, without whom I would have been lost; Charlie Clement, who read over these words with the humor and honesty of a true friend; Doug Kolner and Bill Mahlum, who gave their hospitality when it was most needed;

Acknowledgments

Tony and Clare Doyle, Mark and Holly Heuer, Ed and Nancy Park, Felix and Chris Jaramillo, Bob and Jeanne Bruener, George and Melinda Heathcote, Debbie Navins, Chuck Fox, Anne Georges, Barb Shuster, Ellie Robinson, D. J. Wolf, Pam Luer, Edie Bishop, Mike and Patty Wolf, Lauren Goffen, Christie Riebe, Bob Klein, Sam Rea, Steve Kramer, Julien Tietler, Colette Tietler, Tom Huffman, Koke Winter, Dorothy and Jerry Femrite, and Rod Matthews and Marie Sieker.

Finally, I would like to thank my family, and especially Evelyn Meine, who taught us always to leave our camping places cleaner than when we found them.

Part I

MIDWEST

1

Sources

(1843–1887)

I N 1843, western Missouri was a far outpost of eastern America, and a doorway to the wide-open West. At Independence, in the uplands above the Missouri River, early emigrants congregated, took final stock of their supplies and their situation, loaded their wagons, and struck off for new lands. One main trail, the Santa Fe, led to the Southwest. The other trail, the Oregon, led north to the Platte River and out onto the prairies and high plains further west. As the trails became the principal overland routes of the nation's westward advance, Independence became a primary point of departure.

Liberty, ten miles north of Independence across the valley of the Missouri, was another frontier settlement, the county seat of Clay County. One promising day in the spring of 1843, Charles J. J. Leopold mounted his horse, left his home and family in Liberty, and embarked on a wild scheme. He and several associates planned to drive a great flock of sheep up the Platte River, across the plains, through the Rocky Mountains, and on to California, where they would sell the sheep to the late settlers of that new territory. Leopold met the other men and, with an assortment of horses, mules, and dogs, set the flock, four thousand strong, into motion. The enterprising shepherds and their animal train advanced along the Missouri and then into the prairie territories that would not see statehood for another twenty years.

Charles Leopold was an adventurer. Born in Hanover in 1809, he belonged to a family of Saxon-Dutch, Prussian, and Huguenot ancestry with ties to nobility. He entered the University of Berlin in 1831, but dropped out and came to the New World in 1834, settling in St. Louis, where he helped run a dairy. In 1838, Leopold married Thusneld Runge, whose family had come to America on the same passage and settled in nearby St. Charles. A year later, Charles and Thusneld moved across Missouri to Liberty. Charles began a new career as a rope-maker. They began a family which would eventually grow to include seven children. And then came the idea for the great transcontinental sheep drive.[1]

The drive was ill-fated from its opening holler. Only one bridge and one ferry spanned the rivers along the proposed route west. While fording the Platte, Leopold lost his hat. The hat, with his name inside, was found downstream. Until further news arrived, his friends and family assumed that Charles had drowned. Storms and Indians beset the drive. One night, during a terrible thunderstorm, the man posted as night guard had to take refuge alongside a water barrel. When he ended his watch in the morning, he found a Pawnee arrow impaled in a stave inches from his head. The white men persevered, but the Indians soon discovered the key. They stole and killed the most valuable horses, mules, and dogs. Leopold lost his prize $200 shepherd dog. Without animal assistance, the men could no longer control the sheep, and the drive quickly deteriorated. They had intended to winter the sheep near the Great Salt Lake, but chose instead to go on with the vestiges of the flock to California, crossing the Sierra Nevada during the unpredictable weather of late autumn.[2]

Leopold spent the winter in California and started home the following spring of 1844, eventually returning to Missouri via Panama, New York, and New Orleans. He came up the Mississippi to St. Louis just as an epochal shipment was floating down the great river from its northern headwaters. In July 1844, Stephen Beck Hanks, a first cousin of Abraham Lincoln, guided a raft of logs down from the St. Croix pinelands of Wisconsin and Minnesota, the first raw white pine to reach St. Louis. An obscure moment in history, but one which symbolized the imminent transformation of the upper Mississippi, and of the lives, economies, and landscapes of mid-America. The first of the northern pines were felled, sawed, and rafted south in the 1830s. Before long, every self-respecting river town from Red Wing to Alton would claim a sawmill of its own; conversely, many a riverside sawmill would grow up into a thriving town. Over the next fifty years, the north would be stripped bare of its magnificent pines. As the trees fell, lumber and wealth floated downriver, settled in the valleys, and moved out onto the upland plains. As the towns and farmhouses rose, they would overshadow the open prairie that Charles Leopold, among others, crossed.[3]

At St. Louis, Leopold boarded one of the Missouri-running steamboats and rode up to the landing below Liberty. Thusneld still waited at home with the children. Her husband had been gone a year in search of his fortune. The sheep project, Charles had to report, had been no more profitable than dairying and rope-making, at least not in any financial sense.

$\backsim$

In 1843, when Charles Leopold was rising to his saddle and turning west, Charles Starker was seventeen years old and beginning his career as a civil engineer with the Bavarian government. Starker was born March 11, 1826, in Stuttgart, in the Kingdom of Württemberg. His father Heinrich and his father before him were both furniture dealers, but young Charles followed a different path. He grew up in Stuttgart, attending the Beale School and the Polytechnical School on scholarship, where he received training as an architect and landscape engineer. Such training gave wide play to Starker's considerable natural talents. By the time he left school at seventeen, he could not only design a bridge or building, but just as easily build it, plant the gardens around it, and paint the scene in watercolors. He joined the government and soon assumed responsibilities on a number of projects. Eventually, Starker became the first engineering architect of the Donau-Main River Canal, which connected the watersheds of the Danube and the Rhine; Starker's uncle was the chief engineer in charge of construction of the canal. After four years in Bavaria, Starker left for Italy in April 1847 to work at the marble quarries in Lombardy.[4]

Within a year Europe was collapsing in revolution. At first in the streets of Paris in February 1848, then in all corners of the continent in the months that followed, Europe caved in on itself. Charles Starker decided to leave the uproar of the Old World for the opportunity of the New. Starker was then twenty-two, a tall, robust young man with interests and talents in philosophy and the arts as well as engineering, architecture, and natural history. He sailed from Le Havre on October 22, 1848, and arrived forty-two days later in America.

Starker made his way to Buffalo and found work, at eight dollars a month, with Gray and Company, a firm dealing in hides and leather goods. Like Charles Leopold, however, Starker felt the magnetic pull of the West. Early in 1850 he asked for and received a transfer to the company's Chicago office, and soon after that joined a Chicago architecture firm. Then opportunity knocked. James Wilson Grimes, a prominent lawyer from the Mississippi River town of Burlington, Iowa, journeyed to Chicago in search of an architect to design and build his new home. Grimes, who would later gain fame as Iowa's governor and senator, and as the crucial deciding vote in the impeachment trial of President Andrew Johnson, was advised to hire Charles Starker.

Starker accepted the commission and arrived in Burlington that fall. The town had been founded sixteen years before as a frontier outpost. The native Sauk and fox tribes had once travelled from near and far to gather the high-quality flint that lay embedded in its precipitous limestone bluffs. They called the place Shok-Ko-Kon—"the flint hills." Flint Creek and Hawkeye Creek cut through the limestone, emptying into the Mississippi in the basin where Burlington grew. Starker had little liking for the swamps and mudflats of young Chicago, but he was enamored of Burlington, and of the mighty river that flowed before it. He finished the home for Grimes and decided to stay.

As the only trained architect in town, he found a market rush for his skills. He designed several more homes, Burlington's first public schools, and a number of public and private buildings in town. The initial flood of work receded, however, and Starker had to advertise his services in the newspaper. By late 1851 he realized he would need a more reliable income to stay in Burlington. The need was urgent because he was due to be married. His fiancée was Marie Runge, Thusneld Leopold's sixteen-year-old sister. They were married in St. Charles, Missouri, in February 1852.

Charles Starker was as astute as he was talented. He saw what the future held. Transportation in the valley of the upper Mississippi had built up a full head of steam. Ferries churned back and forth and back across the river, from Burlington to East Burlington, from April to November, carrying emigrants at a rate that rose, by the mid-1850s, to six and seven hundred teams each day. The railroad was taking over the task of the Conestoga wagon. As the network of steel rails spread along and over the contours of the midcontinent, Burlington emerged as a rail-era version of 1840s Independence: a doorway to the West. East Burlington, on the Illinois side of the Mississippi, became the western terminus of the Chicago and Burlington Railroad; Burlington, on the Iowa side, became the eastern railhead of the Burlington and Missouri line.[5] Charles Starker became a retail and wholesale grocer. He borrowed four thousand dollars capital from his family, went into partnership with one Adolph Meyer, and never saw red ink again.

The necessities of business-building forced Starker to sacrifice most of his architectural and engineering interests during the 1850s. He and Marie tried to build a family, but with singularly tragic results. Their first five children all died of "stomach complaint" after being taken off the breast during their second summers. Arthur, born in 1856, was the first to survive; Clara, born in 1860, also lived. Both received their parents' fullest pampering; after losing five infants, Charles and Marie Starker had built up a considerable store of parental affection.

Starker's grocery business rode the high wave of prosperity that came south on the river and west on the rails. In 1868, the consolidated Chicago, Burlington, and Quincy railroad spanned the Mississippi with a new bridge, the first to cross the river at Burlington. The rush to the latest tier of homestead territories — Kansas, Colorado, Nebraska, the Dakotas — was on. The hopeful migrants surged through Burlington, lured by story and broadside to the promised lands of the pushed-back frontier. By 1875, the year Starker and his new partner "Uncle" Hagemann sold the business, their sales had reached a hefty $800,000. Starker had also been active in the Burlington banking community since the early 1860s, where he met with similar success. In 1862, he became a director of the First National Bank of Burlington; in 1868 he became president of the Burlington Loan and Building Association; and in 1874, fearing the prospect of retirement once he sold the grocery, he, with several other prominent citizens, formed the Iowa State Savings Bank, with Starker serving as president.

Such prosperity allowed Starker to devote himself to his primary interests — the community and its development. While living on North Hill, he served as alderman, and initiated rehabilitation of the dilapidated North Hill Public Square. He became director of the Aspen Grove Cemetery, raising funds, donating from his own private fortune, laying out the grounds, and supervising the plantings. His interest in financing made him one of the town's most loved and trusted men. Charles Starker was a capitalist in the best sense of the word, providing capital and credit to young businessmen in whom he saw promise. In the 1870s he made three trips to Germany during which he persuaded some three hundred families to immigrate to Burlington. His proselytizing not only served his banking interests, but gave Burlington a European flavor that is still evident a century later.

ᘓ

Charles Starker was a deliberate settler. He found Burlington, he liked it, he stayed. For other settlers, the process took longer; but like the cottonwood seeds that rode the prairie air, the western pioneers eventually had to alight, there to prosper, or wither, or rise again to the wind. Charles Leopold was simply less deliberate than his brother-in-law Charles Starker. Prompted by the demands of a growing family, or by the hopes of a frontier-bound wife, or by the sheer desire for more society, Leopold moved his family east from Liberty and joined his in-laws at Burlington in the early 1850s, just as Starker was starting in the grocery business. Leopold began another career as a baker and brewer. Thusneld gave birth to their seventh child and fourth son, named Carl, in Burlington in 1858 (an eighth child would die as an infant).

The Leopolds, however, were not yet ready to settle once and for all. When the Civil War broke out, the clan returned to Liberty. Charles enlisted in the state militia, which provided the sole line of defense against the bushwhackers then terrorizing the towns of western Missouri. Leopold was a staunch opponent of slavery, and it is said that he ran a waystation on the underground railroad.

Growing up in Liberty, young Carl found adventure in every tallgrass swell and streamside wood. Once during the war, he was fishing a nearby creek with his older brother Theodore, who was dressed in his Union blues. A band of guerilla bushwhackers rode by. These were dangerous times, and any uniformed stranger was liable to be shot without question or cause. The brothers ducked beneath a bridge, and watched and waited as the armed horsemen rode overhead. Another time, Carl was playing with his friends when the James Gang blazed into town and held up the Clay County Savings Association. It was the first premeditated bank robbery in the nation's history, and the first crime committed by the West's most famous outlaws. The gang left Liberty in a fearful storm of gunsmoke clouds and thunderous reports. Their guns echoed for weeks in the talk of Carl and his playmates.[6]

Inside the Leopold house, the atmosphere was genteel. There was a definite air of haughtiness about the family. Their lineage did include genuine nobility some generations back, but the Leopolds were in free Missouri now, and had no more claim to hereditary distinction than did the Duke and the Dauphin on Huck Finn's raft. Still, the family continued to receive newspapers from the capitals of Europe, and gossiped about the activities of the tangled peerage to which they felt they yet belonged. They were not wealthy. Leopold came to America with money, but he extended many a loan that went unpaid, and his various business ventures never were very lucrative.

Carl was the youngest in the family and developed his own interests, chief of which was hunting. His father was not a hunter, so Carl had to learn on his own or with friends. His quarry was abundant and close at hand. The native grasslands, still not wholly sodbusted, offered quail and prairie chicken, while the woodlands harbored woodcock and turkey. Every field and hill held the promise of rabbit, squirrel, and woodchuck. Skies darkened with the legendary flights of passenger pigeons. Spring and fall brought twenty species of waterfowl in migration, and in numbers that, like the northern pines, seemed inexhaustible.

Carl grew up a hunter; he loved the outdoors, and hunting, whether as cause or effect, took him there. As a consequence, Carl's attitude was different from that of his gregarious family. He retained something of the family's aristocratic bearing, but without its aristocratic affectations. While the others still looked back across the ocean to Europe, Carl looked to what he had—a land of great demands and opportunities, a living frontier right outside the door. A generation later, Carl would tell his own boys stories of Missouri's hardship, of its undiminished bounty, and of how he lined his thin shoes with newspaper so he could go afield in the winter.

~

Clara Starker spent her early years on North Hill in Burlington. She was a bright girl, petite, pretty, and energetic to the point of restlessness. Her father indulged her completely, providing her with a private education as well as his own informal instruction in German culture, gardening, and the fine arts. Her mother passed along the domestic arts, including an extensive knowledge of German cuisine. Although Clara had difficulty with her hearing in one ear, she loved music and played the piano well. While traveling in Europe with her family, she had developed a deep love of grand opera. For years to come, she would make an annual pilgrimage to the opera in Chicago to relive the magnificence.

But all was not drawing rooms and box seats. There was another side to Clara. Her daintiness lasted only as long as her mischievous sense of humor and her outspokenness allowed. She enjoyed the outdoors much as her father did, and eagerly joined in the ongoing planting and gardening. Hardly one to shy away from physical activities, she won several trophies for her figure skating and would to the end of her life remain a devoted sports fan. As a teenager, Clara went east to study music in a Boston finishing school.

At about this time, her father purchased a new home, a large Italianate house on the lip of Prospect Hill at 101 Clay Street. The house had been built after the Civil War by its previous owner, General Isham Gilbert, in an area that supported many of the fruit tree plantations that gave Burlington its early nickname, "Orchard City." The home, "commanding an extensive view of the Mississippi River," was said to be "one of the handsomest in Burlington."[7] It stood starkly on the point of Prospect Hill, to the south of town. Its exterior was extensively trimmed with gingerbread detailing and other ornamentation. Inside, a large formal drawing room dominated the first floor, and three bedrooms the second. An impressive winding staircase with a wide walnut bannister connected the three floors. The most striking feature of the house was its two-story rounded bay, with great curved windows, facing east across the valley of the Mississippi.

When Starker learned that the Gilbert house was available, he decided to move his family there, despite the talk that Prospect Hill was too close to the river and its mosquitoes for healthy living. The view was too enticing to resist. Once there, Starker set about transforming the grounds around the house. At the time of settlement, most of Burlington's blufftops were cleared of their native trees in order to provide an unrestricted view of the Mississippi. Gilbert, following the Victorian style of the day, had kept the landscape formal. Starker, following his own inclinations toward the picturesque landscape tradition, began planting spruces, pines, and larches. He developed a three-block-long footpath, open to the neighborhood, along the rim of Prospect Hill. He nursed dozens of species of flowers in Gilbert's old greenhouse. A Burlington *Hawkeye* article described the Starker compound as a "bird's paradise," and praised this "effort to preserve some of the greatest gifts of nature. . . . Birds that were daily visitors in the long ago, and now but rarely seen, are found nesting on this idyllic spot, returning with the seasons, with the knowledge of security for themselves and their young."[8]

After completing her schooling out east, Clara Starker came back to Burlington. In the 1880s, even a well-educated young lady had little choice but to return home and dutifully assume her place in local society.

Meanwhile, many of the Missouri Leopolds had returned to Burlington, this time to stay. As a teenager in the mid-1870s, Carl Leopold decided to pursue a business career. He went to Burlington and sought advice from his now well-to-do uncle Charles Starker. The wo were of like temperament, and shared an enjoyment of the outdoors, though with different orientations. With Starker's help, Carl enrolled in the Burlington Business College, where he learned the fundamentals of bookkeeping and business organization.

Carl had not seen the last of his prairie hunting grounds. In 1876, he took a job as a travelling salesman for the Donahue and McCosh Iron and Steel Company in Burlington. Carl's sales territory lay in Kansas and Nebraska. His regular trips there gave him another chance to be out on the frontier as well as an important role in the further retreat of that frontier. As a boy in Liberty in the 1860s, Carl had watched the fresh hides of the bison being shipped east off the open range. As a travelling salesman in the 1870s and 1880s, he now saw the gathered bones of the vanquished herds piled high for miles alongside the rails, awaiting shipment east for processing into ceramics, fertilizer, and glue. Carl rode by buckboard out to the isolated farm villages, visiting the general stores to sell barbed wire, the principal product in his sales kit. Invented in 1874, barbed wire was already pinning down the farthest-flung corners of the now bison-free prairie.

Carl had another product to pitch. He was an excellent roller skater, and sold skates with the understanding that when a town had built its new rink, he would return on opening night to hold a demonstration. The young people, starved for entertainment, naturally flocked to see Carl's elaborate spins and tricks, and to receive instructions from the master himself. As Carl told the story, the result was a debacle. The young men, anxious to prove their mettle, donned their new skates and sped off to the far end of the rink. Then they tried to turn. The damage was horrendous. Bruised skaters cried in misery and bemoaned their missing skin and torn trousers. Skate marks on the wall reached shoulder height.

Carl enjoyed his work and did well at it. Among its other fringe benefits, it allowed him to indulge his love of hunting. Along the Platte and in the prairies, much of the game was as abundant as ever. In contrast with the bison, some small game species initially benefited from the white man's arrival and the application of his agricultural techniques. Carl took ample advantage. "I have been chicken shooting twice," he wrote to his sister in

August 1878 from Fairmont, Nebraska, "and had quite a good bit of sport. Last evening three of us were out from 4 o'clock till eight and brought home 60 young birds + mules (Jack Rabbits)."[9] Such a bag would become increasingly rare as the pines housed the new farmers and barbed wire defined their new fields. Carl Leopold was a good man caught in the historical tension of the frontier. He was unknowingly responsible, to a personal degree, for the inroads made against those things he most dearly valued — the wild game and wild places of his youth.

∽

In between his business trips west, Carl boarded with the Starkers. It was then that he and his cousin Clara Starker came to know one another. Besides skating and maternal grandparents, they seemed to have had little in common. Clara was sociable and more than a little sentimental; Carl was a practical young man, self-reliant and hard-working. She liked opera; he liked hunting. Evidently, several years passed before their mutual attraction overcame their mutually exclusive interests. Whether or not they courted formally, they fell in love and were married on February 25, 1886. Marriages between first cousins were not so unusual at the time, and there were no apparent objections from their families.

Carl was still a travelling salesman. Clara no doubt wanted to have him stay in Burlington, a desire underscored when she became pregnant soon after their marriage. Her father looked over the possibilities. He found the Northwestern Furniture Company, a seven-year-old Burlington concern. Starker called on E. D. Rand, an old partner who had made his fortune in lumber (the Rand and Carson Lumber Company was one of the earliest and most successful on the whole Mississippi, taking their pine from the Chippewa and St. Croix). Starker provided the connection, and Rand the capital. In the summer of 1886, they took over the company, and decided to specialize in building desks and other office furniture. Carl Leopold was installed as chief manager. Carl had hardly ever used a desk, much less built one.

Carl was away on company business in St. Louis when 101 Clay Street gained a new resident. On January 11, 1887, Clara gave birth to a son. Carl contributed a first name, Rand, in honor of his new business partner and financier. Clara contributed a second name, Aldo, in honor of Aldo Sommers, an old family friend from Quincy, Illinois. That spring, the Starkers and Leopolds commemorated the arrival of Rand Aldo by planting a small red oak sapling in front of their house on Prospect Hill.

2

Prospect Hill
(1887–1904)

FIVE YEARS before Aldo Leopold's birth, in 1882, Mark Twain undertook a tour of the Mississippi River from New Orleans to St. Paul. When he came to Burlington, he found a "fine and flourishing" city, progressive and beautiful in its Flint Hills setting. "In Burlington, as in all these upper river towns," he wrote, "one breathes a go-ahead atmosphere which tastes good in the nostrils. An opera house has lately been built there which is in strong contrast with the shabby dens which usually do duty as theaters in cities of Burlington's size." The elegant opera house that Twain observed was built largely through the efforts of Charles Starker, whose expertise in financing, the arts, architecture, and construction made him the indispensable man in such efforts. For Twain, the opera house was emblematic of the changes he saw coming to his river, "the great Mississippi, the majestic, the magnificent Mississippi, rolling its mile-wide tide along, shining in the sun."[1]

In the 1880s, the Mississippi River was still a semi-wild stream. Like the pineries and prairies, the river had not yet yielded completely before the pioneers. At Burlington, its waters normally ran about a half-mile across, swelling in springtime, drying down in the summer. The Burlington waterfront resounded with the hornblast arrivals and departures of steamboats — the *Josephine*, the *Libbie Conger*, the *St. Paul*, the *Diamond Joe*, the *Prairie Bird*, the *Sultana*, and a hundred others. Up north, the forests were falling fast. The steamboats had long since assumed the job of transporting the pine, pushing and tugging rafts half a mile long around the twists and through the rapids of the river. Every railhead had its sawmill, and every sawmill came alive when the winter's ice melted and timber poured south. In Burlington, the Burlington Lumber Company had its boom on the riverfront right below Prospect Hill near the CB&Q bridge. There were several other mills upstream. As the mills prospered, the raftsmen that Twain knew as a cub pilot were first replaced and then romanticized. That raftsman, steering by guile, experience, and instinct, drinking and singing as intently as he piloted, belonged to a nation in its childhood. A growing nation could hardly pause to watch as he drifted into memory.

In fifty years, Burlington had grown from a frontier landing to a lively city of the proportions that Twain found. To its 25,000 residents, Burlington was no longer an outpost, or a way station on the route west; it was home. In the new opera house, the citizens of Burlington saw minstrel shows, light opera, burlesques and popular plays, Buffalo Bill's Wild West Show, and Burlington High School's graduation ceremonies. And what the opera house was to Burlington, Burlington and the other river and prairie towns were to the nation: a sign that European culture had come upon the wilderness, adapted itself, and taken root.

The inescapable converse to this fact was that the frontier, and the wilderness before it, had dwindled. In 1890, a report from the Superintendent of the Census in Washington showed that, demographically speaking, the frontier of American settlement had disappeared. The maturing nation was now bound to pause and reflect. In 1893, a young historian from Wisconsin travelled to the Columbian Exposition in Chicago. Frederick Jackson Turner addressed a meeting there of his scholarly colleagues on the meaning of this American passage. He was among the first to seize upon what he called "The Significance of the Frontier in American History." He distilled his idea down to a memorable sentence: "The existence of an area of free land, its continuous recession, and the advance of American settlement westward, explain American development."[2] Later generations of historians would criticize the simplicity of Turner's "frontier thesis," but it was too basic a realization to disregard; it had to be amended and modified, but it could not be denied outright. The roots of the American character could not be understood apart from the virgin soils, the free land, to which they had been transplanted and in which they grew.

Turner went on to confront the question that his idea begged: how would the passing of the frontier affect those characteristics that were uniquely American? He described those qualities he had in mind. "That coarseness and strength combined with acuteness and inquisitiveness; that practical, inventive turn of mind, quick to find expedients; that masterful grasp of material things, lacking in the artistic but powerful to affect great ends; that restless, nervous energy; that dominant individualism, working for good and for evil, and withal the buoyancy and exuberance which comes with freedom—these are the traits of the frontier, or traits called out elsewhere because of the existence of the frontier."[3]

Those traits, evoked in the wilds, nurtured on the frontiers, had too great a hold on the American imagination simply to vanish, but they would have to adapt to the new condition of American life. How would they adapt?

13

Turner was a historian, not a prophet. He did offer a general answer to this "problem of the West," as he called it, when he observed that it would require "original social ideas and social adjustments for the American nation." Subsequent American history would record these ideas and adjustments. The conservation movement was only one such development, but one which was central to the "problem" and which would concern the quality of the land and life for all future generations.

Mark Twain's 1882 journey took him further into the headlands of the upper Mississippi. "The majestic bluffs that overlook the river along through this region," he wrote, "charm one with the grace and variety of their forms and the soft beauty of their adornment. . . . And it is all as tranquil and reposeful as dreamland, and has nothing this-worldly about it—nothing to hang a fret or worry upon. . . . Until the unholy train comes tearing along—which it presently does, ripping the sacred solitude to rags and tatters with the devil's war whoop and the roar and thunder of its rushing wheels—and straightway you are back in this world. . . ."[4]

Harbinger of the frontier's end, the railroad was now well established as Burlington's dominant institution. Charles Eliot Perkins built the Chicago, Burlington, and Quincy into one of the great railroad empires of the West, its rails extending from Chicago to the Rockies. By 1892, the bridge at Burlington had to be rebuilt so it could handle double the traffic. By Pullman car and boxcar, the free land filled in. For farmer and lumberman both, the steel rail provided that vital link between source and use, between the virgin supply and civilization's demand.

From what Clara called "our lofty perch on the dear old Flint Hills," the Starkers and Leopolds enjoyed an expansive view of all this activity during the 1880s and 1890s. That view, now framed by Starker's growing trees, took in forty miles of river and, to the east, an eight-mile-wide flood plain of timber and low meadows, tangled sloughs and swamps, stretching away to the Illinois uplands in the distance. But the physical vista the family enjoyed was no less spectacular than the historical one. The frontier passed before their eyes. At the intersection of these two great axes of American development, the river and the railroad, Prospect Hill looked out over a nation coming of age.

∽

Soon after Aldo was born—his first name, Rand, was never used—Carl and Clara Leopold had two more children, and planted two more trees. Marie was born in 1888, and Carl Jr. followed in 1892. Carl and Clara's kinship caused some initial anxiety about the children's condition, but they all turned out to be bright and healthy ("Well, I guess we got by lucky," Carl would sometimes remark).

The big house was suddenly cramped for space. "Oma" and "Opa" Starker used the front bedroom on the second floor, the five Leopolds used the back bedroom, and two maids had small rooms of their own. After grandfather Starker had had enough of the three restless grandchildren, he approached Clara one day and said, "Liebchen, I think I will build you a house out in the cow pasture. What kind of house would you like?" "Why, you're the architect," Clara replied, "and I don't know what kind of house I'd like . . . but it will have to have good, deep windows, deep enough for my chameleon cage" (chameleons were the fashionable pets of the day). Starker built the house, with suitably deep chameleon windows, to the west of the main house. The Leopolds moved there in 1893. The last of their children, Frederic, was born there two years later.

There was continual traffic between the Starker and Leopold back doors. German remained the household language until the children enrolled in Prospect Hill School. By that time, the Charles Starker influence was engrained. A jovial man, warm and commanding, Starker set the tone of family life with the depth and breadth of his interests. In the afternoon he could be found working in the gardens or taking a glass of his wine. He would offer the grandchildren a little sip and entertain them with a story, lead them around the grounds on inspection, or draw them a picture. Starker still had an uncanny drawing hand; his little trees and squirrels and birds seemed to come alive on the paper.

The land around their two homes served as a common ground of activity and creativity for the entire family. The estate contained about three acres. Its thin calcareous soil challenged all their gardening skills, but the hilltop blossomed under their care. Remnants of the old orchard still produced apples, pears, and cherries. New trees were constantly being transplanted, old ones pruned. The family milk cow provided a reliable supply of rich fertilizer. In the spring, every hand from Charles Starker to little Frederic was out at the garden preparing the vegetable patches, or tending the beds of tulips, lilies, roses, violets, crocus, bloodroots, orchids, and ferns. Even in the winter, the greenhouse was alive with hyacinths and roses, nasturtiums and azaleas, and a prize collection of tropical palms.

The children spent their earliest years in this warm, open, and decidedly Germanic environment. Like Starker's landscapes, the atmosphere in the Leopold home was cultivated but informal, rich in life, but not forced or stuffy. There was always music. In the evenings, while Clara played the piano in the parlor, Charles would explain to Aldo what the music was saying. Sometimes, in the long summer afternoons, the family rode in the wagon out onto the Iowa prairie. Holidays brought the wonders of the candlelit tannenbaum and grandmother's fancy holiday cakes, though none of the family attended church on a regular basis. Starker was ostensibly a Lutheran, but not a churchgoer. Carl Leopold took a dim view of preachers of any ilk. The children were not influenced in any particular direction in their spiritual development, but left to their own devices, and their own conclusions.

Aldo grew to be a bright, inquisitive lad, with sandy hair and striking blue-green eyes. Reserved in company, he was cheerful and outgoing with the family. He had his father's sturdy frame and steady character, but his mother's well-defined features: a broad forehead, precise eyes, a strong nose, prominent lips, and a sharp jawline. Aldo was plainly Clara's favorite. She loved all her children with the keenest devotion, but in her eyes Aldo was something special. The other children recognized the situation, and simply accepted it as a fact of life. Aldo recognized it too, but he could do nothing much about it, except feel embarrassed, and take advantage on occasion. Considering that he could do absolutely no wrong as far as his mother was concerned, Aldo did remarkably little wrong, indulging only in an occasional cake-stealing or school-skipping.

All the children were close, and Aldo would often lead them skating on the river in the wintertime, boating in the summer. Aldo and his brother Carl were especially good pals, exploring the bluffs and the riverbank below, holding midnight snowball fights on the roof, fetching the mail downtown on Sunday mornings, setting traps in the nearby woods, and skinny-dipping in Flint Creek. There was a certain degree of danger in all this: once Aldo and Carl nearly killed themselves slipping over the bluff while playing in the yard after an ice storm. Their father had to come to the rescue. Aldo was inseparable from his other companion, an Irish terrier named Spud. Aldo's schoolmates even nicknamed him, "Spuddo." Spud was only one of several dogs that occupied and sometimes overwhelmed the Leopold home. There was also old Flick, Carl's best hunting dog, and Leo, not so expert as Flick, but almost.[5]

In 1892, Aldo entered Burlington's excellent school system. He was a precocious student, interested in many things, and good at most everything he was interested in. At Prospect Hill School, he learned the basics, and his native curiosity took over from there. Like his grandfather, he was an able artist, and at an early age could turn out a creditable still life or Burlington landscape. His boyhood reading reflected his background: German literature, philosophy, and poetry from Clara, outdoor stories from Carl. Aldo enjoyed the former, but preferred the latter: the adventures of Hiawatha and Daniel Boone, the features of *Outing* magazine, and, later, the writings of Henry David Thoreau, Jack London, Stewart Edward White, and Ernest Thompson Seton.

Leopold's interest in the natural world came easily, an all but inevitable consequence of his family and environment. It is impossible to say just what first caught Aldo's attention, but the sensations common to all children—the flash of color in a bird's wing, the appeal of a tree shape, the smell carried on the wind, the feel of sun and rain—soon began to grow into a deeper aptitude and interest. As an eleven-year-old, he wrote in his school composition book, "I like to study birds. I like the wren best of all birds. We had thirteen nests of wrens in our yard last summer. We hatched one hundred and twenty young wrens last summer. Here are a few of our birds." He listed thirty-nine species that he had identified. "I like wrens because they do more good than almost any other bird, they sing sweetly, they are very pretty, and very tame. I could have caught them many a time if I wanted to."[6] When he was thirteen, his mother and father gave him a copy of Frank M. Chapman's *Handbook of Birds of Eastern North America;* it became the foundation of his lifelong interest in birds.

As the children grew, Carl Leopold taught them to appreciate in a more than casual manner the ways of the natural world. In the years since the establishment of what was now the Rand and Leopold Desk Company, Carl had not made a great, or even consistent, profit, but the company had survived and its reputation was growing. The factory employed some one hundred men, turning out large rolltop desks for use in the nation's offices. The Leopold desk, built with the finest cherry, oak, and walnut wood, became known for its superior quality, and sold nationwide. Carl Leopold was a businessman of the highest integrity. His approach was as simple as it was risky: he wanted to build the best desk he could, and if he could make a profit at it, so much the better. The desk he built was the best, and profits were fair enough that he was able to buy out the Rand interest in the company in 1899. Carl ran the business, renamed the Leopold Desk Company, according to a fundamental credo that graced the heading of the company's stationery: "Built on Honor to Endure."[7]

In his advancement from prairie salesman to head of a business and family, Carl had not changed in at least one respect: his love for the outdoors and the hunt remained as strong as ever. With his long face and bushy, brown, upturned mustache, he was sometimes mistaken for Kaiser Wilhelm, but in his attitudes and interests he resembled no one so much as a man he much admired, Theodore Roosevelt. Like the soon-to-be president, Carl Leopold was a positive, firm man, though perhaps not so bullying; he had an adventurer's passion for the outdoors, but also a naturalist's understanding of it; and in his view of society, he was both conservative and progressive at the same time. Unlike Roosevelt, he was not a student of history, nor did he make history in such a prominent way. But he could read history in what was happening to the natural world he loved.

When the white settlers first came to the Flint Hills, they found abundant game on the diverse terrain. From the upland prairie and oak-hickory groves, down the wooded ravines to the river's islands and braided backwater, the bounty included prairie chicken and passenger pigeon, bobwhite quail, white-tailed deer, wild turkey, woodcock, woodchuck, rabbit, and squirrel. In 1840, there were still elk in the country, and even wolves. Most impressive, however, were the waterfowl. Located in the narrow bottleneck of the Mississippi flyway, Burlington was witness to the incomparable pageantry of their biannual migrations. In the spring, the scattered ducks and geese converged as they reached southern Illinois, flew north along the Mississippi basin, and dispersed again upon reaching Minnesota and Wisconsin. In the fall the flight reversed. The early observer atop Burlington's bluffs gained an eyelevel view of one of the most spectacular wildlife displays the continent has ever offered. The hunter in the marshes below gained one of its most promising shots.

At the time, there were no restrictions on what or how much game a hunter could shoot. He was limited only by what he wanted and what he could carry. Supplying markets and restaurants across the nation, the market hunter was the prime beneficiary of this unrestricted enterprise, gathering literally boatloads and wagonloads of game for sale, playing the role in the wildlife drama that the lumber baron played in the northwoods and the sodbuster on the plains: the reaper of the primeval crop. In the Midwest, the principal targets of the market hunter were waterfowl, prairie chicken, and passenger pigeon. For a time, the commercial value of game birds exceeded even that of the plains bison. In a time of plenty, there was no need to be careful, sparing, or prudent with one's shot. The slaughter of the migratory waterfowl was the most overwhelming. Declines in populations were increasingly evident and progressively worse through the 1880s and 1890s. By the turn of the century, numbers were plummeting and there was still no effective limit on the amount of game one could take.[8]

Carl Leopold was among those who saw the trend and adjusted his hunting technique accordingly.[9] By the time his boys began to hunt, he had a well-developed personal code of sportsmanship. To avoid losing a downed bird, he never loaded a gun until the sun had actually risen. He always used a double-barreled gun so that he could take a second shot at a bird he had wounded with the first. He pursued crippled birds until they were found or at least until a reasonable search had been made. He never would use the new automatic or pump guns, believing that their power was too excessive and tempted the hunter to shoot at game that was out of range. His own gun was a Lefever sixteen gauge, with a range of about forty yards. He never hunted after the sun went down. He set his own personal bag limit, and stopped hunting certain species altogether. Eventually, he gave up all spring hunting of waterfowl, and became an outspoken critic of the legal sale of game.[10]

His sons were not initially bound by these rules that Carl imposed on himself; they were to learn for themselves. Each of the boys in their turn began hunting when Carl thought they were ready. Aldo started when he was twelve or thirteen, but by then he was already well-versed in his father's methods. At first, the boys accompanied their father without a gun, helping to retrieve game and incidentally learning to appreciate the sheer hard work of an all day's outing. Soon they were allowed to carry an unloaded gun, to grow accustomed to its weight and safe handling. Carl sternly admonished them to "never point a gun at anything you don't intend to kill." He started the boys out with a single-barrelled shotgun, figuring that if they had only one shot, it was sure to be a carefully planned and executed one. The gun had no safety; Carl thought this gave a false sense of security. On his first quail hunt with his father, Aldo blazed away his entire supply of shells and took just two birds home. The initiation process was tedious, but effective. Aldo turned out to be a crack shot, as did his brothers after him.

Carl chose his times and places for hunting carefully. He stopped hunting on Sundays, not out of any devotion to the Sabbath, but in order to avoid the hordes of other church-neglecting hunters. Over the years, Carl found a number of choice spots to which he returned with his sons year after year—Viele, Bard, Painter's Valley, Batavia. The closest spots, where the boys took most of their training, were right along the river. The Crystal Lake Hunt Club and the Lone Tree Hunt Club lay to the north and south respectively of the railroad tracks on the Illinois side of the Mississippi. Charles Starker was an early member of the Crystal Lake Club, and Carl Leopold was active in both. On a typical Saturday, Carl, the dogs, and one of the boys (their ages were such that Aldo, Carl Jr., and Frederic rarely hunted together as boys) were up before the sun. After the walk down Main Street to the Union depot, father and son enjoyed a breakfast of milk, a baked apple, and cold, day-old baked pork and beans at the lunch counter; Carl was of the opinion that pancakes and such could hardly sustain a long day's hunt. Then dogs and hunters rode one of the morning locals across the river to the clubs, where the train stopped on request. If Carl reached his limit during the hunt, he would play retriever while his son got in some practice. Aldo's favorite spot was Eagle Swamp at Crystal Lake. His strongest early impressions of the field were of Eagle's quiet waters, its reedy basin, and blue wings topping the trees on cool morning air. He shot his first duck there one winter sunset, after anticipating it for a full afternoon. He never forgot the "unspeakable delight" he felt when his patience was rewarded. After a day afield, the hunters returned across the river with their take.[11]

As often as not, Carl left his gun behind and took the family and friends to the woods on outings and picnics, just to observe the goings-on. He was a very good naturalist, and if he lacked the scientist's special training, he had a lifelong outdoorsman's ability to read the woods. "Those outings," one tag-along friend recalled, "were really lectures on the move about the trees and bushes, the birds and swamp animals, and even how to make a fire and afterward to dispose of it. In it all there was much about the woods in general and how they should be managed and preserved."[12] In young Frederic's eyes, Papa was a wizard pulling surprises out of thin air. "He would open up a decaying hollow log to show us the life dwelling inside, such as mice or large insects. If we came to a certain type of old tree snag he would point out the signs that showed it to be occupied by mink. . . . He might show us where a mink had dug into a muskrat house to kill himself a muskrat for dinner. He pointed out the old raccoon droppings which might be identified by the content of wild grape seeds and skins or of the bleached shell of crayfish he had eaten. We did not need to kill game to have an exciting afternoon in the swamp or field."[13]

Carl Leopold assumed responsibility for the sport he loved; he did not preach it, even to those close to him, but preferred to make his point less directly. One relative who regularly showed up at the Leopold-Starker doorsteps and dinner table was old Uncle Edward Runge. An inveterate hunter who lived a hermit's existence in the river swamps outside of town, he showed up every Sunday in the same dark suit, white shirt, and string necktie, to partake of Clara's pièce de résistance, a huge steamy chicken pot pie. At the dinner table, Edward was given to telling epic tales of his hunting exploits, in colorful detail and with full pantomiming of the action. Clara hid the fine-stemmed glasses on these occasions, for fear that Uncle Edward would sweep them away in his exuberance. One day Carl accidentally shot a wood duck, a species then endangered by overhunting. He had the duck stuffed and mounted hanging upside down by one foot, as if it had just been strung up, and displayed it just so on the dining room wall. Edward, who scoffed at Carl's self-imposed restrictions, saw the duck the next Sunday and commented with relish, "Carl, I see you killed a wood duck. I thought you didn't approve of killing wood ducks!" "Yes," Carl replied, "but I made a mistake and the bird was so beautiful, I had to hang it there for all to see." A week later, the duck was still hanging. "I see you still have your wood duck from last week there," Edward noticed. "Well," Carl replied, "the weather has been cool, so I just left the duck there." The following Sunday Edward could not resist a quick sniff of the still-suspended duck. "Oh, yes," Carl explained, "I just sprinkled a bit of soda on it a few days ago." When Edward came to dinner the fourth week, he went straight for the dining room, and found the wood duck still hanging. Realizing finally that he had been hoodwinked, Edward furled his eyebrow and said not a single word about the bird.[14]

Although Carl Leopold was generally a good-natured, wry-humored man, he had a more serious, self-inquiring side to his personality. When factory concerns or other matters weighed on him, he was apt to turn inward and neglect the outside world. He was known to rise in anger when an obvious stupidity disrupted the factory, and more than one incompetent clerk was fired outright. Such moments, however, were rare. Once, during what he called "the warm days of February," Carl took Aldo up to Schlapp's Run on Crystal Lake to shoot crows that were preying on fish killed by the winter's freeze. The hunters were sitting with faithful Leo in a willow coppice when out of the south flew a sudden flock of pintails, the spring's very first. The flock winged overhead closeby as Aldo looked up to the ducks, then to his father, then to the ducks. Carl by then had given up spring-shooting, but his eyes gleamed, and his trigger finger itched. The ducks continued north unmolested. Carl turned to his son, paused, and then said with a smile on his face, "Just prospecting."[15]

ᔐ

Charles Starker spent the last years of his life working for the improvement of Burlington. He became director of the Des Moines County Agricultural Society, and a founder of the Burlington Public Library. He also served in various positions with the public schools, including a lengthy term as school board treasurer. He helped plan the new park for the Union depot, the impressive Odd Fellows Building, and the city's state-of-the-art sewer system. When in 1894 several of the town's businessmen appealed for a shorter route from the top of Sixth Street to Lower Town, Starker and the city's engineer responded with Snake Alley, a winding series of five half-curves and two quarter-curves that Ripley later immortalized as "the crookedest street in the world." Starker's crowning achievement came in his work on Crapo Park on a bluff downriver of Prospect Hill. He persuaded the German farmers there to sell their land to the city, then served on the park commission and directed the landscaping effort. The result was a park that instantly became the city's pride, and remains one of the nation's most picturesque.[16]

Charles Starker died at home of a stroke on February 9, 1900. The *Burlington Democrat-Journal* reported the next morning that Burlington had lost a citizen "whose like we shall possibly not see again until generations have passed. . . . The news today of his death shocks the whole city. It is not probable that there is another man in this community who was so generally and cordially esteemed alike by all classes of the people. . . . No man more than Charles Starker has earned and merited the confidence of the community."[17] He was buried in Aspen Grove Cemetery, which he had helped design, underneath trees he had helped plant. His wife Marie died a few months later.

Clara's brother Arthur had died in 1893, at the age of thirty-seven. In his will, Charles Starker left his estate and his home to his only surviving child. Carl and Clara moved their family back to 101 Clay Street that spring of 1900.

༄

For the Leopold children, the most important day of the year, apart from Christmas, came early in August. Every year at that time, the family packed up and for six weeks moved its operations to the Les Cheneaux Islands at the far north end of Lake Huron. In order to provide summer relief for Clara's severe hay fever, Charles Starker had bought a membership in the Les Cheneaux Club on Marquette Island in the early 1890s.

In the earliest years, the family would take the CB&Q to Chicago and then clamber aboard the luxurious SS *Manitou* for the ride up Lake Michigan to Mackinac Island. Later, after the Michigan Central completed its northern line, the family made the trip by rail. The train ride from Chicago to Mackinaw City took all night. When the family awoke and looked out the windows, they found themselves in the recently cutover northwoods. Young scrub forests of jack pine, aspen, and paper birch grew on the lands where the slash fires had burned. On the farmsteads that dotted the gaunt landscape, farmers fenced their fields not with barbed wire, but with the massive, upturned stumps of the old white pines. In the final leg of the journey, the steamship *Algoma* ferried the family to Mackinac Island; the SS *Islander* then carried them down the Huron shore to the main dock of the Les Cheneaux Club.

Marquette Island was not wilderness, but it was the next closest thing. A maze of points, bays, spits, and inlets sheltered the island from the main body of Lake Huron. Its thin soil supported a northwoods mix of birch, aspen, poplar, cedar, maple, hemlock, balsam fir, spruce, and scattered red, white, and jack pines. On the Michigan mainland to the north, the lumbermen had removed all of the pine, leaving a legacy of second-growth woods and abandoned logging trails. There were still stands of the "big hardwoods," the rich original forest of sugar maple, hemlock, basswood, and yellow birch that once covered much of the upper Great Lakes. Unlike the midwestern agricultural frontier, the northern timber frontier did not become heavily populated, even when miners joined the lumberjacks. Two small villages, Hessel and Cedarville, served the local loggers and the summer residents of the islands, but settlement beyond the villages was sparse.

The Les Cheneaux Club provided all the amenities of civilization, including tennis courts, nightly dances in the clubhouse, and a rustic nine-hole golf course (where Carl Leopold was able to flaunt his championship form). The refined atmosphere of Mackinac Island was only an SS *Islander* trip away. For Aldo, none of the temptations could compare with the opportunity to *be* Daniel Boone. Marquette Island was of ideal size and definition for exploration: about six miles long and four miles wide, with long points extending into Lake Huron. Aldo produced several intricately drawn maps of the island, carefully illustrated with its typical trees, animals, and landmarks, and showing all its trails, including those that Aldo himself had cleared. When he was not busy exploring, Aldo was camping, or sailing, or swimming, or, most likely, fishing. Split Rock was the preferred smallmouth spot, with St. Ledger's Island a close second. Pike lurked in the weedbeds, while brook trout hid over in the cool cedar springs on the mainland. Carl Leopold's discipline extended to fishing: Aldo never kept a bass under a pound-and-a-half, nor a pike under three pounds. His prize catch in all his Les Cheneaux summers was a fifteen-pound muskie.

One summer day, Aldo was out on Mile Walk, a boardwalk loop built so that the less willing and able club members could get out to the woods. Aldo came upon a skunk ("sachet kittens," his father called them) and, having gun in hand, promptly killed it. He marked this momentous conquest by carving into the crossboards of the walk, in proper Daniel Boone style, the inscription, "Aldo Leopold killed a skunk here on August 20th, 1901."

Most of the club families left after Labor Day. The Leopolds and a few other self-reliant and hay-fever-suffering families stayed behind to enjoy the perfect days of early fall. This was when the serious outdoor activity began. The water was already too cold for swimming, but not for long outings to the wild Huron shore. On the mainland, the old logging trails and second-growth woods provided ideal ruffed grouse hunting. When the worst of the mosquito season was over, Carl led expeditions to the tiny, trout-laden inland creeks. Every fall, around the autumnal equinox, a storm would blow in out of the northwest and drive a stiff wind down the length of the bay. Carl knew that if he could position himself to the windward side of the goldeneye broods that had nested on the bay, he would be assured of a good shot. Goldeneye are deep-water ducks that require a lengthy take-off run before reaching full flight, and with correct maneuvering, the hunter in a boat could force the ducks to fly right by at close range. While Aldo, or the current second-in-command, manned the oars, Carl sat at the stern of the boat directing, and he always brought down at least two birds.

Then it was time to pack up the trunks. On the twenty-sixth of September, the last "Hay Fever Special" left Mackinaw City with the Leopold entourage aboard, and the children started to count again the months and weeks and days until their return.

The lands of the north were poor for most practical purposes except logging and mining. The overbearing hand of the lumber kings had depleted much of its original timber wealth. Agriculture in the north could never approach Iowa standards. Still, it was land rich in the raw material of adventure, and wild enough to inspire the imagination. The lonesome wails of the loons and the fog-muffled horns of the Soo steamers could still evoke a dream. The greatest adventure of all lay just over the northern horizon, at the end of the last logging road, beyond the farthest point of the bay. Looking that way, the young Leopold boys could see the mainland hills in the distance, and beyond that . . . nothing. "In our young minds," Frederic recalled, "we imagined that we were at the jumping-off place where to the north an endless wilderness extended to Hudson Bay and the arctic."[18] The imagined wilderness fueled a specific desire: for many years Aldo yearned to take a canoe trip north, to meet a north-flowing river, and to follow the river until he reached James Bay. The mystery over the horizon was the most inviting one, and Les Cheneaux would have been a very different place were that mystery not there.

∽

One of the summer residents of Les Cheneaux was Dr. Simon McPherson, an eastern educator. McPherson was headmaster of the Lawrenceville Preparatory School in New Jersey, near Princeton, and at some point, probably during the summer of 1901, the idea was broached that it might be to Aldo's advantage to obtain an eastern education. Clara was convinced: she had gone east to school herself and wanted nothing but the very best for her oldest boy. Carl was skeptical: he couldn't see the sense in spending all that money to send Aldo away when Burlington High School and Iowa State University could do just as good a job. He had hopes that Aldo would join him at the factory someday and carry on the family business. Clara was insistent. A decision was postponed until Aldo himself had a firmer idea of what he wanted to do.

In the meantime Aldo entered Burlington High School, which was indeed a superb school, but so overcrowded at the time that students were required to show up only for recitations. That suited him fine. Arranging his classes so that they were all in the afternoon, he could awaken early, take the first train across to Lone Tree and Crystal Lake, and enjoy a full morning afield before showing up at school. Once in the classroom, he proved himself a gifted student. In history class, his notes and essays ranged over topics from the Greeks and Romans to the heroes of American independence, from Chaldea and Persia to the Green Mountains and the Missouri Territory. Carefully prepared maps accompanied the essays. In biology, Leopold was introduced to the disciplined natural science that he would eventually make his life's work. He most enjoyed firsthand field studies, but readily learned, in class, the rudiments of plant and animal biology and the value of the experimental method. His anatomical drawings were rendered every bit as carefully as his maps.[19]

English class with Miss Rogers had the most lasting effect on Aldo. A strict but kindly disciplinarian, she belonged to that order of unheralded teachers whose own names are often forgotten, but whose influence endured in the solid competence and occasional brilliance of the students they taught. With her seemingly endless series of word lists, handwriting exercises, spelling lessons, and literature assignments, Miss Rogers successfully guided even her most reluctant students, and instilled in Leopold in particular a careful consideration for the written word that he would sustain in his own writing and teaching for the rest of his life.

To his classmates, Aldo was something of an enigma. They knew him as an outstanding student, and his family was highly regarded by all the townspeople, but Aldo himself was an unknown quantity. Away from the family, his sharp mind hid behind a wall of shyness, especially when it came to the girls who outnumbered the boys at school by three-to-one. With difficulty, Clara corralled him in dancing school and prodded him to dance with the daughters of family friends. He was trapped, but not broken. Aldo remained solitary in his ways, not antisocial, but nonsocial. His character lay somewhere between the Starker sense of civic duty and the Leopold sense of nobility. "He did not think he was cut from common cloth," his brother Frederic recalls, "and he wasn't."[20] In his school notebooks he collected quotations that impressed him:

Whittier:

> One our faith and one our longing,
> To make the world within our reach
> Somewhat better for our living
> And gladder for our speech.

Tennyson:

> Howe'er it be it seems to me
> 'Tis only noble to be good;
> Kind hearts are more than coronets
> And simple faith than Norman blood.

Emerson:

> Finish every day and be done with it; you have done what you could. Some blunders and absurdities no doubt have crept in; forget them as soon as you can. Tomorrow is a new day. Begin it well and serenely, and with too high a spirit to be cumbered with your old nonsense.

Aldo took the idealistic thoughts to heart. In the absence of any more structured moral training, such secular reflections combined with the family's attitudes to provide the strong ethical base on which Aldo stood. For a reserved teenager with a marked preference for the wild world, that stance made shyness all the more difficult to overcome.

Meanwhile, Leopold's study of birds became more disciplined. He first began to keep systematic records of his observations in 1902. As the migrations began in the early months of 1903, Aldo was up before the sun, out on the blufftop with his notebook in one hand and his grandmother's opera glasses in the other, gazing up into the trees.

The only other person up at that hour was the newsboy, Edwin Hunger. A poor classmate of Aldo's whose family lived on West Hill, Edwin picked up his one hundred and sixty Burlington *Hawkeyes* every morning at 3:45 and ended his delivery route on Prospect Hill. As he cut across the Leopold compound, he came upon Aldo. Edwin had never before seen a serious bird watcher. The boys became birding partners that spring. Edwin became Aldo's closest Burlington friend; Aldo became, in Edwin's words, "the finest and truest friend I've ever had."[21]

All spring long they kept close accounts of bird arrivals and departures. Aldo provided instruction on species and behavior, while Edwin provided the enthusiasm and support of a new convert. On foot they explored the nearby ravines. Bonn's Hollow was a favorite, as was Ransom's Hollow down the street, where Edwin's first big ornithological find was an early flock of evening grosbeaks. By trolley car they rode out to Starr's Cave, or continued on foot to the woods beyond town. By skiff they rowed across the swollen Mississippi to the shady, winding, mosquito-ridden sloughs on the Illinois bottomland. On one boat trip, Edwin was at the oars trying to handle the fast flood current when he spotted a cluster of snakes that had taken refuge in an overhanging tree. Eyeing a huge black snake in the cluster, Edwin rowed close, took an oar out of its lock, and swung wildly at the snake, delivering only a glancing blow as the current nudged the skiff into the trees and snakes. "Damn it," the normally softspoken Aldo cursed, "what did you do that for?!" The snakes dropped around the boat and the big black one lunged for the oar. Edwin managed to replace the oar and then pulled with all his might for the nearby railroad embankment. When calm was restored, Aldo apologized for losing his temper. "Sorry, hell," Edwin answered, "I'm the damn fool who should be sorry."[22]

Leopold revealed the tendency of his conservation attitudes that spring when a squatter cleared and planted corn on several acres of his favorite swamp woods directly across the river from Prospect Hill. Aldo was enraged. When the flood swept away the squatter and his corn, he was delighted. Edwin's expressions of pity for the farmer fell on deaf ears. Yet Aldo was no simple preservationist. He cheerfully shot away at the cats, hawks, crows, squirrels, and sparrows that bothered the birds he favored. He proudly wrote to his parents, who were vacationing in Hot Springs, Arkansas, that he had "shot eight sparrows in a few minutes" that day.[23]

He performed that feat by laying down grain in a long row and firing from one end when the sparrows came to feed. When the ladies of the local bird club came to him for guidance, he begged off, in part because of his debilitating shyness, but also because he regarded the ladies as lightweights, more interested in seeing their names in the *Hawkeye* than in birds. Aldo considered himself no mere birdwatcher, but an *amateur ornithologist*. When the ladies finally recruited Edwin as their guide, Aldo snickered.

Leopold's early study of birds had a pronounced effect on his perception of the natural world and, incidentally, on his writing. Spying the birds trained his eye to concentrate on even the most fleeting phenomena, while identifying them forced him to hone his descriptive talents. In his field notebook he described Bell's Vireo:

This peculiar vireo reminds one of a chat in his actions. In plumage he might be mistaken for a yellow-throat, except for the white throat and more greenish sides. His haunts were saplings and the lower branches of trees, and seen against the light his plumage had a fluffy appearance. His song was a very peculiar sputtering, on a rising scale, and was given during his search for insects. He did not hang by the feet like others of his genus, but kept the head raised and looking above him. He was not shy, on the contrary quite inquisitive, and was not restricted to thickets.[24]

This early study of birds also had an important effect on Leopold's inner self. He was likely thinking of himself when, many years later, he wrote, "I heard of a boy once who was brought up an atheist. He changed his mind when he saw that there were a hundred-odd species of warblers, each bedecked like to the rainbow, and each performing yearly sundry thousands of miles of migration about which scientists wrote wisely but did not understand. . . . I dare say this boy's convictions would be harder to shake than those of many inductive theologians."[25]

On the issue of Aldo's education, Clara's efforts to send him east finally prevailed. Carl still hoped he would return to college in Iowa, but that hope was also diminishing. He talked with his son about the possibility of joining the desk company, but Aldo had other thoughts. Through his reading, Aldo had developed an interest in the new field of forestry. Carl could hardly object. He was as responsible as anyone for his son's inclination. In a business based on a steady supply of lumber, Carl was well aware of the forest situation in the United States, and as an instinctive conservationist he understood the need to correct the predominating wasteful practices. Even a casual observer on Prospect Hill could see that, by the turn of the century, the pine rafts from the north were dwindling in size and frequency. Within a decade or so, the rafts would disappear altogether. There was as yet no demand for foresters, and only one school, at Yale University, that trained foresters. But with Teddy Roosevelt now installed in the White

27

House and arch-forester Gifford Pinchot at his side, the field was about to open wide. Aldo would head east to the Lawrenceville School the following January, and, if all went smoothly, continue on at Yale.

That summer of 1903, the Leopolds did not go north to Les Cheneaux. For some time, Carl had talked about going on a big game hunt with Frank Grover and his son Mortimer, friends from Les Cheneaux. In August, the Leopolds went to Colorado. The family spent a short time together at Estes Park before Carl and Aldo and the Grovers left for Montana. Along the way, they toured the "list of wonders" at Yellowstone. For Aldo this was the highest adventure, rivalling any canoe trip north. The census bureau may have declared the western frontier closed in 1890, but that was hard to believe when one was actually there. Aldo wrote back to the family in Colorado:

We passed through a beautiful country yesterday seeing many antelope and one fine blacktail buck. Woke this morning in 2 inches of snow. The air was damp so to keep our feet warm we walked the 23 miles to Cook through the snowstorm. On the way I found a small lake full of beaver, sign, cuttings, etc., and obtained fine specimens. Passed the foot of Grand Mountain, but could not see the summit on account of snow. Also saw fresh bear + elk tracks. Tomorrow we go to the Gilbert ranch (15 miles) and outfit the pack train for the "Hoodoos." According to natives, this storm will be succeeded by a long Indian summer, which will be very favorable for us.[26]

The natives were wrong about the weather. The snow continued, but the Leopolds and Grovers managed to reach the Gilbert ranch. Gilbert raised cattle, and as a sideline guided hunters into the nearby Hoodoo Mountains. The outfitting operation was a welcome alternative to the main ranch work, which was carried on with little of the frontier romance that so many eastern hunters came west to rediscover.

Aldo struck up a friendship with Gilbert's sixteen-year-old son Clarence. As the snow continued to fall, the three sets of fathers and sons started out for the mountains. From the "Hoodoo Mountain Camp" Carl wrote a note to his "Dear Bonnie" in Colorado. "We are in the hunting Country at last. Delayed by seven days of Continuous snow + guide's illness. May be late getting out on that account."[27] The camp was also beset by Mr. Gilbert's curious fresh bread, which had the consistency of chewing gum. When this was brought to Gilbert's attention, he replied in his broad old country accent, "Ya, it's yuste the vay I like it!" For years to come, Aldo and his father shrugged off many an outdoor disappointment with a firm, "Ya, that's yuste the vay I like it."[28]

Frank Grover killed a black bear, but not the elk he really wanted. Carl missed getting a bear, but did bring down two deer. Aldo considered the trip a complete success. He added dozens of new birds to his lists, and could now identify a total of 261 species. The trip set a standard by which all subsequent outdoor experiences would be measured. Although they were to follow very different paths, he and Clarence Gilbert kept up a correspondence for several years. Clarence led an exhilarating but harsh life on a remote Montana ranch; Aldo, in school, remembered a "fairyland" of natural wonders and adventure.

The family returned to Burlington in October. Aldo began to look ahead to Lawrenceville with a mixture of anticipation and apprehension. In the weeks before he left, Clara primed him on what to do, what to eat, what to wear. She exhorted him again and again to write letters as often as possible on everything that happened. In truth, she was the one who needed most to prepare for his departure.

Part II

EAST

3

Lawrenceville
(1904–1905)

THE MORNING train pulled out of Burlington on January 5, 1904, rolled east over the CB&Q bridge below Prospect Hill, and accelerated past the Crystal Lake Hunt Club. Aldo was downcast at the thought of leaving home, but the nostalgia of the moment soon passed. Even as the locomotive pulled its cars up out of the valley and onto the frozen farmlands of Illinois, Aldo's spirits lifted. New landscapes always enlivened him, and he was especially eager to gain his first view of the Appalachian Mountains. Even if it was the civilized east and not the Rocky Mountain wilds, this was still new country to inspect.

What was an adventure for Aldo was for his mother a loss. Scarcely before Aldo's train had reached Chicago, she wrote him a letter in which she walked the painful line between giving her boy up and giving him the best.

Every day has been precious to us, and your example has been worth so much to the boys. I shall resign myself to our temporary separation if I am only assured of your happiness and welfare.

Surely we should be thankful that you can enter such a fine school, that you are so robust and strong, and that your path is so smooth compared to the struggle your young friend Edwin is fighting every day of his life. And we will be grateful dear, won't we dear, for the comforts Opa's industry has provided for us. Cheer up darling and mother too will smile through her tears.[1]

Writing in her angular Germanic script, she again urged Aldo to write, reported on "his" birds and other items of interest, and then ended her letter in words of characteristic humor, honesty, and devotion: "Tell me frankly too if my writing takes up too much of your time and if I must go to Elliot's for a course in penmanship. I'll do anything in the world for my boy—even return to school—if only he gives his last thought at night

33

to his mother. God bless you my boy and don't forget to mail that letter at Trenton."[2] He would not receive her letter until he had reached Lawrenceville, yet she was reminding him to send a letter before then, at Trenton, where he was scheduled to disembark. She was writing to her son not in his Lawrenceville future, but in his hardly-near-Chicago present, as if they were still sitting together.

Carl Leopold waited two days before sending his first letter to his son. Only rarely did he ever go through the difficult operation of handwriting, preferring to dictate his letters to his secretary at the factory. True to form, Carl's letters were direct and affectionate. His emotions flowed no less strongly than Clara's, but his found a more proper course to command, perhaps because of the dictation, but more because of his character. He reservedly advised Aldo, "Now write us fully my boy as often as you can every detail of your life in school as it will be of interest to us."[3]

Aldo's first letter home, written as his train passed through Pennsylvania, was less than moving: a brief account of the trip, a mention of the mountains and the coal dust, a string of small talk. He admitted, "I cannot think of anything more to write."[4]

Aldo soon thought of plenty more to write. The outpouring of letters to Burlington that began at Lawrenceville would not let up until long after Leopold's college days. Sent off at a rate that sometimes reached four and five letters a week, Aldo's correspondence was his reprieve from schoolwork, his literary training ground, his naturalist's notebook, and his private connection to the family and to Prospect Hill. Heeding Clara's admonition, he would report all: the progress of studies, the activities of schoolmates, exams endured, books read, friends made, athletic accomplishments, social doings, expenses, anecdotes, opinions, hopes, recollections. Most important, Aldo's letters allowed him to explore and express his absorbing relationship with nature. In a hand as smooth as his mother's was severe, he teased, entertained, informed, and warmed his family back home, all the while refining the skills that would one day produce some of the language's most eloquent nature writing.

Aldo arrived at Lawrenceville on January 6, 1904, five days short of his seventeenth birthday. The Lawrenceville School had been preparing Ivy Leaguers since 1810, and had an enrollment of about four hundred young men.[5] Its spacious campus, stately study halls, and handsome dormitories were a far cry from the cramped quarters of Burlington High. Aldo landed there as something of an exotic species. Coming from out west was distinction enough; "I-o'way" qualified as the wild west to his extremely eastern classmates. He was also a latecomer, and faced a demanding year-and-a-half of study if he wished to graduate with his classmates. Bright, serious, and observant, he was unfazed by a study schedule that included classes in English, English history, German, algebra, geometry, Bible study,

Cicero, elocution, and composition. "The instruction in English and History," he wrote to his father after three weeks, "is much inferior to that of the High School."[6]

Overall, though, Aldo was quite pleased with Lawrenceville. His native curiosity took well to the school's opportunities and methods, and he soon gained a reputation around Kennedy House as a "shark." In the gymnasium and swimming pool he followed his father's counsel and his own natural inclination to get regular exercise. In the library he found, among other books, *A Naturalist's Voyage Around the World* by Charles Darwin ("It is very instructive and interesting").[7] At the regular sermons and lectures, Dr. McPherson and others enlightened the boys on everything from "Samaritan Charity" and "Until Ye are All as Little Children" to "Mexico" and "The Joys of the Trail." A lecture by the prominent Native American writer, reformer, and physician Charles Eastman drew Aldo's attention:

Like a true Indian, he talks little, says a great deal to those who have understanding and nothing to those who have not. He ventured no opinions on the present status of his race, holding fast to his subject, or, the education of the young Indian, evidently as it was before the advent of white demoralization, at least he did not mention the latter. Some words and phrases which I have never heard anywhere else impressed me particularly. He said, after speaking of the Indian's knowledge of nature, "Nature is the gate to the Great Mystery." The words are simple enough, but the meaning unfathomable.[8]

High praise, for Aldo was not an easy audience. He panned the next day's offering, a discourse on Abraham Lincoln:

The lecture this morning was not very good. The lecturer was a pretty looking kind of fellow, and hopped about after the manner of a water ousel, unwinding a thunderous oration in a piping voice. His performance was handicapped both by contrast with the Indian *Man* and by his subject, for Lincoln was a *man* if ever there lived one, and is not a suitable subject for a grasshopper.[9]

Leopold's true genius, even then, lay not inside the school, but in the fields around it. Lawrenceville was a quiet, rural crossroad. In a corner of New Jersey bounded by Princeton just to the north, Trenton to the south, and Washington's Crossing to the west, the school offered access to a varied landscape of rich deciduous forest, farm fields and wooded ridges, pastureland and meadow, riverbank and marsh—prime territory for a fledgling naturalist away from home for the first time. Within days of his arrival, he was off on daily "tramps" into the winter countryside, and soon after was being introduced as "the naturalist." Within a month he had acquainted himself with the area for ten miles around, drawn a map, and applied his own labels: Big Woods, Fern Woods, Cat Woods, Owl Woods, Ash Swamp, the Boulders, Grove Country. He typically set aside an hour or two each day, more if his schedule allowed, and took off with a small notebook and his grandmother's opera glasses, later translating his notes into letters home. His first account was dated January 9, two days after his arrival:

I went north, across the country, about seven miles, and then circled back toward the west. Here every farm has a timber lot, sometimes fifteen or twenty acres, so it is a fine country for birds. It is about like Iowa high prairie, but the timber is more like the Michigan hardwood, the commonest trees being oak, beech, ash, hickory, chestnut, red cedar, and some elm. In some places, notably old orchards, young red cedars cover the ground. Nearly all the undergrowth in the woods is saplings and briars. There is little indiscriminate chopping of timber here.[10]

As in Burlington, Leopold's interest focused on birds. As the season advanced and the spring migrations commenced, his cross-country tramps became at least as important as his studies. As the days lengthened, so did the letters home. Sometimes his reports were simple lists of sightings:

Flickers and Blue Jays are beginning to increase in number as the weather grows warmer. Song Sparrows and Meadowlarks are singing constantly, while robins and Fox Sparrows are just beginning to try a few notes. Several migrants, such as cowbirds, Winter Wrens, Hermit Thrushes, and Kingfishers are about due.[11]

Sometimes he described a species in detail. He wrote to Marie about a favorite warbler:

I have seen many birds of beauty, but not one of such dazzling plumage and bearing as the Blackburnian. The upper parts and wings are jet black, with various white markings, especially in the wings and tail, the underparts pure white, heavily streaked with black, and the throat, sides of neck, and head, and middle of the black crown, of deep, rich, fiery orange. I have never seen such a color, soft and beautifully offset by the black, yet apparently about to burst into flame, like a red hot coal. The Blackburnian is a prize for rarity alone, but doubly one for his gorgeous plumage.[12]

Sometimes he launched into a complete ornithological account—as much for his own benefit as for his reader's—of the appearance, behavior, habitat, and migration pattern of a species. A first-time sighting of an American pipit elicited a three-page essay. "In finding new species," he wrote home in mid-May, "I have been also fortunate, thirteen having been added up to date. Inclusive of these I am now acquainted with 274 species of birds in the United States. Of course this is but idle talk and not by any means the end or object of my study of Ornithology, but still rather interesting to note."[13]

Leopold's nature study was not confined to birds. He displayed a sound understanding of forestry and meteorology, a strong interest in all plants, and a basic knowledge of geography and geology. Most significant, Leopold was already able to appreciate the interwoven relationships on his small piece of central New Jersey. He carefully noted the way goldfinches and pine siskins interacted in feeding. He spent a March week closely observing the habits of the phoebe, which he found gathering in unexpected numbers wherever the foul-smelling, early blooming skunk cabbage grew. He theorized that skunk cabbage attracted the earliest emerging insects from the surrounding wetlands, and that the insects in turn attracted the phoebes. After a week of wading through springheads and bogs, he corroborated his theory.

Leopold brought to Lawrenceville more than just his basic enthusiasm for the outdoors; he also brought his father's conservation conscience. While off on the same tramp that introduced him to the American pipit, Aldo came upon a trapped muskrat trying to swim to an escape. After much difficulty, he managed to release the muskrat. He took the trap, and continued on until he came to a second trap, this one containing a muskrat several weeks dead. He took the second trap. A week later, Aldo returned and found a third trap and a third muskrat, dead half the winter. "So you see I have the three traps on my hands, which of course I will by no means give back to the person who traps in the breeding season, and much less if he leaves the carcasses to rot."[14]

At another point, Aldo and a friend found a drained pond on the school grounds. They waded out into the mud and discovered thousands of dead and still-wriggling fish, minnows, and tadpoles. "Why on earth they drain the pond I cannot imagine," he wrote home. "They do nothing to it but towards summer fill it up again. Unless I can find a reason, I intend to speak to Doctor about it. George and I procured some buckets and gathered each a dozen or so fish to keep and restock the pond when it is filled again."[15] Meanwhile, back in Burlington, the annual spring duck harvest began in full force. "I hope the ice will break soon," Carl Leopold wrote his boy, "so the poor birds will have a chance to save their lives."[16]

Aldo's tramps and notebooks and specimens and buckets of fish did not go unnoticed by the members of his own species. Once they got the measure of their serious friend, his schoolmates took upon themselves the moral duty of loosening him up. Aldo was at first a harsh critic of his mates, chastising them in his letters for their lax study habits and their scandalous smoking and drinking. His guard began to melt with the snow. Spring baseball and track seasons began. He quickly made friends at the dinner table: Henry Van Dyke, the ever-plotting prankster; George Orr, the dedicated crow-hunter; Hamilton "Ham" Drummond, the smooth talker; Poittie Page, the shy New Yorker with the ready wit. Aldo's defenses fell before a barrage of tricks and jokes. He was rarely an instigator of mischief, but he became an occasional participant, an appreciative audience, and a good-sport victim. By the time Van Dyke hot-wired a doorknob and shocked the headmaster, Aldo had been won over; his letters began to recount the adventures of Kennedy House and those of the field with equal degrees of perception and enjoyment. His Lawrenceville companions, and the bare fact that he was away from home, were beginning to bring Leopold into the social world that he forsook so easily for his woods, his birds, and his family circle.

The influence was mutual. The fellows, at first bemused, began to wonder what it was that Aldo saw in the woods. By mid-March, Leopold could announce in a letter home that on a recent tramp he "was joined by Kelley and Bullock, who wanted to accompany me on one of my trips. (By the way, it has become a very general amusement here to tramp around the country with a staff and brag miles when returned home.)"[17] His friends became admirers of, if not converts to, Aldo's obvious devotion.

At his core, though, Aldo remained unchanged. This first extended period away from Burlington blurred his moralistic streak and stimulated his sense of humor, but not at the expense of his intensity. Displaying the robust spirit of a young Teddy Roosevelt, Aldo could not abide by the more effete of his eastern schoolmates. "They kick about the food; complain over foul weather instead of being glad of fair; criticize the masters when things don't come their way, and by all such trifles make themselves discontented or unhappy. Of course, not all are so, and you no doubt know what I mean. But if there are any who do not burden themselves with discontentedness over trifles, I believe I am one, and I think I can ascribe the same to yours and Mama's care to have engaged me in manual labor while at home."[18]

In his studies, his amusements, his letters, his responsibilities, his attitudes, Aldo was, above all, earnest. During the spring migrations, "150-duck stories" began to filter east. He wrote home to his mother on March 21, the advent of spring, "I am very sorry that the ducks are being slaughtered as usual, but of course could expect nothing else. When my turn comes to have something to say and do against it and other related matters, I am sure that nothing in my power will be lacking to the good cause."[19] It was a statement, not of prophecy, but of intention. He had simply decided early on where his convictions lay.

Aldo stayed at Lawrenceville through June to complete preliminary college entrance exams, then returned home to Burlington. He arrived early on the morning of the Fourth of July, and woke up Frederic for a predawn blowing-off of fire crackers.

That summer, Aldo bestowed new nicknames on his sister and brothers.

The course in Cicero inspired him: sister Marie became "Cicero," Carl became "Carolo," and little Frederic, naturally enough, became "Kidero."

∽

In order to arrive at Lawrenceville for the opening of the fall term, Aldo had to take an early departure from Les Cheneaux. An intense year of study and an especially vexing algebra course stood between him and his entrance into Yale. A year had passed since the epic journey to Montana, and this autumn there would be no hunting with his father. At one point, Aldo unearthed his western diary and relived the adventure. September this year brought instead a return to the routine of tramping, studying, and letter writing, as well as a new interest in long-distance running and a closer friendship with his fellow runner Ham Drummond.

The fall of 1904 was a memorable one on the Mississippi, and at 101 Clay Street in particular. St. Louis played host to the World's Fair. The Leopolds paid a week's visit to the exhibition, where Clara was especially eager to see the airships. Carl in the meantime became the tickled owner of Burlington's first automobile, a single-cylinder Oldsmobile. "It is a wonderful little machine and I like it very much," he wrote to Aldo, adding an unconscious metaphor for the newly energized and mobilized nation: "It has power to spare and is very easily managed. Of course, having a great deal of power it had to be steered very carefully."[20] Gaily decorated with the German flag and the stars and stripes, Carl Leopold's new automobile was a main attraction in Burlington's annual German Day parade.

Clara Leopold maintained her routine, managing the household, receiving the constant visits of friends and family, attending the functions of Burlington society. She lived for her family, her greenhouse, her shopping sprees with Marie in Chicago, her indulgence in grand opera, and, especially, her letters to and from her firstborn. "Again as so often," she wrote, "your letters are the highlights of my daily routine, when it threatens to become monotonous."[21] She returned the favor. Clara's letters, often accompanied by packages of cookies, candy, and her prized stuffed dates, contained animated tales of life at home, punctuated by motherly advice on everything from clothing to eating to exercise.

Any remaining doubts about where Aldo's interests lay and where they would lead him disappeared in a remarkable final term at Lawrenceville. After a fine Christmas at home, Aldo returned to school with a new resolve to work hard at his studies, and also with Carl's old double-barrelled Lefever. The resolve he needed in order to graduate on schedule. The gun was for shooting crows.

Aldo's tramps began again in earnest. By now, his excursions were part of school lore. His map filled in: The Divide, Crow-Pass Timber, The Woods of Eerie Gloom. The last earned its name "on account of the prevalence of beech in its boundaries. Even in the day-time there is a vague dimness and mystery about the beechwoods."[22] In January, a furious snowstorm raged for a day and a half, burying the school, the town, and the surrounding farmfields beneath twenty-foot drifts. Aldo decided it was a good time for a tramp. "Progress was in some places impossible," he admitted, but he took it as a challenge and concluded that he could "not remember ever enjoying a bit of winter weather more than this of today."[23] Ham Drummond concluded that his friend was beyond hope or help.

On days when the winter winds blew not with snow, but with the large flocks of New Jersey crows, Aldo and George Orr, his partner-in-arms, waged battle against the "sable armies of the sky." Aldo donned his knee boots and winter coat, slipped a glove on his left hand and an opened wool sock on his trigger hand, tied a red bandanna around his head, and headed out to the cornfields. All of his father's methods were brought to bear, and the old trigger itch was thoroughly indulged. His letters home recounted the epic confrontations:

But O how the old gun did shoot! I wish I could describe the whole flight, but suffice it to say that by five o'clock I had *ten* laid out in a line on the snow. Then I stopped (Puzzle: why? Answer: the twentieth shell knocked down a big fellow as clean as a whistle, but shell no. 21 consisted of a stick which I threw at a fellow who flew over at about ten yards distance and nearly got scared to death). You should have seen Henry stand aghast when I brought a festoon of crows into his room, and everybody said the string was the accumulated bag of the whole winter. This makes 25 crows less and 250 rabbits more in Jersey of 1905.[24]

By the end of February, the tally had risen to thirty crows less and, presumably, three hundred rabbits more. Aldo could hardly have been credited with a general reverence for life. Crows, sparrows, even hawks were fair game as long as they posed a problem for even fairer game or for his more preferred birds. Yet Leopold's reaction to the imminent migration and decimation of the ducks back home was as militant as ever. From the beginning, hunting was more than a simple issue of killing versus not killing. It was a complex activity, attended by the whole range of human attitudes from outright greed to sport to communion. Hunting was a measure of both humanity and inhumanity.

In the meantime, Carl Leopold left Burlington in early March for a month-long business trip through the West. He took these trips every several years, in order to keep up with the reactions and requests of his clients. Like his son, Carl Leopold keenly enjoyed long train rides and the views of passing landscapes from the coach window. He reported to Aldo that "the forest in Eastern California [is] in pretty good state of preservation, and not cut down ruthlessly as you see nearly everywhere and would expect here."[25] The lush California springtime delighted him, as did the early season golf, the seafood, and the business prospects. But for all the captivations, he could not escape the concern that was closest to his heart:

Saw more ducks in San F[rancisco] Bay than I have seen for many years. Many Canvas Backs and Red Heads. The waters for miles are spotted with blinds. Great slaughter must be done unless restricted. Goodbye my boy—I am glad you have found more in life to strive for, than the vanities of the thousands who come here to kill time and themselves.[26]

As the spring of 1905 advanced upon Lawrenceville, Aldo entered "a perpetual round of study, reading, baseball, running, and tramping."[27] The warmer the weather turned the more lopsided the round became, with a clear lean toward the tramping end of things. Studies progressed without problems. Most of Aldo's reading was devoted to school books, but Clara tried to interest him in some light fiction, and he made an effort to inform himself on world events, particularly the Russo-Chinese War ("I . . . share your belief that the war is unnecessary," he wrote to his father).[28] Aldo was not an extraordinary athlete, but he was a good and persistent one. Baseball was a pleasurable pastime, running a serious pursuit. He was a long-distance man, and enjoyed the hard training.

On the track and off, Aldo and Ham Drummond became best friends. They made an odd pair. Ham was a naturally outgoing sort, not so bright as Aldo, but not so serious either. Where Ham was an ambitious runner, anxious to "do something" in competition, Aldo believed that "it is more a matter of the training than the prize, or at least ought to be. . . . The track man asks for only one thing at a meet, and that is the chance to do his best. Mud and rain, therefore, are more formidable opponents than a team of champions."[29] As friends, they were complements, quite different personalities bound by a common enjoyment of life and a similarly sly sense of humor.

A change came over Aldo's tramping habits beginning in early March, when he announced in a letter to his mother that he "had no desire to kill crows or anything else, in spite of the favorable conditions. So when the afternoon came, the old gun was left behind."[30] The bird migrations began. Spring fever hit hard. By the end of the month, he wrote home to his father, "I hope you and Carl . . . will enjoy many of these fine Spring days over in the swamps, just *seeing* things; indeed, I cannot imagine wanting to kill anything now when there is so much to see and appreciate out of doors."[31] A week and a half later, while on a bird-watching tramp, he noticed a crow's nest thirty feet up an oak. He shinnied up a nearby hickory and found five eggs in the nest. "Easy to get at, but somehow I did not feel like taking them. Perhaps I ought to, but I can shoot crows much more easily than rob their nests. Even they are attached to their homes."[32] By mid-April, the change was complete: "I was tempted to take some crow's eggs yesterday and make Easter eggs for [Frederic], but I guess he too would rather see the old crows happy on that great day, rascals though they be."[33]

Another factor enriched Aldo's tramps. He hinted in a letter that he could use a new plant collection kit and identification book. Clara insisted he order them at once. The kit arrived in the mail, followed soon after by a copy of Asa Gray's *Manual of Botany*, which he proclaimed "a new intensely interesting work."[34] Gray's work, a key that had already opened the perceptual doors for several generations of young botanists, opened a wide one for Leopold. Birds had drawn him out on most of his previous tramps; now plants became equally fascinating. He went to the woods to find bellworts and anemones, allspice and ground ivy; in the low meadows he found where the kinnikinnic grew, and where the "shad-bush and service berry embower the brooklets in their blossoms."[35]

Most of his classmates spent their final weeks of school in glorious neglect. Aldo Leopold spent his in rapture. Other interests faded away in a gold and green aura of warm sunshine, new sprouts, and familiar birdsongs. He sermonized in a long Easter letter home:

The joy of Easter's Resurrection is today symbolized in as fine a day as was ever given to an unappreciative world. The first Sweet Violets are blooming, and a beautiful flower they are, unsurpassed for the delicacy of their perfume. Bank swallows have arrived and are skimming merrily over the pond all day long. In the woods is a handsome big Towhee, quite alone so far, who arrived Friday. Chimney Swifts are already abundant, the first ones having appeared late on Thursday afternoon. Truly May is drawing near if these birds have already appeared, and I look forward ever with increasing anticipation to this wonderful season of increasing delights. . . . I wonder if the Holy Land is blessed with such a Resurrection of Nature as occurs with us here at this season. For surely it is the most eloquent of all Easter-day sermons to breathe the Spring-breeze laden with the warmth of sunny skies, the essence of April flowers and the joy of a thousand bird-songs, and then to realize that countless centuries would not have prepared such an abode for us if we terminated our existence in the grave. For that indeed would (be) action without an object, and such is not the way of the universe, as we have only to look about us to see.[36]

During the revelrous weeks that ensued, Aldo's tramps accounted for a series of ideal days—a "red letter day" followed by "a perfect day" followed by "as fine a day as I ever spent"—and prompted an intense series of letters home. He celebrated with his family the return of the birds, the blossoming of the woodlands, the discovery of spring-cress and pepperwort, blue flag and sundrops, crowfoot and rattlesnake weed. His writing was often overblown, but just as often inspired and experimental. His prose always carried a smooth rhythm:

Yesterday, for instance, I thought to find kingfishers on Stony Brook. Striking straight across the uplands for several miles I reached the headwaters. Thence I followed it down and on nearly to Princeton, each step further and further from supper, but still no Kingfisher. The course of the Brook is now singularly beautiful, though, with wonderful tree-reflections and grass well advanced on the meadows.[37]

He displayed an unabashed, light-hearted enthusiasm:

Perfectly motionless, a bird with spread tail and greenish back perches on the trunk of a sapling. He turns! a flash of black and gold! and Ye Gods!—A Hooded Warbler! He regards you still motionless, but on the alert for your slightest movement. Nervously you fumble for glasses, get them focussed successfully, and look and look and look. A Hooded sure enough, and O what a beauty![38]

Aldo pressed a hepatica for Marie, and sent it to her with a library card that listed the due date ("spring"), the title of the work ("*Hepatica triloba*"), and the author ("The Giver of every good and perfect gift").[39] He dispatched letters at a rate of one every day, and virtually all of them included a long reference to the day's tramp. As his senses filled up with new impressions, and his mind with new Latin names, he acknowledged an inability to communicate the fullness of the experience. "I almost fear to begin on the news of the woods and fields for the past week," he wrote. "In fact, I sadly fear my attempts are too frequently narrow and dry. We can put on paper that such-and-such flowers are added to the list, that these birds have arrived and those are nesting, but who can write the great things, the deep changes, the wonderful nameless things, which are the real object of study of any kind."[40] Aldo's study provided a wealth of inner rewards, but objective recognition of his prowess came when professors from Princeton and a local ornithology club prevailed upon him to serve as judge for an essay contest.

In the midst of this Elysium, Aldo did not entirely forget the source of his privileges. Back in Burlington, the workers at the Leopold Desk Company went on strike for higher wages in April. Aldo recognized that "in the very secluded sphere of action here at school" it was easy to forget where the pursestrings lay.[41] He was frugal, though, and rarely appealed for funds. Clara warmly chided him for his "tendencies as a Diogenes."[42] Explaining that only "*the* bunch" could afford the extravagance, he skipped the prom. The expense notwithstanding, Aldo had evidently made no further effort nor progress in overcoming his shyness around girls.

While on Easter break, Aldo paid a visit to Yale to arrange his fall housing. He sent the lease home, with an acknowledgment "of how much is being done for me in providing every possible opportunity and advantage, educational and otherwise, and with the determination for new effort in proving worthy of it all."[43] He steadily passed the last of his exams in May, and although he had some coursework and college entrance exams yet to complete, his instructors allowed him to graduate. Ham Drummond, on the other hand, sweated it out. At one o'clock commencement morning, Ham burst into Aldo's room laughing. He had succeeded in a last-ditch attempt to pass an exam, enabling him to graduate. They congratulated one another with hearty handshakes, and talked long into the night.

Lawrenceville left an indelible mark on Leopold. It was there that he first applied his naturalist talents beyond his home territory, and began to chip away at his shell of isolation. He also developed his deeper interest in botany, an interest that would literally change the way in which he saw the world. And in his letters home from Lawrenceville he honed his writing skills. Dr. McPherson, in a graduation letter to Carl Leopold, described Aldo as "a particularly fine fellow, sturdy, intelligent and well-balanced."[44] As Aldo prepared to return to Burlington, he wrote to his father, "I look forward with great pleasure to the trip itself, and the glimpses of new lands which it affords." Then, in a sentence of unusual breadth compared to his previous outpouring of detailed observations, Aldo concluded, "Great lands are they all, the greatest on Earth, but none quite as good as our old native state."[45]

At home and at Les Cheneaux that summer, Aldo's heady preoccupation with the wild world continued. In Burlington, he reexplored the woods and swamps with new insight. At the club, he again devoted himself to birds and botany, to hikes into the "big hardwoods," and to dreams of the great northern canoe expedition; he continued to forego the social diversions of Les Cheneaux life. As at Lawrenceville, his devotion earned him a certain respect. Noting his preference for camping and fishing over golf and tennis, the gang stuck him with the nickname "Adam." Come September, though, Aldo would leave his northwoods Eden to toil in the fields of Yale.

Leopold's grandfather, Charles Starker, about 1895 (Courtesy Steven Brower, Burlington, Iowa)

The Leopold family in front of their house at 101 Clay Street, Burlington, Iowa, early 1890s. The Chicago, Burlington, and Quincy railroad bridge crosses the Mississippi River in the background (Courtesy Steven Brower, Burlington, Iowa)

Leopold's mother, Clara, at the time of her wedding in 1886 (Bradley Study Center Files)

Leopold's father, Carl, about 1900 (Leopold Collection, UW Archives)

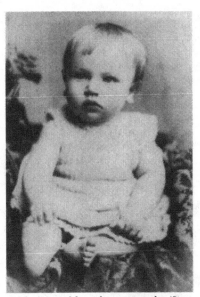

Aldo Leopold at eleven months (Leopold Collection, UW Archives)

Leopold at six years (Leopold Collection, UW Archives)

Leopold with Spud at the Les Cheneaux Club, late 1890s (Bradley Study Center Files)

Clara Leopold with her children, about 1901. *Clock-wise from top left:* Aldo, Marie, Frederic, Carl Jr. (Leopold Collection, UW Archives)

Lawrenceville School portrait of Leopold, 1905 (Leopold Collection, UW Archives)

Leopold boating with friends at the Les Cheneaux Club, about 1907. Marie Leopold is at front left (Bradley Study Center Files)

Leopold on the Les Cheneaux dock (Bradley Study Center Files)

Leopold's portrait, with caricature, from 1908 class yearbook of Yale's Sheffield Scientific School (Yale University Archives, Yale University Library)

The 1909 class of foresters, Yale Forest School. Leopold is seated in front row, second from right (Yale University School of Forestry and Environmental Studies)

4

New Haven

(1905–1906)

YEARS LATER, while jotting down some notes, Leopold wrote that "there are two things that interest me: the relation of people to each other, and the relation of people to land."[1] That, of course, accounted for just about everything; his interests were not narrow. Leopold was eighteen years old when he entered Yale University, with much maturing yet to do. His personal odyssey from amateur hunter and naturalist to trained professional forester would give full play to the tension between his dual interests in society and the natural world. Yale, scene of that transformation, would allow him to combine his interests, but it would also force him to confront the tensions between them.

He arrived at New Haven the first week of September 1905, moving into a room at 400 Temple Street. The ivy-covered walls of Yale, with all their attendant traditions, opportunities, and expectations, seemed at first glance an unlikely setting for the study of forestry. Yet, for Leopold's chosen profession, Yale was not only the best place to be, it was still virtually the only place to be. The Yale Forest School was training the nation's first generation of native foresters, and sending them forth from its Gothic towers to the newly created national forests of the hinterland. The school granted only graduate degrees. Leopold enrolled in the Sheffield Scientific School, which offered a preparatory course of study in forestry for undergraduates. For the first year, that meant a broad, solid foundation of coursework in physics, chemistry, German, English, mechanical drawing, and analytical geometry.

Yale was not Lawrenceville. Geographically, it was not so easy to leave New Haven for nearby woods and marshes, though Aldo announced in his first letter home that he was "immensely pleased" with the country.[2] Educationally, Yale presented a greater challenge to Leopold, and he was determined to meet it. Socially, a whole new sphere of people and activities opened up to him, and he would soon be drawn into the Ivy League rituals of school rivalries, societies, football games, and dances. "Adam" was about to join the human race.

Leopold's tramping habit was the first victim of the new circumstances. At Lawrenceville, he had been out in the woods and fields daily, or at least every other day. At Yale, he went out once or twice a week. He drew a new map, and applied new labels: Marvelwood, Queer Valley, Juniper Hill, The Castle. In the company of new converts—Bosworth, Bunker, Humphrey, Rup—he was soon exploring East Rock, Mill Rock, Pine Rock, and West Rock, high points on the basaltic ridges that stand sentinel over New Haven. In his letters home, outdoor accounts became less frequent, but no less vivid:

The left hillside is rich brown with scrub oak, the bottom mainly yellow and pinkish Sand Grass, while the right hillside is solid dark and green with many hemlocks. The bottom is a gunshot across, suggesting a great rabbit place. But one walks naturally next the hemlocks, for there runs the stream. It is just a big clear brook everywhere else, but in the Valley it feels the spell of strangeness. Swift, dark, and noiseless it glides along the rooty mossy bank and seeks the black shadows that fall from the grim old forest.[3]

Leopold's springtime letters from Lawrenceville had included long lists and inspired descriptions of new discoveries. Now he began to tell more anecdotes and record more impressions. The change reflected a subtle shift in the role of his tramps. Before, his tramping life and school life could hardly be distinguished; his interests indoor and out were mutually reinforcing, and blended into one another. As Aldo entered Yale, they began to grow more distinct. Nature became less a part of his daily routine, and more an alternative to it.

Not that Leopold did not enjoy or thrive in his new setting. He did well in classes, exercised daily in the university's new gymnasium, began training for the cross-country season, attended a Bible study class, and bought tickets for a series of public lectures by, among others, Jacob Riis, Jack London, and Ernest Thompson Seton. His life of self-imposed austerity continued, despite Clara's orders to correct "the scantiness of your wardrobe," and Carl's injunction to "not try to economize too much" when it came to food.[4] Their commands were followed and he gradually began to ease his "tendencies as a Diogenes."

This subject of expenses would be a sensitive one throughout Leopold's college days. He fancied himself as self-reliant as a mountain man or northwoods voyageur, and did not like to admit his dependence on the money from Iowa. Clara insisted that he not shortchange himself: if Aldo wanted something, then he ought to have it. Carl was not so indulgent, but he was pleased, even honored, to provide for his son's education, and asked only that he stick to his schoolwork. Aldo himself might have preferred a less expensive education. He knew, however, that he was being given a great opportunity, one for which even he would be willing to sacrifice some self-reliance. A firm sense of responsibility kept him under rein. He sent home accurate expense accounts, minimized his expenditures, and attended to his studies. He was invited to take board with the Lawrenceville Club, at six dollars per week, but "of course could not pay that. It was very nice of the fellows, but they understand my position."[5] What he bought, he bought carefully. He looked for a new pair of shoes, but reported to his mother that "there is nothing to be had for less than five dollars and so far have found nothing even that high which a good Humane Society would tolerate."[6] And when he paid, he paid painfully: "Will have to get hardened for the day when I fork over $33 for my new suit."[7] He never regretted his circumstances, and in fact considered himself "comparatively well fixed, for some fellows are paying as much as 6 and 8 dollars for a room, not to speak of Theatres, Tobacco, etc., which must count up enormously."[8]

All the details of tramps, studies, exercise, and school affairs were duly reported in Aldo's letters, which became markedly more playful and relaxed. He momentously proclaimed football results:

When the curious medley of yesterday's football scores came in, a very broad grin monopolized everybody's Phiz for the rest of the evening. But curious to say, nobody talked of that unspeakable Columbia game, where *our* team performed such masterful house-cleaning stunts on the New York field. Instead it was all Princeton, the tiger invincible, cleaned up by a little old team that nobody hears of twice a year! And there were many sighs, too, for O how those Princetonites will fight after such humiliation! Verily this is a queer season. Now as to your very kind orders that I go up to see the death of little Johnny Harvard. . . .[9]

Aldo became a storyteller, often with himself as the central figure. To his mother he confessed "one mean trick":

It happened that a certain farmer had not gathered the apples in one of his orchards, which stands a great distance from his house. The coincidence of this fact with the presence of an empty flour-sack in my outfit, made it very obvious that it is necessary to eat a couple of apples after each meal when in training. Accordingly a peck or so of the aforesaid apples which "Der Wind hat umgebläzd," i.e., they were lying on the ground, found their way into the floursack and hence to 400 Temple St. Their numbers will hereafter decrease at the rate of 6 per diem.[10]

He could be satiric, nostalgic, rhapsodic, comedic, epic. When the cross-country team held a practice session drill of "hares and hounds," Aldo ran with the pack of hounds along the trail of shredded paper, and later described the chase in a five-page narrative that only a hunter could have written:

Even though the fresh strewn paper does go up the hill, it cannot cross over. You have been here before and know the eager pack straining on all sides will strike nothing less than the impassible fence of Marvelwood at the summit. This is merely a trick of the [hares]! So you strike off straight to the left on the first cow-path and are alone, save for two who divine "something doing" and follow you. The pack are puffing far above, screened by the brush, as you stride along ahead of the "two," confident of striking the trail coming down again. And sure enough, not two hundred yards, is the plain line of white scent leading down! You make sure, and then in your hunting voice let out a long—Trrail![11]

At home, Aldo's letters were being duly appreciated and answered. An account of the Princeton game had Carl laughing until he cried. He could not contain his pride, and the next morning brought the letter down to the factory and read it to his men. Carl sent back regular news of the house, automobile, factory, dogs, and, especially, hunting trips, but Clara was the real letter writer. Witty and literate, she chronicled for Aldo the ongoing family adventures and nagged him with motherly admonitions. For Clara, writing letters was another maternal chore that she tried her best to transform into an art form. "Today," she wrote to Aldo in early December, "the thought flashed across my mind that I personify prose, while you may stand for poetry. I hate to be always bothering you about little things, but somehow the *rest* of you are too soaring to recall them, so it falls to the lot of your stupid old mother."[12]

In the *Hawkeyes* that his mother sent along, Aldo learned of the lively round of Christmas parties planned for the young people at home. Tongue in cheek, he condemned this "base conspiracy to keep all homecomers dancing during the holiday to which we looked forward with such delight." The job of accepting and rejecting invitations he entrusted to Marie. Then he wrote about the meaning of home:

Home is a queer word. When one speaks it out loud in a far country it is always preceded by "except." We say, "This is the finest country I have seen," and then after a pause, add "except home." After such conversations one either talks or thinks hard. They occur many times, and always comes back the great old river, the rocky bluff, and the big woods on the other side. And last the green lawn, and the trees and all the rest. Even in winter the lawn seems green—that is, from the far country. The far country, too, becomes greater for the fact of being ranked next—to home.[13]

In addition to a normal holiday schedule of family visits, rabbit hunts, and wintertime sports, Aldo, thanks to Marie, faced a forbidding array of social functions. He not only survived the vacation, but enjoyed it beyond all expectations. The late bloomer had opened. Hamilton Drummond, for one, was dismayed. "Woe and alas!" he wrote to Aldo. "I fear, my young friend, you have been inveigled away from the road which you laid out for yourself at Lawrenceville; for you speak of 'having had a great time *with* several balls and a whole week of dances.' Is it possible that you, even you, cannot have a '*great* time without a week of etc. etc.?'"[14] Ham, every bit as gregarious as his friend was solitary, took special delight in Aldo's new interest in females. Aldo's casual mention of a Burlington maiden provided a sufficient target for Ham's needling.

> You see I have been through the stage you are going through and can speak as one having authority. I was the unfortunate swain last summer. Never again will I play that role. I leave it for such — as Mr. Rand of 400 Temple St. "Change and decay in all around, I see" as the old song goes. I changed back into your noble, majestic state of mind — bachelorhood — no cares nor worries. To Hades with Matrimony. While you have decayed into what I used to be — the lover with his ballad: the devoted sweetheart: the passionate letter-writer. Ah me![15]

Well, not quite. On the return trip east, Aldo was still more interested in the passing landscape than in the trainful of returning students. Once reinstalled at Yale, though, he felt the tinge of an unfamiliar sensation: lonesomeness. Such discouragement never lasted long, and always dissolved before Leopold's relentless optimism. "Vacations are so full of new events," he wrote in his first letter of the new year, "and right there lies their value. They freshen and enrich the outlook on the daily round. . . . Stated more concretely, all this means that I have had such a good Christmas as to be really eager for the work ahead."[16]

Aldo's schoolwork proved to be neither very time-consuming nor exciting ("this freshman pipedream," he called it). He performed well, but did not acquire any special mentors. As before, the elements that most significantly influenced him were beyond the classroom. This time, however, they were not exclusively outdoors. He regularly attended lectures, concerts, and debates, and was wangled into the job of collecting funds for the debating team. "Fully 5/6 of the fellows are always 'dead broke' on the spot," he observed, "but by much 'debating' they are, i.e. a very few, led to precipitate fifty cents out of the atmosphere by the wonderful process of delving into an empty pocket. Who says 'Matter is uncreatible and indestructible'?"[17] He found time for his outside reading, which mostly ran to books on forestry and the outdoors — Theodore Roosevelt's *Outdoor Pastimes of an American Hunter,* Samuel Green's *Principles of American Forestry,* Filibert Roth's *First Book of Forestry,* Charles Darwin's *Vegetable Mould and Earthworms* ("of much interest and surprise").[18] Aldo also received and accepted (on his own) his first formal dance invitation. Laura Peasley, a Burlington friend attending Miss Bennett's School in New York, asked him down to "the unknown wilds of Bennett," assuring him that Horace Rand, Marie's sometime sweetheart and son of Aldo's namesake, now out east himself, would also be there.[19] Aldo suspected, with good cause, collusion between mothers back in Burlington. Despite the orchestrations, Aldo accepted the invitation.

As the weather warmed, Aldo reinvaded the woods and fields with unabated interest. Even when a track injury put him on crutches, he couldn't resist a crippled walk to "Juniper Hill":

Hemmed in by monotonous chestnut coppice, its five or six acres are a glory to the eye. Big spreading junipers encroach everywhere upon the smooth green turf, with here and there a slender white birch or a dense thorny matted patch of Barberry, just opening into the softest of green leaflets. Towhees and Thrashers scratch loudly under the bushes, Field and Vesper Sparrows straggle along overhead, the Swifts titter invisible above, and a Grosbeak carols at his meal of birch buds. . . . The sun is gratefully warm, the view takes in everything from the blue sail-dotted sound and harbor to the great half-mountains out Carmel-way, and I wish the kid were here to explain it all to. A Field Sparrow all the while is singing a strange and effective combination of his own song and that of the Black-throated Green Warbler—unmistakable, the V-part. In itself worth the trip. Puzzle—does he do it from memory, accident, or has the Black-throated Green really arrived and been singing? Most probably the latter, he is due. Thus the afternoon passes, and it is five o'clock. Only a few steps to the Trolley-cut on the ridge, and the day is over. Thus one makes rusticate even on a crutch, if one knows the country.[20]

The "old naturalist," as Ham Drummond called him, was drawn again and again out the trolley-line to the edge of New Haven, and into the country beyond. When schoolwork bogged him down, the spring air invigorated him. His father's lessons in sportsmanship always underscored Aldo's observations.

Arrived at the river at noon, and set off down stream. On a sunny grassy bank by the rushing water, with hemlocks and birches all around, we encamped and [ate] a big can of beans and a box of Triscuit. At three o'clock we cut out rods of sweet birch and began fishing. I have never seen a prettier stream so easy to fish, or capable of supporting so many trout if reasonably treated by the public.[21]

In this his first spring at Yale, Aldo had achieved a balance of sorts between the out-of-doors and the indoors. Hard work and hard play, tramps and dances managed to coexist. On occasion, his father still had to chastise him for being so parsimonious. "You must not think it an unpleasant item for us to pay your expenses, because we know they are always moderate, and there is nothing we more cheerfully pay than your bills at Yale, for it is certainly money well-invested, and investments made for you and the other children's benefit are always a pleasure to us."[22] Aldo's seriousness, left unchecked, might have prevented him from embracing human society: misanthropism has always been the naturalist's occupational hazard. But he was blessed with his parent's compensating sense of humor and their keen enjoyment of everyday ironies:

Yesterday morning there was a snowslide off the roof of University Hall, directed by the hand of Providence. For walking below were two of the most sedate and pompous members of our beloved faculty, and across the street some hundred or the like of highly interested spectators likewise bound for an 8 o'clock recitation. The poor profs forgot their degrees for once, and in a very human manner proceeded to clamber out of the mess, humbled in spirit and hat.[23]

Aldo's wit was the counterweight in his character. Without it, there would have been no balance, not even a temporary one, in his personality.

Aldo had been away from home for two years. The interval had only intensified Clara's maternal attachment to him. When one of Aldo's bi-weekly letters failed to arrive, she shot off a worried telegram to New Haven—then embarrassingly apologized two days later. Like her son, Clara was able to check her seriousness with a ready sense of humor. Self-effacement allowed her to turn aside before she crossed the line into parental obsession. "I find that most of my well-meant advice to you is quite superfluous," she wrote to Aldo. "It is just a bad fussy habit I should be broken of. You see in thought I am always with you and am perhaps as much a resident of your college town as where I dwell with flesh and bones (mostly bones), and I know you are always making allowances for your muddling, puttering old mother."[24] Clara practiced the art of motherhood with self-awareness and self-sacrifice, but with extreme possessiveness. That fall, Marie and Carl Jr. were due to follow Aldo east, to the Bennett School and Lawrenceville respectively. "Oh, but it will be lonesome next winter," she sighed in a letter to Aldo. "I shall have to soliloquize or become dumb. Perhaps it will be some relief to strike off the days on the calendar."[25]

Meanwhile, the spring was a busy one for Carl Leopold. Once again there were excursions into the woods with Carl Jr., often with Frederic or Edwin Hunger along. Once again, the ducks ran the gauntlet. Business boomed down at the factory. With restrained pride, Carl announced to Aldo, "We are all busy at the factory. I am much pleased, because we got out an entirely new line in several grades of desks, which appears to be giving the best of satisfaction."[26] The house gained a grand new porch facing the Mississippi River. Burlington chose a new mayor. Papa reported the results:

The campaign was the dirtiest I think I have ever heard in politics, and I trust we will not have another of the kind here. The trouble was the Civic Federation backed by a lot of erratic and overzealous ministers who wanted to make everybody's wings grow in thirty days. The other extreme [was] the saloon and lower element who finally won by a large majority, having a great many people disgusted here with the campaign stories both Republican and Democratic.[27]

Carl Leopold's character dovetailed neatly with his wife's. Where she was emotional, he was reserved. Where she was energetic, he was steady.

They had their differences. Clara constantly pushed for her way with the house and the children; Carl was equally and adamantly practical about such matters. But their quarrels were minor, usually humorous beneath the surface, and always short-lived.

If Carl and Clara Leopold disagreed on means, they never disputed ends. They were proud and devoted parents. In May, Clara wrote to Aldo and assured him "that your whole life is so well balanced and normal that we positively have no unfulfilled wishes, not one change that might add to our absolute satisfaction and contentment in your present life."[28] Their contentment was easy to understand. Aldo had inherited many of their qualities. Clara gave him an aesthetic sensibility and an irrepressible enthusiasm. She could read with sympathy his description of "a find far eclipsing all precedents":

Think of it, a rare new and wondrous Orchid, the Stemless Lady's Slipper! There were two, beauties, in the deep deep woods. On such an occasion one sits down and watches, long and silent and wonderingly, before he plucks, and then, very reverently and carefully, takes just one. Even then it is hard to go away."[29]

Carl, in turn, gave his son common sense and a spirit of independence, as well as a devotion to the joys of outdoor life. Moreover, in Carl's non-doctrinaire approach to economic and political affairs, one finds the germ of Aldo's own independent convictions. After hearing Jack London speak at Yale, Aldo began to read into socialism, "not because I believe in it, but because I want to know what its value is."[30] Darwin's *Vegetable Mould and Earthworms* still fascinated him far more than any political tract.

Leopold completed his first year at Yale having acquired not simply a textbook education, but also a widening circle of friends. Clara was pleased, not to mention relieved, to see this. "You were a born recluse and hermit," she explained to Aldo, "and but for your constant contact with strangers in new surroundings might be in hiding somewhere in the wilderness even now. I don't believe you have any conception of what a shy little fellow you really were."[31] Aldo, despite his "western" ways, was becoming entwined in the Ivy League establishment. Among the closest of his new friends was Tally Ketchum, whose family lived just down the shore of Long Island Sound in Stamford. Before long, Aldo, who a year before had criticized the extravagance of the Lawrenceville prom, was attending, courtesy of the Ketchums, the Opening Dance of the Stamford Yacht Club at the clubhouse on Shippan Point. "Everybody in Stamford, it seemed, was there, and had a remarkably good time."[32] The next morning there was a launch party to attend. The "shy little fellow" had become quite confident in society, no matter what Ham Drummond had to say.

Not all of Aldo's new acquaintances were as well-placed as the Ketch-

ums. One of the oddest and most subtly influential of all his friendships
began during this spring of 1906. There was a custom among Yale students of "adopting" indigent youngsters from New Haven. Aldo's adoptee
was a destitute young Jewish boy named Benjamin Jacobosky. Bennie's
mother and father lived in New Haven, but their constant strife left Bennie
a refugee out on the streets. The dockside kid became the latest and most
unusual of Aldo's tramping and fishing partners. If Aldo was not fully
aware of his own innate cleverness, he became so when confronted with
the pathos of Bennie's first letter.

> Dear Mr. Leopold.
> May 4, 1906
> I am very sorry you are lame.
>   I know you are my best friend.
>   I hope you will feel better
> Don't forget to teach me some examples when I come up
> Yours truely
Bennie Jacobosky[33]

The friendship with Bennie would last through Leopold's college years,
and although they would never become extremely close, both were to gain
from their occasional excursions into one another's alien experience. Bennie was to exercise what Aldo considered every kid's inalienable birthright to fish and picnic and tramp. Aldo was to gain a glimpse of life's
other side.

The ironic juxtaposition of these new friendships was not lost on Aldo.
A week after the yacht club dance and in the midst of final exams, he sat
down to write his usual Sunday letter home. He finished the letter, then
late that night added an unusually hasty postscript:

> The evening has passed with showers outdoors and Byron indoors—both precipi-
> tate. Just now, out in the sweet night-air that one feels after a rain, I passed
> some Jasmine bushes, blooming. Their fragrance in daytime is pleasant in a
> sunny sort of way, but tonight it is an *experience*, and not to be forgotten.
> One remembers the Jasmine bushes at home, and feels that these would make
> one homesick, if any *thing* could do it. But who is homesick in June? with
> all at right with the world, in so far as a boundless future regardless of past
> things may be called right. Even though the course of one has been smooth,
> and that of a second miserable, is *that* a cause for sorrow to the first? I take
> it not so, but in double measure a cause for *action* to him. It is deeds, not tears,
> that *shall*, and some day *will*, give to the oppressed of the earth their due! There-
> fore let us *rejoice* in the June, and *work*. Perhaps, now that this year is over,
> it may be said I have not worked, but this year is gone, and next year is ahead.
> And I look forward to it with the knowledge that work, directly bearing upon
> what I am sent here to study, will begin. Next year, therefore, there is going

to be something doing. Goodnight now, I must [go] out to the Jasmines once more. Love to everybody from

Your Aldo[34]

In some ways this was the same earnest Aldo Leopold — optimistic, forth-right, anxious to get about the *work* of his life, and the studies that "di-rectly bear upon it." In other ways, it was out of character. Rarely did he write so quickly, haphazardly, or abstractly. More rarely yet did he fall into such blatant introspection. In contrasting the smooth course of his own "boundless future" with the rocky way of his friend Bennie, Aldo was led to reflect upon the direction of his education. His definite, if ambigu-ous, reference to the "oppressed of the earth" was an anomaly. Aldo's in-terest in the great human problems had increased since coming east, but he was neither strident nor dogmatic nor zealous. His idealism was show-ing, however, forced to the forefront by the stimulus of new friendships.

ა

In anticipation of his return to Burlington and Les Cheneaux, Aldo had written a letter to ten-year-old Frederic that ranked, in Clara's words, as "classic literature in the Leopold wigwam."[35] In it, echoes of Thoreau, Seton, and Twain blended with those of Longfellow, the Old Testament psalmist, and the New Testament gospels:

My dear Frederic,

Today it seems almost as if spring were coming again — muddy enough for stilts and warm enough for marbles. The snow is melting quite rapidly, and I am hoping that at home too you will soon be able to play baseball and make garden again. Baseball we have here, too, but when it comes gardening weather, I will be wishing I could help you dig again in the rich sweet mellowness of the Spring earth. But if that is not possible we will do the next best — next vaca-tion, cutting the fresh grass and a whole million other delights, all included in "summer."

Do you know, old man, we are going to have high old times next summer! *You and I* are going to try a *new* stunt. We are going to take charge of *Mama* and *Cicero* every alternate day, *both* of us, and there is going to be something doing. On those days things are going to be *moving*. We are going to take them a-blackberrying in the hills of Flint, and a-botanizing in the outermost parts of the — county. We will show them where grow the choicest of gooseberries, and point out the yellow Mayapple on the hillsides. New flowers we shall find in the meadows, and the quails will whistle for us from the green pastures. Of a Sunday we will go a-picnicing, and very often we shall find delight in the reaches of our river. Papa may go along then, and Carolo shall leave his chickens, and with heavy heart accompany us to the Islands of Trumpet-flower. And he shall not go sadly, although he hath great possessions. Then after many glorious days, we will travel to the Isles of Contentment on the shores of Giche-Gumi, by the shining big sea water.

There shall Mama learn how to cast, and Cicero wax mighty in the craft of the fishers. Day by day shall our two boats toss on the waters, and when the south-wind ripples the Channels, mighty and swift shall the big green pike rise to their casting. Again we shall wander in the sunny clearings and burns, mid the Aspens and bracken, and our meat shall [be] locusts and wild raspberries. And again [we shall] sit on the beach where the Bearberries are trailing under the Beachplums, and watch the white water beat on the cobbles. Sweet will be the fresh breezes from over the green waters, and grateful the warm sun on the driftwood. Papa may go along then, and Carolo shall leave his sailboat, and with a hungry gun chase partridges with Spud in the bush. Then shall we seek out the acres of Gentian. Mama shall have bunches of blueness, and for Cicero we will find the wondrous orchid in the cold moss under the cedars, the sweet white Pyrola and Wintergreen, with Harebells and Slender Gerardias from the Muskeg. And at sundown shall follow a royal old perchfry, and other savory dishes withal, with the flavor of camp-fire. Then when the embers of driftwood burn low, and the new-moon rises over the towering balsams, we will embark one and all and wend homeward over the quiet waters.

So shall it go for many glorious days, and when rumors of school-time come from the Southland, and the wildfowl begin to arrive in the bay, our two charges will have imbibed twenty pounds each of the Quintessence of the green earth. Won't that be great?

So long, Kidero, love to all from
Your Brother[36]

5

Forest School
(1906–1909)

A T LES CHENEAUX in the summer of 1906, Aldo got his canoe. Carl Leopold finally gave in to Aldo's requests, and before long a large wooden crate arrived, which they opened right on the dock. Aldo beamed. His dream of entering the unmapped northland was now one long pull-stroke closer to reality. He quickly mastered the canoe, and then taught the rest of the family, treating his mother to moonlit rides on the bay, paddling forth with his brothers on fishing trips and camping expeditions along the Huron shore. The Les Cheneaux gang of teenagers—Aldo, Marie, Carl, Ballard Bradley, Gretchen Miller, the Clark girls—put the canoe to the test. Aldo eventually paid the canoe the ultimate compliment: "When I have paddled in it another year it will attain second honor among all my possessions—first place being, of course, for the old gun."[1]

Aldo and Gretchen became a Les Cheneaux item. She was a member of the upper-class Lexington, Kentucky, contingent that summered at the club. A pleasant, sensible young woman, Gretchen had a down-to-earth quality that appealed to Aldo. She was the first serious object of his romantic intentions, enough so as to cause Clara some consternation.

The "rumors of schooltime" came early for Aldo. He returned to New Haven in early September for a two-week course in surveying, his first forestry-related work. "I am ready to acknowledge now," he wrote to his mother, "that we *did* knock around a bit too much at night during the summer but nevertheless I cannot but call it the best vacation I have ever had."[2] Carl Jr., too, left early for Lawrenceville, and Marie soon followed her brothers east to attend the Bennett School. When the cool equinox winds came over the bay, Carl Sr. was out after the ducks again, now with Frederic as his "head-assistant at the old game." Clara found herself alone in a very quiet shanty on a very quiet island.

True to his resolution of the previous spring, Aldo arrived at New

Haven intent on working hard. He declared the surveying course "exactly to my liking, at least I feel as if I were learning something that counts, and learning it every day."[3] He enjoyed surveying precisely because he was *doing* something, actually studying forestry and not just reading books. He signed up for classes in German, French, and composition, mechanics, mineralogy, and physical geography. He again took up running, and expressed a new desire to join a fraternity. With three Leopolds and assorted friends scattered about the East Coast, a crisscrossing network of correspondence formed to lay plans for attending one another's football games and dances. Elizabeth Clark and Gretchen Miller corresponded regularly with Aldo. He invited Dorothy Clark, another Burlington expatriate at Miss Bennett's School, to New Haven for the Yale-Princeton game. His austerity forgotten, he bought two Brooks Brothers suits, two more tailor-made shirts, and a pair of proper gentleman's shoes. (His mother responded, "Some years ago you were so extremely indifferent as to dress that I encouraged you to attach more importance to the subject. *Now* I am rather aghast at my complete success.")[4]

As the fall progressed, day trips to the woods were squeezed out of Aldo's schedule. Accounts financial and natural disappeared from his letters. What letters he did write were perfunctory. Aldo's natural enthusiasm was missing; he was mired in "lange viele" days. On Thanksgiving, he did take a long walk alone into the rocks behind New Haven, arrived back late for dinner, foraged for leftovers, went to his room, and wrote his usual holiday letter home. It contained the only tramp account of the entire autumn. His mother and father enjoyed this "old-fashioned letter" that had "the same wilderness note as those which came . . . two years ago," but in truth, the similarity was only superficial.[5] The letter contained none of the vivid stories, lively descriptions, or detailed observations of the Connecticut countryside that the old ones did. The new Aldo just said that he found "numberless interesting things—geological, botanical, and what not. Everything went just great. After all one must plug and work twelve hours a day for a while before he can really enjoy things." He ended the letter on an uneasy note, allowing that "I am well content here in my room, apparently lonesome as blazes but in reality enjoying life immensely. I have reason to give thanks."[6] Talk of loneliness is not unusual for one spending a holiday far from home; it was unusual for Aldo, who, if he felt it, rarely admitted it.

As Christmas drew near, Aldo lightened up. He wrote a letter home suggesting that he and his brothers would forsake all womenfolk and holiday dances and instead pursue rabbits through the Flint Hills. But Clara was not about to let Aldo "slip back into the habits of a recluse." "Is there to be no fussing over Cicero and myself even? What then is to become of your poor sister? . . . If Elizabeth and Gretchen were here would rabbit hunts seem less tempting? I know you have a suspicious probing old mother who greatly fears Elizabeth and a score of others as rivals—and loves to tease you about it."[7] Aldo, however, had the last word:

I have a foolish friend named 'Hump' who has a little password which he uses on all occasions: "Girls are weird beasts." I have pondered upon that little phrase, and now believe in the ancient saying about Wisdom coming out of the mouths of Fools. You're darn right, Hump Old Socks, girls *are* weird beasts.

In the first place, whenever you say something that's just a bluff and that any *reasonable* creature can see is just a bluff they take you in deadly earnest and conjure up a string of implications terrible to contemplate. . . .

Then again when you tell them something you really *do* mean in deadly earnest, they won't believe it. But perhaps that is fortunate, anyhow it doesn't bother *me* much. They're weird beasts, that's all.

To be more explicit, let us by all means accept every bid to dances that comes our way! And let me, right now, this seventeenth day of December Annie Domino nineteen hundred and six certify and declare that unless my sister Cicero by name consents and promises to let me her brother take and escort her to every and each dance she goes to for the next two years, there'll be a h--l of a row and I just won't go by jiminy! So there![8]

∽

Back at Yale after the holidays, Aldo threw off the languor of the fall. He applied himself to his studies, which now included courses from the forestry school in timber construction, hydraulics, strength of materials, and plant taxonomy, and even gained the attention of stern Professor Tracy. "[Tracy] even kept me after class the other day, and asked me who taught me how to arrange my work. Then he told me a lot of things, and walked two blocks with me on the street. Think of it, *Tracy!* Yesterday he told me the only thing I had to do was to cultivate speed in my work. All of which is valuable advice and something not easily extracted from the old Outlaw."[9] Although not yet officially enrolled in the Forest School, Aldo joined the Forester's Club ("a landmark in my education"). His outside reading increased—the Bible and *Paradise Lost* ("Don't be startled," he wrote), *Saul of Tarsus, Hiawatha* (again), *Evangeline*, novels, essays, philosophy— and he worked longer hours for the YMCA and the debating society. He even began to take regular hikes again, and sent home several genuinely old-fashioned letters:

Ye Gods! such a night. I needn't try to describe it—the glorious moonlight, the untrodden purity of the snow, the rare sweetness of the cold air. I just went back to my room, donned my boots and woolen shirt, and *walked*. Mill Rock—Head of Whitney—and back over East Rock. I have never seen such a night—from the Rock you could see Long Island, twenty miles away, in every detail. Yes, it was two o'clock when I got back, it was foolish, and all that, but Thank the Lord I went! The verdict of the house was "Either crazy, or in love, or both." What fools these mortals be!: to miss such a night would have been a greater misfortune than either of the lamentable states of mind [with] which I am charged (falsely). So much for the moon.[10]

Then there were dances, lectures, exercise, Bible study, visits with Bennie, concerts. Aldo treasured the variety and declared that he was "enjoying life very uproariously," had "never been so busy, so happy, or so success-ful," was "rolling in satisfaction," and had "never had a more interesting time than lately."[11] Aldo did not merely avoid sluggishness; he drove it off with sheer determination. "I have apparently no time left," he wrote to his father. "More than one of my friends has called me a fool for 'biting more than I can chew' as they put it."[12]

Aldo wrote home in late January about some modest success in a school debate. In his response, Carl took the opportunity to give rare expression to his parental pride and deep appreciation of life:

We have certainly neglected you of late, but you know how helpless I am, in using a pen. Long disuse of that instrument, have about ended my ability to use it, except possibly for signatures in paying bills. In this line practice has made me quite proficient. Your midnight foot trip must have been quite interesting. When I was your age I delighted in such trips, but mine were generally made with a boat on the old Mississippi or a wagon on the plains of Nebraska while on the road commercially. Your interest in your debating club meets with our most hearty ap-proval. Every man should be able to make a speech, and unless you are a natural born orator, practice and study are absolutely necessary to success. Whether you win your debates or not, the value here lies in the *try.* I always regretted it that I never had an opportunity to study oratory. You are now in the most interesting period of your University life. Every day new objects + possibilities are being dis-closed to you + best of all you appear to realize it, and will profit accordingly, we feel sure. When I say "we," you know I mean your Mother and Myself. We discuss you and your promising future, nearly everyday.

We are following the usual "Humdrum" here and still time does not drag, but fairly flies, in fact Sundays come all to fast, and a retrospect reveals the flight of the last few years as in a dream, and we see the afternoon of life come on rapidly— and how little has been accomplished except in that one way, in which so many have failed—We have given + guided in their infancy a new generation, of which the greatest of men could be proud + you my son are one of the first of these whom *we* shall be proud of in *our* declining years.[13]

Meanwhile, Aldo's self-imposed workload led him to adopt a "new rule of study" at Yale. At precisely ten thirty every night, he closed his books, spit in his hand, raised his fist, breathed deeply, slammed the fist down on his desk and roared, "To Hell with Tracy!" (substituting other names of professors when appropriate). The other fellows in the house cursed and complained and told Aldo to go to bed, but that only provoked him to repeat the procedure "mit Fever, not sparing your fist and accenting the second word."[14] The fellows learned to live with it, and then to expect it. Fortunately for all, spring was in the offing.

The dam of intensity broke in mid-March, when Aldo and his friend Reynolds spent a weekend camping on a hill Aldo christened "Diogenes' Delight." "Now we are lying in the warm sun behind the windbreak and taking our ease. Reynolds is sleeping contentedly but I have been listening to the passing Bluebirds and Robins and to the noisy brook down in the hollow, and drinking in the naturalness of it all with a great contentment. It is variety, the spice of life, and tomorrow I will tackle the first of the Easter exams with so much the more energy."[15]

The variety in Aldo's life was never in greater evidence than during the subsequent Easter break. Bennie came for a visit. "He has straightened up, looks rosy and well dressed, is full of schemes and imaginings, and some mischief withal," Aldo wrote. "I feel that I get quite as many new ideas from Benny as he does from me." Aldo proclaimed him "a promising fellow. . . . And what is there in this world better than the promise of great things to come? Perhaps its greatness is magnified to us who have so far received everything and done little, but that is the way it appears to me anyhow."[16] Aldo took a daylong tramp, then spent most of his vacation in New York City visiting with Ham Drummond, Dorothy Carson, and Gretchen Miller, whose family was in New York for the holiday. On his return to New Haven, he stopped off at Tally Ketchum's and took in the Stamford dances. Aldo considered it a "successful" trip, but when the busy week was over, he was anxious to return to his still busier routine. "This confounded loafing gets on my nerves when it comes too thick, and though you wouldn't think it, I'm almighty glad to be back at work again." He professed that "dress clothes and ballrooms are great for a change, but in the end I am always a born simpleton of a farmer, rejoicing in simple things."[17] But Aldo was neither a born simpleton, nor a farmer, and even his joy in simple things did not come so easily at this point. In truth, he was a sophisticated young man, growing more sophisticated by the day, and he had yet to resolve the tensions building in his life.

At home, his father became involved with new legislation intended to establish Iowa's first resident hunting license and fee. "If it becomes law," he wrote to Aldo, "I shall be very much pleased, as the only way to care for our game is through a paid Game Warden System, and this can only be maintained by a low-priced license for every gun that goes out beyond the confines of its owner's property."[18] When he heard of Papa's conservation activities, Aldo renewed his own dormant conviction: "I don't get time to write about it very often but the Woods Fever is still chronic with me, as is also the desire to some day help out our poor ducks and other game in return for what they have been and will be to me. All this sounds pretty sickly on paper, but the time will come."[19]

One day in late April, as the first bloodroots and anemones emerged, Aldo took a walk out to the Maltby Lakes west of Yale. On the way back to Yale, he met a fisherman:

I had an interesting talk with a negro poacher who had slipped out after his day's work was over and was filling his basket with perch for breakfast from the water-company's lake. He was an honest fellow and a good citizen, and cherished many memories of hunting and fishing away down in his native Carolina. 'Down south sure is the place fur huntin and fishin,' he said, with a kind of wistfulness that I could thoroughly understand. We all have our 'Down South' somewhere, our land of simple delight where a man may live close to the soil with contentment in his heart.

It was a comforting thought, a gentle dream to dwell on during times of change, but Aldo was maturing. With more wisdom than he perhaps realized, he continued, "it is only a few of us who may return to that land once in a while, and I am sure we do not fully value the greatness of our opportunity. I am learning, though — every day."[20]

Aldo's second year at Yale drew to a close. Scheduled to attend summer forestry camp in Pennsylvania, he would not be returning to Burlington at all, and instead made plans for a week-long walking tour through the countryside of Massachusetts and Connecticut. He needed the break. His internal strains had begun to show. His friends noticed it. He had lost weight, and was not sleeping at night. While in this state, he received four invitations to join exclusive fraternities, all of which he mysteriously turned down "after full consideration."[21]

When Carl learned about Aldo's hike, he suggested that he might come east and join in if business matters allowed. Carl was deep in the details of a planned factory expansion and implied that he, too, could use a rest. At the same time, he rebuked Aldo, in the mildest terms possible, for turning down the fraternity bids. "You are sometimes too reticent or modest," he wrote, "to really advance your own interests as you properly should. You will find that in all affairs of life, that it is necessary to put yourself forward to a reasonable extent. Modesty is quite a virtue, but it can be over-done, and you are inclined to that extreme."[22]

The prospect of his father's company excited Aldo. "We have always been in the woods together, we understand each other there, and you are still and by far my best companion in the open," he wrote. Aldo gave his father other reasons to come east. He could visit Lawrenceville, and then travel home with Carl Jr. He could see for himself "how and where and with whom we have been spending the years of our dependence upon you

—in hopes, at least, the last years of our dependence." And then Aldo's feelings spilled out.

And finally there is another reason for which I want this visit with you, that is greater than either or any or all of these. I cannot just explain why, but somehow I have come to feel that you and Mama do not really *know* me thoroughly any more. We have seen each other during vacations and all that; but somehow I know that this is true—I have felt it for a long time. In some respects your idea of me is too good, [and] I do not at all come up to your belief in me. In other respects I am equally certain that you under-rate me, because your ideas apply to what I *was* long ago and not to what I have become. Please understand that I do not blame anybody, either you or myself, for this, and also that it is only with pleasure that I look forward to the time when we shall see each other face to face and become even better friends than we are already. For on the whole I think things will balance up all right and there is nothing of which I am ashamed. It is for this reason, then, that I hope you can come. We will have a good visit with each other and part with a better mutual understanding which will be a help to all of us concerned. If I have appeared to be too serious in this, remember that in spite of what I have said I know even better than you do that you and Mama are after all my very best friends and that we also understand each other far better than most people who have never been separated seven consecutive days throughout their whole lives. And for my part let me also say something which has long been in my heart an absolute conviction, and which will always remain an absolute conviction. It is this. That never, in any age, at any time, in any land, has a man been given as many chances to make good in life as *I* have been given, and let me also say with Abraham Lincoln, in whose biography I came across these words: "All that I am, or hope to be, I owe to my angel mother."[23]

A reversal of the Mississippi might have had less effect on Clara Leopold. She was not aware of any such breach of understanding and tried to explain it away as a consequence of her irregular correspondence. "In our old accustomed surroundings," she wrote back, "everything constantly reminds us of the absent ones, and the remark, 'I wish Aldo (Marie or Carl as the case may be) could see this bird, this flower or sunset' arises in a thousand different forms, while to you we must at times drop out of existence, or become shadowy. Then, too, I must confess that your short vacations have not always been what I dreamed and hoped they might be." She scolded Aldo for referring to himself as a "dependent," and suggested that Aldo's letter was the result of a "little touch of homesickness, because I shall never never admit that we can be drifting apart, much less that new interests can displace your loyal old pater and Mütterchen. *You* are my Rock of Ages."[24] Aldo's letter made Carl want to go east all the more, and he wrote back to Aldo saying so.

Despite a bad case of eyestrain, Aldo immediately replied to their letters. He denied the charge of homesickness:

I am *never* homesick. I can honestly say that although there are times when I am impatient, displeased, dissatisfied, or even disgusted with *myself* in some matter or other, I can still honestly say that I have *never* been dissatisfied with my life here, or with anything that it offered me. On the other hand, it is at such times more than any other that I appreciate the opportunities which I enjoy and before long I am always ready to try a fresh start with an ever increasing enthusiasm and love of life. So perhaps there is some good, even much good, in a spell of the blues. Anyhow, don't ever think me homesick! Never. . . . I have the very best that any man can ever have, and best of all my possessions is home.[25]

Then, in one of the most enigmatic passages from Leopold's college letters, he tried to explain his current state of mind:

There is not and never will be any lack of understanding between us. For after all, way down deep we *do* not change, and way down deep we *do* understand each other. It is only in the more superficial matters that we change. I guess that in the old days when I was a kid, in the days when we were together every day, I had just as much desire to live to the Truth as it was given to me to see the truth, as I have now. And perhaps my success in living up to that desire is no greater now than it was then, although I think I can say that it is, and that it grows greater daily in some things, if not in all. . . .

In conclusion, just to show you how far from me it was to entertain any idea of lack of real understanding between us, I will tell you what I had in mind in saying what I did. That is, I will tell you one of the things as an example. It was in regard to the matter of my declining this or that bid to this or that fraternity, and in his letter Papa very properly advised me, that, although he did not doubt that I had sufficient reason for declining as I did, I should still remember my natural *backwardness* and *modesty* and not neglect to "advance myself halfway," so to speak, in social matters of that kind. These are not his words, but it is in effect what he said. Now it is only natural that he should say that in the light of what I *was* years ago, but I could not help but think that he had a wrong idea of me as I am *now* here in New Haven. True it is that in such matters I never "fish" and never have fished, nor do I ever intend to. But it is not true that I am "bashful," or whatever one may wish to call it, here among the *fellows,* whatever I may be anywhere else. On the contrary, I am just the opposite. I make a point of bowing my head to no man, though he be the biggest man in college, and also to be willing and ready to speak to and be seen with the most humble man in my class. My acquaintance extends from the class president to the man who lives in an attic down in the slums and washes dishes behind a lunch counter between recitations. I am on equal terms with the man who spends a thousand a year on clothes and the man who spends a sum total of five hundred; with the YMCA secretary and the man who goes to bed only three or four nights a week and spends most of his leisure in New York. And if I do say it, it is to this policy and nothing else that I owe my comparative success of the past year in the social and official side of college life. What Papa does me the honor of calling "modesty" dates from years ago, and was *not* modesty but something which I cannot tell you here, and which it is my business to forget. "Let us look forward, not back; up, not down" is the motto for me.

Now we are done with this business. Let us, with renewed confidence in each other and renewed appreciation of our opportunity of *having* each other, start out anew and make good, acquit ourselves nobly (these resolutions are for me), and give as has been given to us, generously and with a cheerful heart.[26]

In a time of youthful growth and confusion, Aldo Leopold was not at peace. He had obviously been contemplating his social standing, his school work, and his purpose and values, yet was well aware of the fact that he was receiving every advantage and opportunity one could ask for—a fact brought home by his friendship with Bennie. He was highly sensitive about his dependence on his parents. It became a point of honor to fulfill the obligations he felt not only toward his parents, but toward his world, social and natural, and toward himself and the obscure inner desire that impelled him. His reluctance to join the fraternities may have reflected dissatisfaction with their class-consciousness, though he hinted cryptically of some still deeper reason. What was the mysterious "something" that he was determined to put behind him? A youthful insecurity? A lack of resolve or self-respect? He never again alluded to it.

Whatever its causes, the inner storm that had been so long in the building was quick to dissipate. Once Aldo had aired his troubled thoughts, his optimism returned. The "lack of understanding" disappeared. Ironically, it was the urbane Hamilton Drummond who was swept away by personal pressures. Having burned himself out, Ham quit Princeton in sudden revolt, and took off for the West. "Stick to me, Aldo," he wrote to his old confidant, "for God knows I need you."[27]

Carl sprung loose at the last moment and took the train to New Haven, where he found Aldo in poor physical condition, "worse," he wrote to Clara, "than I have ever seen him."[28] Father and son then enjoyed a week-long New England idyll. They walked up the meadowed valley of the Housatonic River, rode a train into the Berkshires, hiked up into the Green Mountains of Vermont and then back again into Massachusetts, carrying only small day packs, sleeping on the streamsides and in the high forests, and enjoying the constant courtesy of the New Englanders. Aldo, set down in new surroundings, felt his senses come alive.

It is a high climb to our camp, but O how fine after you get here. The country is almost alpine, with sweet fresh pastures and clumps of enormous maples, under one of which is our camp. The breeze blows continually. Fifty yards down the hill a little cold spring, coming out between the roots of a big maple, furnishes our water. We have straw, milk, and eggs from a farm down in the valley. The dog-tent is up, and we are perfectly at home. Yesterday we spent fishing down in the river. . . . The whip-poor-will are with us here also, as they have been at every camp so far. In the evening we sit around our little fire and listen to them, and have long talks together. Both of us are enjoying the trip more and more every day.[29]

Carl wrote home and confessed that "I never before fully appreciated what a relaxation into a semi-barbarous state meant to one's mental and physical being."[30] Along the banks of the Housatonic, up into the white pine hills of Massachusetts, and in the mountains of Windham County, Vermont, the two outdoorsmen took their full measure of verdant pastures and fresh trout. It was a time when one could easily take a trolley to the end of the line, set off on foot, and for at least a while forget one's cares, a time when the land of simple delight was diminishing, but still accessible. Aldo proclaimed the trip "a complete and all around success."[31]

∽

All prospective foresters at Yale were required to spend a summer at the school's camp near Milford, Pennsylvania. The camp was a gift of the Pinchot family, located on lands adjacent to the family's estate in the eastern reaches of the Pocono Mountains. On the train to Milford, Leopold sat with Henry Graves, then head of the Forest School; in later years, as chief of the Forest Service, Graves would be Leopold's boss. Together they botanized from their coach seats.

Free of the tensions that school had brought on, Aldo took great pleasure in the work of camp—surveying, chopping, thinning, mapping, mensuration—and an equally obvious delight in the play—swimming, tramping, fishing, visiting Milford. In regard to the last, he complained that, although the town's summer population swelled with young ladies, "the fussing game here is kind of poor."[32] He christened the hill behind camp "My Hill," and climbed it every evening. "You can see the whole world from up there, and I have built me a stone seat on the very summit. It is nearly sunset when I get there, as we eat at six. I generally stay until the shadow of the hill has crept all the ten miles across the valley and up the Jersey Mountains opposite."[33]

Camp life restored him. He enjoyed field work for the same reason that he had always enjoyed the outdoor life: it gave him a closer understanding of the lay of the land, and of its living things. For the first time, however, he was being trained to manipulate the natural world, and that appealed to him, too. Graves chose him to do some extra work thinning an experimental pine forest. "The White Pine is very pleasant to work in," he wrote home, "and as there is little small brush to cut, the job is a very pleasant one all around. Besides that one learns a great deal about thinnings and about every two minutes I have to stop and figure out the pros and cons of some doubtful step."[34] He also found the atmosphere of camp completely to his liking: late night fires, katydids and hanging moons, mountain streams and unfamiliar forest, good companions and new skills. "Thank the Lord I am not loafing this summer," he wrote to his mother, "and still more that I have taken up this subject."[35]

After two hard months, however, the Milford work began to drag. Aldo looked forward to spending the last two weeks of summer at Les Cheneaux, and to seeing Gretchen Miller. In the meantime, he pronounced himself "well content to pick up the axe again, and while I am biting into the heart of a big pine or chestnut, to think that each chip is like a chip cut out of the interval between Now and Then."[36] When he finally arrived at the club, he missed seeing Gretchen by a day. She too was disappointed, but hoped Aldo would stop in Lexington for a visit with her family on his return east. Aldo was restless again; loafing only made it worse. He decided to leave the club early so he could visit Gretchen. When he told his mother, they both lost their tempers. Aldo left. His stopover in Kentucky was brief, but left an impression. One of Gretchen's friends commented that "he looks and acts like some people on the stage who say exactly the right thing at the right time."[37] Aldo, now a college senior, arrived back in New Haven on September 27, still unsettled, but relieved to be back.

Clara wrote to Aldo and rebuked him for what she considered his inconsiderate early departure. Her frustration and acute disappointment with the apparent erosion of Aldo's loyalty was put into perspective by Carl. "I remarked that the time was evidently near when we no longer could expect to know of your little affairs of the heart. Evidently your mother took this seriously and wrote you I know not what. I am however happy to think we may yet for a while have your confidence in such matters. It will be hard enough for us when this can no longer be so."[38] Carl had calmly pried another finger loose from Clara's grasp, and that grip, though lasting, would never again be quite so strong.

As his classes began, Aldo moved into the Sheffield School's Vanderbilt Hall. Now that his professional direction was clear, he regarded explorations away from that path as mere distractions, or worse. While silviculture, dendrology, and forest botany consumed his time and interest, plant morphology was "an imposing name for a confounded bore. You sit four hours a week squinting through a microscope at a little drop of mud all full of wiggly bugs and things, and then draw pictures of them and label [them] with ungodly Latin names. . . . One cannot help wondering what the *Cyanophycens oscillatorius* has to do with raising timber." Worse yet was French, taught by "a snippy little thing with a faded Van Dyke and curly mud-colored hair. . . . I don't like him, and he doesn't like me, and we both know it."[39] Clara tried to persuade him to enjoy it, but Aldo was uncompromising. "I might also try and cultivate a taste for carpet tacks, but, gee, who wants to pervert nature so ruthlessly."[40]

More important to Aldo were his extracurricular activities — class elections, the debate society, the forestry club, YMCA work, fund-raising efforts for the Extension Committee. The result was class absences, and an official reprimand in the mailbox of 101 Clay Street. His tramps were reduced to a bare one or two for the entire autumn. His social life waned. When he realized that he had no date to the upcoming Princeton game, he invited his mother. Clara declined, but appreciated the offer. "Old ladies," she replied, "enjoy being taken down from the shelf now and then."[41] Aldo indulged in fantasy plans for the great canoe trip, and read with envy Hamilton Drummond's regular letters from out west. Ham had ended up as a singer with a travelling show and wrote to Aldo from Spokane . . . Seattle . . . Aberdeen. . . .

The main news of fall 1907 came from home. Carl and Clara now had three children in expensive eastern schools. The previous spring they had undertaken a costly remodelling of their home. Then, in November, a sudden economic panic caused the demand for office furniture to plummet. As past orders went unpaid, Carl was hard pressed to meet his payroll. Aldo, oblivious to the business conditions, bought yet another new suit. Carl angrily charged Clara with the task of restraining family expenditures. Activity at the factory came to a complete halt. Aldo, Marie, and Carl prepared to remain east over the Christmas holiday. All during these years, the factory had been busy, but barely profitable. More than once, Clara's high-cost wishes for her home and family forced Carl to sell capital assets, including buildings downtown, out of the Starker estate. Now he went to the well once more. They could not afford to buy the more expensive anthracite for heating; it was a period, as Clara put it, of "hard times, soft coal."[42] With Clara monitoring the family budget and Carl holding steady at the factory until money and orders trickled in, the economic crisis eased, but not before the children had had their financial wings clipped. Carl and Clara hoarded enough of their meagre earnings to bring the children home for Christmas.

Carl patiently waited for business to revive, but, cornered by a lack of orders, a restless union, and a backlog of furniture in stock, he was forced to lay off some of his workers. He was on the road trying to drum up business when Aldo's twenty-first birthday rolled around. From a hotel room in Grand Rapids he wrote:

. . . 21 years ago today I received (while in St. Louis) a message that was of importance to both of us. I hope that importance will continue to grow in [the] future as it has in the past, if so the world will [be] the better for a good Citizen + I will feel my life was not entirely in vain. . . . The business situation is not good. Everybody cheerfull + hopeful, but all waiting and little doing.[43]

Both Carl and Clara lived for their children, and invested far more than money in their futures. Still, just as one could build a quality desk and lack customers, so could one present a child with every opportunity and sometimes be disappointed with the returns. Aldo was overextending himself again, and in February 1908 the university put him on probation for missing too many classes. He provided his parents with an off-handed explanation, but this time it did not suffice. Clara sat down and delivered a long, unrelenting upbraiding:

At a time when it had become a serious problem with us to let you continue to prepare yourself for your future career, you seem to give fussing, YMCA, and New [York] preference over your own work, and it is time to call a halt. I no longer understand you it appears. . . . I hoped it was just a passing phase and that you would return to your former earnestness of purpose. . . . You are in danger of losing your former steadfastness of purpose. . . . It is no easy matter for us to furnish you with the funds to complete your course. . . . Even a year ago I should have stoutly declared that *my boy* would never have provoked this letter. . . . If we are ignorant of what you term success at college, we may be in closer touch with the difficulties of real life so far removed from your consciousness. . . . Nothing short of a complete readjustment of your present life to your old time ideals will put you on a safe road.[44]

There were no humorous turns in this letter, and no subsequent apologies.

The letter worked. Aldo sacrificed some of his work load and concentrated on his forestry studies. Springtime arrived without benefit of his annual literary celebration. His tramps disappeared entirely, replaced by the discipline of required field work. Those Lawrenceville outings, once so vivid to his opening mind, became the stuff of nostalgia. "Saw a Blue-headed Vireo up on the Forest School Grounds yesterday—a beauty. Reminds me of the old days."[45] He was outdoors as much as ever, but with a different purpose. He reflected on a day spent thinning the school plantation:

I saw many birds walking out and back that day—and it aroused a kind of regret that I can't get out and just loiter around in the woods any more. One really gets to see nothing in hurrying to and from a certain place—only just enough to remember how much there really is to see on a May morning. Still I think that if I should have to loiter around for a week I would be too restless to enjoy it.[46]

His nostalgic view of the past extended into a wistful hope for the future. All spring he laid detailed plans for the long-anticipated canoe trip, going so far as to plot the route and buy equipment. He and his brother Carl, he insisted, would embark that summer.

Aldo spent his spring vacation in Stamford and in New York City. He paid a visit to his latest interest, a classmate of Marie's named Margery Smith ("Margery never looked better—and that is saying a good deal").[47]

Aldo's other new interest was sailing; he organized a boat party down on Long Island Sound. Following a student fad, Aldo bought himself a canary, which he named "Bunny." He who had glorified the flaming brilliance of the wild warbler now wrote home about the play of his pet canary. Fortunately, Papa was around to provide the necessary tease:

Now the companionship of a Canary bird may be very nice, but it will be interesting to see you come home with a canary, and the only thing you can add is a hat box and a flower pot. You will be strictly in it then. That is the way people travelled west ten years ago when I was on the road. You had better not take a Pullman, but must get up in the front part of the car, take your shoes off and stick your feet up. Then you can feel that you are strictly "Aufait."[48]

Aldo worked himself off probation, performed well in exams, and received his bachelor's degree and diploma. The class yearbook featured a caricature of the foppish forester-to-be looking over his shoulder at a young lady. Its caption: "He passes them all, but not (by)." Aldo's motto: "To hell with convention!"[49] He went home at the end of June.

The family returned to Les Cheneaux that summer. The Canadian canoe trip never did come off. The closest Aldo ever came to fulfilling his dream was a week-and-a-half excursion with his father and brothers along the Huron shore toward the Soo — in a rowboat. His father would have no part of the canoe. The Canadian north that Aldo explored for years in his mind remained there, a blank spot on his mental map, the province of an unfulfilled dream.

∽

In the fall of 1908, Leopold began his final push as a master's student in the Yale Forest School. As such, he would take part in a remarkable educational effort that in the decades to come would literally change the American landscape. These were dynamic times for the conservation movement in America; forestry was at its forefront, and the Yale School was at the forefront of forestry.[50]

When Leopold was born, there was no profession of forestry to speak of in America. There was only the lumberjack's legacy. From New England to New York and Pennsylvania, up through Michigan and across Wisconsin and Minnesota, a trail of slash and ash had followed the lumber baron's exploitation. The bawl and din of emerging nationhood drowned out the isolated voices of protest. The views of men like Henry David Thoreau, George Perkins Marsh, John Muir, and Carl Schurz took on greater relevance only as the frontier retreated and the reality of continental limits emerged. Their conservation intuitions first crystallized into new resource policies in the 1870s and the 1880s as the federal government took tentative steps toward curbing abuses and conserving the nation's forest and wildlife resources. In 1891 Congress passed the Forest Reserve Act that granted the president authority to establish "forest reserves" on the public domain, to be administered by the Department of the Interior. Within a year and a half, President Benjamin Harrison set aside some thirteen million acres of important forest and watershed lands, virtually all of them in the West. Grover Cleveland would add another five million acres.

At the time, those involved in the cause were dedicated outsiders, or migrants from established fields like botany and geography. There was hardly a handful of trained foresters in the entire country, and these were products of the European schools. By the late 1890s, the emphasis in forestry circles had shifted away from the initial protection of forests to the safeguarding and scientific management of the distant reserves. This called for a new breed of forest specialists.

Answering that call with aplomb, the young Gifford Pinchot dominated the early days of the profession. Others had come before and laid the essential groundwork, but it was the forceful Pinchot who brought forestry out of obscurity and transformed it into an important item on the Progressive Era agenda. An 1889 graduate of Yale, Pinchot studied forestry in Germany and France, returned to private practice in America, and in 1898 became chief of the Department of Agriculture's Division of Forestry, forerunner of the modern Forest Service. His goal was nothing less than to convert the public, the lumber interests, and his own government department over to the ways of scientific forest management.

To this end, Pinchot's family donated funds to Yale University in 1900 to open a graduate study program in forestry. Cornell University had established the first American school of forestry in 1898, but it soon became a victim of political controversy. Other schools subsequently opened at Harvard, Michigan, and other universities, but the Yale program, staffed by the foremost professionals in the country and overseen by Pinchot's colleague Henry Graves, quickly became the dominant educational force in conservation.

After Theodore Roosevelt ascended to the presidency in 1901, Pinchot, already a good friend, became a close advisor. Roosevelt added his considerable outdoor experience and boisterous spirit to Pinchot's ardor, and the conservation movement took off. In February 1905, Roosevelt signed the Transfer Act that gave responsibility for the nation's forest reserves over to the Bureau of Forestry in the Department of Agriculture. Five months later, the bureau was renamed the United States Forest Service, and Pinchot became its first chief.

Historians of the American conservation movement regard Pinchot as the foremost exemplar of the utilitarian approach to conservation, according to which man has a right to use natural resources, but also an obligation to use them wisely and efficiently—or as the classic criterion put it, "for the greatest good for the greatest number over the long run." As applied to forests and espoused by Pinchot, this meant that the nation's forest reserves ought not to be maintained as inviolate sanctuaries, but opened to enlightened management. Managed rationally, the nation's forests could provide a sustained yield of timber, safely and indefinitely.

This aim became clear when the new Forest Service issued in 1905 the first edition of its field manual, *The Use of the National Forest Reserves: Regulation and Instructions*. Small enough to fit in a shirt pocket, the *Use Book* was the ranger's indispensable guide to the responsibilities, procedures, and regulations his work entailed. The first edition stated the mission of the Forest Service: "Forest Reserves are for the purpose of preserving a perpetual supply of timber for home industries, preventing destruction of the forest cover which regulates the flow of streams, and protecting local industries from unfair competition in the use of forest and range. They are patrolled and protected, at Government expense, for the benefit of the Community and home builder."[51] In order to emphasize this new doctrine of conservative use, the Forest Reserves were officially redesignated "National Forests" in 1907.

Between 1903 and 1907, Roosevelt, by vigorous employment of his executive pen, would more than double the area of land under Forest Service control, from 63 to over 150 million acres.[52] His enthusiasm was unprecedented. The story is told of one young Forest Service applicant who was asked on a qualifying examination, "Who created the first National Forest?" The would-be ranger replied, "The first national forest was made by God but was afterwards expanded by Theodore Roosevelt."[53] At one point, in 1907, Roosevelt found himself obligated to sign into law a bill with an amendment that would take away his power to establish national forests in the West and Northwest. In the hours before signing the bill, he proclaimed 16 million acres of new forests in those regions. Pinchot hastily helped him lay the boundaries. It is one of the enduring images out of conservation history: Roosevelt and Pinchot on their hands and knees in the White House, busily mapping out the new national forests, the hours ticking away, their opponents unaware of the impending coup. The scene was emblematic of the movement at its zenith.

Roosevelt's part in this expansion may have been the easiest. The adventurous work of examining, surveying, and adjusting the borders of the new forests fell to an elite corps of some two dozen "boundary men" who rode alone across the western wilderness. Facing an exponential increase in his administrative workload, Pinchot in 1908 divided his continental domain up into six districts, overseen by six district foresters. Cadres of Yale-trained officers rode off to man the far forests. Pinchot's influence was pervasive. For the next twenty-five years, a disproportionate number of the major figures in forestry, both in the field and in administrative offices, could trace their professional pedigrees directly back to New Haven. The Forest Service would come to resemble, in one historian's words, "a Washington, D.C., chapter of the Yale Alumni Association."[54]

Yet, even during these high times, the conservation movement was far from unified. In fact, Pinchot's rise only exposed latent tensions, and the movement was soon more divided than at any previous time in its short history. In contrast to the utilitarian view, the preservationist approach denied the assumption that the natural world existed solely to serve man's purposes. Forests might provide for the material well-being of human beings, but they did not exist for this reason alone. As surely as forests provided timber, so did they provide beauty, inspiration, and the renewal of over-citified spirits. Furthermore, they provided a place for the wild plants and creatures to live out their own lives, according to their own purposes. The most prominent preservationist spokesman was John Muir. Inspired by the magnificence of Yosemite and informed by his own natural mysticism, Muir spearheaded the crusade to conserve the natural world in part for its own sake, and not solely for man's. In his passionate regard for all things wild, Muir tapped into powerful sentiments that the practical business of nation-building had all but buried. In Muir's view, no conceivable use of a 3000-year-old sequoia or a unique mountain valley could possibly be wiser than the act of letting them be.[55]

The tension between the utilitarian and preservationist views has always existed not only in society-at-large, but within the individual as well. Aldo Leopold was a special case in point. Like most foresters, he was drawn toward the profession because it allowed him to work with the things he enjoyed most in the places he enjoyed most. There were few channels into which an amateur naturalist could divert his talents and make a living. In part because he held both a Muir-like appreciation of nature and a Pinchot-like intent to use nature wisely, Leopold was destined to lead a life of conflicting desires, constant questioning, and unending effort to better define the meaning of conservation.

For the time being, he put questions aside. Although bothered by eyestrain and restricted by the demands of the technical coursework, Aldo was glad to be back for his final round at Yale, and especially to be back in the company of foresters, "a great bunch."[56] One of the hallmarks of the Pinchot-styled Forest Service was its esprit de corps. The professors hardly had to work to instill it in their trainees; it was a natural consequence of the type of character drawn toward forestry. Leopold was overjoyed when he was elected into the Foresters' Society of Robin Hood, Yale's professional fraternity. It was the only fraternity bid he accepted, and he treasured it, not only because membership was a virtual necessity for the serious forestry student, but because he truly enjoyed the fellowship.

Leopold took a room at 379 Temple Street and settled into his course-work: lumbering, timber management, timber practice, forestry in the West, forest regions, forest law. For a brief interval, while his eyes were on the mend, Aldo began to take long walks again, but time cured both his eyes and his relapse into tramping. What spare time he had he spent compiling a study chart to aid in the identification of trees.[57] The chart was a popular success among the students and the first printing instantly sold out. Even the professors asked for copies. Aldo could be quite a busi-nessman when he wanted to, but, like his father, he first had to believe in his product.

As the autumn passed, Aldo realized that his interests were narrowing, but he had no regrets. "I really have forgotten that there is anything else in this world except our *men* and our *work,* and home. Once in a while I get a letter from somebody and am reminded of other things, but not very often. I don't *want* anything else."[58] There were some outside interests — Margery Smith, Sarah Ernst, and Mary Lord, the last a friend of Marie's whom Aldo placed "in a class by herself"—but forestry and foresters still had priority.

After spending the holidays in Burlington, Leopold boarded the train for his last trip east to school. Aldo was twenty-two, and after six years of making this crossing, he had fashioned a full-blown "philosophy of Christmas vacations":

Heretofore I have come home and experienced a decided sensation of "bigness" as compared with my status at school, due of course for the most part to the fact that I came from Yale and that my name was A. Leopold. This Christmas, how-ever, I feel just the other way. I feel that my heaviest assets are on the "work" and not the "play" end of the line, and that I am more of a man in New Haven than doing Society at home. . . . This is very good for me — it will remind me to beware of the constant tendency towards provincialism which affects a man spending all his time on one pursuit.[59]

The last session of classes was scheduled to last until the first of March, when the entire thirty-five-member class of 1909 foresters was to pull up stakes and move south to Texas for a final field assignment and their Civil Service exams. After that, most would directly enter the Forest Service. "I am getting narrow as a clam with all this technical work," Aldo com-plained. Timber testing, forest regulation, and mechanical properties of wood were not romantic subjects. Foresters at Yale spent at least as much time with numbers, charts, and formulae as they did with trees. Aldo was attracted to the adventure, ruggedness, and social benefits of forestry work, and had "no ambition to be a Tie-pickler or a Timber-tester."[60] Significantly, however, Leopold received at this time his first formal exposure to the national forest system in a course conducted by leading U.S. Forest Service administrators. When he learned about District 3, which included forests in the Arizona and New Mexico territories, he stated, "that is where I want to go."[61] He dreamed of becoming a supervisor on his own forest. One day his friend Rube Pritchard remarked to him, "I'd rather be a Supervisor than be the King of England." Aldo readily agreed.

Leopold received his master's degree at the end of February. As he prepared to leave New Haven, Bennie came around regularly. "He is doing fairly well in a way," Aldo wrote home, "but street life is an awful thing for a kid like that to be up against unless you are willing to judge him by street standards. It is good for a man to think how different his own opportunities have been. It takes the conceit out of me immediately and very effectively."[62] Aldo's concern for Bennie was genuine, and he did what he could to provide him with basic friendship. Later, Carl Jr. would follow Aldo to Yale, and also strike up a friendship with Bennie.

Aldo took no final tramps at Yale. He did, however, express a longing to be "out in the hills" and predicted that, once he had arrived in Texas, "the country of green leaves and spring flowers," he would "be attacked by a most prodigious desire to be lazy and go snooping around the woods."[63]

ᔐ

The class of foresters was due to sail from New York to New Orleans aboard the SS *Comus*. Before his departure, Aldo paid the Ketchums a last visit in Stamford, and then went to New York to spend a day with Mary Lord. He and Mary went for a drive around the city, then took in a Broadway play and dined out that evening. With his usual evasiveness, Aldo told his mother that "Mary . . . is of course the same as ever. Nobody could be, or at least ever has been, any more than that."[64] Then Aldo took a "very reluctant" leave from the East. He wrote from the deck of the *Comus*:

Somehow I felt as if I were leaving civilization and all the pleasant things of life behind me. I must say that in a way I still feel as if I really had. I must own up to a very keen enjoyment of these occasional glimpses of that kind of life—of people like the Lords, of good living, and theatres, and leisurely hours, and all that. I am perfectly aware, however, that it is because these glimpses are occasional that I enjoy them so much.[65]

Thus did Leopold reach a provisional resolution of the tension between his love of nature, nurtured along the Mississippi, in the northwoods of the Great Lakes, and in the settled hills of New Jersey and New Haven, and his love of society, nurtured in the closeness of a tight family, the traditions of privileged education, and a valued circle of friends. The child of the Midwest had made his peace with the culture of the East.

After three days of dismal sailing, the passengers awoke "in Heaven." Aldo's first exposure to a southern climate was memorable. He was taken by the blue of the sea and the glow of the moon. The foresters divided off into two factions while on board: the shuffleboard players on deck, and the card players below. Aldo joined neither. He was busy at the rails, observing the sea creatures in this new place.

There were hundreds of flying fish, large coveys of them breaking water every few minutes and skimming off over the waves like big grasshoppers or dragonflies with gauzy wings. Finally they would drop back into the water with a funny splash. . . . Every few minutes one would see a big brown-yellow hulk a couple of feet under the water, and once in a while one would poke out its head—a huge Sea-Turtle. George, but they looked lazy and comfortable! Some of them must have weighed several hundred pounds. In the afternoon we encountered a shoal of porpoises. They were the real treat of the day. They look like a miniature whale, 4 or 5 feet long, with a sharp nose. George how they do swim! They gambol lazily just ahead of the bow, racing with the ship, and every once in a while breaking water with a graceful spring, apparently in pure glee and good spirits. One by one they tired out and gave up the race, but the more enduring ones kept up for over half an hour. I wish I could swim like that![66]

The *Comus* docked in New Orleans, and Aldo returned to "my dear old native Mississippi." Before heading up to the forestry camp at Doucette, Texas, the boys enjoyed a graduation fling. With an overflowing of southern hospitality, the sponsoring lumber company treated the class to the sights, smells, and tastes of New Orleans and Beaumont. A letter arrived in Burlington announcing the news that "one A. Leopold fell from the high estate of teetotaler and nichtraucher."[67]

Over the next ten weeks, the backslider would be reborn in the spirit of the woods. It was a period of diverse work—surveys, traverses, lumbering, volume estimates, mill work, pacing, timber cruising—in a diverse land of cypress swamps, loblolly pine forests, and river plantations. The vicissitudes of camp grub victimized more than one future forester. Rattlesnakes and insects became their close companions as spring arrived, and snake-killing became as intense a sport as crow-killing had once been at Lawrenceville. Mail service was undependable, but Clara's gingerbread and Carl's spring asparagus managed to arrive safely. The foresters were hard workers, but always ready for an evening in Woodville or a late-night campfire. A convention of distinguished visitors descended upon the camp at one point, including Gifford Pinchot himself. The Civil Service exams came and went, but the postexam "jollification" provided the men with lasting memories.

As the weather grew hotter and the work harder, the romantic mystique of the forester's life melted away. The mosquitos raged, and the swimming hole thickened into murky algal soup, but Leopold's incessant optimism carried him through the camp life blues. "It is really a very beautiful region," he wrote home. "If you could see the full moon tonight, sailing high over the towering pine-trees, you would like it, too. I have decided, again and again, that it is worth all the trouble of the mosquitos and fleas and snakes and pigs, and more too."[68]

The naturalist in Leopold reemerged during these weeks in Texas. Both at work and in his free time, Aldo began to explore the woods with old-time enjoyment and newfound enthusiasm. His letters home were cheerful, witty, and long, and he even described the new birds he had seen. "Everything is at peace," he wrote one night after a cool spring rain had driven off the heat and the mosquito platoons. "I could sit here all night and tell you all about the delights of 'snooping around' in the woods, of how everything I see there puts me in mind of the old days, and of how I would like this minute to begin again on my birds and flowers if I only had time. And I would like to tell you how earnestly I wish that our Frederic shall get started to see and love all these things."[69] With the pressures of school behind him, and the promise of a career before him, Aldo relaxed. His idealistic desire to "live to the Truth," as bold as it was unattainable, had been brought down to the worldly confines of being a forester. In his acceptance of that limitation, he found a kind of mature rejuvenation that displayed itself in a hearty acceptance of the forester's work, an enjoyment of his company, a partial return to nature's sanctuary, and a general cheeriness that had been lacking for so long.

In one of his last letters from Texas, Aldo thanked his mother for the regular packages of cakes, gingerbread, and stuffed dates that allowed him to survive the culinary assaults of the camp cook:

More than once when I have been feeling blue or discouraged, the arrival of a good letter from you, or of some token of your care for me, has made me so ashamed of myself for giving in to mere temporary troubles, that I have straightened up and *made* things go right again. I don't feel blue very often, nor for any reason except the inability to get the most out of my work. But that, with me, means a good deal. Nor is there anything wrong with me just now. But I wanted to take this chance to tell you that your care for me is not wasted.[70]

Aldo's words captured the greater gratitude he felt for the preparation he had received. His parents' devotion had allowed him to explore and follow his interests to their limits, and any bounds he felt were self-imposed — and self-neglected. He was right: he had been given as much opportunity as anyone could desire, and although he occasionally mismanaged that freedom, his sense of responsibility, also taken from Prospect Hill, held sway.

Camp broke at the end of May. Aldo went to Shreveport to conduct a private land survey, then headed north to Burlington for a rest. In a month, he was due to report for work with the United States Forest Service.

∽

The newly minted forester was competent, devoted, and eager. It is tempting, and to a degree accurate, to call Aldo Leopold a disciple of Gifford Pinchot; all the foresters who emerged from the Yale Forest School were. But Leopold did not so much absorb the Pinchot doctrine as adopt it by default. In his professional attitudes, the utilitarian idea dominated because he found confirmation there for his own notions of conservation. Leopold was a naturalist and a hunter who became a forester. Yet, his own attitudes, shaped by a strong father, a devoted mother, a rich experience of natural surroundings, and a strong inner drive, were too independent to be dominated by anyone, or by any idea. He did not often express those attitudes; they were not yet fully developed, the prevailing philosophies sufficed, and, in any case, he was not one to blow his own horn. But Leopold had kept his mind open, thus ensuring that when new light would be needed, he could help to shed it. His greatest asset was not his intelligence, or perceptivity, or spirit, or conviction, although he possessed all of these in abundance. His greatest asset was his independence, and his awareness of the interdependence that allowed it.

Part III

SOUTHWEST

6

Apache: The Breaks
of the Blue
(1909–1911)

O N T H E morning of July 1, 1909, Leopold boarded the Atchison,
Topeka, and Santa Fe at Fort Madison, Iowa, and headed west
for Albuquerque. The train traced a transprairie arc over the route
of the old Santa Fe Trail. It passed near Liberty, Missouri, crossed the
Missouri River at Kansas City, and began its transect of the midwestern
wheatlands. At sunset, the train met the hundredth meridian at Dodge City.
In western Kansas, the austere hills above the Arkansas River rolled away
beneath a widening night sky, and the land flattened out into the treeless
high plains of eastern Colorado. Willows and cottonwoods, confined by
aridity to the rivercourses, left the prairie to the grasses, grains, and homesteaders. The high sky, the sky of the West, dry and deep and light, became luminous with daybreak. At La Junta, with the front range of the
Rocky Mountains coming into view, the train bore south and rode the base
of the Sangre de Cristos into the New Mexico Territory. The hot wind
took on the tangy aroma, new to Leopold, of piñon, sage, and juniper.
     Late on the afternoon of July 2, the train pulled into Albuquerque.
Leopold would not have admitted it to anyone, including himself, but he
was as green as they came. Inexperience was the one trait common to all
new migrants. Each brought along a particular set of values, prejudices,
expectations, motivations, abilities. Leopold brought his notion of the West
as a wild wonderland, as well as a set of acute senses, a restless curiosity,
and an ample young ego. His training as a progressive forester gave him
a new idea to impress on the landscape. Fortunately, he also had enough
common sense to spare him some of the humiliations that newcomers inevitably suffered. And at least he knew how to ride a horse.

The morning after his arrival in Albuquerque, Leopold reported in at the headquarters of District 3 of the United States Forest Service, a row of upstairs offices in the Luna-Stricklar Building. There he first met Arthur Ringland. Ringland, the sharp young head forester of District 3, had criss-crossed the West as one of the Forest Service's "boundary men," became Chief of Boundaries in Washington, then took over as district forester in District 3, which included twenty-one forests in the South and Southwest. Ringland told Leopold to report back for orientation after the Independence Day holiday while a permanent field assignment was arranged.[1]

Leopold and a half dozen other new recruits spent a week in orienta-tion, learning the district's methods and policies on grazing, silviculture, lumber sales, and operations. On July 13, Leopold received orders to re-port to the year-old Apache National Forest in the Arizona Territory, where he would go to work as forest assistant under Supervisor John D. Guthrie.

Three days later, Leopold was aboard the train again, crossing over the continental divide into the expansive mesalands and Painted Desert of north-eastern Arizona. Holbrook, a Navajo trading village, was the rail stop clos-est to Springerville, where the Apache Forest was headquartered. Leopold hired a stagecoach for the two-day, eighty-five-mile journey south to Springerville, upstream on the Little Colorado River.

The desert plain gradually rose toward distant mountains. Above the range loomed the tablelike bulk of Escudilla Mountain and the alpine-tipped White Mountains. Just outside Springerville, the vast, ancient sedi-mentations of the Colorado Plateau gave way to relatively fresh igneous extrusions associated with the Mogollon Rim. Volcanism gave the vista a strange, distinctive beauty. High cinder cones, dark and perfect, pocked the sweep of range. As the stagecoach neared Springerville, the wagon trail ran along a thick sill.

On July 19, Leopold met Supervisor Guthrie in Springerville and be-gan to acquaint himself with his new tasks. In his first two days on the job, he drew up, "for my own use," maps of the Apache.[2] What Leopold etched onto his paper was a land of stunning diversity and beauty. To the north of Springerville lay the plateau lands beyond the Apache Forest bound-ary; to the southwest, the White Mountains, the Mogollon Rim, and the Apache Reservation; to the southeast, the "breaks" of the Blue River and the Blue Range, a confusion of wildlands which an early forest inspector described as "no well-defined mountain range, but rather a chaotic mass of very precipitous and rocky hills."[3] Rising behind Springerville was the purple basaltic mass of Escudilla. Like so many vistas in the West, Springer-ville's was dominated by the mountain on its horizon. And like so many mountains, Escudilla was dominated by a legendary beast, the silver-tipped grizzly bear the locals named "Old Bigfoot."

The gamut of Arizona's forest types grew on the Apache. Cottonwood, willow, and sycamore lined the canyon streambanks. Oak groves, other scrub hardwoods, and the familiar mixture of juniper and piñon covered the higher semidesert range. Above these, a seemingly endless stand of ponderosa pine climbed the mountainsides. Aspen, spruce, and fir grew higher up along the ridgetops. On top of Baldy Peak, at 11,590 feet the highest mountain in the forest, one of the continent's southernmost alpine plant communities survived in the tundralike snow and cold.

Wildlife, though diminished since the arrival of white settlers, was still more abundant on the Apache than on any other tract of land in Arizona. Bison and elk had met their local demise. Antelope and mountain sheep were growing scarce. White-tailed deer were plentiful, but mule deer decreasing. Turkeys were common on the Blue, but declining on the southern end of the forest. Doves, ducks, and geese were seasonally abundant. Large predators—the grizzlies, wolves, and mountain lions—still commanded the ranges in sufficient numbers to draw the fire of encroaching civilization: the era of the bounty hunter and government trapper was at hand, and the campaign against "varmints" reaching its climax.[4]

No roads crossed the Apache National Forest, and few entered it. The train stopped at Holbrook. The automobile had not yet come even that far. The forest was Apache territory until 1886, when Geronimo and the remnant of his Apache nation were subdued, and forced onto nearby reservations. Coronado in 1540 had been the first European to arrive in the area. It is said that he crossed lands west of the Blue River on his epic quest for Cibola and the Seven Golden Cities where the sands sparkled in the sun. There was no gold, but in the centuries that followed, the Hispanic dons and Mexican shepherds braved the Apaches and brought their sheep to the lush grass plains and high interior meadows. In the 1880s, railroads opened the territory and cattlemen began to arrive from the drought-stricken plains of west Texas and Oklahoma to graze their longhorns on the last of the open range.

The Apache National Forest was one of four carved out of the Black Mesa Forest Reserve on July 1, 1908. The original Black Mesa Reserve, established in 1898, took in most of the highlands of central and eastern Arizona. It included the great swath of open ponderosa pine forest that ran 300 miles along the Mogollon Rim from Flagstaff southeast into the New Mexico Territory. Concerns over water supply played a particularly important role in forest policy in the Southwest, and irrigators greeted the new federal reserve with approval. Local miners and stockmen howled, however, sensing a threat to their previously unhindered use of the public domain. The region was spared the more bitter confrontations between old-time users and newly arrived administrators when Pinchot, as part of his effort to open the reserves to use, picked one of their own, a cattleman named Albert Potter, to formulate the Forest Service's grazing policy. Potter's ranch was on rangeland adjacent to what became the Apache National Forest.

Despite grazing pressure from cattle, sheep, and goats, the Apache Forest remained one of the wildest forests of District 3; its rugged topography precluded the intensive overstocking that other forests were experiencing. A new economic force came to bear when the copper mines opened at Clifton, just beyond the southern border of the Apache. The lumber needs of the mines would constitute the first large-scale demand on the forest's standing timber, a project Forest Assistant Leopold would help to plan and initiate.

There was no smooth or unembarrassing way for a tenderfoot to begin his metamorphosis to seasoned local. First, Leopold put away his fancy eastern clothes and outfitted himself in the manner of a true western ranger: boots, leather chaps, jeans, bandanna, and a hat broad enough to shade himself and half the Arizona Territory. He renounced his past as a "nichtraucher" and began his lifelong pipe-smoking habit. Each Forest Service man had to provide and keep his own horses. Aldo went out to Colter's Ranch and, after trying out "Pink" and "Mexico," chose "Jiminy Hicks." At Colter's he received his first lessons in roping. Fitted with a saddle and presented with a regulation set of pistols, Leopold was ready for work.

As forest assistant, Leopold assumed what for him was an ideal position between the rangers in the field and the administrators in Springerville and Albuquerque. While in town he would take part in the official decision-making, but he was to spend most of his time out in the field, implementing the decisions and assisting the rangers. After settling into "Lang 'dobe," the plain house where Guthrie and Deputy Supervisor Viles lived, Aldo rode out into the forest for a month's worth of the work to which he would soon grow accustomed: inspecting private lumber mills, measuring and marking timber for sale, scaling cut logs, surveying and sowing an experimental seed plot. Guthrie was immediately impressed by Aldo's spirit, and approved of his private project: a tentative plan to establish a game refuge on the Blue. During that first month, Leopold rode over most of the northern half of the forest, met all the rangers, and acquired what was known locally as a "rubber butt plate," the one indispensable need in horseback country.

Work was not the only thing for which Leopold had come west. On his first rounds of the Apache, he sampled most of the better trout streams. On his first free Sunday, he did what every even partially romantic spirit had to do—climb the mountain. He rode Jiminy Hicks to the tabletop of Escudilla where, overlooking the green convolutions of the forest below and the tawny flats of the plain beyond, he had reached the symbolic end of his journey west. His means may have differed from those who had come before and those who were yet to come, but the attraction was the same: for Leopold, as for so many others, the open lands of the West revealed themselves as the nation's great repository of promise, adventure, and un-alloyed freedom.

~

After only one month in the Forest Service saddle, Leopold was given his first important assignment. A manpower shortage across the district forced the Albuquerque office to shuffle personnel. Leopold received or-ders to take over as crew chief of the reconnaissance party then at work in the Blue Range.

Reconnaissance was the essential first step taken in establishing new national forests. To administer the forests, supervisors first had to know what they were working with — the amount, location, quality, and charac-ter of the timber. There was only one way to take inventory: parties of timber "cruisers" were sent out on the forest, usually for several months at a time, to survey and map the land, and to estimate the amount of stand-ing timber. The work was the most tedious and demanding in the service, requiring technical expertise, close coordination of effort, sheer physical stamina, and tolerance for one's crewmates and camp conditions.[5]

The first reconnaissance in the Southwest had taken place the previous summer on the Coconino Forest in central Arizona. Its crew was trained by Frank Vogel, an old-school cruiser from Montana who had little re-gard for this new breed of college-trained forester. After Vogel left to in-troduce his methods in Colorado, leadership of that first crew passed on to J. Howard Allison, a 1906 graduate of the Yale Forest School. Allison was to train most of the early reconnaissance leaders and parties of Dis-trict 3. Vogel's method was as straightforward in its conception as it was difficult in its execution. Following the original Land Office survey lines, the reconnaissance crew combed the forest on foot, over all terrain, di-recting by compass, pacing out distances, locating the all-important sec-tion corner markers, erecting markers when there were none to be found. The individual cruiser, his bearings gained, divided his assigned areas into forty-acre blocks. For each block, he was to draw a map of natural and man-made features, note the forest type, measure elevation changes (using semireliable aneroid barometers), and, most important, estimate the amount of timber on the land. On average, the cruiser was assigned forty-eight blocks — three square miles — every two days. He worked alone, carrying only his staff, compass, pace counter, barometer, notebook, canteen, and lunch. "Panting up the canyon," Leopold later recalled, "the cruiser felt a curious incongruity between the remoteness of his notebook symbols and the immediacy of sweaty fingers, locust thorns, deer-fly bites, and scolding squirrels."[6] But it was through such direct means and systematic persistence that the cruiser eventually converted the wild forest into manageable maps and numbers.

The crew chief directed the operation. He was responsible for coordinating, assigning, and inspecting the work of the men. He checked their survey lines and estimates for accuracy, cruised himself most days, and saw that the various maps were in order at the end of the day. In addition, he scouted the location of base camps, secured provisions, and hired the packers and cooks that kept the camp supplied and fed. And he tried to do all this with utmost efficiency; a standing competition existed among parties throughout the district to record the lowest cost per acre on reconnaissance.

Leopold's troubles began about the time he mounted his horse. Before taking over the Blue Range party, he was assigned to another crew on the adjacent Sitgreaves Forest for a week of training. He set out from the CC Ranger Station to find the crew, but soon got lost and had to return. He set out again, got lost again, and had to spend the night in a sheep camp. Finally, after five days, he arrived at the camp of the Sitgreaves crew. One week of training later, on the fourth of September, he was back on the Apache in charge of his own crew.

Leopold's training was hardly adequate for the task. At first his problems were mathematical. In reckoning an important survey base line, his school-day troubles with figures returned to haunt him and he made several crucial errors. His crew, too small to begin with, consisted of three new-growth foresters and two experienced "practical men," local lumbermen who knew the country. The older lumbermen offered advice to their novice crew chief, but Leopold grew defensive, ignored them, and tried to bluff his way through. As the surveying errors compounded, he was forced to stay in camp most days, double- and triple-checking his maps and figures. Consequently, he did little cruising himself. As the party's expenses rose, its pace slowed, and the crew's regard for Leopold sank.

Despite his troubles, Leopold relished the ruggedness of the work and of the country in which he was performing it. He boastfully appealed to his father to pay a visit to "this here Blue Range. . . . I am tired of seeing you slave around that damned office all the year around. . . . Now you and the Kid come out here, get you a small dog and a couple of horses, and just snoop around here for a month. I'll bet you can land some fine hides and some very succulent trout." He challenged his father to take on Old Bigfoot. "There is a big White Bear in here," he wrote, "Come on and show him how to behave. Nobody else can bother him so far, it seems."[7]

Three weeks into the reconnaissance, Leopold received orders to join two "expert lumbermen" on a four-day inspection of the Blue River. The

Forest Service was trying to decide how to deliver the pine of the upper Blue to the towns, mills, and copper mines fifty miles downriver. It was the wildest piece of country Leopold had yet seen, and it was about to be opened up, either by driving the logs down the river or by building a new road up from Clifton. He waxed enthusiastic about moving the timber. "With 15 million a year consumption down at Clifton and the Copper Mines, there will be something doing on this forest before long or I'm mistaken. I am lucky to be here in advance of the big works."[8]

After the inspection, Leopold tried to return to his crew, but the camp was gone. He had left no work outline, and the men had moved on without him. He trailed them and eventually caught up, but the camp was in shambles. Supplies were low. Told that the meat supply had run out, Leopold went out and killed a blacktail buck. The men would have been happier had he just bargained with a rancher for a beef. To make matters worse, Leopold had set ideas about how life in camp ought to be led: it had to conform to his outdoors ideal. He insisted that the cook prepare meals over an open fire instead of a stove, and that the men eat sitting on the ground instead of at the table. The problem was not simply that he was a greenhorn, but that he was confidently inflicting his greenness on the others. He wrote home to Marie on October 4, "two of the men, Lumberjacks to boot, began to grumble this morning about the 'hard life.' And this glorious fall weather too! Why damn their whining souls, wait till it begins to snow. That will take some conceit out of them, or I'm a liar. It would be really laughable if it weren't so unexpected, and liable to become serious. It looks as if it [will] take all the tact and patience I can raise to hold the party together until I finish this job."[9]

He was right about that. Matters progressed from worse to worse yet. In trying to economize, he began to scrimp on food, a serious error in any lumber camp. Charles Heller, a new forest assistant, joined the crew, and he and Leopold took an instant disliking toward one another. Heller was a city-born forester out of Harvard, and so green he made Leopold look like an old hand. Heller arrived in camp saddlesore and promptly took sick, signs of inexcusable delicacy in Leopold's eyes. Then there was the matter of the Apache poachers. For years the Indians had been jerking venison illegally on the southwest slope of the Blue Range. When Leopold saw their signal fires, he resolved to catch them. Twice he pursued them, but twice he returned to camp empty-handed. The men, hard about their work, were annoyed by the antic. The ill-will in camp continued to fester, but the crew and its chief labored on.

It was apparently during this period that an event of lasting import in Leopold's life occurred. He and one of his crew were sitting high on a rimrock eating lunch one day when they noticed movement in the rapids of the river below. They thought it was a doe, but when it made the bank and shook itself off, they saw that it was a wolf. Soon a pack of grown pups, all tailwags and mock assaults, emerged from the streamside willows to greet the old wolf. The men went for their rifles, and hastily blasted away at the wolves from the rock above. After the gunsmoke cleared, they clambered down to the riverside to inspect the results. One pup was crippled, and tried to escape into the rocks. The old wolf was still alive, but unable to move. Leopold saw in the eyes of the wolf what he would describe years later as "a fierce green fire." The men moved closer. Leopold held out his rifle between himself and the dying wolf. In an final, instinctive upwelling of defiance, the wolf gnashed out and grabbed the rifle butt in its teeth. The men backed off. As they watched from a distance, the green fire died, but not before it had burned the moment into Leopold's psyche.[10]

Three months and sixty-five thousand acres after the reconnaissance men began their work, they hobbled into Springerville. They had managed to complete most of their work before the snows came, but at an exorbitant cost. Leopold, preoccupied with his baseline computations, had cruised and mapped only a handful of sections himself. While meticulous in his concern for accuracy and efficiency, it was plain to all that he had taken a serious mismeasure of both his men and the land.

Throughout the reconnaissance fiasco, Leopold remained undaunted and his enthusiasm undiminished. He explained why he liked his work in a letter to his mother. First of all, he didn't have to "fight society and all the forty 'leven kinds of tommyrot that includes. . . . [But] the real reason is that it deals with *big* things. Millions of acres, billions of feet of timber, all vast amounts of capital—why it's fun to twiddle them around in your fingers, especially when you consider your very modest amount of experience. And when you get a job to do, it's yours, nobody to help, nobody to interfere, no precedents to follow."[11] Aldo was indulging in the openness of the time and place. The real frontier had lingered on in the mountains of the Arizona Territory. One could still do "big things" there —and make big mistakes. Leopold later recalled a major event on the Apache, when the very first transcontinental automobilist came through. "The cowboys," he wrote, "understood this breaker of roads. He talked the same breezy bravado as any breaker of bronchos."[12] Leopold spoke his own brand of bravado when he thought about his future on the Apache. "I want to handle these 15-million a year sales when they come," he wrote home. "That would *be* something."[13]

As Leopold's enterpreneurial spirit grew, however, so did his interest in the Apache itself. The land had begun to make inroads on him, as it had done before in Burlington, at Les Cheneaux, Lawrenceville, and New Haven. He wrote to his mother:

I have just about decided by this time about what line of work I want to get into, that is—when the chance comes my way. I want a supervisorship, and I'm "sure sure damned sure" of it. Not *anywhere*, but somewhere that I like as well as the Apache. Of course my future travels may cause me to change my mind, but just now I feel decidedly averse to ever holding down a desk-chair in the Albuquerque office, or to chase myself around the four corners of the earth as Silvical Expert or Reconnaissance man. I was made to live on and work on *my own* land. Whether it's a 100-acre farm or a 1,700,000-acre Forest doesn't matter—it's all the same principle, and I don't think I'll ever change my mind about it.[14]

Back in Springerville, Leopold prepared his reconnaissance report for District Forester Ringland. He discovered that parts of his original base-line were off by a thousand feet; he had been thrown off by a misreading of his transit and subsequently erred in his latitudes and departures. He sheepishly explained in a memo to Ringland that "the computations in which this error was discovered had been triple-checked in the field. I will try and complete the work of correcting it as rapidly as possible."[15]

As much as Leopold relished fieldwork, town did have its benefits. His mother still sent gingerbread. There were parties to attend. Several ranchers and townspeople formed a new literary society, which Leopold joined. And there was always the ongoing game of horsetrading. He traded Jiminy Hicks to an Apache chief even up for 'Pache, a coal black pony. He also acquired Bluedog, a cantankerous, unbroken stallion.

The day after Thanksgiving, Aldo took Bluedog out for some training. Bluedog had been calming down nicely, but was restless as his new master approached. Leopold climbed into the saddle and rode methodically back and forth along Springerville's main street between Lang 'dobe and the Apache Forest offices. All went well until Bluedog suddenly snapped his head down and started bucking. On the first buck, Aldo came loose; on the third, he was pitched off, taking a couple bumps on the hard malpais road. Guthrie and Viles looked on and laughed at the show.

The commotion outside drew an audience. A collection was taken for the man who could tame down Bluedog. The renegade horse was cornered and led by his ears back to the circle of attention, where Fred Oldham, a cowpuncher of local note, tried his turn. The men on horseback released Bluedog's ears, and Oldham let loose with a wild whack to the horse's hind. Bluedog bolted toward the hills with Oldham aboard. By now, the whole town had come alive for the impromptu rodeo, and Springerville's two wildest horses were brought on. Prizes were duly gathered up and the competition began. Leopold was dazzled by one horse, a little bald-faced bay that erupted in unridable kicks, "8 times within a 10-foot circle, 5 feet in the air, turning a complete circle in the air with each pitch."[16] But Oldham was the winner this time, too. He rode the willful bay and went home fifteen dollars richer in the golden dust of the autumn afternoon.

∽

Winter brought no letup in a forest assistant's work. Leopold explained in a letter home what he and Mr. Guthrie had planned:

There are two new timber sales down on the Blue. . . . Then I've got to inspect and reorganize the Cordwood Sales down around Clifton—a good month's job. Then I've got to do some triangulating and make a revised map of the entire Forest —another 2 or 3 weeks. Then a Quarterly Report on Timber Sale Policy—1 week. Then a Mill Report to settle the disputes as to Sale Policy—2 weeks. Then sowing 60 pounds of Spruce Seed up at Alpine—2 weeks, and reporting on the same. Then a trip next spring with Pearson of the Coconino, preparatory to starting a series of Silvical Studies preparatory to the future big sales on the South End—1 month. Then reporting on, posting, and organizing the proposed Game Refuge in the Blue Mountains, and perhaps an additional one on Black River—1 month. Then another Quarterly Report on Relation of Grazing to Reproduction. I am also planning to study up on grasses and get posted on conditions in the field. Last and not least, a report on Bear Wallow and Fish Creeks as a proposed Comparative Watershed Study Site—2 weeks or more. And so forth and so forth. It all sounds good to me, provided I ever get out of this everlasting office once in a while.[17]

The holdup was the reconnaissance report, due on Arthur Ringland's desk in Albuquerque by December 17. Because of his original surveying errors, Leopold had to correct all the maps prior to writing up the report. His office detail would last even longer than he feared, or the district forester expected. Aldo did take a break, however, when his father, travelling west on factory business, visited over the holidays.

All the young foresters lived at Lang 'dobe, which as bachelor quarters go was standard issue. They subsisted on bacon, eggs, biscuits, cheese, and red Mexican beans ("our perennial mainstay"), except when someone got ambitious, or when Aldo went duck hunting on the flats along the Little Colorado. Their mental diet consisted of some thoroughly read periodicals, a book when there was time, and spirited arguments that lasted long into the night. Leopold wrote to his mother, "we seldom get to bed before half past twelve or one, and getting up at seven, the insufficiency of sleep is not theoretical, but *real*. Still—what's a man to do—work all day and sleep all night? In a week I'd feel so mentally stagnated that I'd call myself a fool and be one, too."[18]

His reconnaissance experience notwithstanding, Leopold came to be well liked and respected by his colleagues. Guthrie saw great promise in his assistant; "Mr. Guthrie" epitomized the hardworking devotion for which Forest Service men were known, and he soon became the major influence on Leopold. As Aldo travelled about on forest business, he also gained friends among the cowhands, ranchers, lumbermen, small farmsteaders, and forest rangers that constituted the sparse population of the Apache. The rangers and their families, isolated in their far-flung stations, often took him into their homes (Fred Winn, one of the Apache rangers, would remain a close and important friend for years). On most weekends there was a dance at a local ranch, and competition was keen among the young men for the attention of the scarce young ladies.

At the time, Aldo's attentions were focused on Lilian Johnson, a statuesque blonde from Evanston, Illinois, who was a guest at Les Cheneaux in the summer of 1908. She had a brother in Arizona whom she visited in the summer of 1909. She and Aldo corresponded regularly, and had passed beyond the idle talk stage, although Aldo remained typically tight-lipped in his letters home:

I have sometimes felt that I ought to be telling you more about Lilian and myself, and I have *wanted* to, but really the situation is too much of a puzzle to tell much about. One thing though is certain and I want *you* to know it although *nobody else does,* and that is that Lilian and I are a good deal more than friends.[19]

How much more he would not say, but he hoped for a visit from Lilian the following summer. His mother took it for granted that a full engagement was forthcoming. Aldo only warned her not to assume "what under present force of circumstance is necessarily only a possibility."[20]

Leopold needed all of January and most of February 1910 to complete his reconnaissance report. After that, his desk days waned. Spring was the "busy season" on the national forests, as the sheep and cattle grazers gathered their herds on the low range and moved them up to the high pastures and lambing grounds. Leopold was due for "the out-workin'est time I've had so far."[21] In addition to the normal complement of timber sales and mill inspections, he had overgrazed lands to check, permits and allotments to assign, animals to count, strays to rope and run off, corrals to build, and driveways and crossings to inspect. When Aldo was not out on his horse, he stayed in Springerville as acting supervisor, a title that pleased him to no end. More pleasing yet, though, was his first spring in the mountains. In words that recalled his schoolday tramps, Leopold wrote home about the view from one ranger station:

From Iris one sees 100 miles into the Datils of New Mexico, and in the early morning a silvery veil hangs over the far away mesas and mountains—too delicate to be called a mist, too vast to be merely beautiful—it isn't describable, it has to be seen. And all framed in a little Iris-dotted meadow bordered by the tall orange-colored shafts and dark green foliage of the pines, with a little rippling, bubbling spring, half buried in the new green grass, flowing by the door—Iris is the most beautiful single place I have ever seen in my life.[22]

Meanwhile, Leopold's work on the 1909 reconnaissance had come under fire. Allison, the reconnaissance expert, criticized his report as poorly organized, incomplete, and confusing. Of greater consequence were the complaints, lodged by several members of the crew, that Leopold's leadership had been incompetent. Allegations and rumors had circulated all winter long and, if proven true, Leopold would not be leading the 1910 reconnaissance on the upper Apache and, in fact, could be removed from the service. The most damning charges came from Heller, the Harvard tenderfoot, who had a personal vendetta against Leopold. Somehow, word had spread that Heller's sickness the previous fall was attributable to venereal disease. Heller wrongly assumed that Leopold started the rumor.

Arthur Ringland decided that reconnaissance plans for the upcoming summer would proceed as planned until a full-scale formal investigation was made. "So I guess they're going to risk the Rec[onnaissance] Party with me after all," was Leopold's somewhat relieved comment.[23] Allison ran the investigation. He asked for affidavits from all concerned parties, snooped around Springerville, and planned to rerun the bothersome baseline with Leopold. Leopold for his part wrongly assumed that Allison was part of a conspiracy against him. "I doubt whether he knows anything much about a transit," he sniffed. "I am not in the least afraid of an *unprejudiced* investigation. In fact, the deeper they dig, the better I will be pleased."[24]

Allison received the affidavits in late May. Robert Moak, one of the veterans, thought Leopold's management was "very inefficient," but noted that the crew included only two men who had had any previous experience in the woods. David Adams, a forest officer, charged Leopold with loafing and being too rough on the men, adding that he was "if anything too painstaking in minute details of the work and seemed to be very anxious to have it accurately and well-done." Thomas Longwell, the second lumberman, made the same point, and complained that Leopold "seemed to economize solely on supplies and subsistence, and also in my opinion he was not [as] aggressive in his field work as he should have been." Seward Smith noted that Leopold's attitude was "that of a person suffering from an attack of egoism which made it inadvisable for other members of the party to offer the benefits of their experience. . . . I would add that Mr. Leopold seemed kind-hearted, honest, and continually desirous of keeping the expenses as low as possible." Rex King, one of the student foresters, also vouched for him: "I can remember . . . no important point or act where Mr. Leopold was at fault, except that he was green and inexperienced."[25]

Heller's allegations were the most vitriolic. "The work was slow going, the country exceedingly rough, and food insufficient; consequently the boys were low in spirit; still it did not bother [Leopold] at all. . . . Instead of planning his work in advance he would leave it for the morning when it was to be performed. This meant hasty decisions and also a good deal of unnecessary picking up of scattered work. . . . All the rest of the time he either spent in camp or prowling about in search of semi-fictitious hunters and trappers. . . . In my judgment, there are no good points in his handling of the party. . . . In my opinion, Mr. Leopold considered the Apache reconnaissance as a picnic party instead of a serious matter."[26]

Leopold replied to the charges, denying each in turn. He acknowledged problems in running the base line, but stated that he had checked on them as best he could. To the charge that he spent too much time in camp and too little in the field, he answered that "I used my time in accordance with what, in my judgment, seemed for the best advantage of the work." He sent his notes, work diaries, and files to Allison. He denied outright that he had loafed in camp, "encouraged fast work," or "made things hard" for Heller. As for Heller, Leopold held that they "never had any open misunderstanding. His personal conduct toward me and Mr. Guthrie, however, was such to make it impossible for me to like or respect him."[27]

Allison decided not to pass judgment until he had checked the baseline. He and Leopold would do that together, and then join the new reconnaissance crew gathering in Springerville.

There was plenty of other excitement in town that June. A new phone line opened to Luna, New Mexico. Fires broke out in the hills as a result of a dangerously dry spring. "The ground is like dust," Leopold wrote. "Up on the mountain it is freezing ice every night on account of the extreme clarity and dryness of the air."[28] At least five big fires blazed on the Apache and adjacent forests, and the Springerville force was called into action when nearby Sheep Spring Knoll burned.

Once piece of news that spring outranked even fires, telephones, and Forest Service politics as a topic of local talk. Leopold wrote to his father that the bears "are raising Cain on the Escudilla."[29] A government trapper came to town—"a sort of St. George in overalls," Leopold later wrote, "seeking dragons to slay at government expense."[30] The trapper, a man named Schinn, rode up onto Escudilla after Bigfoot, and for three weeks tried all manner of traps and poison, but could not bring down the old bear. In a small side canyon, Schinn rigged a set-gun. Bigfoot finally found the bait, tripped the trigger, and shot himself. The silver-tipped hide of the great grizzly was so heavy it staggered the trapper's mule, and so large only one barn in town could hold it outstretched.[31]

∽

Among those familiar with the forests of the West, the summer of 1910 has passed into the realm of legend. It remains to this day one of the most storied seasons in the history of the Forest Service. The dryness of spring became the desiccation of summer, and the likelihood of fire was felt along the entire length of the Rockies. The worst realization of the threat came in the Northwest, where forests in Idaho and Montana burned with such intensity that people in Denver, seven hundred miles away, breathed the smoke. The Southwest was spared such epic blazes, but not a plague of lesser ones. Allison and Leopold were checking the baseline when they saw smoke on Stray Horse Divide. They hurried to the scene; anytime fire broke out, a forester's first obligation was to get to it. The reconnaissance crew was supposed to begin its work after the Fourth of July, but another fire on Mt. Baldy delayed them. Fortunately, the seasonal rains arrived and doused the worst fears of fire.

Allison spent a month with the party, watching Leopold and preparing his investigation report for Ringland. Allison was a topnotch man, but rose little in Leopold's defensive opinion. Leopold described his inquisitor as "a pretty efficient worker but otherwise a decidedly small proposition."[32] As for himself, Leopold commented with hard-to-swallow modesty that "it's sure interesting to be the villain."[33] A cool detente prevailed between them. Leopold would later come to admire Allison, but for the time being merely tolerated him. Allison was impartial. In his preliminary report to Ringland, Allison confirmed that the baseline errors were real and substantial, and that Leopold had mismanaged the 1909 reconnaissance as a result of his inexperience. The report noted that "pride also hurt Leopold for he was too proud to own up to the fact that he did not know how to do all the work, and consequently did not take Moak and Longwell into his confidence, while if he had, they could have helped him out."[34] The other charges against Leopold were found to be either wholly unfounded or understandable given the circumstances; the fault lay as much with the Forest Service for giving him the assignment in the first place. In his final report, Allison concluded:

Up to the time Leopold received the criticisms of his report and the request for a statement of his side of last year's work, I think he considered his work entirely satisfactory. . . . The criticism of his report and the attitude various members of last year's party took toward him came to him as a considerable shock. I think he now feels as if he was more or less on trial and that as a result he will try unusually hard to make good. Since he had practically no training last year before being put in charge of the party, I think he should be given another chance.[35]

Leopold made good on his second effort. His new crew was composed wholly of young foresters. R. E. Hopson came from the University of Michigan; three others—G. H. Collingwood, C. W. McKibbon, and Basil Wales—were students at the Michigan State Forest School. Yale was represented by O. F. Bishop and J. W. Hough, and by Raymond Marsh, a 1910 graduate of the Forest School who became a good friend of Leopold's.

Several among this superb group would go on to distinguished careers both within and beyond the Forest Service.

The crew also included several teamsters and a bewildering succession of cooks. Cooks of various and dubious talent came and went no less than ten times over the course of the summer. One of them, Aldo wrote to Marie, "has been trying to kill us all and has succeeded especially well on himself."[36] At one point, the entire crew gathered and, with full funereal pomp and oration, buried a disagreeable loaf of bread. Due as much to their common misery as their common cause, the crew hung together. Leopold noted with amusement that they divided up into two factions: the "Midnight Sons" who caroused around the campfire at night, and the "Hygienic Sons-a-bitches" who practiced Fletcherism, deep-breathing, and abstention. Yet no man was safe from the cook; at one point or another, each one "plumb gave out." Thus did the men become brothers "dwelling together in unity for the present."[37]

The party cruised some of the most breathtaking country on the Apache. On the White Mountain plateau, they surveyed the high virid meadows, the "parks" where clean stands of yellow pine opened up into grassy expanses of glen. The air was fragrant with the pitch of pines—by day in the field, by night at the campfire. Summer storms arose and dispersed quickly in the highlands; sometimes one lingered, and the boys enjoyed a day of rest in camp. On one memorable occasion, Leopold was riding to camp on Baldy through a particularly wild lightning storm. A bolt careened out of the sky, blasted a pine, and drove a fifteen-foot splinter into the ground near the horse and rider. The splinter hummed for a full minute. Reflecting on the storm years later, Leopold wrote, "It must be a poor life that achieves freedom from fear."[38]

The camp moved on to the watershed of the Little Colorado. The men donned their Sunday best for dances at Colter's Ranch. The country, though rugged, made for altogether smoother cruising than the high mountains or the breaks of the Blue, and Leopold was pleased to see his per acre cost drop from two-and-a-half cents in July to one-and-two-third cents in August; well below his 1909 results, and as low as any in District 3.

The crew took a break in September, when all the Apache rangers descended on Springerville for their annual council meeting. Once the horses were pastured and camp set up at Lang 'dobe, the serious work of the meeting began. Discussions covered all the technical subjects vital to the ranger's work: special use permits, cattle counts, range improvement, timber sales, fire-fighting tools, seed-collecting. Topical questions arose. How many horses does a ranger need? Anywhere from two to eight. Should wearing a uniform be compulsory? Most in favor. Were the men getting anything out of the Ranger's Reading Course? Yes. Should an examination be given? A less enthusiastic yes.

The topic of game protection arose. Under a cooperative agreement with the states, Forest Service rangers were allowed to arrest offenders of game laws, but the problem the rangers faced was always the same: the laws were virtually unenforceable, as no jury would convict even an open offender. Leopold felt more strongly than most on the subject. "This is not the time to get discouraged in regard to the condition of things," he told the men. "This is a new country and it takes time to get the people to see the benefit of game laws." He suggested that they try to arrest wealthy tourists first, as a means of gaining public support.[39]

The men also took time to relax. Ranger Pritchard won the prestigious shooting match. Leopold organized the ranger dance. And, behind the able pitching of Raymond Marsh, the forester's ragtag baseball team defeated the Springerville-Eager All-stars, thirteen to eleven. According to Marsh, "It couldn't have happened again in 100 times."[40]

Fresh from the meeting, the reconnaissance crew returned to their task, progressing steadily along the headwaters of the Black and San Francisco rivers, north to Nutrioso Creek, east across the face of Escudilla, and up into the northeast corner of the Apache. Leopold proved to be an able cruiser himself. He quietly confessed to "some absolutely uncanny pacing lately— stepping out a section to the foot by jingo, and over rough country, too."[41] Snows came and the party began to pack up in mid-November, having surveyed most of the northern third of the forest. Leopold had acquitted himself well. He declared it "the best summer I have ever had."[42]

చ

Leopold requested and received a full month's leave time, enough to return to Burlington for the holidays. He enjoyed a full Christmas on Prospect Hill, replete with the candlelit tannenbaum, Clara's special cakes, ice skating on the Mississippi, gossiping with Marie, and rabbit hunting with his father and brothers.

During this leave, Aldo visited Lilian in Evanston and she visited Burlington. Through the summer she and Aldo had kept one another guessing. The family had seen Lilian at Les Cheneaux and gained a favorable impression of her; even Clara withheld her reservations for Aldo's sake. Aldo and Lilian had actually taken some tentative steps toward engagement, but remained noncommittal. "I can promise you," he had written to his mother, "that her happiness is too much to me to gamble with it on what might prove to be a pen and paper fantasy."[43] Now they both seemed to realize that the bond between them was tentative at best. Lilian apparently took the initiative and backed out. Aldo returned west happy with the holiday, but disconcerted over the turn of romantic events.

Leopold turned twenty-four. He was *very very* happy" to be back on the Apache, where local friends gave him a warm homecoming. Guthrie was especially pleased by the return of his able assistant. Leopold's admiration for his boss knew no bounds. "When I think of what he *might* be doing if he chose to—of the salary and luxury he *could* enjoy if he *would*, I am convinced more than ever before that The Service is more than mere work or a mere livelihood; that it is *Service* and *glorious* service too." Leopold did worry about Guthrie's tendency to overwork himself. "I could never work the way he works, because there are too many other things I like to do."[44] For the present, those "other things" included hunting, and reading the collected works of Robert Louis Stevenson that he had received as a Christmas gift. At the office, Leopold welled up with new ideas on forest activities and administration, the latest being a notebook for saving valuable forest statistics that were currently going to waste. "I am sure a dumhead when it comes to memorizing routine procedure," he wrote to his father, "so it's up to me to be useful in some way, I guess."[45]

The Forest Service, meanwhile, had entered a new and more difficult phase of its history. Roosevelt was out of office. Pinchot was no longer head of the Forest Service, replaced as a result of the Pinchot-Ballinger controversy. The service would survive, but with less prominent backing, moral as well as financial, from Washington.[46]

Promotions in those days came quickly to even young foresters like Leopold. One of his superiors reported that Leopold was "well-qualified now for a Deputy Supervisorship in almost any Forest in the District. . . . He is thoroughly interested in all phases of Forest work, more so in fact than almost any Forest Assistant that I have met for a long time."[47] As the busy season commenced on the Apache range, Leopold was called to Albuquerque to attend a reconnaissance conference and to accept a temporary detail in the district offices.

As "acting in charge of operations," Leopold received his first exposure to the business of the district office. He regarded the district officers as "gentlemen of leisure" when compared with the hardworking rangers and forest officers.[48] Nevertheless, he made quick friends of the Albuquerque men, and of Arthur Ringland in particular. Ringland was only a little older than Leopold. Authority in the early Forest Service was based on merit, for seniority was simply lacking. Ringland, a stocky fireplug of a man, was an intelligent, calm, thorough administrator, among the service's best. Leopold's reports from Springerville had impressed him, and he had plans in the works to take Leopold off the Apache. There was even talk of a possible supervisorship.

It did not take long for Aldo to adjust to the relative sophistication of Albuquerque. Ringland and the others often invited him to dinner, and in one month he managed to attend the theater, the circus, several dances, parties, and cotillions, and a genuine wild west show. One night he enjoyed "a very heated argument with two budding lawyers on the origin of matter and kindred highbrowed subjects."[49] Even Teddy Roosevelt came to town, pausing on his way to the dedication of the just-completed Roosevelt Dam near Phoenix.[50]

In contrast to Springerville, Albuquerque was rich with promise for a young bachelor. Leopold was particularly taken with a Miss Rankin, a much sought-after young woman who was Lilian's "very image." She invited Aldo to luncheon with her, and in his subsequent report to Burlington he emphasized the fact that "she is very particular and discriminating in such things — as several slightly fresh town youths have learned to their sorrow."[51] When Miss Rankin left Albuquerque two weeks later, the foresters all gathered at a local cantina to console themselves.

The sorrow was short-lived. Ringland had been talking up the Bergere sisters of Santa Fe. One day, late in March, Anita and Estella Bergere came to town, and Ringland introduced Aldo to them. "Ring" and Leopold gladly accepted an invitation to a weekend party at their family's ranch headquarters at Los Lunas, just down the Rio Grande. Two weeks later Aldo and Ring attended a cotillion at the Bergere hacienda in Santa Fe. At the dance, all the señoritas carried paper lanterns in the shape of birds. The ladies, with lanterns aglow in the night, approached their favored young men for a dance. On the third dance, Estella Bergere presented her lantern, a parrot, to Aldo. Afterward, Arthur Ringland composed a poem for the Bergere sisters:

> Greetings! Anita, Estella, and May
> Many thanks for favors received today
> But we remind you lest you should forget
> We left other favors — our one best bet
> And what is that from which each one did part?
> The best favor of all, my dears — his heart![52]

That same week, Ringland decided on Leopold's new assignment. At one point he thought to make Aldo supervisor of the Chiricahua Forest, on the Mexican border, but changed his mind. Instead, he made Leopold deputy supervisor of the troubled Carson National Forest north of Santa Fe.

On April 28, Leopold rode the train back west to Holbrook. It was still a two-day stagecoach ride to Springerville and the edges of the Apache Forest. Leopold packed his belongings, bid a sad farewell to his friends and colleagues, and sold his horse to Hopson of the summer reconnaissance team.

The Apache would always hold a special place in Leopold's heart, the land where he took and mastered his first job, where he fully learned what wild country was, where the binding power between landscape and mind became an irrepressible factor in his life. The Apache had changed subtly but dramatically in the short two years he had spent there. Like his father before him who sold the barbed wire that subdued the plains, Aldo Leopold was part of a historical irony, taming the very wilderness he most loved. Escudilla was still there, of course, and the White Mountain plateau, and the Mogollon Rim, and the breaks of the Blue. Their absolute wildness, however, was gone: mapped, measured, confined to reservations, shot by a set-gun, rifled from a rimrock, broken and put to bit on a dusty street in Springerville.

7

Carson: A Delightful Turmoil
(1911–1913)

THE ASPIRATIONS of many a New Mexican bachelor focused on the Bergere household in Santa Fe. Before he began his new assignment on the Carson, Aldo found a spare day to call there. He arrived at the Bergere home only to find his friend Alfred Waha, another of Ringland's assistants, already there. The two foresters enjoyed a lively stay in Santa Fe, the social and cultural center of the Southwest. Aldo was even coaxed into attending church for the first time in years. He had never before seen the inside of a Catholic church.

Aldo left Santa Fe, as did every other aspirant, completely charmed. "Estella is a wonder on a horse, and Anita too as far as that goes," he confided to Marie. "But to return to Estella, I am ready to state without qualifications—and you know it's the *qualifications* that are generally the rub—that she is very much of a peach."[1] Pressed for details, Aldo described Estella to his mother:

She must be extremely beautiful, since I do not think she would be called especially pretty. She is very dark, her hair has a reddish glint should you ever see it exactly right, she has very beautiful eyes, aquiline nose, and a very fine mouth. Her voice is very low, she is slender and not tall, and dresses extremely well but very simply. That is as analytical as—with considerable effort and poor success—I am able to be. Miss Anita would be a good deal easier to describe—I think she is the most striking beauty I have ever seen and she is awfully nice too—but she lacks an indefinable something in comparison with Miss Estella.[2]

At the lantern dance, they had exchanged a mutual glance of interest, and it was at that point that Aldo decided to court Estella, despite the fact that she was seeing another. "I am reluctant," he admitted to his mother, "to behave myself at all any more."[3]

On May 12, 1911, Leopold boarded the narrow-gauge Denver and Rio

Grande Railroad for the trip north to Antonito, Colorado, headquarters of the Carson National Forest. The D&RG, "slower'n a burro and about as sorry," was pure mountain railroad, and required eight hours to traverse the hundred or so miles between Santa Fe and Antonito. From his seat, Leopold watched a timber drive on the swollen Rio Grande. As the train came to the broad basin of the upper river, Leopold got a good, albeit distant, look at the forest he would help to administer. To the east rose the magnificent cordillera of the Sangre de Cristos; the Carson took in much of its western flank. To the west were the San Juans, not so prominent, but sprawling in high forest and meadow. The Rio Grande cut a deep gorge through the intermountain plain.

For all its scenic splendor, the Carson was a forest beleaguered. At the time of Leopold's arrival, the upper Rio Grande was probably the most heavily grazed watershed in the entire country. Livestock operations there had expanded continually since the 1850s. By 1900, the range supported some 220,000 cattle and 1,750,000 sheep.[4] The upper Rio Grande became the very heart of the western sheep industry, and the families that for three and four generations had run the sheep outfits there were among the wealthiest in the West. But on the forest and grasslands, the decades of overgrazing were exacting their toll. The vegetation cover was in decline, the forage composition changing, the more palatable species decreasing. The forest trees were unable to regenerate. Soil erosion was gullying the range. Clearly, unless change came soon, the next generation of stockgrowers and foresters would inherit a ruined resource.

The Carson National Forest was established on the same day as the Apache—July 1, 1908—but had since met with less progress in organizing its administration. This was due in part to the cultural differences between the two regions. The Apache was a remote, little-used, sparsely populated wilderness. The people who used it were generally small owners who lived on or near the forest itself. The Carson, by contrast, had been heavily utilized for centuries, most prominently by the large livestock companies whose owners lived far from the forest. Moreover, the population on the Carson was almost entirely Hispanic-American, and the language barrier presented a major obstacle to the men of the Forest Service.

There were also personnel problems. The previous supervisor had done little more than collect his paychecks, and had not issued even a single grazing permit. Rumors of collusion and bribery circulated from one end of the forest to the other. The field force was not much more honorable; three rangers quickly quit the service when they learned that a shake-up was in the offing.

With both the range and regard for the Forest Service deteriorating, Arthur Ringland decided to make a clean sweep of Carson headquarters. He installed Harry C. Hall as the new supervisor. Hall was the right man in the right time and place, a tough-talking troubleshooter who was willing, even anxious, to mix it up for the good of the service. He took the job with the intention of remaining only long enough to put the forest on a sound footing. Leopold, technically proficient but still inexperienced, became Hall's deputy supervisor. The promotion gave him added responsibility and a modest raise to $1400 per year. Ira T. "Nellie" Yarnall, forest assistant, and Lillian Sutherland, forest clerk, rounded out the office force. Together with a dozen or so rangers and guards, they were to bring order to the 950,000 acres of Carson.

The day after Leopold arrived in Antonito, he bought a horse. He already had a name for it, Polly, a reference to the parrot lantern that Estella had carried at the dance in Santa Fe. Aldo faced a considerable logistical disadvantage in his pursuit of Estella. His rival for her attentions, H. B. "Jamie" Jamison, was a bright, young, Yale-educated lawyer who lived in Albuquerque and thus had easy access to Santa Fe. Leopold, even when he was not off in some isolated corner of the Carson, was at best a day-long, semidependable train ride away. His only recourse was the mails. He sent the first of his strategic letters the day he bought his horse:

> My dear Miss Bergere,
>   I must tell you about Polly—he's a beauty—a speckled gray about nine hundred pounds with a dandy chest and withers and slim straight legs, short coupled, and little slender ears and a *soft gray nose*—don't you love a horse with a soft gray nose? I'm sure you would love Polly if you could see his long graceful gliding trot and the pretty arch in his neck—and the soft gray nose would clinch the argument.
>   Of course I'm indulging in first impressions, because I've only ridden Polly up and down the street trying him out—but I've never been very sorry for my faith in first impressions.[5]

Besides serving as symbol, Polly was a strong, dependable horse. Leopold rode him the length and breadth of the Carson in acquainting himself with the rangers and the forest. Aldo was struck by the contrast with the Apache. The overgrazing problem was pervasive and obvious. The worst evidence was out on the Jicarilla district. The Forest Service had just acquired the Jicarilla, a ten-by-thirty-mile rectangle of forest out on the western slope of the San Juans across the continental divide. While inspecting the area, Leopold was forced to backtrack two and three miles around gaping gullies. "If ever a country needed radical constructive protection," he observed, "that's it!"[6] He also noted a further side effect of overgrazing that was closer to his heart. "There is practically no game in this country. Of course the sheep have run out all the deer; there are a few turkeys, and I saw one place with bear-sign. Two elk were seen here two years ago."[7] As impressive as the country looked, Leopold concluded that it "can't hold a candle to the Apache—any of it."[8]

The new officers wasted no time in disturbing the status quo. It was too late to do much about the current grazing season, but Hall instructed Leopold to draft a plan for the 1912 season. Hall also decided that the forest needed cohesion, what with its guards, rangers, and officers scattered over two mountain ranges and nine thousand square miles of the New Mexico Territory. In June, accordingly, the first issue of the *Carson Pine Cone* rolled off the presses. Under the banner, "A Square Deal for Everybody, Special Favors to None," the *Pine Cone*'s stated purpose was "to scatter seeds of knowledge, encouragement, and enthusiasm among the members and create interest in the work. May these seeds fall on fertile soil and each and every one of them germinate, grow, and flourish. . . . This is one of the most beautiful forests in this country and we should strive to make it one of the best organized and conducted forests in the country."[9] Among his other responsibilities, Leopold became chief editor, reporter, and illustrator of the *Pine Cone*. After a month on the Carson, Leopold wrote home to his father that "We are beginning to think we've made a start in putting this Forest on a working basis. Certain it is 'times has changed'—everybody says that."[10]

Antonito, though, was too far removed from most of the field activities for efficient administration. Hall and Leopold decided to move headquarters south to Tres Piedres, a village along the D&RG tracks, on the high side of the Rio Grande basin across from Taos. For the service, it had the advantage of being as close as possible to the heart of the discontinuous Carson. For Leopold, it had the advantage of being thirty miles closer to Santa Fe.

Leopold's rivalry with Jamison was good-natured. In later years they would become close friends and hunting partners, but for the time being, Aldo was determined to block his adversary. After several more "Polly letters," Leopold travelled to Santa Fe to spend the Fourth of July holiday with Estella, Jamison, and other assorted sisters, foresters, and gentlemen callers. On the Fourth, several of them decided to attend a baseball game. Walking to the field, Aldo gave Jamie his due, allowing him to accompany Estella. After the game, however, Jamison insisted on clinging to her. "He hung on like a leech," Aldo complained.[11] Exasperated with Jamison, Estella stopped in her tracks; with one deft maneuver, Aldo assumed Jamie's place at Estella's side.

After the holiday, Leopold returned to Tres Piedras. The small house where he lived was crammed with reconnaissance men preparing for the summer's survey of the Carson. Amid the din, Aldo sat down and wrote a letter of admission to his mother:

It is *all up with me*. Five minutes after I saw Estella this last time I could have told you what I *know* now—and that is that I love her. The fact that I put it in so many words will do away with the necessity for any elaboration as to how much. . . . I have said nothing yet. But *somebody* is going to have to show their cards very soon—and with Jamie on my mind I can't promise to wait any longer than my next chance.[12]

The next day, Aldo wrote to Estella:

My dear Estella,
    This night is so wonderful that it almost hurts. I wonder if you are seeing the myriad of little "Schärfchens volken" I told you about—do you remember the "little sheep clouds"?—I have never seen them so perfect as they are to-night. I would like to be out in *our cañon*—I don't know how to spell it so you will have to let me call it that—and see the wild Clematis in the moonlight—wouldn't you?[13]

꙳

When Aldo Leopold fell in love with Estella Bergere, he did so with the same intent concentration that a deep interest always provoked in him. The object of that interest, however, had never before been another person. Neither Gretchen Miller nor Lilian Johnson had touched him so profoundly. He still lived, essentially, in isolation. While he had gained friends and respect in the Forest Service, he still had a way about him, a combination of perceptivity, refinement, ego, and wit, that tended to distance him from many of those with whom he associated. His incurable passion for wild places only reinforced those tendencies. Now he had fallen in love; and only one who so valued solitude could be so strongly attracted to another in compensation.

María Alvira Estella Bergere was born August 24, 1890 at Los Lunas, New Mexico, the second surviving child in a family that grew to include seven sisters, two brothers, two half-brothers and one half-sister.

Her father, Alfred M. Bergere was among the most prominent men in Santa Fe. Born in Liverpool, England, to a Franco-Milanese father and a Venetian mother, Bergere had been a musical prodigy, studying piano until he was sixteen, when he left Europe to seek his fortune in America. He arrived in New York in 1874, and eventually worked his way to the Southwest, where in 1884 he made the acquaintance of Don Solomon Luna, the leading sheepman and powerbroker in the New Mexico Territory. Two years later Bergere married Luna's widowed sister Eloisa Luna Otero. "Don Alfredo" had four consuming interests in his life: music, finance, politics, and his large family. He played a major role in bringing classical music to New Mexico, and the Bergere home became the region's unofficial recital hall. As a realtor, sheep owner, and insurance executive, Bergere enjoyed only middling success, and never reached the lofty plateau where his in-laws stood. As a political figure, though, he was more successful. An absolute

Republican, he held a number of prominent positions in the state party. As the 1912 election approached and the Republican ranks split into the Roosevelt and Taft camps, Bergere lined up solidly behind Taft; he regarded Roosevelt and his Progressive disciples as political heretics.[14]

Estella, through her mother Eloisa Luna Otero Bergere, belonged to a family embedded deep in the history and lore of the Southwest, Spanish America, Mexico, and Old Spain. The family name Luna, bestowed over the ages upon any number of descendants and places, dated from the year 1091, when a young Spanish capitano led his fleet into the Mediterranean and achieved a great victory over the occupying Moors. On the captain's orders, the battle was waged not at dawn, the usual time of attack, but by the light of the quarter moon. In honor of the victory, the king conferred upon the captain a coat of arms and the title "de Luna." In the centuries that followed, the family ensconced itself in the nobility of Aragon, Castile, and Segovia; a Luna became Pope Benedict XIII during the Great Schism; another was de facto ruler of Castile until an envious queen accused him of witchcraft and had him beheaded.

The first of the family to come to the New World was Don Tristan de Luna y Arellano of Castile. Primogeniture deprived him of an estate in Spain, and in 1530 he sailed with Cortez (who had married his cousin) to New Spain. Two other Lunas were captains under Cortez. Another cousin became first viceroy of New Spain. Don Tristan himself became one of the storied conquistadores, and served as second in command to Coronado on his epic expedition of 1540; he and Coronado are believed to have built the first bridge in the New World, across the Rio Pecos in what would become New Mexico. In 1559, Tristan de Luna became the governor of Spain's Florida colony.

After the 1693 reconquest of New Mexico, a branch of the Lunas settled in the province, and eventually acquired claim to eighty thousand acres of the San Clemente Grant, between the Rios Grande and Puerco (another cousin, the Duke of Albuquerque, settled a claim just to the north). A century later, this land became the seat of one of the great sheep empires of the West. Don José Enrique Luna, in the early 1800s, acquired the land titles and established the flocks. His son Antonio José Luna took over in the mid-1800s and became the largest sheep owner in the Southwest. During the 1850s, Antonio José drove several large flocks to California, in much the same manner as Charles J. J. Leopold. Estella's grandfather met with a better fate than Aldo's; he made an immense fortune. That fortune passed to the children of Antonio José, one of whom was Estella's mother Eloisa. The Luna sheep operation continued to expand under her brothers Tranquilino and Solomon, and by 1900 it was said to be the largest sheep outfit in the United States.

In old New Mexico, the lines between family, business, and politics were tangled in a complex web of intermarriage among the powerful families. Eloisa Luna, well educated and renowned as the most beautiful woman in the Southwest, married Don Manuel B. Otero, who carried a name and ancestry as illustrious as her own. Together they had three children. But a noble name was poor protection in the yet wild west; Manuel Otero was shot in a land title dispute at Estancia. After three years of widowhood, Eloisa married Alfred Bergere, and they began their own family.

Estella Bergere was two months shy of her twenty-first birthday when Leopold fell in love with her. Unpretentious, playful, self-motivated, independent-minded, and always gracious, she taught first grade in a Santa Fe school. She was a devout, but not intransigent, Catholic. Although already spoken for by Jamison, she was not committed to him. In any event, she neither discouraged nor encouraged Aldo's attentions; at first, she merely accepted them. Aldo was drawn to her intelligence, poise, and lighthearted manner, but it was not her character alone that attracted him. He was riveted by her distinctive Spanish features. She was, in his eyes, simply beautiful.

Accustomed to sharing his inner self only with his mother and father, and then only sparingly, Aldo saw in Estella one with whom he felt able, even compelled, to share all. As she began, tentatively, to respond in kind, it was as if Aldo's ties to society, stretched taut even to the top of Escudilla and the remoteness of the Blue, suddenly yanked him back. "I have made up my mind," he wrote to his father. "I know what I want and what I need to get it, and by Jove I'm not going to be standing on one foot the meanwhile!"[15]

Between Leopold's resolve and reality stood seventy miles of mountain ranges, a heavy work load, and Jamison. Aldo regarded Jamie as "an enthusiastic hard-working brilliant fellow, and likable in lots of ways," but nevertheless "not good enough for Estella." He suspected that Jamison had eyes on Estella's inheritance and social connections. "Jamie's soul," he wrote, "is about like a silk-covered brick."[16] He could say what he wished, but Jamison was still closer to Santa Fe, in love with Estella, and making more money than he.

In his favor, Leopold had Arthur Ringland, all-purpose advocate, spy, and matchmaker. He also had a personal connection, having found Estella's nineteen-year-old brother Luna a summer job on the Carson; they bached together in "Mia Casita," Aldo's tiny bungalow. Finally, Leopold had his epistolary skills, and he drew on them as he hadn't since his school days.

To tell you the truth, Estella, the luckiest thing that ever happened to Polly is his name. . . . I have been *proud* of horses, and *grateful* to them, and I have *pitied* them—but Polly *only* has had my *respect* and a little corner in my heart. So I want you to know him, and tell me whether you really like him too. He is not a horse that most girls would notice at all—because he is a sort of speckled gray color, and girls as a rule have an eye for "snow-white chargers" and shiny chestnut bays and coal-black parade horses. But then there are mighty few girls that understand horses. Besides, Polly's mane is very unfashionable—it falls partly on one side and partly on the other—and his homely speckles make one look twice to notice his beautifully straight legs and solid round little hoofs and the wonderful arch of his chest. Besides one does *not* see Polly until he strikes his gliding trot and pricks his little pointed ears at something interesting. In short, Polly is *my* horse, and money—why I would *laugh* at anyone so blind as to think they could buy him.[17]

Meanwhile, there was a national forest to organize. Three extra crews went to work during the summer of 1911: a telephone crew strung wire between headquarters and the ranger stations, a boundary crew established official forest borders, and a reconnaissance team under Raymond Marsh surveyed the Amarilla division north of Tres Piedras. Leopold went to work on the details of the new grazing plan, and performed the normal variety of chores that fell to the deputy supervisor—inspecting ranger stations, erecting a flag pole at headquarters, firing a good-hearted but incompetent ranger, coordinating the nomadic field crews.

Aldo, in his romantic condition, became a favorite target of wisecracks and jokes from one end of the Carson to the other. During one of Leopold's visits with the boundary crew, the field men decided to play a trick on their tender officer, taking him along on an all-day excursion into the bejungled canyons of the Rio Brazos. The heat of early August was baking the rocky draws. "The surveyors fully expected to walk my legs off I know —and I chuckled with sheer delight when I dragged them all into camp by moonlight and watched them doubled up exhausted by the fire. After all it's a pretty interesting old world."[18]

Estella learned, once and for all, the true depth of Aldo's affection when he sent her a pin. Not just any pin, but the pin signifying his membership in Yale's Society of Robin Hood. "In that little pin," he emphatically explained to her, "is more than half my life. Not only because it has every ounce of loyalty that the Lord ever put into me, but it is more than that —it was a *turning point* in my life, Estella, because before that time I had *done* little and *was* less to be proud of—in fact I was beginning to be branded with that burning letter F which is the ghost of failure. But when that came it was *up to me*. Loyalty one can give, but honor and success one must *earn*."[19] He had never given the pin to anyone else. Estella, taken aback by the gesture and the words, stopped corresponding with her ardent admirer.

While Aldo's heavy workload left him with no time to resolve his romantic dilemma, it did keep his mind off it. Day by day he was growing more proficient at the job, and enjoying it more. "It is absolutely absorbing, this game of handling people, and I'd rather know how to do it than to handle millions of dollars."[20] After only two months, Supervisor Hall had had a noticeable effect on his deputy. Leopold did not wholly admire Hall by any means, but he did respect what Hall was accomplishing on the Carson, and the manner in which he was accomplishing it. "The oilier processes of diplomacy and persuasion," he wrote to his mother, "are unknown to [Hall], and he rules men not by knowledge, though he has some; not by experience, though he has had a great deal, nor by reason, of which he has little—but by the sheer fighting force of his personality. . . . Obstacles and impediments alike are swept away by what is stronger than they. Many a time I have called him, to myself, a roughneck, a barbarian, and worse—I have hated him enough to kill him—but it has always come back to his better qualities, which I must admit that I admire enough to find them, as a kind of surprise to myself, growing in *me*."[21]

On August 8, Arthur Ringland came to Tres Piedras to confer on the placement of a new ranger station. Afterward, he gave Leopold the lowdown: Jamie had apparently played his hand, proposed formally to Estella, and then left to spend a month in the East with his family. That evening, Aldo sat in his house, smoking his pipe, burning candles long into the night. The time had come to make his play. He decided to go down to Santa Fe at the next opportunity. "I think you would have done the same some time long ago," he wrote to his father. "I've not a sufficiency of saintly qualities to wait forever and then lose out for my trouble."[22]

Leopold confronted Hall and told him he needed a day off to visit Santa Fe. Hall understood. On August 19, Leopold railroaded down the Rio Grande to Santa Fe and proposed to Estella Bergere.

⌇

"Santa Fe has quite an attraction for Leo," the *Pine Cone* deadpanned. "Wonder what it is?"[23]

Estella Bergere had known Aldo Leopold only four months, mostly through letters. He had visited Santa Fe only three times. She couldn't say yes—but she didn't say no. She had much to consider: her family, and her stern father Don Alfredo in particular; Aldo's position and prospects; and, of course, Jamison. She asked, understandably, for time to think. She promised him an answer by November. Behind her delay, however, there was a vague apprehension about the force of Aldo's feelings and an acknowledgment that, although she was fond of Aldo, something was lacking between them. She came forward with this admission, and trusted Aldo to understand . . . which made him love her all the more.

Aldo returned to Tres Piedras to await Estella's decision. "There is a reasonable hope," he wrote to his mother, "and an *un*reasonable confidence that *some* day it will all come right."[24] In his next letter to Estella he was more passionate: "If I could only make you understand how the last two days have *changed* my love for you Estella, changed it to none the less of admiration and respect but O so much more of just simple sweet human desire for *you, all* of you, and *always.*"[25]

Few if any Anglo-Americans had married into Estella's family network of historical ties, political influence, and large land holdings. If the New Mexico Bergeres and Lunas were somewhat surprised by the possibility of one in their family, the Burlington Leopolds were equally nonplussed by the possibility of an Hispanic addition to theirs. Once Clara learned the full extent of Aldo's intentions, she helped in every way she could, sending notes and small gifts to Estella. Carl, more hesitant, was concerned about Estella's ethnicity and, probably more, her Catholicism. Estella's family apparently included some Jewish forebears as well—a consideration that Carl may have fretted over, but which Aldo ignored. He wrote to his mother, "Some have it that the Lunas are partly Jewish—in a left-handed way—I'm sure I don't know."[26]

The Leopold family's attitude toward racial matters was one of naive indifference tinged by Saxon insularity. Burlington was a river town, but a northern river town. Former slaves had not settled there in significant numbers. The only nonwhites Aldo Leopold had encountered as a boy were native Ojibwe at Les Cheneaux, maids, and "Black Peter," whom Carl Leopold hired as a gardener and yardman during Aldo's school years. (Carl was at first reluctant to hire a black man, but when Peter proved to be a better worker than any of the others, Carl kept him on, and often shared his hunting take with him.) Aldo probably knew of blacks at Yale, but they were not foresters; blacks worked in the nation's sawmills, but not yet in its schools of forestry. Once in the Southwest, Leopold was exposed to the region's pervasive cultural complexity. Although his fellow foresters were Anglo-Saxons almost to the last individual, Leopold in the course of his work became accustomed to dealing with the full range of Navajos, Apaches, Hispanics, Mexicans, Texans, cowboys of all colors, and lumbermen from all corners of the country. He had not anticipated, however, falling in love with a Spanish-Italian Catholic.

In the weeks that followed his proposal to Estella, Leopold lost much of the composure and self-assurance that had generally been the hallmarks of his character. "A sort of restless discontent is gnawing at me," he wrote to Estella. "I am not exactly on the right side of my nerves."[27] He had plenty of work to do—field chores, the *Pine Cone,* an important letter to the rangers outlining strategy on the grazing situation—but his heart was not in the work. Unable to do anything but wait for Estella's verdict, he began to lose sleep, just as he had during his tense college days. "I wish I could turn all my mental energy into my work," he wrote to his mother in October, "but I'm naturally two d__ lazy I guess. But what else to do with it is the problem. One's head feels about to explode sometimes—but what is one going to do about it?"[28]

There was one thing to do. As in the past, when he was unable to share his problems with other people, he turned to the world around him. His weekly horseback rides into the mountains became his release. As fall emblazoned the aspens, he wrote to Estella:

San Antone Mountain was a great glory of bronze and gold—and the Taos Mountains—sixty continuous miles of main range under the eastern sky—ablaze with great masses of orange and crimson. I can hardly tell you what a blessed peace I find in my Sundays in the hills—I wouldn't be able to get along without them—something would break, I know.[29]

Aldo's letters to Estella during his weeks of flustered waiting revealed the possessive streak long latent in his personality. Estella had tipped the scales that balanced his desire for wildness and his desire to *hold*. And he regarded as his own anything and everything that he loved—including Estella. "I have been wondering at what a wonderful little word that is— 'mine'. . . . there were a thousand little things about *you* which I saw and felt—and something told me that in some way they were *mine,* Estella— and the world can never grow old enough to make me forget a single one, or to keep them from flooding my memory with sweetness, whenever I *let* myself think."[30] This possessiveness was a powerful aspect of Leopold's psychological constitution, and it would affect everything from the way he wanted to build his house to the way he wanted to build his life. It might have degenerated into simple selfishness but for his comprehensive sense of self and for the sensations that Estella evoked:

Tonight I took a little ride with Polly and Spud—back around the rock again. There are a lot of porcupines back there eating off some little pine saplings which are *mine* because they make the rock look so beautiful—last night I killed an awfully big one. Every one of those little pines is mine, and the great old rock, and the little ferns growing on it—everything even to the sweeping plains that one sees from there, and the purple mountains where the indigo shadows rise at Sunset. It is *all* mine, but I don't want it much longer for myself, Estella.[31]

Marriage, Aldo was beginning to realize, is a state of mutual and reciprocal possession, and as that understanding registered, his own individuality reared up to give its last kicks. He wrote to his mother in early October, "I was thinking yesterday as I rode in the hills what a price in Liberty one has to pay for success. If it were not for necessity, and a certain elusive something else—I rather believe I would have to flip a quarter to choose."[32] His was a case not so much of cold feet as itchy feet, the old urge to wander confronting the present need to settle. Two weeks later, he explained:

What in hell is success to a man but that his friends may be proud of him?—for my part I don't give a *damn* for myself—if I were trying to please myself alone I would be in Canada and Siberia & South America seeing the world—and to *hell* with sticking around to one job! I get it badly these fall days, and if it were not for Estella, and you all, and about three others I would pull up stakes and dig out. When you get down to it there is mighty little *interest* in this country here—it is very beautiful but there are no traditions—no romance—no flavor of the wilds— like on the old Apache—and there is nothing that holds me but that fact that it is a big job undone, and up to me.[33]

All such doubts to the contrary, Leopold's desire reached new heights as the day of Estella's decision drew near. He and Hall were scheduled to attend a meeting of D-3 supervisors in El Paso beginning November 10. Leopold planned a stop in Santa Fe along the way. The closer the day came, the higher Aldo raised his emotional stake in Estella's answer. On November 1, he declared in a letter home that, "the world would be more likely to come to an end, than that anything would go wrong. If you knew Estella, you would know that I am not boasting, either."[34] Aldo was setting himself up for either the greatest joy, or the greatest disappointment, of his life.

Estella, having weathered the initial unforeseen wave of Aldo's affection, was deeply touched, and her hesitations began to wane. Her feelings were not as vehement as Aldo's, but they overcame her steadily and strongly. Yet, Estella did have an impulsive side. Jamison had long ago asked her to the Montezuma Ball, the main social event of the fall in Santa Fe. Seventy miles away, Leopold swallowed the pill like a man. After the ball, at 4:30 in the morning, Estella sat down and wrote her own letter, which convinced Aldo that she was his.[35]

On November 10, Aldo stopped in Santa Fe. Estella said yes. Don Alfredo said maybe; he wanted another week to consider it (and to complete a discreet check of Aldo's family background). Estella declared that nothing, not even her father, would make her change her mind.

Leopold spent the week in El Paso at the supervisors' meeting. He joined in the professional debates, met his old professor and new Chief Forester Henry Graves, and heard all manner of praise for Estella, "the most loved and respected girl in New Mexico."[36]

When he returned to Tres Piedras, he found a letter from Alfred Bergere, granting approval and offering congratulations. A wedding date was arranged for the following October. When he tried to explain to his mother how he felt, Aldo admitted that, "somehow, *this* time, I don't seem to be able to write."[37]

◊

Carl Leopold came to visit his son and future in-laws that Christmas. Whatever reservations he may have had concerning the marriage had been swept away by Aldo's ceaseless commendations of Estella. "I have known many young men under similar conditions," he wrote to Estella, "but never such exalted confidence and belief in *you* as being the *one* girl for him, that he never expected to find or win."[38] When Carl arrived in Santa Fe, he was given a warm and generous Latin reception. Before they had even allowed their guest to catch his breath, the seven Bergere sisters, arrayed in gay holiday dresses, arranged themselves into a giggling line—Anita, Estella, May, Consuelo, Dolores, Rosina, and Isabel—and ordered Carl to pick out the one that Aldo had chosen. Carl made the wrong choice, but Aldo, he soon learned, had made a good choice. Carl wrote to Clara that "I have *never seen quite* such a *lovely family* relationship in my whole experience."[39] William C. MacDonald, the newly elected governor of New Mexico, came to call on Don Alfredo and his family while Carl and Aldo were there. Carl proudly noted that even the governor had not received so warm a welcome as he.

On January 6, 1912, New Mexico became the forty-seventh state of the Union, due in no small part to the efforts of Estella's uncle Solomon Luna. The inauguration of MacDonald on the fifteenth gave Santa Fe unprecedented cause for celebration. Two thousand attended the reception at the Palace of the Governors. Aldo and Estella attended the gala Inaugural Ball. Aware of the fact that his progressive views did not jibe with those of Estella's family, Leopold steadfastly refused to discuss politics, and warned that "the first man who tries to spoil things for me through politics gets his block knocked off."[40]

After the festivities, Leopold returned to Tres Piedras. He and the other Carson officers and rangers now faced the chief challenge of their mission: putting into practice the grazing policies of the service. The legal authority to do so had been secured once and for all the year before, when the Supreme Court decided, in cases originating in California and Colorado, that the Department of Agriculture had acted within the Constitution in regulating grazing on the public forests. Even before that, though, most forests were well along in making the transition to conservative use. The Carson was only beginning.[41]

The main tool in the Forest Service's organizing kit was the Individual Allotment System, which assigned every stock owner an area of forest and permitted him to graze an assigned number of stock. Applications began to arrive at Carson headquarters in January; by the end of February, over a thousand had come in, seeking permission to graze 220,000 sheep. Leopold's task was to sift through the applications and help Hall cut back the number of sheep to 198,000.

By and large, the sheepmen cooperated; they were coming to realize the necessity of cooperative measures to maintain the health and long-term productivity of the range. But, as in many other parts of the country, there were pockets of opposition. The San Antone district north of Tres Piedras was the critical area on the Carson. "The sheepmen themselves are all right," Leopold observed, "but it's the demagogues, the big crooks, that think they can bluff us."[42] Applications for that portion of the forest came in slowly, and as the lambing season approached more direct action had to be taken. Hall called a meeting of sheep owners at the ranch of Antonio Ortiz, the largest of the Carson users. The confrontation was loud and angry, but Hall emerged on top, delivering a bluster of threats that left the stockmen mumbling in scorn.

As it turned out, however, the task of making the threats stick fell largely on Leopold's shoulders. Hall left the Carson in March to take an assignment near his home in Oregon. With some bluster of his own, Leopold proclaimed that, "By God, the Individual Allotment and every other reform we have promised is going to *stick*—if it takes a sixshooter to do it. We can't *afford* to back down on a single point or all those agitators will be down on me like vultures and the fight will be all to do over again."[43]

Leopold and his rangers kept their six-shooters close at hand. The Carson force stood firm, but above all their task demanded diplomacy. At one point, the flocks were already moving when Leopold received orders from Albuquerque to close the main mountain pass to the lambing grounds. The sheepmen had received no advance notice. The order was plainly impossible to carry out, and Leopold sent a message back to Albuquerque asking that it be rescinded. Meanwhile, it had to be enforced. Leopold rode up to the sheep camp to explain the situation. This time, he left his pistols on the saddle, and walked into camp unarmed. To do otherwise would have invited certain trouble. As it was, there was much fingering of six-guns as he explained that the sheep could not proceed until the order was reversed. Tense moments ensued as the camp waited for word from Albuquerque. Finally, a ranger rode in with the message that the flocks would be allowed to continue.[44]

The resolve of the rangers made the grazing plan stick. The March *Pine Cone* reported that "payments are coming in at the rate of about a thousand dollars a day, and it is believed that the policy of insisting on prompt and business-like attention to the grazing business by the permittees, as well as by the Forest Officers, is beginning to produce results."[45]

The *Pine Cone* also noted the departure of Supervisor Hall, praising his "sincere courtesy and firmness." Arthur Ringland recommended that Leopold be appointed Hall's successor. The appointment was the high point in Leopold's young career. He proudly informed Estella that "of all the men in our class from Forest School there are only *two* of us Acting Supervisors, and none are Supervisors yet."[46] The dream from his Yale days, his dream of becoming a supervisor, responsible for his own forest and his own men, had come true. In comparison, the king of England seemed poor indeed.

Springtime brought the usual onslaught of work to the Carson and to its acting supervisor. "This," he wrote home in the midst of it all, "is such [a] delightful turmoil of a world."[47] Leopold added twenty men to the force, including Ray Marsh, back for another round of reconnaissance. The Forest Service appropriated funds, "six-hundred-and-fifty large round silver dollars, coin of the realm," to build a new supervisor's quarters at Tres Piedras.[48] After discussing the matter with Estella, Aldo drew up blueprints. He planned the house to face east over the thirty-mile-wide valley to the snow-capped Sangre de Cristos. It had to be done just right — simple, elegant, of necessity small, and set amid the granite boulders and piñon pines of Tres Piedras. And, of highest priority, it had to have a great fireplace. The supervisorship brought Leopold's annual salary up to $1600, but he was at a loss for furnishings until his mother and father came through with an offer to provide furniture. Construction began in May. Aldo and Estella jointly agreed to call the house "Mia Casita."

As before, Aldo's letters spanned the distance while work prevented him from visiting Santa Fe. Careful though Aldo was with words, he was as blissfully susceptible to gushing declarations of love as any man. And Estella received his letters with blushing appreciation. "It has been such a happy playful spring-like day," he wrote at one point, "as if some wild spirit were at play up there in the scudding clouds, flinging down madly whirling peltering little gusts of snow and then bursting suddenly into golden floods of joyful sunshine. I love it all so, Darling, and I wished that *you* were here and that we could smile at that wild spirit up there together, and feel the springtime in our hearts, and in all our beautiful world *together,* darling."[49]

If Aldo wrote to Estella of his desires and joys, he also shared with her his fears about his work, his responsibilities as supervisor, his inability to provide her with all she deserved, and, not least, the power of his own emotions. He told her of a dream he had while falling asleep to the song of a mockingbird. "I dreamed you and I were listening to him singing, and that we walked down to where he was and that — when we came to 'The River' somebody said — 'please' — and . . . the river was very very wide, and deep, and . . . dry. It wasn't *my* fault that the river was dry, though — was it? I wish—I would give anything—if I could ask you. Will you tell me the next time whether it was my fault?"[50]

That summer, Estella and Anita visited Burlington and Les Cheneaux, while Luna Bergere and Frederic Leopold came to Tres Piedras to stay with Aldo and work on the forest. Frederic stopped first at the Bergere home in Santa Fe, and immediately developed an attachment to one of the sisters; Aldo had to go down to Santa Fe to fetch him. Aldo, Frederic, Luna, and Yarnall shared the rooms above the office that summer while work on the new house progressed. On August 10, Leopold officially became supervisor of the Carson. There were constant pressures on him that summer, and he lost his temper on several occasions, but by and large Leopold considered himself "an awfully happy poverty-stricken improvident foolish lucky man."[51]

As the days of his bachelorhood waned, Leopold never wavered in his absolute love for Estella. He allowed himself to philosophize in a letter to his mother:

. . . there are so many things that my logical mind is forced to admit that I *don't* know, even yet. Life is so different, in retrospect. I thought that love, the beginning of it—was a great and sudden *perception* of beauty behind a beautiful mask, but now it seems like a *blind daring* guess, all the more wonderful *because* it is blind, and always *more* and *more* wonderful if right. My blindfold is being taken off now. I said "guess"—*Faith* is better—blind instinctive faith—sought for years—held for years, all blindly—and then of a sudden justified. . . . What I have said here is just the logical—the contemplative side, as I see it now. There is *much* more than that —that transcends logic and is beyond words—O so *much* more.[52]

Had Estella, for whatever reason, rejected Aldo, he would have been shattered, and his life would have followed a far different route. When Estella said yes, she sensitized him to an extreme degree. She inspired him in his thought, in his senses, in his work, and in his ambitions, and she would continue to do so for thirty-six years. Aldo pronounced himself, in the same letter to his mother, as "very grateful just to *Be*."

While preparing for the wedding, Estella's family was struck by tragedy. Late in August, Solomon Luna, the family patriarch, the most powerful man in the Southwest, the man Leopold described as "a kind of king to New Mexico," died at the age of sixty-three. His demise was not heroic: while taking some air one evening, he fell into a vat of sheep-dip, apparently knocked himself unconscious, and drowned. Estella's half-brothers Eduardo and Manuel Otero now assumed the financial and political reins of the family.

Aldo and Estella were married on October 9, 1912, at the Cathedral of Saint Francis in Santa Fe. As a non-Catholic, Aldo had to vow not to interfere in the spiritual upbringing of any children that he and Estella might have. Aldo was annoyed, but took the vows. Only the immediate families attended the ceremony; otherwise, half of New Mexico would have come. Aldo and Estella had little time for a honeymoon. The Forest Service called.

‿

The Leopolds settled into their house overlooking the great valley of the upper Rio Grande. Estella, otherwise a practical young woman, could not cook, but learned quickly. Neither could she cut hair, but Aldo willingly placed himself in her hands rather than make the special long journey to the nearest expert. Life in high, remote Tres Piedras was not easy, but such was the lot of Forest Service couples throughout the country. Aldo and Estella shared "a somewhat shy but quite sizable sense of humor."[53] Given the circumstances, that was not a luxury, but a necessity. Among her other newly acquired talents, Estella learned to hunt, and proudly displayed her first rabbit to her even prouder husband. She was not prepared though, for the mountain lion that materialized outside the kitchen one day and laid claim to one of Tres Piedras' granite outcrops.

As the early months of married life passed, Aldo Leopold could look on his life with deep satisfaction. He had the modest but tastefully appointed home he had envisioned. He was supervisor of his own forest, and had helped make that forest a viable proposition. He had even received another raise, to $1800. He had only to stand on his porch to partake of a landscape as beautiful as any on the continent. Twenty-six years old, he had found and won the one deep love of his life, a devotion Estella returned in equal measure. By the time the aspens budded out and the 1913 grazing applications began to come in, Estella knew that she was pregnant with their first child. For a sweet interval, he had attained his ideal: his land, home, family, and work, his fireplace, pipe, and books, and time for the contemplation of his days. Leopold enjoyed the best of all worlds. Like the Carson Forest itself, he had ached his way through a long period of change to emerge secure and established.

On April 7, 1913, Leopold left Tres Piedras to iron out some problems on the Jicarilla district. The ewes were on their way to the lambing grounds, and local sheepmen had petitioned against the Forest Service's placement of the driveways. Several had trespassed. Estella went to stay with her family in Santa Fe, while the Carson's new deputy supervisor, Ray Marsh, kept an eye on the office.

Reaching the Jicarilla was a chore in itself, requiring a roundabout train ride over the continental divide toward Durango. Leopold then hired a horse and rode up into the interior of the Jicarilla. For five days he attended to the various disputes, spending most of his time outside during the worst high-elevation weather of early spring. On April 16, he camped out, sleeping in a soaked bedroll. That night a hailstorm hit. The storm continued for two days, changing back and forth from sleet to rain to snow. The arroyos of the Laguna Seca Mesa flooded (Leopold noted in his work diary: ". . . suggested checking incipient erosion").[54] On April 20, he started back to Tres Piedras, but instead of returning the way he came, via horse, ferry, stage, and rail, he decided to take a shortcut. He began riding east across the Apache Reservation toward Chama, where he could meet the train. That night he got lost in the dark and stayed with an Apache Indian. The next day he crossed back over the continental divide, rode via Stinking Lake to El Vado, but there had to quit riding. His knees had swelled up so badly that he was forced to slit his riding boots. He was able to take a stage to Chama, where a doctor diagnosed his problem (wrongly, it would turn out) as rheumatism, and gave him a prescription.

Normally, a supervisor stayed in close touch with headquarters while in the field. Ray Marsh had received not a word of Leopold's whereabouts during his entire two-week absence. Leopold showed up at Tres Piedras without warning on the morning of April 23. Marsh was stunned. Leopold's face, hands, arms, and legs were all swollen. "He emphatically insisted that nothing was seriously wrong," Marsh recalled, "and seemed to think that with a few days rest he would be all right."[55] Marsh and Lee Harris, the Carson's stalwart land examiner, insisted that he take the next train to Santa Fe. That evening, Aldo jauntily wrote to his father that he had just returned from "one devil of a trip on the Jicarilla. Great trip—will write you about it later. All kinds of adventure. Mighty nice to get home again now. Estella will probably be up tonight. It seems years since I left home. Am feeling exceptionally well but have a bad attack of rheumatism which amuses me greatly but which I am going to take good care of."[56]

His condition worsened steadily over the next forty-eight hours. On the twenty-fifth, he boarded the train, rode down the valley of the Rio Grande, and arrived, dreadfully swollen, barely alive, in Santa Fe.

8

On Top
(1913–1915)

HAD LEOPOLD remained in Tres Piedras, he probably would have died. The doctor in Santa Fe correctly diagnosed his case as an attack of acute nephritis, known also as Bright's disease. Two days prior to the Jicarilla inspection tour, Leopold had mentioned in his work diary that he was "sick." This unspecified illness, combined with the subsequent exposure to the Jicarilla elements, seems to have brought on the attack. In effect, Leopold's kidneys had failed, and for eight days lymph and toxins accumulated in his body tissues. The errant prescription he received in Chama may have exacerbated the inflammation. Leopold was immediately ordered to bed, buried in blankets, fed "sweating pills," and restricted to a special diet.

He survived the initial attack, but his fate was unclear. Nephritis was poorly understood at the time, and its treatment uncertain. The medical wisdom of the day held that overexertion could lead to a relapse, and that a relapse would almost certainly be fatal. Still critically ill, he was ordered to remain in bed for six weeks and entrusted to the care of Estella and the Bergere household.[1]

Outwardly, Aldo maintained a cavalier attitude of composure. "I am very cheerful & confident that all will be well," he wrote to Arthur Ringland. "Drop me a line when you have time—it will be hard work keeping me on my back for six weeks."[2] Ringland had an uncommon concern for his men, personally and professionally. He paid a visit to Santa Fe, and reported back to an assistant in Albuquerque, "I hope [Leopold's condition] is not as serious as I am inclined to believe."[3]

Beyond Leopold's guard of optimism were more honest expressions of concern, relief, and gratitude. His encounter with death was at fearfully close range, and he knew it. He had plenty of time while lying in bed to ponder it. Estella became both his nurse and his reason to be nursed; his

124

life, he realized more than ever, was no longer his alone. "I'll *make* it sure," he wrote to his father, adding with his usual protectiveness, "with a little wife like mine I want to use every resource to make *sure*."[4]

Raymond Marsh took over as acting supervisor of the Carson. Leopold requested six weeks' sick leave. He was "restless to do something," but obediently stayed in bed, following doctor's orders and swallowing pills. As the weeks passed, he lost weight and failed to regain his strength. It became plain that his recovery, still not assured, would be slow at best. The doctor recommended that he travel to Burlington's lower altitude. Leopold asked for an extension of his leave without pay until August. He made it clear to Ringland that the decision was not his own. "My plans about going east were made *by the doctor,* Ring. I would like to return to work sooner, but I had a narrow escape and had better behave. Am 'progressing splendidly'—all or practically over my attack, but getting *stout* is really harder than getting *well,* it seems."[5]

On June 6, 1913, Leopold gingerly arose from his bed. He and Estella boarded the train and went to Burlington.

∽

Up until his harrowing ride out of the Jicarilla, Leopold had always enjoyed fine health, never suffering anything more serious than eyestrain, nervous tension, and an occasional cold. He was, of course, an indefatigably active outdoorsman, and never more so than during his years on the Apache and Carson; the intermittent adversities had always been a slight price to pay for the compensatory thrills. Now, in the middle of his twenty-sixth year, drained of his strength and under dire orders not to overexert himself, Leopold faced an indefinite period of complete inactivity. Turned inward by circumstances, Leopold was now presented with the opportunity to reflect on, assimilate, and undoubtedly to appreciate, his intensely outdoor experiences and values.

Aldo, a month and a half disabled, and Estella, five and a half months pregnant, were welcomed into 101 Clay Street. Aldo was yet, as much as ever, Clara's favorite concern in life. With his return, and Estella expecting, she turned mother again. Carl Leopold was now fifty-five years old, still going down to the factory every day, still golfing and hunting and tending the spring asparagus beds. His factory burdens had eased since Carl Jr. had graduated from Yale and joined him in managing the company. The rest of the family was also home; Marie was being courted by a Chicago banker and Frederic was back from Lawrenceville for the summer.

For three years, late spring and early summer had been for Aldo the "busy season," a time of constant work and splendid mountains, of lambs and cattle, rising desert winds, horses in meadows, and eyes on the lookout for fire. Back in green and humid Iowa, the season brought rest. Leopold spent his sedentary days sitting on the east porch of the house, reading, smoking his pipe, and looking out over the familiar panorama of his childhood: the Flint Hills, Burlington below, the yawning curves of the Mississippi, the river traffic, the Illinois lowlands opposite. His thoughts, however, darted back to the Carson National Forest. Leopold wrote a long letter, dated July 15, 1913, to his colleagues on the Carson. Ray Marsh included it in that month's *Pine Cone*. Leopold explained that his enforced leave of absence did have certain benefits:

After many days of much riding down among thickets of detail and box canyons of routine, it sometimes profits a man to top out [on] the high ridge leave without pay, and to take a look around. Most of us always *have* envied the lookouts, anyway. When your "topping out" is metaphorical and prescribed by the doctor—that is a circumstance which merely augments your envy, without decreasing your profit. But be that as it may, I will crave your indulgence while I attempt to describe what I now see from my point of vantage.[6]

He then shared his thoughts on conservation in general and on the duties of the Forest Service in particular. He took a remarkably broad and prescient view of the service's responsibilities, and of the resources for which it was responsible:

We are entrusted with the protection and development, through wise use and constructive study, of the timber, water, forage, farm, recreative, game, fish, and aesthetic resources of the areas under our jurisdiction. I will call those resources, for short, "The Forest". Our agencies for this development are: first, the Forest Users; second, our own energies, labor, and example; and third, the funds placed at our disposal. . . . It follows quite simply, that our sole task is to increase the efficiency of these three agencies. And it also follows that the sole measure of our success is the *effect* which they have on *the Forest*. . . . In plainer English, our job is to sharpen our tools, and make them cut the right way.

The daily details of administration, Leopold continued, sometimes prevented the forest officer from keeping in sight his long-range goal. "We ride in a thicket. We grapple with difficulties; we are in a maze of routine. Letters, circulars, reports, and special cases beset our path as the logs, gullies, rocks, and bog-holes and mosquitos beset us in the hills. We ride—but are we getting anywhere?" The measure of success, he reiterated, "is THE EFFECT ON THE FOREST."[7]

He was warming up to his main point. As a supervisor, Leopold was frustrated by this tendency of policy details to take precedence over even the principles of conservation the policies were intended to serve. His men were having to spend more time and effort on the routines of work, and less on the effects; the means were overwhelming the ends. The proper role of policy was "to guide our daily task, and . . . *not* to confine our minds.

And the Forest Officer who lets it do so is burying his talents." In trying to avoid ever more tangled thickets of detail, Leopold pointed out "the necessity for clear, untrammelled, and independent thinking on the part of the Forest Officers." Such thinking had to guide the Forest Service if it were to succeed in its purpose. And the man in the best position to gauge success was not the forester in Washington, nor the district forester in Albuquerque, nor even the supervisor, but the individual forest ranger. "The ranger is the man on the ground. He lives there. He is in the position to see the effects of our work at all seasons and under all circumstances, and it is these effects, and nothing else, that counts. His is the task of applying our principles in detail, and it is not until they are applied in detail that they have any effects. His is the opportunity to apply and measure and hence to study and improve."[8]

Leopold's distant view of forest administration was a logical extension of that advocated by Gifford Pinchot and his predecessors in government forestry. Decentralized authority had always been the key to managing the diverse and scattered forests of the United States. Now, with the Forest Service well established and taking on the qualities of a true bureaucracy, Leopold felt the need to reemphasize the idea that the ranger's job was, and always would be, to range, and not fill out forms.

Leopold's advice to the men on the Carson initiated a theme in his writing and thinking that would emerge, time and time again, in variations, throughout his life. In recognizing and emphasizing both "the Forest" and the place of the ranger in the field, Leopold was in fact addressing the relationship between the two. He was arguing for a more democratic approach to land management: let those who live on, work on, and know the land assume, to as great a degree as is feasible, the responsibilities and privileges for implementing policy. Only their best judgment and input could ensure success in a broad-scale conservation effort. At the time he wrote his letter, he was thinking only of his friends back in New Mexico, the rangers on horseback. In the decades to come, he would elaborate this idea—and its internal complexities—and apply it to fields far from forestry.

In August 1913, Aldo and Estella travelled with the rest of the family to Les Cheneaux. Four years had passed since Aldo's last vacation in the northern woods and waters. Frederic, now eighteen, rowed him out to a favorite fishing spot every morning, and picked him up every afternoon. That was the extent of Aldo's outdoor activities. "It's a hard lot," he complained in a letter to Ringland, "to be up here where I used to do so much but can now do nothing at all. I am allowed to fish a little, but not very much. Am getting along fairly well, though. At this time, however, I see no definite prospect of returning this fall. . . . I regretfully remind you that [my leave without pay] must again be extended, if convenient."[9]

Through letters to and from Ringland and monthly issues of the *Pine*

Cone, Leopold was able to stay abreast of forest matters. An early return, though, grew less and less likely as the summer passed. "My doctor is absolutely non-committal," he wrote to Ringland in early September, "except to say that I will probably *not* be permitted to work this winter."[10] Ringland tried to encourage him. He was anxious to start up a public relations branch in the district office, and thought Leopold an appropriate man for the job, especially since it would require little or no field work. Leopold had no desire to return to a desk in Albuquerque; the work on the Carson was unfinished. The longer his recovery took, however, the narrower his choices grew. In October, after the family returned to Burlington, Leopold's doctor advised him not to resume work until spring.

As Estella neared the end of her term, Aldo occupied himself as best he could. He edited the *Pine Cone* from afar and rendered special etchings for its cover. His reading increased. "It's pretty poor pickin' without the salt of reality," he wrote to the rangers, "but so be it."[11] He reviewed his parents' back issues of *Atlantic Monthly* and *National Geographic.* Teddy Roosevelt had a particularly provocative piece, an account of a hunt along the Grand Canyon, in *Outlook. A* new book of interest was Will Barnes's *Western Grazing Grounds and Forest Ranges.*[12] He reread one of his childhood favorites, Stewart Edward White's *The Cabin,* and leafed through Thoreau's *Journals,* a wedding gift from his mother.

But the book that had the greatest effect on Leopold was *Our Vanishing Wild Life,* by William Temple Hornaday. Newly published, Hornaday's book was among the first wholly devoted to the plight of endangered wild game populations. Leopold bought it for his father, but doubtless read it himself first. The book galvanized Aldo's conviction. Never before had the case for game protection been so alarmingly stated. Never before had the argument been made so strongly that people bore a moral responsibility for the preservation and perpetuation of threatened game species. The facts and fears had been long known, but Hornaday's uncompromising polemics gave new urgency to the issue. The message sank in as Aldo's long months of recuperation continued. His focus began to shift, slowly, certainly, and irreversibly.[13]

Aldo became a father on October 22, when Estella gave birth to a boy, whom they named Aldo Starker Leopold. The news was greeted with rejoicing in both Burlington and Santa Fe. Starker was the first grandchild for both families. Don Alfredo Bergere's joy (and ink) overflowed in a letter to Estella:

. . . I ran back hollering at the top of my voice, and of course your Mother, Miss Lizzie, Anita ran out, May was not downstairs yet, but ran down in her nighty, and immediately your Mother, Miss Lizzie, and Anita began to laugh, but before I knew it Anita had her head on my shoulder crying, and of course your Mother and Miss Lizzie followed suit, well after a few minutes so that we could get our breath, I rang up Manuel and Lucy, and told them, and then Anita commenced phoning to all her friends, and congratulations came pouring into Granma, Grandpa, and Auntie's, well I went down town, and had to fill up all my pockets with cigars, and everyone I met got a cigar. . . .[14]

The proud father wrote to Herman Chapman, one of his professors at Yale, and boasted that "A brand new Forest Supervisor arrived here."[15] The December *Pine Cone* carried the news to the high mountaintops of the Carson National Forest.

That *Pine Cone* carried another item of special interest to Leopold. Ranger Elliot Barker, who had joined the Carson force in 1912, reported killing four bobcats and four mountain lions in the space of a few November days. Leopold, in the January 1914 *Pine Cone,* applauded this feat and praised Barker for "some shooting."[16]

Leopold's fundamental concern for wild game was resurfacing during this interval away from the forests of the Southwest. Barker's success and the writings of Roosevelt and Hornaday prompted another long letter from Leopold to his officers, his first lengthy discussion of the issue of game protection in the national forests. Leopold believed that "the moral and aesthetic arguments on this question are readily appreciated by every right-minded man," and so he did not argue on these grounds. Rather, he reminded his colleagues of the economic benefit to be gained. He calculated that an abundant supply of big game "would bring $33,000 into the Carson country annually, equal to the net profit on one-third of all the sheep on the Forest. . . . It would even bear comparison with our total timber receipts under sustained yield, and it might easily be that the sum would in actual practice be doubled, due to my very conservative figures." The Forest Service had done little to take advantage of this opportunity. "The United States," Leopold concluded, "are richer in possibilities for a permanent game supply than their feeble efforts to preserve such a supply deserve. In Europe a man must be very rich to enjoy hunting at all. Here we have hundreds of National Forests, which if well stocked would afford as good sport for the man of moderate means, as for the rich."[17]

Significantly, that same *Pine Cone* included another item on cooperation between the Forest Service and the U.S. Bureau of Biological Survey, forerunner of the modern Fish and Wildlife Service. These two agencies, together with the National Park Service, would provide the main thrust in early federal efforts to protect native game populations, efforts in which Leopold would soon become deeply involved.[18]

Not all of Leopold's contributions to the *Pine Cone* were so heavy with thought. The New Year's issue listed ten "Resolutions of a Ranger," courtesy of the absent supervisor. A sampling:

1: I will love mine enemies. Yea, though their goats abide in my pastures, though they tell the Super I am a sonofagun, I will love them alway.

3: I will collect all the weeds on my District, and cherish them in mine Herbar-i-um, that their ways shall be known of men, and their latin names, and the length thereof.

8: In the month of fires I will drape my cayuse with shovels; with rakes of steel and pickaxes of iron shall my mule be laden, and I will dwell in mine Lookout many days.

10: I will honor the Super all the days of my life, and the Working Plan for ever and ever.[19]

Leopold would not allow the *Pine Cone* to become a "dry-as-dust publication." He held that "a pipe and a sense of humor are two of the essentials for a good Forest Ranger."[20] He also continued to furnish etchings for the cover: a ranger station burdened deep with winter snow, a ranger on horseback waving a New Year's hello. For the March cover, Leopold drew a portrait of a snarling mountain lion.

In February 1914, the doctor finally agreed that Leopold could return to the Southwest, but not to the Carson, and not to work. Aldo, Estella, and four-month-old Starker returned to Santa Fe and the Bergere fold. It was still unclear when Leopold would be able to return to active duty. He had to request yet another extension of his leave without pay.

Soon after Aldo and his family left Burlington, Carl Leopold began to experience medical difficulties of his own. He developed problems with his prostate, and had to turn most of the daily operations of the factory over to Carl Jr. He recovered, but not completely. "I am getting out to the office now every day," he wrote in March to Frederic at Lawrenceville, "but I am pretty badly crippled. . . . My muscular or nerve pains have disappeared, but I am not much better off otherwise, and it is going to be some time before I will be [in] anything like normal condition again." Though serious, Carl Leopold's condition did not prevent him from appreciating another spring's migrations. "I notice the Birds are coming in right along. It is cold and blustery but there were several Robbins in the yard, Meadow Larks and Blue Birds. Last Sunday was a beautiful day and I took your mother for a ride. . . . We got out in the country several miles North of the city. We heard and saw a good many Spring arrivals among the birds."[21]

∽

Six more months would pass before Aldo Leopold returned to work. The Santa Fe spring helped. He reported to Ringland some improvement in his health, but it was "slow as all 'get out.'"[22] He was allowed to move about on his own now, though not to any great degree. At least he could begin to think about returning to the Carson. He still harbored hopes that he could return there as supervisor. Sometimes he rode over to the Santa Fe headquarters of the Pecos Forest, where he kept posted on District 3 matters and on the excitement Pancho Villa was stirring up along the Mexican border. In the meantime, he recuperated at the Bergere home, playing pinochle with Don Alfredo, rooting about in the garden, and tinkering in a makeshift workshop. Aldo and Estella were no match for energetic young Starker. "Teddy Roosevelt is as placid as a mill pond before a rain, compared with that little Dickens."[23]

Matters bleakened for Leopold at the end of May. After one year of unpaid leave, he had to be "separated" officially from the Forest Service. Ray Marsh, with Leopold's full trust and support, was made supervisor of the Carson while Ringland scrambled to find Leopold a position in order to keep him on the payroll. Aldo was ready to return to work when, on June 7, he was again ordered back to Burlington by his doctor. Disheartened, Leopold retreated, with the realization dawning that he might never return to the Forest Service, much less to the physically demanding job of supervisor. He went back to Burlington, alone this time, to spend another three months reading, watching the Mississippi, resting with his father, and considering the possibility of another line of work.

Arthur Ringland was not going to let go of Leopold, even after an absence of more than a year. Ringland was thinking of combining two forests in southern Arizona and New Mexico, the Coronado and the Chiricahua, and appointing Leopold supervisor. The prospect excited Leopold, who was no longer so choosy about an assignment. "If I were free to go to Tucson this minute I'd be off so fast you wouldn't see me for the dust. In other words, I'm d__ anxious to get back to work at *anything*."[24] It was not to be. The consolidation of the two forests fell through, and Ringland had to search for another opening. At the end of August, Leopold returned to Santa Fe, well enough to resume office work, though still not wholly reconciled to the fact that his romantic days as a ranger were over.

A few days later, on September 3, Estella's mother Eloisa passed away after a brief illness. She was fifty years old.

On September 14, 1914, after sixteen and a half months on leave, Leopold was reinstated by the Forest Service. Ringland needed a man to assist John Kerr in the district's Office of Grazing, but he also had an ulterior motive: eventually he wanted to use Leopold in work on publicity and game protection. Aldo, still forbidden even to walk far, gratefully accepted the position. He returned to Tres Piedras to supervise the packing of his household goods. This was a less self-assured Leopold than before, his idealized life of rustic civility now being packed into boxes and moved down to Albuquerque. He would never relinquish the desire to be back in the forests, but he was well satisfied to be back at work and self-sufficient again. "It will be a great relief," he wrote to his father, "to have a roof of our own, and makes me feel pretty near like a U.S. citizen again."[25]

Ironically, a modern doctor might not have placed such tight restrictions on Leopold's activities during his illness, nor made such dire predictions about the results of a relapse. Leopold was obviously incapacitated, but the treatment he received was probably, and understandably, overcautious. Psychologically, these measures could only have deepened his already acute awareness of and sensitivity toward his surroundings. Henceforth, his response to conservation matters in particular would be both more direct and more thoughtful. In a sense, his own physical frontiers had narrowed abruptly, and driven him to contemplation. The return to reading that began on the porch in Burlington would never end. That second summer of recuperation, he began to keep for himself a small notebook of favorite quotations from selected readings. The summer's collection included wise words from Ralph Waldo Emerson, Robert Louis Stevenson, and Samuel Johnson, among others. The first entry came from an article by Henry Seidel Canby in the June 1914 issue of *Atlantic Monthly,* entitled "Redwood Canyon":

It all depends upon the results. To make two blades of grass grow where one grew before is surely no achievement unless the grass is good grass.

The final quotation culled that summer came from the August issue of the same magazine:

With the inhabitants of the air, as with the inhabitants of the earth, necessity increases friendliness.

Leopold then invented an adage of his own and jotted it in the notebook, the only bit of his own wisdom that he ever included:

Necessity is the mother of friendship.[26]

∽

The Leopolds moved to Albuquerque on October 4, settling into a small house on South Ninth Street, near the Rio Grande. Aldo took his place in the Office of Grazing, where his chief duties were to run the office and process paperwork when John Kerr was out in the field. As it turned out, Kerr was almost always out in the field, and Leopold unexpectedly found himself acting head of the office. He was plainly ill-suited to work under Kerr, an old-time cattleman-turned-administrator, but the clash of their personalities was muted by Leopold's determination to return to a working routine. He was encouraged by the special assignments that Ringland gave him. Within two weeks of his reinstatement, he and Ringland met to discuss the district's fish and game policies. Leopold was to take charge of all the work on game protection, and to "[build] a fire under some field men who don't sweat much in these matters."[27] For the time being, though, there was little time to concentrate on that much more appealing job. There was a thicket of paper, worse than any Leopold had encountered before, waiting to be thinned: grazing claims, trespass cases, fence complaints, maps, appeals, refunds, reviews, and reports.

At home, Estella took care of Starker, now a year old, and tutored her husband in elementary Spanish. Aldo rested, read, tinkered, and gazed longingly at the golden aspens in the Sandia Mountains, and at the ducks against the sunset over the Rio Grande. "Neither you nor I," he wrote to his ailing father, "have worried the ducks much lately, have we? Doubtless they think you and I have grown to be a pair of good hombres. I wish I could be on hand so we could *talk* ducks, anyhow, but so goes it."[28]

Late in November, Carl Leopold travelled to Chicago to undergo an operation, the third since the troubles with his health began. In Burlington, Clara and Frederic nursed him as best they could, but the nine months of fighting had taken the struggle out of him. On December 8, Aldo wrote his father about young Starker: "He's a puzzle. Showed him a photo of a fish and he looked puzzled and then the idea hit him—Agua! Agua! Devil knows how he knew unless it was from a little celluloid fish he had in his bathtub months ago. He's a wonder in interpreting pictures. Knows all the prints on the wall and what kind of critters are depicted in each one."[29] On the nineteenth, Aldo ended another letter with a discussion of the developments overseas:

I am still amazed at the astounding unintelligence of the American comment on the war. I am not referring to its trend of sympathy, but [to] the general lack of understanding. Seems to me Elliot knows less than the rest. The most sensible comment I have read is Bernard Shaw's. As for the philosophers, they are all making fools of themselves, including, I am sorry to say, some of the German ones.[30]

It was the last letter that Aldo would write to his father.

Carl Leopold died on the night of December 22, 1914. Immediately after receiving the news by wire, Aldo left for Burlington. The train ride home brought him back across the Kansas plains where his father had hunted prairie chickens, through the Missouri hills near Liberty, where his father had learned to shoot. Carl Leopold was a man of many admirable qualities: honesty, integrity, adventurousness, flexibility, kindness, humor. Years later, his son would memorialize him as "a pioneer in sportsmanship." The quiet paradox in that phrase captured well Carl Leopold's experience and contribution. Born in a time when pioneering and sportsmanship were mutually exclusive pursuits, when bison lay rotting and forests disappeared, he adopted, as a matter of purely personal honor, a new code of conduct aimed at preserving the wealth of nature's store as well as posterity's opportunity to use and enjoy it. Not an unsophisticated man, yet his fullest pleasures were always those of the outdoors: the hunting fields, the country roads, the picnic grounds, the prairies and woodlands where he tried to show his children how the other creatures lived. He left his children a name, a family business, and a concern for and enjoyment of life in the wild.

◌

After the sad holiday, Leopold returned to Albuquerque and the tedium of work in the grazing office. Kerr was in the field most of January, again leaving his assistant to the paperwork. At the end of the month, Ringland bestowed upon Leopold a "spiritual raise," allowing him to sign his official correspondence as "Acting Assistant District Forester." The flow of claims and appeals slowed enough to allow Leopold to devote some time and thought to game protection. The loss of his father may have motivated him, for within a week of his return from Burlington (and two days before his twenty-eighth birthday), Leopold prepared a long memo that outlined "plans for improvement of game protection work for which I have been gathering data for a long time."[31] He conferred with Alfred Waha, then sent the memo to Assistant Forester Leon Kneipp in Washington. Kneipp, who had begun his Forest Service career as one of the early rangers in Arizona, was due to visit the District 3 offices in February.

The problem of game protection on the national forests had only worsened since Leopold arrived on the Apache in 1909. The forests still supported the nation's most significant populations of wild game, but the service still had not taken any major steps to maintain those populations. In part, the problem was jurisdictional. The states, in accordance with common law traditions that dated back centuries, were responsible for game laws; the forests were federally administered units. Moreover, the Forest Service had no statutory mandate to manage wildlife on its lands, although the *Use Book* did call it to the attention of the foresters. What efforts the service did make were local and more or less voluntary. Arizona and New Mexico had entered into cooperative agreements with the service—probably through Arthur Ringland's efforts—dealing with the enforcement of game laws. Under these agreements, forest rangers were deputized as state game officials, the states themselves being unable to provide the manpower to patrol the vast lands within the national forest borders. The rangers, it was reasoned, could enforce state game laws in the normal course of their duties. In practice, the arrangement was simply not working. There was no incentive from within the Forest Service, and no encouragement from beyond, to concentrate on enforcement. Not a single case had been prosecuted by the Forest Service since the agreements were signed.[32]

Leopold met Kneipp on the sixth of February. His memo had been essentially an argument for greater service-wide attention to the situation. Its one specific recommendation was that rangers be compensated for time spent on game protection. Kneipp did not concur. In a subsequent note to Ringland, Kneipp pointed out that "existing statutes do not recognize wild game as a Forest product. . . . There is a possibility, and in the mind of the Forester a hope, that perhaps in the course of time the public opinion will so change and statutes [be] amended . . . so as to concede that game animals . . . are . . . Forest products." In the meantime, Kneipp argued, game protection should be a matter of public duty. Other districts had enjoyed greater success than District 3, due not to favorable public sentiment or economic incentive, but to simple application of effort. "There ought not to be any false pretenses about this game protection work," Kneipp concluded. "The rank and file of the Service should regard it as a duty to be thoroughly and effectively discharged, or else we should disavow the responsibility for the game and refuse to be connected with its protection."[33]

Partly in response to this opinion, Ringland began to look for ways to take advantage of Leopold's obvious interest in the matter. Over the next few months, Leopold took on several game-related chores in the district, including plans to cooperate with the Bureau of Biological Survey on predator control. For his part, Kneipp came away from his meeting with Leopold disagreeing on specifics, but impressed by the need for greater involvement in the cause. In this regard, Leopold, Ringland, Alfred Waha, John D. Guthrie, Ray Marsh, Elliot Barker, and others in the Southwest were in the vanguard of the agency's growing concern for wildlife. Within months, Forester Graves would himself come out with an article entitled "The National Forests and Wild Life," among the first public indications of the agency's new push in the matter.[34]

Leopold continued to work in the grazing office through the spring, but it became increasingly clear that he would not be able to function freely there. When Kerr was out, he had to take up the slack work. When Kerr was in, friction inevitably arose between them. More than once, Kerr deliberately slighted his assistant. Leopold did not complain openly, but registered subtle gibes in his work diary: ". . . worked up plan for Tonto reduction *for* [Kerr] . . . ," ". . . helped [Kerr] figure out corrections. . . ." Theirs was a clash, not only of personalities, but of conservation philosophies. Leopold was a member of the new guard, pushing for lower numbers of livestock on the heavily grazed ranges. The need that was obvious to him was not obvious to Kerr, who instead concentrated on maintaining the cooperation and compliance of the stockmen, many of whom were his friends. To Leopold's credit, he did not make the same mistakes he had made under similar circumstances on the 1909 Apache reconnaissance. Assuming nothing, he kept his peace, did his job, and tolerated with patience his more experienced superior.

By the middle of March 1915, Ringland sensed that Leopold was chafing under Kerr and was ready to assume other duties. He called Leopold into his office to discuss his future with the Forest Service. The primary concern was Leopold's health. Although slowly regaining some of his former vigor, he was still under orders to guard against overexertion or fatigue. Leopold told his boss that he was willing "to undertake anything which, after full understanding of my physical limitations re field work, he desired to have me tackle."[35] Two months later, after another round of disagreements with Kerr, Leopold was told that he was being taken out of the Office of Grazing and assigned to the district's new work on fish and game, recreation, and publicity.

The nine months' detail in the Office of Grazing was, despite its grind and irritation, a valuable experience for Leopold. In a purely technical sense, he had become well versed in the business of grazing. His administrative experience, combined with his prior field knowledge, now made him as proficient a range manager as forester. He also became fully acquainted with the term and concept of "carrying capacity"—in its grazing application, the number of stock a given range could support without deteriorating. The discovery would reverberate through his work for the rest of his life. Leopold's experience with office routines also proved useful. In subsequent years he would make no small contribution to the increased efficiency of the district offices. Finally, the job gave Leopold a chance, quite literally, to get back on his feet. He had finally resigned himself to the fact that he would not, for the forseeable future, be leading the strenuous life of a horseback forester, the life that originally drew him into the profession. His nine months of on-the-job therapy gave him time to see that there were other fields to range.

In the meantime, the house on Ninth Street had become a home. Leopold's salary had not risen above the $1800 plateau, and was unlikely to given the appropriations problems the Forest Service was having in Washington. "We just stumble along over the cost of living from month to month," he wrote to Burlington. "However, paid bills are more comfortable than new clothes."[36] Aldo bought eight new chickens to provide eggs. When spring arrived, so did the greatest joy a semimobile Leopold could have asked for—a return to the garden. On Sundays, the whole family was out to the garden, putting in the vegetables. Rio Grande mosquitos and New Mexico sandstorms were no deterrent. Even after the chickens raided the sunflowers and linnets mowed the lettuce, Aldo was not discouraged. "All of (this)," he wrote to his mother, "is the struggle with nature, without which I should wilt like a transplanted cabbage."[37] For a long time, the joys and disappointments of that struggle had ceased.

On June 8, 1915, Leopold left the Office of Grazing. Ringland, in a note to Forester Graves explaining Leopold's new assignment, wrote that, "As a general rule I like to foster any particular interest a member of the Service may have in certain lines of work on the ground that with his deep interest he is more apt to succeed."[38] That management philosophy had made Ringland a successful district forester and had pointed not only Leopold, but dozens of others, in directions where they were able to make lasting contributions to the profession. Even Aldo was not so sure about this new assignment. "I don't trust this new job to last, much less like it. However, I'm so d__ glad to be making a living that I gladly waive the fine questions."[39] With Ringland's encouragement, Leopold had ridden out the worst of his illness, come through the thickets of detail, and now stood poised, ready to enter another newer, larger territory.

The staff of the Apache National Forest, 1910, including Forest Supervisor John D. Guthrie *(seated, second from left),* Deputy Forest Supervisor Fred Winn *(crouching, with hat, on Guthrie's left),* Forest Assistant Aldo Leopold *(seated, with pipe, fifth from right),* and District Forester Arthur Ringland *(seated, on Leopold's left)* (Photo by Raymond Marsh. Leopold Collection, UW Archives)

Leopold with Guthrie's dog, Flip, at the abandoned Irwin claim on the Apache National Forest, 1910 (Photo by John D. Guthrie. Bradley Study Center Files)

The crew of "Camp Indigestion" buries the cook's bread during the 1910 reconnaissance of the Apache National Forest. *Left to right:* Leopold, G. H. Collingwood, R. E. Hopson, C. W. McKibbon, O. F. Bishop, J. W. Hough, Basil Wales, Raymond Marsh (Photo by J. H. Allison. Leopold Collection, UW Archives)

Officers of the Carson National Forest at forest headquarters in Tres Piedras, New Mexico, 1911. *Left to right:* Deputy Forest Supervisor Leopold (riding Polly), Forest Assistant Ira T. Yarnall, Forest Supervisor Harry C. Hall (Photo by Raymond Marsh. Leopold Collection, UW Archives)

Estella Bergere in 1913, at the age of 21
(Bradley Study Center Files)

Estella with family, about 1907. *Clockwise from rear left:* Alfred Bergere, Eloisa
Luna Otero Bergere, Manuel Otero, Estella, Nina Otero, Consuelo, Rosina, Dolores,
Luna (Leopold Collection, UW Archives)

Estella and Aldo on wedding day in Santa Fe, New Mexico, October 9, 1912 (Bradley Study Center Files)

"Mia Casita," Aldo and Estella's house and Carson National Forest supervisor's headquarters, in Tres Piedras (Bradley Study Center Files)

Leopold toting the *Binnacle Bat II* on the Rio Grande, 1918 (Leopold Collection, UW Archives)

Ward Shepard, Luna, Starker, Flick, and Aldo after a day of hunting doves and yellowlegs at the Tomé Gun Club, 1921 (Bradley Study Center Files)

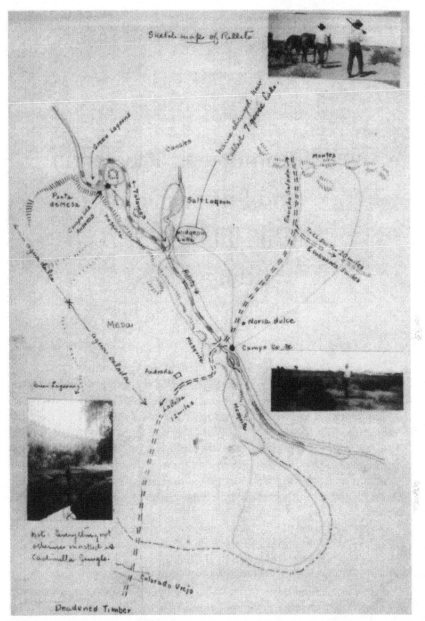

Leopold's journal map of the Rillito on the Colorado River Delta, 1922 (Leopold
Papers, UW Archives)

9

"To Promote the Protection and Enjoyment of Wild Things . . ."

(1915–1919)

O N JUNE 16, 1915, one week after leaving the Office of Grazing, Leopold stood on the south rim of the Grand Canyon. He was now responsible for District 3 recreational policy, and his first assignment was to investigate conditions at the Canyon, then a national monument administered by the Forest Service as part of the Kaibab and Tusayan National Forests. Leopold would visit the Canyon several times during the next two years, and collaborate with Tusayan Supervisor Don P. Johnston on a working plan for the Canyon. Theirs became the first such comprehensive plan for the public enjoyment of this greatest of natural wonders.[1]

Leopold knew enough basic geology to appreciate what he saw: two billion years' laminations of limestone, sandstone, shale, and schist, lifted and faulted, cloven and exposed by the Southwest's great red river. Through all its previous ages, the Canyon had seen no species to compare with the one now scratching away at its layers of time. European man had come upon it only 350 years prior to Leopold's visit. John Wesley Powell had made his epic exploration down the Colorado less than fifty years before. A steady influx of tourists, speculators, exploiters, scientists, and artists had followed. In 1893, the Canyon and its pine-laden rims drew protection within one of the first forest reserves. In 1903, President Roosevelt visited the Canyon, and implored his fellow citizens to "leave it as it is. You cannot improve on it; not a bit. The ages have been at work on it, and man can only mar it. . . . What you can do is to keep it for your children, your children's children, and for all who come after you, as one of the great sights which every American, if he can travel at all, should see. Keep the Grand Canyon as it is."[2]

In the thirteen years that had since passed, the inheritors had not responded very nobly to Roosevelt's call. Gaudy electric advertisements lit up the rimtop nights. Hawkers for competing travel companies squalled through megaphones at the break of dawn, persevering until the tourists surrendered their patronage. Shifty concessionaires continually feuded, with visitors caught in the cross fire. The campgrounds and stables were unsanitary; wastes went untreated and garbage uncollected. The Canyon, in short, was feeling the initial effects of the changes in American society: more wealth, more leisure time, and, above all, more mobility.

By June 1915, outdoor recreation was a topic of high priority on the conservation agenda. John Muir, seventy-six years old, disappointed by the failure of efforts to prevent the damming of Yosemite's Hetch Hetchy Valley, had died the previous December (three days after Carl Leopold's death). Muir's concerns endured, however, in growing sentiment for the creation of a consolidated National Park Service. The Forest Service, anxious to accommodate the public and, incidentally, to hold on to its lands, responded by giving greater attention to recreational needs.

Leopold's new responsibilities in the district were threefold: to oversee these new recreation efforts (paying particular attention to the sanitation problem), to handle all information and publicity work, and to coordinate the nascent fish and game program. His brief visit to the Grand Canyon involved all three. His main objective was to gain firsthand knowledge of conditions there as base data for the new working plan. He also wanted to gather information for a public guidebook to the Canyon. Finally, he was interested in the state of game protection efforts there. The Canyon had not only been part of one of the nation's first forest reserves; Roosevelt, by a 1906 executive order, had also declared it one of the nation's first game refuges. Leopold spent five days looking over the campgrounds, trails, and Forest Service facilities, and conferring with rangers and officers on conditions in the area.

Leopold returned to Albuquerque and, after clearing his desk of initial publicity and recreation work, turned his attentions to his fish and game assignments. He worked on a tentative outline of game refuges for the district—despite the fact that the Forest Service had as yet no congressional authorization to establish such refuges. He wrote a report recommending that Stinking Lake (the same lake he had passed two years before on his fateful return from the Jicarilla) be set aside as a national bird refuge, and began to gather data on the status of game in the district. Every visitor to the Albuquerque offices had to face a battery of questions about their local game situation. By late July, Leopold had enough information to begin work on a game handbook for the forest rangers and officers.

Leopold spent a month and a half preparing the handbook, his first substantial written work on game conservation. The Forest Service had never before issued anything like it. Leopold gathered together all information pertinent to the fish and game resources of the southwestern forest lands, from laws and regulations to the proposed refuge system, from species descriptions to fish-planting procedures. The influence of William T. Hornaday was evident in Leopold's introductory discussion of the "biological value" of wildlife:

North America, in its natural state, possessed the richest fauna in the world. Its stock of game has been reduced 98%. Eleven species have been already exterminated, and twenty-five more are now candidates for oblivion. Nature was a million years, or more, in developing a species. . . . Man, with all his wisdom, has not evolved so much as a ground squirrel, a sparrow, or a clam.[3]

Leopold added to his argument a discussion of the potential economic value of southwestern game. Maine, he pointed out, took in $13 million from its hunters; Arizona and New Mexico could not even be compared due to the scarcity of game. But even in his economic arguments, Leopold did not think solely in terms of dollars returned. "The breeding stock must be increased. Rare species must be protected and restored. The value of game lies in its variety as well as its abundance."[4]

Other aspects of Leopold's early attitudes toward game were evident in his handbook. He hardly mentioned predators, and certainly did not include them among the species to be protected. He emphasized the need for more information, more data, more research. And, already, Leopold was highlighting the inherent diversity of the Southwest. He singled out the ptarmigan as the emblem of this regional richness: "No better proof could be found of the valuable diversity of climate of the Southwest than the presence of this purely Arctic bird on the high peaks of the Carson and Pecos. Unfortunately, it is doubtful whether any still survive. They have not been seen for some years."[5]

Leopold completed his *Game and Fish Handbook* in September and distributed it the following month. The handbook soon garnered praise, not only from district personnel, but from the national office as well.

Meanwhile, the national offices had plans for Leopold. Forester Graves had previously expressed interest in bringing Aldo to Washington. Now Graves was pressing. Arthur Ringland covered for his friend. Shortly after Leopold's handbook came out, Ringland wrote to Graves, "I have gone over the situation carefully with Leopold and find that it would simply cripple our work to have him detailed to Washington this fall. When I talked to you I thought this would be feasible but now find, quite without regard to Leopold's health which is still unsatisfactory, that the work laid out for him here will fully engage his time."[6] The "work laid out for him" was, first and foremost, game protection. Leopold was to take the initiative in organizing the sportsmen of Arizona and New Mexico into cooperative game protection associations.

An eventful month lay ahead. On September 18, Leopold dictated letters to twenty persons in Albuquerque interested in game protection. On October 5, he sent his handbook to the field men. On the eighth, Estella gave birth to their second child, a son whom they named Luna Bergere Leopold. And on October 12, Albuquerque received a visit from William Temple Hornaday himself.

∽

The personal shift in Aldo Leopold's career, away from forestry proper and toward the protection of game, paralleled a shift in the direction of the conservation movement as a whole. The highly visible battles of the 1890s and early years of the twentieth century primarily involved the nation's land resources—its forests, parklands, grazing grounds, and waterways. Wildlife conservation always figured importantly in these battles, and sportsman-naturalists often spearheaded the skirmishes, but renewed concentration on wildlife itself came only after the debate over these broader land-use issues subsided. Through the 1910s, 1920s, and into the 1930s, the wildlife proponents would increasingly draw (and sometimes dissipate in internal squabbling) the movement's energies.[7]

Since the 1870s, conscientious sportsmen across the country had been organizing themselves into clubs and associations committed to the local preservation of fish and game. These groups, numbering in the hundreds, played a quiet but significant role in fostering discussion and encouraging public understanding of the fate of America's wildlife and its habitat. Their local efforts were reflected in the growing attention paid to fish and game by the state and federal governments.

By 1915, most states had enacted laws for the protection of fish and game, and had authorized administrative agencies to oversee and enforce the laws. Real protection, however, did not necessarily follow. More often than not, the laws simply went unenforced. The agencies were only as effective as local politics allowed. To qualify as a state warden or commissioner, an appointee generally required only an interest in the outdoors and proper political connections, with an emphasis on the latter. Even when competent administrators manned the state agencies, they were constrained by a chronic lack of funding. There were exceptions. Especially in the Northeast and in progressive pockets of the West, game protection efforts were beginning to gain strength.

At the federal level, progress was sporadic, but gaining momentum. The dozen or so national parks were closed to hunting, and harbored some of the nation's healthiest remaining herds of bison, elk, deer, and bighorn sheep. During his presidency, Theodore Roosevelt had established individual wildlife refuges—fifty-one before he left office—with the same vigor that he had employed in creating national forests. On the legislative side, Congress in 1900 had passed the landmark Lacey Act, prohibiting the interstate shipment of illegally taken wild birds and mammals. In 1913, Congress passed its most comprehensive piece of wildlife legislation yet, the Weeks-McLean Migratory Bird Act, which asserted federal jurisdiction over migratory game birds and conferred upon the Bureau of Biological Survey unprecedented enforcement powers. The constitutionality of the act was unresolved in 1915; a new effort was afoot to secure its goals through international treaty.

Behind these advances lay the influence of a number of prominent and well-placed eastern conservationists, acting in groups and as individuals. The most potent of the groups, small in numbers but selective in membership, was the Boone and Crockett Club. Founded by Theodore Roosevelt and George Bird Grinnell in 1887, and based in New York City, the Boone and Crockett Club counted some of the most distinguished public figures of its day as members, including Henry Cabot Lodge, Carl Schurz, Gifford Pinchot, Francis Parkman, John Lacey, General William Tecumseh Sherman, and Albert Bierstadt. Grinnell, the standard-bearer and main strategist in many a conservation crusade, had also founded the first Audubon Society in 1886. Although that initial group faded, the Audubon movement did not. In 1905, thirty-six state groups, led by the Massachusetts Audubon Society, joined forces to form the National Association of Audubon Societies.

By 1911, commercial interests were ready to join the cause. The Winchester Repeating Firearms Company, acknowledging that a decline in game meant a decline in business, approached the Audubon Association with an offer to fund game protection programs. After much internal debate, the Audubon group declined the offer. Winchester then led a consortium of gun companies in funding and creating, in September 1911, yet another organization, the American Game Protective and Propagation Association, the aim of which was to preserve and restore wild game populations (the group shortened its name in 1913 to the American Game Protective Association, or AGPA).

Winchester had initially approached William T. Hornaday with its funding offer. The crankiest, most eccentric, and in many ways the most effective of the eastern conservationists, Hornaday was an outspoken opponent of sport hunting. He refused to accept industry money, and pressured the Audubon board of directors into its turn-down. Infused with the righteousness of his cause, the crusading Hornaday was the most widely known wildlife conservationist of his day, with the possible exception of Teddy Roosevelt himself. Hornaday began his career as a taxidermist, and in that capacity had hunted as many rare animal species as any man alive. He eventually became chief taxidermist for the U.S. National Museum in Washington, and later accepted an appointment as director of the New York Zoological Society. From there, Hornaday waged his highly personal campaigns on behalf of wildlife. Profits from *Our Vanishing Wild Life* helped fund his own one-man brigade, the Permanent Wild Life Protection Fund. Hornaday was sixty years old, with a biblical voice and countenance to match his zeal. Tact and forbearance were not among his virtues. A gadfly to his company of polite gentlemen conservationists, he was, in one historian's words, "a knight in shining armor rising to the defense of wildlife and swinging a mighty sword with such vigor that he often laid open his allies along with his enemies."[8] It was a role that Hornaday enjoyed playing, and it was just the kind of agitation that the established, eastern-based wildlife movement needed. In print, at meetings, on lecture tours, he forcefully issued his dire warnings and spread his wildlife message. "I have been a sportsman myself," he wrote in *Our Vanishing Wild Life,* "but times have changed, and we must change also."[9]

A speaking tour of the West in the fall of 1915 brought Hornaday to Albuquerque. Leopold had been anticipating his visit for weeks. On the evening of October 13, Hornaday presented a fiery lecture, replete with lurid slides of slaughtered game, to the concerned sportsmen of Albuquerque.[10] The sportsmen gave Hornaday an enthusiastic reception. Hornaday, in turn, encouraged them in their new organizing effort and backed up his words with several hundred dollars from his Protection Fund. Before leaving town, he gave Leopold a copy of his latest book, *Wild Life Conservation in Theory and Practice.*[11]

The sparks that emanated from Hornaday's orations fell on Leopold's own highly combustible convictions. On October 19, he led the organizational meeting and was elected secretary of the Albuquerque Game Protective Association. A week later, he was in Taos, lecturing and organizing a second local GPA there. The next day Leopold, Ray Marsh, and Elliot Barker, to advertise the seriousness of their intentions, investigated an illegal deer kill. Within twenty-four hours, the offenders were arrested, tried, convicted, and fined. Leopold was able to do all this on official time. The Forest Service already maintained cooperative relations with such groups as the New Mexico Cattle Growers Association; Ringland gave Leopold a free hand to organize sportsmen in the same manner.

Leopold proved to be a compelling organizer and speaker, adept at enlisting the support of diverse, apathetic, and even potentially hostile factions. In November, he spoke to the sportsmen of Magdalena and organized a third Game Protection Association. This was a particularly vital meeting. Magdalena sat at the eastern end of the magnificent Plains of San Augustin, the vast grassland basin where the Luna family operated the N-Bar Ranch, headquarters of its sheep empire. Leopold gained the backing of his brother-in-law Eduardo Otero, who not only ran that empire, but presided over the New Mexico Wool Growers Association, a crucial ally in the sportsmen's cause. In Magdalena, Leopold also met J. Stokely Ligon of the Bureau of Biological Survey, an enthusiastic game protector and perhaps the most knowledgeable man in the Southwest with regard to wildlife. This time, Ligon accompanied Leopold on the example-setting arrest of a local game-law violator.[12]

Leopold had only begun. He put together a new bulletin for the sportsmen of Albuquerque. Borrowing his title from the old Carson Forest newsletter, Leopold distributed the first issue of *The Pine Cone* in December. Its purpose was "to promote the protection and enjoyment of wild things. As the cone scatters the seeds of the pine and fir tree, so may it scatter the seeds of wisdom and understanding among men, to the end that every citizen may learn to hold the lives of harmless wild creatures as a public trust for human good, against the abuse of which he stands personally responsible. Thus, and only thus, will our wild life be preserved."[13]

The Pine Cone would become, over the next five years, the main educational tool of the GPAs. The first issue included articles on the law enforcement efforts of the Forest Service, the proposed Stinking Lake refuge, the endangered Mexican Mountain Sheep, and Hornaday's books (*Our Vanishing Wild Life* was "the most convincing argument for better game protection every written"). Another article, entitled "The Varmint Question," called for "the reduction of predatory animals . . . the wolves, lions, coyotes, bob-cats, foxes, skunks, and other varmints." Leopold argued that stockmen and game protectionists ought to cooperate in a "practical, vigorous, and comprehensive plan of action" to meet this "common problem."[14]

Writing to his mother in the midst of this rush of activity, Leopold explained the paucity of his correspondence:

To make a long story short, I have been entirely tied up in this game business, and so pleased with the results we are getting that I really haven't enjoyed doing anything else. We can pretty nearly say now that we have the whole state sitting up and taking notice, and *most* of the state falling off the fence on our side. It's a fascinating game. Every so often, however, I awaken to the fact that I am fighting on crutches after all, and must make myself sit down and take it easy for a while.[15]

In December, another memo from Washington arrived, hinting again that Leopold might be transferred to the national offices. Leopold responded by tallying the recent successes:

> On June 1, 1915, after two years of work under cooperative agreements with both states, we had not a thing to show except considerable time and money put into periodical reports and a few streams stocked in a haphazard way. The State Wardens, and to some extent the public, were complaining, and with good cause. Two valuable species were on the verge of extinction, all game was decreasing, and Forest Officers had prosecuted not a single case.
>
> On December 1, 1915, we have initiated 12 prosecutions, won 8, lost 1, pending 3. We have a complete handbook to work under, which has been commended by schools, Foresters, and authorities. We have stocked more waters than ever before, including three heretofore empty ones. We have a complete census of the two threatened species; we have definite plans for saving them, and we have organized the forces to put these plans through. . . . We have the promised support of both governors, both game wardens, one chamber of commerce, the state of Texas, and dozens of influential citizens for our program. We have forced both game wardens into unprecedented activity without losing their cooperation. Almost every issue of every important newspaper has something on game protection. A majority of Forest Officers have been converted from a passive or even apathetic attitude into activity and alertness.[16]

"The progress of this work," Leopold wrote, "has convinced me that with another year's time, I can have well under way a movement which will revolutionize conditions in Arizona and New Mexico." No other district in the Forest Service could make such boasts, and Leopold had still only begun his efforts. He, Estella, two-year-old Starker, and two-month-old Luna spent the holidays in Santa Fe. As the year drew to a close, Leopold took the opportunity to organize the Santa Fe Game Protective Association.

ᔐ

In January 1916, Leopold embarked on a major organizing tour across southern New Mexico. First stop was Silver City, where Leopold conferred with Miles W. Burford, leader of the Sportsmen's Association of Southwestern New Mexico. The beginning of the game protection movement in New Mexico actually predated Leopold's campaign. Burford, in 1914, had single-handedly organized the hunters and fishermen near Silver City, and converted local cattle ranchers and miners over to the cause. His group now included a hundred members. Burford was, in Leopold's words, "a direct man . . . endowed with that highest and finest form of diplomacy, militant fairness."[17] They discussed the possibility of a state-wide confederation of game associations. Later, Leopold delivered an illustrated lecture to Burford's group.[18]

Leopold set forth from Silver City, preaching the gospel of game protection. Travelling by train and coach to Rincon, downriver to El Paso, around the white sands to Alamogordo, up to Cloudcroft in the Sacramento Mountains, through the Valley of Seven Rivers to Carlsbad, Leopold carried the word: if the hunters of New Mexico continued along their same path, they would kill off not only the game, but the sport itself; organize and work at it, and the "game hog" would be the only victim. Three hundred showed up at the meeting in Roswell. "The curious thing," Leopold wrote to his mother, "is that this thing has been tried time and again right here in New Mexico, and as promptly failed. I therefore can simply state that my plans and methods are delivering the goods."[19]

While Leopold was busy proselytizing, Arthur Ringland was up in Salt Lake City attending a meeting of the nation's six district foresters and Chief Forester Henry Graves. Graves was adamant this time: he needed Leopold in the Washington office, and issued personal orders to that effect. Leopold's reaction bordered on insubordination. He had no interest in what he considered a dead-end Washington detail. He declined to follow the orders, and offered to resign rather than abandon his efforts in New Mexico, which were to culminate in a state convention of GPAs in March. He also expressed concerns about the effect on his health of a Washington assignment. A flurry of telegrams blew back and forth between Salt Lake City, Albuquerque, and points south, Graves growing more insistent, and Leopold likewise. Graves naturally questioned how Leopold could plead health problems when he was running around to all corners of the Southwest.

Leopold made his case in a personal letter to Ringland. "I must, when it comes to figuring out my future, consider my [physical condition] chronic. This means that, however much I may improve, I will never be able to meet the physical requirements of a job involving regular field work. If I overdo just once, I am done for, no matter how well I may be feeling or looking beforehand, a second relapse being considered fatal in all cases."[20] This was news to Ringland. Leopold had not confided even to his friend and boss the full nature of his doctor's orders. Leopold continued:

To speak plainly, I do not know whether I have twenty days or twenty years ahead of me. Whatever time I may have, I wish to accomplish something definite. Unless, however, I can settle down to one thing, I have small chance of such accomplishment. This "one thing" for me is obviously game protection. . . . I think you will agree with equal readiness that to abandon a chance at a live field in favor of a sure job at nothing at all would be playing quitter.[21]

Graves was put off by Leopold's disobedience, and unconvinced by his claims about his health. Still, the forester was impressed by Leopold's obvious devotion to his cause, and offered to bring him to New York in March to attend a meeting of the nation's leading wildlife experts. Even this temptation would not sway Leopold, who felt that his presence at the upcoming state convention was crucial. Having fueled the new movement, Leopold took a proprietary interest in its success:

The fact is that I have stirred up plenty of force and energy, but it has needed constant "steering." Above all, the convention must be "steered." If I am not there, there will be a squabble or somebody will run off hog-wild on some entirely impracticable proposition, and the whole movement will be "queered." I say this not from theory, but experience. I know everybody who will be there, and I know what each one will want to do. They are fine men, but they are too new at this proposition to be "rounded out."[22]

Leopold was not the only one stirring up New Mexican dust in the early months of 1916. On March 9, the day before the GPA delegates met in Albuquerque, Pancho Villa alarmed the nation with his raid on Columbus, on the border south of Silver City. Even Leopold, adept by now at public relations, could not prevent the convention from assuming second position in the day's headlines.

The convention was an unqualified success. The confederated groups now constituted the New Mexico Game Protective Association, with a membership of a thousand, Miles Burford serving as president, and Aldo Leopold as secretary and "committee of one in charge of the educational and publicity work." The NMGPA also became, overnight, an important force in New Mexico politics. Leopold himself displayed a tinge of political ambition. He did not foster, but neither did he discourage, loose talk about his possible appointment as state game warden.

The New Mexico Game Protective Association had three main goals on its agenda. Law enforcement was its top priority, and this meant that the process of choosing and backing the state game warden had to be taken out of the hands of politicians. "Why is the big game of the West disappearing today?" Leopold wrote at one point. "Principally for the reason that the game laws are not enforced. And why are they not enforced? *Politics.* Paper game laws and political game wardens are inseparable."[23] New Mexico's current warden was not opposed to the new movement; he had cooperated with Leopold and the GPAs, and attended the state convention. But it was not enough to be merely competent or sympathetic; a proper game warden had to be *inspired.* "We need a super-Game Warden, a man fired with an intense personal enthusiasm for the cause of game protection. He should, moreover, be directly responsible to the sportsmen of the state, as well as to the governor. More important still, he should be responsible to neither political party, because there are no political issues involved in game protection."[24] The process of choosing a warden, Leopold insisted, had to involve the sportsmen. "Man really prizes only those things which he has earned by the sweat of his brow. Sportsmen do not *really support* a game warden until they have had to *roll up their sleeves* in some common disinterested effort to get a good one."[25] The opportunity to do so would soon arise, as the 1916 New Mexico gubernatorial campaign began. Leopold's own interest in the state wardenship faded as quickly as it had emerged. Having felt the flush of popular support, Leopold resumed the behind-the-scenes work with which he was most comfortable. His intent did not diminish, however; in *The Pine Cone* and in news releases he would continue to emphasize the NMGPA's political role in this supposedly non-political issue.

Leopold had a special interest in a second goal of the NMGPA: the establishment of game refuges on the national forests. Bills to authorize national refuges had been introduced in Congress before, but without success. The current effort was the Chamberlain-Hayden Bill, which embodied the so-called Hornaday Plan. This plan—named by none other than Hornaday himself—called for the creation of a national system of game refuges, superceding the previously haphazard method of creating preserves by executive order. Hornaday was stumping the country for support. Leopold took up the fight locally. Despite their common cause, Leopold and Hornaday differed in their thinking on the purpose of refuges. A refuge, in Hornaday's mind, protected game from hunting; in Leopold's, it produced game *for* hunting (Leopold distinguished between a refuge and a sanctuary, which protected endangered species from all hunting).[26] This conceptual difference, however, did not affect Leopold's support of the plan. At the March convention, he spoke on its behalf in his official Forest Service capacity. Although the bill was destined to wither in Congress, Leopold would continue to press hard on the local level for the establishment of refuges.

Predator control was the third flank in the battle for game protection. The convention passed a resolution "urging and fostering by all possible means a systematic campaign against predatory animals destructive to game and livestock."[27] To this end, it proposed the creation of a cooperative commission, involving stock-raisers, sportsmen, the State Game Department, the Forest Service, and the Bureau of Biological Survey, to pursue "the wise control" of wolves, mountain lions, coyotes, bears, bobcats, foxes, and birds of prey.

For many, if not most, "wise control" meant "extermination." The situation in the Southwest was ready-made for the ensuing emotional crusade against predators. The depletion of wild prey, the shrinkage of native habitat, and the easy availability of domestic sheep and cattle had, over the years, altered the range and feeding, behavioral, and reproductive habits of most predators, and of wolves in particular. On the Carson Forest, where hunters had taken a mere eight deer in 1915, wolf depredations on stock were rising, as were the tempers of stockmen and sportsmen. The

predator found few friends in the pioneer's world. Even as staunch a pre-
server of wildlife as Hornaday, for instance, could advocate that the pere-
grine falcon be shot on sight. An economic stake, centuries of cultural indoctrination, and an almost complete lack of scientific information on the
role of predators in natural systems only bolstered the immediate observation of both stockman and sportsman: that varmint takes my food.

New impetus in the battle against predators and other "pests" came
in 1914, when Congress authorized the Department of Agriculture to intensify control efforts. A year later, the Bureau of Biological Survey received
funds to initiate a large-scale predator control effort. "Control districts"
were organized throughout the West, and professional "wolfers" went to
work in the mountains. J. Stokely Ligon was put in charge of the Arizona–
New Mexico district, and methodically began to discharge his professional
duties. Cooperation among the Biological Survey, the Forest Service, the
State Game Department, and the NMGPA soon made New Mexico an
acknowledged leader in the drive to rid the West of predators once and
for all.

And that was the goal, particularly in these early years. Leopold was
not the most vehement advocate of extermination; some were more rabid
than he, others less so. But as designated propagandist, Leopold enthusiastically railed against "vermin," "varmints," and the "skulking marauders
of the forest." Leopold did none of the actual hunting and trapping; ironically, he was not as yet hunting at all, due to his doctor's orders. His main
contribution was to generate cooperation between ranchers and sportsmen.
The best that can be said of Leopold's initial attitude toward predators
can be said of the prevalent attitudes of the day: they were not based on
scientific understanding, nor did they foresee the day when many predatory species would reach the brink of extinction. Although Leopold was
fired up enough, on occasion, to call for total eradication of predators,
he could still express admiration for the wildness they represented. In *The
Pine Cone,* Leopold reported the demise of a famous grizzly of the Mount
Taylor country, at the hand of Ligon and an associate:

He was a famous bear, notorious throughout the land. Many hunters had tried
their luck on him, and went their way with a fat pay-check but nary a bear. We
think that every true and keen sportsman will subscribe to our confession of a
weakness for big bear, and a secret temptation to wish them a long life and a merry
one. But the king of Mt. Taylor was a cow-killer from away back. He was a bad
egg. He ate a thousand dollars' worth of beef a year. The destructiveness of cow-
killers is intolerable, and it is highly desirable that they be destroyed on sight.[28]

Leopold was still an officer in the United States Forest Service. Having
laid the foundation for the NMGPA, Leopold now stepped aside. But not
very far. He temporarily left his post as secretary of the statewide group,

but continued to serve in that capacity with the Albuquerque GPA. He would remain the most prominent individual in the movement as he lectured, churned out news items, and assembled the quarterly *Pine Cone.*

In April 1916, Arthur Ringland was transferred to Washington. The war in Europe was expanding, and Ringland went to work on contingency plans for the Forest Service should the United States have to enter the conflict. Leopold lost his closest friend and staunchest supporter in the district. Ringland had given him the chance to innovate and to follow his enthusiasms; he worried now about the progress of his work, and about losing the kind of trust that Ringland had placed in him. "I don't know how the new D.F. . . . will look at the game business," Leopold wrote to his mother. "I'm sorry to see Ring go—he's given me a free ride, which is the best kind of supervision there is."[29]

He needn't have worried. The new district forester turned out to be Paul G. Redington, who was also deeply interested in game matters. In the months that followed, Leopold continued to divide his time between his official duties and his quasi-official game protection activities. His health was improving, enough so that he could go into the field for the first time in three years, to survey recreational lots. The year before, on March 4, 1915, Congress had passed the Term Permit Act, authorizing the Forest Service to approve private recreational facilities—cabins, lakeside resorts, summer homes, and so forth—on suitable forest lands. Part of Leopold's duties included the siting, mapping, and surveying of these lots. Much of the spring and summer of 1916 he was on the road again: in April, to Flagstaff and the scenic Coconino Forest; in May and June, to Silver City and the wild Gila; in July, to the Apache and the Sitgreaves, where he saw his old friends John D. Guthrie and Fred Winn. When the day's surveying was over, Leopold often held a meeting or led a conference on game protection. He helped organize the first GPAs in Arizona, at Flagstaff and Springerville. He spoke to a large crowd at the Empress Theater in Flagstaff. And, as always, Leopold gleaned information from the rangers on local wildlife.

Between travels, Leopold made the most of his time at home. Leopold's income still hovered at its 1913 level, which was hardly adequate to support his growing family. Redington recommended a raise for Leopold. Graves, as something of a disciplinary move, turned it down. Aldo and Estella hoped for a larger home, with more room inside for the children, and more room outside for the garden and chickens, but that, in Aldo's words, was "a long way off."[30] He gratefully accepted, but never requested, money from Burlington. Recreation was accomplished cheaply, and was perforce restrained. He now had enough confidence in his health to take out the bicycle, sit Starker on the handlebars, and pedal down to the Rio

Grande for a try at the catfish. At night, Leopold worked on *Pine Cone* copy and news items. Often he and Estella read aloud to one another, an activity that became a lifelong habit for them.

The family did move into a new house that fall. With Clara Leopold's help, Aldo and Estella financed a move to 135 South Fourteenth Street in Albuquerque, a large lot with backyard access to the Rio Grande. The Leopolds would live there for the duration of their years in the Southwest.

In September 1916, Leopold began yet another long trip, this time to southern Arizona, to survey Term Permit lots on the Crook and Tonto Forests. At Nogales, he consulted with the army border patrol on sanitation techniques, and convinced the soldiers to stop using the endangered bighorn sheep of the nearby Patagonia Mountains for target practice. He organized two new GPAs at Tucson and Payson. Then, after five weeks of surveying, traveling, and lecturing, Leopold suffered a minor recurrence of nephritis. He immediately cut short his trip, returned to Albuquerque, and took two weeks' leave.

Aldo's illness put a scare into him, and forced him to let up on what had been a workhorse schedule. He recovered from his relapse, but confined himself for the time being to office work. He spent most of the fall completing a first draft of the Grand Canyon Working Plan with Don Johnston. Calling the Canyon "the most important single administrative unit within the National Forests," the plan described prevailing conditions at the Canyon and outlined broad changes in its administration and development. The plan was premised on the notion that there was "discord" between the "great spectacle of nature" that drew people to the Canyon and the "material services and conveniences" that the public "needs and demands" once there. "It should be the first object of an efficient administration," the report stated, "to reduce this necessary discord to a minimum." The plan recommended establishment of a zoning system, called for a crackdown on "repugnant" business practices, and suggested a number of specific improvements of the Canyon's recreational facilities. The plan was ready for review in December.[31]

Meanwhile, New Mexico was electing a new governor. By election day, November 7, Burford, Leopold, and the 1000-member NMGPA found themselves the center of much attention. Leopold followed his progressive bent and led the NMGPA down the high road. "The movement for the conservation of American wild life," he had written in the July *Pine Cone,* "is a fight between reaction and progress."[32] In a spate of news releases, Leopold pressed for the principle: the need for an "efficiency" game warden. "Scrupulous care," he would later write, "was exercised to make the whole question one of *progress for the future,* avoiding discussion of the shortcomings of the past administrations. Justice, tact, and expediency made this precaution a very necessary one. . . . There being no 'charges', there was nothing for reactionaries to attack, except the principle of the proposed change, and that principle was of course unassailably sound."[33]

The approach worked. Before the election, both candidates pledged their support for the NMGPA and offered to work cooperatively in choosing a new warden. Leopold was determined to keep them to their promises. Governor-elect Ezequiel de Baca emerged from the election to face an NMGPA-orchestrated blitz. "All available organizations in the state, including civic, livestock, commercial, educational, and scientific bodies were asked to pass resolutions, while private citizens of both parties lent their personal backing. The aid of eastern game protective organizations was freely asked for, and freely given. 'Independent' candidates [for Game Warden], who were legion, and included all manner of persons, from altruistic lady-conservationists to pie-eating politicians, only helped to advertise the issue. By Inauguration Day every intelligent person in the state knew about 'Efficiency Game Wardens', and wagers pro and con were laid by onlookers in many sporting centers."[34] In the end, de Baca double-crossed the sportsmen and appointed an unsatisfactory warden; but de Baca promptly died, and his candidate was never confirmed. The strength of the game movement was only underscored when the new governor, Washington E. Lindsey, a member of the opposite political party and under no obligation to the sportsmen, appointed the NMGPA's candidate for warden, Theodore Rouault, Jr.

News of the New Mexican successes spread along the conservation grapevine. In little more than a year, the organized sportsmen had awakened their state and turned it into one of the most progressive in the nation in terms of game conservation. In January 1917, shortly after his thirtieth birthday, Leopold received an unexpected letter that undoubtedly he prized:

> My dear Mr. Leopold,
>   Through you, I wish to congratulate the Albuquerque Game Protective Association on what it is doing. I have just read the Pine Cone. I think your platform simply capital, and I earnestly hope that you will get the right type of game warden. It seems to me that your association in New Mexico is setting an example to the whole country.
>
>   Sincerely yours,
>   Theodore Roosevelt[35]

ᔐ

Though far removed from the ranges of the American West, the war of attrition in Europe permitted no illusions of isolation. The Forest Service was to play a critical role in the Great War. The United States entered the conflict in April 1917; in June, the Tenth Engineers of the U.S. Army, comprised wholly of foresters and led largely by Forest Service men, landed in France. The Allied forces needed lumber for barracks, trenches, and aircraft. The Americans provided the men and the know-how. A second regiment, the Twentieth Engineers, was formed shortly after the first. National forests throughout the country lost many of their rangers and administrators to the war effort. Many of Leopold's colleagues, including Ringland and Guthrie, would play significant roles overseas.[36] Leopold himself, because of his age, his family, his uncertain health, and the need for his presence at home, was exempt from the draft.

The war also brought about a shift in Forest Service priorities. In May, orders came down from Washington to stock the ranges to their fullest capacity. For the cattlemen, it was time to cash in their conserved chips. They put more cattle onto the ranges than ever before. The *Arizona Star* editorialized:

To the spirit of the Forest Service the nation is indebted for the prospect of increased herds of beeves at a time when the country needs more beef—needs it for the manpower which it will sustain; manpower which must sustain principles of government far removed from thoughts of beef. Yet it but shows to what extent we are committed in this fight against the world menace of German domination.[37]

The war also postponed many of the plans for recreational development of the national forests, though not all. Anticipating the day when returning soldiers would seek out the solitude of the forests, and goaded into action by the establishment of the National Park Service within the Department of Interior the previous August, the Forest Service in 1917 commissioned one of the nation's foremost landscape specialists, Frank A. Waugh, to prepare a report on the recreational possibilities of the forests. His tour of the country brought him, in May, to the Grand Canyon, where he met Leopold and several others for a review of the Canyon facilities and the revised working plan.

Leopold's first trip to the Canyon had included only a brief excursion into the chasm itself. This time, he spent a full week below the rim. He described the experience as "a curiously pleasant and also a very sad one."[38] Before descending into the Canyon, the party suffered the usual harassment of the rimtop solicitors. The Canyon, Leopold wrote, "would be a pleasant place to loaf but for the 'improvements.'"[39] Once below the layer of human development, however, the power of the wilderness overcame him. Leopold declared the field inspection of the inner gorge "a whooping success. The shrubs and the flowers down in the Canyon are a regular botanical garden now, the weather was perfect, the whole party extremely congenial. . . . We were out on muleback three days—one day of 24 miles I weathered with equanimity. Moreover, the Canyon is best from the bottom—it beats the rim twenty ways for Sunday. My only disappointment is that we saw no Mountain Sheep." Leopold greatly enjoyed his company on the trip, especially Waugh, who besides being an expert landscape engineer was, in Leopold's words, a "regular humorist—or rather irregular—anyhow I have seldom laughed so hard."[40]

Back on top, the committee members went at their work: laying out a future for the Canyon. Long days and nights of arguing ensued. Waugh regarded the working plan as creditable, but inadequate. He initially had plans for the Canyon "on a huge scale—a dozen hotels—thousands of cottages—a tramway to the bottom—a $100,000 water development—and 1000 tourists a day. . . . He is opposed to making a National Park since the Park Service is no good, he says." Leopold was deeply impressed by Waugh's expertise and aesthetic judgment, and had no outright objections to Waugh's grandiose plan. "The whole thing is very inspiring in the abstract, and I believe his scheme is both practicable and justified. But in the meanwhile we have the messy little job of clearing the way."[41] Part of that "messy job" involved putting small operators out of business—easy "in the abstract", but difficult in practice:

Sometimes I doubt my capacity for following the cold light of reason, even when I earnestly believe I am right. One old livery operator stormed at us all morning, which was not so bad, but this afternoon he brought a frail worn-out wife and four children to do the tear act, which was worse. There is no getting away from the fact that the "public interest" is sometimes cruel to individuals—and I would rather saw many cords of wood than be on hand when it [is].[42]

Leopold returned to Albuquerque in mid-May. With the game protection movement now on track and ready to move ahead, and the Forest Service converting to wartime operations, Leopold would be staying closer to home. The pattern there was beginning to emerge. Aldo's devotion to his work was matched by Estella's devotion to their home; each was exceeded only by their devotion to one another. Five years and a family had only strengthened their marriage. Leopold was an inveterate carpenter, building houses for birds, pens for the chickens, cold frames for the vegetables. His masterpiece was the windmill behind the house, which provided water for animals and the garden. Gardening took over as the season advanced. Once an enjoyable amenity, the garden was now a personal and national necessity. Leopold's skill was such that, for the duration of the war, he became something of an extension agent, advising the public on war gardens and aiding in irrigation plans.

Leopold's reading also increased at this time. His interests ran of course to wildlife, and, increasingly, to the accounts and journals of early explorers. He began to read, in company with Estella, more literature and philosophy: Jefferson, John Stuart Mill, Carlisle, Butler, Hugo, William James, Kipling, Epicurus, and, especially, the Bible. Their literary appetites were wide-ranging and, over the years, omnivorous. Leopold began to quote from these works in his own speeches and articles.

At night, Leopold worked on his writing. He now shared responsibility for *The Pine Cone* with Ward Shepard, a wildlife enthusiast who left his ranger station on the Datil Forest the previous autumn to join the Albuquerque staff. Shepard would become Leopold's closest friend and chief influence during these years. Through many a shared hunting trip and editing session, Leopold and Shepard exchanged and developed their conservation ideas, and provided the guiding philosophy of the local game protection movement.

Leopold's game work was garnering national, and even international attention. In July, he received a letter of inquiry from a Boris Zakharov of Kharkow, Russia. That same month, Hornaday's Permanent Wild Life Protection Fund awarded Leopold and the NMGPA its Gold Medal for progress made on behalf of wildlife. In an acceptance speech before the Albuquerque Rotary Club, Leopold explained that the NMGPA was "working toward an exceptionally high ideal by the use of exceptionally practical every-day methods. . . . As per the great philosopher's instructions, we have hitched our wagon to a star, but we are using just ordinary axle grease to speed it on its stony way." The ideal, Leopold told the businessmen, was

"to restore to every citizen his inalienable right to know and love the wild things of his native land." We conceive of these wild things as an integral part of our national environment, and are striving to promote, restore, and develop them not as so many pounds of meat, nor as so many things to shoot at, but as a tremendous social asset, as a source of democratic and healthful recreation to the millions of today and the tens of millions of tomorrow. But in striving we do not preach — too much — of social assets and other philosophical tenets and concepts. We go to the common man and say: "Here, if you want to have anything left for your kid to shoot at, it's time to get busy." He knows what we mean. . . . It is our task to educate the moral nature of each and every one of New Mexico's half million citizens to look upon our beneficial birds and animals, not as so much gunfodder to satisfy his instinctive love of killing, but as irreplaceable works of art, done in life by the Great Artist. They are to be seen and used and enjoyed, to be sure, but never destroyed or wasted.[43]

Leopold was a complicated, indivisible mixture of the practical and the ideal, of utilitarianism and aesthetic appreciation. In the months to follow, he would return to these themes — the role of man the hunter, the place of hunting in a modern age, and the definition of progress — as he and his fellow GPA members moved toward the next phase of their movement.

The war deepened through the summer. More rangers left the Southwest to man the sawmills of France. The officers at home worked overtime. When in the field, Leopold and the other foresters found themselves with new responsibilities. "We had lots of duties that were directly connected with the war effort," Elliot Barker recalled. "We'd work all day and travel all night to make speeches and help sell bonds and to reconcile the people to the fact that their sons were being drafted to go to war. It was pretty tough going."[44]

Although the service was handing out fewer promotions, Leopold finally received one that summer, his first in four years. "Mr. Leopold," the evaluation read, "is a very brilliant man and an accomplished all-around Forest officer. He is considered one of the brainiest men in the District. . . . He is an indefatigable worker and largely interested in community welfare problems. His health is considerably improved and is in such shape that he will be able to do the commensurate amount of field supervision necessarily incident to his work."[45] In August 1917, Aldo and Estella became parents for the third time when their first daughter, Adelina, was born.

That same month saw another significant development: Leopold began to hunt again. He had not hunted with any regularity since his days along the Little Colorado at Springerville. On August 16, 1917, he took Starker down along the Rio Grande flats and shot three doves. Afterward, Leopold sat down and recorded the day's take. "Shot poorly."[46] This concise comment was the first entry in Leopold's hunting journals. The journals, through various permutations and in various locales, would continue for the rest of his life. He kept a careful record of his hunts: the date, weather conditions, bag, weights, sexes, shots fired, cripples, etc. From the outset, however, his journal was far more than a ledger of postmortem numbers. By the third entry, Leopold was jotting down observations peripheral to the game itself. Over time, the journal would become more of a field notebook, a systematic record of the habits of the wild plants and animals he encountered. It would chronicle the raw data of his experience, the impressions of the natural world on a man whose particular genius was an ever-expanding intimacy with that world.

In October, duck season opened. The Migratory Bird Act of 1913 and the follow-up Migratory Bird Treaty with Canada, enacted in 1916, had already had a positive effect on waterfowl populations. Hunters noted larger flocks during the autumn migrations. One Sunday, Leopold joined several friends, including his former rival Jamie Jamison and Ward Shepard, for a hunt on the Rio Grande. They built their blinds on the sandbars south of Los Lunas and enjoyed an uncommonly gratifying day. Leopold shot fifteen ducks (five short of the legal limit) by ten o'clock, then quit and "watched the show—which was magnificent—the best I have seen in years. . . . It is great to have real shooting again—I missed Carolo and old Dad —anybody could work like the Devil with such Sundays ahead."[47]

During this period, the pages of *The Pine Cone* provided Leopold with an opportunity to put down on paper his early ideas on the ethics of sportsmanship. These discussions not only anticipated Leopold's later philosophical development, but addressed an issue long divisive among conservationists: the seeming inconsistency in being both a hunter and a protector of game. "People's notion of sport varies a good deal," Leopold noted in *The Pine Cone.* "It begins with killing a beef or sticking a hog, and runs from there on up. Sportsmanship differs from gunning merely in the extent to which the individual's notion of sport has advanced beyond the hog-sticking stage." "But times change," he wrote, echoing Hornaday, "and so do standards."[48]

To Leopold, the title of "sportsman" was the highest honor to which a hunter could aspire. "It is an honor to win, by enterprise and skill, the reputation of being a keen and successful sportsman. But to acquire a reputation for killing limits is a doubtful compliment, at best."[49] Sportsmanship was a personal matter, referable by the individual to his God, mediated by the human conscience. Leopold's hunting habits would change during his lifetime but this code of honor would not, except to expand and include interests broader than hunting.

Leopold was not always patient in his appeals. Logical arguments sometimes gave way to barbed satire, as when Game Warden Rouault caught up with two Las Vegas hunters who had killed a "ferocious doe" at a salt lick: "What marvelous skill it took to pot her, from a dead rest, at fifty yards! What elemental pride must have stirred in their breasts, when they removed her mangy summer hide, and heard her orphan fawn bleating hungrily nearby! Hail! Intrepid pioneers! Hail! Conquerors of the wilderness! Behind the bars, we salute you!"[50]

Leopold had a favorite quotation which he found in *Harper's* magazine, and which he used from time to time in his talks: "We . . . want culture, by which I mean no mere affectation of knowledge, nor any power of glib speech, or idle command of the fopperies of art and literature, but, rather, an intelligent interest in the possibilities of living."[51] In many respects, this became Leopold's credo, and it characterized his hunting practices. He saw hunting, not as an abomination, nor as an inconsistency, but as active participation in the drama of life, to be conducted in a civil manner.

Economics and technological advances, however, were changing the practice of hunting. In regard to the former, Leopold remained steadfastly progressive. He thought it vitally important to maintain, in the face of increasing (and increasingly concentrated) wealth, the democratic opportunity to hunt. The advancement of culture demanded that the privilege of sport not be monopolized by the fortunate few. A classic example of this was the political storm brewing over Stinking Lake, the waterfowl breeding ground that Leopold hoped to have declared a national bird refuge. A group of wealthy Coloradans was attempting to lease the lake as a private shooting ground. The lake was on government land, adjacent to the Jicarilla Indian Reservation. *The Pine Cone* rose up in indignation. "There is nothing vicious about private clubs as such, but to clamp one of them on Stinking Lake would be exactly analogous to giving them the Grand Canyon, or the Yosemite, or any other superlative natural wonder, for the delectation of the select few at $100 per look—the impecunious public to enjoy the crumbs. The principle of the thing is wrong."[52] This idea of a democratic allotment of opportunity would arise again and, in a similar manner, stimulate Leopold's later pioneering efforts in wilderness protection and game management.

The effect of new technologies on hunting was an even more complex issue. The world was in the process of learning a tragic lesson: technological advances made the old rules of conflict obsolete. The unleashing of horror in Europe was a consequence of more powerful tools and less effective rules for restraining them. The swift decline of America's wildlife was attributable, though on a different level, to the same causes. In fact, the conservation movement itself, despite ongoing internal divisions, remained unified by its historical genesis: it was the urgent reaction to unrestrained destruction and wastefulness. Leopold, imbued since childhood with the lessons of fair play, saw the rules of sportsmanship as the only reasonable response to technological innovations that had outstripped their reasonable application.

Leopold, Shepard, and Jamison were not considering the abstractions of culture or the "possibilities of living" when they sat in their cold blinds, watching the wedges of geese and sords of mallards fly over the sandbars of the Rio Grande. It was their love for the outdoors, for the cottonwoods and willows, the winds and waters, the sandstone rims and sandy bottoms of the river valley, that brought them there. Hunting was an expression of love for the natural world. In the context of the times, the gulf between love and barbarity was so great that the philosophical point of difference between shooting game for sport and shooting men in war was not even considered.

Perhaps Leopold's consideration of that question, and many others, was deepened by events overseas. During this period, Leopold sent to his mother a poem he had clipped out of *The Literary Digest* entitled, "A Lost Land (to Germany)." The poem bemoaned the perversion of German culture:

> Slave nation in a land of hate,
> Where are the things that made you great?
> Child-hearted once—oh, deep defiled,
> Dare you now look upon a child?
> Your lore—a hideous mask wherein
> Self-worship hides its monstrous sin:—

Music and verse, divinely wed—
How can these live where love is dead?[53]

∽

Throughout 1917, Leopold worked with a number of Albuquerque civic groups on war-related activities. Late in the year, the newly reorganized Albuquerque Chamber of Commerce offered him a position as secretary. Although the job hardly seemed to suit Leopold, the Chamber of Commerce recognized his talents for organization and public relations. The job would bring Leopold a substantial raise in pay, at a time when his family could most use it. Leopold also saw room in the job for continued work on game protection at a time when the Forest Service had more pressing concerns. On the other hand it meant leaving the Forest Service, and in Leopold's mind, as in the mind of all foresters, that was a question of loyalty. Moreover, Leopold was not particularly devoted to the type of work the new job would entail.

Leopold accepted the Chamber of Commerce position. From the start, he meant to keep the job only until the war was over and the Forest Service ready to resume its peacetime priorities. Even then, Leopold was prepared to turn down the offer if Forester Graves thought the needs of the service came first. After receiving approval from Washington, Leopold left the Forest Service in January 1918.

Leopold took to the new position with high spirits and fresh ideas. Just nine years before, on the Apache, he had stated his disdain for society "and all the forty 'leven kinds of tommyrot that includes." Now he was on the move for civic improvement. Albuquerque was only a small city of twelve or thirteen thousand, but Leopold saw it as "spiritually alive, typically American, and 'upon its toes,' which after all is just as important [as] the numbers of ciphers in our population."[54] Immediately, he began to push a number of his own pet projects. He wanted the city to employ, through the chamber, a professional city planner, and argued for the inclusion of labor groups in the chamber. He encouraged builders to feature indigenous Spanish architecture in new construction projects. His forestry background proved valuable when he supervised the removal of cotton-bearing female cottonwoods in the city and led an effort to secure parkland along the Rio Grande.

Several months after taking on the job, Leopold spoke to a local women's club on "The Civic Life of Albuquerque," explaining what he saw as the role of the Chamber of Commerce in the community. He viewed the chamber not merely as a voice promoting the town's commercial interests, but as "the common center—the clearing house . . . of all public spirited effort in Albuquerque." "Public spirit" he defined as "year-round patriotism in action. . . . It means that a democratic community and its citizens have certain reciprocal rights and obligations, and for the efficient discharge of any or all of them the intelligent citizen is alternately and absolutely responsible."[55] Leopold's choice of words was important: he had absorbed the progressive spirit, not only as it applied to natural resources, but also to human society. He was out to reform civic affairs just as he was out to reform attitudes toward game.

Leopold cited the rise of Albuquerque's "public spirited" organizations — its business clubs, professional societies, women's clubs, "cause" groups. "The cynic sees in these organizations a medley of 'lost causes'—they seem to him a chaotic host of 'cranks', 'highbrows', and 'reformers.' But to the optimist, this welter of public-spirited activities is one of the most inspiring features of American life, each and every one representing a separate manifestation of the indefatigable idealism of the American people." Leopold, his organizing instincts emerging, saw great promise in the unification of these groups. There were, however, great difficulties to overcome; in particular, the "unnecessary cleavages in our population . . . between businessmen, as such, and all other persons. To remedy this, the trade, craft, and labor organizations should be represented in the Chamber of Commerce. . . . I know of not one project of our Chamber in which the farmer, the carpenter, and the brick mason is not just as vitally concerned as the banker or merchant."[56] A group of businessmen had previously considered Leopold's "remedy," but "declined to try the experiment."

Albuquerque's greatest defect, to Leopold's thinking, was that "it is just like other western cities of its size." Despite two hundred years of history and tradition, the city had made no effort to preserve or enhance its distinctive culture and natural setting. Santa Fe, by contrast, had made such an effort, to its commercial and aesthetic advantage. At one point, Leopold had suggested to a local businessman "the absurdity . . . of our street names, pointing out New York Avenue [as an example]. I also suggested that the proposed Civic Centre [be built according to the] Spanish or Pueblo type of architecture." The businessman replied that he wanted "nothing but plain American." "Is Boston UnAmerican because she is proud of her Pilgrim Fathers?" Leopold asked. "Is New Orleans UnAmerican because she is New Orleans, and proud of it? . . . Where is our native Spanish American artist? Our native poet? Our native novelist? The real flavor of the old Southwest is bound to disappear—another generation and it may be too late. Would it be hoping too much to predict that Albuquerque — through an Hispanic Society—might be the means for producing one or two men who could interpret—from the inside out—New Mexico culture to the world?"[57]

The reaction to Leopold's efforts was consistently lukewarm. Finding unified support for game protection was relatively easy; there he faced an obvious need and a concerned citizenry. Finding such support for civic ventures and idealistic experiments was more difficult. But where progressivism and commercialism met, there was success. During the summer of 1918, Leopold helped organize a conference to discuss draining the Rio Grande Valley to aid agriculture. In a press release he wrote, "If we don't drain, then what? The handwriting is on the wall. A rising water table, a rising crop of salt grass, alkali, and mosquitos, and an agricultural area gradually approaching zero. If we do drain, then what? One of the richest valleys in the West—every acre worth $200, and if properly farmed, paying a profit on that valuation."[58] In later years, Leopold would view indiscriminate wetland draining as a primary factor in the destruction of wildlife habitat. In 1918, such draining was another aspect of progressive conservation: the wise management of a natural resource to provide a common good.

Leopold's new job soon proved to be more time-consuming than expected, and his GPA activity was limited to producing *The Pine Cone*. At the same time, however, Leopold's writings began to appear regularly in journals and periodicals.[59] Although Leopold had temporarily left his Forest Service job, he had not abandoned his intent to devise a system of game protection for the service as a whole. As early as November 1916, he had begun work on a book defining the role of the Forest Service in game conservation. Due to the war, the press of work, and the underdeveloped state of his ideas, the book was never completed. He revised several of the sections, however, for publication as articles. These articles, and several others that appeared in the years 1918–1920, were Leopold's first published attempts to chart a future course for the conservation of wildlife in America, and to explain his view of the role of wildlife in modern society.[60]

Through Hornaday, Leopold was acquainted with the editor of *Outers Book—Recreation*, a sportsman's magazine based in New York. In January 1918, the month Leopold joined the Chamber of Commerce, the magazine published his article, "The Popular Wilderness Fallacy." Once again, the central theme was progress as viewed through the eyes of a game conservationist. Leopold took to task those who believed that, in building a society, one had to choose between civilization and wildlife. There was a time, Leopold pointed out, when the same was said of civilization and forests, when "a stump was our symbol of progress. We have since learned, with some pains, that extensive forests are not only compatible with civilization, but absolutely essential to its highest development." The time had now come, Leopold explained, to learn the same lesson with regard to wild game. Civilization had squandered the primeval abundance, but that was not to say that such waste was inevitable, or that wildlife could not now coexist with human settlement. Leopold cited the forests of long-settled New England, which were producing four times as many deer as the "wild" forests of New Mexico. "Who shall say," Leopold asked, "that only a wilderness can raise deer? . . . Progress is no longer an excuse for the destruction of our native mammals and birds, but on the contrary implies not only an obligation, but an opportunity for their preservation."[61]

In another article from this period, entitled "Forestry and Game Conservation," he wrote, "The American people have already answered, in a vigorous affirmative, the question of *whether* our game shall be conserved. Game conservation is ready to enter its second stage, and even the layman is beginning to ask *how* it shall be accomplished. . . . The time has come for *science* to take the floor *prepared to cope with the situation.*"[62]

Leopold described the analogies he saw between scientific forestry and the as-yet-undeveloped science of game *management.* Timber reconnaissance corresponded to game censusing; timber trespass to poaching; fire damage to predation; sustained annual yield to sustained annual kill; growing stock to breeding stock; and so on. There was one major point at which the analogy failed; importantly, Leopold distinguished between the two when he discussed diversity:

Forestry may prescribe for a certain area either a mixed stand or a pure one. But game management should always prescribe a mixed stand — that is, the perpetuation of every indigenous species. Variety in game is quite as valuable as quantity. In the Southwest, for instance, we want not only to raise a maximum number of mule deer and turkey, but we must also at least perpetuate the Mexican Mountain Sheep, bighorn, antelope, white-tail deer, Sonora deer, elk, and javelina. . . . The perpetuation of interesting species is good business, and their extermination, in the mind of the conservationists, would be a sin against future generations.[63]

Significant in this passage was Leopold's omission of predators and other nongame wildlife from his list of "interesting species." His conception of wildlife management at the time was flexible enough to embrace certain "unprofitable" game species, but not to include apparently useless or harmful species.[64]

But why was all this important? Assuming that these species could be perpetuated in the face of human economic progress, why was it important to do so? Leopold's reasoning had gained focus. He still did not emphasize moral sentiments. He could agree with John Muir, who championed even the despised rattlesnakes that were "loved only by their maker. . . . As if anything that does not obviously make for the benefit of man had any right to exist; as if our ways were God's ways."[65] Leopold wrote down Muir's words in his notebook. Such philosophy, however, he was not yet introducing directly into his professional work. At issue, in Leopold's mind, were the preservation of natural diversity and the quality of the hunting experience. Systematic, scientific management of game had to take root, or the increasing pressures on game would result in "a wholesale commercialization of hunting privileges."[66]

The national forests played an important role in this regard, inasmuch as they constituted "the last free hunting grounds in the nation," and were sure to be inundated by those who could not afford to join exclusive hunting clubs, or who found it distasteful to shoot artificially reared game. This last point was an especially sore one with Leopold. He had little regard for what he called the "radical game farmers," whose stake in hunting was purely and openly materialistic, and who advocated the selling of game on the open market and the abolition of restrictive game laws. "To grant the wishes of the radical Game Farmers," Leopold wrote,

would be tantamount to adopting the European system of game management. A wide-open market, almost universal game farming, commercialized shooting privileges, and some incidental overflow shooting for the poor man—is this not the sum and substance of the European system? It is. And the European system of game management is undemocratic, unsocial, and therefore dangerous. I assume that it is not necessary to argue that the development of any undemocratic system in this country is to be avoided at all costs.[67]

Hunting clubs—such as Lone Tree and Crystal Lake—had once provided opportunities to the nation's sportsmen. "The dues were low; the membership was local; anybody joined, from the bricklayer to the bank president." Then, as game dwindled, "dues went up and democracy went down." Now society had an obligation to set aside public lands and manage them for the common good. "Cannot the public see that a pond which furnishes inspiration, rest, and health to a score of tired workers has a higher social value than a patch of corn which furnishes feed for an equal number of hogs or steers? Of course not, if only millionaires can enjoy the pond! When we take away the democracy of sport, we take away the only chance for fair public consideration of the sportsmen's interest."[68]

By 1918, then, Leopold had a rationale and a plan for game management as advanced as any in the Forest Service. The times, though, were not right. Game protection as a cause was a far simpler undertaking than would be game management as a policy and a science. The former required only political change; the latter would require years of research, public education, and hard thinking. The easy part was over.

The April 1918 *Pine Cone* neatly captured these trends. The lead story advertised a motor expedition to the proposed refuge on Stinking Lake (which was soon thereafter renamed Burford Lake, in memory of Miles Burford, who had died unexpectedly the previous autumn). The other front-page story reported the NMGPA's opposition to a bill before Congress allowing the sale of big game in Alaska. Another article outlined the GPA's next major effort—reform of the state game laws. And for good measure, Leopold called again for "A Cleanup on Varmints."

Two feature articles by Leopold illustrated the fundamental rule of resource management that researchers, including Leopold himself, would have to learn the hard way in the decades to follow: that environmental interactions were far more complex than suspected. One of the articles, "Boomerangs," described a novel situation. Local stockmen were complaining because their cattle were eating downed pine boughs, causing miscarriages of calves. The cows were able to eat pine boughs because tassel-eared gray squirrels had become abnormally abundant, and cutting off pine boughs was one of their habits. The squirrels were abnormally abundant because predatory hawks were growing scarce. Hawks were scarce because people (including the stockmen) were slaughtering them by the thousands during migrations. "If you must kill hawks," *The Pine Cone* coyly advised, "try to distinguish between the harmful and the beneficial."[69]

The other article dealt with the problem of elk protection, an issue which forced Leopold to lay his conservation cards on the table. For virtually all other species of native big game, conservationists could rationalize their efforts as a sure good, since they had no detrimental effects on the human economy. Elk, however, did damage to crops. "Even a small number of elk," Leopold admitted, "will work wonders with an alfalfa patch or an orchard, six-foot fences to the contrary notwithstanding." In this instance, Leopold came down on the side of human utility, and in the interest of a unified game protection movement: "loose elk on the range are liable to be a standing menace to the conservation of game in general. We are glad to state that both the cowmen and the sheepmen of New Mexico agree in this view, and have so stated in resolutions passed at their recent conventions."[70] Evidently, further progress in game management, like progress in civic affairs, was bestrewn with unforeseen prejudices and conflicts of interest.

On the back page of that *Pine Cone,* Ward Shepard contributed an item that revealed Kaiser Wilhelm as a slaughterer of game as well as men. According to the article, the Kaiser had personally accounted for the demise of some sixty-one thousand game animals over a lifetime of hunting.

Apparently his withered arm is merely the physical counterpart of a withered soul —a soul that is too withered to see, through haunted nights, the avenging eyes of the millions of God's creatures—men and women and children and the harmless beasts—whom he has done to death. Even in a world whose tragic history for a hundred thousand years has been traced in a flaming river of blood, Wilhelm II stands out, in stark and ghastly horror, as the Incomparable Killer of Living Things.[71]

The war had come closer to the Leopold home. Estella's father Don Alfredo Bergere, now sixty years old and a widower, sailed overseas to work with the Knights of Columbus in France, providing comfort to wounded Americans. Frederic Leopold, now twenty-three years old, sailed in July 1918, and within weeks was at the front near Souilly, just south of Verdun. In his memoirs, Frederic recalled the battleground:

At night the sky to the north was illuminated by artillery fire of the Argonne Forest front lines where American troops were advancing to the northward. On several nights I hopped the ammunition truck bound for the lines and got right up to the front trenches. These were located in a formerly forested area. Now the trees had been reduced to stumps by artillery fire. I got back to our shack by daylight. Finally the rumor of "Armistice" spread one day and November 11th arrived. The firing ceased all at once in a great stillness.[72]

In November 1918, New Mexico elected a new governor, and the NMGPA again waded into the political waters. With the passing of Miles Burford, Leopold was now clearly the leader of the state's organized sportsmen. In general, Leopold had little regard for party politics and politicians. The aftermath of the war had not altered his opinion. "I devour the papers recently on the Peace news," he wrote to his mother, "and cannot say that I have much respect for the Republican obstructionists. It seems to me they are deliberately sacrificing the League of Nations. . . . I consider no other issue, internal or foreign, to be even remotely comparable in importance to the League of Nations as the agency to *make* and *keep* the Peace Treaty. On the other hand, the Democratic internal policy seems to me to grow worse daily."[73] Leopold considered himself, at the time, a progressive-turned- "self-respecting liberal," without a home on the current political landscape.

The game protection movement had slowed during the war. Now it was time, in Leopold's words, "to go after results, to undertake actual constructive measures which will produce more game."[74] In December, NMGPA delegates convened in Albuquerque to plot strategy. They gave top priority to reforming state game laws, exterminating predators, and securing the reappointment of Rouault as state game warden. The next issue of *The Pine Cone* cockily asserted that sportsmen viewed the reappointment of Rouault not merely as a favor, but as a right: "The stockmen are never saddled with a sanitary board unsatisfactory to them. Likewise, the organized sportsmen should not be saddled with a Game Warden whom they do not approve."[75] The new governor, Octavio Larrazolo, was unimpressed, and ignored the sportsmen's avalanche of resolutions, telegrams, letters, and endorsements.

In January 1919, the NMGPA appointed a forty-man committee to meet with Larrazolo and explain the sportsmen's position. Leopold, having resumed the position of secretary of the NMGPA, was named spokesman and Elliot Barker his deputy. The committee gathered in Santa Fe and crowded, en masse, into the governor's office. Leopold did the talking.

Over the course of an hour, he explained in polite terms and persuasive manner the logic of the game protection argument—the importance of protection, the need for an "efficient and sympathetic" game department, Rouault's notable achievements during his two-year wardenship. The governor sat quietly at his desk throughout Leopold's presentation, never looking up, scribbling on a pad of paper the full hour.

When the committee had exhausted its time, Leopold pressed the governor for an expression of his views. "Gentlemen," Larrazolo announced, rearing back in his chair, "when I was elected governor, I asked for no additional prerogatives. By the same token, I shall surrender none! Good day!"

Leopold and the forty stood stunned. Leopold's rage rose. After gathering himself, he replied, "Governor, we appreciate your letting us talk to you. Now, I only want to say that you have just announced that it is impossible for you to run for a second term as governor!" Leopold indignantly led his forces out of the office. Elliot Barker recalled it as the only time he ever saw Leopold boil over.[76]

The sportsmen were fiercely proud of their leader, but Aldo's histrionics had no effect. Larrazolo dispatched Rouault and installed his own man, Thomas P. Gable, as game warden. Leopold did not take the move sitting down. Chamber of Commerce work brought him to Santa Fe on a regular basis. During one trip, Leopold, acting in his capacity as secretary of the NMGPA, placed on the desk of every legislator a blank pledge requesting that, when the time came, they not vote for the renomination of Larrazolo. He issued a special edition of *The Pine Cone* with a similar pledge for the state's sportsmen, advising them to gird up their loins for the campaign of 1920. ("When the sportsmen of New Mexico have mobilized and used their votes—then, and not sooner, will they obtain a 100 per cent Game Warden"). Angry though he was, Leopold still kept to the high road, and reminded his men to pay due respect to the governor and his warden. "Let the sportsmen remember that hindsight and resentment are vain things for safety. Let the sportsmen remember that O. A. Larrazolo is governor and Thomas P. Gable is warden, and as such both are entitled to all the respect and to all the cooperation and backing that they will take and that we can give." Gable, the new warden, was not especially antagonistic toward, nor supportive of, the sportsmen. He had some knowledge of game matters. What galled Leopold was the system that allowed party politics, rather than the sportsmen, to dictate his appointment. "That system remains a millstone around the neck of progress. It must be changed, and will be changed, we hope in 1920."[77]

Leopold's reformist streak ran back into his Chamber of Commerce activities. When he began a similar, if more subtle, campaign to remove the appointment of the state university president from politics, the staid *Albuquerque Morning Journal* blasted Leopold on its editorial page, accusing him of advocating government by special interests. There was sting in the charges, and the admonishment cooled Leopold's irrepressible activism. In a reply to his critics, Leopold stuck to his guns, but kept them holstered. The GPA, he admitted, had organized its voting power, but "did not anticipate that it will be necessary to call on these votes."[78] He was confident that, as public awareness rose, reform would come from the bottom up. In the meantime, the NMGPA would shift its emphasis and go to work to change the machinery of the State Game Department.

By early 1919, as all this was taking place, Leopold was considering leaving his position with the Chamber of Commerce. The job had not afforded him the expected opportunity to pursue game work, and he was encouraged by word from Washington that Graves was returning the service to peacetime plans. Graves was anxious to reenlist Leopold. An opportunity came several months later when District Forester Redington recommended that Leopold be appointed Assistant District Forester in Charge of Operations, declaring that "there is no man available either in or out of the Service so well adapted by special training and experience to fill the position."[79] Several more months would have to pass before the paperwork was properly routed through Washington and Leopold had fulfilled his contractual obligations to the Chamber of Commerce.

In the meantime, Leopold redevoted himself to civic affairs, and to the Rio Grande drainage project in particular. He bought the family's first automobile. "With all extra fixings," he wrote to his mother, "it cost us $652."[80] In July, while Estella and the children visited relatives in California, Aldo's brother Carl came to New Mexico for a long-postponed fishing trip. Now twenty-eight years old, and not yet married, he was well known in Burlington for his warmth and leadership. In the years since Carl Sr.'s death, he and Frederic had taken over the family business interests; Carl was now president of the Leopold Desk Company. He and Aldo drove away in the new Ford for their first fishing trip together since their summer days at Les Cheneaux. "I am tickled as a small boy to be off," Aldo wrote.[81]

&

Leopold would remain an active public figure throughout his life, but he would never again be as energetic an activist as during these early game protection days. As an organizer, publicist, administrator, civic leader, and budding scientist, he had devoted himself to the cause that most deeply concerned him. As the cause matured, and the protection of wild things became policy, Leopold too would have to change. The steadfastness necessary to win the cause was one thing; the suppleness necessary to sustain success another. Like most visionaries, he was not lacking in the former. Unlike many, he also had the savvy and common sense to make the shift to the latter. Although his opportunity to work strictly with wildlife would be delayed for another decade, he was already looking ahead to the day when game management would be as solidly established a field as was forestry.

Four years had passed since Leopold's first visit to the Grand Canyon. The interval had wrought great changes in the world. Theodore Roosevelt was gone. He died early in 1919, and was buried near his beloved home at Sagamore Hill. A month later, on February 26, 1919, the Grand Canyon became a national park, thereby assuring that man would at least try to "leave it as it is." Overseas, an autocrat with delusions of domination had led his nation and the world into the abyss of the Great War; freedom-loving peoples, in a conflict that would forever redefine the meaning of war, suffered and triumphed. While humanity on the rim tried thus to adjust to itself and to the natural world, the Colorado River carved itself infinitesimally deeper into the rock, and carried the rock to the sea.

The July 1919 *Pine Cone* provided, on its back page, a moral to the times:

> The truth is, that in spite of all religion and all philosophy, mankind has never acquired any real respect for the one thing in the Universe that is worth most to Mankind—namely Life. He has not even any respect for himself, as witness the thousand wars in which he has jovially slain the earth's best. Still less has he any respect for other species of animals. He slays the last of a species with as little compunction as he crushes a worm. . . .
>
> The trouble is that man's intellect has developed much faster than his morals. His machines get away from him. He is still the "Fool with a gun." His cunning mind equips him with tools whose frightful possibilities are not evident to him. Bombs are all right, but not in the hands of a half-baked fanatic. Guns are all right, but not in the hands of a maniac.
>
> What possible relation has all this sermonizing to such a practical thing as game conservation? Merely this, that game conservation will never succeed merely through repressive laws. It must be founded on a respect for living things. No man who would rather see a dead deer than a living one, no man who has not a profound belief in the doctrine of "Live and let live," has any right himself to live in a world so full of glorious living creatures.[82]

10

Chief of Operations
(1919–1922)

L EOPOLD rejoined the Forest Service as Assistant District Forester in Charge of Operations on August 1, 1919. Ten years after arriving in Albuquerque, Leopold now occupied the second highest position in the district. He was responsible for overseeing and evaluating the day-to-day functions — personnel, construction, fire control, roads and trails, other permanent improvements, public relations, recreation, timber management, land acquisition and exchange, supplies and equipment, grazing and watershed maintenance — on twenty million acres of Forest Service land. The work was far greater in scope, both professionally and geographically, than any he had previously undertaken. As Leopold grew into the job, his interest in game management would continue, but it would be overshadowed by the emergence of new conservation concerns, and by an extraordinary personal endeavor to understand the changes taking place on the vast but fragile landscape of the American Southwest.

Leopold was not welcomed back to the Forest Service by all. His prominence in the game protection movement brought pride to some of the officers, but annoyed other more conventional foresters. Many in the District 3 force felt that Redington was playing favorites with Leopold and Ward Shepard. Even before Leopold left the USFS, they felt he had been advanced ahead of his experience. The discontent became open when Redington brought Leopold back and placed him in a position that required, above all, experience, judgment, and tact.

The chief of operations had three main tasks: to conduct inspection tours of the individual national forests, to report on his findings, and to recommend changes. Inspection was a still-evolving art in the Forest Service. There was no standard method for inspecting a forest. Tours generally lasted a month or longer. An inspector could expect to examine, at the most, three forests per summer. The resulting reports usually reflected less on the forests than on the inclinations of the individual inspectors, who often had little patience for such bureaucratic formalities. While the inspector's work was rigorous, and often thankless (especially when it came to evaluating personnel), it also afforded unmatched opportunities to range the forests, and to see the district as a working whole.[1]

By now, Leopold's health no longer caused him great concern. He had regained his former strength, although he would never be as animated as before. In August, just a week after beginning his new job, Leopold conducted a brief inspection of the Taos District of the Carson Forest. In September and October he toured, by Ford, the ranger stations of the Datil Forest. The mountains of the Datil, rising above the Plains of San Augustin, covered with oak, piñon, and yellow pine, included some of the best deer and turkey range in the Southwest, and some of the best trout streams. While on inspection, Leopold took a Sunday to fish the high headwaters of the Gila River on the southern border of the forest. The Gila would soon assume a critical place in his conservation thinking.

Leopold's reports on the Carson and the Datil were skeletal in comparison to the full-fleshed reports he would later submit. He did give a tantalizing hint of the direction in which he was heading. Leopold found a "surprising lack of initiative" in the ranger force on the Datil. "They do not have the air of men who have been given a definite responsibility, a free hand to find their own ways and means for carrying it out, and a word of encouragement for meeting responsibility successfully, or for evolving a new idea."[2] Leopold was as concerned as ever about the preponderance of detail in the ranger's work, and still pushing for independent thinking on the ranger's part. Now, however, he was responsible for both rangers *and* details.

Leopold nearly lost his new position just as he was settling into it. In November 1919, Redington was transferred out of District 3, and Frank C. W. Pooler took over as the new district forester. Pooler was among those who had been critical of Leopold's appointment. He and Leopold had been colleagues in the Albuquerque offices under both Ringland and Redington, and were in fact neighbors, the Poolers living just two houses away from the Leopolds on Fourteenth Street. Nonetheless, Pooler did not hesitate to inform Leopold of his objections. Pooler considered him the wrong man for the job, and felt he could be of greater service in some other capacity. Pooler also saw a practical problem in retaining an inspector who did not have the full support of the district force. He informed Leopold, in no uncertain terms, of the sentiment against him on the part of some of the supervisors and other field men. They agreed to discuss the matter again after the upcoming annual meeting of district foresters in Salt Lake City. Estella was about to deliver another child (their fourth in just over six years), but insisted that Aldo attend the meeting.

At Salt Lake City, Carl Stahl, assistant district forester in District 2, told of a recent policy development regarding Trappers Lake in the White River National Forest of Colorado. Stahl had just received a recommendation from one of his assistants, a landscape architect named Arthur Carhart, that the shoreline of Trappers Lake be kept free of road construction and summer home sites.

Arthur Carhart was twenty-seven years old. Another native Iowan, he had joined the Forest Service just nine months before, the first landscape architect and the first full-time "Recreational Engineer" to be employed in the service (he was immediately dubbed "Beauty Engineer" by his fellow foresters in D-2). Carhart spent July of 1919 on assignment at Trappers Lake, source of the White River and a site of incomparable alpine splendor. Carhart's job was to survey out several hundred summer home lots along the lakeshore for leasing by the Forest Service under the Term Permit Act (the same work that Leopold had performed at various locales in D-3). By the end of the summer, Carhart had reached a conclusion: the best way to serve the public at Trappers Lake was to leave its shoreline unimproved.[3]

Some state lands, notably the Adirondacks of New York, were maintained as wild preserves, but the question of *wilderness preservation,* a new question with different implications, had not yet arisen in regard to the vast federal holdings of the West. The wilderness sentiment had indeed inspired creation of the nation's first national parks, and of the new National Park Service; now, that success was forcing further definitions of the idea behind it. The act establishing the NPS had not explicitly directed it to maintain wilderness conditions within the parks, and the trend of the times was to develop them to the hilt. Neither the Park Service Act, nor any other act, protected wildlands beyond the parks.

Stahl agreed that Carhart's recommendation merited further discussion. He brought it up at Salt Lake City. When Leopold expressed interest in the matter, Stahl arranged for him to meet with Carhart.

The thought of preserving portions of the national forests in their wild state seems to have occurred to Leopold at least as early as 1913.[4] He did not advertise the thought. It was, quite simply, a radical notion, and it developed only slowly. It is difficult to say how far it had advanced in his mind by 1919. He was not alone in his thinking. He had discussed it, or would soon after, with a number of his GPA and D-3 colleagues—Jamie Jamison, Fred Winn, Elliot Barker, Ward Shepard, M. W. Talbot, Hugh Calkins, Charles Cooperrider.[5]

On December 6, en route back to Albuquerque, Leopold visited the D-2 offices and spent the full day in discussion with Carhart. Theirs was a meeting of kindred concerns, destined to assume an important place in the history of the American wilderness. Carhart explained why he thought

Trappers Lake was best left undeveloped. Leopold encouraged him to broaden his reasoning.

At the end of the day, Leopold asked Carhart to commit to paper the main points they had covered. The resulting memorandum stands out as an important early statement on the need for wilderness protection on federal lands. "The problem spoken of in [our] conversation," Carhart wrote, "was, how far shall the Forest Service carry or allow to be carried man-made improvements in scenic territories, and whether there is not a definite point where all such developments, with the exception perhaps of lines of travel and necessary sign boards, shall stop." Carhart's words echoed Leopold's progressive disdain for the monopolization of nature's wonders: "There is a limit to the number of lands of shore line on the lakes; there is a limit to the number of lakes in existence; there is a limit to the mountainous areas of the world, and in each one of these situations there are portions of natural scenic beauty which are God-made, and the beauties of which of a right should be the property of all people." These areas, Leopold and Carhart agreed, "in order to return the greatest total value to the people, not only of the Nation, but of the world," ought to be protected from the "marring features of man-made constructions." Should the Forest Service fail to do so, the memo warned, "severe criticism will some day be meted out by the collective owners of this territory, the public." Carhart, sounding very much like Leopold, stated at the end of his memo that "the question of how best to do this is perhaps the real question, rather than shall it be done."[6]

Leopold was undoubtedly spurred on in his thinking by the action of his younger colleague; Carhart was conversely led to consider the greater implications of his recommendation. Although it did not specifically mention "wilderness," the "Memorandum for Mr. Leopold, District 3" based its argument on the aesthetic value of wild lands, in this case the spectacular beauty of the Colorado Rockies at Trappers Lake. This was primarily a reflection of Carhart's motives, but it was also the starting point of Leopold's lifelong battles on behalf of wilderness. Leopold would later write, under different circumstances, that "our ability to perceive quality in nature begins, as in art, with the pretty. It expands through successive stages of the beautiful to values as yet uncaptured by language."[7] He had begun an irreversible trek outward through those successive stages. Carhart's initiative would soon gain approval, and Carhart too would carry his convictions on to new battles over other vestiges of wilderness. He and Leopold were not the first to voice concern for wilderness, but their meeting gave birth to a new endeavor within the Forest Service: to act on those concerns before the wilderness was gone.

Leopold arrived back in Albuquerque on December 7. He had a series of career decisions to make in the days that followed. As a further outcome of the Salt Lake City meeting, Graves offered to make Leopold chief of operations in D-1, in the northern Rockies. The move would allow him to begin anew, without the burden of lingering reputations. Leopold and Pooler talked it over. Pooler did not mince words. He laid out to Leopold "the handicaps and prejudices he unfortunately must face and live down in District 3 and the personal tendencies he is going to have to overcome to make me a successful Chief of Operations."[8] Leopold declined the transfer and asked for an opportunity to make good in his current position. In a subsequent letter to Graves, Pooler wrote:

[Leopold] understands that I consider him a Chief of Operations *in the making,* not the rounded out product of years of experience, and the consciousness of this, to a man of Leopold's make-up, is going to put him on his mettle rather than discourage him. I think I have without unkindness disturbed his complacency somewhat. . . . There is an extraordinary amount of ability and originality stored up in this man. The FS can hardly afford to lose it. It will be my business to try to draw it out and get it properly applied, just as it will be his business (and I have told him so in so many words) to *win* my confidence as an operations man.[9]

Leopold was determined to prove himself. Another job offer presented itself several weeks later when E. W. Nelson, head of the Biological Survey, asked Leopold to take charge of the nation's seventy-four bird and game refuges. Leopold declined that opportunity as well.[10]

On December 18, Estella gave birth to their fourth child, Aldo Carl Leopold.

∽

Early on the morning of December 26, 1919, two Albuquerque shipbuilders launched their vessel into the ice-ridden waters of el Rio Grande del Norte. Aldo and Ward Shepard had constructed their mighty scow two days before, in six hours, at a cost of five dollars. "With her hold full of sowbosom, seabiscuits, and sandwiches, her rigging covered with ice, and the waves dashing over the crow's nest, she will present a spectacle of gallant intrepidity," the newspaper reported. "She will be manned by A. Leopold, captain, deckhand, and cabin-boy, and by W. Shepard, first and second mate, boatswain, pilot, chief engineer, gunner, cook, coxswain, stoker, stevedore." The *Binnacle Bat III* sprung numerous leaks soon after its christening, but performed nobly after makeshift patching by the crew. The hunters on board drifted at a leisurely pace for five days, camping on sandbars, bagging ten ducks and a goose before debarking at Bernardo, forty miles downriver.[11]

As usual, Leopold watched with interest the passage of the river's life. Near Belen, he noted his northernmost sighting of mesquite; below Sabinal, his southernmost sighting of a magpie. As Leopold's detailed journal accounts and hunting records accumulated, he began to work them into formal articles, his earliest published scientific writings on wildlife: "Relative Abundance of Ducks in the Rio Grande Valley," "Differential Sex Migration of Mallards in New Mexico," "A Hunter's Notes on Doves in the Rio Grande Valley," "Weights and Plumages of Ducks in the Rio Grande Valley," and so forth. Most of these appeared, starting in 1918, in *The Condor,* the bulletin of the Cooper Ornithological Society. Some of his contributions simply described interesting natural phenomena. Once, while hunting during a hailstorm, Leopold sat in puzzlement when a flock of pintails turned to face the hail, pointing their heads and bills up into the storm. He postulated that the ducks were doing so to protect their sensitive bills from a direct hit. Another time, he sighted a red-headed woodpecker, a species previously seen only further east. After hearing several other reports of this new arrival, he noticed that they occurred mostly along transcontinental railroad lines. He theorized that the woodpeckers crossed the plains by following the adjacent telegraph poles. Just as birds and hunting had led Leopold into the profession of conservation, so now would they lead him deeper into the *science* of conservation.[12]

The NMGPA's perennial efforts to reform the state's game and fish administration sprouted anew in the spring of 1920. The March *Pine Cone,* under the banner headline "EXTERMINATION OR REFORM," warned that "drastic house-cleaning [is] needed in [the] whole theory and practice of game management." The proposed program had some new twists. Having learned that their regular efforts to elect a friendly governor (and thus secure a trustworthy game warden) only bogged them down deeper in politics, the leaders of the NMGPA switched tactics. They now pushed to reorganize the State Game Department by establishing a permanent commission "which will have authority to hire [the] State Game Warden, to close seasons on game when and where needed, to establish state refuges, and to exercise all other powers necessary to the efficient management of game."[13]

The second item on the new agenda was a refined version of the game refuge plan. Every year, new bills came up before Congress calling for the establishment of a national system of game refuges; every year, western representatives claimed state's rights and batted the bills down. The latest attempt, the Nelson Bill, had the full support of the NMGPA, reflecting as it did Leopold's own increasingly sophisticated ideas on a proper game refuge system.[14]

Finally, the NMGPA supported a quantitative regulation of kill. Heretofore, limits had been placed only on the amount of game each hunter could take; there was no limit on the number of hunters who could take game. The result, despite every effort to the contrary, was still diminishing game populations.[15]

The NMGPA convened at Santa Fe on April 23 and 24, 1920, to take action on these new initiatives. Most significant, they prepared a tentative draft of a bill to establish a game and fish commission. Leopold was, again, at the center of the effort. He called the convention "the most successful we've had" and felt confident that, finally, a nonpartisan state game policy could become a reality.[16]

At the convention, the topic of predator control was conspicuous by its de-emphasis. Ligon and his men had pursued their predatory quarry with deadly success. The "easy" wolves were all but cleared out by 1920. Only the most remote, wily, and persistent survived. Ligon estimated in 1919 that no more than a dozen wolves remained in New Mexico. A colleague in Arizona guessed that there were few or none left in that state.[17]

These figures, however, were no cause for complacency. Just a few weeks prior to the convention of the NMGPA, Leopold had travelled east to New York to attend the Sixth American Game Conference (his first appearance at the AGPA-sponsored national conference, which brought together the foremost figures in game conservation). In a report on game conditions in the Southwest, Leopold said of predator control efforts that, "as the work progresses, the remaining animals become fewer, more sophisticated, and more expensive to catch. It is going to take patience and money to catch the last wolf or lion in New Mexico. But the last one must be caught before the job can be called fully successful. This may sound like a strong statement," he allowed, "but if any of you have lived in the West and seen how quickly a piece of country will restock with wolves or lions, you will know what I mean. . . . No plans for game refuges or regulation of kill will get us anywhere unless these lions are cleaned out." With a zealot's faith, he predicted that "when they are cleaned out, the productiveness of our proposed refuges and plans for regulation of kill, will be very greatly increased."[18]

The newly promulgated measures of the NMGPA met with varying degrees of success. In July 1920, the leaders of the NMGPA sat down with state legislators and hammered out a plan to reorganize the State Game Department. The resulting bill called for the creation of a three-man State Game and Fish Commission to oversee the work of the Game Department, the state game warden to serve at the commission's behest. The NMGPA played that fall's election coolly (Leopold's threats of 1919 notwithstanding). The new governor, Republican Merritt Mechem, pledged to support the reorganization plan. A bill was finally passed in 1921, after one key compromise on the sportsmen's part. In order to get the plan passed, they agreed that the governor would retain the power to appoint the state warden.

In the meantime, the Nelson Bill met the same futile end in Washington as had all the previous refuge bills. In New Mexico, at least, the new commission rallied to the cause. Soon after its establishment, the commission implemented a system of state refuges that closely followed Leopold's plan. He took great pride in the system, but continued to write and speak for the creation of refuges on the national level as well.

The success in securing a reorganized game department, a system of refuges, and the nearly complete eradication of predators brought to a close Leopold's most active period with the NMGPA. Even *The Pine Cone* was discontinued in 1920. Hunting again became primarily a personal activity, and, above all, a family affair. Seven-year-old Starker joined his father on most hunts now. Luna, two years younger, was beginning to tag along as well. Sibling conflicts naturally arose. Once, when only one of them was allowed to accompany their father, they drew straws for the opportunity. Luna won. Starker went into a crying fit that subsided only after he had bargained away his finest pencil in exchange for Luna's hunting privileges. Luna soon owned all of Starker's pencils. Estella joined in on the hunts as well, and masterminded the family's regular camping and fishing excursions.[19]

For Leopold himself, hunting and the study of nature were activities not merely enjoyable, but absolutely vital to the conduct of life. Only reading came close to being as important a way to spend free time. Both were crucial elements in Leopold's evolving ideas on the quality of life. In October 1920, Leopold addressed a group of students at the University of New Mexico on "A Man's Leisure Time." He delivered a lighthearted but earnest defense of nonconformity. Leopold challenged the students to avoid "the tragedy of prescribed lives" by making judicious use of their leisure hours. "I confess my own leisure," he told them, "to be spent entirely in search of adventure, without regard to prudence, profit, self-improvement, learning, or any other serious thing. I find that these serious things are a good deal like heaven; when they are too closely pursued as conscious objectives, they are never attained and seldom even understood." Adventure, to Leopold's thinking, was one of six "necessaries of life," the other five being work, love, food, air, and sunshine. To be real, he argued, adventure required "untrodden ground," be it geographical or metaphorical. "It is because the vast majority of people do not have the courage to venture off the beaten path that they fail to find [adventure], and live lop-sided lives accordingly." Leopold gave examples of successful explorers: a doctor who took up fishing, and became enthralled in the study of the optical powers of trout; a bank president who "adventured in roses"; a taxi driver who "romances in sweet corn"; the old German merchant who spent years chipping away at the limestone bluffs of Burlington in search of fossilized crinoids, and became a world authority as a result. Few would attain that kind of fame, but fame was unimportant to the true adventurer. And in the pursuit of adventure, Leopold reminded his student audience, formal education was at best irrelevant. "A good healthy curiosity is better equipment with which to venture forth than any amount of learning or education." In such a world of vast horizons, he said, "the beaten paths of conformity are literally a prison."[20]

～

Leopold's love of literature focused during this period on the Bible. Although as recalcitrant as ever on matters religious, he had become no mean student of the Bible through his own reading. He had a particular fondness for the Old Testament prophets, proverbs, and psalms. Ever on the lookout for historical evidence, he also found the Old Testament an abundant source of information on natural history. In April 1920, as the forest inspection season began, the *Journal of Forestry* published an article by Leopold entitled "The Forestry of the Prophets." Drawing on references to forests in the Books of the Prophets, Leopold appraised the Hebraic knowledge of forest fires, timber use, and silvicultural practices. He considered Isaiah "the Roosevelt of the Holy Land," and the author of the book of Job "the John Muir of Judah." Joel was "the preacher of conservation of watersheds, and in a real sense the real inventor of 'prevent forest fires.'" Solomon was indeed wise, but only in an urban sense. "The nearest he comes to a forest is the fig tree and the cedar of Lebanon, and I think he saw more of the cedars in the ceiling of his palace than he did in the hills." Ezekiel described the use of cedar chests. Isaiah and Solomon referred to wooden idols. "Graven images, if one is to believe the prophets, must have been an important product of the wood-using industries of the day."[21]

Leopold's article was more than just a playful combination of Bible study and natural history. The Bible, like the explorers' journals he was also reading at this time, rendered real lessons about the relationship between man and his environment over time. Leopold wondered, for example, whether modern Palestine had forest cover dense enough to support the spectacular fire described in Joel. The Holy Land had evidently changed over the course of the centuries. Perhaps modern forestry could learn from the example. Perhaps we could understand what the prophets could not. "I think it is quite possible," Leopold wrote, "that the effect of forests on streamflow was known empirically to a few advanced thinkers like Joel, but it is quite certain that their knowledge went no further or deeper. The habit of thinking of natural phenomena as acts of God instead of as cause and effect prevails to this day with a majority of people, and no doubt at that time prevailed in the minds of all."[22] Leopold, though, had praise for the common sense of the ancients. He cited with approval Ezekiel's "doctrine of conservation": "Seemeth it a small thing unto you to have fed upon the good pasture, but ye must tread down with your feet the residue of your pasture? And to have drunk of the clear waters, but ye must foul the residue with your feet?"[23]

In this same article, Leopold used, for the first time in print, a new word in his vocabulary. He noted a passage in Ezekiel that indicated some knowledge of "forest types and the ecological relation of species" as well as "the succession of forest types." Leopold had picked up the word "ecology" in his professional reading. At the time, the term was known only to a few people. The *science,* in fact, was known only to a few people, and just emerging from its infancy. The word itself was first used in the late 1860s by a German adherent of Darwin, Ernst Haeckel. Continental biologists, in their efforts to describe and organize the distribution of plant species according to physiological characteristics, were the first to explore systematically the new science. Many of the most significant strides, however, were taking place not in the revered halls of long-established academies, but in the minds and landscapes of frontier America. A few scientists, primarily at the universities of Chicago and Nebraska, were interested in the characteristics and dynamics of plant communities. On the dunes of Lake Michigan and in the prairies of Nebraska, they described patterns in space and time in the ways plants grew, competed, reproduced, and died. The American Southwest, too, had made its contribution to the new field. C. Hart Merriam, E. W. Nelson's predecessor at the Bureau of Biological Survey, studied the plants of the San Francisco Peaks above Flagstaff, and was the first to describe in detail their distribution according to elevation.[24]

Leopold was likely familiar with these early studies, but certainly showed no dramatic signs of conversion to this new way of seeing patterns in nature. In a sense, it was just a new label for a way of understanding that was at least as old as Ezekiel. With his inspections of 1920, however, Leopold would begin to apply this understanding to the patterns he himself observed on the southwestern landscape.

Early in April, Leopold met with two of his superiors from Washington — Roy Headley, the new chief of the Branch of Operations for the Forest Service, and his assistant, Major Evan Kelley. Headley and Kelley had come to meet their new man in D-3 and to inform him of the serious budgetary restraints the Forest Service was facing. "We are all lambs for the slaughter," Leopold wrote to his mother. "Considering the rising cost of everything, it is a fact that, if the Forest Service did not meet the growing stringency of the situation with a growing amount of ingenuity and effort, the whole organization would fall in pieces. This ingenuity must come from O[perations]—wherefore my scanty letters."[25] Leopold began the year's inspections with this aim in mind. The efficient use of manpower had to become as important as the efficient management of forests. Leopold's unwillingness to sever these two—the men and their work, the means and the ends—would lead him to redefine the meaning of efficiency in conservation, to consider the deeper social implications of conservation, and to amend in his own work the progressive tradition from which he was emerging.

In April, Leopold conducted a week-long inspection of the Tajique District of the Manzano Forest, southeast of Albuquerque. The forest that spring was buffeted by winds laden with topsoil lifted up from the valley below. "One day," he wrote to Burlington, "we came home with cakes of mud a quarter of an inch thick surrounding our eyes—stuff that had blown into our eyes and was 'teared' out so you had to pull off the lumps every few minutes."[26] In his official report he stated, "One of the most serious conservation problems in this general community is the 'blowing' of cultivated lands in the Estancia Valley. The winds this spring on land which has not been properly cultivated have blown away an incalculable amount of very fine soil, thereby not only detracting from the permanent value of the agricultural lands but also destroying roads, fences, and other improvements."[27] In years past, Leopold had taken note of soil erosion, but he had not shown any compelling interest in it. Now it was part of his official responsibility, and he began to look upon it more carefully.

Soil, of course, was not only carried off by wind, but by water. That, too, was a natural process, but one liable to be exacerbated by indiscriminate use, and in particular by indiscriminate grazing practices. Leopold did not have to go far to see the effects of poor range management. The Bosque ranch, high on the crest of the Manzano Mountains, was "badly cut up" by goats and cattle. At Priest Canyon, Leopold and two rangers took advantage of some spare time to build three experimental brush dams, in hopes of retarding the spread of incipient arroyos.

In May, Leopold was off to the opposite end of D-3: the Prescott National Forest in west-central Arizona. Upon his arrival, Leopold was deeply impressed by the boundless oak woodland, famed among foresters, that cloaked the mesas of the Tonto Basin:

Granite Basin, where we rode today, is a jumbled mass of pink granite mountains with a good deal of pine but the oak is everywhere—Live oak, Gambel, Blackjack, and a dozen other kinds, with great fields of Manzanita sprinkled in, and lots of little running streams. The manzanita and snowbrush [are] in bloom and the ground covered with carpets of tiny yellow flowers fragrant as a grape thicket. I almost wished I were vacationing instead of inspecting.[28]

After a week of hard riding over the forest, he began to see beneath the beauty of the oak veneer. Serious soil erosion problems were evident throughout the forest and range, and especially so in the narrow agricultural valleys. In a letter to his mother from the Prescott, Leopold announced, "I have a new hobby. I am seriously thinking of specializing in erosion control. The problem is perfectly tremendous here in the Southwest, and I seem to be the only one who has any faith in the possibilities of tackling it successfully. Don't you think one more hobby would keep me out of mischief?"[29]

Leopold's subsequent report on the Prescott reflected his attention to his "new hobby." He devoted an entire section to the erosion situation. The Prescott rangers and officers had depended solely on adjustments of grazing allotments to check erosion. This was in line with the official policy of the Forest Service, which viewed soil erosion as a watershed problem and assumed that, because the lack of range control caused erosion, the inauguration of range control would cure it in due course: reduce grazing pressure and the sod cover would restore itself. On the Prescott, that policy was not working. Gullies were invading pastures that still had luxuriant sod. The continual concentration, and not just the number, of livestock seemed to instigate the gullying process. Moreover, the incentive to keep as many cattle as possible on the forest was strong: grazing kept down the forage grasses which spread fire through the beautiful, but highly inflammable, woodland. Leopold recommended that the Prescott personnel actively initiate artificial means of erosion control—check dams, willow plantings, gully plugging—in specific problem areas:

The progressiveness of the local population and the scarcity and high value of agricultural valley land make remedial measures more than usually practicable. I consider *actual work* on erosion as a major problem on this Forest, and further "investigative work" of the kind previously done by our office as a waste of time. What is needed is a series of actual demonstrations, to test and improve techniques and to serve as examples to private interests.[30]

Leopold spent a week and a half in June inspecting the Jemez Division of the Santa Fe Forest, in the Jemez Mountains west of the Rio Grande. There the forest lands adjacent to the Rio Las Bacas also showed recent signs of increased gullying. In his report to Pooler, Leopold stated conclusively, "The range does not appear to be overstocked. Here again is an example to prove that erosion is inevitable on many ranges, and cannot be checked except by artificial works. Many valuable cienegas are being drained by these gullies and the bottomland is being torn out."[31]

Years later, Leopold described "the perpetual feeling of attending a funeral which beset me when I first became erosion-conscious in [the Southwest]."[32] By the end of his first full season of inspections, he had begun to grasp the regional nature of the problem. A regional perspective would be needed to understand the process behind it.

The investigation of erosion was not the sole purpose or product of

Leopold's inspections. He devoted himself equally to such matters as personnel, finances, roads and trails, construction projects, fish and game, and public relations. His reports began to fill out, showing a greater confidence in his own judgment and in his command of the various forest functions. He had made no enemies, a noteworthy accomplishment for inspectors in any bureaucracy. On Christmas Eve, 1920, Frank Pooler wrote a note to Leopold:

In the closing days of my first year as District Forester, I want to express my appreciation for the loyal assistance you have given me and for the perfectly splendid way in which you have run your office. It was not an easy thing to take up Operation work when you did, with a change of District Foresters in the air, but you have overcome these difficulties in a way that has unqualifiedly won my fullest confidence. . . . It is with a great deal of personal satisfaction that I can write to you in this way at this time.[33]

ဢ

Erosion, of course, was hardly a new phenomenon. As long as wind and water have confronted rock, erosion has sculpted the distinctive vistas of the Southwest, carving away the spires of Monument Valley and fashioning the depths of the Grand Canyon, laying plain the basins and leaving aloft the sandstone arches.

But erosion works on different scales. Leopold was concerned with the process, not on a geological scale, but on a human, historical scale. A major difficulty in studying the phenomenon was deciding where to draw the line between the two, where to distinguish between an age-old process and a humanly aggravated one. As Leopold took on the problem, he had only a slight scientific foundation on which to stand. Information on the area's hydrologic properties was scant, derived mainly from work on the recent water reclamation projects. Scientists were only beginning to gain insights into the region's climatic past, the most significant (and elusive) piece of the greater puzzle. Only a handful of pioneering scientists were at work on such questions. Even fewer foresters were asking them.[34]

Leopold explored his new interest quietly at first. His ideas and conclusions were closely tied to the observations he made during his inspection tours. There was much to see. The wartime order to stock the ranges to the limit had backfired badly. The war was over long before the cattle were ready for market; when they were ready, the market collapsed. Ranchers, unable to sell, had to keep their stock on the public domain and the national forests. The range deteriorated and the markets languished. More than one cattle grower committed suicide. All the while, the land base suffered.

Leopold was not alone in his concern. Others in the Forest Service, from rangers to officers, collaborated with him, and stimulated his thinking. Important in this regard were his colleagues in the Office of Grazing—John Kerr, Paul Roberts, M. W. Talbot, and, especially, Charles Cooperrider. Cooperrider was a range expert whom Leopold would later describe as "a prophet. He saw that unkindly land-use was leading the Southwest toward disaster, and he devoted his career to the creation of techniques whereby we might use the western lands, and also keep them." Apart from his technical prowess, Leopold also admired Cooperrider's "warmth and kindliness," his "extraordinary tolerance and patience," and "his ability to not only criticize the stockman as a land-user, but to understand and sympathize with him as a human being."[35]

Though necessarily homespun in its science, Leopold's study was leading him to conclusions about conservation in the Southwest that substantiated John Wesley Powell's original thesis that these were arid lands, and could only be successfully settled with that fact in mind. Leopold's first public expression of his ideas on erosion came in an address entitled "Erosion and Prosperity," delivered January 18, 1921, during the observance of Farmer's Week at the University of Arizona. He opened his talk with one of his earliest general discussions of *land* as the fundamental resource:

> All civilization is basically dependent upon natural resources. All natural resources, except only subterranean minerals, are soil or derivatives of soil. Farms, ranges, crops and livestock, forests, irrigation water, and even water power resolve themselves into questions of soil. Soil is therefore the basic natural resource.
>
> It follows that destruction of soil is the most fundamental kind of economic loss which the human race can suffer. With enough time and money, a neglected farm can be put back on its feet—if the soil is still there. With enough patience and scientific knowledge, an overgrazed range can be restored—if the soil is there. By expensive replanting and with a generation or two of waiting, a ruined forest can again be made productive—if the soil is still there. With infinitely expensive works, a ruined watershed may again fill our ditches or turn our mills—if the soil is there. But if the soil is gone, the loss is absolute and irrevocable.[36]

Leopold was still a good utilitarian conservationist: soil erosion was bad because it adversely affected human use of the land. But he had to deal with the inevitable conclusions drawn from his observations: that erosion was, in part at least, a *result* of human use, and that conservation as practiced by the Forest Service had so far been unable to check it.

The problem was most acute in the mountain valleys, which Leopold regarded as "key resources" because they supported the hayfields, vegetable gardens, poultry farms, and small communities that in turn supplied the ranches, mines, and sawmills of the forest interiors. Leopold's records showed that seven of thirteen such agricultural valleys in Arizona with which he was personally familiar were in danger of deterioration through streambank erosion. The root of the problem, as Leopold saw it, was not floods, which had always come and always would, but weakened resistance to floods. It happened in this manner:

Even on the best managed range, a certain concentration of stock at watering places, salt grounds, drive-ways, shearing pens, and roundup grounds is unavoidable, and in rough country most of these are perforce located along water courses. Because of the resulting local overgrazing, the sod is weakened, stock trails start gullies, and the brush holding up the creek banks is consumed. Then comes a cloudburst and the creek bottoms begin to go out. . . . In all of the eroded creek valleys previously mentioned, the damage seems to have started since the range began to be used for stock, and the case of Blue River indicates that an entire valley can be ruined within a decade.[37]

The most sobering aspect of this process was that, once it began, even cessation of overgrazing on the upland watershed did not seem sufficient to stop it. Immediate steps had to be taken to build up resistance to floods. Leopold offered examples of inexpensive, practical techniques that a ranger or rancher could employ: preserving and planting willow thickets, anchoring downed tree tops to the creek banks, damming gullies with brush and rocks.

Two months later, the *Journal of Forestry* published Leopold's "A Plea for Recognition of Artificial Works in Forest Erosion Control Policy." As befitting his technical audience, Leopold gave a more sophisticated, but also more outspoken version of his Arizona address. His paper was a direct challenge to Forest Service policy and to its underlying arguments. To Leopold's thinking, these arguments quite literally did not hold water, at least not when applied in the Southwest. Range control was necessary, but it was not enough. "The truth of the matter," he wrote, "is that (1) any system of grazing, no matter how conservative, induces erosion, (2) no system of range control, no matter how conservative, can be relied upon to stop erosion already started, and that (3) erosion can only be controlled by a proper system of grazing control, supplemented by artificial erosion control works." The last point was sure to rile the watershed experts. The need for artificial techniques amounted to an admission of failure that range control worked. Leopold took strong exception to such defensiveness. "Our function," he wrote, "is not to prove the infallibility of our initial forest policies, but to conserve the Forests."[38]

The hallmark of Leopold's argument was its practicality and its reliance on his own observations. For this paper, he tabulated twenty-five creek bottoms in his experience throughout D-3. Fifteen exhibited signs of beginning or advanced bank erosion. He reemphasized the point that these valleys were vital "not only to the prosperity of Forest industries, but to decent social conditions and the building up of Forest homes." He recognized the problem in differentiating between "normal and abnormal" erosion, but regarded that as "a question of academic rather than practical interest. If erosion is taking away land heretofore untouched, at a rate which will destroy that land within a generation, and if that erosion looks in any degree preventable, the first step is to prevent, not classify."[39]

In both his address and his article, Leopold described the case of the Blue River. Having worked there, and knowing personally many of the old settlers of the valley, he was able to trace its history in detail. In the mid-1880s, the riverbottom supported groves of hardwoods and pine, intermixed with stirrup-high fields of grama grass. The riverbank was lined with willows, and the waters abounded with trout. As cattle ranchers moved into the valleys and foothills of the Blue Range, peach orchards replaced the native groves, and alfalfa the native grasses. The soils might have withstood this change in vegetation, but not the attendant concentration of grazing. In the exceedingly jumbled terrain of the Blue, cattle naturally converged on the most accessible spots, eating clean the main valley and the tributary watercourses as well. Floods began to cut an ever-widening channel about 1900. A series of floods in 1905 and 1906 ripped out some three-quarters of the valley bottom. When Leopold first visited the Blue, during the 1909 Apache reconnaissance, it was plain that the proposed lumber road from Clifton to Springerville could not be built up the valley. Another devastating flood in 1916 tore out much of the remaining bottom land. In 1917, the Forest Service and Greenlee County finally decided to build, at considerable expense, a road that would twist over and around the wild barrancas to the west of the river.[40] "Today," Leopold wrote in 1921,

Blue River valley is mostly boulders, with a few shelves of original bottom land left high and dry between rocky points. Farming is practically at an end because the land is gone, and because it is nearly impossible to maintain headgates to lead irrigation water upon such land as is left. The population about 1900, as estimated by an old cowman, was 300 people on 45 ranches. The present population is about 95 people on 21 ranches. In other words, erosion has destroyed about two-thirds of the homes, and part of the remainder have lost their irrigated land. The loss of land still continues.[41]

Leopold would soon have another opportunity to see the valley of the Blue. He was scheduled to inspect the Apache Forest that summer.

In March 1921, Leopold spent a week in consultation with William B. Greeley, the new head of the Forest Service, and Roy Headley, reviewing operations procedures and discussing the summer's inspections. Evidently, Washington was not satisfied with the state of the forests in the Southwest, nor with the system of inspection. Headley planned to dispatch Evan Kelley to the district to help Leopold and the forest supervisors tighten up their methods. Despite their dissatisfaction, Greeley and Headley left their meetings impressed with Leopold and his self-motivated research into the erosion problem. Not long afterward, Greeley offered him a position at the Forest Products Laboratory, the main research facility of the Forest Service, in Madison, Wisconsin. Leopold declined the offer. Such a move, he felt, would not constitute much of an advance. He wanted to see through his work on game management and erosion control, and a move would "take me away from the ground, and from a force to work through on the ground." Leopold also declined for reasons of personal pride. He explained that, "the question as to my ability to make a success of my present job, which I found existed in this District after I accepted it, is still only partly answered."[42]

Leopold took most of May and June of 1921 to inspect the Apache and Sitgreaves National Forests. It was a turning point in his life, in terms of both his professional development and his personal attitude. Kelley met Leopold on May 14 and accompanied him for ten days on the rounds of the two forests. On horseback they rode the trails, visited the ranger stations, and camped out in the mountains where Leopold had first worked. As they rode, they talked over the methods and aims of inspection, and argued the politics of forest administration. A plain-spoken man dedicated to his work, Kelley kept a close eye on Leopold. While Leopold inspected the forests, Kelley inspected Leopold.

In a subsequent report to Headley, Kelley made no bones about it: he thought Leopold was too haughty in his manner, too confident in his approach to inspection, and too careless in his attention to detail. Leopold did not so much acquire humility as he had it thrust upon him by Kelley, who wrote that, "Mr. Leopold's discoveries in the field were a genuine surprise to him. . . . Now he feels chagrined. He frankly admits that until this season inspection methods followed failed to give him a glance into affairs as they actually prevail." This fact was especially true, Kelley felt, in the way Leopold handled field personnel:

Mr. Leopold has always held the opinion that training or educational courses like those of Dist[rict] 2 were not necessary. The main object to accomplish as he has seen the job is to cultivate a man's imagination by permitting him to choose reading matter; for example, he thought and is right to certain degree that if a ranger reads a thesis on mythology (?) he would develop imagination to assist him in his daily work. After getting his first real insight into administration as it actually prevails he says what we need is primer stuff, not only for rangers but for some supervisors. He is now planning to develop for use next winter telephone courses, grazing courses, etc. He frankly says that this trip had been a revelation to him. Highbrow ideas have been blasted by seeing affairs in their true aspects.

Kelley's unsparing criticism did not prevent him from admiring Leopold's tenacity. "Personally," Kelley concluded, "I think Leo had done well in light of his experience and the handicaps under which he works, but you know that I also believe he moves along with his feet somewhat off the ground. But he lowered several inches during the past month."[43]

Leopold's Apache and Sitgreaves reports reflected Kelley's advice. They were better organized, more comprehensive, and crammed with details. Leopold carefully evaluated the readiness of firefighting tools, and proposed wholesale reforms in fire protection plans. He painstakingly analyzed the forage and travel expenses of the individual rangers, and rated the conditions of ranger stations, tool-houses, and outhouses. He criticized lookout towers on the Apache that were so shaky that they could not be used during high winds, recommended crop rotations in ranger station pastures, and pored over diaries to ascertain the efficiency of the personnel.

Leopold's newfound diligence did not keep him from paying special attention to the quality of the country itself. On the Apache, he was able to compare range conditions to those he had found upon his arrival in 1909. Not all the ranges were damaged; erosion was not a predetermined effect of settlement. In localized areas, however, the situation was bad and getting worse. The high country on Mt. Baldy had "deteriorated badly, and has certainly been severely overgrazed. Many of the draws show signs of washing. . . . The old stockmen with whom I talked all said the mountain was going downhill." Near the Malay Corral, Leopold was able to compare overgrazed rangeland with adjacent land on the Apache Indian Reservation; he found the contrast "painful and humiliating." The green cienegas of the Blue Range had begun to wash out; "all the open draws and parks which were grass in 1910 are now mostly weeds, and even the burns are nearly bare, whereas they used to have quite a lot of grass and wild oats."[44]

Leopold did not mention the Blue River itself in his 1921 inspection report, although he spent time there during his tour. There was one moment on the river, however, that left a lasting image in Leopold's mind. An unusually dry spring had arrived on District 3. The heat and the parched range began to take their toll on the all-too-numerous cattle. While riding among the sunbaked rocks of the Blue River ravine, he came upon a cow dead in the sand. What he then saw stayed with him for a year before he finally wrote it down:

I reined up, not sure whether the old cow was dead, or just dying. She had come down out of the drouth-stricken hills to drink, I guess. And now she lay there, quite still, on the hot sand bar. A swarm of brilliant green flies buzzed about her head, and plagued her mouth and eyes. She had craned her neck—the mark was there in the sand—as if for one last look up into the cruel cliffs of Blue River.

I was reflecting on this—especially the ghoulish flies—when it happened. A flash of vermillion, a soft bubbling warble, and a little red bird hovered over the old cow's head, snapping up flies right and left, one after another, for each a cry of ecstacy, in very joy of living. And then with one quick crimson sweep of wing, it disappeared into the green depths of a cottonwood.

Did the old cow see the bird? No. Her dead eyes stared up into the cliffs. Her calf was somewhere up there.

For a while I looked at the old cow, and thought about the little red bird. Then I rode on down Blue River.

At the bottom of the page, Aldo added a note to Estella: "Do you think this is any good? It happened last year on the Blue. I've been thinking for a year how to write it. Afraid it can't be done. Bird is the Vermillion Fly-catcher. I've told you about them."[45]

〜

In July 1921, Aldo's brother Carl married Estella's sister Dolores, thus further entangling two already uncommon family trees. Carl was more emotive, less absorbed than Aldo; Dolores was not so high-spirited as Estella. Carl and Dolores had known one another for years, but their romance had only recently bloomed. He had paid a visit the previous holiday season and at that time, apparently, proposed to Dolores. Aldo and Carl, always close, became even closer by virtue of their being brothers-in-law as well as brothers.

Leopold completed one more inspection that summer, on the Lincoln Forest in south-central New Mexico. The Lincoln was among the smoothest-run forests in the district, with one of the best ranger crews. By now, Leopold's own work had attained a high level of clarity and fullness. He had mastered the aims of inspection, and was ready to revamp his methods to put them on a more orderly, standardized basis. By this time, too, Pooler had high esteem, both personally and professionally, for his once-suspect assistant.

The end of inspection season neatly coincided with the opening of dove season. That fall Leopold joined the Tomé Gun Club, just downriver from Albuquerque, where he leased a tiny one-room adobe hunting cabin near the river flats. The Tomé Club became Leopold's main hunting grounds. For Starker and Luna, it was the equivalent of Aldo's Lone Tree Club on the Mississippi: the place where their father took them to hunt, to learn about woodsmanship and the ways of wildlife. The latest in a long line of spaniels named Flick joined the outfit. Aldo indulged in a new shotgun, a beautifully engraved, .20-gauge, double-barrelled Ainsley-Fox that cost the princely sum of three hundred dollars ("Three hundred dollars," Estella would later point out, ". . . and I needed a washing machine.")[46]

Aldo's brother Frederic came out from Burlington that December (though *not* to court a Bergere sister; he was already married). He, Aldo, and Starker took a week-long canoe trip down the Rio Grande. Ducks that season were particularly abundant, but the Leopolds were after geese. One week and seventy miles later, the party arrived in Socorro, "gooseless but well content with their trip." On the last day of the waterfowl season, Aldo was up scouting the river for birds well before the others were even rousing. He had an insatiable appetite, not for killing, but for the game fields. "At noon," he wrote in his hunting journal, "found the boys wanted to go home so had to pull my decoys and call it another season."[47]

∽

Two years had passed since Leopold and Arthur Carhart met in Denver. Carhart's efforts to protect the shoreline of Trappers Lake from development had met with success in early 1920. Carhart then turned his attentions to the wild canoe country of northern Minnesota. In formulating recreational plans for the Superior National Forest, Carhart took the first steps in preserving what is today the Boundary Waters Canoe Area.

Leopold, for his part, continued to share his concern for the passing of the wilderness with his friends and colleagues in the Southwest.[48] There was increasing cause for concern. The federal government itself posed the greatest threat to what remained of the Southwest's, and the nation's, wildlands. The National Park Service, saddled with its paradoxical mandate to both protect and open up to the public the nation's scenic wonders, was concentrating with zeal on the latter, feverishly building new roads and visitor accommodations on the parklands. If great stretches of the American wilderness were to be maintained, the effort would have to come from the nation's other major conservation agency, the Forest Service. The USFS, however, was hardly pointed in that direction. As thoughts of wilderness protection emerged in the minds of a few individual foresters, the service as a whole was simultaneously embarking on the so-called good roads movement, a copiously funded effort to expand the road system in the national forests.[49] Leopold, in fact, as part of his operations work, helped oversee this work in the Southwest.

By mid-1921, Leopold felt that the time had come to broach publicly the subject of wilderness protection in the nation's forests. The November 1921 issue of the *Journal of Forestry* carried his seminal article, "The Wilderness and Its Place in Forest Recreation Policy," the profession's first formal discussion of the topic. As such, Leopold's article was a fulcrum point in the 150-year history of America's public domain, and in American civilization's shifting view of its land, its development, and its own values.

The American frontier had reached the far ocean. It had not moved west like some great, symbolic, crashing wave. It was not the grand unfurling of a manifest destiny. Ineffable images had not crossed and settled the land; conversely, images had not retreated and bled before that advance. The white settler's frontier was defined by the movements of quite real people: natives who had their birthright seized, and newcomers who derived their justifications from a very different past. The immigrants dispersed along a few major and a thousand tentative paths. These outbranchings, following the demands of impulse, rumor, and geography, met degrees of resistance from the first occupants, and reached assorted ends: some branches were abruptly lopped off; some turned back on themselves; some simply ran out; some found fertile ground and established themselves. In time, the network of settlement extended itself over the land. The river landings, wagon trails, railroad lines, telegraph wires, and, now, highways, were the visible links between new lives come to inhabit an old place. As the maps filled in, the blank spaces shrank. The spaces of mountain, mesa, and basin were still great in reality, a mockery to the scrawny abstractions laid upon the maps, but a few individuals, possessing no extraordinary amount of wealth, intelligence, or moral virtue, but perception, foresight, and a healthy sense of adventure, could see that those lines on the map represented something still greater. The main energy of European expansion had reached a climax on the North American continent. It was a special point in history, a window in time during which whole futures, of people and land, would be influenced. Aldo Leopold, who had played his own role in that expansion, would emerge from the moment as a voice of restraint, arguing for a preservation of the past in the present, so that the future might have an approximate sense of its own roots.

One could argue the case for wilderness from a variety of directions. Scientists in the new Ecological Society of America were calling for preservation for science's sake.[50] Arthur Carhart's approach was primarily aesthetic: he saw wilderness as a scenic resource whose grandeur ought to be kept for future generations to enjoy. Leopold's *Journal of Forestry* article argued from a recreational standpoint, and that implied reserves of greater extent than the others had advocated. One could find rare plants and animals, scenery, hunting, fishing, and isolation within a mile of a paved road, but if future generations were to understand and experience "a real wilderness trip," then something more was needed: "a big stretch of wild country."

Leopold's stated purpose in his article was "to give definite form to the issue of wilderness conservation, and to suggest certain policies for meeting it, especially as applied to the Southwest." He opened with a statement that turned the progressive conservation movement back on itself:

When the National Forests were created the first argument of those opposing a national forest policy was that the forests would remain a wilderness. . . . At this time, Pinchot enunciated the doctrine of "highest use," and its criterion, "the

greatest good to the greatest number," which is and must remain the guiding principle by which democracies handle their natural resources.

Pinchot's promise of development has been made good. The process must, of
course, continue indefinitely. But it has already gone far enough to raise the question of whether the policy of development (construed in the narrow sense of industrial development) should continue to govern in absolutely every instance, or
whether the principle of highest use does not itself demand that representative portions of some forests be preserved as wilderness.[51]

Leopold's statement was rich in irony. He was saying that the highest use
to which some wilderness land could be put was no use at all, or at least
uses of minimal impact—hunting, fishing, canoeing, camping. "Highest
use," Leopold wrote in a marvelous concentration of conservation philosophy, "demands its preservation." What those interested in outdoor recreation needed, he surmised, was "some logical reconciliation between getting back to nature and preserving a little nature to get back to."[52]

Leopold offered an initial definition of wilderness: "By 'wilderness' I
mean a continuous stretch of country preserved in its natural state, open
to lawful hunting and fishing, big enough to absorb a two weeks' pack
trip, and kept devoid of roads, artificial trails, cottages, or other works
of man."[53] Such areas, he assumed, would be limited in size and number,
ill-suited for ordinary development, and representative of country with
distinctive recreational values. The Forest Service, he emphasized, had here
a special opportunity to display foresight. There was still time and room
enough to meet the recreational needs, not only of those who demanded
modern conveniences (a majority, Leopold granted), but of the minority
who did not. Time and space, though, were rapidly shrinking. The opportunity had to be seized. "It will be much easier," he observed, "to keep
wilderness areas than to create them. In fact, the latter alternative may be
dismissed as impossible."[54]

Leopold concluded his argument with an example. He proposed setting aside the headwaters of the Gila River, high in the Mogollon Mountains of west-central New Mexico. It met the criteria. The whole area was
within the boundaries of the Gila and Datil National Forests. It included
nearly half a million acres, isolated by mountain ranges and box canyons.
Neither railroads nor automobile roads had breached its natural borders.
It contained little agricultural land of any value. The native wildlife populations were relatively intact. Some cattle grazed there, but Leopold considered this an asset in that frontier grazing operations were themselves
of recreational interest. The cattlemen, too, would benefit by the exclusion
of new settlers and hordes of motorcars. The only economic loss would
come from the prohibition on large-scale logging.

Leopold acknowledged that his proposal might seem "rank heresy to
some minds," just as timber conservation had been heresy a generation

before. There were many in his own forests of District 3 and in the Albuquerque offices who opposed the idea. With stalwart conviction, he included in his defense a favorite quotation: "The truth is that which prevails in the long run."[55]

The article had its intended effect: it opened the subject for discussion within forestry circles. Greeley himself had advised Leopold to publish it, implying some degree of sympathy. Kelley planned to mention it in his new "Roads and Trails Manual" for operations men throughout the Forest Service. Pooler agreed to entertain proposals for its application on the Gila, which Leopold was due to inspect that summer. Veteran forester Austin Carey spoke for many when he wrote to Leopold, "In my opinion you are entirely right and have brought out a point in National Forest Policy that needs to be looked after."[56]

Leopold and his colleagues based their argument for wilderness preservation on a simple desire: they wished to keep a place where it would remain possible to travel, hunt, and fish under frontier conditions. That desire, however, was premised on something more enduring and universal. By their efforts, they hoped to ensure that wilderness could continue to feed a culture's idea of freedom. In an earlier day, it was the abundance and newness of the land that nurtured that idea. Now it would become the test of America's maturity whether it would have wisdom and conviction enough to preserve, to at least some extent, the fountain of its own inspiration, and by so doing continue to replenish itself.

ᔑ

In January 1922, Assistant Forester Roy Headley jotted down some notes to himself on Aldo Leopold. Headley's notes gave a full picture of Leopold as he turned thirty-five:

1) Possesses splendid imagination; handles theory with ease and skill of a master. Has a theory to explain nearly everything which comes up.
2) Has passion for scientific determination of things; wants to test things—wants to be sure not to stand alleged facts which are actually composed usually of prejudice, fragmentary observations, and a desire to have something to say. Wants to make an investigation project of nearly every question that comes up. May carry this too far.
3) He is teachable to an extraordinary degree. Instances are, the way he digs into detail because he has been taught that his former method of flying too high for detail was wrong; probably no man has learned more readily from [Evan] Kelley's teaching than Leopold. . . .
4) Is a tireless worker. Has an enormous range of interests and knowledge.

In Headley's estimation, Leopold's greatest weakness was his manner of handling difficult personnel cases:

5) Is perhaps a little inclined to dodge the disagreeable necessity of calling a spade by its right name. If crowded a little bit he evidently talks over with men their serious as well as their minor failings. I suspect, however, that one of Leopold's inherent weaknesses is a slight tendency to avoid, unconsciously, those lines of thought and those lines of handling a subject which, while logical and desirable from the standpoint of the development of the Forest Service, are nevertheless likely to lead to the soul-searching experiences which an administrator encounters if he is ready to take the bitter with the sweet.

Headley summed up Leopold's prospects:

6) What would happen if Leopold were made a District Forester after he thoroughly learns his lesson that no man in the Forest Service is big enough to neglect details?
   (a) As to his leadership—he would inspire a group of men unless they doubted his practical judgment and skill.
   (b) Could he make others work as hard as he worked himself? Doubtful.
   (c) Would he crowd matters in personnel cases? Doubtful.
   (d) Would he work very hard himself? Very.
   (e) His judgment on such things as personnel would be a little theoretical; on questions of forestry, watershed protection, and game, it would be sound and penetrating.[57]

Leopold was an uncommon forester. His resolute view of forests—as sources not only of our material well-being, but also of our psychological and spiritual well-being—was enough to distinguish him. His willingness to take the lead in incorporating that view in policy decisions made him unique. Although he was an innovator and always open to new ideas, Leopold was not quick to change. His growth, in general, came not through instant conversion but through incremental evolution.

By 1922, Leopold had begun to outgrow the Roosevelt-era conservation mold. He was now opposed, for instance, to the unnecessary drainage of river basins. It was the idea of wilderness preservation, however, that truly signalled a departure from the Pinchot path. Although couched in traditional utilitarian terms, Leopold's arguments contained the seeds of a new, more sophisticated conservation philosophy. Times were changing, as were the needs and realities of conservation. Progressive-era conservation had been an admixture of economic aims, social ideals, and scientific information. In post–World War I America, all three ingredients were in flux.

The root of Leopold's thinking would not change. Anchoring his conservation faith like a willow on a streambank was a deeply held concern for the land itself. The condition of the forest remained the measure of effective Forest Service management. This objective stance was admirable, but Leopold still had many misunderstandings and outright biases to overcome before even he, much less the Forest Service, could attain such an attitude.

In the meantime, the task of the Forest Service was enormous: coordinating manpower across the breadth of a continent, conserving to the best of its ability a major portion of the nation's natural resources, and doing both on limited funds. Leopold still professed that the ranger's intuition was the most important factor in effecting real conservation, but as chief of operations he now saw that, first, the work had to get done. The more quickly and effectively it got done, the better. Accordingly, Leopold and his operations colleagues in other districts began to study and apply the time-and-motion theories of Frederick Winslow Taylor and other specialists in industrial management. After the 1921 inspection season, Leopold sat down and devised a new method of inspection that would be more thorough, and fairer to the field force. His main innovation was a notebook of tally sheets that allowed the inspector to record field observations of everything from the eyesight of the fireguards and the tension of telephone lines to the readiness of pack animals and the mileage of motor vehicles. Leopold acknowledged that this method could result in "mechanical inspections," but reasoned that the unambiguous categories would keep the inspector alert. The new system had its first trial when the 1922 inspection season opened, on the Gila Forest.

Refined theories of management seemed inconsequential when Leopold arrived on the Gila on May 22, 1922. The seasonal rains were not due for several weeks, and the Gila was being overwhelmed by wildfires. Leopold had seen the telltale orange glow in the sky the night before, from fifty miles away. A southwest wind carried the ashes and aroma of burning timber. Dry lightning lit the mountaintops. Fred Winn, now the supervisor of the Gila, was leading his men at the most disastrous of the blazes, in Curtis Canyon. "If we can hold the line today," Winn wrote in his diary, "and God Almighty will not send a gale but give us a westerly wind, we will have it."[58] Leopold met Winn at the Kingston Ranger Station. They discussed the situation. The fire crews were exhausted. Supplies were arriving slowly. Leopold decided to delay his inspection until the situation was under control. Even as they talked, another fire broke out on the top of Mogollon Baldy.

The next morning, Winn and Leopold rode up to the fire line in Curtis Canyon. The blaze there was being held, so they began normal inspection rounds. Then fires broke out all over the forest — one up on the Datil boundary, another to the east on Diamond Peak, two more on Granite Peak in the Gila interior. Leopold and Winn had just begun a pack trip north to look over the area of the proposed wilderness when they spotted a large plume of smoke rising above Little Creek. They turned around.

More fires were reported at Lookout Mountain and at the head of Mogollon Creek. The next ten days were, in Winn's words, "one continual 'go' all the time." He stayed in the fire camps to organize the crews and supplies while Leopold went out to plan strategy. When Leopold's horses and mules got too leg-weary, he and Winn switched. Conditions remained volatile: dry and windy, with lightning striking continually in the high ranges. None of the fires crowned out, but they stubbornly persisted, repeatedly flaring up and jumping the fire lines. June 2 was the worst day. Leopold and Ranger Conner rode to extinguish one blaze in Rocky Canyon while yet another rose on a flank of Lookout Mountain. Winn dispatched what men he could. Exasperated, he noted that there was "nothing else to be done in view of conditions." In ten days, forty-one fires had broken out on New Mexico forests, the worst fire season since 1904. The extent of the spring drought was unprecedented.[59]

By June 5, most of the fires were contained. Leopold and Winn rode off to restart their inspection in the Black Range. They toured the ranches, canyons, and ranger stations for a week, scrutinizing range conditions, tool box inventories, and lookout towers, fishing when there was a free evening, and discussing the wilderness plan. On the night of the thirteenth, they split up at the old Gila Flat Road, Winn to return to Silver City, Leopold to continue on to the north and west parts of the forest, where the heart of the wild country lay.

On June 18, a new fire broke out near Whitewater Creek, one of the Gila's headwaters. Leopold again interrupted his inspection to lead the crews. Two days later it was out. Leopold then returned to Silver City, where he praised the local citizenry for their vigilance during the emergency. "I have seen fire fighters of many kinds in many places, but I believe the settlers and range men of the Gila Forest, with good equipment and supervision, are the most efficient men on a fire line that I have ever seen."[60] In Silver City, Leopold sat down with Winn and the other officers of the Gila for a conference, and they drew on a map the boundaries of the proposed Gila Wilderness Area, to encompass some 750,000 acres in the Mogollon Mountains.

Before returning to Albuquerque, Leopold also took note of the Gila's erosion problem.[61] On the entire forest, only the upper reaches of a few watercourses were unaffected; all of the bottomlands in the mountain country were deteriorating. For a graphic example, Leopold had to look no further than downtown Silver City and "The Ditch," a fifty-five-foot chasm where Main Street used to be, gouged out by a series of deluges that began in 1895. A 1903 flood climaxed the destruction, scraping the ditch to bedrock and carrying downstream not only tons of soil, but the judge's house, a Steinway piano, several "entertainment parlors," and a host of barnyard creatures.

In July, Leopold completed his Gila inspection report. The section on "Lands" contained the Wilderness Area recommendation. The area was outlined on the accompanying map by a red line, "which marks the limit of automobile accessibility." The tentative policy for this area suggested that "no additional permits for any but grazing uses . . . be given. This excludes permanent improvements like summer homes, hunting lodges, hotels, etc." The plan hardly provided for a "pure" wilderness. Grazing would continue at a "very conservative" level. Trails and phone lines for fire protection would, of course, be retained. Predators would be given "special attention" by the Biological Survey. These recommendations were to be outlined in further detail in a new recreational plan for the forest.[62]

Immediately following the wilderness proposal in his report, Leopold turned to its antithesis: the erosion problem. His comments were his strongest yet. "I am now convinced that while tearing out of watercourses is undoubtedly *made worse* by burning or overgrazing of the general watershed, neither of these is nearly so potent or universal a cause as the *overgrazing of the watercourse or canyon bottom itself.* . . . Continued acceptance of the current theory that only overgrazing damages the country constitutes *glossing over* an unpleasant but to my mind now undeniable fact, and it is not the tradition of the Forest Service to gloss over unpleasant facts."[63]

Leopold's new tally sheet format had worked well. Pooler was pleased with the results and praised Leopold for "the painstaking detail and at the same time comprehensive work you are doing in inspection."[64] He approved the Gila report on August 3, and asked Leopold to prepare a full report on the Wilderness Area proposal for discussion at the next winter meeting of district foresters.

∽

Every new inspection added to Leopold's knowledge of the landscape, while simultaneously teaching him how little he really understood the dynamics of that land. Southwestern foresters knew silviculture, but they were groping for answers when it came to range and watershed management, fish and game, recreation, and erosion control. The result of such ignorance was inefficient, often ineffective conservation work.

Leopold tried to address this shortcoming in a manuscript he called "Skill in Forestry." He wrote that, "the only thing I am sure of is that policy is being written much faster than research can illumine the path, that huge values are at stake, and that there are neglected possibilities in personnel management that might be useful in telling us what to do until research forges abreast of the times." What Leopold had in mind was some means of harnessing an illusive human quality, a combination of intuition, native talent, and specialized judgment, that he termed "natural skill." "Natural skill" was a rare quality, usually limited to a single field, but which if recognized and utilized could save foresters many a headache. As an example, Leopold naturally chose the erosion question:

Who, for instance, has set down the laws governing erosion in the Southwest? And when will they be set down? Maybe our grandsons will have them, but by that time the best parts of the Southwest bid fair to repose in the Gulf of California. We must have "something to go by" now. Are there not, perhaps, some persons with such a "natural skill" in this particular subject, that they have anticipated and carry in their minds substantially what the scientists will say when they get around to it a decade or half a dozen decades hence? If such can be found, it may save some fiddling while Rome burns.[65]

Leopold passed the paper around the office in Albuquerque. It was a little too mystical for most of his colleagues. John Kerr asked, "It's merely the difference between inductive + deductive reasoning, is it not? . . . Is there really anything to 'natural skill' except common sense and close observation?" Ray Marsh wrote, "I conceive our fundamental job to be growing timber. This means forestry. . . . Why concentrate on a new complicated piece of machinery while we are not anywhere near reaching the possibilities of our present equipment?" Morton Cheney, who worked in the Lands Office, did express interest. "We spend too much time proving the obvious," he wrote, "[but] you will accept it from the man of 'natural skill' + still *prove* the result by collection of data and study."[66]

Leopold dropped the idea. Significantly, however, the manuscript reflected the way Leopold's own mind worked, and the direction in which it was turning. His thought was exquisitely balanced between the analytical and the intuitive, the rational and the imaginative working side-by-side. Both qualities would become more focussed and would nourish each other in the years to come. Neither would completely dominate.

In August 1922, Leopold returned to the Prescott National Forest in Arizona. Conditions on the Prescott would provide ample fuel for these thoughts on forest conservation, forest administration, and the connection between the two. The timber there was in good shape, reproducing well, in fact spreading to previously nonwooded areas. The fire control record was likewise good, but the overgrowth of thick brush constituted a serious fire hazard, a problem Leopold was specifically told to investigate. Agricultural land was "rapidly disappearing." Range and watershed damage was so extensive and so widely recognized that Leopold hardly dwelt on it; it was common knowledge. In trying to understand how this combination of conditions had arisen, Leopold would have to ask what impact they had had on one another.

Leopold toured again the mesas whose beauty and deterioration had so impressed him two years before. He visited the rangers on their districts, and asked old-timers about the history of the vegetation cover. In his notebook he recorded pieces of evidence. The extensive brushfields—the oaks, manzanita, mountain mahogany, ceanothus—had grown in height and density. Old-timers recalled the time prior to heavy grazing, when thick grass was interspersed with the then-thinner brush. Amid the present-day brush, there were old, charred stumps of juniper; under the brush, young juniper was coming in. Manzanita was known to be highly combustible. Leopold also showed that it was highly *dependent* on fire for reproduction. He pointed out that, in areas where insects, not fires, had killed pines, the manzanita did not reproduce; he deduced that it was fire, and not just the opening of the forest, that manzanita required. And the heavier the burn, the more abundant the reproduction.

These were clues in an environmental mystery. The mystery, in Leopold's words, was "when, how, why, and what kinds of brush constitute a fire hazard." The question was a timely one; the Prescott, like the Gila, had suffered extensive fires that dry spring. Leopold ventured only a few speculations. He kept notes on the behavior of fires on the Prescott. He, Supervisor Wales, and Ranger Oldham performed experiments on the inflammability of the various brush species, but their tests did not yield much insight. "Inflammability of the Prescott (and probably other) brush fields," he concluded, "happens to be complex, and requires more refined methods for successful solution."[67] To ascertain the factors involved, he advised the Prescott personnel to keep a careful record of the habits of the fires they fought.

But there was a question behind the question, a mystery behind the mystery: when, how, and why had the vegetation cover of the forest changed so as to constitute a fire hazard in the first place, and what would the answers mean in terms of management strategies? As usual, Leopold had a theory:

In its virgin state, large parts of the brush type were probably thinner than now, with much more grass. Grass fires and grassroot competition kept the brush down, and the grass probably checked the wholesale spread of manzanita through fire. . . . This virgin state was in itself temporary, the soil or at least large areas of it, being a forest soil, tending to come back to woodland whenever fires allowed. This accounts for the widespread occurrence of [scattered] Juniper stumps. . . . The reappearance of woodland on a large scale, after removal of sod and grass fires . . . dovetails into this hypothesis. . . . So do the various phenomena of erosion.[68]

Leopold admitted that his examination had been too superficial to substantiate this interpretation. It was nonetheless a remarkable first stab at an answer. He had focussed in on ground fires and grazing as the fundamental factors influencing both the rate of erosion and the change in vegetation since settlement. The very process of settling the land had unwittingly exacerbated both the fire and the erosion problem. Leopold would bolster and refine his reasoning over the next two years, but the hardest step has already been taken. He had connected fire to grazing to vegetation change to erosion, and realized the need to study formally those connections.

This new view of conditions in the brush fields had definite policy implications for fire control, forest management, and range management. Grazing had previously been encouraged as a fire-control technique: it kept down grass, thereby retarding fires, thereby protecting trees, thereby preserving the watershed. The result after two decades of this policy was a denuded grassland, a greater fire hazard, and unspeakable erosion problems. Easing up on grazing would encourage grasses and, thus, fires. On the other hand, maintaining heavy grazing would only make bad erosion problems worse. The aims of forest and range conservation seemed to be working against one another.

The Prescott had been established originally as a watershed forest; that is, it was set up primarily to protect the watershed values of the forest, and not merely the timber itself. That being the highest conservation objective, Leopold wrote, "we should restore the grass, which all the evidence indicates is better watershed cover than either brush or woodland."[69] He was prepared to accept the greater risk of fire rather than the certainty of a deteriorating watershed. That in itself was a revolutionary recommendation for a Forest Service employee, and one that Leopold ventured only reluctantly.

These intricacies of vegetation change and policy options led Leopold to question the manner in which the Forest Service was going about its business on the Prescott and other southwestern forests. While on the Prescott inspection he wrote some notes to himself on the topic. The service, he explained, had always set standards for itself. Heretofore those standards had been applied only to the machinery of administration: so many days per year had to be spent on grazing work, so many general inspections had to be made on so many units of range, and so on. What would be the result, Leopold mused, if standards were applied, not to the machinery of administration, but to the objectives that machinery was meant to serve? Such standards Leopold labeled "standards of conservation." They were needed because, as he succinctly put it, "natural resources are a complex affair."[70]

Leopold gave an example. While on inspection on the Prescott, he talked with one ranger who for years had striven to stock his district with as many cattle as possible. The ranger's idea was to force them to eat the nonpalatable ceanothus and thus reduce the fire hazard. Leopold pointed out to the ranger that the heavy grazing pressure was destroying the willows in the watercourses, resulting in serious bank erosion. "Here were two men, both anxious to conserve, but with opposite ideas as to what most needed conserving, and hence with opposite plans of administration." The situation demanded a clearly defined ultimate goal, and not merely "machinery standards" that, over time, were liable to become "a subterfuge to cover up the absence of scientific thinking in analyzing the objectives of conservation."[71]

On both the biological and administrative levels, Leopold was seeking answers to questions that others would not be asking for years. While plant ecology was building its jargon and theoretical base back in midwestern universities, Leopold was exploring it (though still not using the term "ecology" with any regularity) in a functional way in the diverse forests of Arizona and New Mexico. Here his personality and professional training held him in good stead. He was endeavoring to understand the Southwest and civilization's effect on it sooner, and with greater latitude, than were "purer" naturalists, or foresters, or scientists. His thoughts on resource administration and his appreciation of the fact that forests serve multiple uses—including wilderness—were, at minimum, half a century before their time. As for "standards of conservation," they would remain poorly defined, and conservation itself would be hard pressed to gain credence before the simpler, shorter-term standards of our human economic enterprise.

∽

On October 2, 1922, Leopold submitted to Frank Pooler his report on the proposed Gila Wilderness Area.[72] The object of the proposal was "to preserve at least one place in the Southwest where pack trips shall be the dominant play." He reported favorable reaction to the plan from the Gila officers and from the public. Both the state and local Game Protective Associations had gone on record in favor of the proposal. But, Leopold added, "I expect some opposition." The issue was not high on Pooler's list of priorities. It would be taken up in discussions with the supervisors.

About this time, Leopold put down on paper some of his earliest thoughts on the greater meaning of wilderness in his own life and in the life of his civilization. He spoke of maps. Like many an ordinary thing, a map was "common or sublime depending on by whom possessed." He recalled an early experience:

Once in school I was staring up at a map of Brazil. I was bored with school, and maps, and all this ilk. My eyes fell on that great blank place behind the Amazon, and there I saw a name. El Rio del Madre de Dios—[the] River of the Mother of God! That name was electric. It stung like the fall of a whiplash. It seared my consciousness; the memory of it quickens me to this day. Some unknown soldier of Spain, whose very bones mayhaps have been devoured by the Jungle these four centuries, named that river, and left unnamed the score of rivers roundabout.[73]

That river, issuing forth from the blank spot on the map, seemed to Leopold "the perfect symbol of the Unknown Places of the earth. And its name, resonant of the clank of silver armor and the cruel progress of the Cross, yet carrying a hush of reverence and a murmur of the prows of galleons on the seven seas, has always seemed the symbol of Conquest—the conquest that has reduced those Unknown Places, one by one, until now there are none left. . . . No doubt it was 'for this the earth lay preparing quintillions of years, for this the revolving centuries truly and steadily rolled.' But it marks a new epoch in the history of mankind, an epoch in which Unknown Places disappear as a dominant fact in human life."[74]

He wrote of the influence of unknown places on paleolithic man, on the Sumerian tribes and Phoenician sailors, on Hanno, Ulysses, Eric, Columbus. Would something be lost from the human character, he wondered, now that such places were lost from the human environment? Not necessarily. Just as the prehistoric chase was preserved in sport, so could the feel of wilderness travel be preserved in outdoor adventure:

It is [the] reaction against the loss of adventure into the unknown which causes the hundreds of thousands to sally forth each year upon little expeditions, afoot, by pack train, or by canoe, into the odd bits of wilderness which commerce and "development" have regretfully and temporarily left us here and there. Modest adventurers, to be sure, compared with Hanno, or Lewis and Clark. But so is the sportsman, with his setter dog in pursuit of partridges, a modest adventurer compared with his Neolithic ancestor in single combat with the Auroch bull. The point is that along with the necessity for expression of racial instincts there happily goes that capacity for illusion which enables little boys to fish happily in wash tubs. That capacity is a precious thing, if not overworked.[75]

Given that the human values of wilderness adventure could and would endure, was it possible to preserve some remnant of unknown places in which to exercise them? Could it be done "without undue loss in economic values?" Leopold answered yes to both questions, provided action were taken quickly. Suitable areas existed on America's public lands. "The one thing needful is for the Government to draw a line around each one and say: 'This is wilderness, and wilderness it shall remain.'"

Leopold then took on the economic nay-sayers. He stated that such a wilderness policy "would not subtract even a fraction of one percent from our economic wealth, but would preserve a fraction of what has, since first the flight of years began, been wealth to the human spirit." He asserted that, unlike the dinosaurs and all other creatures before and since, man has gained the capacity to direct his own evolution. He is "the first creature, in any spiritual sense, to create his own environment. Is it not in that fact, rather than in mere ciphers of dollars or population, that we have grown? The question of wilderness playgrounds is a question in self-control of environment." Wilderness, Leopold emphasized, was the one thing, perhaps the only thing, that man could never create. "To artificially create wilderness areas would overwork the capacity for illusion of even little boys with wash-tubs."

What I am trying to picture is the tragic absurdity of trying to whip the March of Empire into a gallop. Very specifically, I am pointing out that in the headlong stampede for speed and ciphers, we are crushing the last remnants of something that ought to be preserved for the spiritual and physical welfare of future Americans, even at the cost of acquiring a few less millions of wealth or population in the long run. Something that has helped build the race for such innumerable centuries that we may logically suppose it will help preserve it in the centuries to come.[76]

The wilderness, in short, was not just a place to hunt, but a place to know the freedom of adventure, the joy of self-expression, and the value of self-restraint, without unduly insulting our capacity for illusion. The significance of wilderness was not merely recreational, but cultural.

Leopold's own passion for the wilds remained undiminished. Its most poignant demonstration came that same fall of 1922, when he and Carl vacationed on the delta of the Colorado River at its confluence with the Gulf of California.

On October 25, Carl and Aldo Leopold ("gentlemen-adventurers" in Aldo's playful journal account), accompanied by Flick, began their "Voyage of Discovery" into "the Mythical Straits of Annian, the Jungles of the Rio del Pescador, & the Environs of the Vermillion Sea."[77] They drove down to San Luis, on the international border, where they made the acquaintance of several local officials. "It being agreed that we were harmless hunters, and not the conspirators of a new revolution, we all repaired to the saloon and had some real beer." There the gentlemen-adventurers heard tales of the terrible tidal bore, the crashing wave that came in off the gulf during flood tide. Their host, Alexandre Sortillon, and his friend, Major Gomez, predicted certain destruction of the frail canoe and its inhabitants. With visions of roaring waters on their minds, the brothers went to sleep on the floor of Sortillon's restaurante.

They decided to start their trip by camping and hunting deer on the upper delta. Within a day they had received their "first lesson in arrow-weed thickets." They would have many more. The cachinilla, "a tall spear-like shrub," grew in dense impenetrable groves throughout the delta.[78] They also got a glimpse of the impressive breadth of the verdant basin by climbing a hill from which "we could see the whole delta and even the mirage-like mud flats of Santa Clara. A howling wilderness is the only name for it." For a week they accustomed themselves to the country, taking no deer, but subsisting on the abundant ducks and quail, and on Aldo's speciality, sourdough bread.

Gradually, the country took ahold of them. At one point, Aldo and

Carl looked above to see "a huge 'chimney' of cranes wheeling high in the sky over the punta. When they got the glint of the sun, they showed *pure white* and looked like a huge skyrocket bursting into white sparks. . . . like great draped strings of pearls against the blue. At no time did they utter a sound." They heard geese everywhere, but it was impossible to see them, or to get a shot at one. (Carl remarked that their to-do sounded like a girl getting home from college.)

Sortillon met them after a week. They were anxious to get to the geese, and Sortillon took them to the head of the delta. "The tide was in," Leopold wrote. "It did look bad for canoe work. They say sharks come up this far." But they were resolved to put their canoe to water, and to explore the brackish sloughs. They backtracked some and then embarked on the Rillito.

There followed ten days of immersion into the delta wilds. No distinct route guided them. There was no telling, in the confusion of waters, which river was which. Every lagoon and backwater possessed what seemed like absolute calm: glassy surfaces over green-tinted pools. Travel, however, was by no means easy. Beaver dams forced portages. Cachinilla forced *very careful* portages. "I used to talk pretty brave," Leopold wrote, "about wiggling through the Labyrinth of the Colorado, of which this is probably the head. But we learned something on the Rillito."

Gliding their canoe over the green lagoons, Aldo and Carl noted, above all, the unexpected abundance of the fertile delta. While walking through stretches of leguminous brush, Aldo was surprised to find that "one can gather quite a lot of beans by simply holding the hands cupped and letting them rain in from overhead."[79] The mesquite and tornillo were heavy with pods. On the mud flats grew an annual grass, the "grain-like seeds of which could be scooped up by the cupful." Calabasilla, a wild melon, flourished in great patches on the flats.[80] Doves and quail feasted on the bounty; Aldo and Carl feasted on the doves and quail. Water birds shared the lagoons: cormorants, avocets, herons, willets, yellowlegs, pelicans, teal, widgeon, mallard, and the elusive geese. Clouds of white egrets alighted on the green willows. Hawks and owls and coyotes and buzzards lurked overhead and underbrush. Still on the lookout for varmints, Aldo and Carl killed and skinned a coyote and a bobcat. They sensed, too, the presence of the jaguar; el Tigre filled their thoughts and their campfire talk, but not their gunsights. And circling overhead, splayed out in an aerial array, the distant sandhill cranes were pearls in the sky. Leopold wrote, from a perspective of two decades, that, "we all reveled in a common abundance and in each other's well-being. I cannot recall feeling, in settled country, a like sensitivity to the mood of the land."[81]

On November 14, their trip came to an end. Hidalgo, an old rancher, had agreed to bring them back to San Luis. They climbed out through the cachinilla and reached his ranch by noon. In his journal, Leopold recalled the luncheon they enjoyed with Hidalgo:

The wind blew gusts of sand through the wattled walls of his dining hall as we ate tamales and drank coffee. The pet pig, Flick, 2 dogs, 5 children, and a black mare stood guard by the door, watchful for the crumbs of the master's table, and sortied into the hall when the crumbs failed to materialize. A little white-toothed, dusky-faced boy haunted Flick's side trying to feed him watermelon, and repeating over and over again some kind of assurance that sandias were fine food for dogs. A little sick girl, wrapped in a shabby overcoat, sat in a dim corner and watched us with great soft eyes. And all the while our host poured coffee and recounted with gusto and large gesture brave tales of the days when he was a free-lance vaquero seeking fortune and adventure on the Arizona frontier. Of adventure he found great store, of fortune many a fair beginning. Meanwhile the wind blew gusts of sand, the little boy chanted to Flick of watermelons, and the little girl looked with great eyes upon us. Finally the coffee pot went dry, and we started.[82]

〜

Three weeks later, Leopold attended the annual meeting of the New Mexico Association for Science. There he presented his most forceful analysis yet of the soil erosion situation in the Southwest. He entitled his address, delivered on December 4, 1922, "Erosion as a Menace to the Social and Economic Future of the Southwest."[83]

Leopold restated his proof. He now tallied thirty creeks in his experience, twenty-one of which were eroding away their banks at an accelerated rate. "The proof," he said, "is manifest to anyone who will ride the country, especially the mountain districts, with his eyes open." Not everyone had the opportunity, the inclination, or the eyes to do so. Leopold had the responsibility to do so. The canyons and arroyos of his travels, from the Tajique to Walnut Creek, from the Tusas to the Blue, told him the story of recent human habitation. Where modern human influence was absent, erosion was normal; where it was moderate, erosion was unavoidable; where it was heaviest, erosion was economically and ecologically unacceptable. "It is not an act of God," he stated, "but the direct result of our own mis-use of the country we are trying to improve."[84]

Leopold's discussion of the causes, results, and remedies for erosion was much fuller than his earlier attempts, reflecting the expansion of his historical and environmental knowledge. The more arid the climate, he summarized, the less resistant the land-base was to abuse. In the Southwest, as in the Holy Land, the soils, the forests, the range forage, the wildlife all were more fragile than in wetter regions. Echoing John Wesley Powell, Leopold emphasized that water was the key to understanding, and to wise inhabitation of, the Southwest. "The total possible acreage of tillable, irrigable land, the total possible acre-feet of accessible water, and the total storage capacity of dam sites set the limit for the total future development of decent homes in the Southwest. . . . We are dealing with the question of whether we are here to 'skin' the Southwest and then get out, or whether we are here to found a permanent civilized community with room to grow and improve."[85]

Under his discussion of remedies, Leopold reiterated the various steps that land users could take: maintain grass cover on the watersheds, especially on the watercourses; try to keep and restore the willows along the streambanks; use inexpensive artificial works to clog channels; work with other landowners on a unified plan. He added a condemnation of the rampant overgrazing of the unreserved public domain, beyond the jurisdiction of the Forest Service. He added something else: a belief and a prediction that "the day will come when the ownership of land will carry with it the obligation to use and protect it from erosion so that it is not a menace to other landowners and the public. . . . The privilege of grazing use carries with it the obligation to correct and offset its effects by artificial works as well as the obligation to minimize and control those effects by more skillful and conservative methods."[86] With that, Leopold signalled an expansion in his conservation philosophy: a conservation ethic was not just of concern to sportsmen in pursuit of their quarry, but to landowners and landusers in general. This was a new idea for Leopold, one he would continue to explore for the remainder of his life.

During his address, Leopold turned once again to the bitter history of the Blue River as an example of the wrong way to develop the Southwest:

We the community have "developed" Blue River by overgrazing the range, washing out half-a-million in land, taking the profits out of the livestock industry, cutting the ranch homes by two-thirds, destroying conditions necessary for keeping families in the other third, leaving the timber without an outlet to the place where it is needed, and now we are spending half-a-million to build a road around this place of desolation we have created. And to replace this smiling valley which nature gave us free, we are spending half-a-million to reclaim an equal acreage of desert in some place where we do not need it nearly as badly nor can use it nearly so well. This, fellow citizens, is Nordic genius for reducing to possession the wilderness.[87]

11

Pioneers and Gullies
(1923–1924)

EOPOLD turned thirty-six in January 1923. His sandy hair had thinned a little, and he had begun to wear spectacles. He remained slender and solid in frame, and the lines coming to his face made his already sharp features seem only more severely defined.

Estella was thirty-two, in good health, lively and cordial in character. Her appearance was classically Spanish: jet-black hair, high cheek bones, dark eyes, smooth bronze skin. She followed Spanish tradition, too, in her role as mother and wife, keeping their home running smoothly so as to keep Aldo free of distractions. She remained Aldo's most trusted critic and sounding board, primarily responsible for the singular advances he was making during these crucial years of his life.

Starker, Luna, Nina, and Carl now ranged in age from nine to three. The genetic dice had endowed them with distinctive variations on the Latin and Germanic themes. Aldo was not the sort of father to wrestle around on the floor with the children, but he was continually with them in the workshop or the garden, or leading them on picnics and hunting and fishing expeditions. Even during the busiest times of his later years, he was careful to keep sacrosanct the family's time together on weekends and holidays.

In his professional life, Leopold was a responsible maverick. His ideas on erosion, wilderness, outdoor values, administration, leisure, wildlife, and economics were all beyond the scope of forestry as then generally practiced. A more reflective man now, he was no less willing to take an independent stand, but able to do so with a greater sense of his own authority. His work as chief of operations had sharpened his thinking and his reasoning abilities. He had always displayed an innate sense of curiosity; now he was acquiring the methods and discipline to translate that curiosity into knowledge. Three years of observing and evaluating forest personnel had also made him a keen judge of human character, and he was no longer too proud to turn that critical eye back on himself.

For the D-3 operations staff, winter was a time of plans, meetings, and conferences. The nation's six district foresters and their assistants gathered for their annual meeting in March 1923, at Ogden, Utah. There Leopold reported to the Forest Service hierarchy on his game work and pushed his proposition for wilderness protection. The latter apparently did not go over well. On March 9, Aldo wrote to his wife:

Stella Dearest,

A rather noteworthy day. I felt pretty blue this afternoon, because I'm pretty sure to be voted down on my Wilderness Policy—although everybody commended my speech. But I guess I must stick to my crazy ideas in spite of turn downs. I'll put it thru yet.

This evening we were given a banquet by the Chamber of Commerce and I did a mean trick—slipped out after they had darkened the room for some moving pictures. You know I get that hankering to be alone—and I haven't been alone since I left you—which you know is the same thing.

Well, I strayed into a movie, and that is the reason for this day being noteworthy. Maybe you'll enjoy the joke with me—for it really is a joke—to know that my heart is still pounding like a 21-year-old. In short, I saw a perfectly beautiful creature—which must be after all the most wonderful thing in creation, because as you know I get thrills out of everything in creation from ducks to cabbages and books to dogs.

It is a mercy—a great one—that wonders are not denied even to an old wheelhorse like me who has to use specs and twenty 'leven kinds of gargles to keep from falling to pieces, and it's probably also a mercy that some of this kind are better seen than possessed, but others like you are better both.

Don't laugh too much at your old but young husband, sweetheart. I wish I were with you, but since I can't be it's good to write. I wonder if I ever forget to be thankful that I may always either have you or write to you. But I don't forget to be thankful that you love me in spite of the gargles and specs.

Always,
Your Aldo[1]

༄

Leopold's special interest in erosion, far from narrowing his focus, had proven to be a pathway to a broadened outlook on the southwestern environment. He had progressed through a series of discrete steps. He began by observing conditions on the ground, which led him to question the official policy of range control as a sufficient solution to the problem, and to advocate artificial control works. The further he explored the complexities of landscape change, the more he realized that simple interpretations and patchwork policies would not suffice to manage the resources at hand.

One could not deal adequately with soil erosion without also taking into account geology, plant ecology, forestry, range management, fire policy, history, and economics.

Leopold took a further step in the early months of 1923, when he prepared a draft of an article he called "Some Fundamentals of Conservation in the Southwest." Here he made an abrupt leap, and dealt not with erosion per se, but with erosion as a symptom of an overall conservation problem. It was Leopold's most ambitious attempt yet to integrate what he had seen and learned with what he believed.

He opened with a survey of the Southwest's resource base, grimly concluding that "the deterioration of our fundamental resources—land and water—is in the nature of permanent destruction, and the process is cumulative and gaining momentum every year." What was the cause of this deterioration? Was erosion an act of God, over which man had no control? Was it simply a geological process, in which case, again, man had little say? It was the old question of normal vs. abnormal erosion, the key to which was climatic change. Two years had not offered much new insight on the issue. The scant evidence of the day, based on tree ring measurements, archaeological relics, and shifts in vegetation types, gave no clear indication of climatic change over the last three thousand years. The tree rings did suggest, however, a fairly regular eleven-year drought cycle, and, in Leopold's words, "the eleven-year wave is the one that swamps the boats." Range management had not adapted to this cycle. Instead of stocking the ranges only to their drought-time capacity, or arranging to move or feed stock when drought came, stockmen tended to fill the ranges to normal or maximum capacity, "and when drought comes the stock eat up the range, ruin the watershed, ruin the stockman, wreck the banks, get credits from the treasury of the United States, and then die. And the silt of their dying moves on down into our reservoirs to some day dry up the irrigated valleys—the only live thing left!" In sum, Leopold wrote,

Our organic resources are not only in a run-down condition, but in our climate bear a delicately balanced interrelation to each other. Any upsetting of this balance causes a progressive deterioration that may not only be felt hundreds of miles away, but may continue after the original disturbance is removed and affect populations and resources wholly unconnected with the original cause. Erosion eats into our hills like a contagion, and floods bring down the loosened soil upon our valleys like a scourge. Water, soil, animals, and plants—the very fabric of prosperity—react to destroy each other and us. Science can and must unravel those reactions, and government must enforce the findings of science. This is the economic bearing of conservation on the future of the Southwest.[2]

The responsibility for accelerated deterioration, then, lay not with God or nature, but with people. Leopold was leading up to a discussion of the philosophical issues that conservation raised. "In my opinion," he wrote, "one can not round out a real understanding of the situation in the Southwest without likewise considering its moral aspects."[3] Under the heading "Conservation as a Moral Issue," Leopold ventured his most extensive ideas yet on the ethical bond between mankind and the earth.

Philosophy, Leopold suggested, offered two reasons why mankind could not ruin the earth with impunity. The first of these was based on the notion that the earth itself, far from being inanimate, possessed "a certain kind and degree of life, which we intuitively respect as such." Were we able to see the earth as a whole, he continued, and to view the whole over a great length of time, we might recognize it as a living thing, endowed with coordinated functions not unlike our own life processes. As humans, we are not physically able to see the earth in this manner, but we are nonetheless able to sense it:

Possibly, in our intuitive perceptions, which may be truer than our science and less impeded by words than our philosophies, we realize the indivisibility of the earth—its soil, mountains, rivers, forests, climate, plants, and animals, and respect it collectively not only as a useful servant but as a living being, vastly less alive than ourselves in degree, but vastly greater than ourselves in time and space—a being that was old when the morning stars sang together, and when the last of us has been gathered unto his fathers, will still be young.[4]

This intuitive sense of a living earth had always been a part of Leopold's psyche. Over the years he had found support for it in the words of many poets, naturalists, and philosophers: the Bible, Emerson, Thoreau, Bergson, Whitman, Muir, Burroughs, Bailey. The strongest influence on him during this period was the Russian philosopher-mystic, Piotr Ouspensky. Ouspensky's *Tertium Organum* had been translated into English in 1920, and made something of a splash in American philosophical circles. Leopold had read it by 1922. He did not adopt Ouspensky's philosophy outright—he did not adopt anyone's philosophy outright—but he did recognize elements in it relevant to the conditions he was observing on the ground.

In *Tertium Organum*, Ouspensky tried to reconcile Western science with Eastern mysticism. He professed that all matter, regardless of its level of organization, was alive with consciousness, and only "our limited power of communion" makes it appear lifeless. Ouspensky's words no doubt struck a responsive chord in Leopold: "Sometimes we vaguely feel an intense *life* manifesting in the phenomena of nature. . . . There are days brimming with the marvelous and the mystic, days having each its own individual and unique consciousness, its own emotions, its own thoughts. One may almost commune with these days. And they will tell you that they live a long, long time, perhaps eternally, and that they have known and seen many, many things. . . . There can be nothing dead or mechanical in nature. If in general life and feeling exist, they must exist in all."[5] Ouspensky's animism challenged Newtonian mechanics and the Cartesian view of nature; it accepted the latest advances in physics and evolutionary biology as further proof of the indivisibility of the cosmos — and indivisibility was the essential attribute of life. "In organic nature where we see life it is easier to assume the existence of a psyche. But life belongs not alone to separate, individual organisms — anything indivisible is a living being."[6]

Leopold recognized the discrepancy between this intuitive, organismic view of a living earth and the mechanistic view of a "dead" earth that the sciences generally provided. He regarded the discrepancy as a linguistic one, "the very words 'living things' having an inherited and arbitrary meaning derived not from reality, but from human perceptions of human affairs. But we must use them, for better or worse." With characteristic practicality, he suggested that "the essential thing for present purposes is that both [views] admit the interdependent functions of the elements."[7]

Leopold also recognized that this mystical notion of communion with the earth might not appeal to everyone as a sound reason to practice conservation: "Possibly, to most men of affairs, this reason is too intangible to either accept or reject as a guide to human conduct. But philosophy offers another and more easily debatable question: was the earth made for man's use, or has man merely the privilege of temporarily possessing an earth made for other and inscrutable purposes?"[8] Most religions, and most science, presupposed the former: the earth existed for the benefit of man, who was the end and purpose of creation. Leopold chose not to argue the point. "It just occurs to me, however, in answer to the scientists, that God started his show a good many million years before he had any men for [an] audience — a sad waste of both actors and music — and in answer to both, that it is just barely possible that God himself likes to hear birds sing and see flowers grow." Even granting the primacy of our species on the earth, Leopold pointed out that other human cultures had flourished in the Southwest prior to our occupation, and had done so without inflicting massive damage on the earth. Leopold ended by asking,

if there be, indeed, a special nobility inherent in the human race — a special cosmic value, distinctive from and superior to all other life — by what token shall it be manifest? By a society decently respectful of its own and all other life, capable of inhabiting the earth without defiling it? Or by a society like that of John Burroughs' potato bug, which exterminated the potato, and thereby exterminated itself? As one or the other shall we be judged in "the derisive silence of eternity."[9]

Leopold never published "Some Fundamentals of Conservation in the Southwest." He did pass the draft around for comments. Frank Waugh praised it and encouraged Leopold to continue working on it. Others were more critical. Morton Cheney, Leopold's colleague in the D-3 Lands office, argued that standard geological interpretation sufficed to explain what was happening in the Southwest, and that the effects of erosion were simply more noticeable now that settlement had taken place. Leopold's philosophical presentation may have drawn similar criticisms.[10] In any event, he would avoid the deep waters of philosophy for some time after this. Turning his attentions back to the southwestern land, he would continue to denounce "economic determinism" as a guide to forest management, but he would not return for another ten years to the question of humanity's moral responsibility for the well-being of the earth.

∽

Leopold returned to the mountain trails in April 1923, on inspection in the Manzano Forest with Evan Kelley. Leopold's innovations had by now drawn service-wide attention. Roy Headley in Washington received a copy of Leopold's 1922 Prescott report, and neglected a morning's work in order to read it. "I regret the dissipation of the morning's time," Headley wrote to Pooler, "but feel that I have gotten my time's worth . . . in the suggestions and inspiration I have gained. . . . We are, of course, revising our inspection outlines and methods in preparation for the coming season's work and I shall not only be influenced by what District 3 and Leopold have developed—I shall copy quite shamelessly a number of the methods Aldo used."[11]

Leopold went from the Manzano to the Santa Fe. In August, he conducted his first inspection of the Tonto National Forest in central Arizona. The Tonto, exhibiting all the changes and pressures that had been brought to bear on the southwestern forests, presented Leopold with the opportunity to pull his ideas together. The Tonto was similar to the Prescott in that it was a "watershed forest." Lower in elevation than the belt of yellow pine, and higher than the Sonoran Desert, most of the Tonto wore the same extensive cover of brush and hardwoods as the Prescott. The fire hazard was the same. Tonto Creek drained much of the forest, emptying into the Salt River at the Roosevelt Dam (which was within the forest). The Tonto range was badly damaged. A 1914 inspection had shown fifty thousand head of cattle on the Tonto, far more than it could handle. The district decided to reduce the burden. Then the war came and, in John Kerr's words, "[we] reduced all the way up to 82,000 head!"[12] In the worst years following the war, some ranchers lost as much as half their stock to starvation. The Forest Service finally had to demand reductions. One rancher near Pine decided that his cattle and horses were too weak to sell or drive. He had to shoot those animals he was obligated to remove. "It makes you get down and think," the local ranger recalled, "when a man is willing to see that done."[13]

Leopold's inspection of the Tonto was a model of ecological inquiry. He spent several days at the Roosevelt Dam, making extensive notes, taking down available figures on acre feet, siltation rates, and storage capacities, in order to work these in with his knowledge of conditions on the watershed. From local sources he was able to compile a history of grazing and vegetation change over the previous forty years. By carefully examining, dating, and correlating fire scars on old junipers—Leopold was among the first to use this technique—he was able to determine with some accuracy the fire history of the forest. He saw the same vegetation trends he had noted on the Prescott the year before: dense oak brush blanketed the mesas where once a cow could be seen from three miles away; grass was absent from all but the most cattle-proof recesses of rock; young brush and yellow pine crowded out the old fire-dependent manzanitas; vegetation types were "moving downhill," yellow pine encroaching on what was once oak-juniper woodland, oak and juniper encroaching on what was once open grassland. Range erosion was "bad but not much worse than the average Forest. I incline to think not much Tonto silt is as yet in [Roosevelt] Lake. But a stupendous acreage is *on the way.*"[14]

Much would come of the Tonto inspection. In the months to follow Leopold would revise and refine the theory he had formulated on the Prescott. For the time being, he stated unequivocally the problem for administrative policy: after forty years of Anglo settlement and twenty years of federal stewardship, "the timber resource on the Tonto has undergone a vast improvement, while watershed and range values have undergone a vast deterioration."[15]

The Tonto made one point clear. Fire played a greater role in maintaining presettlement patterns of vegetation than even the Prescott had suggested. Fire as a primary factor could no longer be avoided. Leopold, like all foresters, had been conditioned to a simple response: fire was evil. Fires were to forests what wolves were to game and livestock—natural agents of destruction that had to be eliminated at all costs. To those timber and railroad interests that advocated "light-burning" techniques akin to the traditional practices of the Indians, Leopold replied, in 1920, "this proviso is the very negation of the fundamental principle of forestry, namely, to make forests productive not only of a vegetation cover to clothe and protect our mountains, but also of the greatest possible amount of lumber, forage, and other forest products."[16] By 1923, Leopold still regarded fire as "the scourge of all living things," but admitted that forest fires sometimes caused an increase in vegetation beneficial to game. "For this exception to an otherwise black record," Leopold allowed, "let the fire devil have his due."[17] Forestry practices, he hastened to add, could bring about the same end without the attendant destruction. Conditions on the Prescott and the Tonto were forcing Leopold to amend his thinking. In his Tonto report, Leopold went so far as to say, "there is no evidence that even the severe fires of pre-settlement days destroyed the equilibrium of the watershed. . . . The Tonto bears out my observation on the Prescott: that there is a lot to be learned about the behavior of brush fires."[18] Beyond that, Leopold would not venture. He was willing to accept the increased risk of fire for the sake of the watershed, but not to admit its possible role as a management tool. Nevertheless, in recognizing the important role of fire in the semidesert woodland ecosystem, he had surmounted a major obstacle in his effort to understand how that system functioned.

❧

Hunting took on new relevance in the Leopold family when, a few weeks before this tenth birthday, Starker received his first 20 gauge shotgun. His father took him out to Alameda, north of town, for a dove hunt. They bagged twelve birds.[19]

Waterfowl season opened in October. On one hunt, with Fred Winn and Luna, Aldo lost one of his veteran live mallard decoys. "A greenhorn sneaked up behind Fred Winn's haystack and potted my old hen. Offered to pay but I told him that hen was not a matter of money. Wanted me to take the carcass but I told him I would as soon eat my dog. Starker cried when I told him about the old bird being no more."[20]

During another hunt with Starker and Luna at Tomé, Jamie Jamison came by in the afternoon, carrying two geese he had bagged with a single shot. "Jamie wasn't speaking of ducks," Aldo wrote in his journal. "He was expanded into the fourth dimension."[21] The reference in his quip was to a basic postulate of Ouspenskian philosophy. Those fortunate souls who made it to the fourth dimension, via goose-hunting or other means, could expect to experience, according to Ouspensky, "a new concept of time. . . . Flashes of cosmic consciousness. The idea and sensation of a living universe. A striving toward the wondrous. Sensation of infinity. . . . Possibility of personal immortality." Aldo had to content himself that day with eleven ducks and three dimensions.

Deer season opened on November 20. Aldo and Estella turned the children over to relatives and joined Jamie and his wife on a pack trip into the interior of the Gila. They rode up Black Canyon and pitched camp on Diamond Creek, within the area that had been proposed for wilderness designation. For Leopold, this was not only a vacation, but an opportunity to see the NMGPA game policies in action. Throughout the Mogollon–Black Canyon area, the NMGPA was trying an experiment. Several of the new state game refuges had been situated there, and now the integrity of those refuges had to be established. The GPAs of Silver City, Deming, Magdalena, and Mogollon, in cooperation with the Forest Service, the Biological Survey, the State Game Department, and local cattlemen, put twenty wardens on the Gila Forest to monitor the hunt and to ply the hunters with talk about the need for law enforcement and inviolate refuges.

The Leopold-Jamison party saw plenty of does at first, but only a few fleet bucks. On the second day of the season, Aldo had a point blank shot at a spike buck, but passed it up. On the fourth day, he and Ramon, a visiting friend, spotted a large herd above camp and were eyeing them with binoculars "when three horseback hunters from Black Canyon came along shouting and shooting and scared out 8 bucks and a whole herd of does." On the fifth day Aldo saw two bucks. The first vanished behind a Douglas fir. The second was in heavy brush, and Aldo's two shots missed. Aldo was returning to camp about sundown when he came up over a pine mesa. "I suddenly saw a big [white-tailed] deer standing broadside to me by an oak tree. Couldn't see any horns but put the glasses on him and immediately saw he had very good ones. (He was directly against the sun and hard to make out.) Dropped to my knees and found both an oak limb and the grasstops in my way but there was no time to be lost so I let fly. He didn't move—I must have shot over. I again fired quickly and this time he went down, while the other deer nearby (I never looked to see what they were) jumped away."[22] The eight-point buck scaled just over two hundred pounds. It was the second deer that Leopold had killed, the first being the blacktail that fed the 1909 reconnaissance crew.

The party continued to see an abundance of does, fawns, and yearlings, but few bucks. Snows fell in the highcountry and made tracking possible, but no other shots were fired. The Leopolds and Jamisons packed out at season's end after a wholly memorable hunt. The number of deer seen was encouraging from a management standpoint. Doe killing was reduced, and hunters abided by the refuge boundaries. Moreover, the wardens were able to gather some sorely needed statistics on the deer herd. The final tally showed that 450 bucks were killed, but the refuges had apparently worked as hoped, providing refuge for the bucks and an overflow for the hunters. On one refuge, the cowman-warden counted forty-eight bucks in just a few hours.

Aldo, Estella, Starker, and Luna celebrated New Year's Day with a goose hunt on the Rio Grande near Los Lunas. Aldo bagged four ducks for dinner, but no geese. On their way home, they met a friend who was looking for promising hunting grounds. Aldo lent him his decoys and directed him to his blind. Later in the evening, the friend showed up at the house with Aldo's decoys and two great swans he had mistaken for snow geese. Guilt-filled, he asked Aldo for advice. Aldo advised him to see the game warden and to turn the skins over to Stokely Ligon for preservation. Before he left, though, Aldo carefully examined and measured the two swans. In his journal he wrote, "They were the hugest fowl I have ever laid hands on."[23]

༄

In the late months of 1923 and early months of 1924, Leopold produced three statements that, taken together, summarized his recent concerns.

In December, Leopold completed a *Watershed Handbook* in which he assembled all his previous work on the erosion problem in D-3. The purpose of the handbook was to teach field personnel how to diagnose and respond to watershed problems. In this sense, it was the culmination, not only of his erosion research, but of his concern for "standards of conservation" and "natural skill" in forest administration.[24]

The handbook revealed how far Leopold had come since taking on his "new hobby." In 1920, he had criticized the range control policy of the Forest Service as an inadequate response to erosion problems, and emphasized instead the need for artificial means of control. By the end of 1923 he had come full circle, stating that the use of artificial techniques "must not be allowed to obscure the fundamental fact that they are merely supplementary to conservation of vegetative cover through proper forest and range management."[25] Leopold had arrived back where he began, but with a deeper knowledge of the landscape and a far different standard of conservation. The Forest Service had held that more livestock could be kept on a given range as long as there was forage enough to feed them and as long as heavy grazing helped to reduce the fire hazard. Leopold, with the experience of the Prescott and Tonto behind him, considered those criteria not only inadequate, but downright dangerous in the case of the Arizona brushfields. He held that the number of livestock permitted ought to be determined by the overall condition of the watershed itself. It was the difference between managing cattle and managing the forest and range as a whole. And, to a large degree, that was the difference between Progressive Era conservation and a conservation movement that now had to deal increasingly with the complex nature of the resources themselves.

As Leopold was compiling the *Watershed Handbook,* he was also preparing an address that he called "A Criticism of the Booster Spirit." Delivered before the Ten Dons Club of Albuquerque, the address was a direct broadside against what Leopold regarded as an "unholy wedlock between the moral principle of loyalty and the technique of billboard advertising."[26] It seems Leopold had been reading Sinclair Lewis' *Babbitt;* "Babbittian" would long remain one of his favorite adjectives. Leopold knew the boosters of Albuquerque. He had worked with them. He had been one himself when he worked at the Chamber of Commerce. But he had lost patience with the materialism that now seemed to dominate civic life in Albuquerque. He deplored the booster aversion to self-criticism, the blind addiction to quantitative measures of growth, the narrow-minded fear of nonconformity. He had no end of examples to cite:

Just now the boosters are lashing the latent patriotism of the Nation to build by public subscription a huge memorial sanatorium to the War Mothers of America — in Albuquerque. The sweep and daring of this idea is as splendid as its avowed motive is sordid and miserable. Would you want the Marble Manufacturer to conceive the splendid idea of passing the hat among your friends, in order that he might build, for cost plus ten per cent, a monument to *your* mother? What is the difference? Will this splendid monstrous scheme find favor where stand the crosses, row on row, in Flanders Field? But, say the boosters, while the scheme is selfish for Albuquerque, it will give expression to unselfish and lofty motives throughout the Nation. Indeed! Was the Statue of Liberty thus conceived? Did the Westminster Chamber of Commerce boost the Abbey? And why not charge a fee of admission for the battleground at Gettysburg?

One boosting editor had advocated the preservation of the Pueblo Indian communes because they drew tourists and thus added to the wealth of New Mexico. Leopold regarded this cynical reasoning as "the ultimate impertinence of boosterism in the Southwest. . . . [It] betrays a fundamental disrespect for the Creator, who made not only boosters, but mankind, in his image."[27]

Leopold naturally lamented the booster's "unintelligent and irresponsible" attitude toward natural resources: "Growing away from the soil has spiritual as well as economic consequences which sometimes lead one to doubt whether the booster's one hundred percent Americanism attaches itself to the country, or only to the living which we by hook or by crook extract from it. . . . A hundred percenter in making the flag fly and the eagle scream, he is awkward in self-government. Worshipping commerce, he is slow to regulate its own abuses."[28]

Still, Leopold was willing to give even this devil his due. "Sincerity," he reminded his listeners, "is never ludicrous."[29] He admired the spirit and energy of the boosters, if not the ends to which they were applied. He concluded with a wish that their enthusiasm might be put to nobler purposes: "Is it too much to hope that this force, harnessed to a finer ideal, may some day accomplish good as well as big things? That our future standard of civic values may even exclude quantity obtained at the expense of quality, as not worthwhile? When this is accomplished [we shall] vindicate the truth that 'the virtue of a living democracy consists not in its ability to avoid mistakes, but in its ability to profit by them.'"[30]

Having previously expressed doubts about Judeo-Christian orthodoxy and Western civilization's approach to the natural world, Leopold was now on record against rampant commercialism as well. His fondness for Lewis' *Babbitt* was no anomaly. In an oddly parallel fashion, the maverick forester was doing what his sophisticated urban contemporaries were doing in their literary circles: challenging the status quo, questioning cultural myths, penetrating the veneer of postwar prosperity. But it would be stretching a point to group Leopold with the expatriates and the literati. His concerns grew from very different roots, and bore very different fruits. In the cafes of Europe a lost generation escaped the American myth. In the mountains of New Mexico, Leopold endeavored to understand what that myth had wrought on the land.

In the early months of 1924, Leopold prepared his most comprehensive interpretation yet of the southwestern environment. The previous summer's tour of the Tonto provided him with enough new evidence to publish what he had thus far advanced only in his inspection reports. In "Grass, Brush, Timber, and Fire in Southern Arizona," which appeared later that year in the *Journal of Forestry,* he neatly summarized his theory:

Previous to the settlement of the country, fires started by lightning and Indians kept the brush thin, kept the juniper and other woodland species decimated, and gave the grass the upper hand with respect to possession of the soil. In spite of the periodic fires, the grass prevented erosion. Then came the settlers with their great herds of livestock. These ranges had never been grazed, and they grazed them to death, thus removing the grass and automatically checking the possibility of widespread fires. The removal of the grass relieved the brush species of root competition and of fire damage and thereby caused them to spread and "take the country." The removal of grass-root competition and of fire damage brought in the reproduction.[31]

Five circumstances supported the theory: the behavior of "fire species" like manzanita and piñon pine; the downhill movement of vegetation types; the existence of the grassy parks, attributable only to fire, in the mountain forests; historical evidence that the original grass cover was indeed thick enough to transmit fires; and the occurrence of fire scars on widely scattered old junipers. The theory, in short, was hinged on a significant role for fire in the evolution of the forests.

In regard to erosion, Leopold's hypothesis implied that "at least in this region, grass is a much more effective conserver of watersheds than foresters were at first willing to admit." In regard to forestry, it implied three things:

First, 15 years of Forest administration were based on an incorrect interpretation of ecological facts and were, therefore, in part misdirected. Second, this error of interpretation has now been recognized and administrative policy corrected accordingly. Third, while there can be no doubt about the enormous value of European traditions to American forestry, this error illustrates that there can also be no doubt about the great danger of European traditions uncritically accepted and applied, especially in such complex fields as erosion.[32]

This Emersonian call to free American forestry from its European roots was fundamental to Leopold's expanding philosophy. What had worked in Germany, in France, at the Yale Forest School, and even in other Forest Service districts, was not entirely appropriate to the arid Southwest. The challenge to forestry, as Leopold saw it, was "to conserve the benefit to timber and minimize the damage to watershed and range in so far as technical skill and good administration can do it. Wholesale exclusion of grazing is neither skill nor administration, and should be used only as a last resort. . . . We are dealing right now with a fraction of a cycle involving centuries. We can not obstruct or reverse the cycle, but we can bend it; in what degree remains to be seen."[33]

"Grass, Brush, Fire and Timber in Southern Arizona" was a notably early demonstration of ecological reasoning in Leopold's work and in the literature of forestry. By careful consideration of the climate, geology, topography, soils, plants, animals, people, and history of the Southwest, Leopold had pieced together the story of the brushfields. His synthesis was remarkable for its time, but not yet complete. The jury had not yet gathered, much less reached a decision, on the question of long-term climatic change; more information was needed on the fire history of the area; and Leopold was unaware of the full impact of the fires set by Apache Indians during their 300-odd years of occupation. Despite these gaps, the essay remains a solid accomplishment in terms both of science and of Leopold's life.[34] The effort that went into it, the striving for objectivity and comprehension, was every bit as important as the original speculations that came out of it.

In all of these works—the *Watershed Handbook,* "A Criticism of the Booster Spirit," and "Grass, Brush, Fire and Timber in Southern Arizona" —Leopold discussed in detail the ideas, stripped of the philosophical extras, that he had implied in "Some Fundamentals of Conservation in the Southwest." These later expressions, full, buoyant, and precise, actually gave better, if less lofty, expression to his evolving ideas about conservation and the quality of life.

∽

In March 1924, the New Mexico Game Protective Association gathered for its eighth annual convention in Albuquerque. The NMGPA had made stupendous progress since its organizational meeting in 1916. Sixteen local GPAs now represented a combined membership of some sixteen hundred sportsmen. Violators of hunting laws now faced more than just a wink and a smile from the judge. The New Mexico Department of Game and Fish had been reorganized and largely removed from politics, at least in theory. The state had a system of demonstrably effective game refuges;

most were located in the more receptive southwestern part of the state, but the NMGPA was pushing for an extension of the system to the northern and eastern counties as well. And in 1924, by Ligon's estimation, there were only twelve wolves remaining in the state, most of these stragglers from Mexico, none of them east of the Rio Grande. In other respects, the NMGPA still had a fight on its hands. The struggle to secure a federal refuge system had made little progress. The State Game Warden still served at the governor's discretion, even after eight years of concerted efforts to change the law (a 1925 amendment would finally grant the power to appoint and remove the state warden to the Game and Fish Commission). The 1924 convention passed resolutions reiterating their positions on these issues.

Due to a shortage of time and funds, no *Pine Cone* had rolled off the presses since December 1920. After the 1924 convention, Leopold published an eighteenth issue. He reported the convention's unanimous vote in favor of retaining the Gila headwaters as a "Wilderness Hunting Ground," the first public report of the proposal. Leopold wrote, "New Mexico is justly proud of its vast outdoors. Surely we can afford to dedicate one little corner of it to maintaining the physical and spiritual welfare of those who retain the instincts of the wilderness hunter, and are better citizens by reason of that fact."[35] The *Silver City Enterprise* reprinted Leopold's article, and predicted that the proposal would "meet with the approval of sportsmen in this part of the country. No doubt it will [also] meet with opposition."[36] Progress on the wilderness initiative had been slow. Leopold's 1922 report had been misplaced in the office files. Other work took priority. Finally, in March 1924, Leopold and Morton Cheney completed a Recreational Working Plan for the Gila Forest which, if approved, would establish a wilderness area of 755,000 acres. John D. Jones, Chief of Lands, and Ray Marsh, now Chief of Forest Management in D-3 and no great fan of the wilderness idea, prepared a short statement of limitations the Forest Service would observe on the Gila. All the plan needed now was the endorsement of Frank Pooler.[37]

Besides convention news, Leopold's latest *Pine Cone* also contained a report from the NMGPA's Quail Committee, which consisted of Leopold, Jamison, and R. Fred Pettit, an Albuquerque dentist who was a long-time hunting partner and GPA member. The report outlined a twelve-point program of "detailed steps toward quail production." It was Leopold's earliest attempt to formulate a management plan for a specific wildlife species. The plan may have been connected to yet another of his many projects. Since late 1922, he had been planning to gather into a book his voluminous notes on wild game in the Southwest. He tentatively titled the book "Southwestern Game Fields" and enlisted Pettit and Stokely Ligon as co-authors.

That issue of *The Pine Cone* also included brief biographical sketches of the new and retiring officers of the NMGPA. Leopold did not mention himself, but before the issue went to press his fellow sportsmen inserted a word of appreciation "to the man who, they feel, has done more for game protection in New Mexico than any other man. . . . Mr. Aldo Leopold is known as the past, present, and future Secretary of the State G.P.A. . . . and we have never met a man who does not hope that we will never have another during his life time."[38]

Unbeknownst to the sportsmen, the career of their leader was about to take a major turn. On March 18, 1924, Greeley wrote Frank Pooler a letter stating his desire to have Leopold assume the job of assistant director at the Forest Products Laboratory in Madison. The current director of the Lab, Carlile P. Winslow, was expected to resign within the year. Greeley explained that the new assistant director

must be one of the outstanding leaders of the country in forest research. While the particular province of the Laboratory is research in forest products, it is essential that its activities be correlated more and more closely with the whole forest conservation movement. . . . I have felt that Leopold has rather exceptional qualifications for this position, notwithstanding his lack of intimate contact with forest products work. This is because of his executive experience and ability combined with his interest in investigation, his ready grasp of a new problem, and his ability to represent the Forest Service effectively in contacts with the public. . . . In the nature of things, it should be a stepping stone to the Directorship sooner or later. It is probable, though not certain, that the opportunity to become head of the organization will materialize in no very great length of time.[39]

The job was important, coequal with district forester in the USFS hierarchy, but Leopold was reluctant to accept it. He had reservations about leaving the field and taking up work that was necessarily more confined and technical. In April he traveled to Madison and to Washington for a series of meetings with Greeley, Winslow, and Earle Clapp.

The decision was undoubtedly a difficult one. For Leopold, such a move would involve far more than transporting one's effects; it was more akin to dismemberment, a severing not only of family ties, but of ties to the land itself, to the places he had worked, explored, fished, hunted, studied, written about, shared with his family and his closest friends. In late April, Leopold, for reasons he never fully explained, accepted the position. He was instructed to report to Madison as soon as possible. Winslow wrote to welcome him to the laboratory and to express confidence that they could work well together. Leopold replied, "I entirely share your conviction that you and I will be able to work together in the best sort of way. I hope, however, that everybody will remember that I will be decidedly green for a long time and make no pretense of being anything else."[40] Leopold had made that mistake before.

The reaction in New Mexico was one of surprise and regret. His friends and colleagues had come to regard Leopold himself as a fixture in the southwestern landscape. Pooler wrote to Leopold "to tell you how deeply I shall feel your loss in D-3 and yet how honestly glad I am that this opportunity has come your way. . . . Your service to D-3 has been monumental and the District will miss you sorely, but the cause of forestry is the gainer in the broader sense."[41] Another D-3 officer wrote, "I had learned to love you as a coworker + some of the most enjoyable moments of my F.S. life have been [during] a social chat with you."[42] Fred Winn, who as a boy had partially lost his hearing in an ice-boat accident on one of Madison's lakes, predicted that he would have good duck hunting and would enjoy Madison, "a fine town but with nine months of winter." Winn, though, could not hide his dismay over the departure of his old friend:

Who is going to take your place for the pack trips and the hunting and fishing trips? What is to become of our game situation and the wilderness plan in view of the open hostility to the latter on the part of the majority in the D[istrict] O[ffice]? . . . We shall have some one in Operation of course but he won't fill your unique position. After 14 years down here, dating from the Apache days, one is inclined to think you were under obligations to stay with it and not go chasing off to strange places. Rest assured, no one will miss you more than I.[43]

On May 23, the Albuquerque Game Protective Association hosted a smoker in Leopold's honor at the Chamber of Commerce. Over one hundred attended.

On June 3, five days after Leopold left Albuquerque, Frank Pooler unceremoniously initialed the Recreational Working Plan that established the Gila Wilderness Area, the first such area in the national forest system, and thus in the nation, to be so designated.

ᔆ

During Leopold's years as chief of operations in District 3, his interests in soil erosion and wilderness protection had advanced along a dual track. Both grew out of his observation of human settlement in a region whose ecological equilibrium was, in his later words, "set on hair-trigger." If abnormal erosion was a result of unwise use of land, wilderness protection was an effort to exercise wisdom before it was too late. The same month Leopold left for Madison, *Sunset* magazine published a new version, designed for broader public consumption, of his 1922 address, "Erosion as a Menace to the Social and Economic Future of the Southwest." He called the article "Pioneers and Gullies." The title provided a fitting symbol for his years in the Southwest. Leopold's experiences there would leave him with a sensitivity to the causes and effects of landscape change that he might never have gained elsewhere. One incontrovertible conclusion would issue from this, and resonate through his later work: that human beings could maintain a healthy quality of life on the land they inhabit only if their economic system worked with, and not against, the underlying natural system. There was no longer a choice. There was no longer a wilderness in which to begin all over.

Leopold was thirty-seven. At some point he had ceased to be a child of the East. He was now a full veteran of western mountains, western ranges, and western rivers. As he returned to the Midwest, he left behind an impressive record of achievement. Leopold was a capable, well-experienced field man, the leader of a region-wide game protection movement, a pioneer in national forest policy on recreation, soil erosion, wilderness, and game management, an innovator in administrative methods, and a self-motivated researcher in a new kind of science. As a leading spokesman, in print and in person, for conservation, he had gained a reputation as an original thinker in all these areas.

Land is never static and neither are people, nor would be the relationship between them that Leopold sought to understand and influence. Soil erosion would continue to be an intractable problem. Game management was taking its first tentative steps; it would soon encounter many new possibilities, and new difficulties. The designation of the Gila Wilderness Area was hardly the end of a battle; it was just an opening volley. The Gila itself, for all its ruggedness and grandeur, was only marginally more secure than it was before. Its protection was by administrative fiat only, and assigned it merely to another category of land use. Washington had had no say in its establishment, and the designation could be altered at any time. Opposition to the whole idea remained, both within and beyond the Forest Service, and Leopold would continue to be the leader in the fight for its acceptance.

When Leopold arrived in Springerville in 1909 as a naive and adventurous forest assistant, much of the Apache National Forest, and much of the Southwest, was de facto wilderness. As he left Albuquerque in 1924, wilderness was something rare. It was inspiring and splendrous, yet clearly diminishing. Above all, to a growing number of people, it was something worth keeping. Aldo Leopold was one player in a signal turn of events. The natives of this land had no word for wilderness. All this was *home.* The pioneer had no home in the new world, and all too few kind words for what he found here. All this was *wilderness.* By officially designating the Gila "a wilderness," western culture had in fact taken final possession of the wilderness. It was a conquest, albeit a conquest of the gentlest kind. It conquered by recognizing that there is a point beyond which the spoils of conquest are no longer commensurate with the value of the vanquished. For all the settler's energy and impertinence, here was a sign of cultural foresight, a willingness to let a wild place be. While serving the self-interest of those, including and especially Leopold, who enjoyed the experience of untamed country, it was, in the larger view of history, a quiet act of national magnanimity. No European nation ever could, or ever would, proclaim such a wilderness.

Part IV

WISCONSIN

12

A Fish out of Water

(1924–1928)

EOPOLD left Albuquerque on May 29, 1924, eastbound on the Atchison, Topeka, and Santa Fe. Ten-year-old Starker and eight-year-old Luna travelled with their father. As the train pulled out onto the high plains of eastern New Mexico and Colorado, Leopold would have concentrated his view along the long crest of the Sangre De Cristos. On the other side of the jagged line of mountain peaks was the Carson Forest, and the valley of the upper Rio Grande, and Taos, and Tres Piedras. The train barreled eastward, and left the sun to set on that far side of the Rockies.

On June 1, the train rounded the Flint Hills, and pulled into Union Station in Burlington. On Prospect Hill, the Leopold compound was in its spring glory. Clara still lived in the big house. She was now sixty-four years old, a Burlington matriarch, increasingly hard of hearing, but as lively as ever. In her widowhood she had built a second life for herself, centered around her clubs, her cooking, her family, her active circle of friends, and her love of gardening. She had become an expert gardener, and that June, as every June, the wildflower beds around the grand old house blossomed to their best advantage. To her grandchildren, she was an imposing figure, affectionate but distant, a figure from Burlington's gilded age.

Carl and Dolores Leopold lived in a new home across the yard from Clara. Frederic and his wife Edith lived in the house Charles Starker had built in the 1890s. Marie was married to a Chicago banker and lived in Evanston, Illinois. Aldo's brothers continued to run the Leopold Desk Company, which still produced the finest in office furniture.

Aldo's appointment to the Forest Products Laboratory was not due to become effective until July 1. Given this open time, he and his brothers made plans for a two-week voyage into the renowned canoe country of the Superior National Forest, along the Minnesota-Canada border. Luna lost out this time. He would have to remain in Burlington. Aldo planned to meet Carl, Frederic, and Starker in Ely, Minnesota, after first travelling to Madison to find a house for his family.

Leopold arrived in Madison on June 5. After a full day of house-hunting, he wrote to Estella and declared Madison "an awfully dolled-up town," notably lacking in such Albuquerque amenities as chicken coops, woodsheds, fences, windmills, and spacious backyards. What it lacked in backdrop mountains and grand rivers, however, Madison made up for in freshwater lakes: four of them, strung together in their ice age basin, blue against the June green of the surrounding hills. Soon Aldo was describing to Estella the "cool sparkling morning on the lake" and a visit to Wingra Park, where "dozens of boys (from 6 to 60) . . . [were] catching sunfish and almost all of them had a mess of nice big ones. I must say there are a lot of things like that which are going to please our boys very much."[1] After two days of searching, Aldo rented a house near the Lab that would suffice until Estella arrived with Nina and little Carl in July.

Leopold left for Minnesota a few days later. On June 11, the four Leopolds put their two canoes into Basswood Lake and plunged paddle toward the international border and the Quetico beyond. For fourteen memorable days they canoed the complicated maze of cold rivers and wild lakes. On June 14, Leopold wrote in his journal:

We camped on a beautiful rock point full of reindeer moss and backed by pines. Hermit thrushes serenaded us at supper, and a loon called from a far bay. Starker, as usual, started to fish, and from the canoe landing hooked what we supposed (from his spots) to be a small pickerel, but he fought as no pickerel ever did. On landing him we found him to be a beautifully spotted lake trout. This was on a barbless spoon—which we shall use hereafter. Starker got two more trout. We have had two big ambitions—seeing moose and catching trout, and have now solved the trout problem. After supper, Fritz stumbled upon a hen mallard setting eight eggs right in the pine forest. The number of adventures awaiting us in this blessed country seems without end. Watching the grey twilight settling upon our lake, [we] could truly say that "all our ways are pleasantness and all our paths are peace."[2]

Leopold had recourse to his biblical references more than once in the Quetico. On this trip he composed his "Loon Island Decalogue," a set of commandments for voyageurs. Among them:

Cuss not thine ancient backlash, for the poor cast we have with us always.
Cherish thine hat on the portage, that it may be with thee to the end of thy trip.
Stack not tortillas without flour, lest they cleave together and thy brother gather up thereof seven baskets full.
If thou wouldst bump the tent in a rainstorm, do it over thine own bed.
Six days shalt thou paddle and pack, but on the seventh thou shalt wash thy socks.[3]

Leopold wrote somewhat more reverently of the loon, the plaintive siren of the wilderness: "The Lord did well when he fitted the loon and his music into this lonesome land."[4]

Leopold's final journal entry of the trip hearkened back to his boyhood days at Les Cheneaux. "It has been a memorable trip," he wrote, "maybe the best we ever made—and we have made some that are hard to beat. It is the first trip we have made together since we went to Drummond Island with Dad about 1906 or 7. How Dad would have loved it! I am reminded of Isaac [sic] Walton's terse but loving tribute—'An excellent angler, now with God.'"[5]

Aldo and Starker returned to Madison at the end of June, and were soon joined by Estella and the other children. For Aldo, the move to Wisconsin was difficult, but it was at least softened by the fact that he was returning to his native Midwest. For Estella, the move was absolutely wrenching. She was accustomed to the music and atmosphere, the light air and sunshine, of her ancestral New Mexico, and dreaded Wisconsin's cold, its unpredictable weather, its lack of family and friends. She wept often during her first weeks and months in Madison, but never questioned the decision once it was made. Even in the years that followed, she seldom returned alone or for long to the Southwest.

At the end of July, the Leopolds bought a comfortable but undistinguished gray stucco house at 2222 Van Hise Avenue, a short walk away from the Forest Products Laboratory and the University of Wisconsin campus. Aldo immediately led the family in fixing up the yard. They planned vegetable gardens, planted wildflowers, new trees, and native bushes, erected bird houses, and put up feeders. Aldo hauled some glacier-transported boulders from a nearby field and dropped them onto the front lawn.

Coincidentally, remarkably, Van Hise Avenue gained another new resident that summer. Frederick Jackson Turner, then sixty-two years old and perhaps the nation's most prominent historian, retired from teaching that same June, left Harvard, and returned to Madison to continue his research and writing at the University of Wisconsin. In early July, Turner moved into a Cape Cod house two doors east of the Leopolds. Turner's daughter and son-in-law, Dorothy and John Main, lived one house further down. Although Turner himself remained in Madison only a few years before moving on to work at the Huntington Library in California, the Leopolds and Mains would remain good friends, as well as neighbors, for years to come. Thus did Turner and Leopold—two men for whom history, frontiers, and wilderness defined the very contours of their lives and their work, and whose work in turn defined the contours of history, frontiers, and wilderness—come by chance to meet on a quiet residential street in Wisconsin.[6]

ᔕ

Forest conservation, as envisioned by Gifford Pinchot and his circle of founding foresters, entailed not only the protection and management of the nation's living forests, but also the wise use of the harvested tree — the wood itself. To this end, the Forest Service, in cooperation with the University of Wisconsin, established in 1910 the nation's main facility for timber research, the U.S. Forest Products Laboratory. In its formative years, the Lab conducted basic investigations of the mechanical properties of native woods and tested new techniques in wood preservation, seasoning, fireproofing, byproducts, and construction. Under Winslow's predecessor, Howard Weiss, the Lab worked during World War I to bring this knowledge to bear on military needs, traditional and modern: gunstocks, artillery wheels, and support structures, airplanes, munitions, gas masks, and medical supplies. By the time Leopold arrived as assistant director in 1924, the Lab had redirected itself to meet the needs of the peaceful, prosperous 1920s. The war had stimulated research into new glues, veneers, plywood, and drying and shipping methods. After the war, Winslow and his staff worked to strengthen the Lab's relations with the wood-using industries and to encourage these emergency-spawned advances in wood use. The industries, generally suspicious of research and theorists prior to the war, responded with enthusiasm.[7]

Aldo Leopold was, in one colleague's words, a "fish out of water" at the Lab. "We were scientists, engineers; Leopold was a forester."[8] Although practically born and raised on wood, Leopold was not a technician, and made no effort to hide the fact. But he was chosen for good reason. His probing mind was well-suited to the guidance of research. His organizational abilities, well-proven as chief of operations in D-3, were needed as the Lab broadened its programs. His flair for writing and publicity would be valuable as it reached out to foresters, industrialists, and the general public. By talent, if not by temperament, he was the right man for the job.

Leopold assumed responsibility for several key items on the Lab's agenda. He began to promote closer cooperation with the national forests around the country, a chore that would take him back out to the field at least a few times each year. Leopold also oversaw the Lab's effort to reduce the wastage of wood by industry — estimated to be as high as 66 percent — and to encourage the use of "inferior" species of trees and nonstandard size stocks of lumber. In addition to such special assignments, Leopold assisted Winslow in coordinating the rapidly expanding research schedule. As a student in the Yale Forest School, Leopold had once declared that he had "no ambition to be a tie-pickler or a timber-tester." He was now the nation's number two tie-pickler, with every expectation that he would soon be number one.

In September 1924, two months after beginning his new assignment,

Leopold went to the Mayo Clinic in Rochester, Minnesota, to have minor surgery performed on his upper jaw and antrum. It was an unremarkable episode, but for the series of letters Aldo sent to Estella. The letters revealed his first renewed impressions of the Midwest's people and landscapes, impressions gathered virtually in George Babbitt's own backyard. At the clinic, Leopold met another patient, a Texas cowman. "He looked so lonesome among all these 'foreigners' that I introduced myself. Alligator boots with square toes and a big stetson and a Pecos Valley drawl—tell him a mile off. Doubtless lived on fried beef and biscuits and coffee so long he had to come here for repairs. I've seen thousands. He was so pleased to see somebody who could talk cow sense and read a brand. So was I."[9]

Leopold then turned his eyes to the Minnesotans. In between delays and complications in his treatment, Leopold did what he always did: walk.

I like to walk and just soak in perfectly idle and footless impressions. The most vivid impression I had was of a little Elk. You could see the tusk dangling on his round little tummy a block away as he trudged up the street with his grip, evidently returning from a long trip selling—well, I should say floor-wax, or clothespins. He was short and pink and very shaven, and wore the most beatific smile, as if he were about a block from home and expected a very dolled-up child to rush out and hug him. The smile haunted me. I admired it, and rather felt gratified that this system of ours should provide so limited a person with sufficient thrills to engender it. In spite of his limitation there is something worth while in his existence. . . . Whether his innermost ambition is to become Exalted Ruler or a Rotarian I am not quite sure, but it doesn't matter nearly as much as that smile, which was more important than either. This fall he will vote for Coolidge, and some day he will build him a Dutch Colonial house with canvas on the front lawn, and drive a little Packard. But these too, if he only knew it, will be much less important than his smile.[10]

As smug as Leopold could sometimes be, he could be every bit as sensitive and compassionate. One of his Rochester walks took him past the state home for the aged:

On the big lawns were several old women, in striped cotton uniforms, over which each wore an old jacket, or a shawl of her own—in subtle refutation of uniformity. One tall old lady stood by an elm tree. She pulled down a drooping bough and held it in her arm as one would hold a child, passing her hand—back and forth—over the thick shining leaves in a kind of caress. I thought at first she was blind, but it was not that—she was just looking far away across the prairies as she caressed the leaves. I hurried off, full of crowding thoughts. Elm leaves! And after all, why shouldn't they be caressed? Thick shiny leaves, elm or Magnolia, have the same kind of physiological poetry as a young woman with dark shining hair. And she had been young once—"A woman straight as a hunting knife, and trim as a Salem-Clipper."[11]

Leopold had apparently just read Stephen Vincent Benét's "The Ballad of William Sycamore," for he referred to it in several letters. He continued his stroll along the Zumbro River:

Once a pretty prairie river—"unheard of streams were our flagons." Now a noissome polluted thing, full of old cans and discarded tires, which the willows and arrow-roots valiantly try to hide in a green bower, only the town won't let them. And on a little sandbar, oblivious of this tragic conflict of filth and green leaves, were three little boys, joyfully building ponds and dams and canals, that forthwith filled with oily water. They must have been told "not to wade in that dirty creek," for they had their shoes on. I wonder if the irony of this is known to William Sycamore or his tall straight wife? To what end did they conquer this prairie? After all, they did their part—it is we who are not doing ours. We who like animals in a cage cannot keep out of our own filth! We—who "develop"—we who "boost," and brag, and swagger over "our" conquest, and send our boys to play in sewers![12]

Leopold's disdain for Babbitt's mores and materialism was at its highest pitch during his earliest years in Wisconsin. In its best expressions, it was a rejection of the insularity and shallow-mindedness that prosperity brought, willy-nilly, to middle America in the 1920s. In its worst expressions, it revealed a streak of arrogance that still colored Leopold's attitude. Yet his conservationist convictions had always been, and would always remain, stronger than his social or political views and would ultimately subsume them. Leopold's beliefs about humankind's relationship to the natural world would expand to take in his beliefs about social relationships. His Wisconsin years may be read, in part, as a steady transformation of his highborn tendencies, from a merely social to a more natural sense of aristocracy. His letters from Rochester in 1924 belied a still-roiling inner tension between the aristocratic and the democratic. He would play out in his own life this peculiarly American tension, one that has been on the nation's mind at least since Thomas Jefferson and John Adams addressed it in their classic exchange of letters.

Returning to Madison, Leopold enjoyed his first midwestern hunting season in twenty years. The territory around Madison was not altogether different from that of Aldo's Iowa boyhood. He, Estella, and the children explored the country at every opportunity. After work, Aldo led them to nearby marshes and ponds and to the Madison lakes, in pursuit of ducks, snipe, and partridge. On weekends, they hunted together along the bluffs and bottoms of the nearby Wisconsin River. Aldo and Estella searched that autumn for a permanent hunting camp along the Wisconsin, and on Lake Waubesa, but without success. For the present, city life and frequent hunts would have to suffice.

By the end of November, Leopold was fitted into his new work. He travelled to the National Conference on Utilization of Forest Products in

Washington to deliver the keynote address, entitled "Wood Waste Prevention." After six months on the job, though, he had not yet received his expected promotion. Cap Winslow had shown no further inclination to step down as director.

⟳

Leopold's new position, although confining, was also a blessing in disguise. His official duties did not engross him as had his previous assignments in D-3. He would gain in technical expertise during his four-year tenure as Winslow's assistant, but his most valuable contributions to conservation would come in an unofficial capacity. The move to Wisconsin was, in this sense, an auspicious one. It brought him to an area of the country where the public interest in new conservation initiatives was as strong as the need was urgent.

Advancing civilization had dealt harshly with original Wisconsin. The state divided naturally into three broadly defined regions. Prior to European settlement, southern Wisconsin was oak savannah and prairie land, the northeast edge of the tallgrass expanse that stretched from Ohio to Kansas, and from Arkansas to Alberta. The north was forest land, the green realm of the white pine, but also of mixed hardwoods, cedar swamps, spruce-fir forests, bogs, and marshes. Between the prairie and the forest, running along a generally northwest-southeast diagonal, was an area of overlap, a transition zone where the flora and fauna of the north and south extended, intermingled, halted.

These regions hardly constituted three uniform stripes. The southwestern third of the state had escaped recent glaciation, leaving it with a topography of picturesque ridges and valleys—"coulees," the new immigrants called them. Onto the remainder of Wisconsin's landscape the Pleistocene glaciers had gouged, scraped, deposited, washed, and deluged many particulars. Humping moraines, sinuous eskers, teardrop drumlins, conical kames, sunken kettle holes, pitted plains, and outwash flats covered much of the state. Myriad lakes dotted the green forests of the north; boulder-strewn streams drained the forests into the Mississippi, Lake Superior, and Lake Michigan. Another great lake, Lake Wisconsin, once inundated the middle of the state; when it burst its ice dam and emptied around the Baraboo Hills, it left behind its sedimentary bed, the central sands. On the low soppy flats of these "sand counties" formed the wide marshes to which the immigrants gave such singing names: Buena Vista, Roche a Cri, Endeavor, Shiprock, Pilot Knob, Germania, Great Swamp, Dancy, Leola, Cranberry Creek, Little Yellow.

By the mid-1920s, virtually all of this territory had been altered by European occupation. Only remnants of the original prairie remained. The south was now Wisconsin's agricultural stronghold. Even after a misadventurous concentration of wheat-growing following settlement, and a fractious farm economy at the turn of the century, the soil's raw fertility could still sustain the immigrant farm communities. The marshlands, so vital to waterfowl and other wildlife, had disappeared rapidly, ditched, drained, and dried up in the early years of the century, with the blanket encouragement of land speculators and agricultural college experts. In dry years, wide stretches of peatland burned and, as often as not, the owners abandoned them. Wildlife had been depleted throughout the state. Pollution was a new distress along the industrial corridor south of Milwaukee and in the Fox River valley, home of Wisconsin's major paper producers. The state's greatest problems were in the deforested north. The great pine was gone by 1900; the big hardwoods would be gone by 1925. As the lumbering boom passed, most of the logging companies fled to new forests, their barren land holdings—the "cutover" as it was known—reverting to the counties when the taxes went unpaid. Fires burned regularly, often spectacularly, consuming the leftover slash and even the soil itself.

Although new to the area, Leopold was still a forester, and well aware of the wastefulness that characterized the taming of Wisconsin. In an October 1924 speech to an association of resort proprietors, he compared the state's resources to the goods in a department store:

Our original stock was as good as the world had to offer, but our present stock is another matter. . . . We have considerable of what the uncritical call forests mainly in spite of, rather than because of, our way of using them. We have a considerable number of lakes mainly because forest fires were not able to burn them up. We have some fish and game mainly because wild life in this region has a lot of "come back." But by and large it is no exaggeration to say that on all these counters we are selling damaged goods. We get by with it mainly because the other states are doing the same thing. Maybe it is unprofitable to lament the fact that our goods have been damaged, but it is a very practical thing to consider which state will be first to put them back in good condition.[13]

Wisconsin had made halting moves in that direction in the early years of the century, passing game laws, employing a state forester and game warden, establishing a fish commission, authorizing a handful of state parks. These efforts were consolidated in 1915, when Governor Emanuel L. Philipp created a three-person conservation commission consisting of the heads of the Wild Life, Parks, and Forestry agencies. This commission worked well in view of its limited funds, but, as was the case in so many other states, it was constrained by politics. As of 1924, Wisconsin had made little further progress in any conservation direction: soils and waters were widely mistreated, forestry and fire protection existed only in speeches, outdoor recreation was unorganized, game protection was still wholly ineffective, and nongame wildlife was ignored or, in some instances, facing extinction.[14]

Fortunately, Wisconsin's political climate was conducive to reform. The state already had a solid tradition of progressive politics, sustained for over three decades under the leadership of Robert M. La Follette. La Follette's progressivism was not so intimately associated with conservation as was the Teddy Roosevelt brand, but it did recognize conservation as a significant part of its firebrand reformist crusade. An important link between the two progressive camps was Charles Van Hise, president of the University of Wisconsin during the first two decades of the century, and a friend to La Follette, Roosevelt, and Gifford Pinchot. In 1910, Van Hise wrote one of the classic tracts of the early conservation movement, *The Conservation of Natural Resources.*

Referring to this latent potential for change, Leopold told the resort association in 1924 that "Wisconsin has an almost international reputation for her ability to get effective public service when she sets about it, and has proved that ability [in] many fields, notably agriculture. The time is now past due for her to adequately support and expand her public service in conservation."[15] Among the first opportunities to show that support came a week after Leopold's speech, on that election day of 1924, when Wisconsin voters overwhelmingly approved a referendum that made it possible for the state to go into forestry by levying a property tax, an important first step toward the restoration of the ravaged forests of the north.

The election result was no accident. In the years just prior to Leopold's transfer, an active force of conservation-minded citizens had emerged in Wisconsin. Among the Madison contingent were several who would become Leopold's lifelong friends, colleagues, and hunting and fishing partners: Ed White, an engineer at the Forest Products Lab; Bill Schorger, a chemist at the Burgess Laboratories in Madison with a passion for wildlife history and ornithology (in later years, he would turn to wildlife exclusively); Ray Roark, a mechanical engineer at the university; William J. P. Aberg, a prominent Madison attorney; and Thomas E. Coleman, a manufacturer active in state and national Republican Party politics. Sworn conservationists all, they linked up with one another and with equally dedicated citizens around the state to push for major reforms in conservation policy.[16]

The main agent of change in Wisconsin was the newly created Izaak Walton League. Established in January 1922 by a group of Chicago businessmen and professionals, the IWL had become overnight a national conservation phenomenon. In an area of public policy dominated by trained professionals, academics, entrenched interest groups, and bureaucrats, the league was by 1924 the most effective, dynamic, wide-open conservation organization in the country. Under the roller-coaster leadership of Will

Dilg, a Chicago advertising executive, the IWL gained its ascendancy by adopting the recruitment techniques of the fraternal organizations of the day, and adapting them to the cause of conservation.[17]

Cap Winslow, Ed White, and others at the Forest Products Lab helped organize an early Madison chapter of the IWL in 1923. Other chapters organized in Milwaukee, Fond du Lac, Green Bay, and other towns, large and small, north and south. The first statewide convention was held at Janesville in October 1924. The officers and members, as one of their first public initiatives, stumped the state in support of the 1924 forestry referendum.

By the time they held their second convention, in Green Bay in October 1925, Leopold had been recruited and quickly pushed up through the ranks. He addressed the convention on "Forestry in Wisconsin": "The Izaak Walton League of Wisconsin has clearly expressed its determination that the forests of this state shall be given an opportunity to grow up instead of burn up. We have heard some very interesting discussions on how this change shall be brought about—on what practical means shall be used to accomplish forest conservation on the ground. It seems to me that . . . these ways and means are a matter of pioneering in new fields of knowledge."[18] During the mid- and late-1920s, the Izaak Walton League would lead the way into these new fields in Wisconsin.

Although Leopold was paying close attention to Wisconsin's needs, he by no means neglected his southwestern and national conservation activities. In December 1924 he travelled to New York to address the annual American Game Conference on "Ten New Developments in American Game Management." Foremost among these developments was the very *idea* of management. In a field still dominated by game farming, unscientific hunches, and internal bickering, the possibility of actual management seemed distant, but no less necessary for that fact. "We have learned," Leopold told the conference, "that game, to be successfully conserved, must be positively produced, rather than merely negatively protected. . . . We have learned that game is a crop, which nature will grow and grow abundantly, provided only we furnish the seed and a suitable environment."[19]

Through 1925, Leopold continued to gather information from his southwestern contacts for "Southwestern Game Fields." As envisioned, the book was to survey the history, range, and condition of all species of southwestern game, and to lay out how these species could be managed "to grow and grow abundantly." Among Leopold's informants on the southwestern forests was S. B. Locke, a forest examiner with the Forest Service. In the summer of 1924, Locke and E. A. Goldman, senior biologist with the Biological Survey, had surveyed the burgeoning herds of mule deer in the forests of the Kaibab Plateau. Their findings would bring to the fore one of history's most celebrated cases of game *mis*management.

Hunting on the Kaibab had ceased in 1905, when Roosevelt included the area in the Grand Canyon Game Preserve. Government predator hunters had cleaned the range of thousands of coyotes, lions, bobcats, and wolves. Sheep and cattle were excluded from the preserve. The deer population, unchecked and apparently unable to check itself, grew until, in the late 1910s, a few foresters began to notice signs of an overrun range. The population continued to grow, the range continued to deteriorate, and the official policy simply continued. By the time Locke and Goldman surveyed the range, the situation was critical, and on the brink of disaster. On December 16, 1924 novelist-adventurer Zane Gray led an ill-conceived attempt to save the herd. His plan was to have dozens of men on horseback drive the deer down into the Grand Canyon, across the Colorado, and up to the South Rim. The result was an utter fiasco. Not a single deer made it anywhere near the river. Several of the men got lost, others simply gave up. Clearly, frontier spirit and methods alone, however well-meaning, would not suffice to avert an ecological problem twenty years in the building. That winter, and the winter of 1925–26, an estimated 60 percent of the herd was removed, intentionally through reinstituted hunting and unintentionally through mass starvation.[20]

Although now far from the scene, Leopold was kept abreast of developments on the Kaibab. He received a copy of the report by Locke and Goldman in October 1924, and apparently conferred with Locke during a business trip to Utah four months later. The Kaibab crisis would ultimately force Leopold to reexamine the very basis of his thinking on the aims of game management, but not until science and management techniques caught up with experience—and that would take another two decades. The nature and extent of the crisis would never be precisely ascertained; accurate survey methods and deer range analysis were nonexistent. All that was known at the time was that there were too many deer. Interested humans could only critically reexamine or stubbornly defend the methods and beliefs that had invited disaster.

Meanwhile, discontent with the federal government's official predator policy emerged, quietly, at the 1924 meeting of the American Society of Mammalogists. A small group of zoologists, led by Joseph Grinnell of Berkeley's Museum of Vertebrate Zoology, argued on scientific and economic grounds that the Biological Survey was causing more harm—real and potential—than good in carrying out its large-scale, intensive campaign against predators.[21]

Leopold was aware of these inside discussions. Whether the influence was direct or indirect, by the end of 1925, Leopold took his first tentative steps away from the belief that the only good predator was a dead one. And once again Evan Kelley was party to the shift. In November, Kelley and Leopold were assigned to a joint inspection of the Wichita National

Forest in Oklahoma. Leopold subsequently prepared a memo for Kelley that heavily emphasized the nontimber attributes of the Wichita. Game management was obviously on his mind:

It is amazing how little is known about the life histories of game.

About the role of wild life in the ecology of the forest, we know even less. Yet we cannot manage either game, forest, or forage without such knowledge.

The Wichita obviously presents exceptional opportunities for such studies, and can contribute enormously valuable facts to forestry, game management, and science in general if these opportunities are utilized. . . .

The proposed ecological studies need not, in fact cannot, be confined to game. They must cover the flora and fauna as a whole, as well as all the factors affecting them, such as fire and grazing.

To facilitate ecological studies, the introduction of exotics should be carefully avoided, except insofar as may be necessary to cultivate exotic food plants for the game management studies suggested. . . .

For the same reason, it is important to avoid the extermination of predators, but there is no danger of this as yet.[22]

In his hunting journal, Leopold still talked of "vermin." He would not rush to conversion, and neither would he go any further than necessary in admitting the possible value of a varmint. Nevertheless, his innate sense of reason could not deny what his eyes saw, what his ears heard, and what history was beginning to tell him.

એ

Aldo, Carl, and Starker returned to Minnesota's canoe country in the summer of 1925. This time Luna joined them.

August 15
As I sit against a mossy rock writing up the sequel to yesterday's adventures, a cool breeze fans the blueberry bushes which dangle big dewy fruit over the very page of this journal. Starker and Luna, after being prodded through the job of dishes and beds, are organizing the fishing tackle for the day with thoroughness and enthusiasm. Carl is trying a new way of putting the tumpline on the boys' packs. Gentle waves are lapping the canoe in invitation for the days' travel. Down the lake a loon calls, and back in the aspens, a pine squirrel tells us to get the hell out o' here. We will![23]

Their nine-day vacation refreshed them for a return to what Aldo called "the land of neckties and boiled shirts."

Leopold's published articles during the years 1924–28 fall neatly into three categories: game management, technical forestry, and wilderness. The first reflected Leopold's growing, but still avocational, interest in advancing the management idea: "Quail Production: A Remedy for the 'Song Bird

List,'" "The Way of the Waterfowl," "The Next Move: A Size-up of the Migratory Bird Situation." The technical articles were written for professionals and laymen alike, their subjects closely connected with Leopold's work at the Forest Products Lab: "Wastes in Forest Utilization—What Can Be Done to Prevent Them," "Wood Preservation in Forestry," "Short Lengths for Farm Buildings," "Forest Products Research and Profitable Forestry," "The Home Builder Conserves." The wilderness articles were the most significant. A half dozen of them, appearing in professional and popular forums, established Leopold as the nation's foremost spokesman for the preservation of wild country, and sparked a national debate over what became known as "the wilderness idea."

The explosion of interest in outdoor recreation, foreseen by Leopold years before, had come to pass. The most conspicuous expression of this social development was the government-sponsored National Conference on Outdoor Recreation, first held in Washington in 1924. Although conservation leaders representing a broad range of groups and interests attended, no mention was made of wilderness areas such as Leopold and his cohorts envisioned. Irked by this exclusion, Leopold first took his case to the public in two articles, "Conserving the Covered Wagon" and "The Last Stand of the Wilderness," published in March and October 1925 respectively. "Can we not for once use foresight," he asked, "and provide for our needs in an orderly, ample, correlated, economical fashion?" What professionals like Leopold could see on a nationwide scale, the public could not: that the nation's wild expanses were disappearing so rapidly that any debate over their fate would soon be rendered pointless. Leopold pleaded for "a definite expression of public opinion on the question of whether a system of wilderness areas should be established in our public Forests and Parks."[24]

In October 1925, the *Journal of Land and Public Utility Economics* published "Wilderness As a Form of Land Use," an article tailored more carefully for a professional audience. It marked a distinct shift of tone in Leopold's public discussions of the wilderness idea. Heretofore he had stressed primarily the recreational value of wilderness; "Wilderness As a Form of Land Use" built on this and stressed the broader cultural and historical values implicit in wilderness preservation. "Our system of land use is full of phenomena which are sound as tendencies, but become unsound as ultimates. . . . The question, in brief, is whether the benefits of wilderness-conquest will extend to ultimate wilderness-elimination."[25]

Leopold thought not. He viewed wilderness as a hedge against "the inexorable molding of the individual American to a standardized pattern in his economic activities." With his experience of American history, not as the dead past, but as alive in the present, he dreaded the day when "the pack-train will be dead, the diamond hitch will be merely rope, and Kit

Carson and Jim Bridger will be names in a history lesson. Rendezvous will be French for 'date' and Forty-Nine will be the number preceding fifty." Leopold had no desire to see Americans follow the European path in outdoor recreation or in culture generally. "Europeans do not camp, cook, or pack in the woods for pleasure. They hunt and fish when they can afford it, but their hunting and fishing is merely hunting and fishing, staged in a setting of ready-made hunting lodges, elaborate fare, and hired beaters. . . . The test of skill is confined almost entirely to the act of killing itself. Its value as a human experience is reduced accordingly."[26]

In all of this, Leopold echoed the words of his neighbor on Van Hise Avenue. Although there is scant documentary evidence of their paths crossing, Leopold and Frederick Jackson Turner plainly shared many backyard and dining table thoughts. To Turner's scholarly presentations, Leopold added the vitality of his western experience. At certain points in his writing, Leopold sounded very Turnerian:

There is little question that many of the attributes most distinctive of America and Americans are the impress of the wilderness and the life that accompanied it. If we have any such thing as an American culture (and I think we have), its distinguishing marks are a certain vigorous individualism combined with ability to organize, a certain intellectual curiosity bent to practical ends, a lack of subservience to stiff social forms, and an intolerance of drones, all of which are the distinctive characteristics of successful pioneers. . . . Many observers see these qualities not only bred into our people, but built into our institutions. Is it not a bit beside the point for us to be so solicitous about preserving those institutions without giving so much as a thought to preserving the environment which produced them and which may now be one of our effective means of keeping them alive?[27]

Perhaps Leopold could not have appreciated so fully this implicit cultural value of wilderness until he had returned to the Midwest. In any case, wilderness, in the four years since he openly began his campaign to protect it, had come to stand for far more than just a place where one could take a two-week pack trip without crossing one's trail. Leopold ended his article with a ringing call to reflection and action:

If we are unable to steer the juggernaut of our own prosperity, then surely there is an impotence in our vaunted Americanism that augurs ill for the future. The self-directed evolution of rational beings does not apply to us until we become collectively, as well as individually, rational and self-directing.

Wilderness as a form of land use is, of course, premised on a qualitative conception of progress. It is premised on the assumption that enlarging the range of individual experience is as important as enlarging the number of individuals; that the expansion of commerce is a means, not an end; that the environment of the American pioneers had values of its own, and was not merely a punishment which they endured in order that we might ride in motors.[28]

244

The public response to Leopold's argument was strong, and generally positive. In January 1926, he was invited to speak on the subject of wilderness protection at the second session of the National Conference on Outdoor Recreation. His presence may have been facilitated by none other than Arthur Ringland, who, after spearheading the postwar food relief program in Europe, was chosen executive director of the conference. Leopold reiterated his points before the delegates:

I am asserting that those who love the wilderness should not be wholly deprived of it, that while the reduction of wilderness has been a good thing, its extermination would be a very bad one, and that the conservation of wilderness is the most urgent and difficult of all the tasks that confront us, because there are no economic laws to help and many to hinder its accomplishment. . . . We insist that the average American is entitled to these things as a privilege of citizenship rather than as chance crumbs from the economic table.[29]

Although Leopold had struck a responsive chord, not all were pleased by it. Critics within and beyond the Forest Service assailed Leopold and the wilderness idea. One efficiency-driven forester indicted the wilderness "enthusiasts" for being "anti-road." Leopold strongly denied the charge, drawing again on his gift for metaphor:

It is not a question of how many roads, but a question of distribution of roads. . . . Roads and wilderness are merely a case of the pig in the parlor. We now recognize that the pig is all right—for bacon, which we all eat. But there no doubt was a time soon after the discovery that many pigs meant much bacon, when our ancestors assumed that because the pig was so useful an institution he should be welcomed at all times and places. And I suppose that the first "enthusiast" who raised the question of limiting his distribution was construed to be an uneconomic visionary, and anti-pig.[30]

Another critic went straight for the jugular, raising the familiar charge that wilderness was only a playground for wealthy, misanthropic elites: "Perhaps if one closely analyzes the arguments of the true 'wilderness' advocate it will become apparent that it is not roads but people that he objects to. Perhaps he wants the 'wilderness' to himself and the elect few, and objects to roads because they inevitably bring other people."[31] Leopold did not mince words in response. "Why 'perhaps?' I would say *surely* it is people." He related an incident that occurred the previous summer in the Quetico. While on a portage, Aldo and Starker came upon five backcountry guides, each grunting beneath a canoe and heavy pack. Then came five tourists panting along behind with their cameras and fishing rods. "Now we objected to those people. Why? Because they invaded our wilderness? Not at all—they had just as good a right there as we had. We objected because they had bought their way instead of working their way into our wilderness. . . . All that we wilderness cranks are asking for is a few roadless areas where we can go once in a while, and where we will at least have a chance of escaping the man who buys his way."[32]

The imputation of an "unholy alliance with wealth" was the most galling to Leopold, for it was precisely that tendency he was fighting to reverse. "It is the opportunity, not the desire, on which the well-to-do are coming to have a monopoly. . . . The American of moderate means can not go to Alaska, Africa, or British Columbia. He must seek his big adventure in the nearby wilderness, or go without it."[33]

Those who accused the wilderness supporters of "locking up" resources were, in Leopold's eyes, completely missing the point. Leopold, at this stage of his advocacy, was actually willing to allow skillful, regulated timber cutting when extensive road systems were not involved, as in the watery wilderness of the Superior region. But beyond this, he argued that the preservation of intangible wilderness values far outweighed in importance whatever fractional economic benefits might be squeezed out of the remaining wilderness. America, he held, had yet to show that it could use its settled lands wisely; would we have to extend our ignorance to the final strongholds of unsettled land before learning, too late, that "good use is largely a matter of good balance—of wise adjustment between opposing tendencies"?[34] This was the essence of the wilderness idea that Leopold, as chief spokesman, tried to communicate. "The measure of civilization," he wrote in early 1925, "is in its contrasts. A modern city is a national asset, not because the citizen has planted his iron heel on the breast of nature, but because of the different kinds of man his control over nature has enabled him to be." If on occasion a person can visit or even imagine visiting great wild places, then "he is just that much more civilized than he would be without the opportunity. It makes him one more kind of man —a pioneer."[35]

"While it would be theoretically possible to overdo the wilderness idea," Leopold allowed, "the actual present question is not whether the establishment of wilderness areas will be overdone, but whether it will be done at all."[36]

That question was heating up in the case of Minnesota's canoe country. To theorize a wilderness idea was one thing; to implement it, another; to implement it after the sequence of commercial development had already begun was still another. There were serious obstacles to a Gila-type designation in the area. State and private land holdings within the Superior National Forest hindered large-scale plans. Manning and managing the forest was already difficult; without roads it could only remain so. Moreover, there were said to be potentially significant mineral deposits in the forestlands near the international boundary. On the other hand, the proximity of the region to midwestern outdoorsmen made it especially desirable as a wilderness area. Its suitability for canoe travel was unique within the U.S. National Forest system; only in Maine was there a comparable labyrinth of canoeable waters.

In the summer of 1926, Arthur Carhart's historic 1922 recreation plan for the Superior Forest, which restricted roads in favor of canoe travel, was still nominally in place. But the plan had no sooner been approved before local boosters and forest officers began campaigning for a system of new roads. By 1923, the sides had polarized. The newly formed Izaak Walton League was the strongest and least compromising of the groups opposed to roads. A conference of interested parties in April 1923 failed to settle the issue. The wilderness proponents organized a Superior National Forest Recreation Association. The Forest Service, as a gesture of reconciliation, ceased building roads on federal land. On state lands, however, the pressures remained, and in July 1925 a major new highway to Ely opened. In May 1926, the Forest Service issued a new recreation plan, allowing roads in certain sections of the Superior Forest. The recreationists objected, but by now they too had split into two factions. The Superior Recreation Association was willing to accept certain roads, with restrictions. The Izaak Walton League would not budge, and wanted the entire forest to remain roadless. Chief Forester William Greeley personally intervened in the dispute, but to no avail.[37]

The situation was stalemated in August 1926, when Secretary of Agriculture William Jardine arranged a September conference of all parties involved. In anticipation of the conference, Leopold quietly bridged the gap between the Izaak Walton League and the Forest Service. He travelled to Chicago in mid-August to consult with the IWL's national conservation director, Seth Gordon, who had just left the post of Conservation Commissioner of Pennsylvania under Governor Gifford Pinchot. Leopold emphasized the point that there would be no wilderness of any kind unless the private lands in the forest were first purchased and the forest consolidated; the Forest Service needed the backing of the Waltonians for this to take place. The Forest Service plans for keeping a large part of the area roadless were not as extensive as the league wished, but there could never be a secure wilderness without service approval. Leopold advised Gordon that it was more important "for all to agree upon the Service Plan and back it up with action than to force through a more ambitious one without any provision for making it effective." It was "absurd to fight about something that doesn't exist, instead of getting together to bring something into existence."[38] Leopold reported the results of the meeting to District Forester Allen Peck, who in turn reported to Secretary Jardine. The issue was largely settled prior to the September conference.

After the conference, Jardine issued a policy statement that expressly recognized the unequaled value of the Superior as a setting for "a virile and wholesome form of recreation off the beaten paths." Among the earliest indications of a service-wide shift in policy, this statement led to accelerated movement within the Forest Service for the wilderness idea. By the end of the year, Greeley was encouraging other forests to follow the Gila and Superior in reserving primitive areas; in 1927, he ordered them to. A 1928 study of recreation on federal lands by the National Conference on Outdoor Recreation quoted Leopold for two pages on the need to retain wilderness. In 1929, Leon Kniepp, now the Forest Service's recreation specialist, established the "L-20" regulations that gave the agency, and the nation, its first official wilderness policy.

Leopold's public advocacy of wilderness protection subsided after the activity of the mid-1920s. It would reemerge with startling new urgency in the thirties and forties, but after 1927 his leadership position was assumed by others. The Superior-Quetico area faced decades of future controversy, and Leopold remained a staunch defender of its integrity, but leadership in that arena would fall to Ernest Oberholtzer, Sigurd Olson, and others closer to the scene. They and others who would become national leaders in the fight in the 1930s found much of their inspiration in Leopold's early efforts and words. Benton MacKaye regarded Leopold's wilderness thesis as "one of the very few contributions thus far to the psychology of regional planning."[39] Robert Marshall, in his first communication with Leopold, referred to him as "the Commanding General of the Wilderness Battle."[40] Frank Waugh was another admirer. He and Leopold had maintained a correspondence ever since their 1917 trip together in the Grand Canyon. "The first loud protest I heard," Waugh wrote in 1930, "came from Aldo Leopold. . . . When Leopold's trumpet call rang through the forest, echoes came back from every quarter. Thousands of foresters and hundreds of common nature lovers felt the same way about it."[41]

ᔕ

The tedium of Leopold's work at the Forest Products Lab increased with the passing months. Cap Winslow was a skillful, but by no means compulsive, administrator. An ever deeper and swifter stream of paperwork flowed toward Leopold's desk. There was still no indication that Winslow was ever going to leave, but Leopold remained a loyal assistant director throughout. Although his work mounted and his attempts to influence research went nowhere, he expressed no frustration. He and Winslow always remained good friends, as well as co-workers.

Leopold had an opportunity to leave the Lab early in 1926. In March he was offered the directorship of the Roosevelt Wild Life Station at the New York State College of Forestry at Syracuse University, the only institution of its kind in the country. Such a move would have put him at the vanguard of the earliest work in game management. After much urging, Leopold declined the offer. "To build it up to a leading institution," he explained, "is a 10 or 20-year job and a job that would entail a radical change in the line of work I have followed so far. I have changed my line of work so often already that I doubt the wisdom of doing it again."[42] Only after two more years of frustration at the Lab would Leopold be ready to make such a drastic move.

In the meantime, Leopold's outside activities and family provided his chief alternatives to Lab life. In early 1926 he began the actual writing of "Southwestern Game Fields." During that year, too, the family romance with archery began. It began as Leopold's own personal diversion; it was to become his, and the family's, primary hobby. He had read the 1925 edition of Saxton Pope's classic *Hunting with the Bow and Arrow.* Bow hunting was an arcane sport at the time; few practiced it, and the necessary equipment was hard to come by. Leopold built his own. Working at the nation's foremost wood research facility had its fringe benefits, including access to exotic woods and expert engineers. In his basement, he began his private experiments in bow and arrow construction, using osage orange from the Midwest, yew and Port Orford Cedar from Oregon, and Sitka spruce from the slopes of Alaska. That November, Starker and Luna joined their father in his first field trial of the gear, a rabbit hunt in Ashton Woods near Madison.

The interest in archery only added to the closeness of the family. "Dad worked down in the basement on his equipment every night. Mother would sit down there with him knitting, and it was a cold, dismal place." Aldo and Estella's obvious devotion to one another impressed the children. "You could really feel it, and all of us did. Dad would walk in the door [after work] and give mother a hug, and they would just go on and on. It was a very lovely relationship, even the mundane things."[43]

Aldo was a patient and even-tempered father, caring but not overly indulgent. He never took the antics of his growing sons too seriously—even when they hoisted a neighbor's lawn furniture up the school flagpole. Except on extreme occasions, disciplinary action was Estella's responsibility.

"I think we were perfectly normal kids," Nina remembered, "except when Dad was home; then we were all very quiet and good. Initially, when we'd see him coming down the sidewalk on his way home, boy, everybody would sit up, clean up the mess, straighten up the lamps, put on Beethoven and take off the jazz, put away the funny papers. I think Mother had us all completely conditioned. Yet, it was not out of fear—it was out of respect. The boys were real roughnecks. I can remember their knock-down drag-outs, running around the dining room table trying to catch one another. Luna and Starker really went at it. I remember running up and hiding under the bed, scared to death that they would kill each other. But this didn't ever happen when Dad was home."[44]

By and large, Aldo and Estella led a happy home life. Their children grew up much like other children, although, as might be expected, they spent a significant portion of their time in the outdoors. In 1927, a fifth child was born. She was named after her mother. One of daughter Estella's earliest memories is of a camping trip with the family in a pouring rain. Inside the tent, as the rain dripped off the flaps, she sat and blubbered endlessly, refusing even to drink the warm milk her father prepared. When her whimpering showed no sign of letting up, Dad finally broke out with an insistent, "Quit your whining!" She did.[45]

∽

1926 was an election year in Wisconsin, and one which would lead to significant changes in the state's conservation policies. Once again the impulse for change came from the spirited members of the Wisconsin Izaak Walton League. The leaders of the league were determined men: Haskell Noyes, a Milwaukeean "whose heart and soul was dedicated to conservation"; Frank Graass, the league's untiring secretary, a legislator from Door County, and "a brusk, forceful hard driver. . . . When legislators wouldn't go along with him, he rode right over them . . . but he did accomplish things and he knew the inner workings and the fighting that goes on in legislative matters"; Lou Radke, who led the fight to restore the famed marsh at Horicon. There were dozens of other like-motivated men throughout the state; together they made the Wisconsin chapter of the IWL one of the most effective in the nation. Even when national membership began to drop off, the Wisconsin division was held together by its active leadership and its legislative agenda. By the late 1920s, there were some 12,000 members in over 100 chapters around the state.[46]

Leopold played a significant, though background, role within the league. By 1926, he was a state director and served on several key committees, most notably those assigned to publicity and legislative matters. It was in the latter capacity that Leopold applied most effectively his national influence and wide experience.

The top item on the IWL's agenda was one long familiar to Leopold: the removal of state conservation administration from arbitrary political considerations. The situation in Wisconsin was precisely what it had been in New Mexico. Conservation policy, requiring above all continuity, skill, and autonomy, was dictated by the political whims of every new governor and legislature. By 1926, the old conservation set-up was plainly inadequate, especially in coming to terms with the forestry problems of the north.

Leopold and Bill Aberg, the legal brain of the IWL, were assigned to the task. Aberg complemented Leopold well. An intense, private man, he had an insider's understanding of Wisconsin state politics. They worked with four or five other members in formulating ideas for a new system of administration. Leopold did the bulk of the research, drawing heavily on his New Mexico experience. He and Aberg also surveyed the conservation departments of Michigan and Pennsylvania, two of the country's most progressive. They consulted with Seth Gordon. By the fall of 1926, they had a program outline and an early version of a bill to put before the Wisconsin legislature. The main provision of the bill directed the governor to appoint, with the state senate's approval, a six-member unpaid conservation commission, who in turn would choose a trained director to run a new Wisconsin Conservation Department. The commissioners were to serve overlapping six-year terms, a schedule that kept in check the influence of any one governor.

The conservation constituency in the state had grown to the point that it played a decisive role in the 1926 gubernatorial race. One of the progressive hopefuls, Herman Ekern, the state's attorney general and a friend of Aberg's, feared the political repercussions of the suggested reforms. Another candidate, Republican Fred Zimmerman, embraced the program and capitalized on it during the campaign, declaring in speeches and in print his full support for the new measures. He promised to choose his six commissioners from a list of twenty to be prepared by state conservation groups. This played well throughout the state, particularly in the north, and helped Zimmerman overcome three other candidates in the general election.

The battle, however, had only begun. Through the early months of 1927, Aberg and Leopold worked through a half dozen revised drafts of the bill before it was introduced in the Wisconsin senate in March. Leopold and his colleagues brought Gifford Pinchot in to speak to the legislators.[47] Several key compromises had to be worked out. The original bill gave the Conservation Commission authority to fix seasons, set bag limits, and enact other specific regulations; the representatives were not about to concede such powers. They also demanded that the commission include three members each from the north and south, a move by the northerners to retain the disproportionate share of power they enjoyed at the time. Senate Bill 404 was approved in May, only to face a still rougher ride through the assembly. Factions within the state's political cauldron haggled incessantly over the bill until July 13, 1927, when the assembly voted in favor of the bill by a margin of 78–6. Governor Zimmerman approved the law on July 21.[48]

Zimmerman had now to appoint the six conservation commissioners. As promised, he asked the state's conservationists to compile their list of twenty qualified candidates. The Izaak Walton League, garden clubs, Rotary Clubs, Kiwanis Clubs, the American Legion, and miscellaneous other organizations cooperated in selecting the twenty. The IWL was hoping to have its labors rewarded with the appointment of Haskell Noyes to the commission. There was also a general expectation that Aldo Leopold would be chosen director of the department.

List in hand, Zimmerman promptly turned against the conservationists and used the commission to pay off political debts. He ignored their recommended candidates and nominated six men who, in Frank Graass's words, "didn't know a carp from a herring."[49] The six included two lawyers from Madison and Milwaukee, a labor leader from Green Bay, and a casket manufacturer from Fond du Lac. While not antagonistic toward the conservation movement, they were simply uninformed. Only one, a teacher from Ladysmith who also ran a tree nursery, had shown any previous interest in conservation.

The turnaround stunned the Waltonians. Leopold was in northern California at the time, inspecting logging camps in the redwood country. "Apparently," he wrote to Estella when he received the news, "we are entirely sold out and worse off than before we started. I feel pretty sick about it—especially about egging on my friends to do such a terrible lot of work for nothing. When I think of Bill Aberg I almost feel as if I had misled him. Well—it may be all right in the end but it's evidently to be a long slow grind just as it was in New Mexico."[50]

While in California, Leopold paid his only visit to the Yosemite Valley, high temple of the American outdoors, but lately turned jazz-era den of thieves, tacky concessionaires, and tourists attracted more to the night life than to the range of light. Leopold's lament carried uncharacteristic shades of introspection:

I can't say whether it was more pleasure to see Yosemite than pain to see the way most people see it. It's a struggle for me sometimes to play ball with the crowd at all. How much to compromise is a question on which there is no such thing as advice, or consolation. Every man is a lone wolf when he faces real realities. . . . We went through the Sierras for two days. If the Lord made another country like that it wasn't on this particular star. . . . The tourists all gape at Yosemite, but what none of them see is the fifty miles of foothills on the way in. They are almost a relief after the highly frosted wedding-cake (and the wedding guests) on the other end. Especially the quail, and the live oaks "joyously uttering dark green leaves." You never have read my nickel volume of Whitman. We must read some of it together when I get back.[51]

On this trip, Leopold also took the opportunity to meet Dr. Joseph Grinnell and other zoologists at Berkeley, who were still deeply embroiled in the controversy over federal policies on predator control.

Back in Wisconsin, there was still a hope that Zimmerman's appointees would choose Leopold as the director of the reconstituted Conservation Department. The 1927 bill explicitly stated that the commission was to choose "a person having executive ability and experience, special training and skill in conservation work." Leopold was eminently qualified for the position. His experience and dedication were beyond reproach. Tom Coleman rallied a group of influential businessmen to insist on Leopold's appointment. The Izaak Walton League pulled its collective strings. The *Wisconsin State Journal* heard the rumor of Leopold's availability, and proclaimed it "too good to be true. . . . Here we have, as though made to order, a technical conservationist of seventeen years' experience, schooled in the handling of large funds and in the employment of large numbers of people, prepared for his work from both the practical and the research viewpoint, his life definitely committed to the great task of conservation."[52] Leopold did not campaign for the job, although he plainly hoped for it. It was his ticket out of the Forest Products Lab situation.

A Leopold appointment was not in the heavily stacked cards. In October 1927, after granting Leopold a token interview, the conservation commission chose Louis Nagler, an assistant of Governor Zimmerman and utterly inexperienced in conservation, as director. Newspapers across the state inveighed against the choice, or at least against the method. The anti-Zimmerman progressives rejoiced at this clear indication of the governor's unworthiness; they smelled political blood.

Apart from his purely personal disappointment, Leopold must also have felt another pang of disillusionment with politics. He had invested time, thought, and friendships in an effort that, far from taking conservation out of politics, only drove it into politics more deeply. His relations with the conservation department he had helped create would not smooth out for years. Already independent-minded, he would never align himself with any political party.

Recriminations were soon to follow. Zimmerman was trounced in a 1928 reelection bid. Nagler, his ineptitude showing, was out of the director's job after a year. Haskell Noyes of the IWL did become a commissioner in 1928. Zimmerman appointed him in a belated act of penance.

∽

By November 1927, Leopold had readied drafts of the two opening chapters of "Southwestern Game Fields." The first, entitled "Elements of Game Management," was Leopold's initial attempt to explain the foundations of the science he envisioned. "We have ventured into a new field," he wrote, "with no guide except our conviction of its importance, no training except our experience as outdoorsmen, and no resources except that dwindling amount of spare time which the professional man can spare from bread-and-butter pursuits."[53] Leopold did have, however, an abundant backlog of ideas, and a compulsion to lay them out.

"Game management," he wrote, "does not consist of farming game.

It consists of so regulating the natural factors of productivity that game farms ˙self." Leopold identified nine "factors of productivity" and placed them in two groups: those environmental factors which directly limited a species' natural rate of increase ("hunting, predation, starvation, disease, parasites") and those which affected the welfare of the species and thus indirectly its increase ("food and water supply, availability of coverts, and other 'special' factors"). The interplay of these "decimating factors" and "welfare factors" determined a given species' productivity. In a natural state, these factors tended to maintain populations in a more or less balanced condition. "But nature is not undisturbed; civilization has upset every factor of productivity for better or worse. Game management proposes to substitute a new and objective equilibrium for the natural one which civilization has destroyed." By isolating "certain prevalent combinations [of factors] and by manipulating a factor here or another there," game management could "bend the resultant to its own ends and uses."[54]

Leopold could have written a full book on the subject; eventually he would. As yet he had neither the depth of knowledge nor the intention to do so. The chapter was to serve only as the foundation for a study of southwestern game. He followed with a second chapter—"The Virgin Southwest and What the White Man Has Done To It"—that was a further refinement of those theories of landscape change he had formulated during his inspection days. For the first time, however, he brought game and other wildlife into the picture. Not without difficulty. This inclusion forced Leopold into some uncomfortable stretches of logic, for he had to admit that, in certain cases, the very changes that had disrupted the range had also benefitted game species. Grazing, for example, had ruined the vegetation on some watersheds, but had brought about predator control and improved deer habitat. Erosion had torn away a mountain valley, but created a sandbar oasis for quail. Even in its genesis, game management would admit of no easy answers. As a result, in part, of these conceptual difficulties, "Southwestern Game Fields" progressed only intermittently, when Leopold had enough time and information. These difficulties were compounded by the fact that his coauthors, Stokely Ligon and Fred Pettit, were fifteen hundred miles away.

In November 1927, Leopold returned to the Southwest on vacation, a two-week bow hunt in the Gila backcountry with his friend Howard Weiss. He met with Ligon and Pettit before taking to the field. Since early 1926, Leopold had been aware of a possible Kaibab-like overabundance of deer on the Gila. In the summer of 1927, Ligon conducted an official inspection of the situation for the New Mexico Department of Game and Fish, and corroborated the reports. He estimated a surprising thirty-eight deer to the square mile on certain portions of the Black Canyon watershed, much higher than expected.

Leopold and Weiss camped upriver from Canyon Creek, beneath Loco Mountain Mesa, and for two weeks stalked deer and turkey with their long bows. The return to his former haunts exhilarated Leopold. On November 13, he returned to camp via a high mesa rim. "Walking along this high prairie in the sombre sunset with a howling wind tossing the old cedars along the rim, and a soaring raven croaking over the abyss below, was a solemn and impressive experience. Jumped three whitetails right out on the prairie but it was too late to see horns. They were very pretty bounding over the sea of yellow grama grass with the wind blowing them along like tufts of thistledown."[55] The next day he saw some two dozen deer on Lily Mountain. Leopold managed one shot at seventy yards, but the buck bolted at the flash of the bow, and the arrow struck the rocks the buck had just vacated. "I also jumped the turkeys again and counted about forty as they sailed back to the south side of the canyon. I never saw such a flock, or such a hunting ground."[56]

A day later, Leopold's aim was better. He saw a buck in a pine thicket at fifty yards. "I moved to avoid a bush, drew to the barb at point blank, and let fly. The unmistakable thud of the arrow striking flesh told me I had hit—as nearly as I could tell in the fore ribs or shoulder. The buck plunged like a pitching bronco and disappeared over the hogback."[57] Leopold searched desperately for the wounded buck over the remainder of the trip, but never saw it again. He was disappointed with himself for losing it, but his spirits recovered as the abundant deer presented ample further opportunities. The archers returned to Madison empty-handed, but well satisfied with their experience.

Vacations, for Leopold, were never merely vacations, but semiofficial field trips. His observations inevitably found their way, weeks or months later, into essays, reports, and addresses. Several months after the New Mexico hunt, "Pineries and Deer on the Gila" appeared in the *New Mexico Conservationist*. The article was the first to reflect the new emphasis on habitat that he had anticipated in his work on "Southwestern Game Fields." Instead of stressing the role of such decimating factors as poaching and predation, he concentrated on the welfare factors—the cover provided by pines that had grown up with the advent of fire protection, and the need for proper management of deer forage. That shift in emphasis reflected, in many ways, the emerging difference between game *protection* and game *management*.

Leopold had some distance to go, however, before he could arrive at some notion of what "new and objective equilibrium" was appropriate for game populations. He lauded the "admirable recuperative capacity" of the Gila deer herd, and displayed no deep concern that the Gila was going the way of the Kaibab. In this respect, Leopold was not nearly as concerned as his friend Ligon, who warned that "a considerable portion of the inner

Gila watershed is now over-populated with deer. . . . Unless the surplus game is taken out, a very serious situation will ultimately develop."[58] By this time, Leopold had further modified his views on predators. He was voicing concern for certain predators on certain areas, and acknowledging that "we have overdone control on some of the National Forests, especially with respect to bear."[59] Nevertheless, on an area such as the Gila, where refuges were small and hunting was permitted beyond their borders, Leopold saw no need to consider predators in the formula for equilibrium.

∽

Leopold turned forty-one in January 1928. The Conservation Department job had passed him by. The longer he remained at the Forest Products Lab, the slimmer his chances for advancement seemed, and the more anxious he became. In February he took a month's leave to work on the manuscript of "Southwestern Game Fields," and to consider his options. The direction of his interests was clear. In an address to the national convention of the Izaak Walton League, he spoke on "Science and Game Conservation." "Game management research," he warned, "is a job of continental proportions. It involves every acre of rural and forest land in the country. This job is not going to be done, or even scratched, in the spare time of a few enthusiasts, or by a dribbling appropriation here and there."[60] Despite the enormity of the task, Leopold clearly wanted to devote himself to it.

In April, Leopold openly announced that he had "no intention to continue in my present place."[61] Once word of his availability filtered through the conservation community, job opportunities arose. Ovid Butler offered Leopold a staff position with the American Forestry Association. There was talk of an opening at the University of Wisconsin. Greeley's successor as chief forester, Robert Y. Stuart, hoped to hold on to Leopold by offering him a position as chief of public relations for the service.

Among those approaching Leopold was a consortium of industry representatives known as the Sporting Arms and Ammunitions Manufacturers' Institute. Representatives of the institute came to Leopold early in 1928 with an offer to fund a national survey of game conditions, to be overseen by Leopold. Leopold met with their board, drew up a proposal, and on May 22 accepted their contract. It took no small amount of courage to make such a move. Leopold, in mid-career, with a wife and five children to support, was entering a field which did not even exist. A survey of the type proposed was unprecedented. The contract gave Leopold a healthy raise in salary, but with the provision that SAAMI could terminate the arrangement after a year if they were dissatisfied with the results. Leopold, however, had supreme confidence in his own abilities. On June 26, 1928, he officially took his leave from the United States Forest Service.

Shortly after beginning the new job, Leopold received a letter from John D. Guthrie, his old boss on the Apache. Guthrie warned him that difficulties undoubtedly lay ahead:

. . . it will be a big job, and a much needed one. I don't know how effective any conclusions you may reach will be with certain of the state game people; they may regard them as something handed down to them, and so unwelcome. Then again, you may have to keep dark the fact that you are a forester and former employee of the Forest Service. I hope that such a feeling may be rarely encountered, but State Game Commissions are at times particularly narrow and bigoted, you know. . . . I suppose that there will be some clear-cut publicity about it. I believe that the point must be made clear as to *why* the ammunition and small arms people are financing this movement; it may readily be misunderstood by the average man, you know, as more propaganda.

Guthrie also took the opportunity to offer Leopold his opinion of the wilderness idea. "The principle," he wrote, "is away from forestry. Forestry is not aesthetics, is not 'natural areas,' nor wilderness areas, per se, but the putting to use, and *commercial use* at that, of all the resources of the country. We are too much getting away from the real forestry idea in this country, and more and more making the national forests into half-baked national parks."[62]

On that issue, at least, Leopold had not budged. The day before Leopold left the Forest Service, the *Service Bulletin* published his reply to yet another critic of the wilderness idea. Leopold's response provided a fitting valedictory to his years at the Forest Products Lab and to his nineteen-year career as a U.S. forester:

The issue is whether any human undertaking as vast as the national forests can be run on a single objective idea, executed by an invariable formula. The formula in question is: land + forestry = boards. We need to use it more than we do. But can we run the national forests on it alone?

. . . Whether we like it or not, national forest policy is outgrowing the question of boards. We are confronted by issues in sociology as well as silviculture—we are asked to show by our deeds whether we think human minorities are worth bothering about; whether we regard the current ideals of the majority as ultimate truth or as a phase of social evolution; whether we weigh the value of any human need (like recreation) wholly by quantitative measurements; whether we too have forgotten that economic prosperity is a means, not an end.

. . . The wilderness idea is a small but significant outgrowth of the idea of national forests. Its importance is that of a test case. The decision, in my opinion, will indicate whether the U.S. Forest Service is tending to become a federal bureau which executes the laws, or a national enterprise which makes history.[63]

If Leopold was deeply disaffected by his four-year stint at the Forest Products Laboratory, he never stated so openly. Typically, once he left, he never looked back. At one point, however, near the end of his life, he did write that he had disliked "the industrial *motif* of this otherwise admirable institution."[64]

13

"Game Methods: The American Way"

(1928–1932)

I N T A K I N G charge of the game survey for the Sporting Arms and Ammunition Manufacturers' Institute, Leopold stepped into a conservation movement maelstrom.

There was no science of game management to speak of in the United States. Zoologists studied game and nongame wildlife, but rarely with an eye toward conservation. "Wild life" itself was still a two-word term used mainly by sportsmen, naturalists, and outdoor writers. Animal ecology was only a rudimentary science, and barely connected to its sister science, plant ecology.

Although lacking a solid scientific base, wildlife conservation did not suffer from a lack of interest. On the contrary, interest was so great that the major conservation groups argued long and bitterly over the best way to pursue it. In one corner were the established east coast organizations, led by the National Association of Audubon Societies, the American Game Protective Association, and the U.S. Bureau of Biological Survey. In the other corner were the so-called protectionists, still led by that indomitable scourge of polite discussion, William T. Hornaday.[1]

Throughout the 1920s, the clash of their philosophies focussed on the question of how best to protect waterfowl. After the passage of the Migratory Bird Treaty Act in 1918, waterfowl populations experienced a sudden, but brief, rise in numbers. The treaty eased the gunfire, but it could not moderate the economic boom of the 1920s, nor counter the attendant loss of waterfowl habitat. Prosperity brought good roads, automobiles, improved firearms, more leisure time, and millions of new sport hunters. Simultaneously, agricultural expansion expropriated breeding, feeding, and resting grounds across the continent. The shrinkage of habitat was especially acute in the northern wet prairies, where vital marshes, potholes, river bottoms, and peatlands were being drained off the map. Whatever gains the 1918 treaty had yielded were being overwhelmed by these sweeping environmental modifications. To make matters worse, drought was beginning to dry up the northern breeding grounds.

In the absence of facts—no one knew the exact extent of these changes—opinions ruled debate. Hornaday was the most outspoken, sounding his trumpet and warning of imminent extinctions, but he still knew how to play only one note: the solution was to restrict hunting. He ignored considerations of habitat and regarded basic research as a waste of time. His approach, however simplistic, was effective; Hornaday always made for good news copy and the public could easily grasp his argument.

The major conservation groups, led by the American Game Protective Association, championed the alternative view that the fate of the waterfowl depended on preservation of habitat. Accordingly, these groups cooperated in support of federal legislation to establish a system of national game refuges. Their perennial efforts had still not succeeded as of 1928, when Leopold began his game survey, but they had been cause for some spectacular internecine bloodletting. The conservation groups pushed for a combined refuge-public hunting ground system; Hornaday pressed for reduced bag limits and shortened hunting seasons. When the smoke finally cleared, Hornaday was out of his position as director of the New York Zoological Society, John B. Burnham, the head of the AGPA, had lost credibility, and neither faction's efforts had gone anywhere. In the course of events, Hornaday had produced documentary evidence revealing the blatantly "unsportsmanlike and selfish purposes" of the arms and ammunitions companies in their connections with the AGPA. In the fall of 1926, the companies withdrew their financial support of AGPA, in part to improve the association's image, but also to back out of a losing proposition. After fifteen years of pouring money into the AGPA, the sponsors had yet to see any real returns, whether counted in dollars or ducks.

Meanwhile, the game situation remained precarious. Populations continued to decline, habitats continued to shrink, and solid facts were still lacking. The human observers, Leopold included, quite literally had no real idea what they were talking about.

Leopold watched these battles from afar. First in New Mexico, then in Wisconsin, he tried to split the difference between the two factions, arguing in support of both the refuge plan and reductions in the federal waterfowl bag limit.[2] Living in the Midwest, he was able to avoid personality clashes—a good thing since he knew most of the parties involved. On the other hand, he saw a continuation of the pattern evident in the Quetico-Superior case: as conservationists bickered, their nonconservationist opposition did not pause to wait, and the resource in question continued to diminish.

Leopold's acceptance of SAAMI's offer in May 1928 thrust him into a position of national prominence. The institute had taken up where industry support for the AGPA left off, cooperating with the AGPA aboveboard. Through their Committee on Game Restoration, the companies embarked on a program to propagate waterfowl, small game, and upland birds. The game survey was to be their largest investment to date, and their riskiest: nothing like it had ever before been attempted. Ideally, the survey would reveal some of the basic facts that were so sorely lacking, and employ them in the new endeavor to manage game.

SAAMI could not have chosen a more able man for the job than Aldo Leopold. His reputation was strong, his expertise unquestioned, and his interests unboundable. Moreover, Leopold was sensitive to the views of protectionists and could help smooth relations among the various groups. Leopold, in turn, could not have imagined a more appropriate job. It was an opportunity, as he sometimes put it, to turn his hobby into his profession. SAAMI expected him to investigate on-the-ground conditions throughout the country, to report on the status of game conservation efforts, to recommend and direct promising research projects, and otherwise to set his own agenda. SAAMI did not attempt to hide its openly commercial interest in his work, but neither did they place any restrictions on Leopold that might have compromised his personal motives. All parties, regardless of their particular stakes, were genuinely and primarily interested in advancing the cause of game management.

In June 1928, Leopold travelled east for a series of preliminary meetings with his overseers and with representatives of the major conservation groups.[3] He was first given a tour of the Game Conservation Institute at Clinton, New Jersey, a school and experimental station for aspiring game breeders. Leopold would never be comfortable with this aspect of game conservation, but in his new position he was obliged at least to be more tolerant. After the tour, he met with SAAMI's Committee on Game Restoration in New York City.

A day later, on June 7, Leopold made a special trip to Stamford to visit William T. Hornaday. Hornaday, now seventy-three and confined to his bed, was persona non grata in wildlife circles. Leopold, however, still felt a personal debt to the man who had stimulated him to action thirteen years before.

I told him that I wanted him to know first hand about my intended connection with the Game Survey. He was very sympathetic with the whole project and gave me valuable advice and information. I told him I was not asking for his advance approval of the findings of the Survey; I was asking that in the event anything came up which met with his disapproval that he give me a chance to come and see him before making his disapproval public. I do not think the Survey, if rightly carried out, need have any concern about Mr. Hornaday. I think his organization can later contribute valuable help in getting the support and approval of the school of thought of which he is the leader.[4]

Hornaday was no closer to Leopold's position than ever. He still scoffed at the idea that research could reveal anything of practical value. He still advocated tighter restrictions on hunting as the only solution to the game shortage. Their meeting, in fact, symbolized the evolution of philosophies in wildlife conservation. The old idea of game protection rested primarily on the control of hunting; the new idea of management rested on the control of the species' environment, in which hunting was but one factor. Despite their differences, Hornaday and Leopold held one another in mutual respect. Apparently, the old warrior had something of a soft spot in his heart for his one-time footsoldier.

Leopold's first official day on the job was July 1, 1928. The next day he began his first field trip, a two-and-a-half-week swing through Michigan and Minnesota. Obviously, there were major logistical obstacles in an effort such as Leopold's: one could spend a lifetime studying game conditions in a single county and never know the full story. To suppose one could do the same for a state, much less a country, much less in a few years, was simply preposterous. Leopold's situation was in many ways parallel to that which he faced a decade before as chief of operations of District 3, when he was given an expansive task, with no precedent to follow and only his own internal compass to guide him. "I must have an instinct for poker," he wrote to Estella soon after the work began.[5] At best, he hoped to gain a general view of conditions for a limited number of species, to ascertain trends in habitat change, and to lay a solid foundation for more specific research.

Through trial and error, Leopold eventually built up a standard field method. He began by visiting the state capitol and university in order to gain a general impression of local conditions and problems. By consulting records, libraries, officials, and faculty members, he learned what to look for in the field, and compiled lists of persons to contact. He plotted the locations of particular problems and persons on a map, rented a car, and began his travels. In the course of his surveys, he would meet hundreds of people, from all walks of life: sportsmen, scientists, foresters, politicians, journalists, professors, farmers, administrators, conservation officers, wardens, museum curators. The game survey thus became an important landmark in the further democratization of Aldo Leopold. His southwestern qualities showing, Leopold was keenly adept at communicating with farmers and other rural citizens; he understood the need to shoot the breeze for a while before getting down to business. Once in the field, Leopold's list of people to see and problems to investigate naturally grew. As he traveled, he kept detailed notes, tabulations, charts, and maps, "the objective being to perceive trends during, not after, the completion of field work, and to end up the field work with the foundations of a report already completed." After making his rounds, Leopold usually returned to the capitol and university to check up on information, and to seek out advice on its interpretation.[6]

The limits of Leopold's methods soon became plain. Obviously, he could scout only a fraction of a state's land area, and consult only a fraction of its informants. He had to ration his time, sometimes out of proportion to a particular area's promise of information. Inevitably, the mental picture he gained was, in his own words, "seasonally lop-sided"; there was a world of difference between a game environment in the summer and in the winter. But one had to begin somewhere.

Leopold learned quickly that conditions varied from state to state, and even within states. In Michigan, the decrease in cover was depressing quail populations. Woodcock and jacksnipe numbers were at best remaining stationary. In Minnesota, ruffed grouse were at the low point of their long-recognized, but little understood population cycle. Pheasants were firmly established, and able to withstand regular open seasons. In Iowa, woodcock were "practically gone"; jacksnipe "low, and decreasing on the Mississippi side"; prairie chickens "nearly gone with no hope of reestablishment as huntable game."[7]

No one generalization could cover all the conditions of all species, but after Leopold's first months on the job, he began to find evidence of the most important trend of the times: the intensification of agriculture was eliminating food and cover plants required by upland game species. Fence rows, borders, woodlots, and wetlands were disappearing from the midwestern landscape, and the quail, prairie chicken, grouse, snipe, woodcock, and in some localities even rabbits and squirrels, were disappearing with them. This was not a new realization, but Leopold had begun to give it factual substance, breadth, and definition.

Before the summer of 1928 was out, Leopold had surveyed and completed his reports on Michigan, Minnesota, and Iowa. These first reports were experimental, nowhere near as detailed as they would become with experience, but from the outset Leopold paid attention to far more than the game per se, providing descriptions of each state's peculiar geography and vegetation as it related to game. He summarized land use patterns, described the status of research and education, outlined government administration, and gauged local conservation sentiment.

Leopold returned briefly to Madison in September 1928, to set up headquarters for the survey. The University of Wisconsin offered him office space in its chemistry building. He hauled in his sturdy Leopold desk and file cabinets and hired a secretary, a freshman named Vivian Horn, at the going student rate of fifty cents an hour. Vivian Horn was an intelligent, attractive young lady, and at six feet she stood two inches taller than Leopold. She recalled her first meeting with him:

Since I was shy and had never been any good at bluffing, I told him frankly that I'd had no experience, that this would be my first job. This did not seem to discourage him, and he took me on. That was a lucky day for me. For no awkward beginning stenographer ever had a kinder and more considerate boss. He was the kind of boss who complimented me when I did well, and passed over my mistakes lightly, or overlooked them altogether. No wonder I grew devoted to him, and talked about him so much that I know I became a real bore at Anderson House, the cooperative rooming house where I lived.[8]

It was a lucky day for Leopold as well. Vivian Horn became the first of several highly competent and dedicated secretaries with whom he would work over the next twenty years. Horn did have to adjust to Leopold's peculiar schedule. When he was out of town, her work dried up to a trickle; when he returned, she was swamped. She noted immediately Leopold's complete devotion to his task. "I was astounded," she recalled, "at the amount of data he could collect, and how steadily he could work assembling the data and turning out his reports after his return."

In October, Leopold travelled to Ohio to survey the state and to set into motion SAAMI's plans to establish research fellowships for studies in game management. His partner in this was Herbert L. Stoddard, on loan from the Biological Survey. It was an important meeting for Leopold. Leopold has been inevitably dubbed the "Father of Wildlife Management," but he personally held that Stoddard was the true pioneer. Stoddard's classic study of bobwhite quail in Georgia, begun in 1924, was the first to examine a game species in detail and to utilize that information in a restoration effort. While Leopold was evolving an abstract framework for the science, Stoddard was providing its first concrete example.[9]

In Stoddard, Leopold found one of his closest professional colleagues and personal friends. "I could see at once that we were kindred spirits," Stoddard wrote years later in his memoirs. "We shared almost identical interests, from ornithology and game-bird life-history studies, to hunting and outdoor life. I was impressed by his mental capacity, his tremendous enthusiasms, and his high ethics and ideals. He had a stimulating personality, and in conversation he was able to draw out the thoughts of others, as well as freely sharing the depths of his own brilliant mind. He would think deeply and quietly a few minutes, marshaling his thoughts in logical sequence, and then express them clearly, forcefully, and eloquently."[10]

Over a period of three weeks, Leopold and Stoddard visited seven states, and enjoyed, in Stoddard's words, "a most interesting and rewarding journey. . . . meeting with groups of professors; visiting laboratories; making field trips with ecologists, ornithologists, mammalogists, botanists, entomologists, and horticulturalists; looking at land and talking to farmers, graduate students, and teachers; formulating ideas; and evaluating terrain and men. Aldo specialized in surveying the personnel and facilities, I in looking over the land near each university and the game birds frequenting it."[11] Their work resulted the following year in SAAMI's first endowed research projects.

Leopold completed his report on the Ohio survey in November 1928. The situation there was the most dismal yet. Virtually all small game— pheasants, partridge, quail, grouse, waterfowl—was suffering from the loss of habitat. Whether measured in terms of social utility, efficient conservation, or esthetic and scientific value, Ohio's "system" of depending on accidental preservation of wild game had "broken down." Leopold summarized his findings:

The basic reason why the present system fails on all three counts is that it deals with stocks only, and ignores the preservation and improvement of environments. Now that accidentally favorable environments no longer prevail, they must be deliberately made favorable, or game conservation will fail. The outstanding problem is [how to foster] and release . . . social and economic forces which will conserve environments without the undue sacrifice of democracy in sport and without interference with other forms of land use.[12]

With that, Leopold had focussed in on the issues that would most deeply concern him as a pioneering theoretician and practitioner of game management.

In December 1928, Leopold travelled to New York to attend the annual American Game Conference. He reported on "The Game Survey and Its Work," and before the conference was over was chosen chairman of a new committee to discuss and draft a national game policy. This policy, the first of its kind, was to outline the goals and priorities that anchored the new approach to wildlife conservation. Under Leopold's supervision, the committee over the next two years would draw up the policy with the utmost care and deliberation. Serving on the committee were many of the foremost figures in game conservation, and several of Leopold's old colleagues: Paul Redington, now chief of the Biological Survey, John B. Burnham, Seth Gordon, Carlos Avery, P. S. Lovejoy, Fred Pettit, John C. Phillips.[13]

After the conference, Leopold met with his sponsors in SAAMI to report on his progress. They jointly agreed that, for the time being, Leopold would scale down the scope of the survey and concentrate his efforts on just the north central block of states: Ohio, Indiana, Michigan, Illinois, Wisconsin, Minnesota, Iowa, and Missouri. After covering this territory, he would publish a full, integrated report of his findings.

To gain a taste of conditions beyond the Midwest, however, Leopold decided to try out his methods in a totally unfamiliar state. He went to Mississippi in January 1929 and found there "a widespread and intense popular interest in game and hunting . . . [excelling] any other state so far surveyed," but only the rudiments of a conservation movement—no state game department, no refuge system, little law enforcement, and no public desire for game management.[14] By this time, he had no more illusions about the enormity of his task. A farmer-trapper from New Jersey, eager to share his fifty-years' experience in the outdoors, wrote to Leopold at length on his state's game history. Leopold wrote back to express his gratitude, but bemusedly added that "I [have] found out . . . that the United States is rather a large place and I cannot at this moment even set a date on my undertaking any work on the Atlantic Coast."[15]

In February and March of 1929, Leopold delivered an important series of lectures on game management through the University of Wisconsin, his first official connection with the institution that would ultimately play such a significant role in his life. Leaders from Madison's civic, university, and conservation communities attended, including many of Leopold's closest friends.[16]

In his lectures, Leopold laid out the concepts of game management as they had evolved in recent years: the underlying rationale of the new approach, the interplay of "factors of productivity" in determining game populations, the uncertain status of various species, the utility of management techniques. These ideas had grown in Leopold's mind largely through field excursions and hunting trips, in letters and conversations with friends, and in his published articles and unpublished manuscripts. The game survey, though only in its early stages, had added the crucial missing ingredient: extensive field inspection. He was now accumulating facts to support the theoretical framework. By March 1929, Leopold was envisioning a book, to be written in the indeterminate future, that would draw this information together.

Leopold was fortunate to have in the University of Wisconsin an unusually supportive institution. Academia, in general, presented a serious barrier to the new profession. Game conservation was a suspect area of study. It had no scholars, no recognized experts, no method of research; neither did it have a Pinchot (nor the bequest of a Pinchot family's money). Joseph Dixon, a colleague of Joseph Grinnell's in California, complained to Leopold at the time that "the *orthodox* Zoology Depts. are loathe to accept such problems as life histories, or general problems involving game management, as being sufficiently *academic* to qualify for an advanced degree, particularly in [the] case of a Ph.D. . . . Of course the questions of parasites, disease and life histories are all biological problems, but there seems to be an ingrained feeling against such problems being handled with a viewpoint of their being applied to present problems [in] game management."[17]

The Sporting Arms and Ammunition Manufacturers' Institute initiated its fellowship program specifically to counteract this prejudice, and to provide at least a foot in the academic doors. Stoddard and Leopold chose the first recipients. Leopold's work had begun to reveal many pertinent findings, but three stood out: in the forest belt, population cycles violently affected such species as the ruffed grouse and snowshoe hare, but the cause, degree, and extent of the cycles were virtually unknown; all game populations in the agricultural belt were shrinking as their coverts disappeared; and the planting of exotic species was giving mixed results, often resulting in a complete waste of time, money, labor, and the creatures themselves. The first three research projects, begun in 1929, addressed these questions. On June 1, Ralph T. King began work on ruffed grouse at the University of Minnesota, designed to shed light on the cycle phenomenon. On July 1, Paul Errington began his work on bobwhite quail at the University of Wisconsin, focussing on the restoration of habitat in the dairy region of southern Wisconsin. In October, R. E. Yeatter opened studies at the University of Michigan on pheasants and Hungarian partridges, aimed at identifying the reasons for success or failure of introduced species. (The following year a fourth project was set up at the University of Arizona, where David M. Gorsuch investigated the life history and needs of Gambel's quail.) Stoddard and Leopold oversaw these projects, checking up on their progress and reporting results back to the Institute sponsors.

Leopold's own field work resumed in the spring of 1929. He spent four weeks in March and April surveying Illinois ("By and large, Illinois game will continue to suffer a net shrinkage as long as the present approach to conservation problems is continued. On the prairie, this shrinkage will approach actual zero"). He spent May and June in Indiana ("By and large, the future of game in Indiana will be determined by what is done in the next five years. Under a continuance of the present system of merely regulating seasons and planting seed stock, the ultimate closure of everything but pheasants and rabbits is more than probable").[18]

Despite such dire forecasts, Leopold's reports and predictions were not exercises in doom and gloom. His immense and growing collection of facts always led to an objective appraisal of the social and biological potential for restoration. By now he was putting the big pieces together. The concepts of "game range" and "edge effect" were emerging as the building blocks of game management, particularly in the farm belt. Game range was another term for habitat; a habitat was suitable when it afforded places to feed, hide, rest, sleep, play, and breed, all within a given animal's "cruising radius." Every species had its particular range requirements, and these requirements varied from season to season. These habitat needs had to be met, not only in particular quantities, but in the proper place, for optimal game populations to exist. Generally, the more interspersed food and cover types were—woodlands, brush, grasses, cropland—the better for the game. The larger and more solid the areas of vegetation, the poorer the habitat became. All hunters knew that edges—of forest and cropland, woodlot and pasture, oak wood and pine wood, marsh and hayfield, young and old growth forest, fencerow and cornfield—were the places to expect a good shot. This "edge effect" explained why the agricultural boom of the recent years played havoc with game. Clean farming not only appropriated more land, but reduced the diversity of its plant cover and took away its rough edges—its fence rows, for instance. Management was a matter of determining a species' habitat needs and cruising radius, and then manipulating the composition and interspersion of the required vegetation types.

Through the summer of 1929, Leopold conducted an exhaustive survey of Wisconsin. Every new report was thicker than the last with details on individual species and land practices. His Wisconsin report, completed in early October, paid particular attention to waterfowl, rare species, the organization of the Wisconsin Conservation Department, and game cycles (the last reflected the important influences of Wallace Grange, superintendent of game for the WCD, and of Alfred O. Gross, a zoologist from Bowdoin College in Maine who was studying prairie chickens in Wisconsin). Leopold identified, in summary, two fundamental trends affecting the game resource, not only in Wisconsin, but throughout the Midwest: an increase in human population and, thus, the demand for hunting opportunities; and a decrease in both the ability of land and the incentive of landowners to produce game. He explained in his Wisconsin report:

We have thus two fundamental opposing forces bearing on game as a recreational resource, both growing stronger with time, and each pulling harder against the other. Which one is gaining in Wisconsin? Where? When? Why? What statesmanship can alter the balance for the common good? How? These questions—not barbless hooks or closed seasons, campaigns or creeds—constitute the subject matter of the conservation movement.[19]

In October 1929, the overarching force that gave conservationists this dilemma—their own human economy—was shaken to its foundations. The failure of the stock markets on Black Thursday did not affect Leopold directly, at least not immediately. The arms and ammunitions industry was among those best insulated from the economic shockwaves, riding out the Depression's earliest perturbations with little damage done. For Leopold, as for most Americans, the most bitter fruits would not fall for another year and a half or so. The revived game conservation movement had achieved much in a short time, but these advances were destined to be radically redirected in the impending, uncertain social environment.

∽

Ironically, Leopold's extensive work on the game survey cut into the time he spent on his own outdoor activities. Starker and Luna, sixteen and fourteen years old respectively, no longer required their father's supervision on outings. Madison was then a compact city, easy to leave behind, and there were plenty of hunting, fishing, and exploring grounds nearby: the Madison lakes, the marshes of Lake Waubesa, Dunn's Marsh out the Verona Road, the woodlots and morainal hills beyond Middleton, the Wisconsin River bluffs to the northwest, all within easy walking, bicycling, or train-riding distance.

The whole family had caught the archery bug. Leopold corresponded regularly with a number of the country's prominent archers and equipment makers, including Roy Case of Racine and Cassius Styles of California. Leopold himself was a meticulous craftsman. Aided by whatever hands were present, he spent many of his evenings in his dank basement workshop. The basement now resembled a laboratory more than anything else. Clamps held bows-in-progress. Concoctions for mixing glues sat on shelves. Materials for everything from quivers and bowstrings to broadheads and armguards lined the workbench. Above the bench, Leopold rigged a device to measure the tensile strength of the bows. On the walls, graphs and charts plotted out weights, densities, stiffness, specific gravity, deflections. He kept a detailed record of the performance of all his bows and arrows.

The bows and arrows were not just for show. Starker did most of the hunting, but the whole family took part in target shooting and "roving" picnics at Wingra Park. In roving, one chose a distant target, loosed one's arrows in its direction, chased after the arrows, then chose another target. Target shooting became a favorite way to pass the long, pleasant afternoons of Wisconsin's summers. In 1929, the Wisconsin Archers began holding annual tournaments, in which the Leopolds regularly participated. These were lively occasions for the state's eclectic collection of archery devotees, and presented a valuable opportunity to compare gear and techniques. The true master in the Leopold family, as it turned out, was Estella. After she won the women's championship in the first state tournament, Aldo concluded that "my role is that of a coach rather than a shooter."[20] Estella became Wisconsin's women's champion for five years running, and in 1930 placed fourth at the nationals in Chicago—achievements of which Aldo was immensely proud. Estella also taught archery in the university's physical education department.

What time was left over after work and archery, Aldo devoted to his writing. "Southwestern Game Fields" had gone through a number of changes. Leopold sent a preliminary draft of the manuscript to Charles Scribner's Sons (which was planning to publish Herbert Stoddard's quail study), but it was turned down as "too regional." By March 1929, "Southwestern Game Fields" was dropped in favor of a revised version entitled "Deer Management in the Southwest." The narrower focus may well have reflected Stoddard's influence. "Southwestern Game Fields" had plainly been a too ambitious effort; by concentrating on deer alone, Leopold and his collaborators, Ligon and Pettit, hoped to keep their study down to reasonable proportions.

Even this hope, however, was unrealistic. Leopold prepared a complete outline of the proposed book, and the authors produced drafts for many of the chapters, but their project soon stalled. Distance made communication difficult. More important, ever since the Kaibab situation came to light, developments in the Southwest had complicated Leopold's basic assumptions about deer productivity.[21] Unable to investigate these conditions in person, Leopold had to rely on indirect impressions. Frank Pooler wrote to Leopold in March 1929, informing him that the overabundance of deer on the Gila was acute, and growing worse. "We are meeting some difficulties in connection with the increase of deer for localized areas under somewhat the same conditions as developed on the Kaibab."[22] Moreover, as the deer population as a whole was rising, so was the number of does relative to the number of bucks. This, Leopold noticed, was similar to the situation that had come to pass in Pennsylvania, long regarded as the model for effective deer management but now experiencing its own problems with excess deer.

Leopold's analysis of the condition constituted an important milestone along his road to an appreciation of the role of predators in natural systems. He wrote back to Pooler:

It has occurred to me that this condition is not necessarily due, as usually supposed, to the over-killing of bucks, but may rather represent an accumulation of barren does, due to the killing off of too many of the large as distinguished from the small predators.

I would not like you to accept this as anything more than a half-baked theory, but it is certainly true in both the Gila and in Pennsylvania that the remaining predators are largely those preying on fawns and yearlings, rather than grown deer. It might follow from this that there is nothing to remove the old does, and hence they overgraze the range all out of proportion to the productive power in the form of mature bucks.

I would not like to have this theory given wide publicity because it might lead to a demand for an open season on does. It is not clear in my mind that this is the real remedy. Concentrating the predatory animal work on coyotes and letting the lions alone for a while might be a better remedy.[23]

Leopold was still not able to comprehend the full ecological value of predators. Nor, as yet, was anyone else; even on the Kaibab, predators were still being hunted down as zealously as ever. Leopold advocated the control of coyotes, who blithely prospered in the face of civilization's feverish persecution.[24] In suggesting to Pooler, however, that mountain lions might serve some constructive role in the Gila, Leopold gave away a large portion of his argument—even though he himself would not know it for some years to come. He had ceased advocating predator extermination some years before. By 1925 he was advocating preservation of some large predators for scientific reasons. By 1927, he was privately voicing concerns for certain predatory species. Now, in 1929, he was implying that lions, in this one area, might be allowed to increase. He had crossed over an intellectual divide.

Meanwhile, the practical problem of overabundant deer on the Gila had to be addressed. The Forest Service was not going to allow another Kaibab to develop. A special committee, several members of which were long-time colleagues of Leopold, was formed to look into the problem. It recommended that more research be conducted to facilitate better management; that hunters temporarily be allowed to increase their take; that the pressure on lions be eased; and, finally, that a road be opened into the Gila Wilderness. Hunters, it had turned out, would not go into the wilderness unless it was made more accessible. The committee suggested that the North Star Road from Mimbres to Beaverhead, a wagon trail unused since the Apache wars, be reconstructed. In June 1929, Frank Pooler approved the recommendation. The road opened in 1931, cutting off about one-third of the Gila Wilderness. Ironically, the integrity of the wilderness was not violated from without—although private commercial interests had never let up in their opposition to it. Rather, the Gila was diminished by a threat from within, and by a limited human conception of what it ought to be: a place to grow deer and turkey and pine trees. Leopold would not soon forget this hard lesson in wilderness management.

In November 1929, Leopold managed to leave the game survey behind to join his brother Carl and Starker for a two-week deer hunt on the Gila. It would be his last such adventure there. Carl took his .30-30 Winchester, while Aldo and Starker used their osage and yew longbows respectively. They packed into an area east of Leopold's 1927 site, under the southern flanks of Black Mountain. There they hoped to avoid some of the abundant hunters and find some of the abundant deer. They succeeded on the latter count at least. In ten days they saw well over two hundred deer, does outnumbering bucks by three-to-one, fawns and yearlings scarce. Carl took an eleven-point, 175-pound buck on opening day, Aldo performing the autopsy and taking measurements. Over the next several days, Aldo and Starker found numerous targets in the ridges, canyons, and juniper breaks of the Gila, but their arrows missed their marks. Then, on the next-to-last day, Aldo saw three deer coming down a hill toward him through the brush.

When directly opposite me, and about 60 yards distant, they stopped, seemed to ponder the fate of nations, and then to my utter surprise, plunged squarely down the hill and directly at me, but still obscured by brush. As they filed across a very small opening I made out that the first two were does, while the last seemed to be a spiker. I drew on a clear opening under a juniper where I knew they would pass, about thirty yards to my left, and in a moment the two does filed by in that peculiar hesitating trot which makes it uncertain whether the next instant will bring a total stop or a terrified leap. Then came the spiker. I was not yet sure whether his horns were 6 inches (the legal minimum) and devoted the first instant of clear vision to verifying this fact, instead of to a final appraisal of distance and aim, as I should have. Then I shot. The arrow passed over his back and splintered harmlessly on the rocks. I had held only 2′ under instead of 3′. . . . More perfect chances to make a kill do not occur, except in deerhunters' dreams.[25]

Aldo returned to Madison without a deer, but with a collection of "Maxims of an Unsuccessful Deer Hunter": 1. A deer never follows anything. If he can cross a ridge, a rimrock, a ravine, or even a prairie, he will do so, especially if it is into the wind. 2. The doe always comes first—the buck after. 3. A whitetail will lie in his bed and let you pass. 4. A deer will not jump from scent close by, but he will sneak out as far as the scent will carry. . . .[26]

As for the Gila, even the numerous hunters that fall could not more than barely trim the deer population. The New Mexico Game and Fish Department, still awash in controversy and torn by factionalism, was unable to deal adequately with the problem. Although never reaching as critical a state of deterioration as the Kaibab, the Gila would remain chronically overstocked for years to come.

∽

The Sixteenth American Game Conference was held December 2–3, 1929, in New York. Leopold delivered a report to the two hundred delegates on his committee's progress in formulating the national game policy. Actually, Leopold up to that point had done most of the work himself. As was typical on a Leopold-chaired committee, the members were content to allow Leopold, increasingly recognized as one of the finest wordsmiths in conservation, to lay the groundwork himself. By July he had written a rough draft of the policy statement, which he subsequently circulated among the committee.

Leopold did not expect the 1929 conference to vote on this early draft. Several of the policy statements called for major departures from the existing order, and Leopold well understood that these moves would not be popular. He went to great pains to explain that "these criticisms are impersonal and . . . they apply just as much to us fellows who have signed the report as they do to anybody else."[27] The most controversial provision tried to address the growing problem of posted farmland. As hunters increased and game decreased through the 1920s, farmers began to post their lands against hunting, not only to protect wildlife, but to retain their own hunting privileges and to discourage the obnoxious element of undisciplined hunters. Posting, along with loss of food and cover, was the main threat to abundant, inexpensive hunting in the agricultural areas of the country. Leopold proposed to address both problems by offering the farmer an incentive to foster game on his lands. "Instead of trying to persuade the farmer not to post (which is futile and negative) the public ought to urge him not to stop at posting, but to also practice management and sell the privileges of hunting the excess game crop."[28]

As logical as this step seemed, it was not likely to sit well with a majority of sportsmen. Many of them were in conservation to begin with because of their devotion to the American tradition, as deeply engrained as the pull of the frontier and the rights of the individual, of free access to shooting grounds. Abuse of that freedom and an altered environment, however, had made reform necessary. Leopold spelled it out:

All of this may look like cold water for the American sportsmen to jump into, but it is not as cold as the other two alternatives, which are,

    1. Outright adoption of the European system for farm game, with all its abuses.

    2. Eventual complete closure of open seasons on farm game. The American farmer will insist on complete closure if the American sportsman does not find some remedy for the present situation, which is rapidly becoming intolerable, not only to farmer and sportsman alike, but also to the protectionist or non-shooting nature-lover, who is on the increase, and whose rights and opinions must be taken into account.[29]

Although the pay-for-the-privilege provision would apply only to certain classes of game on certain kinds of land, many saw it as a first move toward the much-hated "European system," wherein the landowner retained full ownership and all the rights of property when it came to game and hunting. Apparently, however, the sportsmen had begun to realize the inevitability of Leopold's point. "The crowded program prevented discussion," he later reported to his committee, "but the attitude of the conference as a whole seemed not unfriendly."[30] Leopold's draft report was published as a basis for further discussion. The committee members were to share their thoughts and present a final document for consideration at the next annual meeting.

After the conference, Leopold travelled to Missouri to complete the last of the surveys that would go into his report on the north-central states. On the road in a January ice-storm, Aldo wrote home to Estella, "This evening I drove through the 'Irish Wilderness'—I guess the wildest remaining spot east of the plains. It was quite impressive to look across miles and miles of ice-covered oak timber from the summit of the Ozarks. . . . I don't know when I'll get home Dearest. . . . I think of you all the time and the long visit we're going to have all of Feb., March, & April. . . . Goodnight Dearest and love to all of you."[31] The field work, with its long weeks on the road, was not easy for Aldo, nor for the family.

Among Leopold's findings in Missouri: "Predators show no alarming trends. All past and present ideas about predator-control seem inadequate. A rational policy must be built up on a foundation of scientific facts yet to be determined." He paid special attention to the fox. In the case of Missouri, where fox-hunting was a long-established custom, foxes could be classified as both game and predatory animals. In some localities, the object of the hunt was to kill the fox. In others, the opposite sentiment prevailed; the worst that could be said of a man was that "he would shoot a fox." "In spite of the fact that conclusions about the habits of foxes date back to the time of Aesop," Leopold wrote, "I have never learned of any competent investigation on which such conclusions might be based. . . . The question at issue is not really whether foxes do more harm than good. But rather what fox population of what species affords the best balance between harm and good in each region, all interests having been considered."[32]

While in Missouri, Leopold located a small cabin that he would use for quail hunting vacations over the next several years. The first of these trips came the following December with Ray Roark, Howard Weiss, four dogs, Starker, and a friend of Starker's.

The completion of the Missouri survey on January 28 drew Leopold's field studies to a close, at least for the time being. He spent most of 1930 back in Madison writing up his findings, working on articles, and revising the game policy statement. A considerable amount of concentration went into this work. In the game policy revision, Leopold was attempting to forge a game and wildlife program that would give the entire movement a direction while easing the tensions among the various conservation factions. In his articles, addressed primarily toward farmers and foresters, he was trying, in a sense, to enact the policy, encouraging the actual managers of the land to take steps toward game management. In his work, begun in February 1930, on the *Report on a Game Survey of the North Central States,* he was condensing his field work so as to give the sustenance of facts to the fledgling profession.

Leopold's closest associate at this point was probably Paul Errington, who had received one of the SAAMI research fellowships. Errington was not formally a student of Leopold's; his work on quail was actually performed under Leon Cole, a friend of Leopold's whose specialty—genetics—often yielded to a strong personal interest in birds. Errington, however, was a frequent visitor in Leopold's office, where they discussed the progress of the study and mulled over the latest numbers from the field. Foreshadowing his future role as a professor, Leopold gave an inordinate amount of his time to Errington, and especially to Errington's writing. Errington later gained fame as a scientist and writer in his own right; his talents, to a great extent, were honed in Leopold's office, and in laborious, late-night editing sessions at the Leopold home.

At the time, Errington later recalled, he was impressed by Leopold's self-discipline. "Aldo's own alertness and powers of synthesis were very evident from the beginning of my relations with him. Even when beset by great fatigue, he could somehow continue to think effectively." At one point, in October 1930, Leopold was hospitalized for ten days. Facing a deadline, he dictated whole chapters of the *Report on a Game Survey* from his hospital bed. Errington considered this "one of his most impressive intellectual performances."[33] By the end of October, ten of the report's thirteen chapters were finished.

Throughout the year, Leopold consulted with his fellow committee members on a final version of the game policy. In the process, he tried steadfastly to solicit as broad a range of opinion as possible. The issue of predator control was a case in point. While one of his committee members, Paul Redington, was trying to quell growing protests against the Biological Survey's predator program, Leopold asked one of the main protesters, Dr. Harold Bryant of the National Park Service, to contribute to the policy. "The recent widespread discussion of predator control policies," Leopold wrote to Bryant, "has made me anxious to include something on this subject and to seek the cooperation of the protectionists in drafting it."[34] On a variety of issues, Leopold endeavored to find common ground on which the factions could stand. Although openly promanagement, Leopold realized that the policy's success depended on a broad base of support within the conservation community.

Even within the hunting segment of that community, the division between those leaning toward the European system and those trying to retain the American system threatened to stall progress. While the reality of game depletion forced Leopold toward the European system, he was unwilling to move any further in that direction than absolutely necessary. That said, however, he and like-minded sportsmen faced a dilemma: however noble the notion of preserving the democracy of sport, the American system was admittedly less effective than the European as a means of preserving game; the average hunter of the day, the "one-gallus" shooter, showed little inclination to bear the burdens of conservation. To compound matters, the dispute had overtones of class conflict, with the wealthy, enlightened sportsmen lined up against less sophisticated hunters.

The situation culminated in September 1930 with the formation of the More Game Birds for America Foundation. Organized by New York publisher Joseph Knapp, More Game Birds proposed a large-scale, well-funded program to propagate game along European lines: private ownership and captive breeding. At this same time, Leopold was laboring to arrive at diplomatic wording in the game policy. He was also trying to extract additional funds from SAAMI to support a demonstration project in Michigan where farmers and sportsmen could work together to manage game, the first such experiment in cooperative planning. When Knapp solicited his suggestions for More Game Birds, Leopold was not sparing in his criticisms. In contrast to his own fragile gains on behalf of a more traditional American system, More Game Birds was an attempt to impose its methods and smother all alternatives. "It so happens," Leopold wrote to Knapp,

that I am personally opposed to the system of individual game ownership, and its logical corollaries, open markets and unlimited bags. . . . However, what I personally favor is beside the point. Even if . . . the Foundation [were committed] to my particular "system," I would still consider it a mistake for the Foundation to espouse it to the exclusion of all others. . . .

By and large, the country has wasted several decades already debating about conflicting theories, instead of trying some of them out. The Foundation, by its advance commitment to one of them, now threatens to prolong the debate indefinitely, instead of ending it by trying all of them, and letting experience be the umpire.[35]

Leopold's objections to More Game Bird's program were both practical and philosophical. He disagreed in principle with their aims, but he also doubted the utility of such large-scale schemes. "The United States," he wrote with the authority of experience, "is a large place, geographically in miles and acres, morally in folkways and traditions, biologically in fin, feathers, and fur." To commit the country to the private ownership of wildlife would be to prescribe a single, unproven cure to a multifaceted problem. "Reforms," Leopold held, "are attained by evolution, not by prescription, of ideas. Real reforms are always home-made."[36]

Leopold summarized his views on this issue in an article entitled, "Game Methods: The American Way." He defended his committee's game policy as ultimately more efficient, cheaper, less intensive, indigenous, and better suited to the aesthetic sensibilities of Americans, who were accustomed to truly wild game. Leopold also hoped that by evolving their own system, Americans might avoid "the ruthless suppression of predators which goes with game management in most European countries. . . . European predator-policy is empirical, not scientific. Its standards were set before biological science was born. Our standards can be better. This is not Europe's fault, but our own good luck, in that our biology preceded our management."[37]

Leopold carried these arguments with him to the Seventeenth American Game Conference in New York on December 1–2, 1930. The final version of the game policy called first and foremost for a commitment to game management. "Game," it stated in its opening paragraph, "can be safely hunted only when the stock on each parcel of land is protected against overkilling and provided with cover, food, and some protection from natural enemies." It placed the responsibility for management in the landholder's hands. It identified four main classes of game—farm, forest and range, wilderness, and migratory—each with its own peculiar management needs. It called for the recognition of game management as a distinct profession, with appropriate training programs. And it emphasized the need for cooperation within the conservation movement:

> The public, not the sportsman, owns the game.
> The public is (and the sportsman ought to be) just as much interested in conserving non-game species, forests, fish, and other wild life as in conserving game. . . .
> No game program can command the good-will or funds necessary to success, without harmonious cooperation between sportsmen and other conservationists.
> To this end sportsmen must recognize conservation as one integral whole, of which game restoration is only a part. In predator control and other activities where game management conflicts in part with other wild life, sportsmen must join with nature-lovers in seeking and accepting the findings of impartial research.[38]

"We believe," Leopold wrote in the introduction, "that experiment, not doctrine or philosophy, is the key to an American Game Policy. . . . We are convinced that only bold action, guided by as much wisdom as we can muster from time to time, can restore America's game resources. Timidity, optimism, or unbending insistence on old grooves of thought and action will surely either destroy the remaining resources, or force the adoption of policies which will limit their use to a few."[39]

The policy still faced considerable opposition from the conferees. An amendment was introduced that would strike out the key provision, that the landowner be somehow compensated for the privilege of hunting on his land. Without that incentive, Leopold countered, the entire policy would be "unbalanced and incomplete." A delegate from Virginia concurred; "free hunting eventually means no hunting. We might as well face that fact." John Burnham remarked, "this American Game Policy is not drawn up against free shooting at all. . . . I never would have signed that policy if it had been drawn up on that basis. The point really is this: we are up against a condition, not a theory." An opponent answered, "the game does not belong to the farmer; it belongs to all the people alike. . . . We have got to take that provision out of this policy. . . . Let's adhere to the old public policy and maintain it."[40]

After debate, the crippling amendment was rejected, and the policy adopted by a comfortable margin. It was the most far-reaching document yet put forth by conservationists concerned with the fate of American wildlife. Its passage, *American Forests* editorialized, "invests the . . . Conference . . . with the historic importance of a constitutional convention."[41] *Time* magazine reported the story, alongside a photograph of Leopold. The policy garnered praise from interested observers throughout the country. Even the More Game Birds group expressed support for the policy, without disclaiming its own focus.

The passage of the policy opened a new chapter in the history of American wildlife conservation. For the first time, a coherent national strategy directed the previously disparate activities of sportsmen, administrators, researchers, and (its framers hoped) landowners. The Game Policy would prove to have amazing staying power; it remained the wildlife profession's guiding statement for over forty years, until a revised policy was adopted in 1973.[42] Leopold's reasoning was sound. While necessarily sacrificing a degree of individual freedom for the good of the resource, the policy ensured that the foundation of that freedom—whatever one's attitude toward it—would not continue to erode without counter efforts. Perhaps even more significant, it gave pause for many to consider the subtle but pervasive connections between freedom and resources.

ᔄ

Leopold's *Report on a Game Survey of the North Central States* was published and distributed in the spring of 1931. No one had ever packed so many facts about game and habitat into a single book. The report contained thirteen chapters: one describing the types of game range in the upper Midwest; eight devoted to big and small game species, waterfowl, and predators; one discussing the game cycle; two on administration, research, and education; and a concluding chapter that reiterated the proposals put forth in the game policy. Leopold would later express dissatisfaction with certain aspects of the report. It was hastily compiled. As a pioneering effort, it contained a number of loose ends and blank spots. Leopold's love of maps and graphs overflowed to a fault; some readers found them incomprehensible without a magnifying glass and an hour's effort to decipher them. Nevertheless, the book was a groundbreaker, an empirical companion to the ideals of the game policy.

Praise for the *Game Survey* came in from game and wildlife men around the country. William Riley of the University of Minnesota lauded Leopold's "lack of dogmatic assertions and the obvious desire to get at the facts in the matter."[43] P. S. Lovejoy predicted that "game management in America is going to 'date' from it."[44] Joseph Grinnell criticized Leopold's relative lack of attention to predators, but approved of "the principles so forceably and convincingly enunciated in your book."[45]

William T. Hornaday thought the book "very excellent," and then proceeded to damn it. "I have been impressed," he wrote to Leopold, "by the final and outstanding fact that uprears its head like the Peak of Teneriffe. It is the absolute hopelessness of either *restoring game,* or *maintaining* game, without a great volume of new help from new measures to now reduce the excessive killing of game. . . . Your people should be mighty glad, and profoundly thankful, to me and my allies for what we have done . . . in contributing to your success." Although blinded by his own zeal, Hornaday accurately identified the main obstacle in the path of the new generation of game managers: "The importance of *farmer activities and expenditures* to the success of what you are trying to work out is vital. The difficulties that confront you in your efforts to secure your objectives are colossal." Hornaday could not resist tossing a final bucket of cold water on Leopold's work: "Your efforts are scientific, scholarly, and fine; but you are bucking against the impossible. Your results through farmer help will be so scattered and so *trivial* that it will not amount to shucks! Fifteen years from now, remember this warning."[46]

Other preservationists were not so apocalyptic. Willard Van Name of the American Museum of Natural History, a leader in an insurgent effort to reform the Audubon Society, wrote to Leopold, "Those of us whose main interest is in preserving our native wild life from extinction rather than merely saving such species as can provide sport (although I used to shoot myself) have been coming to feel for a good many years past that not much help could be obtained from sportsmen. . . . It is a bright spot in the midst of a dark outlook to find a sportsmen's organization and the arms and ammunition manufacturers joining a real effort to get at the truth of the game situation, and to tell it, whether it is agreeable or not."[47]

Publication of the *Game Survey* brought Leopold a new measure of respect in the conservation community. While previously acknowledged for his writing ability and for his leadership in forestry, wilderness preservation, and wildlife protection, Leopold was now recognized as the most informed game expert in the nation. His command of facts was formidable, his network of friends and colleagues continental. His office became something of a national clearinghouse of information on research, personnel, and publications, an advisory service for federal administrators and dirt farmers alike.

For the rest of his life, Leopold would wear this mantle of leadership with integrity and forbearance. A change had overcome his personality since beginning the game survey. Wildlife had always been his deepest interest, the motive force of his conservation impulse. When he made it his full-time profession, it took the edge off his youthful egoism. He once wrote to his friend Fred Pettit that "the fundamental weakness of the game movement so far has been that its leaders gradually come to value their personal prestige more than the game. It has happened to every one of them so far, although they are of course unaware of it."[48] Leopold was aware of it, and he was determined not to make the same mistake. He was far ahead of his contemporaries in his comprehensive understanding of the environment and in his approach to environmental problems — far enough ahead that few could even appreciate the level on which he was thinking. Such enlightenment isolated him, yet it was no longer an excuse for condescension. Of the reaction to his *Game Survey* report, he complained that he had received "quite a stack of commendatory letters, but it is rather noticeable that they come from the intellectual vanguard of the sportsmen's movement rather than from the rank and file."[49] In a letter to Seth Gordon, he warned against the tendency "to make technical game men a self-contained class" and "the all-too-prevalent trend toward 'priestcraft,' i.e., toward making a 'mystery' of the subject requiring a special 'caste' to explain such mystery to the lay public."[50] Only by making game management a matter of common knowledge among the public, the outdoorsman, and the landowner could such tendencies be countered.

Over the years, impressions of Leopold would fall into two categories. Some found him cool, aloof, definitely not one of the boys; he was impatient with jealousy, foolishness, and pettiness. Most, however, knew a humbler, unusually kind Leopold who went out of his way to listen and to offer advice. This side of Leopold seems to have gained the ascendancy once he began to carve out his niche in game management. It took a large task to balance out Leopold's own high opinion of himself.

The penchant for acting as peacemaker in conservation quarrels seems, however, to have emerged from within. The external conflicts between aesthetes and utilitarians, sportsmen and preservationists, academics and outdoorsmen, managers and observers, were personal matters for Leopold, for the factions reflected in many ways his own internal composition. He was all of these. His inner gyroscope helped him to maintain his philosophical equilibrium, but the torque of changes — social and ecological — in the outside world was shifting his general position. He did not always find himself in a comfortable place. At one point, one of the companies in SAAMI ran an advertisement encouraging hunters to use their products to kill hawks and owls . . . period. Leopold, midway in his shift of attitude toward predators, wrote a well-reasoned letter to his sponsors, pointing out that "some [of us] doubt the wisdom of killing the natural enemies of game" and that "others contend that sportsmen are often inclined to kill any and all possible enemies of game, without first getting substantial

evidence of just which species are harmful, and under what conditions."
He asked that such advertisements at least specify species, and include
only those proven to be "harmful."[51]

With the *Report on a Game Survey of the North Central States* behind
him, Leopold turned to his next project: completion of a textbook on game
management. He had been planning such a book ever since abandoning
the "Southwestern Game Fields" manuscript. The 1929 series of lectures
at the University of Wisconsin provided the rough outline for such a text,
and he now had the field background and professional connections to complete the task.

He envisioned the book as a companion to the *Game Survey,* and for
a while he had actually worked on them simultaneously. He devoted the
first six months of 1931 to the new book. Conceived as a unifying text on
the history, theory, and practice of the profession, *Game Management,*
unlike the *Game Survey,* would not be confined to a particular region; and
unlike Herb Stoddard's *The Bobwhite Quail,* it would not be concerned
with a single species and its habitat. It was intended, rather, as a guide that
game researchers, administrators, and other conservationists could apply
to any species in any habitat.

Leopold worked tirelessly on the book. It was a measure of his dedication that he applied himself so single-mindedly to it even as the nation
slipped toward the nadir of its economic condition. As the arms and ammunition industry began to feel the effects of the Depression, Leopold's
sponsors began to consider ways to scale down the survey program. Leopold persevered, though, and by June 1931 the book was nearly complete.
Vivian Horn kept pace, not only with the manuscript, but with Leopold's
rapidly growing mail pile. At home, the children were pressed into type-
writer duty at the dining room table. Leopold finished writing in July 1931,
but given the unstable economic conditions, finding a publisher would
prove to be difficult.

By mid-1931, SAAMI was looking to curtail completely the game survey. Leopold, hoping to salvage the promising research fellowships, recommended that his own set-up be rearranged so as to allow the individual
states to share the burden of travel and publication expenses. SAAMI approved the plan, and began to accept applications from the states.

During the summer of 1931, Leopold became involved in a local venture that allowed him to put into practice the provisions of the new game
policy. Leopold was travelling in western Dane County one Sunday, looking for promising hunting grounds for the upcoming season. He ended
up in Riley, a mail stop on the Chicago and Northwestern line that consisted of a church, a general store, and a small stone cheese factory. "I
stopped at a farmyard for a drink of water. The farmer, [Reuben] J. Paulson was washing milk cans at the well. We talked game. He needed relief

from trespassers who each year poached his birds despite his signs; I needed a place to try management as a means of building up something to hunt. We concluded that a group of farmers, working with a group of town sportsmen, offered the best defense against trespass, and also the best chance for building up game. Thus was Riley born."[52] Paulson organized eleven neighboring farmers. Leopold organized a small group of his Madison hunting partners—Ray Roark, Tom Coleman, Bill Schorger, and Howard Weiss. Together they formed the Riley Game Cooperative, the farmers providing the land and some materials, the town members furnishing operating funds, and both contributing labor. They began restocking and winter feeding that fall.

Riley immediately became one of Leopold's favorite hunting spots, not only because of the improved habitat, but because he and the Riley farmers became good friends—once they realized he was as comfortable in a barnyard as he was in town. One day Luna and his father went to Riley and, before going off to hunt, stopped at Paulson's for a chat. They walked into the barn and passed the time of day with Paulson, who was shoeing a horse. Paulson was just about to drive a nail in when Leopold said, "Mr. Paulson, that nail is going in the wrong direction." Paulson paused, put down the horse's hoof, stood up, turned to Leopold and said, "Where did you learn to shoe a horse?!" Aldo replied, "Well, I've done quite a lot of that."[53]

That same summer, Leopold took part in one of the most intellectually significant events of his life. Earlier in the year he had received an invitation to attend an international conference of biologists in Quebec. The conference was planned by Copley Amory, an American official who had a long-standing interest in the occurrence of natural cycles. Amory spent his summers at his Canadian retreat, a converted trading post on the Matamek River north of the Gulf of St. Lawrence. He was impressed there by the profound effect of periodic natural fluctuations, particularly in the populations of cod and fur-bearers, on the local economy of Labrador. This interest led him to the idea of a general conference on cyclic phenomena, to be attended by a broad range of researchers.

Leopold's interest in cycles was itself at a high point. In the *Game Survey of the North Central States,* he had concluded that, "until science discovers the cause and mechanism of the cycle, all efforts to manage and conserve the cyclic species must necessarily grope in darkness."[54] Leopold may have been convinced of the importance of such research, but persuading his SAAMI overseers was not so easy, and the hard times did not make it any easier. Responding to Leopold's request for travel money, the chairman of the Game Restoration Committee asked him "to tell me as frankly as you are able what commercial benefit will accrue to the Sporting Arms and Ammunition Manufacturers' Institute as a result of your attendance at the Labrador conference."[55] Hard-nosed businessmen were not keen on the practical value of such pure research, especially when it involved as wispy a notion as invisible global rhythms. Nevertheless, Leopold argued convincingly for the theoretical and practical value to be gained, and his sponsors sent him off to Canada.

The Matamek Conference, as it came to be called, brought together an extraordinary collection of specialists: mammalogists, entomologists, ornithologists, marine biologists, foresters, fisheries experts, bacteriologists, meteorologists, astronomers, and an assortment of legislators, administrators, and journalists (Leopold was listed in the program as an "editor"). Their aim was to exchange information from their various fields, and perhaps to show some general correlations between such diverse phenomena as sunspot activity, climatic patterns, cod populations, bacterial outbreaks, and national economies. As one newspaper account put it, "who would suppose that the whole world, including man, would be upset by booms and crashes in the lives of some of the rat family?"[56]

The participants arrived at the Matamek River on July 22, and for nine days compared notes, heard and presented a variety of reports, and took advantage of the salmon and trout fishing opportunities. Leopold forged several important and enduring friendships in the course of the conference. Harrison Lewis, of the Canadian National Parks Branch, promised Leopold a copy of an article he had written entitled "The Philosophy of Wildlife Conservation"; the article stimulated Leopold to rewrite the end of *Game Management*. Leopold also met William Rowan, a waterfowl expert from Alberta, for the first time. He and Rowan remained close friends, and would later collaborate in supervising some of the earliest research on waterfowl habitats and life histories.

Of all the new friends Leopold made at Matamek, none was so important as Charles Elton, Professor of Zoology at Oxford University. Elton, thirty-one years old at the time, was easily the guiding force at the conference. At the age of twenty-six, he had written *Animal Ecology*, a classic in its field and the one book that more than any other ushered in the modern approach to functional ecology. He came to Matamek to explain the results of his study of the records of the Hudson's Bay Company. By analyzing fur-trading records, which stretched back over a period of several hundred years, Elton was able to identify distinct cyclical trends that corroborated more recent data. It was Copley Amory's meeting with Elton that had precipitated the Matamek Conference.

It is hard to say when Leopold first became aware of Elton.[57] He had likely read *Animal Ecology* by early 1931, but Elton's ideas had not yet permeated his approach to wildlife management. He was still a manager first, and a scientist second.[58] The reverse could be said of Elton. A quiet, brilliant young man, he had arrived at ecology not via the rough and tumble route of American conservation, as had Leopold, but out of the rich British tradition of natural history; "Ecology," he wrote in the opening lines of *Animal Ecology,* "is a new name for a very old subject. It simply means scientific natural history."[59] In writing his book, Elton shot a lasting dose of intellectual vitality back into the veins of that tradition. *Animal Ecology* outlined many of the concepts—trophic layers, food chains, food webs, the "pyramid of numbers," population dynamics, and so forth—that underlay the new science, and that would help usher in a revolution in conservation philosophy.[60]

It is unlikely that Elton had heard of Leopold prior to the Matamek Conference. Despite their differences, and possibly because of them, they struck up an immediate friendship. It was a fortuitous convergence. They complemented one another superbly. Elton was abstract, a theorist whose field experience was accurate, but relatively limited. Leopold was above all a field man who knew enough theory to give his observations broad application. Elton was laying the foundations of ecology; Leopold was attempting to apply the science even before its foundations were set.

Although the Matamek Conference ended without any sweeping conclusions, promising connections did emerge between sunspot, game, and disease cycles. No one had expected any easy explanation for the great waves and pulses that rocked the earth from time to time. All went away invigorated by the discussions, and eager to perform follow-up research. Leopold and Elton would maintain a steady intercontinental correspondence. Their influence on one another was mutual and, again, complementary. Elton's ecological ideas would influence ever more deeply Leopold's maturing philosophy. Elton's writing, in turn, would increasingly bear the mark of Leopold's conservation thinking. Leopold, writing to Herb Stoddard, called the Matamek Conference "the best thing of its kind that I have ever attended."[61]

∽

The state of Iowa created a new Fish and Game Commission in 1931. The commission had hardly taken its seats when, following a legislative directive, it began to prepare a comprehensive, twenty-five year plan to guide its conservation activities. SAAMI, under its new arrangement, loaned Leopold to the state to help coordinate the plan and to direct its section on game. This was a visionary project, and just the sort Leopold liked. Not only would it allow him to return to and apply himself in his home state, but he was given six full months in which to do so. Furthermore, it was an opportunity to update his original 1928 survey of the state, which he now looked back on as "very sketchy. . . . It rather embarrasses me to have the work I did there called a game survey at all."[62] On October 7,

1931, Leopold was back on home ground, "the fat black loam of Iowa."[63]

After an initial three-week tour, Leopold reported mixed game conditions: pheasants were thriving, rabbits plentiful, quail abundant in the south but absent from the prairie regions. The waterfowl situation was "pitiful." Farmer relations were "approaching a crisis. . . . In [some] counties farmers are so sore about corn damage and hunter damage that they deliberately trample nests and shoot off the breeding birds in spring, hanging them on the fences along roads for everybody to see." Loss of habitat was still the fundamental problem and it was growing worse. "The devegetation of Iowa is spectacular," he wrote, "even since 1928 when I was here before." Still, he reported that he had "never encountered as much interest in any state, or as much willingness to try anything that promises to deliver results. . . . Generally speaking, the game situation is ready for a revolution, constructive or destructive. The degree to which it is constructive will depend on the local leadership."[64]

Leopold returned to Madison in November to find he had been awarded *Outdoor Life*'s gold medal, which was presented annually to two individuals, one from the east and one from the west, in recognition of their service to conservation. In presenting the award, the magazine (published by the Izaak Walton League) called the *Game Survey of the North Central States* an "outstanding contribution" to the cause of game restoration.

But in the Depression autumn of 1931, a medal and a dime bought a cup of coffee. Between trips to Iowa Leopold tried to find a publisher for *Game Management*, but hard times had hit the industry, and publishers were reluctant to put out a book on a subject that was still, by and large, nonexistent. Leopold was confident. "The need for such a book," he wrote to one prospective publisher, "has grown so rapidly that it might be a moderate success in spite of the depression. . . . I am willing to make a substantial contribution personally to its publication, and while I cannot prove it, I feel that there will be a better demand for it than the average publisher is able to appreciate."[65] The manager of the company was not convinced. "It seems," he replied to Leopold, "that we are of the same opinion as submitted to you by other publishers. . . . Taking our own experience in book sales, things are dull, very dull indeed! It would be wiser, perhaps, to await the return of prosperity, or at least a renewal of confidence in our economic system."[66]

In December, while attending the game conference in New York, Leopold visited the office of Charles Scribner's Sons. They offered to publish *Game Management* if Leopold would make certain changes to reduce production expenses, and if he would contribute five hundred dollars to help offset the cost. Leopold agreed to the terms and signed the contract on January 11, 1932, his forty-fifth birthday.

Since completing the manuscript the previous summer, Leopold had distributed drafts of *Game Management* for comment and review. This process would continue for another six months, before Leopold sent off the final version to Scribner's. Most of the nation's foremost wildlife experts were consulted at one point or another, including Stoddard, Walter P. Taylor, P. S. Lovejoy, and John C. Phillips; E. A. Goldman, W. L. McAtee, Stanley Young, and Wallace Grange, all of the Biological Survey; and the SAAMI fellows and their advisors, including R. G. Green of Minnesota, a pioneer in the study of wildlife diseases.

In general, Leopold's correspondents had particular specialities — species, regions, population dynamics, physiology. Thus, Leopold was rarely faced with the dilemma of reconciling conflicting information or positions. Such was not the case when it came to predators. When Leopold returned from Iowa in November 1931, the *Outdoor Life* award was not the only thing he found waiting on his desk. He had also received a letter from Olaus Murie, a Biological Survey researcher in Wyoming. Murie, a scientist-naturalist of tremendous talent, had joined the survey in 1920, and spent a number of years travelling the far northern expanses of the continent on various research outings. In 1927 he was assigned to Jackson, Wyoming, where he was to perform classic early studies of the famous elk herds of Jackson Valley. Murie was, and remained for years, a leading critic of his own agency's hate-ridden campaign against predators.

After reading Leopold's *Game Survey* and his article on American game methods, Murie "noted a sense of fairness" in Leopold's discussion, and decided to write to him on the question of predators. "Personally," Murie wrote, "I have felt that too much attention has been given to the predatory animal factor." This was notably true, he believed, in the case of coyote predation on elk, a relationship Murie had intensively studied for over three years. "I do not find the coyote a bad fellow at all," he concluded. "As far as the elk are concerned he is not nearly as big a factor as several other things. I will not go into detail here, but would point out that a considerable number of people enjoy the coyote in the hills, he is a part of the environment, and his entire removal would make elk hunting less attractive to some people. I feel that if sportsmen and non-shooting conservationists could get together, progress would be so much more rapid. If sport could be placed on a higher plane, and some recent plans might work in that direction, nature lovers in general would be more likely to help in game matters. We all have the same interests and must work together to accomplish anything."[67]

Leopold, sensing a kindred spirit, replied with obvious gratitude. "I have had a good many commendatory letters about my recent publications which said this, that, and the other thing, but I do not prize any of them as highly as I do your letter which makes a point of the question of fairness. None of us, of course, ever attains complete fairness, but it gives one no end of encouragement to have your spontaneous comment on this point. I would like very much to discuss these matters with you sometime in person."[68]

Murie's supervisors in Washington were not entirely pleased with his coyote findings, and neither were they confident that Leopold would treat the issue fairly in his forthcoming book. E. A. Goldman, senior biologist at the survey, reviewed Leopold's chapter on predators. Leopold had written that overcontrol of predators "is almost invariably followed by" excessive increases in prey populations, particularly in "buffer" species (those small animals, such as rodents, that serve to "divert the attention of predators" away from game species). Goldman took exception to such a blanket statement. "Our work," he wrote to Leopold, "is essentially a campaign against coyotes. . . . Under normal conditions rodents are so abundant and [their] breeding rate is so enormous that coyotes and probably most predatory animals have comparatively little effect upon them. On the other hand, the effect of coyotes upon large game and upon game birds in general . . . may be very vital." He cautioned Leopold to "avoid including material that might convey wrong impressions in regard to this highly controversial subject."[69]

Another voice in the debate was W. L. McAtee, in charge of food habits research for the Biological Survey, and a man whose work Leopold respected greatly. McAtee wrote to Leopold in January 1932, and explained his belief "that natural enemies should not be sacrificed merely to insure sport. . . . I continually try to maintain a sane middle-of-the-road position, economic values being recognized, but the words and deeds of many sportsmen make it hard for me to do so."[70]

Like McAtee, Leopold tried to maintain a middle-of-the-road position, but the general direction of the road was changing. In December 1931, the American Society of Mammalogists, still the leading institutional critic of the Biological Survey's policies, asked its members to petition the year-old special Senate Committee on Wild Life Resources on the issue of bear protection in Alaska. In 1930, the Alaska Game Commission had lifted restrictions on the killing of bears. The mammalogists were leading an effort to establish a bear sanctuary on Admiralty Island. Leopold wrote to Senator Frederic Walcott of Connecticut, a personal acquaintance and chairman of the Senate Committee:

I personally lack first-hand knowledge of Alaskan conditions but I strongly lean to the belief that where commercial interests conflict with bear conservation, the former have been given undue priority. I favor the sanctuary and will strongly support any policy which your committee or others may evolve to not merely perpetuate the species, but to assure such perpetuation on the largest range in the largest possible numbers.[71]

The issue raised itself time and again in the early 1930s, Leopold shifting from concerned sportsman to practical manager to preservationist according to the circumstance. But always he returned to the starting position of inquiring scientist. He had the benefit of close contact with Paul Errington, who, it was now evident, was born to study predators. Errington's research was ostensibly on quail management, but he had taken it far beyond that. His studies of quail at Prairie du Sac, near Madison, provided some of the earliest hard data on predator-prey relationships, and called into question many of the assumptions prevalent among biologists. According to Errington's observations, quail were far more sensitive to food and cover conditions (Leopold's "welfare factors") than to the depredations of hawks, owls, and foxes. Or, as Leopold inimitably put it, "better food and cover represent, in many instances, the cheapest and most effective predator-insurance."[72]

Leopold's final version of the predation chapter in *Game Management* would draw heavily on Errington's findings. At the end of the chapter, Leopold commented on the general issue that confronted all parties to the debate:

If [the sportsman] emerges from this review with the idea that the whole play is hopelessly complex, he will have missed the point. If on the other hand he feels his curiosity intrigued and his fairness challenged to gain a better understanding of his local problems, then our purpose is accomplished. There is only one completely futile attitude on predators: that the issue is merely one of courage to protect one's own interests and that all doubters and protestants are merely chickenhearted.[73]

Leopold returned to Iowa during the first three months of 1932 to make a further field survey of game conditions for the conservation plan. At this time, too, Errington completed his studies at Madison and agreed to head up a new wildlife research station at Iowa State University. Jay "Ding" Darling, Iowa's Pulitzer Prize–winning cartoonist and a dedicated sportsman and conservationist, provided the moral and financial support for the setup, which later became a model for the nation's wildlife research system. Leopold and Darling had first met in 1928, during Leopold's original game survey of Iowa, and renewed their acquaintance during Leopold's second stint. Both were destined to play key roles in the development of wildlife conservation in the years shortly to follow.

By March 1932, Leopold's support from SAAMI had dried up completely. The institute had been reimbursing him $1250 a month until the previous December, when the economy finally forced the gun companies to cut back. With the end of his field work in Iowa, Leopold was "discontinued" from SAAMI. Iowa continued to pay him a consulting fee of $700 per month until he finished his report in May. After that, Leopold was on his own with nothing but his vast experience and a letterhead that proclaimed his services as "consulting forester."

&

As Leopold completed his field work in Iowa, there appeared in the pages of *The Condor* a diatribe from T. T. McCabe criticizing both Leopold's *Game Survey* and the program of the More Game Birds Foundation as "a framework of pernicious doctrines."[74]

Leopold's response was penetrating. After first disavowing himself of the alliance with More Game Birds, Leopold defended his approach as the most workable way out of the present deadlock, "from which the sharpest pens gain much glory, but the game gains nothing except a further chance to disappear." The arch-protectionists were, to Leopold's thinking, unrealistic:

Does anyone still believe that restrictive game laws alone will halt the wave of destruction which sweeps majestically across the continent, regardless of closed seasons, paper refuges, bird-books-for-school-children, game farms, Izaak Walton Leagues, Audubon Societies, or the other feeble palliatives which we protectionists and sportsmen, jointly or separately, have so far erected as barriers in its path? . . . I have tried to build a mechanism whereby the sportsmen and the ammunitions industry could contribute financially to the solution of this problem without dictating the answer themselves. . . . These things I have done, and I make no apology for them. Even if they should ultimately succeed, they will not restore the good old days of free hunting of wholly natural wild life (which I loved as well as Mr. McCabe), but they may restore something. That something will be more native to America, and available on more democratic terms, than "More Game Birds" pheasants, even though it be less so than [in] Mr. McCabe's dreams of days gone by.[75]

His critic's nostalgic vision, Leopold wryly noted, "might be realized if America consisted of 120 million ornithologists"; his own approach, however, was designed "to fit the unpleasant fact that America consists largely of business men, farmers, and 'Rotarians', busily playing the national game of economic expansion. Most of them admit that birds, trees, and flowers are nice to have around, but few of them would admit that the present 'depression' in waterfowl is more important than the one in banks." One could courageously deny this state of affairs, "and die heroically under the heels of the mob." "But," Leopold asked, "have we not already compromised ourselves?" His poignant answer to that question directly addressed the rub that confronts all reformers, whether conservationists or not: that one must live in, take part in, enjoy, and make contributions to the same world that one works to change:

I realize that every time I turn on an electric light, or ride on a Pullman, or pocket the unearned increment on a stock, or a bond, or a piece of real estate, I am "selling out" to the enemies of conservation. When I submit these thoughts to a printing press, I am helping cut down the woods. When I pour cream in my coffee, I am helping to drain a marsh for cows to graze, and to exterminate the birds of Brazil. When I go birding or hunting in my Ford, I am devastating an oil field, and re-electing an imperialist to get me rubber. Nay more: when I father more than two children I am creating an insatiable need for more printing presses, more cows, more coffee, more oil, and more rubber, to supply which more birds, more trees, and more flowers will either be killed, or what is just as destructive, evicted from their several environments.

What to do? I see only two courses open to the likes of us. One is to go live on locusts in the wilderness, if there is any wilderness left. The other is surreptitiously to set up within the economic juggernaut certain new cogs and wheels whereby the residual love of nature, inherent even in "Rotarians," may be made to recreate at least a fraction of those values which their love of "progress" is destroying. A briefer way of putting it: if we want Mr. Babbitt to rebuild outdoor America, we must let him use the same tools wherewith he destroyed it. He knows no other.[76]

Aldo Leopold was not a naive man. He saw clearly into the complexities of the human condition as well as the natural world; he was committed now to a realistic reconciliation of the two. He had always been aware of the tensions that drove people, and that drove himself, but not until the time when he first devoted himself completely to his chosen field of wildlife conservation could he begin to encompass those tensions, accept them, and employ them toward a greater end. That end was not just more quail, or Alaskan bears, or continued days afield, but fullness of life, and fit environments in which such fullness was no accident, but a birthright.

14

Consulting Forester
(1932–1933)

THERE WAS scarce demand for any sort of work in the spring of 1932, much less for that of a consulting forester. The Depression held Madison, a small city with its economic base in agriculture, education, government, and small businesses, in a dull grip of stagnation. At the government's end of State Street, politicians tried to legislate a way out of the crisis; at the university's end, economists tried to theorize a way out. In the Greenbush, the concentration of ethnic neighborhoods on the south side of town, old world resourcefulness carried the city's newer immigrants through the hard times. At hobo camps along the shores of Monona and Waubesa, the dispossessed waited for trains to leave the downtown yards, eastbound to Chicago, westbound to the switches at St. Paul, and thence to points west.

Leopold's credentials, impressive though they were, would not bring him work for some months to come. Few states, industries, private groups, or individuals had dollars to spend on such luxuries as conservation. Undeterred, Leopold returned to work on *Game Management*. In May, he began to revise the manuscript, hoping to ship it off to Scribner's by the end of the summer. Meanwhile, he had to provide for a family. He had invested an inheritance of $7,000 that his father had left him, and he still held stock in the Leopold Desk Company. Returns on these, plus whatever savings he and Estella had accumulated, were enough to see them through the toughest months, though not without sacrifices. They always managed to find eight dollars per week to keep Ida and later Martha, their live-in maids, employed. Neither Aldo nor Estella, it seems, considered turning to their families. In fact, Clara Leopold had lost her financial security when the banks collapsed. Only quick manipulation of her accounts by her children kept the remnants of the Starker estate intact.

Paul Errington later described this period of personal crisis, when Leopold was "without income for months during 1932 and 1933 in the worst of the Depression. He took this punishment most creditably, kept up the standard of living of his family as well as circumstances allowed, worked on the manuscript of *Game Management,* and made plans with courage and realism. He was offered desirable positions, including a professorship at a prominent state college, but those would have entailed moving his home from Madison, which he was reluctant to do."[1]

Leopold wanted to stay in Wisconsin for several reasons, chief among them the fact that both Starker and Luna were now attending the university, and extra room and board costs would have been prohibitive. The boys had inherited their mother's handsome Spanish features and their father's sharpness of mind and love of the outdoors. The similarities ended there. Starker and Luna were two quite different young men. Easygoing and cheerful, Starker had a ready sense of humor and his father's sartorial tastes. He was sixteen when he enrolled at the university in 1929. Luna was more serious, no less spirited or tastefully dressed than Starker, but tremendously self-disciplined, especially when it came to his studies. Luna entered the university prior to his fifteenth birthday, aiming at first for a career in civil engineering, but ultimately following a natural interest in geology.

Aldo and Estella did not push the children into any particular field. In fact, Aldo seems to have made a conscious effort to avoid instilling biases in them. All the children eventually gravitated toward personal and professional involvement in the natural sciences, but they were not led there blindfolded. If Aldo did lead them, it was not through outright coercion, but through the subtler arts of campground and dinner table conversation. "He treated us with considerable dignity," Starker recalled. "I suppose that had as much as anything else to do with our being so intensely interested in what he had to say."[2] Always an eager listener, Aldo inevitably began conversations by asking the children what they thought about this or that. At the dinner table, he would routinely inquire of each of the five in turn, "What happened today in your life that was interesting?" The discussions veered unpredictably into the subject of the day—boats, horses, books, archery, history, birds.

If Aldo did not prod the children along, neither did he express undue worry about their difficulties. Estella was the family worrier. Aldo simply assumed that, given time, they would exercise proper judgment. When the time came for the family to buy a new car, Aldo gave Luna, a mechanically inclined sixteen-year-old, the responsibility for selecting it. Such trust was not always rewarded, but Aldo was an unusually patient man. After Starker discovered coeds, fraternities, and alcoholic beverages during his freshman year at the university, his grades plunged. At first, Aldo barely mentioned the subject. When Estella expressed her dismay, Aldo took Starker to lunch and explained calmly, "Now, Starker, your mother is worried about you. . . ." One day, however, Starker surpassed the limits of his father's patience. The new Chevrolet was only a month old when Starker took it to a poker game. A young lady whom Starker was seeing at the time borrowed the car to drive to her sorority house, and proceeded to flip it over into a ditch.

Hearing of the accident over the phone, Aldo asked, "Is Aggie all right?" The answer was yes, apparently she wasn't hurt. Then he turned to Estella. "Estella, you'd better ask Aggie to come to dinner. She might think we're angry at her for wrecking the car."

When Starker returned, he endured a stern fatherly rebuke, with no nonsense. "That's it!" Aldo intoned. "We're not going to buy another car. And furthermore, your grades, son, are so poor that we're going to take you out of school." Aldo decided to send Starker off to the state game farm. "I'm going to get you a job and you can work out there until you show yourself to be man enough that we might consider putting you back in school—or maybe you'll have to support yourself."[3] Shades of Yale.

It was about time for Starker to try his own wings anyway. By their seventeenth or eighteenth summers, the children were expected to learn to fend for themselves out in the world. In the Depression summer of 1932, Starker went into exile at the state game farm in Poynette, while Luna landed an unpaid position at the federal government's new Soil Erosion Control Station at La Crosse, on the Mississippi. The boys did not know it at the time, but both had found the fields in which they would eventually make their own substantial contributions.

∽

Leopold scrambled through May, June, and July, 1932, to complete the revisions of *Game Management*. He updated the manuscript to include the most recent field results and bibliographic references, to take into account professional criticisms, to simplify the maps and tables, and to "lighten up" heavy parts of the text.

As he worked the book into final shape, Leopold was also coming to terms with the greater questions his work addressed: the philosophical context in which management techniques would be applied. *Game Management* was the most extensive collection of information on wildlife conservation yet assembled, a masterful synthesis of management theory and techniques. But Leopold went further. He sprinkled the technical explanations of population dynamics, game range, winter cover, and refuge patterns with his own sense of humor and irony, his knowledge of history, and his approach to conservation. *Game Management* was to provide its readers not only with a knowledge of the field, but with a management philosophy as well.

Game Management was clearly oriented toward the utilitarian. It explained how the natural world could be manipulated and controlled to produce more game. The first sentence of the first chapter defined game management as "the art of making land produce sustained annual crops of wild game for recreational use." In this sense, Leopold was trying to do with game what Pinchot thirty years earlier had done with the nation's forests. Yet, just as Leopold was never a purely utilitarian forester, growing board feet instead of forests, neither was he a mere game farmer. He aspired to management that grew natural species "in an environment not greatly altered for the purpose in hand, relying on partial control of a few factors to enhance the yield above what unguided nature would produce."[4]

"Guiding" nature meant using natural processes to produce more game. Ideally, a manager's work would hardly be noticed: fencing out cows here, planting patches of brush there, downing strategic oak limbs, keeping a close eye on the activities of predators, perhaps providing feeding stations in the winter. The hoped-for result—more game and better game conditions —could not be measured in dollars and cents, or even in numbers, alone. In a chapter on "Game Economics and Esthetics," Leopold wrote, "It is not merely a supply of game, in the strictly quantitative sense, that is in question. The conservation movement seeks rather to maintain values in which quality and distribution matter quite as much as quantity. Like most other really important things, this conception of quality eludes definition. We might, if we chose to spend the money, release each year millions of artificially reared birds, and thus 'maintain' a supply of game in the quantitative sense. But would we thus maintain value? I think not."[5]

Game Management captured Leopold in a state of transition. It was his crowning work as a pioneer in game management, as well as his fullest indication yet that he was seeing far beyond the utilitarian conservation philosophy. The idea of controlling nature, albeit with low-intensity techniques, dominated the book, but Leopold's concession was not to the utilitarian philosophy per se, but to the simple reality of the "wild life" situation:

There are still those who shy at this prospect of a man-made game crop as at something artificial and therefore repugnant. This attitude shows good taste but poor insight. Every head of wild life still alive in this country is already artificialized, in that its existence is conditioned by economic forces. Game management merely proposes that their impact shall not remain wholly fortuitous. The hope of the future lies not in curbing the influence of human occupancy—it is already too late for that—but in creating a better understanding of the extent of that influence and a new ethic for its governance.[6]

His last point was crucial, for *Game Management* also marked the beginning of a renewed attempt by Leopold to define more fully his own conservation philosophy. For some time, he had been growing impatient with conservation's reluctance to address the larger questions it raised. "Understanding" and "ethics" were seen as the province of scholars, yet few philosophers and historians showed any interest in conservation, and they too often labored in utter ignorance of natural history. Leopold began to explore this void as much out of frustration as desire.

His exploration began, as usual, in the field. As early as 1930, if not earlier, he was speaking of ecology as "the rock bottom of game management."[7] He concurred with his friend S. Prentiss Baldwin, an ornithologist from Ohio, who encouraged him to broaden game studies to include "the whole field of wild life, as game preservation cannot be intelligently studied or controlled without consideration of all other wild life."[8] Leopold was prescient enough to see that game management techniques could be applied to nongame wildlife, a point he repeatedly made in his efforts to mollify preservationists; but he was practical enough to realize that such opportunities might never arise unless those techniques were first perfected and put to use on game species.

Not only other wildlife, but other aspects of land use had to be considered if conservation as a whole were to avoid lopsidedness. This point was always inherent in Leopold's thinking, but it was driven home by his recent experience in Iowa, where his game management plan had to be coordinated with a broader, overall conservation plan. Iowa had also stimulated another line of thought in Leopold's work. Due perhaps to his personal attachment, or to the comprehensive survey he was able to conduct there, or simply to his maturing intellect, Leopold began to emphasize more than ever the historical aspect of conservation. The early portions of Leopold's "Report of the Iowa Game Survey" appeared in *Outdoor America* in the fall and winter of 1932–33. The first installment, entitled "The Fall of the Iowa Game Range," opened with a pointed criticism of history as usually taught:

In studying the behavior of human populations—which we call history—we were once taught to memorize the names of kings and the dates of battles. He who could recite the longest list of such facts was accredited a scholar, who might one day be entrusted with some post in the prediction or control of population behavior—which we call sociology and politics.

It is now apparent that such "knowledge" gave no clue to the underlying forces which caused races to rise and empires to perish; that we were studying merely the froth on the surface of a swirling tide, the cause and direction of which remained unknown. The real task of the historian is to explain the tide; of the statesman to control it for beneficial ends.

In short, history too often ignored the physical foundations of human culture—the soils, waters, plants, and animals that, like bedrock itself, shape and condition, quietly but completely, the civilizations that subsist on them. His own field of natural history, Leopold was quick to note, was no better than any other: "For too long," he complained, "it has been a matter of baptizing species and describing feathers and bones."[9]

Leopold worked with these thoughts as he revised *Game Management.* At one point, he wrote some extensive notes to himself on "The Social Consequences of Conservation." Not since 1923, when he wrote the abortive "Some Fundamentals of Conservation in the Southwest," had he tried to fence in his broader thoughts on conservation. Beyond the immediate impact of his Iowa work, other factors were influencing him: the nation's economic woes, his wide-ranging travels during the game survey, his recent readings in history and conservation philosophy (including sources as diverse as Charles Beard, H. G. Wells, José Ortega y Gasset, and Liberty Hyde Bailey).

The most important stimulus, however, seems to have been the one Leopold felt most personally: the ongoing disputes between the two schools of wildlife conservation—the "wild-lifers" and the "gunpowder faction," as Leopold now called them. "The psychology of the leaders," he wrote in his notes, "has gradually become a war psychology, and lost the aspect of friendly debate as to the best way of achieving a common end. The situation is extremely serious. Neither faction can initiate any action without being attacked by the other, even when such action is obviously beneficial."[10] Each faction, he pointed out, liked to consider itself the antithesis of the other. "The nature student is at small pains to conceal [the belief] that he is superior to mere atavistic blood-letting, while the sportsman sees a lack of Rooseveltian robustness in hunting with field glass or camera."[11]

By now, Leopold had reconciled this dilemma, at least in his own mind and practice. "Hunting and nature study," he wrote, "are merely the beginning and the end of a cycle normal to advancing age in each individual. . . . Just as the evolution of the species is repeated in the pre-natal history of each individual, so the evolution of the nature-lover is being repeated in each boy keen for the hunt. It is conceivable that the hunting stage could be eliminated by educational pressure on the youth, but it seems equally probable that too much pressure of this kind might cut off or subvert the whole process, nature-lover included, and thus sever the last personal tie which binds the city dweller to the land."[12]

Thus, game management was a means of insuring that this "whole process" could continue indefinitely. His work on the game survey, on *Game Management,* and especially on the American Game Policy, were efforts toward this end. At this point, Leopold again raised the specter of the European system: Europeans had preserved hunting and some wildlife, but only by sacrificing the democracy of the sport. Europe's expanding population had resulted in narrower opportunities, more stringent regulations, and, most disconcerting to Leopold, a highly intensive system of game management. Leopold brought the point home: "The gunpowder school and the wild-lifers are in very fact irreconcilable, provided an indefinite and uncontrolled increase in population is assumed as a fixed premise. . . . The important point is that the two systems can be combined to accomplish the objectives of each up to a certain point of population pressure."[13]

These ideas had been incubated in the context of game management, but now Leopold was beginning to see how they applied to the conservation movement in general. The tension between conservationists of different persuasions had its reciprocal within the single individual who "on Monday . . . attends a meeting of his Chamber of Commerce" to boost and boast of economic expansion, then "on Tuesday sends in his membership check to the Izaak Walton League 'to preserve for his boy the outdoor America of his ancestors.'" What to make of this dilemma? Leopold could not provide a ready answer, but only a clear statement of the issue:

The thesis of economic expansion is as old as human history, and in simpler form as old as evolution itself, but never before in biological history (as far as we know it) has any species evolved the *conscious* antithesis that its success, like Shakespeare's "virtue grown into a pleurisy," may "die of its own too much." In the lower animals, too much success is automatically cured by disease or predators, without any conscious effort on the part of the "patient." The antithesis of expansion in these lower forms is an external force, which comes into play automatically. The conservation movement in modern America is a new kind of antithesis arising from an internal force — an idea. A species for the first time in history foresees and fears the consequences of its own success. Can it formulate a synthesis between its biological momentum, as expressed in its Chambers of Commerce, and its fear of going too far, as expressed in its Izaak Walton Leagues? Within what limits is that synthesis workable? By what devices can ideas of snythesis be executed as facts?[14]

These were profound ideas, and far-reaching questions, yet Leopold always returned to what he saw and valued on the land. He gave a clue to the trend of his thought when he mused that "an understanding of these ideas requires a certain moral and esthetic competence. There must be born in the public mind a certain fundamental respect for living things, and for the epic grandeur of the processes which created them. Society must see itself not as the terrestrial end-result of a completed evolution, but as the custodian of an incomplete one. In its ultimate analysis, the conservation movement may prove to be a denial of the anthropocentric philosophies. The real threat to the future of 'outdoor America' lies not in the agencies which destroy it, but in the multiplication of people who think they can live without it."[15]

297

Several months would pass before Leopold organized these thoughts. He did, however, rewrite the memorable ending of *Game Management,* in which he described the "social significance of game management." The final paragraphs read:

It promulgates no doctrine, it simply asks for land and the chance to show that farm, forest, and wild life products can be grown on it, to the mutual advantage of each other, of the landowner, and of the public. It proposes a motivation—the love of sport—narrow enough actually to get action from human beings as now constituted, but nevertheless capable of expanding with time into that new social concept toward which conservation is groping.

In short, twenty centuries of "progress" have brought the average citizen a vote, a national anthem, a Ford, a bank account, and a high opinion of himself, but not the capacity to live in high density without befouling and denuding his environment, nor a conviction that such capacity, rather than such density, is the true test of whether he is civilized. The practice of game management may be one of the means of developing a culture which will meet this test.[16]

Leopold sent the final draft manuscript of *Game Management* to Scribner's on July 16, along with illustrations rendered by Allan Brooks, a wildlife artist from British Columbia who was referred to Leopold by John C. Phillips.[17] Although Leopold was not obligated to cover his end of the publishing costs until the job was done, he forwarded his check for five hundred dollars on July 19. "There is still some uncertainty as to banking conditions here," he explained to Scribner's, "and I wanted to make this payment while I was sure that I had money."[18]

With *Game Management* now out of his hands, Leopold returned to his erstwhile consulting business. "I have a few odd bits of work ahead for the state of Iowa," he wrote to Charles Elton on August 1, "but otherwise I am unemployed. Of course I have worlds of things to do, but the question is [how] to get paid for them."[19]

꙳

For Leopold, and for the country at large, the hardest times came during the fall and winter of 1932, and into early 1933. As the economy withered and withdrew into itself behind a cold barrier of closed bank doors, Leopold looked into a number of possibilities: game surveys in Minnesota, New Jersey, and Pennsylvania; a lecture series at Yale; funds from the National Research Council for independent game studies; work on the important Copeland Report, which would redirect U.S. Forest Service policy for years to come.[20] All fell through.

Leopold was hesitant to work for a state department or a bureau ("that means fighting politics in the former case, or defending the intellectual rut of two generations in the latter"), but his options and his income were running low. In October he went to work for the Wisconsin Conservation Commission, setting up a statewide system of game management demonstration projects—refuges, farmer cooperatives, a quail experiment area, and the state's first public hunting grounds. He conducted field inspections across the state in November and worked intermittently over the next several months in bringing these projects to fruition.

Simultaneously, a development of crucial importance to conservation took place. Although its effect would not be felt until the following spring, and not fully appreciated for several years, the election of Franklin Delano Roosevelt that November was destined to change forever the scope, direction, and flavor of the conservation movement in America. Conservationists, along with almost everyone else in the country, were not sure what to expect, but the feeling of change in the offing was unmistakable.

Leopold was out of steady work in this interim, but he was never idle. At the end of November, he travelled to New York for the Nineteenth American Game Conference. In a speech to his policy committee on the issue of predator control, he gave some indication of how far he had moved in his thinking:

All through history tyrannical majorities have condoned their acts of violence on the grounds of punishing "wickedness." The hawk which kills my pheasant is wicked and cruel, and hence must die. Some hawks in some situations doubtless should die, but let us at least admit we kill the hawk out of self-interest, and in doing so we act on exactly the same motives as the hawk did.

Bird-lovers would have scant complaint if predator-control were resorted to reluctantly, selectively, and only after other measures fail to restore the game. As a matter of fact, however, predator-control campaigns are usually indiscriminate, and are resorted to before anything else has been tried. I could name a dozen states using public money for wholesale "vermin" campaigns which have never lifted a finger to bring about wholesale food or cover improvements.

Conferences like this present a danger, as well as an opportunity. As we sit in our compact circle of mutual understanding, we may possibly forget that there is such a thing as a sporting attitude toward other groups, as well as toward game and toward each other. Above all, it is the essence of both sportsmanship and science habitually to doubt our own ability to truly understand all that we see in nature.[21]

In December Leopold returned to Iowa for a week, where he evaluated the state's week-long training program for game wardens. For better or worse, unemployment also gave Leopold more time to hunt that season than he had had in years. He, Starker, and Luna took advantage of their membership in the Riley farm cooperative, and in December Uncle Carl joined them on their annual quail hunt in Missouri.

Meanwhile, in Madison, a behind-the-scenes move was afoot to secure Leopold a position at the University of Wisconsin. Talk of such a move had been in the air for several years, at least since Leopold's days at the Forest Products Lab, when he first made the acquaintance of Harry L. Russell. Russell had been dean of the university's College of Agriculture for twenty-five years before he became, in 1931, the first director of the university's research-funding affiliate, the Wisconsin Alumni Research Foundation. Leopold and Russell both belonged to the Getaway Club, a jovial group of Madison outdoorsmen who gathered once a month in members' homes to swap tales of the wilderness, discuss conservation concerns, and share prohibition home brew. In an official capacity, Russell and Leopold had collaborated on joint research projects between the university and the Forest Products Lab. As early as 1927, Russell had expressed interest in establishing a game management program under Leopold within the College of Agriculture. Russell was also the likely instigator behind Leopold's 1929 lecture series at the university. Because of a shortage of funds, no action was taken at the time to firm up a university connection.

Russell was not Leopold's only supporter. Another of the Getaways, Colonel Joseph W. Jackson, a codirector of Madison's Jackson Clinic and a leading catalyst in Madison society, was the driving force behind an effort to establish a university Arboretum and Wild Life Refuge on land surrounding Lake Wingra. An outgoing, determined man, Jackson tirelessly organized dinners, wrote letters, and enlisted support for his plan from anyone who would listen—the U.S. Forest Service, the Wisconsin Conservation Commission, business leaders, journalists, university administrators, and politicians. Part of Jackson's plan was to establish a "chair of conservation" at the university, the responsibilities of which would include serving as director of the arboretum and refuge. Jackson's intention was to have Leopold assume this new position. These plans reached a climax in the early months of 1933.

In January, Leopold conferred with Harry Russell and Howard Weiss and then drafted a memo outlining the functions, objectives, organization, and financial needs of the proposed chair. Leopold naturally weighted his proposal to emphasize wildlife, but also recognized the need to coordinate with other university activities, "to the end that they may serve the Conservation Movement, the Conservation Commission, and the owner of the land on which conservation is to be practiced."[22] Leopold sent the memo to Jackson, who pulled the appropriate strings. The proposal cleared its first hurdles in February when university president Glenn Frank and Chris Christensen, Russell's successor as dean of the College of Agriculture, approved the plan, provided it could be financed. Given the chaotic economic conditions of those weeks and months, that was still far from a foregone conclusion.

On March 1, 1933, Leopold wrote to William T. Hornaday in regard to *Game Management*. The book was in its final stages of publication, and Leopold had instructed Scribner's to forward a copy to Hornaday as soon as it was available.

> I want you to get it promptly, partly in acknowledgement of the fact that my whole venture into this field dates from your visit to Albuquerque in 1915, and your subsequent encouragement to stay in it.
>
> I do not by any means assume that the book will meet with your approval, or that its appearance is an event of importance. It is of importance to me because it summarizes the chain of thought which I have developed. This is a freer expression than my *Game Survey*, because the survey was a compilation of facts, not a discussion of principles, and as such left little room [for] philosophical interpretation of the facts described. This then should be a better basis for judging whether the tangent I have been following has any long-term merit or not.[23]

Despite their philosophical differences, Leopold still held Hornaday in high regard. In the opening chapter of *Game Management,* Leopold referred to Hornaday cryptically as "the Crusader" and praised his achievements: "He insisted that our conquest of nature carried with it a moral responsibility for the perpetuation of the threatened forms of wild life. This avowal was a forward step of inestimable importance. In fact, to any one for whom wild things are something more than a pleasant diversion, it constitutes one of the milestones in moral evolution."[24] Leopold's letter to Hornaday was more than a gesture of respect, however. While Colonel Jackson sought out donors to support the university chair, Leopold was again looking for work. Leopold mentioned to Hornaday this "purely personal matter":

> The time and expense involved in getting out this book have pretty well exhausted what I had laid by while with the Ammunition people. Accordingly I am available for any sort of work, permanent or temporary, regardless of location, which will advance wild life conservation. I would dislike, of course, to tie up with anything politically dominated. I would prefer that my situation be not widely discussed, but if you happen to hear anything, I would appreciate your telling me about it.[25]

It was a time of deep frustration for Leopold. At forty-six, he was among the nation's best-informed men in wildlife conservation, and yet could find no way to support himself and his family. He had labored the better part of a lifetime trying to counteract the ravages which an unrestrained economy had wreaked on its own resources, and with that economy now floundering, he could not find work.

On March 4, 1933, Franklin Delano Roosevelt became president of the United States. Within days of his inauguration, Roosevelt initiated a plan that he had experimented with in New York: putting the unemployed to work on reforestation and other conservation projects. By the end of the month, the legislative whirlwind of Roosevelt's first hundred days kicked out the bill that established the Civilian Conservation Corps. Overnight, the CCC became the single greatest application of manpower the conservation movement had ever seen. Eventually, half a million unemployed young men, many of them city-born and gaining their first experience in outdoor work, would join the CCC to plant trees, construct trails and campgrounds, build cabins, ranger stations, and firetowers, and perform whatever other tasks the New Deal conservation agenda assigned to them.

Veteran conservationists, including Leopold, were both caught off guard and invigorated by this sudden influx of energy. Leopold was asked to assist in the CCC work shortly after the agency's inception. At the end of April, he returned to Region 3—the old "Districts" had been renamed "Regions" in 1930—of the Forest Service, where he was to spend the summer supervising the erosion control work of the CCC camps in New Mexico and Arizona. Estella stayed in Wisconsin with the children.

The first week of May was unusually active for Leopold. *Game Management,* at long last, came off the presses. Leopold dedicated the book to his father, whom he simply memorialized as a "pioneer in sportsmanship." He later gave a copy to Starker as a Christmas present, and inscribed it with these words: "The materials for this book were gathered from the four winds, but the conviction that it should be written comes largely out of our trips together on the Rio Grande. The greatest fortune I can wish you is that you and your son may someday find such a river, and that there may still be mallards to fly when the dawn wind rustles in its cottonwoods."[26]

That same week, Leopold delivered no less than four major addresses in his old haunts along the Rio Grande. At the University of New Mexico in Albuquerque, he spoke on "Ecology as an Applied Science"; at Santa Fe, he addressed a group of anthropologists on "The Virgin Southwest"; at Las Cruces, he discussed "Wildlife and Soils."

The Las Cruces talk was given at the annual meeting of the Southwest division of the American Association for the Advancement of Science. Earlier in the year, Leopold had been asked to present the John Wesley Powell lecture, the highlight of the annual gathering. Leopold responded with another paper, among the most important of his career, entitled "The Conservation Ethic." In *Game Management,* Leopold had spoken vaguely of "that new social concept toward which conservation is groping." In "The Conservation Ethic," he defined more precisely what he meant: where conservation was going, what it needed, and what it had to offer to civilization in the broadest sense.

Leopold proposed that the study of history revealed a gradual expansion of the social sphere in which human ethics operated. The Ten Commandments, for instance, had given individuals a set of ethical guidelines within which they could successfully cooperate. Later, such developments

as Christianity and democracy offered means by which the individual and
the greater social organization could adjust to one another. This idea of
evolving ethical criteria was not new to philosophy. Leopold, however, gave
the idea a new biological twist. He suggested that an ethic could be viewed
as a natural phenomenon that had its origins in "the tendency of interdependent individuals or societies to evolve modes of cooperation . . . [that]
enable them to exploit each other in an orderly way." As human societies
grew in numbers and complexity, and as our technological prowess increased, cooperative measures necessarily had to expand as well. "It was
simpler," Leopold suggested, "to define the anti-social uses of sticks and
stones in the days of the mastodons than of bullets and billboards in the
age of motors."[27]

Leopold's central thesis was that economic expediency, long since discarded as an uncivilized guide to human relations, was no longer adequate
as a guide to humanity's relationship to *land*—the next sphere in which
people, because of increased numbers and technological advances, needed
guidelines to follow.

There is as yet no ethic dealing with man's relationship to land and to the nonhuman animals and plants which grow upon it. Land, like Odysseus' slave girls,
is still property. The land-relation is still strictly economic, entailing privileges but
not obligations. . . . Individual thinkers since the days of Ezekial and Isaiah have
asserted that the despoliation of land is not only inexpedient but wrong. Society,
however, has not yet affirmed their belief. I regard the present conservation movement as the embryo of such an affirmation.[28]

Leopold's purpose was to place the conservation movement at the forefront of this historical trend. In his attempt to explain the biological foundations of ethics, Leopold was treading unsure ground, and his wording
was confusing. When he turned to his forte, however—the ecological interpretation of history—he found firmer footing:

A harmonious relation to land is more intricate, and of more consequence to civilization, than the historians of its progress seem to realize. Civilization is not, as
they often assume, the enslavement of a stable and constant earth. It is a state of
mutual and interdependent cooperation between human animals, other animals,
plants, and soils, which may be disrupted at any moment by the failure of any of
them. Land-despoliation has evicted nations, and can on occasion do it again. As
long as six virgin continents awaited the plow, this was perhaps no tragic matter—
eviction from one piece of soil could be recouped by despoiling another. But there
are now wars and rumors of wars which foretell the impending saturation of the
earth's best soils and climates. It thus becomes a matter of some importance, at
least to ourselves, that our dominion, once gained, be self-perpetuating rather than
self-destructive.[29]

"In short," Leopold summed up, "the reaction of land to occupancy determines the nature and duration of civilization. . . . We inherit the earth,

but within the limits of the soil and the plant succession we also *rebuild* the earth—without plan, without knowledge of its properties, and without understanding of the increasingly coarse and powerful tools which science has placed at our disposal."[30]

The continued stability and advancement of civilization, then, depended on some means of adjusting the relationship of people and land. Self-interest, as expressed in economic incentives, was one such means. Legislative compulsion and greater public ownership was another. But Leopold was unconvinced that these alone could suffice, and he had plenty of discouraging examples from his own experience to illustrate the point. Self-interest could spur action in certain instances (this was, after all, a main premise of the American Game Policy), but "the economic cards are stacked against some of the most important reforms in land-use." Public ownership, on the other hand, "while highly desirable and good as far as it goes, can never go far enough"; advocates of large-scale public ownership regarded conservation merely as "a means to an end, but not the end itself." The real end, Leopold proposed, "is a universal symbiosis with land, economic and esthetic, public and private."[31]

In Leopold's opinion, there was no recourse for this dilemma in the standard political philosophies of the day. His disaffection for politics emerged in a discussion of "the economic isms":

As nearly as I can see, all the new isms—Socialism, communism, Fascism, and especially the late but not lamented Technocracy—outdo even Capitalism in their preoccupation with one thing: the distribution of more machine-made commodities to more people. They all proceed on the theory that if we can all keep warm and full, and all own a Ford and a radio, the good life will follow. Their programs differ only in ways to mobilize machines to this end. Though they despise each other, they are all, in respect of this objective, as identically alike as peas in a pod. They are competitive apostles of a single creed: *salvation by machinery.* We are here concerned, not with their proposals for adjusting men and machinery to goods, but rather with their lack of any vital proposal for adjusting men and machines to land.[32]

Leopold was searching for foundations, for root sources of problems and fundamental principles for change. He suggested that the seeds for such a new approach might be found in conservation. Not in the brand of conservation that boosters used to lure tourists, or that politicians hitched for a ride, but in the practical conservation measures he had tried to promote in *Game Management.* The hallmark of this approach was "a positive and affirmatory ideology, the thesis of which is to prevent the deterioration of environment." It was as simple and as complex as planting bushes on an Iowa fencerow. And at the core of this approach was (in a fascinatingly paradoxical phrase) the idea of "controlled wild culture." Applied not just to game, "but to any living thing from Bloodroots to Bell's Vireos," this idea had the potential to show "that bread and beauty grow best together. Their harmonious integration can make farming not only a business but an art; the land not only a food-factory but an instrument of self-expression, on which each can play music of his own choosing."[33]

Leopold waxed enthusiastic about "the sweep of this thing," and then took a breath. "I will not belabor the pipe dream," he told his audience. "It is no prediction, but merely an assertion that the idea of controlled environment contains colors and brushes wherewith society may some day paint a new and possibly a better picture of itself." Leopold granted that economic obstacles could stall the realization of this vision, but he denied that the motives affecting individual economic decisions were preordained and immutable.

Neither was Leopold forgetful of the fact that, during hard times, many viewed conservation as a luxury. He concluded his talk on this point.

It may seem idle to project such imaginary elaborations of culture at a time when millions lack even the means of physical existence. Some may feel for it the same honest horror as the senator from Michigan who lately arraigned Congress for protecting migratory birds at a time when fellow-humans lacked bread. The trouble with such deadly parallels is we can never be sure which is cause and which is effect. It is not inconceivable that the wave phenomena which have lately upset everything from banks to crime rates might be less troublesome if the human medium in which they run *readjusted its tensions*. The stampede is an attribute of animals interested solely in grass.[34]

There is no record of the immediate response to "The Conservation Ethic," but after its publication in the *Journal of Forestry* several months later, it became widely distributed among conservation professionals. It was a landmark statement for many who were beginning to think more deeply about the philosophical aspects of resource issues.

"The Conservation Ethic" brought together a number of important forces in Leopold's life. The lessons in responsible sportsmanship that Carl Leopold passed along to his children provided an ethical base. The fundamental devotion to wise land management was second nature to all who were nurtured on the philosophy of Gifford Pinchot and whose convictions were tested on the forest ranges. Leopold's personal experiences in the Southwest left him with an unusual degree of insight and foresight. On the aerie of Escudilla and in the torn valley of the Blue, from the overgrazed ranges of the Carson to the wild recesses of the Gila, Leopold had watched history at work. His powers of abstraction and his native curiosity gave philosophical breadth to that experience. His work in Wisconsin reaffirmed both the possibility of and the political impediments to change, while his game survey of the Midwest impressed upon him the urgent necessity for conservation work by individual landholders. The Depression added a full measure of realism, while simultaneously activating Leopold's thoughts on social changes and consequences. Finally, the internecine disputes among conservationists leavened Leopold's thinking, and produced a need, at least in his own mind, for some sort of unifying statement.

"The Conservation Ethic" was not a final product, but the first expression of an idea that would gain depth and urgency in the remaining years of Leopold's life. For, as far-seeing as it was, it would prove to be lacking in one important regard. Its call for an ethic was based on ecology; yet, as a science, ecology was still in a premature state, while Leopold, as a scientist, was still consolidating his own foundations. He had come a long way since 1923, when in "Some Fundamentals of Conservation in the Southwest" he made a similar ethical argument for conservation based on Ouspensky's mystical earth-as-organism abstractions. Now he was basing his argument on the evidence of history, and, increasingly, on the ability of the natural sciences to reveal and interpret that evidence. "The Conservation Ethic" was the full flower of his thinking as a conservationist, but it was only the early bud of his thinking as an ecologist.

〜

Leopold spent the summer of 1933 retracing his footsteps in the southwestern forests, putting the CCC machinery to work on erosion control measures, and revising his decade-old handbook on erosion. The experience was not altogether encouraging. The hasty deployment of the CCCs resulted in too much make-work, and not enough effective conservation. The crews too often worked at cross-purposes to one another. Leopold wryly noted the discrepancies. "There was, for example, the road crew cutting a grade along a clay bank so as permanently to roil the trout stream which another crew was improving with dams and shelters; the silvicultural crew felling 'wolf trees' and border shrubbery needed for game food; the roadside-cleanup crew burning all the down oak fuel wood available to the fireplaces being built by the recreation-ground crew; the planting crew setting pines all over the only open clover-patch available to the deer and partridges; the fire-line crew burning up all the hollow snags on a wildlife refuge, or, worse yet, felling the gnarled veterans which were about the only scenic thing along a 'scenic road.'" This was just the kind of uncoordinated effort that rankled Leopold, and the summer left him a lasting skeptic of the New Deal's grand, but poorly thought-out, conservation plans. He did not blame the CCCs, who were simply following instructions, but did blame those, including himself, who failed to foresee the administrative complexities of the new program.[35]

While awaiting word on developments at the University of Wisconsin, Leopold received a number of job offers. Ovid Butler suggested that he be named head forester for the new Tennessee Valley Authority. The Department of Interior considered him for the post of director of a proposed "Navaho Reservation Authority."

On June 26, Harry L. Russell informed Leopold that the Wisconsin Alumni Research Foundation had approved funds to support a game management program within the university. This unprecedented grant gave Leopold $8,000 per year for five years, out of which all expenses for the program were to come, from Leopold's salary to travel costs. After the five-year trial period, the program would be evaluated and, if found worthwhile, funded thereafter by the state of Wisconsin. On July 16, Leopold accepted the position. As finally worked out, the chair of conservation was narrowed down to game management, and placed within the Department of Agricultural Economics. Leopold thus became the first instructor in the country to wear the title of Professor of Game Management.

The announcement of the appointment in August made headlines around the country and brought Leopold a shower of congratulatory letters. Even William Temple Hornaday expressed approval — and perhaps even pride — when he wrote to Leopold:

My Dear Ally,

I salute the University of Wisconsin, for its foresight and enterprise in establishing the first Collegiate Professorship of Game Management created in the United States.

I congratulate the Wisconsin Alumni Foundation on its correct initiative in the choice of the Best Man for the new foundation.

Finally, I congratulate Professor Leopold upon the appreciation that his merits and his activities have received thus early in his career. It is all a helpful gesture in the struggle to save American game and sport from finally going over the precipice, A.D. 1940.

Very Sincerely Yours,
W. T. Hornaday[36]

15

The Professor

(1933–1934)

A FEW days after joining the faculty of the University of Wisconsin, Leopold gave a short talk for the state's farmers over WHA radio, the university-sponsored station. His topic was "Building a Wisconsin Game Crop":

At this season when the frost will soon be on the pumpkin, and the first sumacs are turning red, many a young man's fancy turns to thoughts of game birds. The trouble is that in most places game birds have become scarce. The city dweller interested in game can do little about it except to make speeches about conservation. The farmer, however, can actually raise a game crop on his farm, which is much more useful service to conservation than making speeches. Anybody can deplore the passing of the good old days, but to help bring them back is the special privilege of farmers.[1]

In these pithy talks, delivered once or twice a month, Leopold gave the farmer instructions on basic wildlife management strategy—"Feeding Winter Birds on the Farm," "Feed Early to Keep Game at Home," "The Farm Woodlot and the Bird Crop."

Over-the-airwaves talks were only a small part of his new duties. He was responsible for teaching a short course for young farmers, conducting a graduate seminar in management theory and technique, directing research at the new arboretum, overseeing graduate student progress, assisting in special projects throughout Wisconsin, and taking on assorted other extension work. For Leopold, it was a new beginning to his work, an opportunity to encourage activity, disseminate information, and guide research across a state that was a waiting laboratory. Far from ascending to an ivory tower, he now had an institutional base on which to build his ideas. For the remainder of his life he would be "The Professor," and a natural resource himself for the people of Wisconsin.

Leopold had operated on the periphery of the University of Wisconsin ever since he and his family moved to Madison. In formalizing the bond, Leopold joined an institution that already had a notable conservation legacy. In the 1860s, John Muir travelled to Madison, often on foot, from his family's pioneer homestead near Portage, and took his first formal studies in the natural sciences. Bernard Fernow, whose important efforts to promote forestry in America predated even Gifford Pinchot's, was named a special lecturer in 1896; his were the first lectures on conservation at the university. Charles Van Hise, president of the university at the turn of the century, was an eminent geologist as well as a nationally known figure in conservation; his commitment to the cause permeated the university. Early studies of Lake Mendota in the 1910s and 1920s by Edward Birge and Chancey Juday provided many of the fundamental concepts in the new sciences of limnology and aquatic ecology, and made Lake Mendota one of the most studied lakes in the world. At the same time, the innovations of Stephen Babcock, Harry Steenbock, and Harry L. Russell built the College of Agriculture into a dominant force in agricultural research, revolutionizing the dairy industry in the process and securing Wisconsin's milky place in the nation's folklore. Beyond such prominent figures as these, a host of distinguished geologists, geographers, biochemists, botanists, and zoologists made the university a major center for study in the natural sciences.

As the university rose to a position of international prominence, it was guided by an ideal that came to be known as the "Wisconsin Idea." Under it, the university gained a worldwide reputation for progressive scholarship. The Wisconsin Idea conceived of the university not as an insular community of scholars, but as an institution whose walls extended (as the image had it) to the borders of the state. The expertise of the faculty found its proper, and highest, expression in the service that was given to the people of Wisconsin. The privilege and duty of scholars was to promote the well-being of the commonweal. President John Bascom, sensing the imminent social changes that wealth and science were bringing, endeavored to instill this ethic into his faculty and students. "The University of Wisconsin," Bascom wrote in 1887, "will be permanently great in the degree in which it understands the conditions of the prosperity and peace of the people, and helps to provide them; in the degree in which it enters into the revelation of truth, the law of righteousness, and the love of man, all gathered up and held firm in the constitution of the human soul and the counsel of God concerning it."[2]

Bascom's lofty sentiments found practical expression on a dozen fronts: in an active agricultural extension service, in a close alliance with the state government, in a commitment to social reform and academic freedom. The university's Departments of History, Political Science, and Economics were among the nation's best, and one result of the cross-pollination of these fields was the creation of the nation's first Department of Agricultural Economics in 1909. Historian Merle Curti writes, "The Wisconsin combination of theory and practice was exemplified in the organization of the new department. . . . The outstanding work of the Wisconsin specialists in the economic and social problems of rural life won, in the years following 1925, international recognition."[3]

Such was the academic environment that Leopold entered in the fall of 1933. Leopold was an unorthodox figure in a suspect position. He was not an academic, and lacked the requisite Ph.D. Game management, he himself acknowledged, was still "a sort of stepchild in that austere family known as The Sciences. Nay, we are perhaps a sort of foundling left on the doorstep by unauthorized enthusiasts."[4] Leopold declined to use the more apt metaphor: game management was widely viewed as a bastard science, an illegitimate mingling of applied zoology and blood sport. Those outside of wildlife conservation had little sense of the directions in which Leopold and his colleagues were trying to lead the profession. Appropriately enough, Leopold and his loyal secretary Vivian Horn were relegated to a dingy, cramped office in the basement of the university's Soils Building.

Leopold knew that his steps would be watched, but he also knew that he now had a unique opportunity to advance the cause of game management, both in academia and on the land. Wisconsin typified the situation in the Midwest. Farms were not producing game because most farmers, even if they were willing, did not know how to go about managing for it. The Conservation Department had no money (or desire) to conduct basic research; all their funds went into law enforcement and game farms. The fewer farmers managing their lands for game, the less game there was; the less game there was, the louder the call for more restrictive laws and game farms. "Thus," Leopold wrote, "we have the sad spectacle of one obsolete idea chasing another around a closed circle, while opportunity goes begging." In the university, unbeholden to sportsmen, politicians, or private interests, the scientist might now begin his work of extracting the facts required by the landowner and land manager.

Leopold's appointment would have statewide, nationwide, and even international implications. His focus, however, was always the local piece of land and the life, human and otherwise, it supported. "Conservation," he wrote at about this time, "is not merely a thing to be enshrined in outdoor museums, but a way of living on land." Leopold would increasingly promote wildlife management, not only as a way to restore game, but as a factor determinant in the quality of rural life. He was certain that, once science disclosed the needs of wildlife, many—not all, but many—farmers could be counted on to do the rest. "If all farmers were actuated solely by the profit-motive," he wrote, "few would continue to be farmers."

It takes all kinds of motives to make a world. If all of us were capable of beholding the burning bush, there would be none left to grow bushes to burn. Doers and dreamers are the reciprocal parts of the body politic: each gives meaning and significance to the other. So also in conservation. Just now, conservation is short of doers. We need plants and birds and trees restored to ten thousand farms, not merely to a few paltry reservations. I would rather see a few feathers flying in the well-stocked fencerows of the future, than to see the paths of young men lead forever through these phantom coverts, grassless, foodless, birdless, inviolate, and desolate.[5]

That was the essence of Leopold's creed at this point in his life. He had applied it throughout his years as a forester, game researcher, and writer. Now he would carry it forward into his new career as a teacher.

∽

Letters of praise for *Game Management* and "The Conservation Ethic" arrived throughout the fall. Joseph Grinnell was "very enthusiastic" about Leopold's book and expressed surprise "that anyone working on game management should have such a comprehensive grasp on ecology, life history and fundamental needs of game." "Why is it," Grinnell's colleague Joseph Dixon wrote to Leopold, "that people *jump to the conclusion* that you are *only interested* in raising birds to be shot?"[6] John C. Phillips, the grand old man of New England wildlife conservation, requested fifty copies of "The Conservation Ethic." "It is a corker," he wrote to Leopold, "the finest thing you have done yet. You have the wonderful gift of presenting the same old basic problems in new and attractive ways, a new sauce on the same old goose, every time you write. How you do this I surely don't know but this is a most valuable gift."[7]

Word of Leopold's activities even reached distant ports. Herbert Jones, one of Leopold's Lawrenceville tramping pals, wrote from London that he found *Game Management* "over my head . . . but very good reading none the less. It is always interesting to listen to a man who is a master of his subject, and an enthusiast."[8] From New Haven, a "Benjamin Jacobs" wrote to inquire "whether you . . . are the Aldo Leopold from Burlington, Iowa . . . who attended the Yale School of Forestry some years ago?" Aldo replied to his former charge, "I am delighted to have a word from you and to know that you still remember our pleasant visits in New Haven. I have done a good deal of jumping around since I last heard from you, and have not been back to New Haven since 1909. If I ever get there, I will try to give you a ring."[9]

More material acknowledgment of *Game Management* also began to arrive. By November, nineteen hundred copies had been sold—not an insubstantial number for such a book during the Depression—resulting in a royalty check for $675. As the profession expanded through the 1930s and 1940s, and *Game Management* became the required text for wildlife conservationists across the country, a modest royalty check came in the mail once or twice each year. Aldo invested these first returns in a "much-needed blowout for my family."[10]

Leopold did not begin classroom instruction until January 1934. In the interim, he had to organize the new academic program. Money to support prospective graduate students was still scarce; Leopold did not take on any students until the following spring, after he had drummed up the funds. Plans for the university Arboretum and Wild Life Refuge took firm shape. Its backers held a series of meetings that fall to lay out its organization. In October, Leopold drew up a wildlife management plan for the arboretum's five hundred acres. He foresaw the arboretum serving not only as a field research station, but as an educational exhibit of management techniques, as a refuge for rare species, and as a "seed" area from which surplus wildlife populations might spread to farm lands south of Madison.

Leopold's reputation and new position tended to give his activities a life of their own. One assignment inevitably led to a dozen others; one personal contact involved him in that individual's entire organization. This would be the case for the remainder of his life. He would take part in a hundred organizations, serve on dozens of committees, write up an untold number of reports and memos, dictate hundreds upon hundreds of advisory letters.

One result of this intense activity was that Leopold not only had his irons in a remarkable number of conservation fires, but he was generally in on the original stoking process. In the fall of 1933, he began to devote time (it is unclear whether he initiated the idea) to a plan to establish on 100,000 acres of tax-reverted lands in Wisconsin's central sand counties a public "Conservation District." The lands were to be restored with New Deal labor and then administered by the state. Meanwhile, Wisconsin's Conservation Department was being reorganized, and given legislative authority to set seasons and bag limits on game (a landmark in the history of state fish and game administration); Leopold agreed to serve on the department's new game and fisheries committees.

About this same time, Leopold became involved in one of his most important long-term game management projects. He was asked to advise a group of farmers near Lake Mills, east of Madison in Jefferson County, on the prospects for increasing wildlife on their farms. The lands turned out to be ideally suited for management experiments, containing cropland, pastures, hardwood forest, tamarack swamps, river bottom, and a valuable tract of virgin prairie. Just as important, the farmers of the area, led by octogenarian Stoughton Faville, were enthusiastic about the idea. Faville, one of the area's early homesteaders and a leading dairyman in Wisconsin, was an accomplished naturalist, and his strong interest in Leopold's work was instrumental in making the project a success. Leopold greatly admired Faville, and the Faville Grove farms were to exert a major influence in Leopold's thinking about land use and the people behind it.[11] Management began that winter with a simple feeding program for upland game birds, but within a few years the farmers joined together to create the Faville Grove Wildlife Experimental Area. Like the Riley farms, Faville Grove originated as a cooperative game management area, but as Leopold began taking on graduate students, both became vital research sites, training grounds for the university's first generation of wildlife managers.

A bit of work that gave Leopold particular satisfaction during this period was the new federal project to control soil erosion in the Coon Valley watershed in the driftless area of southwestern Wisconsin. The entire driftless region, with its maze of picturesque valleys and ridges and its dendritic network of creeks draining into the Wisconsin and the Mississippi, was highly susceptible to soil erosion. The thin limy soils and steep slopes washed away easily when the first wave of white settlers indiscriminately applied their plows, cows, and saws. Coon Valley, sadly, was typical of the region; Leopold described it as "one of the thousand farm communities which, through the abuse of its originally rich soil, has not only filled the national dinner pail, but has created the Mississippi flood problem, the navigation problem, the overproduction problem, and the problem of its own future continuity."[12]

The plethora of New Deal bureaus that Franklin Roosevelt signed into being in the early months of his presidency included a consolidated Soil Erosion Service within the Department of Interior. Under Hugh H. Bennett, whose evangelistic fervor made him soil conservation's answer to William T. Hornaday and Billy Sunday, the SES opened up a whole new area of activity in the nation's conservation movement.

The SES chose southwestern Wisconsin as the ground on which to begin its crusade. Coon Valley became the nation's first soil conservation demonstration area. Leopold, in his role as extension advisor, was involved in the project from its inception, contributing to the revegetation and game management portions of the conservation strategy (Ernest Holt, a good friend, was in charge of the project). The ambitious goal of the SES was not just to save soil, but to reverse the tradition of disintegrative land use that wasted it in the first place. This implied a coordinated approach to Coon Valley's resources—its soils, waters, forests, wildlife, scenery and other recreational opportunities—so that "they collectively comprise a harmonious balanced system of land use. . . . The crux of the land problem is to show that integrated use is possible on private farms, and that such integration is mutually advantageous to both the owner and the public."[13] Leopold hoped that this approach could prevent the sort of cross-wiring that had short-circuited the work of the CCCs in the Southwest the previous summer.

The farmers of Coon Valley worked together on a voluntary basis in a watershed-wide plan to encourage contour plowing, strip cropping, regular rotations, gully repair, exclusion of livestock from steep slopes, and other restoration measures. The government contributed CCC manpower, wire, fertilizer, seed, and planting stock. Leopold personally contributed two sons to the Coon Valley project. Luna was increasingly interested in the technical aspects of soil erosion. Starker, having reentered college only to flunk out, was now banished to work in the SES. Aldo visited Coon Valley several times that fall, gathering information from farmers on the area's history and field characteristics.

Leopold was never a convert to the New Deal approach to conservation, but in his regular visits among the farmers, technicians, and CCC crews at Coon Valley, he found two things that greatly impressed him: a healthy combination of private initiative and unobtrusive government assistance, and a spirit of enthusiasm that reminded him of his own youth. He especially enjoyed the nightly bull sessions of the technical staff, where, he later wrote,

one may hear a forester expounding to an engineer the basic theory of how organic matter in the soil decreases the percent of run-off; an economist holds forth on tax rebates as a means to get farmers to install their own erosion control. Underneath the facetious conversation one detects a vein of thought—an attitude toward the common enterprise—which is strangely reminiscent of the early days of the Forest Service. Then, too, a staff of technicians, all under thirty, was faced by a common task so large and so long as to stir the imagination of all but dullards. I suspect that the Soil Erosion Service, perhaps unwittingly, has recreated a spiritual entity which many older conservationists have thought long dead.[14]

The heady air of activity on the conservation scene sometimes left those involved dizzy. Alignments were changing, both within and beyond the government superstructure. New programs, new personalities, new precedents, and a rush of new federal funds caused more than their share of turmoil. One center of discontent was the Bureau of Biological Survey. Wildlife conservationists of all stripes were upset with the survey, and in particular with its inability to address the problem of dangerously low waterfowl populations. The Migratory Bird Conservation Act of 1929 had authorized the establishment of federal refuges, but funds were never appropriated due to the Depression. All the efforts at refuge legislation and all the dollars of the More Game Birds group could not slow the encroachment of civilization on the breeding grounds in the northern prairies, nor bring rain when the droughts of the early 1930s turned the marshes into thick mud, and then dried the mud to hard clay ("If only waterfowl could swim in ink," Leopold joked grimly. "If only they could feed on the broad acres of paper we have dedicated to guesses about their welfare!").

Paul Redington had acted in the fall of 1929 to forestall a crisis, dropping the daily bag limit on ducks from twenty-five to fifteen. But, as if to prove the point that restrictive actions alone could not ensure viable wildlife populations, the migratory flocks continued to dwindle. Criticism mounted, the brunt of it directed toward Redington and the survey. Bitter infighting broke out among aspirants to Redington's position. By December 1933, even an outsider such as Leopold could see that "what [the survey] needs is a radical overhauling of program and policies by radically strengthened personnel."[15] Then Leopold received an opportunity to influence, at least indirectly, such a change.

In October 1933, Thomas Beck, editor of *Collier's* magazine, chairman of the Connecticut State Board of Fisheries and Game, and a founder and current president of More Game Birds, had met with President Roosevelt and presented a plan to divert federal relief funds into a new wildlife program. Beck was a personal friend of Roosevelt, and his "restoration" plan was expedited to Secretary of Agriculture Henry Wallace. "Restoration," to Beck's thinking, meant a system of captive breeding projects, administered by a new, independent agency. His plan made no provision for refuges, for regulating annual kill, or for research into habitat requirements. It also implied that the Biological Survey could not be relied upon for new initiatives in wildlife conservation.

Despite criticisms from Redington and others in the government, Beck's plan gained the backing of Wallace and of Roosevelt himself. On December 15, Wallace asked Beck to serve as chairman of a special three-person committee to outline methods for implementing the plan. The other two appointees were to be Jay "Ding" Darling and Dr. John C. Merriam of the Smithsonian Institution. By December 20, the president had amended the original idea, promising to set aside a million dollars of relief funds to acquire refuge grounds, and to put the CCCs to work developing them. Over the next two weeks, the committee and its objectives continued to evolve. By the time formation of the President's Committee on Wild Life Restoration was announced on January 2, 1934, it had an expanded responsibility: to fashion a national wildlife conservation plan that would coordinate with the president's $25 million program for purchasing submarginal agricultural lands. The committee also had a new member. Merriam was unable to serve, and Aldo Leopold took his place.

Although Leopold was not a Roosevelt supporter, the prospect of contributing to such a potentially influential effort, and of meeting and serving the president, excited him. The family was thrilled. It meant a wildly busy month of work. In addition to the normal load of work, Leopold's short course for farmers was due to commence the same day that formation of the committee was announced in Washington.

The work of the Beck Committee, as it became known, would not be dull; the personalities of its three members assured that. Leopold and Darling had been loosely associated for several years now. Their work together on the committee added a bond of friendship to an already high mutual regard. They were very different characters. Leopold was calm, meticulous, and dry-humored; Darling was high-spirited, gregarious, and more politically inclined. Different though they were, they shared Iowa backgrounds, a complete devotion to their respective crafts, a fundamental love of the outdoors, an uncommonly broad view of the relationship between civilization and natural resources, and an overriding devotion to conservation. When Darling donated the funds to establish Iowa's program for wildlife research in 1932, he chose Leopold as his "designated representative." Leopold, in turn, appreciated the role that Darling played in the conservation movement. Darling's cartoons, which regularly employed conservation themes, were familiar to newspaper readers nationwide, and said as much in one insightful panel as whole books on the subject.

Leopold's appointment to the committee might well have come at Darling's suggestion. In any case, the committee was predisposed to head-knocking. Leopold and Darling were closely aligned in their approach to the work of the committee, and opposed to the views of Beck. "Generally speaking," Darling recalled later in his life, "Beck advocated the theory held by the 'More Game Birds' crowd—that the way to restore ducks was to hatch them in incubators and turn them loose into the flight lanes, in other words restocking by artificial methods. Leopold and I held to the principle that nature could do the job better than man and advocated restoring the environment necessary to migratory waterfowl."[16]

Tolerant though he was, Leopold was not one to budge on matters of principle, especially conservation principle. Beck was just the sort to push Leopold to his limit. Well-connected and headstrong, Beck went to Washington expecting to have his way as chairman. He found the wildlife professionals there uncooperative, and sensed "some little peevishness, some little jealousy, some little selfishness about my coming in on this work. Some of the master minds probably resented the intrusion of a new man."[17]

Busy with teaching, Leopold was at first unable to attend to committee business, but he did meet with Darling in Chicago for a comparison of notes. At the Twentieth American Game Conference, held in New York on January 22–24, rumors circulated that the Biological Survey was about to be closed down. Roosevelt's Bureau of the Budget had already proposed massive funding cuts for the survey, and a complete extinguishment of all its game research activities. On top of this, Beck was out to abolish the survey, terming it "a semi-scientific organization, inadequately manned [or] equipped for large administrative tasks." Leopold and Darling absolutely opposed Beck on this point; they held that beneath the surface turmoil, there was a growing corps of competent scientists in the survey whose work was becoming ever more, not less, important. A cut in funds, especially in research funds, would paralyze state and private efforts around the nation. And to do so while millions were being doled out to buy up farmland was simply incomprehensible. Leopold told the conference that, "the issue is a wholly artificial distinction between going work, which we abolish in the name of economy, and new work, which we finance on a large scale in the name of agricultural relief. I cannot believe that the conservation movement is naive enough to stomach such an absurdity."[18]

After the conference, the three members of the President's Committee went to Washington and met FDR. (Luna recalls, "I can remember Dad coming back from that trip and telling the family that he was asked to come in and talk with Franklin Roosevelt. He thought that Roosevelt was one of the most impressive men he had ever talked to, even though he didn't agree with FDR.")[19]

Leopold, Darling, and Beck retired to a backroom in the Department of Agriculture building for a series of turbulent meetings. Darling served as moderator between Leopold and Beck. The committee did manage to make progress on its top priority: identifying submarginal lands suitable for government purchase and conversion to refuges for waterfowl, upland game, big game, and nongame birds and mammals. To accomplish this, they hastily solicited advice from every state in the nation, from state agencies, Audubon clubs, gun clubs, and Izaak Walton Leagues. "The response," Darling noted, "was magnetic." They also sought the advice and cooperation of the Biological Survey, which responded with a half-baked report that Darling called "a very poor thing."[20]

The lackluster attitude of the survey only fueled Beck's antagonism toward it, which in turn added further to the committee's internal gnashing of teeth. By the end of January the three members split up without having agreed on a report. Darling "took the whole batch of stuff home and wrote what I hoped would be a compromise between Leopold and Beck." Leopold's objections were three. He disagreed with Beck's attitude toward the Biological Survey; he "doubted the wisdom" of Beck's plan to create an interdepartmental "Restoration Commissioner"; and he favored state rather than federal administration of refuges. Leopold explained in a letter to Darling on January 29:

The shaping of a new policy, and the building of an agency to execute it, cannot be done in a hurry by a committee. It can be done by a broad-gauge administrator, who shall take at least a year to [do] it, and [who] makes his moves one by one as they become clear. . . . To sum up: we must not delude ourselves by seeing this job as merely a heaven-sent chance to buy some game lands. It is, whether we will or no, the chance to make or break federal leadership in wild life conservation. Every step has far-reaching implications. The fact that the rank and file of conservation enthusiasts are unaware of those implications makes us all the more responsible for foreseeing them, hence my solicitude over what may seem trivial details in our report. If we could be sure of a qualified administrator, with this broad conception of his duties, I would not care what the report said, or whether we submitted any at all.[21]

The final version of the "National Plan For Wild Life Restoration" (complete with one of Darling's cartoons) was submitted February 8, 1934. Despite his reservations, Leopold wrote to Beck that he was "well satisfied with it"; "I appreciate your attitude most sincerely," was Beck's response.[22] With time, in fact, Beck would grow more sympathetic to Leopold's wildlife outlook.

The final report listed nine recommendations. Most important, it called for federal purchase of some twelve million acres, at a cost of $25 million; another $25 million would be allotted from the Public Works Administration and other New Deal relief programs for restoration and improvement of refuges. This was a far more extensive plan than anyone except Beck—who assumed he had a minimum committment of $25 million from Roosevelt—had planned. Secretary Wallace read the report and reported to Roosevelt that it was "too ambitious to be feasible in the immediate future." But Wallace also read the Biological Survey's disappointing contribution; "The contrast," according to Darling, "was too evident to be ignored."[23] Wallace gave Redington and the survey an opportunity to implement the report of the Beck Committee. Redington declined. His health faltering, his professional reputation crumbling, and his bureau in deep trouble, Redington resigned within the month.

The President's Committee disbanded after submitting its report. For a time, the fate of the nation's wildlife and its main wildlife agency hung in limbo. The report had made some important points, but it was a patchwork plan, hastily drawn up; it needed a strong administrator to guide it. Beck's pet plan for a "Restoration Commissioner" went exactly nowhere. Clearly the choice of a new chief for the Biological Survey would determine the direction of the nation's wildlife committment. "In my opinion," Leopold wrote to a friend at the time, "it does not matter much what is in our report. The only thing which really matters is what kind of men are appointed to execute the program. I have reason to believe that the Secretary [of Agriculture] is trying to make the kind of an appointment that you and I would approve [of], but it is too early to be sure."[24]

Leopold seems to have played an advisory role in the choice of that appointment. In any case, when Roosevelt on March 1 chose Darling to take over the Biological Survey, Leopold was apparently the only one in the country, including Darling himself, who was not surprised. Leopold expressed "utmost confidence" in Darling's ability, a sentiment not shared by all conservationists. Many wondered whether a cartoonist (albeit a Pulitzer Prize winner) could run the U.S. Biological Survey. Politicians were even more skeptical. Darling's biographer writes, "FDR was asking a rock-ribbed conservative Republican political cartoonist to join the Roosevelt administration at an influential level, and Darling was not sure he wanted to 'aid and abet' the opposition. Roosevelt was also asking this outspoken critic of his administration to forego a six-figure income to become an $8000-a-year member of the New Deal team. It was an unlikely prospect at first glance."[25] Darling weighed the cost against the great opportunity to benefit posterity. After receiving assurances that he would be free of interference from the "hunting clubs crowd," and that the wildlife refuge program would receive immediate funding, Darling accepted the position on a temporary basis.

He hit Washington with his feet running and his direction clear. In short order, he proceeded to revive, revamp, and strengthen the beleaguered Bureau of Biological Survey. Within a month Congress passed and Roosevelt signed the Duck Stamp Act of 1934, providing for a one-dollar federal hunting license, proceeds from which would go toward the acquisition and improvement of waterfowl habitat. The first stamp was designed by Darling himself. His tenure as head of the survey would be brief and rocky, but it would redirect the force and course of wildlife conservation in America.

∽

Self-criticism was always a hallmark of Leopold's professionalism. In a field where myth, generalization, and enthusiasm were often liable to outweigh real results, he was constantly pushing himself and others to examine and reexamine their aims, means, and results. Sometimes it seemed as if he were more critical of those within conservation than he was of those beyond it.

In the spring of 1934, Leopold began to turn his critical eye back on his experiences of the previous year. By now he was something of a veteran New Deal conservationist—as much a veteran as one could be in an administration barely a year old. He had served in the Southwest with the CCC, in Wisconsin with the SES, and in Washington on the Beck Committee. Like Darling, Leopold was not a New Dealer by nature. Essentially, he had been a man without a party ever since Teddy Roosevelt bolted the Republican ranks in 1912. His progressive streak still ran deep, especially when it came to conservation and his broad economic outlook, but he could best be described as a moderate. According to his son Luna, Leopold saw no promise in the major party candidates for president in the 1930s and 1940s, and voted, as did many disaffected intellectuals, for Norman Thomas. Yet, one of Leopold's closest and oldest friends in Madison, Tom Coleman, was a staunch conservative, and a mover and shaker in the Republican Party. Leopold was simply not a political animal, a trait only reinforced over the years by his sour tastes of state politics.

On March 1, 1934, Leopold gave a talk to the Taylor-Hibbard Economics Club at the University of Wisconsin entitled "Conservation Economics." It was a major address for Leopold, one of his first public expressions on the New Deal way of doing conservation. As such, it took on the yet greater question of the responsibility of individuals and governments in dealing with vital environmental problems. Leopold thus saw it as a companion piece to the pre–New Deal "Conservation Ethic."

Leopold described the advent of New Deal conservation in astronomical terms. "A mighty force," he dryly explained, "consisting of the pent-up desires and frustrated dreams of two generations of conservationists, passed near the national money-bags whilst opened wide for post-depression relief. Something large and heavy was lifted off and hurled into the galaxy of the alphabets. It is still moving too fast for us to be sure how big it is, or what cosmic forces draw rein on its career. My purpose is to discuss the new arrival and his prospects in life."[26]

Leopold did not issue a blanket criticism of this new entity. In fact, he regarded it as a "natural consequence" of the nation's past abuse of resources, and its mixed success in correcting that abuse. That said, however, certain problems inhered in conservation-by-agency. First and foremost was simple geography. Increased public ownership of land was a main premise of New Deal programs. Leopold had advocated this in the report of the Beck Committee. But this "stampede for public ownership" could only go so far; resources were everywhere, and so was abuse. Conservation, in the broad sense that Leopold now understood it, could never be achieved by buying up odd parcels of abused land. For wildlife, for forests, for recreation, and especially for soil erosion control, this was simply an untenable solution. "The disease of erosion," he warned, "is a leprosy of the land, hardly to be cured by slapping a mustard plaster on the first sore. The only cure is the universal reformation of land-use, and the longer we dabble with palliatives, the more gigantic grows the job of restoration."[27]

Leopold did not oppose public ownership in principle. He did, however, challenge the assumption that "bigger buying is a substitute for private conservation practice." He wrote in another context that, "It is easy to side-step the issue of getting lumbermen to practice forestry, or the farmer to crop game or conserve soil, and to pass these functions to government.

But it won't work. I assert this, not as a political opinion, but as a geo-graphical fact. It's not in the cards. The basic problem is to *induce the private landowner to conserve on his own land,* and no conceivable mil-lions or billions for public land purchase can alter that fact."[28] This em-phasis on individual responsibility was now a firm cornerstone in his philo-sophical construction. It grew out of his lifetime of conservation field work, but now he was beginning to see it in its larger social context. Private con-servation was simply an expression of "that first theorem of social justice: The Lord helps those who help themselves."[29] Moreover, to hand the job over to government was to lose many of the rewards and challenges—"the social disciplines"—formerly reserved for the individual. This was the basic rationale behind both the Riley and Faville Grove experiments in farmer-sportsman cooperation.

A second problem raised by the New Deal approach was that which Leopold experienced in the CCC camps of the Southwest: lack of coor-dination. "The instructive part of this experience," Leopold said, "is not that cub foremen should lack omniscience in integrating conservation, but that the high-ups (of which I was one) did not anticipate these conflicts of interest, sometimes did not see them when they occurred, and were ill-prepared to adjust them when seen. The plain lesson is that to be a practi-tioner of conservation on a piece of land takes more brains, and a wider range of sympathy, forethought and experience, than to be a specialized forester, game manager, range manager, or erosion expert in a college or a bureau."[30] Compounding this on-the-ground confusion was the fact that a tangle of legislative acts seemed almost to mandate it. A dozen acts, laws, agencies, and incentives, each with their own standard, had to coexist on the same piece of turf.

Leopold concluded that, in the broadest economic terms, the New Deal's emphasis on wholesale public expenditures amounted to a taking over, by the taxpaying public at large, of the bills incurred by the private landowner who abuses land. "Abuse," it followed, "is no longer merely a question of depleting a capital asset, but of actually creating a cash liability against the taxpayer." The environmental chickens, in other words, were coming home to roost on the taxpayer's doorstep. In a way, it had always been thus, but under the New Deal programs, they had begun to roost en masse. Leopold summed up his point:

The thing to be prevented is destructive private land-use of any and all kinds. The thing to be encouraged is the use of private land in such a way as to combine the public and private interest to the greatest possible degree. If we are going to spend large sums of public money anyhow, why not use it to subsidize desirable com-binations in land use, instead of to cure by purchase, prohibition, or repair, the headache arising from bad ones?

I realize fully that such a question qualifies me for the asylum for political and economic dreamers. Yet I submit that the proposal is actually less radical politically, and possibly cheaper in economic cost, than the stampede for public ownership in which our most respectable conservatives have now joined.[31]

"Conservation Economics" reflected not only Leopold's experience inside the New Deal, but his deepening appreciation of the biological and economic complexities of successful land-use reform. Between the lines, one reads the influence of George Wehrwein, a colleague in the university's Department of Agricultural Economics whose original work on the economics of land reform, soil erosion, and rural taxation would have a steady impact on Leopold. Another influence, in a reverse way, may have been Bob Marshall. Marshall, an out-and-out socialist, had stirred up a good deal of dust with his recent book *The People's Forests*, in which he made the case for vastly increased government involvement in administration of the nation's forest lands. The important Copeland Report, released in March 1933, similarly called for the government to undertake a sweeping program of public forest acquisition, and recommended that the Forest Service be granted powers to regulate cutting on private timber lands. Leopold undoubtedly followed the debate over these issues in the *Journal of Forestry,* and may have intended "Conservation Economics" as his own contribution.

Herb Stoddard praised "Conservation Economics" as "a very keen paper. . . . I only wish that a copy could be sent to every conservationist, farmer, and citizen of the country."[32] Darling thought it "the finest thing I have ever read, seen, or heard on the subject. It ought to make you President."[33]

Leopold's views hardly found unanimous acceptance. In fact, as conservation expanded under Roosevelt, the unanimity which Leopold had long tried to advance receded further and further. But Leopold was gaining a wide reputation for disinterested criticism, for his ability to clearly define issues, and for making provocative points. Ironically, where he had always fought against land-abuse problems, now he was also fighting the New Deal's proposed solutions. In his own way, he was still fighting the same battle.

"Conservation Economics" inaugurated a period in Leopold's life, concurrent with the rise of the New Deal, when he began to explore in far greater detail the social and economic aspects of conservation that he had summarized in the previous year's "Conservation Ethic." The exploration would continue for the remainder of his career. He was not a scholar on social or economic issues, but neither was he an ideologue. He almost never used such words as "class" or "the masses" in his speeches; he never wrote about "the people" in the folksy collective sense. His experience of urban problems was vicarious at best, naive at worst. He appreciated the problems of urbanized man, but he was not a social activist, and offered no strong opinions on such topical matters as civil rights. His focus was always the natural environment within which social forces operated; if he had any particular view to expound, it was that the one could no longer be understood without reference to the other.

On a personal level, Leopold was not only an individualist, but dealt with people on an individual basis. "He had an uncanny ability to talk to anyone in their own terms," Estella remembered. "He was just completely open."[34] This was a quiet quality, and expressed itself unobtrusively. Luna remembers one hunting trip to Missouri when he and his father were laid over at the train station in St. Louis. Aldo suggested they have their shoes shined during their wait. Aldo had a lengthy, animated discussion with the shoe man, drawing him out, questioning him on his business. At heart, Leopold was interested in anyone from whom he could learn.

As for social welfare, Leopold seems to have held to the same attitude that guided his friendship with Bennie Jacobosky at Yale—do what you can when the opportunity arises. One winter's day during the Depression, Aldo and Estella were feeding birds in an orchard west of Madison. They met the impoverished owners of the land, who lived in a run-down, drafty farmhouse. That Christmas, and for many thereafter, they played Santa Claus for the couple, and offered to foot medical bills for their daughter ("I talked my folks out of that," the daughter later recalled. "I was afraid of doctors").[35]

Conservation, in Leopold's view, was not bound to any particular social philosophy. From his earliest days as a forester, he was concerned with keeping ends and means balanced. This meant adherence to principles, but not resistance to change—as amply demonstrated in his innovative ideas and in his shifting views on predation, game management, and the utilitarian attitude toward forests. Thus Leopold was able to avoid the trap that pits concern for people against concern for the natural world. Leopold's work, though still in its formative stages in many ways, was based on the sound premise that the welfare of species and individuals—be they man or beast—depended on the suitability of habitat. When applied to the human economy, especially that of an industrialized culture, this meant that the accumulated costs of private environmental abuse must in one manner or another be borne by the public at large, to the detriment of the general quality of life. Only by "readjusting the tensions" in society could the knot of poorer land, greater government, and fewer freedoms be relaxed. The Depression, the New Deal, and the conservation response had brought these issues together in Leopold's mind.

The *Journal of Forestry* published "Conservation Economics" in May 1934. As if to verify Leopold's points, that same month brought an early warning that land-use problems were too extensive to be addressed by mere legislative fiat. On May 9, out on the sprawling flats of Montana, Wyoming, and the Dakotas, the winds from the north gathered up an immense cloud of dust. The same drought that had dried the prairie marshes had baked the overworked sods. When the rains refused to return and the winds swept down from Canada, the topsoil rose to darken the western skies. It was the first of the thirties' continental dust storms.

∾

Meanwhile, Leopold had begun to teach. Eighteen young farmers signed up for the month-long short course in January. The results were revealing. Leopold was surprised to find that half of the students, although raised on farms, were completely unfamiliar with game species. He immediately resolved to add more fieldwork to his presentations.

In March 1934, Leopold offered Game Management 118 for the first time. The course would evolve with Leopold throughout his teaching career. Those students who wandered into it, knowingly or unknowingly, tended to emerge, literally, with a new view on life. For many, the course was a turning point in their own careers. It began as a half-semester orientation course for all levels of students, with heavy emphasis on field techniques and basic principles of game management.

Leopold began to take on graduate students that spring. His first was an intelligent, introverted field biologist named Franklin Schmidt. Schmidt was a taciturn fellow, more at home in the marshes of central Wisconsin than in an academic cage. His studies concentrated on the prairie chicken, a species whose fate in Wisconsin and elsewhere was threatened by the disappearance of the native prairies through plowing and fire suppression. The studies of the prairie chicken pioneered by Alfred Gross had subsequently passed on to Wallace Grange, and then to Schmidt.

In the early days of wildlife studies, researchers had none of the radio transmitters, coded tags, and four-wheel-drive vehicles of their present-day descendants. Work was much more basic. In the summers, Schmidt packed up his instruments, his bedroll, and his notebooks, and disappeared into the backcountry for weeks at a time. Eventually, he emerged with data. "He was very intense," one fellow student recalled. "He couldn't bear being cooped up. Wherever he went, he insisted on sleeping outdoors. When he came out of the bush, all he needed was a drainage ditch to take a bath and he came out clean and respectable."[36] When Schmidt began his graduate studies at Wisconsin, Leopold held that he "knew more about the life history and ecology of the prairie grouse than any living man, and as much as any living ecologist knows about any American game bird."[37]

Initially, Leopold also supervised privately supported work by Grange on the cycle phenomenon in wildlife populations. Grange's funding arrangement, however, fell through, and the work on cycles was taken up in the fall of 1934 by the second of Leopold's students, Leonard Wing. Wing was more urbane than Schmidt. With his thick black hair and Latin features, Wing looked "like Mephistopheles without the mustache. And he could put the fear of God into a timid type, just by sheer force of personality."[38] He was not the naturalist that Schmidt was, but his strong mathematical mind suited him perfectly for cycle research.

In addition to instructional chores, Leopold was busy with his own continuing research on quail (in cooperation with Paul Errington), final touches on the establishment of the university arboretum, and the aftershocks of the Beck Committee. He cosupervised a survey of marshlands for the Wisconsin Conservation Commission and the Biological Survey, hoping to stimulate progress on the proposed Central Wisconsin Conservation District. He organized the training of several men for work on trout-stream improvement, continued his advisory work with the erosion project at Coon Valley, and gave a lengthy series of speeches, talks, and informal presentations—to the Wisconsin Academy of Science, Arts and Letters, the Dane County Sportsmen's League, the Shriners of Madison, the Science Advisory Board in Washington, the Nakoma Welfare League, the Lake Mills High School, the Stoughton Rotary Club. In August, he spoke coast-to-coast on NBC radio on "The Game Cycle" ("Nineteen hundred thirty-four will go down in history for something more than droughts, strikes, and blood-purges. It is a year of biological eclipse").

In June 1934, Leopold accepted the chairmanship of the National Research Council's Committee on Wild Life (again taking over for John C. Merriam). Leopold was one of twenty individuals in on the formation of the committee in 1931—he and Leon Cole had proposed its formation in 1930—and had served on it ever since. His appointment as chairman, however, was controversial. Two prominent members of the committee protested that the position required a "broader perspective" than Leopold's. Their objections were not intended as a personal slight, but reflected the general low esteem in which game management was held by "pure" zoologists. Ivey F. Lewis, head of the NRC Division of Biology and Agriculture, defended the selection of Leopold. "[His detractors] seem to fear that under Leopold the whole Wild Life program will be turned over to the sportsman. . . . If members of the Wild Life Committee who fear over-emphasis on game had been active as members of the committee I would be more disturbed than I am about the difference of opinion. However, the only sign of activity I saw in the committee came from Leopold."[39] Leopold retained the chairmanship until 1936. The committee during that time stepped up its promotion of research activities and played an advisory role in creating a national program of "cooperative wild life research units," an idea then hatching in Jay Darling's mind.

At the end of May 1934, Leopold and Darling again crossed paths. After two months in Roosevelt's administration, Darling was climbing the walls in Washington. The funds that Roosevelt had promised him for purchase of refuge lands were plugged up in the office of Harry Hopkins (Hopkins' comment at a crucial meeting: "I don't know if we're interested in the relief of birds").[40] By mid-May, Darling was ready to resign, an inclination backed up by impatient newspapermen who reminded Darling that he was still under contract to them. Secretary of Agriculture Wallace and his deputy, Rex Tugwell, consulted a number of informed figures, including the president and Darling himself, and offered Darling's post to Leopold in a letter dated May 16, 1934.

Darling wrote to urge Leopold on:

I doubt if again within our time we will see such an effort to place intelligent selection ahead of political considerations. It has not happened before within my memory. It seems to me the one opportunity that may occur in many years to make of this Bureau the force in the country which you and I know it should be.

Under these circumstances to do less than the best within our vision in unthinkable. I know your heart is given to the work you have created [at the University], but I would be less than honest if I did not say that in relation to the Biological Survey your Wisconsin possibilities are as one to forty-eight.[41]

John C. Merriam added his influential pull. "I do not know of anyone in America," he wrote to Leopold, "who has your view of this situation, or anything like comparable views coupled with scientific and practical experience. As far as my knowledge reaches, you have the friendship and support of leaders throughout the country."[42] Back in Madison, though, Bill Schorger reminded Aldo that "The 'powers that be' would be very much displeased if you should leave here to take the position at Washington. The feeling is that much effort was spent in creating this [University] position and finding the money; that it is a pioneer attempt for a University; and that your resignation at this stage might discourage attempts to continue through." Schorger appreciated Leopold's dilemma. "Every man has but one life to live," he concluded. "And it is sometimes hard to decide where he can spend it most usefully."[43]

Daughter Nina recalled the mood at home:

Who knows what competing goals Dad was nurturing? . . . He became moody and silent. He sat and looked up at the wall, lost in thought, or paced up and down. He wrote to Washington for more information and continued to think about it. We could all feel the strain of a major decision in the making and kept out of his way.

Who knows what Mother thought? It is a fact that she was the one who had to wrestle with the skimpy budget and try to make ends meet. She would have been less than human if she had not yearned for a more comfortable margin of security.

Finally one evening Dad walked to the telephone and through the operator made contact with his brother, Carl, in Burlington. In those days a long distance call was a major budget item but Carl, being nearest in age, was Dad's closest confidant and it was normal for them to make contact before an important decision. From my bed off the first landing of the stairs I listened carefully to the conversation, which went something like the following:

"Hello. . . . Hello Carolo! Yes this is Aldo . . . in Madison. . . . I have just had an offer from D.C. to head up the Biological Survey. . . . Yes, we would have to move to Washington, but that would be just a base for operation all over the country. . . . Yes, I would have supervision of wildlife research for the United States. . . . Yes, quite exciting—marvelous challenge, good staff. . . . What? Salary? Umm, I'm afraid I forgot to ask."[44]

Financial considerations had to play a part in the decision. A professor's salary, even at a major university like Wisconsin, was meager, and the family budget was still recovering from the hard times of 1932–33. (Starker was back in college and, according to Nina, he and Luna "had dreams of fraternity life and wardrobes to fit the pattern of new social challenges.") Leopold replied to Wallace on May 23, asking for further details and promising a decision by June 1, after he had conferred with Dean Russell. Darling managed to intercept Leopold's reply in Washington. "Please Oh Please don't send such explosive material unless marked 'personal' into this shaky old building," Ding warned. "The hint of such an impending change would likely blow it from its foundations."[45]

Darling wrote again to Leopold on May 29, under the heading "Something to read on your way to Washington": "My newspapers are getting pretty ugly over my neglect of them but that can't be helped until this thing is out of the way. I feel like a man out in the middle of a rushing trout stream with a big salmon on the end of my line—down stream—and about all my line out. I never handled this kind of a fish before and I need advice—please hurry!"[46]

Leopold chose to remain in Wisconsin. After mulling it over, he felt that he could best serve wildlife management by guiding fundamental research at the local level. "It boils down, in my mind, to a choice between policy-making and research," he wrote to Darling on May 29. "In short, there is at least a doubt in my mind whether bringing research to actual fruition in one state is not, at this moment, just as important as starting it in many states." Leopold came to his decision with much personal and professional regret. "Jay," he wrote, "I am exceedingly sorry to disappoint you. You have been very generous of your time and talents—more so than I. I can say, quite impersonally, that you have a finesse in handling the public which I lack, and which is a very important qualification. I would fast four days and nights to cancel those [newspaper] contracts of yours."[47]

In retrospect, Leopold's decision worked out for the best. Darling, his early difficulties behind him, took his bureaucratic bull by the horns and turned it around, modernizing its divisions, implementing the refuge plan, and enacting the national system of cooperative wildlife research. Leopold remained in Madison, and never again gave serious thought to leaving. Having found his ground, he concentrated on building up his educational program.

◡

On the morning of June 17, 1934, civic leaders and university officials gathered in a barn on the south edge of Madison and officially dedicated the University of Wisconsin Arboretum and Wild Life Refuge. The university had acquired five hundred acres of typical postsettlement Wisconsin farmland: pasturelands, grazed woodlots, plowed prairie, marshes, and fens. Indian burial mounds dotted the perimeter of Lake Wingra, on whose southern shore the lands lay. Now those lands were to become a living laboratory for the study of Wisconsin's biological legacy.

Leopold was one of several speakers that morning. In his talk he described what he and the other faculty overseers envisioned for the arboretum. It was not going to be just a collection of trees, like other arboreta, but "something new and different"—a collection of landscapes, a re-creation of the land as it once existed. It would be replanted not simply with individual species, but with entire plant communities: prairies, hardwood forest, coniferous forest, marsh. "Our idea, in a nutshell, is to reconstruct, primarily for the use of the University, a sample of original Wisconsin—a sample of what Dane County looked like when our ancestors arrived here during the 1840s." There were limits to such an undertaking. Leopold predicted (somewhat optimistically) that it would take fifty years to do the job, and even then it could never regain certain elements of its original state. Wolves, for instance. Even its possibilities for wildlife research were modest. Yet, Leopold was enthusiastic about the aesthetic and scientific potential for the area. In showing what Wisconsin *was,* the arboretum could offer insights into "what it is, and what it expects to become."[48]

"Why worry?" Leopold asked rhetorically. "Why try to discover the exact processes by which the Wisconsin of 1840 became the Wisconsin of 1930?" His answer bore the mark of the times:

Because we are just beginning to realize that along with the intentional and necessary changes in the soil and its flora and fauna, we have also induced unintentional and unnecessary changes which threaten to undermine the future capacity of the soil to support our civilization. . . . The function of the Arboretum [is] to serve as a benchmark, a starting point, in the long and laborious job of building a permanent and mutually beneficial relationship between civilized men and a civilized landscape.[49]

Leopold's measured words impressed the audience, and provided a lasting sense of purpose for a wild institution that remains a valued asset in Madison's more urbanized landscape. But according to accounts, the most poignant moment in the ceremony came when Chief Albert Yellow Thunder, a native Ho-Chunk, appeared in full ceremonial regalia, and addressed the gathering. "My people are like the trees," he said, "a dying race, leaving behind them as their only monument the natural forests and streams of America."[50] The natives, like the wolf, might not return to the land, but the arboretum could at least remind future generations that they were once there.

Within a year, the arboretum's restoration work was in full swing. State and federal relief crews, supervised by Leopold, horticulturalist Bill Longenecker, and botanist Norman Fassett, began remaking the land. In 1935, the CCC established Camp Madison at the arboretum, a major step in assuring the success of the venture. "Camp Madison," according to the arboretum's historian, "was soon known as the only CCC camp on a university campus, and was selected for the privilege of flying a special banner of honor from the flagpole."[51]

The value of "a sample of original Wisconsin" was never so plain as during the spring and summer of 1934. The drought that seared the western plains also hit locally in the central sands, and when the May 9 dust storm ripped out of the west, it tore loose a layer of central Wisconsin's soils as well, burning young crops and burying fields. In Waushara County, thirty thousand acres of cropland were ruined. In Adams County, sand drifts had to be broken with snowplows. In Wood County, a fire broke out in the dehydrated marshlands, rode the driving wind onto higher ground, and eventually burned twenty thousand acres.[52] Fortunately, the rains began to fall again in June. The strong-willed farmers of the area were quick to learn from the experience, showing notable flexibility in adopting soil conservation measures. Wisconsin would not regularly receive its normal annual allotment of thirty-odd inches of rain again until the forties, but the sensitive sand counties would manage to avoid the general catastrophe that was building up out on the southern plains.

Leopold visited the central sands a number of times that summer. The parade of alphabetic agencies was arriving in full force—the CCC, the AAA, the FERA, and SES, the RA—and Leopold occasionally was sought out for consultation. He also looked in on Franklin Schmidt, who spent his summer studying the prairie chickens at Shiprock Marsh in Adams County.

In July, Aldo, his brother Carl, and Starker took a week-long trout fishing trip to Waushara County. Starker left early for Coon Valley, but Aldo and Carl dawdled on their way back to Madison. Aldo had heard reports of a remnant band of sandhill cranes breeding in the Endeavor Marsh near Buffalo Lake, a wide water on the upper Fox River. The marsh, lying at lake level, had escaped the drainage mania of the previous decades. If there were cranes, birds of impressive proportions and solitary ways, Endeavor Marsh was a likely place to find them.

Leopold had not previously shown any marked interest in the great birds, and his knowledge of their biological characteristics was limited. On July 16, Aldo and Carl stopped to talk with a farmer who lived near the marsh. The farmer, W. J. Somerton, pointed them toward an oak grove along the marsh's edge. "We went over there," Leopold wrote in his journal, "and were standing under the oaks, scanning the marsh with glasses, when with loud trumpetings the pair flushed from the edge of the woods not a gunshot away. It was a noble sight."[53] He had probably never before seen a crane in Wisconsin. Their populations had plummeted during the agricultural expansion of the 1910s and 1920s, and Leopold estimated at the time that there were no more than twenty breeding pairs in the entire state. Back at the farmhouse, Leopold interrogated Somerton, who had lived on the marsh for sixty years, on the history of his farm and his observations of cranes over the years.

Leopold's curiosity was piqued, and he began to inquire among friends and colleagues around the country about the life history, food habits, and habitat needs of cranes. At the end of September, on a weekend grouse hunt at Pilot Knob Marsh with his three boys, Tom Coleman, and Bunker Schlatter, an undergraduate assistant, Aldo again encountered the cranes: "A fine bright sunny morning with the brush full of quail and about the same number of birds as the day before. A big migration of sharpshins this morning, also some larger hawks higher up. But the big event of the day was the continual aerial evolutions of cranes, of which Bunker Schlatter counted 59 at one time. Many small detachments alighted near us. (I later learned Franklin Schmidt had flushed 80 cranes from the Roche a Cri Marsh, and these were doubtless the same birds.)"[54]

The sandhill crane flipped a mental switch in Leopold's mind. Over the next few years he continued to search out cranes, in marsh and library, and he devoted much thought to their role in nature's scheme. But his pursuit of the crane went even beyond this. As he learned more about the tall, gray denizen of the wild marshes, Leopold explicitly drew the connection, heretofore only implicit in his appreciation, between a natural object's beauty and its evolutionary history. The value of the creature lay not in its appearance alone, but in its story as a species. By the time he composed his memorable essay, "Marshland Elegy," in 1937, he wrote of cranes with a respect approaching awe:

Our appreciation of the crane grows with the slow unraveling of earthly history. His tribe, we now know, stems out of the remote Eocene. The other members of the fauna in which he originated are long since entombed within the hills. When we hear his call we hear no mere bird. He is the symbol of our untamable past, of that incredible sweep of millennia which underlies and conditions the daily affairs of birds and men.[55]

The crane itself was "a sample of original Wisconsin," a symbol of a past which could never be regained, but which contained values that were alive, and could contribute in the present and future. Although the crane was not a game bird, Leopold's interest in it was closely connected to his devotion to game management as a profession. Game management—which was even then rapidly evolving toward *wildlife* management—was an attempt to retain for the future an aspect of America's historical past. The crane was a living reminder of America's *evolutionary* past, a quality which had never before struck Leopold so directly about any creature. The naturalist's motive had not changed; only his time-scale.

Leopold holding catch during 1924 Quetico canoe trip (Leopold Papers, UW Archives)

Carl Leopold, Starker, and Luna canoeing the Quetico, 1925 (Photo by Aldo Leopold. Leopold Papers, UW Archives)

Luna and Aldo "roving," about 1930 (Bradley Study Center Files)

Leopold with daughter Estella in front of their home,
1927 (Bradley Study Center Files)

The Leopold home at 2222 Van Hise Avenue, Madison, Wisconsin (Leopold Collection, UW Archives)

Portrait of Leopold, taken as he began his
game survey work for the Sporting Arms
and Ammunitions Manufacturers' Institute
in 1928 (Bradley Study Center Files)

The route of Leopold's game survey of the north-central
states, 1928–30 (From Leopold's *Report on a Game Survey of the North Central States*)

335

Leopold, Charles Elton, and William Rowan at the Matamek Conference in Labrador, 1931 (Leopold Collection, UW Archives)

Leopold and fellow foresters en route to Europe aboard the *Europa*, 1935 (Bradley Study Center Files)

Nina, Aldo, and Estella rehabilitating the shack in
1936, the year after Leopold purchased the property (Bradley Study Center Files)

Spring planting at the shack gate, 1936. The shack is in the background, and the
Wisconsin River is just beyond it (Bradley Study Center Files)

Aldo and Estella, with Flick trailing, haul firewood at the shack, about 1936 (Bradley Study Center Files)

Estella (with daughter Estella in background) carrying red pines up sandhill west of the shack, 1937 (Bradley Study Center Files)

Leopold taking a rest during hunt along the Rio Gavilan in 1938 (Photo by A. Starker Leopold. Leopold Papers, UW Archives)

Campsite on the Rio Gavilan, 1938 (Photo by Aldo Leopold. Leopold Papers, UW Archives)

16

The Value of Wilderness
(1934–1935)

THE WISCONSIN Conservation Commission declared a bow-and-arrow-only deer season in Sauk and Columbia Counties, north of Madison, for the fall of 1934. It was the first archery-only season in recent American hunting history. "Look Out Mr. Buck!" read the headline on the November 21 edition of Madison's *Capital Times;* "Fair Huntresses Will Stalk Deer with Bows and Arrows." The *Times* interviewed Estella Leopold: "Mrs. Leopold doesn't hope to have much luck in bringing down a deer. 'We are going for the fun of seeing the deer more than anything else,' she said. 'You see it will be very difficult to get close enough to hit them with an arrow, but we'll try.'"[1] The novelty of the season, and of women archers, was enough to merit notice as well in the *Chicago Tribune* and *Daily News* (the *Daily News* labeled Estella "Diana of the Hunt").

For four days, Aldo, Estella, Starker, Luna, and assorted friends and students stalked the bucks on a farm north of Lodi, and along the Baraboo River in Sauk County. A light snowfall on the second day made for good tracking. The party spotted twelve bucks altogether, but none of their arrows hit the mark. "By and large," Aldo concluded in his journal, "deer hunting is a continuous series of mishaps. If you persist long enough, there comes a time when the hap takes place without the miss."[2]

The hunt was so enjoyable that several of the participants decided to make it an annual event. This required a base camp. Leopold still owned the cabin in the Ozarks, but Ripley County, Missouri, was a long (and, during the Depression, expensive) drive from Madison. Ever since moving to Wisconsin, Aldo and Estella had considered buying land closer to home. Their children now ranged in age from twenty-two to eight. Aldo wanted a place outside of town where the family could spend time together. The need for an archery camp clinched the idea.

On January 12, 1935, a day after Leopold's forty-eighth birthday, he and his friend Ed Ochsner paid a visit to an abandoned farm on the Wisconsin River in Sauk County.[3] Ochsner, a taxidermist from Prairie du Sac, had joined in on the autumn bow hunt, and was a longtime friend of Herbert Stoddard, who had lived in the area years before. (As young men, Ochsner and Stoddard had shared many a specimen-collecting adventure on the Wisconsin River and in the precipitous sandstone bluffs near Prairie du Sac. They once faced the ultimate challenge when the Ringling Brothers Circus, headquartered in nearby Baraboo, allowed them to skin and stuff a deceased bull hippo. The hippo remained an attraction at the Milwaukee Public Museum for years.)

By virtue of his taxidermy business, Ochsner knew the country in and around Sauk County as well as any man. He and Leopold drove along the Baraboo Hills, quartzite remnants of an ancient mountain range. The hills wore a quilt of snow, stitched by the fencerows of solvent, if not prosperous, farms. Sauk County, at the southern extremity of Wisconsin's central sands, had escaped the worst of the previous years' agricultural trials, though it had its fair share of tax-reverted farms and overworked soils.

They came to a bend in the road near the Wisconsin River, and turned onto a two-rut trail. The trail had once been the main pioneer wagon route west out of Portage. Leopold's hopes must have risen as he and Ochsner passed a grove of old white pines, but when they stopped, at a forlorn site along the river, there were few pines in sight. Clumps of aspens sprouted along the margin of a frozen marsh. A haggard row of wind-swept elms lined a driveway. The fields, poor and sandy even in the summer, seemed even more barren when gripped by winter. The spent soils supported only sand burrs, their dried heads held out above the snow. The farmhouse at the end of the line of elms had burned down; all that remained of the house was a dug-out foundation. To one side there was a small but sturdy chicken coop, the only structure still standing on the property.

Leopold and Ochsner tramped around the orphaned farmland, over a sand ridge and down along the icy riverbank. They took a look inside the chicken coop and found a year's accumulation of manure piled up against one wall ("When we carry it out and put it under your garden," Aldo later encouraged Estella, "you'll be very glad it was there").[4]

Despite its obvious flaws, Aldo was apparently taken with the site. He asked Ochsner to arrange for a lease on the property. Returning to Madison, he gave an approving report to the family. In the months that followed, Aldo and the children paid several visits and went to work on the chicken coop. In February, he, Starker, and Luna cleaned it out and began to build a fireplace (the first chapter in what would become a long saga of fireplace construction). In April, they raised a new roof. The first visitors came — Paul Errington and his wife, and two of Errington's students, Frederick and Frances Hamerstrom. That same month, Leopold bought eighty acres of surrounding land for next to nothing (in later years, he would purchase another forty). He began a new journal, and recorded his first field observation on April 27: "Violets and Indian Sweet Grass blooming."[5] No earthly paradise, the Wisconsin River bottoms nurtured nasty hordes of mosquitos that came out in full force that summer. "Run out by mosquitos," Leopold noted in July. "Went to tourist camp for night."[6]

The family visited the new place—they referred to it variously as the "the elums," "Jagdschloss" ("Hunting Lodge"), and, finally, just "the shack" —infrequently over the remainder of 1935. In fact, it was more or less ignored during what proved to be a very busy year for Leopold.

There was no open deer season in the fall of 1935. That December, Leopold would join Ray Roark, Howard Weiss, George Bryan, Starker, and Luna on a fifth quail hunt in Missouri; it was their last at the Ozark mountain cabin. From that point on, the outdoor activities of the Leopold clan focussed on the worn-out alluvial farm on the Wisconsin River.

༄

Wilderness protection received little attention during the early years of the New Deal. In part, this reflected Roosevelt's conservation priorities. Of all the fronts on which the movement advanced—wildlife, parks and recreation, forestry, range management, soil and water conservation, land reclamation—wilderness was the issue that concerned Roosevelt least. Since Leopold's activism of the mid-twenties, and into the early years of the Depression, concern for the remnants of wilderness receded, or at least expressed itself more quietly. The Forest Service continued to designate and maintain "primitive areas" under the L-20 regulations adopted in 1929, but these regulations did not have the force of law, imposed no minimum size limit, and made no explicit prohibition of development. The National Park Service, however, was showing renewed interest in wilderness under Secretary of the Interior Harold Ickes. In 1934, Ickes told a convention of CCC workers that "We ought to keep as much wilderness area in this country as we can. . . . I am not in favor of building any more roads in the National Parks than we have to build. I am not in favor of doing anything along the line of so-called improvements that we do not have to do."[7] Ickes' motives were not wholly pure, according to some. An ambitious, covetous administrator, he saw in the advocacy of wilderness a chance to wrest acreage away from the Forest Service. This rivalry between the Departments of Interior and Agriculture would continue to escalate throughout the 1930s.

Occupied with putting game management on a sound footing, Leopold himself had written and spoken little about wilderness since his campaign of the mid-1920s. By late 1934, however, a small corps of advocates had again begun to sound the wilderness call. An October 1934 convention of the American Forestry Association in Knoxville, Tennessee, brought together four men who were concerned about new road construction in the Shenandoah and Smoky Mountains National Parks: Robert Marshall; Benton MacKaye; Harvey Broome, a Knoxville attorney active in a local hiking club; and Bernard Frank, a Manhattan-born forest economist at work for the TVA. Through various personal and professional connections, the four had discovered their common concern. They were riding in a car together, en route with the other conventioneers to a nearby CCC camp, when Marshall presented his thoughts on a constitution for a new conservation group, to be devoted solely to the preservation of wilderness. Their discussion became so animated that they had to pull off the road. As the other cars whizzed by, they sat on the bank of Coal Creek near Knoxville and thrashed out the details of Marshall's ideas.[8]

The four decided to keep the new group small and undiluted. They invited six others to become founding members, four of whom eventually assented: Harold Anderson, a Washington accountant and a mutual friend of MacKaye and Marshall; Ernest Oberholtzer, still holding the fort on the Quetico-Superior; Robert Sterling Yard, seventy-four years old, the former head of the National Parks Association, and a leading critic of National Park policies; and Aldo Leopold.

Marshall wrote to Leopold on October 25, 1934. "We want no straddlers, for in the past they have surrendered too much good wilderness and primeval areas which should never have been lost." Included in Marshall's letter was an "invitation to help organize a group to preserve the American wilderness." The group's principles were uncompromising. "The time has come, with the brutalizing pressure of spreading metropolitan civilization, to recognize this wilderness environment as a serious human need rather than a luxury and plaything."[9]

Leopold replied on October 29 that he was "more than glad to serve" in the new "Wilderness Society." As an indication of the philosophical shift that was taking place in Leopold's thinking, he questioned whether the society should include "only those interested in wilderness from the esthetic and social point of view, or whether it should also include those desiring wilderness for ecological studies."[10]

On January 20 and 21, 1935, five of the founders met at the Cosmos Club in Washington and formally organized the Wilderness Society (Leopold was unable to attend because of the concurrent meeting of the Twenty-first American Game Conference in New York). Bob Marshall was elected president. "It was my strong belief," he later wrote to Leopold, "that you would make a better president than I." Marshall was reluctant to serve due to the fact that he was working at the time in the Department of Interior in the Office of Indian Affairs. A conflict of interests was inevitable, a point which Harold Ickes soon reiterated. In March, Marshall wrote to Leopold to "request, urge, and implore you to accept the presidency of this Society."[11]

Leopold, burdened by academic responsibilities, dozens of other organizational activities, the new farm, various writing projects, consulting chores, and sheer geographical distance, did not wish to assume the presidency, but offered to serve if absolutely necessary. "I would much prefer not to take it on," he wrote to Marshall. "In this particular matter, however, I do not feel like flatly refusing to take on the obligation." He proposed that Yard, a long-time resident of Washington and one well familiar with its political channels, serve as president. By April, Leopold was convinced that accepting the presidency "would simply be an absurdity. It necessarily involves a lot of lobbying on current departmental actions and bills of which I know nothing whatsoever, and I lack both the time and desire to find out. My only utility, if any, is in connection with general policy, and that function I can perform without any office." "Yard," he again advised, "is the logical president."[12]

Later that spring, Robert Sterling Yard did become president, although Marshall continued to provide most of the group's financial backing, policy direction, and moral suasion. The group grew quickly in its early months, but radical as it was, even among conservationists, it remained relatively small and tight-knit. And effective. Its members, though few in number and diverse in personality, were headstrong, well-placed, and knowledgeable in the ways of land-use politics. In just a few years, the Wilderness Society established itself as a dynamic new influence on the national conservation scene.

Leopold, busy in the hinterlands, played a background role within the Wilderness Society, serving mainly as a senior advisor, as go-between to other conservation groups, and as the society's intellectual statesman. For the first issue of *Living Wilderness,* the organization's new magazine, Yard asked Leopold to contribute a brief statement on "the fundamental need or purposes of the Society."[13] Leopold responded with an article that exhibited his emerging ecological viewpoint.

"Perhaps it is a truth," he began, "one day to be recognized, that no idea is significant except in the presence of its opposite. This country has been swinging the hammer of development so long and so hard that it has forgotten the anvil of wilderness which gave value and significance to its labors. The momentum of our blows is so unprecedented that the remaining remnant of wilderness will be pounded into road-dust long before we find out its values."[14]

For a quarter century Leopold had been defining the values of wilderness. His thoughts were layered like the strata of sedimentary rock. At the base was the purely esthetic value of wilderness, the simple thrill to beauty evoked by wild places. The wilderness also had biological value, as a place to conserve wildlife. Connected to this was the recreational value for hunting, fishing, and backcountry travel that Leopold emphasized in the early 1920s. Above this, there was the cultural value of wilderness that Leopold had put forth in Turnerian terms after his move to Madison. Now, in 1935, Leopold was emphasizing yet another value of possibly profound importance—the scientific value, which, he admitted, was "still scantily appreciated, even by members of the Society. . . . The long and short of the matter is that all land-use technologies—agriculture, forestry, watersheds, erosion, game, and range management—are encountering unexpected and baffling obstacles which show clearly that despite the superficial advances in technique, we do not yet understand and cannot yet control the long-time interrelations of animals, plants, and mother earth."[15]

Wilderness, in short, was the control against which we could measure our experiment in civilization. As an example, Leopold cited (for the first time) the research of John Weaver on the native prairies of Nebraska. Weaver's work was showing how the stability of prairie soils was affected by the intensive cropping of exotic plants. This was work with far-reaching implications. "But how shall it be followed up," Leopold asked, "if there be no prairie flora left to compare with cultivated flora? And who cares a hang about preserving prairie flora except those who see the values of wilderness?"

"The Wilderness Society," Leopold concluded in a statement recalling "The Conservation Ethic," "is, philosophically, a disclaimer of the biotic arrogance of *homo americanus*. It is one of the focal points of a new attitude—an intelligent humility toward man's place in nature."[16]

Between his lines, Leopold had captured the changes that he and many in his profession were beginning to sense. The social and economic rationale behind conservation had always been its selling point. Now, conservationists were finding that even those foundations rested on a yet more fundamental bedrock of biological and ecological facts of life. And science, for all the advances it was making in other spheres, had hardly begun to scratch the surface of this one.

While the other founders of the Wilderness Society were meeting in Washington, Leopold made these points in an address to the American Game Conference. His topic was the progress of the American Game Policy in the four years since its adoption. Leopold reported that the focal point of the policy, the idea of rewarding the landowner for game cropping, had made "some headway," but he was no longer convinced that shooting revenues provided sufficiently powerful incentive. "I now incline to believe," he said, "that the full development of game cropping on farms, as well as most other kinds of conservation, must await some rather fundamental changes in rural culture and in land economics. . . . Conservation, in short, is at direct variance with the moral and esthetic standards of our generation, and until those standards change, we can have only such fragments as happen to 'come easy.'"[17]

Conservation as a social policy was far more complex than it had seemed four years before. So, too, was the science behind it. Schools that trained land managers—farmers, foresters, game men—had failed to impart "that perception of dynamic ecological forces, without which damage to land remains invisible until after it has occurred. [But] let no layman crow over this statement as an indictment of technicians, until he himself learns how hard it is to foresee and prevent the abuse of land. . . . We know almost as little about the ecological mechanism of these United States as a hen knows about the cosmic chemistry which controls her life and her productivity."[18]

At the conclusion of the conference, Leopold was elected chairman of the next annual meeting.

ဢ

When Leopold returned to Wisconsin, he found over one hundred students signed up for his short course, an encouraging development, but too many for effective teaching. Prospective managers of game were growing in abundance, even if game itself was not.

Franklin Schmidt had completed most of his exhaustive—and exhausting—fieldwork, and was about to work his backlog of data on prairie chickens into a definitive series of scientific papers. Leonard Wing's work concentrated on the possible connection between wildlife and solar cycles.

A third student had joined Leopold's fold. Arthur Hawkins was a bright, lanky, affable ornithologist from Cornell, and came to Wisconsin to investigate the rise in quail populations across the southern part of the state. Hawkins knew next to nothing about quail, and had never set foot west of Buffalo. He had heard of Leopold, but did not know what to expect when he walked into Leopold's office for his first interview with the Professor. Leopold often screened prospective students by engaging them in a lengthy conversation, designed to ascertain in detail the extent of the student's knowledge of natural history; it was a subtle but accurate test. "My initial worries about the encounter proved to have been wasted energy," Hawkins remembered. "I was treated like a visiting dignitary, even an old friend. There was no breaking-in period. We chatted informally until nearly noon, as though the Professor had nothing better to do and I was a trusted advisor. He insisted that I have lunch at his home so that I could meet some of the family. By then, I'm sure, he knew a great deal about my strong points and shortcomings, but the way he gained this information was painless to me."[19]

Across the state, several of the projects that Leopold had helped instigate were beginning to produce results. Planting at the arboretum proceeded in earnest. The Riley and Faville Grove arrangements were working well, both in terms of game bird production and farmer satisfaction. Out in Coon Valley, a game census showed that, in just one year, the quail population had doubled and the pheasant population quadrupled. The Biological Survey finished its survey of the central Wisconsin marshes and recommended three areas for purchase and reflooding as waterfowl refuges. The Resettlement Administration moved ahead with its own plans for marshland restoration. (The first actual work in reflooding drained marshes, however, came about without the aid of the federal government. At a rather wet meeting of Milwaukee sportsmen, Franklin Schmidt asked the men to contribute a hundred dollars to build a dam to demonstrate the potential benefits of reflooding. They agreed to give the money, provided Schmidt would drink a glass of whiskey. They thought their money safe, Schmidt being as chary of alcohol as he was of human society. Rising to the challenge, Schmidt downed the double shot in a gulp, and the dam was soon built. The ducks soon followed.)

Leopold felt encouraged that the science he had helped to foster was reaching the point where it could support itself. Interest in game and wildlife management had picked up around the nation. Research on a dozen species was underway, as opposed to just one (Stoddard's quail study) a decade before. And he himself was now able to devote time to basic research on game population dynamics, life histories, and habitat characteristics. "I like it," he once wrote, "because it is like riding to hounds—a perpetual quest for something seldom found." In a playful mood, he described his "specifications for a perfect research enterprise":

First and foremost, the field of inquiry must promise to yield no gainful knowledge. Any field holding out a prospect of new facts which some inventor might patent and sell, or some manufacturer use to build a new machine, or some Chamber of Commerce endorse as a contribution to progress, or some preacher hail as uplifting, or some editor headline in an extra, or some advertiser blazon on a billboard, is disqualified thereby. The perfect quest must seek something entirely useless to all practical men, such as why a sunset is red, or how a dog finds a covey.

Second, and of like importance, the quest must be so difficult, and promise such long and devious paths, as to hold out no assurance of ultimate success. It must demand the keenest research nose, set in the stoutest and most highly trained hounds of science.

Thirdly, the quest must lie in no single field of science. Like a cold trail laid at random across a thousand hills, it must transect with contemptuous abandon all those little patches which the priests of knowledge have labelled, fenced, and preempted as separate "sciences." Should by any chance the fox be one day run to earth, no bureau or department or learned society must strut or crow as the successful master of hounds. Rather should men marvel at how little each had known or done, over what wide horizons a single quest can lead, and even then be but a single spider's skin, laid on the panorama of the unknown hills.[20]

Leopold's disregard — some would say disrespect — for disciplinary boundaries would only increase with time. His frustration with academic categories had both a theoretical and practical basis. The ecological science toward which he was moving could not, by definition, be as neatly categorized as more traditional fields of inquiry. In practice, he had seen and taken part in too many conservation efforts that floundered and even backfired on account of their narrow outlooks. Accordingly, Leopold soon began to push for a new "general cultural course in conservation" that could tie together university experts from George Wehrwein in land economics to Edward Birge in aquatic ecology.

Beyond these promising fields of investigation, however, there were starkly real clouds on the horizon.

The spring had come hot, dry, and early to the southern plains. Once again the farmers and ranchers banked on rain. Once again, the rains held back. The busted sod of an entire region lay waiting for water, and received only wind. Nature made a disaster possible; human misuse of the land made it all but inevitable. The storms began in February, in Kansas, Oklahoma, and Texas. On March 6, soil from Colorado sifted into the halls of Congress in Washington, where hearings were being held on the question of whether to give the Soil Erosion Service permanent official status. Hugh Bennett, alert to the drama, was scheduled to testify before a Senate committee. Bennett drew out his testimony until the storm reached its height and dust darkened the committee room. "This, gentlemen," he intoned, "is what I have been talking about!" Congress quickly passed the bill that established a Soil Conservation Service within the Department of Agriculture, with Bennett as its chief.[21] The dust flew unrelentingly through March. On the fifteenth, Kansas was blacked out, engulfed by its own swirling soil. A journalist reported that "Lady Godiva could ride thru streets without even the horse seeing her."[22]

On March 21, 1935, Leopold received a letter from Paul Roberts, a former colleague in the D-3 Office of Grazing. Roberts was head of FDR's new Plains Shelterbelt Project, an ambitious program to plant a hundred-mile wide strip of trees across the Great Plains, from North Dakota to Texas, to provide a line of defense against wind erosion. Roberts went at the project with gusto, setting up headquarters in Lincoln, Nebraska, hiring labor, starting nurseries, and planning planting strategies. By that March, the first saplings were in the ground.[23] "I presume," Roberts wrote to Leopold, "[that] you have read of the severe dust storms which have been occurring in the Shelterbelt States this spring. I am enclosing an interesting clipping in regard to the flights of prairie chickens, in this connection." The clipping from the March 21 *Nebraska State Journal* reported unusual flights of hundreds of prairie chickens, flying low out of the western sandhills, driven by dust storms and the scarcity of food. "You no doubt would be interested in such a phenomenon."[24] Leopold often received such reports through letters from friends around the state and country.

The storms reached their climax on April 14, a day that victims subsequently referred to as "Black Sunday." Out of the high, dry plains of eastern Colorado and western Kansas, in the long rain shadow of the Sangre De Cristos, the worst of the dusters rose into the sky, an immensity of grit and topsoil moving south in a rage. It did not let up for hours. Driving was impossible. Those caught outdoors had only a few minutes to find shelter, and no shelter could stop the blows of driven dust that penetrated even the finest cracks. Livestock and wildlife perished, their lungs plastered with mud, their hides sandblasted. On the Monday after Black Sunday, a Denver reporter gave the area a label and the nation an icon: the Dust Bowl.

On that same day Aldo Leopold spoke to the Sigma Xi chapter at the University of Wisconsin. The title of his talk was "Land Pathology." There was still dust in the air of Madison, and the events of the recent days lent added poignancy to his words.

Philosophers have long since claimed that society is an organism, but with few exceptions they have failed to understand that the organism includes the land which is its medium [in the margin of his manuscript, Leopold pencilled in the name "Ospenski"]. . . . We may never put society and its land into a test tube, but some of their interactions are discernible by ordinary observation. . . . Conservation is a protest against destructive land use. It seeks to preserve both the utility and beauty of the landscape. It now invokes the aid of science as a means to this end. Science has never before been asked to write a prescription for an esthetic ailment of the body politic. The effort may benefit scientists as well as laymen and land.[25]

Leopold came back to the main point he had made in "The Conservation Ethic" in 1933: that America had yet to evolve any "vital proposal for adjusting men and machines to land." Remedial practices were being worked out, but could be applied only on public land, or at public expense; there was still no sufficient solution to what was a universally dispersed phenomenon. America's social structure, with its roots in preindustrial Europe, a land and time different from our own, contained "no suitable ready-made mechanisms for protecting the public interest in private land." With one eye, perhaps, on central Wisconsin, and the other on the southern plains, he noted that "the unprecedented velocity of land-subjugation in America involved much hardship, which in turn created traditions which ignore esthetic land uses. . . . Rural education has been preoccupied with the transplantation of machinery and city culture to the rural community, latterly in the face of economic conditions so adverse as to evict the occupants of submarginal soils."[26]

What developments could bring stability to the landscape?

One is the formulation of mechanisms for protecting the public interest in private land.

The other is the revival of land esthetics in rural culture.

The further refinement of remedial practices is equally important, but need not here be emphasized because it already has some momentum.

Out of these three forces may eventually emerge a land ethic more potent than the sum of the three, but the breeding of ethics is as yet beyond our powers. All science can do is to safeguard the environment in which ethical mutations might take place.[27]

It was one of the first uses of the phrase "land ethic" to appear in Leopold's articles or speeches. Although Leopold would later become identified with the "land ethic," he himself rarely used the term, and then only at the end of his life. He first had to overcome a nagging tension within himself. Leopold was not a preacher. He despised demagoguery, and chafed under social conventions. Ethics were a personal matter, weighed by the individual, not dictated by authority. An individualist to the core, he was confronting the complex reality of twentieth-century environmental problems, with the quality of life, for both people and land, held in the balance. Leopold was not yet ready or willing to go further in defining a "land ethic," but "Land Pathology" was an important speech for Leopold. In an atmosphere dark with dust, he began to consider again the foundations he had laid so pointedly and, he thought, so *finally,* in "The Conservation Ethic."

Leopold's concluding remarks that day spoke, not only for himself, but for the many scientists, administrators, and landowners who, all of a sudden, felt the tragedy of an agricultural economy at odds with its own basic resource:

Every American has tattooed on his left breast the basic premise that manifestations of economic energy are inherently beneficent. Yet here is one which to me seems malignant, not inherently, but because a good thing has outrun its limits of goodness. We learn, in ecology at least, that all truths hold only within limits. Here is a good thing—the improvement in economic tools. It has exceeded the speed, or degree, within which it was good. Equipped with this excess of tools, society has developed an unstable adjustment to its environment, from which both must eventually suffer damage or even ruin. Regarding society and land collectively as an organism, that organism has suddenly developed pathological symptoms, i.e., self-accelerating rather than self-compensating departures from normal functioning. The tools cannot be dropped, hence the brains which created them, and which are now mostly dedicated to creating still more, must be at least in part diverted to controlling those already in hand. Granted that science can invent more and more tools, which might be capable of squeezing a living even out out of a ruined countryside, yet who wants to be a cell in that kind of a body politic? I for one do not.[28]

∽

Leopold's work was changing, its center shifting, its scope expanding. This growth took many forms: a renewed interest in nongame wildlife; emphasis on the biotic values of wilderness; the by-now complete change in attitude toward "our magnificent predators"; a concern for the stability of land "as an organism"; a recognition of the absolute necessity of coordination in conservation activities; a view of game management as not only an end in itself, but as a means toward a yet greater end. These points were about to come into alignment under unexpected conditions, in an unexpected setting.

On June 24, 1935, Leopold received an exciting letter. The Oberlaender Trust, a fund operating under the auspices of the Carl Schurz Memorial Foundation, had issued invitations to Leopold and five other foresters to conduct a study of forestry methods in central Europe. Leopold was asked specifically to study "the various ramifications of game management in relation to forestry."[29]

The Schurz Foundation had been established in 1930 to honor the visionary German-American forester and statesman. A "strictly non-political organization," its aim was to promote the development of cultural relations between the United States and the German-speaking countries. In keeping with the legacy of its namesake, the foundation was particularly active in promoting discourse in the field of forestry. Ward Shepard, Leopold's old friend and coeditor of the *Pine Cone,* spent fifteen months observing Germany's forestry system in 1932–33 under a foundation grant. In 1934, the Oberlaender Trust brought Franz Heske, director of the Forestry School at Tharandt and one of the world's leading forestry authorities, to the United States, and sent a group of twelve American lumbermen on a tour of private forests in Germany and Czechoslovakia.

The Oberlaender Trust attached no strings to its invitation. Leopold was encouraged to devote as much time overseas as was necessary ("three months at least"), and to spend it as he saw fit. The trust would pay all living and traveling expenses, from Madison to Madison. Leopold eagerly accepted the offer, pending an okay from the university. Since he was not scheduled to be in the classroom that fall, his way was cleared in early July, and he found himself packing for what was the only overseas trip he ever made. He was due to sail out of New York on August 3.

Aldo's opportunity would be Estella's trial. In their twenty-two years of marriage, they had never been separated for so great a length of time, nor by so great a distance. While he was taking advantage of the chance of a lifetime, she remained behind to run the household.

Leopold left Madison on July 30, bound for New York via Washington. While on the train, he met Bob Marshall for the first time. Their meeting was testimony to the ecumenism of the wilderness brotherhood. Leopold was an Anglo-Saxon midwesterner, nonpolitical, nondoctrinaire; Marshall was an ungainly-looking man, a New York–born Jewish socialist, son of a renowned attorney, with a passion for civil liberties and social justice that matched his convictions on wilderness. Leopold strolled observantly in the field, slowing down the older and more inquisitive he became. Marshall was drive personified; his idea of wilderness travel was to climb a dozen mountain peaks in a day, or to hike sixty miles with hardly a pause to rest. There is no record of their conversation, but no doubt they discussed the Wilderness Society's agenda and the latest developments in the Washington bureaus. In a letter to Estella, Aldo described it as an "interesting" talk.[30]

In Washington, Leopold caught up with a number of friends: John D. Guthrie, Arthur Ringland, Ward Shepard, Ovid Butler, Ding Darling. "I have a growing affection for all of these," he wrote to Estella, "and it was a real satisfaction to get to see them." Darling was again threatening to step down as head of the Biological Survey. "I told him NO," Aldo wrote, "so don't worry." Aldo also made a bon voyage request of Estella. "I wish you would ask Miss Horn to order Frederick Turner's 'History Of The American Frontier,' as soon as she gets ahead enough. We ought to have it, and the boys should read it. Be sure and call Miss Horn once in a while. She is really an important member of our 'economy,' and I'm afraid we tend to take her for granted too often."[31]

On August 3, Leopold and his fellow grant recipients boarded the ocean liner *Europa* and sailed out of New York Harbor. The other five were all Forest Service men: Senior Forest Economist William N. Sparhawk; Edward E. Carter, Assistant Forester in Charge of Forest Management; Clarence L. Forsling, director of the Appalachian Forest Experiment Station; Hardy L. Shirley, a silviculturalist at the Lake States Experiment Station; and Leopold's old friend Leon Kniepp, now serving as head of the Division of Lands (in which position he had become one of the service's most outspoken advocates of wilderness protection).

The ocean passage was safe and luxurious, with perfect weather and delicious food that arrived in "mountains, five times a day." "All of us," Aldo reported to Estella, "have developed a capacity for loafing which would surprise you." Aldo whiled away the time trying to resurrect his childhood German, observing seabirds, measuring the swells of the sea, and attending informal briefing sessions with the other foresters. He called the ship "an admirable mechanism," but he found the trip a little dull. "A boat like this," he wrote to his mother Clara, now seventy-five, "is so big and perfect that there is little sense of risk or adventure. It must have been vastly different in 1848. This is just like a temporarily isolated hotel."[32]

The Germany toward which they sailed was still in the early expectant phase of Hitler's Reich. The foresters, as unsuspecting of the imminent cultural degeneration as any, would take little notice of the political atmosphere (Leopold's first comment on the situation came shortly after landing, when he described in a letter the "notably good-looking . . . young men, thousands of which are in uniforms of 57 varieties.")[33]

Leopold and the others were more interested in the status of German conservation than in politics. The German love of forests was engrained in their history as a people. Long before there was an American conservation movement—long before there was an America—the landed noblemen of central Europe had not only practiced both forestry and game management, but, especially important for Leopold's purposes, maintained historical records of their efforts. As the touring foresters soon learned, the result of the long centuries of land manipulation was a mixed bag of environmental effects, with plenty of lessons for the United States.

This devotion to conservation was readily apparent to Leopold, who noted that "the people in general retain a hankering for doing things with soil which we seem to have 'outgrown.' . . . Most people, even in the middle of Berlin, have the look of living outdoors."[34] Outside the cities, however, modern-day Germans were paying for mistakes made long ago. In the early 1800s, German foresters discovered that pure plantations of spruce and pine outyielded the naturally occurring, less-intensively managed forest of mixed conifers and hardwoods. Coming on the heels of a century-long timber famine, this discovery caused, in Leopold's words, "a general stampede toward the planting of spruce. . . . Never before or since have the forests of a whole nation been converted to a new species within a single generation."

The "spruce mania" continued into new generations. Spruce was planted far and wide, often beyond its natural range. Foresters reaped the promised increase in yields, and planted new spruce seedlings. By the second and third rotations, however, the superior yields had failed to recur, and began to decline. Leopold later described the long-term consequences for the forest:

Litter failed to decay, piling upon the forest floor as a dry, sterile blanket which smothered all natural undergrowth, even moss. Roots ceased to penetrate the soil, lying in a tangled mat between the soil and the litter, with so many root grafts that cut stumps formed healing calluses by reason of their connection with nearby uncut trees. The topsoil developed excessive acidity, became bleached, and was separated from the subsoil by a dark band. These conditions became known as "soil-sickness," and are now technically understood as podzolization — an accumulation of surface acids due to the lack of hardwoods to pump up bases from the subsoil. Windfalls increased, due to shallow anchorage. Insect epidemics swept through the unbroken regiments. In short, pure spruce, the precocious child of timber famine and "wood factory" economics, grew up into an unlovely and unproductive maturity.[35]

The reaction to this situation began in the 1910s, when forestry officials began to follow, at first under their own inclination, later by law, principles that came to be labelled "Dauerwald" ("permanent woods"). Foremost among these measures was the reintroduction of beech, oak, and other hardwoods into the spruce forests. By 1935, the first measurements had come in, and a revised understanding of forests was taking hold. "In general," wrote Leopold, "it is now conceded that mixed forest, naturally reproduced, outyields pure conifers in the long run. Speed of reproduction, decay of litter, self-pruning of trees, rate of stump rotting, and other indices to ecological health are speeded up to an almost phenomenal extent."[36]

Germans loved their game, especially deer, as much as they loved their trees. But the hundred-year speculation in spruce had been as disastrous for wildlife as it had been for the forests. The conversion to spruce had damaged native bird life, reducing the variety and density of birds, upsetting the species composition, and virtually excluding hole-breeders. Generations of gamekeepers had preserved viable game populations for the hunting class, but nongame wildlife had suffered or prospered according to happenstance. Centuries of control had reduced predators to a precious and valued few.

The deer were a special case. They were hard put to subsist in the solid spruce forests. In the acidic soil beneath the closed forest canopy, the herbs, shrubs, and hardwoods on which deer depended could not survive. What palatable plants did remain were subject to heavy browsing pressure. In order to maintain abundant deer, the Germans turned to artificial feeding, which by keeping deer numbers high only further increased the pressure on natural plants in the forests. Over time, many of those plants were eradicated (to the detriment, in turn, of other wildlife). Deer predators had long since been removed from the scene. Even with the advent of Dauerwald and mixed forest planting, the Germans still insisted on feeding their deer artificially. To protect hardwood plantings and even young spruce from damage by deer, the Germans had to resort to expensive means of protection, erecting fences and wiring bundles of dead twigs to the trunks of young trees. "The Germans," Leopold surmised, "would rather put up with damage than forego their pleasure in having and seeing deer."[37] Ironically, this situation was not even good for the deer. Generations of artificial feeding and selective hunting of the prime males had damaged the stock. The deer found themselves caught literally between one fence that excluded them from the new "permanent forests" and another that excluded them from cropland, doomed to walk to their feeding stations on soil-sick forest floors. The problem was familiar to Leopold: one well-intentioned conservation motive at loggerheads with another.

These were generalized tendencies, and not every locality was experiencing the deadlock. Nevertheless, a widespread disenchantment with overartificial land use had taken hold in the form of the "Naturschutz" movement, a program of active wildlife restoration which paralleled in some ways the Dauerwald policies, and which also bore similarities to the preservationist wing of the American wildlife conservation movement. Under Naturschutz, German conservationists had succeeded in protecting and reintroducing a number of rare birds and mammals, including raptors and other predators. Success, however, was hard won in the face of too many deer, too much spruce, and long traditions of intensive game and forest management.

The Naturschutz movement, while aspiring to many of the same goals as the "naturalism" movement in American conservation, was fundamentally different in two important ways. In America, Leopold noted, the need for more natural approaches to land use arose because we had adopted sensible conservation policies too little, too late, or not at all; in Germany, the need arose because "conservation" of a sort had been practiced too recklessly, for too long. Germany was trying to escape a deadlock; America still had enough time and space to avoid its own. Second, the Naturschutz movement in Germany was strongly connected, in the German mind, to nationalism. The Third Reich embraced and strongly supported conservation in general, and Naturschutz in particular. Thus the historical paradox: while many Germans revolted against policies that would regiment nature, many simultaneously paraded toward the regimentation of their own culture. American conservation was not immune to similar strains of nativism and even outright racism.[38] But with its recent origins on a democratic frontier, and not, as Leopold phrased it, "encrusted with the political and economic barnacles of feudalism," American conservation as a whole was not receptive to the deadly political mixture of nativism and nationalism.

None of this was yet apparent to the six Americans when the *Europa* arrived at Bremen on August 9. The group travelled together for the first month of their stay, meeting with forestry officials in Berlin, visiting the Tharandt School near Dresden, and touring state forests in Saxony, Czechoslovakia, Bavaria, and Württemberg. Impressed though Leopold was with the official and popular interest in conservation, he was repulsed by the artificiality of the German system. He wrote for his departmental newsletter back home, "One cannot travel many days in the German forests, either public or private, without being overwhelmed by the fact that artificialized game management and artificialized forestry tend to destroy each other."[39] After touring the school forest at Tharandt, he recorded in his notebook a "preliminary impression that there is a mutual aggravation between game and silviculture: the game precludes natural systems of regeneration, and the unnatural fencing of regenerating areas cuts down the carrying capacity for game."[40] The pattern repeated itself at the Colditz Forest southeast of Leipzig, at the great Spessart Forest in western Bavaria, along the Rhine near Freiburg, in the Bohrnerwald near Krumau in Czechoslovakia.

Leopold's German picked up quickly after the first few days, and he became unofficial translator for his group. Against his own better nature, he occasionally found himself becoming a tourist. He greatly enjoyed the museums, films, castles, and shops, and indulged in Bohemian glassware for Estella, a camera for Carl, and wool clothing for himself. He described Freudenstadt, in west Württemberg, as "a picture-book German village and the country round about is the prettiest we have yet seen. We walked all morning in the town forest, and this afternoon, it being Sunday, we went to a movie which was bad even though German (many of the German films are good). This evening we were received by the Burgermeister and a committee of citizens—and of course had to drink much beer."[41] Leopold was in his grandfather Starker's territory, though he had no time to investigate his own roots. He was most impressed by the countryside of the upper Bohemian plain in northern Czechoslovakia. "It is a magnificent landscape, calling to mind the best of our sub-montane basins of the Rocky Mt. region. . . . Of all the parts of Mitteleuropa I have so far seen, this is inherently the most beautiful, and ecologically the richest, most varied, and most interesting."[42]

After his first month of travelling, Leopold concluded that "there is an almost uncanny mixture of the admirable with the false in everything one sees here."[43] As much as he was enjoying the expansion of his cultural horizons, Leopold could not shake his vague feeling of discontent. Here was a nation practicing conservation on a scale American conservationists could only imagine, yet something was lacking. Trying to pinpoint it, he wrote that "we have here the unfortunate result of what might be called a too purely economic determinism as applied to land use. Germany strove for maximum yields of both timber and game, and got neither. She is now, at infinite pains, coming back to an attitude of respectful guidance (as distinguished from domination) of the intricate ecological processes of nature."[44] He kept these points in the back of his mind as his visit continued.

In August, Leopold received tragic news. Franklin Schmidt had been killed in a fire at the home of his parents near Stanley, Wisconsin. Schmidt had escaped the blaze, but when he reentered the house to save his mother, a room collapsed and he perished. Leopold had lost not only the kind of young researcher he most admired, but a good friend as well. A world away, he sadly wrote to Estella that "I'm pretty much knocked out about Franklin, so will not attempt to write you much of a letter."[45] In an obituary he later wrote, Leopold paid tribute to Schmidt as a "rare and inspiring" biologist whose death was "the first fatality in that young profession known as wildlife management. He has set for that profession a high standard of devotion, modesty, skill, and thoroughness."[46]

Through most of September, Leopold worked out of the Forest School at Tharandt. He concentrated his study on the history of forest and game management in the region. With the benefit of the school's impressive library and the well-maintained records of estate-holders, he was able to retrace that history back through nine centuries. He was a guest at the estates of several local noblemen. The Prince of Hohenlohe hosted Leopold and Professor Heske on a partridge hunt at Rothenhaus. Later he joined a Baron von Riebnitz for a field trial at Wohrlau. This taste of European hunting, with all its ceremony and ritual, impressed Leopold, but again he found something lacking in the experience. "The successful participant in such a hunt," he wrote, "needs endurance and especially marksmanship, but no woodcraft—indeed, he has no opportunity for the exercise of hunting skill, even if he possesses it. He has no part in working the dogs, and no choice in the selection of ground."[47] Leopold's confrontation with the European system of sport only reinforced his faith in what he and others in game management were trying to preserve in the United States. One night, while walking along the brook that flowed through Tharandt, he heard a "really big trout" rising not far from his hotel. Upon inquiring, he learned that all the fishing in the brook was leased to two Dresden businessmen. "Nobody here in Tharandt can fish in his own creek," he complained.[48]

One experience he enjoyed without qualification was an exciting display of falconry by the Baron and Baroness von Vietinghoff-Reisch of Saxony. Leopold watched enthralled as the birds stooped after partridge above the potato fields on the estate. He took extensive notes for his son Carl, who had developed an interest in the sport. The Vietinghoffs were also well informed on the bird life of local forests, the Baron being fond of songbirds. They became the closest friends Leopold made on his trip.

In October, Leopold took a further field excursion through Silesia and Brandenburg and began to write up his findings. He took advantage of the opera season in Berlin (". . . we heard Lohengrin and Madame Butterfly. I enjoyed Butterfly, but Siegfried was too fat to hug his girl and I can't preserve the illusion of reality under such circumstances"). He even delivered a "very elementary" speech in German over the radio.

At home, Estella read Aldo's accounts of his adventures with a mixture of loneliness and envy. The older children being able to take care of themselves, she spent part of the summer with her family in Santa Fe. Together with Estella Jr., she made the long cross-country drive to New Mexico, through the very center of the Dust Bowl. They returned to Madison in time for the start of the school year.

Aldo had been gone for two and a half months. On October 22, he wrote about his "best and busiest week," describing a hunt, a walk in the country, and a congenial dinner. One evening, after a day in the field near Breslau, he found himself far from his hotel. The game warden suggested he stay at the nearby estate of his cousins, the Count and Countess—or, as it appeared in Aldo's letter to Estella, "[I] stayed over night with a cousin of his, Countess Von Holdenberg, who is a veritable Countess out of a picture-book—slim, blonde, 25, etc. I also liked the Count very much."[49] Aldo's unfortunate wording did not strike the right note with Estella. She read into it a lot more than Aldo had intended. Confused and frustrated, she fretted for several weeks over a transgression which Aldo had not even committed. In all the smooth years of their marriage, this was one of the few obvious rough spots. Meanwhile, the effects of the long trip on Aldo had also begun to show. In his next letter, his last from Germany, he sweetly appealed to Estella to meet him in New York upon his return. He knew well that Estella not only made his work more meaningful; she made it possible.

Leopold did not dwell on the political situation in Germany, but he could hardly avoid it. He was initially impressed with the appearance and bearing of those in the new order, particularly the German youth. "The German *regular* army is the finest looking bunch of young men I've ever seen anywhere," he wrote at the end of September, adding, "I do not apply this to the brown-shirts."[50] With time, however, his admiration dropped. In October, he was a guest at the family estate of Alfred Schottlaender in Silesia, where he met Schottlaender's "very nice wife" and his "perfectly charming old father," a professor of oceanography at the University of Breslau. Schottlaender was a Jew and had relatives in the newly established concentration camps. Leopold likely learned then of the dread reality of the camps; if not then, soon after. Typically, he did not write of it in his letters. On weighty matters, he always preferred to wait until he could talk in person. All he wrote to Estella was that "there is a tragic story behind this family of which I will tell you when I get home."[51]

To a degree, Leopold's return to his ancestral homeland forced him to confront the cultural division within himself, although he probably did not view it in those terms. He expressed no outward remarks to this effect, but he did not have to; it was evident in his reactions to what he saw and heard. At times, the juxtaposition was deeply ironic. At one point, he wrote of the German rivers which, "confined in their strait-jackets of masonry, will bear for centuries the scars of that epidemic of geometry which blighted the German mind in the 1800s. Some of those distortions of nature were necessary, but not many."[52]

Leopold's achievements as a naturalist and conservationist owed much to what one of his students once described as his "Teutonic sense of logic" — his passion for detail and thoroughness, his ability to find order in complexity, his mindfulness of potential weaknesses, his marvelous concentration. But even this kind of truth held "only within limits." Confronted directly by an outward landscape—and by a political landscape as well—that bore these traits to a fault, he was now obliged to look on America's land in a new light, and with new alarm.

In any event, by the end of his trip Leopold had come to realize what was lacking in Germany: wildness. Not wilderness, per se, but wildness. He did not expect to find real wilderness areas. "Such monuments to wildness," he wrote in an essay he never completed, "are an esthetic luxury which Germany, with its timber deficit and the evident land-hunger of its teeming millions, cannot afford. I speak now of a certain quality which should be but is not found in the ordinary landscape of producing forests and inhabited farms." In the slick-and-clean forests he had seen, he detected the lack of "a certain exuberance which arises from a rich variety of plants fighting with each other for a place in the sun. It is almost as if the geological clock had been set back to those dim ages when there were only pines and ferns. I never realized before that the melodies of nature are music only when played against the undertones of evolutionary history."[53] The lesson was now clear. "We Americans," he wrote in one of the five articles that came out of his trip, "have not yet experienced a bearless, wolfless, eagleless, catless woods. We yearn for more deer and more pines, and we shall probably get them. But do we realize that to get them, as the Germans have, at the expense of their wild environment and their wild enemies, is to get very little indeed?"[54]

Sitting in a hotel room one evening in Berlin, Leopold jotted down some notes to himself under the heading "Wilderness":

The two great cultural advances of the past century were the Darwinian theory and the development of geology. The one explained how, and the other where, we live. Compared with such ideas, the whole gamut of mechanical and chemical invention pales into a mere matter of current ways and means.

Just as important as the origin of plants, animals, and soil is the question of how they operate as a community. Darwin lacked time to unravel any more than the beginnings of an answer. That task has fallen to the new science of ecology, which is daily uncovering a web of interdependencies so intricate as to amaze — were he here—even Darwin himself, who, of all men, should have the least cause to tremble before the veil.

One of the anomalies of modern ecology is that it is the creation of two groups each of which seems barely aware of the existence of the other. The one studies the human community almost as if it were a separate entity, and calls its findings sociology, economics, and history. The other studies the plant and animal community, [and] comfortably relegates the hodge-podge of politics to "the liberal arts." The inevitable fusion of these two lines of thought will, perhaps, constitute the outstanding advance of the present century.[55]

Leopold sailed out of Hamburg on November 7, carrying several articles on Dauerwald and Naturschutz, a few new game management techniques, gifts for the family, and a wooden cane for himself. All the foresters had lightheartedly bought walking sticks for themselves in Freudenstadt. Along with his pipe, the cane became a Leopold trademark.

Leopold also returned to America with the sober realization that, unless change came quickly in Germany, the world was headed for war. He was, in Luna Leopold's words, "very conscious and very worried" about the rise of German militarism and oppression, and talked about the situation often after coming home. He was "fearful of what was happening." When war did come, Leopold was not surprised.[56]

Aldo arrived in New York on November 15. He and Estella stayed at the Hotel Astor for a weekend, and took in the Broadway performance of Paul Robeson in "Showboat."

∽

1935 was a landmark year for Leopold. With the purchase of the property on the Wisconsin River, the reality of a conservation disaster on the western plains, the formation of the Wilderness Society, and the eventful trip overseas, Leopold was forced to redefine many of his prior assumptions more carefully and more broadly. Three statements he made that December illustrate this reorientation.

On December 19, Leopold delivered a lecture to the Madison chapter of Phi Sigma on "Deer and Forestry in Germany." He concluded his talk by stating that "One cannot divorce esthetics from utility, quality from quantity, present from future, either in deciding what is done to or for soil, or in educating the persons delegated to do it. All land-uses and land-users are interdependent, and the forces which connect them follow channels still largely unknown."[57]

On December 20, Leopold wrote a letter to Karl T. Frederick, president of the National Rifle Association, protesting an article on "Eagle Shooting in Alaska" that appeared in the *Rifleman*. The author had called his killing of eagles "the purest of all rifle sports." "We gun enthusiasts," Leopold wrote, "are constantly complaining of restrictive legislation on firearms. Is it likely that the public is going to accord us any more respect and consideration than we earn by our actions and attitudes? . . . I would infinitely rather that [the author] shoot the vases off my mantelpiece than the eagles out of my Alaska. I have a part ownership in both. That the Alaska Game Commission elects to put a bounty on the eagle, and not on the vase, has nothing to do with the sportsmanship of either action."[58]

Also on December 20, Leopold responded to an editorial in the *Journal of Forestry*. The editorial had referred to the Wilderness Society as nothing more than a faddish cult, and reminded foresters that esthetic judgments were not their responsibility. "I think I disagree with you," Leopold wrote to the editor (who was also a friend of his). "I suspect there are two categories of judgement which *cannot* be delegated to experts, which every man *must* judge for himself, and on which the intuitive conclusion of the non-expert is perhaps as likely to be correct as that of the professional. One of these is what is right. The other is what is beautiful. The question of the 'highest use' of remaining wilderness is basically one of evaluating beauty, in the broadest ecological sense of that word."[59]

17

Toward a Biotic View of Land
(1936–1939)

W HILE LEOPOLD was in Europe, a revolution in wildlife conservation was occurring back in the United States. Ding Darling
provided the spark. On April 24, 1935, Darling sat down with
a group of industrialists at the Waldorf-Astoria Hotel in New York, a meeting that in the following months gave rise to a number of new conservation initiatives. At some point in the process, "wildlife" itself became one
word, and replaced "game." The old American Game Association was disbanded, its activities assumed by the American Wildlife Institute, which
incorporated that summer. Darling succeeded in persuading the business
leaders to support, through the institute, a national program of Cooperative Wildlife Research Units modeled on the Iowa prototype. Under the
plan, the AWI, the Biological Survey, and the state wildlife agencies were
to share costs for research and training programs in nine land-grant col-
leges around the nation.[1] Darling also pushed for the creation of a national organization of local sportsmen's and conservation clubs. With
AWI's assistance, a "General Wildlife Federation"—later the National Wildlife Federation—came into being, and quickly became the largest single
organization in conservation. Finally, the Twenty-second American Game
Conference, which Leopold was to have chaired, was cancelled; President
Roosevelt instead called for an expanded North American Wildlife Conference, to be held in February 1936. Having permanently altered the course
of wildlife conservation, Ding Darling left the Bureau of the Biological
Survey in November 1935, and Ira T. Gabrielson took over as chief.

Leopold was in Breslau when he learned of plans for the big February
conference. Seth Gordon, now secretary of the new AWI, asked Leopold
for suggestions in connection with the conference. Leopold responded with
a lengthy review of wildlife conservation, detailing his thoughts on
everything from the effects of the tax system on farmers to the problems

of migratory bird administration. He also added one of his clearest statements on the general direction of conservation, one which reflected his German experiences and foreshadowed the emphasis of his own work in the latter half of the 1930s:

Any program, to be effective, must be premised first of all on a revision of the national attitude toward land, its life, and its products.

The basic assumption that land is a merely economic commodity, and that land-use is governed wholly by economic forces, must be definitely discarded. The ownership and use of land entails obligations and opportunities of trans-economic value and importance, just as the establishment of a family does. Until this concept of land becomes an integral part of the national philosophy, conservation can be nothing but a makeshift.

Economic forces, especially the forces of a mechanized society, tend to obstruct and defeat such an attitude toward land. To this extent economic development has become, from the viewpoint of conservation, a pathological process. The ways and means to conservation, then, must deal primarily with arresting these pathological tendencies, and with the removal of economic obstacles to better land-use.[2]

Leopold's points were blunt. He sent a copy of his suggestions to Darling, who replied that "you are getting us out into water over our depth by your new philosophy of wildlife environment. The end of that road leads to socialization of property which I could only tolerate willingly if I could be shown that it would work."[3] In truth, however, Leopold was as true a conservative as Darling, and saw in the "revision of the national attitude toward land" the only ultimate means of avoiding a greater role for government in private land use.

Over the next three and a half years, in many ways the most complex years of his life, Leopold would strive to define accurately this new attitude toward land, and to apply it in his work. Over the course of his career, Leopold had grown into and out of a number of labels: Naturalist. Forester. Game Protector. Game Manager. Wildlife Manager. The subtle distinctions in this progression of titles reflected changes in the purview of conservation generally and of Leopold personally. Without discarding either the techniques or perspectives he had gained in these previous roles, he was now ready to bring them to bear in a still broader calling, as a land manager, a land ecologist, and a teacher of both.

૭

The First North American Wildlife Conference was held February 3–8, 1936. Open to all interested parties, the conference was a rousing success. Twelve hundred attended. Even Leopold, who was generally wary of high expectations unbacked by realistic plans, expressed hope that conservation's factions "have virtually agreed to do their contending face to face across the conference table, rather than at long distance by the war of the inkpots."[4] Leopold spoke at the conference on "Wildlife Management by Private Agencies," and on "Farmer-Sportsman Set-Ups in the North-Central Region."

At the conference, those involved professionally in wildlife research formed a tentative "Society of Wildlife Specialists"—later renamed the Wildlife Society. Its main task was to establish a new journal of wildlife management. Leopold and Herb Stoddard agreed to serve as counselors to the first president, Ralph T. King. Leopold also accepted an invitation to serve as chairman of the American Wildlife Institute's Technical Committee, which supervised the AWI's research activities.

Leopold returned to Madison and resumed his teaching chores. Thirty-seven signed up for the short course, and thirty-five more for the regular survey of game management. These were healthy figures for relatively obscure courses in the College of Agriculture; Leopold was always a popular professor, and drew students from a dozen departments within the university. Three graduates now worked directly under Leopold: Art Hawkins, Leonard Wing, and a new addition, Douglas Wade. That semester, Leopold initiated a series of biweekly seminars where students and guest speakers could present and discuss their work. The nighttime meetings soon became an important part of every student's experience.

That spring the family began to visit the Sauk County shack on a regular weekend basis. On March 1, Aldo and the boys took their bedrolls, a new saw and axe, went to the shack, and made a supply of wood (the winter was an abnormally hard one, and especially hard, as Leopold and his students were learning, on game birds around the state). On March 7, Aldo, Estella, children, and dogs spent their first weekend together at the shack, hiking in the last few miles over the miry, spring-thawed road. At the end of March, they finished work on the one essential addition—an outhouse that Starker proclaimed to be "as sturdy as the Parthenon." The nickname stuck.

Aldo, Starker, and Luna had toyed around with the idea of "building a little forest for ourselves" on the property. The two-year-old plantations at the university arboretum provided a personal precedent for Leopold. His trip to Germany sold him on the idea. He ordered a thousand white pines and a thousand red pines from a nursery in Madison. "Oh, Aldo," Estella said in surprise, "that's going to be so much work." "You couldn't order less than that," Aldo explained. "You have to get a certain minimum or you can't get any at all." Aldo hired a neighbor farmer named Webster to plow some furrows in the sandy soil. In April, during the university's spring break, the family moved up to the shack and planted two thousand pine trees and dozens of shrubs—mountain ash, juneberry, nannyberry, cranberry, raspberry, plum.

That spring was one of the driest on record. By May, most of the shrubs had dried out. On May 17, Leopold noted a "very dry hot wind" in his shack journal. That day, Aldo, Estella, nine-year-old Estella, and Ray Roark, up for a visit, organized a bucket brigade to water the pines. Despite an unpromising start to the forest-planting project, Aldo was beginning to enjoy the weekend getaways. His journal entry on May 21 ended with the note, "Regretfully went home."[5]

Spring warmed into summer, and still no rain fell. The river, usually three hundred yards wide, was so low one could wade it without getting one's ribs wet. Leopold recorded the tree mortality figures:

Norway Pines	95% dead
Whites	99% dead
Mt. Ash	100% dead
Tamaracks	50% dead
Grapes	All alive but 1

They would have to try again the following spring.

During these months, Leopold gave further evidence that his entire conservation orientation had shifted, only slightly in degree, but significantly in impact. He published his first article devoted wholly to the plight of nongame species threatened with extinction by man. "The immediate needs of threatened members of our fauna and flora must be defined now or not at all," he wrote. "The new organizations which have now assumed the name 'wildlife' instead of 'game', and which aspire to implement the wildlife movement, are I think obligated to focus a substantial part of their effort on these threatened forms."[6] As chairman of yet another committee, the Committee on Forest Game Policy of the Society of American Foresters, Leopold pressed for a broadening of policy "in the interest of non-game, rare, or threatened species" such as the grizzly bear, Mearns quail, California condor, and spruce hen.[7] By no means was everyone in the profession comfortable with the shift from the tried-and-true "game" to the indefinite, new-fangled compound "wildlife." Leopold seems to have adopted it without hesitation, and in a number of letters to and from colleagues around the country, debates ensued on the meaning and implications of this new label.

On the subject of predators, Leopold had completed his conversion, and was even beginning to think of predators in terms of positive management. A Wisconsin Conservation Department forester from Ladysmith wrote to Leopold about the damage that field mice were inflicting on hardwood timber during the winter. Mammalian predators had been trapped out; deep snow protected the mice from owls. Leopold explained that periodically high mouse populations were probably inevitable, but that the effects might be mitigated by a "better" policy on predators, "and even by the deliberate 'management' of the most effective predators."[8]

And, yet, even Leopold's faith in management had been shaken. In 1933, Leopold and everyone else thought game management was a matter of working with farmers, setting up demonstration areas, planting food and cover, and tallying the gains. It had not been that simple. He and his graduate students were coming up with unexpected results in their research. Populations did not always respond as anticipated. Other factors impinged. Other land-uses had to be coordinated. It was supposed, for example, that quail could avoid violent fluctuations in their populations if provided with adequate food and cover. When the harsh winter of 1935–36 came, however, Leopold and Art Hawkins found their managed quail areas hit just as hard as unmanaged areas. Moreover, the lessons of Germany and the Kaibab loomed. Early hints of instability in the Wisconsin white-tailed deer herd had come to light, yet basic research on their food habits and life history had hardly begun. Even less was known about threatened species and predators.

Leopold had once spoken of game management as a means of establishing "a new and objective equilibrium" in place of the natural one that civilization had upset. He no longer believed that such a goal was possible, or even worthy. On May 5, 1936, he spoke at Beloit College on "Means and Ends in Wildlife Conservation." Wildlife management, he said, had advanced to the point where it recognized "the invisible interdependencies in the biotic community." It had "admitted its inability to replace natural equilibria with artificial ones, and its unwillingness to do so even if it could." The new approach, he emphasized, was based on both economic and esthetic arguments, and its implications were far-reaching: "When some women's club protests against the 'control' of game-killing hawks, or the poisoning of stock-killing carnivores, or of crop-eating rodents, they are raising—whether they know it or not—a new and fundamental issue in human land-use."[9] That "new and fundamental issue" was humankind's role and responsibilities within the community of life.

At the end of the summer of 1936, Leopold was asked to prepare a report to the Wisconsin Alumni Research Foundation on the progress of his game management program after its first three years. "In general," he wrote, "game management has spread in geographic area, in scientific area, and in social significance. It has ceased to be a separate thing. It has become a slower, harder, but vastly more important job than it was. It will succeed, or fail, not by and of itself, but as part of the whole problem of land and people. The Chair will succeed or fail not by and of itself, but as a part of the whole University relationship to Wisconsin resources."[10]

〜

In September Leopold returned with his friend Ray Roark to the Southwest for a two-week bow-and-arrow deer hunt. Instead of hunting Leopold's familiar Gila range, however, they planned a trip into the wild interior of the Sierra Madre Occidental in northern Mexico. On September 3, they met their guide, a Chihuahuan rancher named Clarence Lunt, at El Paso, and spent the day acquiring licenses and permits.

The next day, they were off to Lunt's ranch in the arid hills on the eastern slope of the continental divide. Leopold took note of the condition of the landscape, the ancient Indian checkdams in the draws, and the recently established "resettlement lands," where the Mexican government had, as Leopold phrased it, "scattered landless voters over many a nonirrigable mountain valley, to dryfarm if the Lord sent rain and to get along somehow in any event." To Leopold, the situation was all too reminiscent of the early efforts to settle homesteaders in the national forests north of the border. "I recognize the land pressure which forces the adoption of such a policy," he later wrote, "but I also recognize the inevitable ruin which will follow. . . . Just so were our own dry canyons sent to their death."[11]

These settlements, however, were but pinpoints on the map. To the west of Lunt's ranch, the Rio Gavilan ran through an endless backdrop of dry woodlands, one ridge and canyon after another of live oak and juniper, pine and side-oats grama. In the canyons, trout streams coursed clearly amid sycamores and cottonwoods. To Leopold, it came "near to being the cream of creation."

The Gavilan was a virtual counterpart to the Blue and the Gila in terms of its topography and native vegetation, but not in terms of its recent history. The mountains of Chihuahua had been the stronghold of the Apache, and the mutual antipathy between Apaches and Mexicans had precluded settlement. Pancho Villa's bandits and economic depression had limited human incursion ever since. As a result of this benign neglect, the landscape presented, in Leopold's words, "a picture of ecological health." In two weeks of hunting, he found no evidence of overgrazing; livestock raising had been confined to a few scattered Mormon colonies. The vegetation exhibited none of the instability that had so puzzled Leopold in his southwestern days. The watercourses were intact. Fires burned regularly in the mountains, once every several years at least, but Leopold noted "no ill effects, except that the pines are a bit further apart than ours, reproduction is scarcer, there is less juniper, and there is much less brush."

The wildlife of the Sierra Madre was in a similarly stable condition. Mountain lions and wolves were still common, and coyotes rare. The large predators did not seem to affect adversely the game animal populations. Deer and wild turkeys were "abundant, but not excessive." Leopold and Roark saw 187 deer in nine days of hunting (once again, though,

Leopold's arrows missed their mark; in his journal, Leopold recorded his ten shots by date, target, distance, result, and "alibi").

The creature that most impressed Leopold on the Gavilan was not a game animal. Squawking gangs of guacamaja, the pigeon-sized, thick-billed parrot of the Chihuahua, accompanied the hunting party throughout their backcountry travels. Every morning, the harlequin parrots performed a riotous welcome to the day, a show that delighted Leopold. Shortly after returning to Madison, he wrote an unusually rhapsodic account of his observation: "Like squadrons of cranes they wheel and spiral, loudly debating with each other the question (which also puzzles you) of whether this new day which creeps slowly over the canyons is bluer and golder than its predecessors, or less so. The vote being a draw, they repair by separate companies to the high mesas for their breakfast of pine-seed-on-a-half-shell."[12]

The trip to Chihuahua left Leopold with more than just the echoes of the whirling parrots. It provided a striking contrast to Leopold's experience in Germany. In less than a year, Leopold had caromed between the opposite poles of human impact on land: the fully civilized, and the fully wild. Opposite approaches to conservation were in evidence: centuries of intensive management in Germany, and centuries of natural controls in Mexico. Leopold now realized that in all his years of work to preserve wilderness, he had never actually understood what wilderness in the full sense entailed. "The Sierra Madre," he wrote, "offers us the chance to describe, and define, in actual ecological measurements, the lineaments and physiology of an unspoiled mountain landscape." That chance had been lost on our own side of the border.

Leopold returned to Chihuahua in 1937 with his brother Carl and Starker. These two trips would have a positive and profound effect on his thinking about land. Toward the end of his life, Leopold recalled that it was in the Sierra Madre that he "first clearly realized that land is an organism, that all my life I had seen only sick land, whereas here was a biota still in perfect aboriginal health. The term 'unspoiled wilderness' took on a new meaning."[13] In his lectures and articles, the phrases "land sickness" and "land pathology" began to fade, as he became increasingly concerned with defining the qualities of what he called "land health."

Almost immediately this new emphasis began to emerge in Leopold's work, and, as was so often the case in Leopold's career, the struggle to convert ideas into practice was played out in the arena of deer management.

By the mid-thirties, wildlife researchers had arrived at a general principle that Leopold deemed of utmost importance: in the absence of predators, browse-eating game can and will ruin its own range, while seed-eating game will not. Leopold proposed, then, a general rule for guidance in wildlife administration: "overstocking range with game birds carries no invariable penalty in loss of future carrying capacity, but overstocking range with browsing mammals does." This rule was implicit in Leopold's reaction to the German deer forests. After Germany, he began to argue that the aim of management must be to provide a safe margin between deer numbers and the capacity of the range to support them; that managers must become "generous in building up carrying capacity . . . and stingy in building up stock."

This was a highly important redefinition. Failure to keep that safe margin between habitat and population would result in one of two ends: a ruined range or a highly artificial management strategy—the Kaibab or Germany. The Kaibab, as it turned out, was not an isolated incident. By 1936, Leopold began to receive reports of similar deer problems in vastly different habitats around the country. In Wisconsin, evidence of overbrowsing and starvation in the regenerating forests of the north emerged as early as 1930, when Ernie Swift noticed deer damage in the forests near Hayward. Game men in the Forest Service discovered an acute overpopulation of deer on the Chequamegon National Forest in north-central Wisconsin at the end of 1935, but, like Swift, they were unable to persuade officials in Madison to take necessary reduction measures. The state legislature's only response was to authorize a winter deer feeding program.

Reflecting on his trip to Mexico, Leopold wrote that "the Sierras present to us an example of an abundant game population thriving in the midst of its natural enemies." He challenged conservationists to consider whether "a normal complement of predators is not, at least in part, accountable for the absence of irruption? If so, would not our rougher mountains be better off and might we not have more normalcy in our deer herds, if we let the wolves and lions come back in reasonable numbers?"[14]

Securing normalcy in "our rougher mountains" was one thing; managing deer back in the settled Midwest quite another. Nevertheless, the principle was the same. In October 1936, Leopold was hired as a consultant by the owner of a private estate near Rockford, Illinois. The owner was not a hunter, but enjoyed having and seeing deer on his property. Leopold welcomed the opportunity, not only because research on deer was so spotty up to this point, but also because the area was situated on what was once prime deer range, the prairie–oak savannah border.

Later that month, Leopold inspected the estate and wrote an initial report. He found that deer were plentiful enough to be readily seen, and that, while the area did not as yet show signs of damage, the threat was there. The summary of his findings was also a summary of his own recent experiences:

The whole history of deer herds from California to Massachusetts and from Minnesota to Georgia shows that heavy stands of deer on ranges free of natural enemies may suddenly "irrupt" and not only spoil their range but their own physical vigor. After a range has once flared up in this way it becomes impossible to secure either an abundant or a healthy stand of deer. The obvious lesson is not to let a good herd irrupt. To prevent an irruption this herd must be kept trimmed down to a safe margin, and the carrying capacity of the range built up so there is a safe margin of capacity above population. [15]

He recommended planting wild foods, dispersing agricultural feeds to prevent overconcentration of deer, and implementing, if necessary, selective culling of the herd. He also recommended that the area be used for research. [16]

The Rockford report was Leopold's first attempt to put his emerging ideas on land health into practice. As a manager, his tools had not changed, but his goals had. He was now working to manage, not the species, but the *species in its environment*. It was a vastly more complex undertaking, in which success would be measured not in numbers alone, but in the healthy interplay of components within the entire system.

For the duration of 1936, Leopold returned to an augmented teaching load. Three more graduate students—Ellwood Moore, Orville Lee, and Irven Buss—were on board. At the shack, only sixty trees out of two thousand had survived the summer drought. The grapes managed better. The family picked three bushels for wine-making. For the first time, Aldo hunted extensively with sixteen-year-old Carl. Starker and Luna had graduated from college the previous spring, and were now graduate students at Yale and Harvard respectively. That Christmas, the entire family reassembled and spent four days together at the shack. Leopold's record of the visit in his journal read simply: "Too good a time to make note in journal." [17]

〜

Leopold realized now that there were no miracle cures for the symptoms of "land pathology." The only effective treatment was preventive: the long, laborious task of teaching the public, professional and layman, to appreciate the dynamics of land. As a teacher himself, Leopold addressed this challenge of conservation education time and time again, beginning in earnest in 1936.

Leopold's approach to education was closely tied to his broadening conception of "land" in the late 1930s. In a book review that appeared in the Audubon Society's *Bird-Lore* magazine in early 1937, he wrote, "We are embarked on two large-scale experiments. One is premised on the notion that conservation is something a nation buys. The other is premised on the notion that conservation is something a nation learns." [18] Learning conservation meant something more than learning the names of plants and animals. Leopold drew a distinction between "static" natural history and "dynamic" ecology. In his view, a conservationist who knew only the names and habits of species was akin to a politician or economist who had a wide circle of acquaintants, but no knowledge of business: "Both lack an 'inside' picture of the struggle for existence. Ecology is the politics and economics of animals and plants. The citizen-conservationist needs an understanding of wildlife ecology not only to enable him to function as a critic of sound policy, but to enable him to derive maximum enjoyment from his contacts with the land."[19] As he struggled to define his own sense of land, Leopold was always striving for realism. He resisted the nationalistic appeals that he had witnessed in German conservation, and made no sentimental references to "the heartland." Conflict, paradox, and irony were part of conservation's "authentic human drama"; without them, conservation "falls to the level of a mere Utopian dream."[20] Education was the necessary means of conveying this reality to the citizenry.

In his own field of wildlife, the rise of interest around the nation was threatening to inundate what few competent training programs existed. Leopold warned that the boom market for wildlife managers was liable to dilute the quality of instruction. Already universities were rushing into the field with hastily built programs and with personnel who, as he put it, "arrived on the previous train." If the trend continued, the likely result would be an oversupply of mediocre managers, a shortage of well-trained researchers, and a neglected nonprofessional public.

This situation was doubly dangerous in view of the ecological complexity that new field evidence was revealing. At the Second North American Wildlife Conference in March 1937, Leopold cautioned that "selling professional training without a research base is like selling securities without a property base. The right to teach must be earned, not seized."[21] Arguing for scientific investigations that were more intensive ("deep-digging research," he called it), and less concentrated on farm game, he told those at the conference that "no advance ever attains an even front, but good generals remove kinks when they can. Our front is full of kinks, especially in the non-gunpowder sections."[22]

Leopold deemed nonprofessional education to be just as important as professional training, and perhaps more important in the long run. At the conference he warned that "we face a future marked by a growing public zeal for conservation, but a zeal so uncritical—so devoid of discrimination —that any nostrum is likely to be gulped with a shout. . . . Under these conditions is it wise for our universities to focus their teaching on overstocking the market with professionals? Should they instead stock their farms and offices with citizens who know what it is all about?"[23]

Within the University of Wisconsin, Leopold was working to establish an interdisciplinary instructional program, the purpose of which was to "build up a critical comprehension of conservation problems in the public at large." As chairman of an intrauniversity committee that included Leon Cole, Norman Fassett, and Chancey Juday, Leopold wrote in early 1937 a report on "The University and Conservation of Wisconsin Wildlife." The report recommended that three new professorships be created in fields that dovetailed with his own program (only one of these was quickly filled, by botanist-ecologist John T. Curtis). The university, the report stated, ought to encourage students with an interest in natural history "to develop that interest as a field of personal scholarship and as a source of personal recreation."[24]

Beyond the universities, Leopold noted the need for educational materials that combined "sound science, sound policy, and sound pedagogy." This, he admitted, "is a task calling for very uncommon mental powers, not to mention time and funds. It is a task at least as exacting as the scientific fact-finding which underlies it."[25] The Dust Bowl had stimulated public schools nationwide to introduce conservation into their curricula. The Wisconsin state legislature passed a law in 1935 mandating the teaching of conservation in schools, but materials were scarce and instruction for teachers virtually nonexistent. Teachers from around the state regularly wrote to Leopold for ideas, and he always responded with a letter and a list of references (he specifically suggested for school use Paul Sears's topical classic *Deserts on the March*). In particular, he recommended that students be exposed to the literature of all sides in conservation disputes, "as illustrations of how divergent conclusions can be drawn from identical facts." This would allow students to confront these differences, and, in essence, formulate their own conservation ethic in response. "The end result of conservation teaching must be, I think, to show the prospective citizen that conservation is impossible as long as land-utility is given blanket priority over land-beauty. In short, it is his personal philosophy of land use, as well as his vote and his dollar, which will ultimately determine the degree to which conservation is converted from preachment into practice."[26]

As much time and effort as Leopold dedicated to the progress of conservation education, he realized that the effort had its inherent limitations. A healthy interest in the workings of nature could not be injected from without; it had to well from within. Staid teachers, reform-minded evangelists, and overspecialized academics were as likely to douse an interest as to fuel it. "An understanding of ecology," he would write, "is by no means co-extensive with 'education'; in fact, much higher education seems deliberately to avoid ecological concepts."[27] Thinking back, perhaps, on his own class-dodging days at Burlington and Lawrenceville, he wrote in 1939, "Prudence never kindled a fire in the human mind; I have no hope for conservation born of fear. The 4-H boy who becomes curious about why red pines need more acid than white is closer to conservation than he who writes a prize essay on the dangers of timber famine."[28] For Leopold's tastes, a good scholar, like a good area of land, had to be part-tame, part-wild.

Leopold tried to retain these values in his own classroom. He always arrived well-prepared, organized, and attired in his neat, tailor-made tweed sportjackets. A polished lecturer, he spoke in an informal voice quite distinct from his carefully honed literary prose. He was also a great advocate of audio-visual aids in class and used his sizable catalogue of slides from the field to illustrate his lectures. Above all, students recall his endless questions. In class, he masterfully applied the Socratic method to situations one might encounter in the field, drawing on the students' unsuspected powers of reason, training them to think in terms of interrelationships as well as objects. "He kept asking questions! Sometimes he didn't really want the students to answer them. They were rhetorical questions. He would then begin to reason out the answers for you. He would present material that way: he'd frame the question first, then go after specifics."[29] Once, the topic of overbrowsing of shrubs by deer came up. After ten minutes of delicate questioning by the Professor, a perplexed student discovered that deer do not "browse" with their eyes, but with their teeth.

As effective as he was in the classroom, Leopold was truly in his element in the field. Field trips were the highlights of every course. There were a number of favorite venues—the arboretum, familiar farms, research demonstration areas, the shack property. He had initiated field trips as a means of exposing students to game management techniques; in time, the trips became exercises in reading landscape: looking at the features of the land and extrapolating from current conditions its history and destiny.

Leopold was not the sort of nature guide who tried to reveal God in Nature. His aim was to teach others how to take a given field situation, recognize and weigh the variables on display, and connect those variables in time and space. His method was not to stuff students with facts, but to use facts to entice their curiosity. It was reading sign in the woods, on a grand scale. He showed his class a gully. How old was it? Over fifty years, judging from the age of the cottonwood growing in it. . . . Probably made while the loess bluffs were still being cropped exclusively for wheat. How high was this pond before drainage ditches drew it down? A line of birches marked the old shore. Why are there long-eared owls here? Because there are pines here. Why are there pines in such an isolated area? Because the native sandstone is exposed above the glacial overburden. Only by mulling over these "mental whetstones," Leopold felt, could students get beyond the type of conservation teaching that lined up statistical horrors end-to-end and told the student "what has happened, but not how or why." At its best, conservation teaching taught the pupil to think independently; it addressed "the social causes for misfortune, rather than merely describing the misfortune or feeling sorry about it."[30]

By the spring of 1937, six graduate students were under Leopold's tute-lage. Leopold kept a relatively loose rein on them. Logistics alone demanded self-reliance on their part. In the early years, Leopold required his students to live on and assume responsibility for a demonstration area, acting as game managers while conducting research. At any given time, half of them were away at Faville Grove, or the Riley farms, or Prairie du Sac, or at Elkhorn in Walworth County. Once a semester, more often if necessary, Leopold met with each student individually to offer suggestions, encour-age interpretation, and bring up deficiencies in data.

Every so often, Leopold visited his students at their study areas. Art Hawkins remembered this as "a high point in the scholastic life of his stu-dents." Leopold often brought other students and professors along on these outings, "which were, more than anything else, a contest in perception. . . . The field trip became a test of observational skills among all par-ticipants. There were no losers; everyone learned through this process."[31]

Leopold was concerned foremost with the accuracy of his students' data and the clear exposition of that data in well-written scientific papers. Every student was required to produce a publishable thesis, and most came away with stories of the dozen revisions a thesis had to go through before Leo-pold deemed it publishable. In the spring of 1937, Leopold's first four stu-dents received their degrees. Leonard Wing received a doctorate for his work on wildlife cycles and went to work for the Tennessee Valley Authority. The others earned their master's degrees: Harry Anderson graduated in zoology and game management after studying the avifauna of the univer-sity arboretum; Ellwood Moore, a forester on leave from the New Jersey Conservation Department, returned east; Art Hawkins decided to stay with Leopold for further research into game foods.

As an educator, Leopold was facing a disconcerting, but challenging dilemma: the need for conservation education was increasing even as the subject matter was growing more complicated. In a report to WARF filed in June 1937, Leopold confessed that, while his program was making head-way, "if anyone hoped for research to produce a set of simple formulae which could be blindly followed by laymen, that hope is gone glimmer-ing." He pointed out, though, that wildlife management was opening up "entirely new vistas of cultural value," and predicted that "the time is com-ing when education which omits to picture man's infinitely delicate sym-biosis with land will not be considered education."[32]

⌒

In April 1937, the Wilderness Society held its first full-membership meeting in Washington. Leopold passed up even this event in order to have another try at tree planting at the shack. Over spring vacation, the Leopold crew put in cedars, junipers, crabapples, witch-hazel, raspberries, mountain ash, and three thousand red, white, and jack pines. Then they hoped again for rain.

The Leopolds and their friends now visited the shack virtually every weekend. They chinked the walls of the shack, and battened them with fugitive planks cast up by the river. Aldo rarely bought lumber; the spring floods always provided. They completed a small side addition to the shack. The shack exterior was plain—unpainted sideboards, a foundation of field-stones, the roof protected by wood shingles and tarpaper. The interior was no fancier—unadorned walls, a clay floor, some shelves and cabinets, a sturdy wooden table, a woodbox, several benches and chairs, a large bed that consisted of a straw-filled mattress supported by snowfence (later they built some bunks). A hefty tool box doubled as a bench. Other tools hung neatly on the wall (Aldo, his experience as a forest inspector yet showing, was an absolute stickler for well-maintained tools). Cooking was performed in the large hearth, or outside over an open fire. Water came from a pump just outside the door.

That spring, Leopold's interest in wildflowers expanded significantly. His close association with Norman Fassett undoubtedly spurred him on. In many ways, Fassett was Leopold's equivalent in the university's botany department: a sensitive man, sometimes withdrawn, a brilliant plant tax-onomist, a superb naturalist, and a resolute conservationist. Their work together on the early woodland and prairie restoration experiments at the university arboretum was now extended to the shack. The family began propagating and transplanting Dutchman's breeches and pasque flowers, violets and trillium, spring beauties, lady slippers, and puccoons.

Estella had herself absorbed a formidable knowledge of plants and ani-mals and knew as well as Aldo the name of every flower in the field. At the shack, she was treated regally, as her husband and children assumed domestic chores for the weekend. Although shack visits interfered with her obligations as a Catholic, she brushed the conflict aside. "Oh, it's no mortal sin to skip church to go with your father," she assured the children. "It's OK. Those are the church's rules, not God's rules."

"They loved going to the shack," Vivian Horn recalled. "I used to no-tice that, frequently, the children preferred going to the shack to some other activity they had an opportunity to do over the weekend. Their family ac-tivity seemed to have more attraction. What was the secret? I didn't know, but it made for a happy and congenial family life. All I knew was that this family seemed to think it was a lot of fun to spend a vacation together doing the hardest kind of work."[33]

The Leopold children were maturing in shifts. Luna and Starker were less frequent visitors now that they had embarked on their separate lives. Aldo had always shown a certain bias toward his two oldest. Now he spent more time in turn with Nina and Carl, who were nineteen and seventeen respectively. Little Estella was a puckish ten-year-old, and her father's pride and joy. Her self-appointed responsibility at the shack was to build and rebuild a log bridge across the narrows of a nearby slough, and to do it all over again after floods swept it away.

"On the few weekends that mother and I would be in Madison," Estella Jr. recalled, "I would go to church with her and go to confession. What can you tell the priest? I very lucidly described what wonderful weekends we had for the last six weekends since I'd been in church, at an abandoned farm; that we were bringing it back by planting and so forth, and we saw a lot of wild birds and game. The priest would ask me about this in very worried tones and then pronounce *enormous* sentences and I would have to do penance."[34]

Aldo remained absolutely mum on the subject of religion. Estella did not send Starker or Luna to the local parochial schools, but did enroll Nina and Carl in alternate years — not always with pleasant results. The nuns were a grim bunch and the priest notoriously generous in his assignment of Our Fathers and Hail Marys. For the most part, Aldo hid his misgivings about the Church. The children could sense, however, that he took a dim view of it. The spiritual aspect did not bother him; it was the sober discipline and oppressive orthodoxy, so foreign to his own upbringing, that he could not abide. But Leopold did not have to speak to his children about religion. Through his daily attention to the natural world, his weekend work at the shack, and his career-long efforts to address human dilemmas through conservation, Leopold managed to accomplish through the back door what he had vowed not to broach through the front. The children were gaining an awareness of life's processes, of creation itself, that was unencumbered by middlemen.[35]

The 1937 plantings at the shack managed well their first months, but by July the skies again turned dry, hot, and windy as drought and dust storms swept across the Midwest. At the shack, no rain fell for five weeks. On July 30, Leopold recorded the results in his journal: "Many weak pines watered by hand last week [are] dead this week. Losses to date: Triangle 70%, Sandhill 50%, Birch Row and Ring Around 15%, woods 10%. Many more will go this week. Big tamarack planted last fall suddenly died."[36] Clearly, tree planting was not going to be a one-time event, but a continuing process. That fall, in fact, they decided to plant three thousand more pines.

For the first time in years, Leopold's work did not require extensive travelling, and through the remainder of 1937 he stayed close to home, conducting business from Madison. He always woke early, busied himself in the kitchen, and went to work before the rest of the family had risen. Early morning was his most productive period. He was usually at the office well before Vivian Horn arrived, working on papers, lectures, letters, field data. Most days he walked home for lunch and a brief nap before the afternoon's work. Nights were normally reserved for basement activities, and for reading with Estella. Through Estella's lively reading club, Aldo kept abreast of current literature. On Sunday nights, the family gathered around the radio to listen to the broadcasts of the classics on the Ford Hour.

Aldo and Estella belonged to a town-and-gown dinner club, and often entertained small groups of friends and students at home. The wife of one of Leopold's students remembered that these invitations were "valuable for other reasons than keeping us from going hungry. There was a certain quality about the atmosphere at the Leopold home not easy to define. There was family affection and loyalty. There was good talk that left me thinking along unaccustomed lines."[37] Leopold himself tended to shun cocktail parties and university functions. Estella teased him. "Come on," she would say. "You always end up enjoying yourself when you go." Aldo would finally relent and invariably he had a delightful time. Likewise, he went with Estella to movies ostensibly to please her, but found himself captivated by them. He loved movies — even bad ones — and often treated the children to matinees downtown at the Orpheum or the Capitol.[38]

By 9:30 in the evening, Leopold was usually in bed, resting for the next busy day.

More than ever, he needed that self-discipline. In addition to his university activities, he was serving on and advising two dozen agencies, committees, and organizations. He was writing almost constantly: committee reports, feature articles, book reviews, technical papers, conference addresses. Several of the articles he wrote at this time exhibited the more lyrical style that would soon begin to dominate his output. In October, *American Forests* published "Marshland Elegy," his classic celebration and lamentation of Wisconsin's sandhill cranes. (Owen Gromme, then a taxidermist and artist at the Milwaukee Public Museum, and a friend of Leopold's, wrote to him that, "Only a man who has worked with these noble birds can possibly grasp the full import and depth of your written words. There is *no sound on this earth* that stirs the primitive in me like the indescribable wild rattle of the Sandhill Crane. Well, I guess that you understand. You said it all.")[39]

The fall of 1937 brought several new graduate students into Leopold's remuda. Hawkins, Wade, Buss, and Lee remained from the earlier group. Hans Albert Hochbaum arrived from the National Park Service, intent on studying hole-nesting birds. Hochbaum was burly and gentle, essentially quiet and immensely talented, equipped with a keen mind, a skilled drawing hand, and an honest, direct manner (". . . with all that gentleness, he wouldn't put up with any guff either"). Frederick and Frances Hamerstrom began their formal work under Leopold that fall. They were Boston Brahmins who left their patrician pasts behind them to study wildlife. Frederick was an Ivy Leaguer, handsome and liberally educated; Fran a high school dropout who became a highly paid fashion model. Together they had gone to Iowa in 1933 to study wildlife under Paul Errington, and came to central Wisconsin when Frederick took a job supervising the conservation work of the Resettlement Administration in the sand counties. They had remained close to Leopold and his work ever since. In 1937, they took over the prairie chicken work of Franklin Schmidt and officially became students of Leopold. Frances Hamerstrom thus became one of the first women in the profession, a fact that hardly mattered one way or another to Leopold. In judging applicants, Leopold looked first for enthusiasm, dedication, and a certain indefinite quality that made a person a *wildlifer.* Usually his hunches were right. Lyle Sowls, another new arrival, was a case in point. Sowls was an unassuming young man with an ambition to be a forester. After working odd jobs in Leopold's program, be enrolled in game management. As much as any of the students, he benefited from Leopold's methods and became not only an able game manager, but a highly competent researcher.

At fifty, Leopold was like a veteran sled dog newly energized by the companionship of young pups. A spirit of good-natured competition prevailed among this dynamic and gifted group of students. Most of the time they were out at their separate field stations, but they all gathered in Madison for special presentations and for the biweekly seminars. The seminars were informal but electric gatherings, and, for many students, the highlight of their years under Leopold. Discussions always lasted late into the evening, long after the supply of beer or apples was exhausted. The student who gave a seminar found himself in a crucible. "Those seminars were so powerful because you either had it or you didn't have it," Frederick Hamerstrom recalled. "And if you didn't have it—*pow!* It was not done with any meanness. It was simply that we were all there, all learning, and we were all trained with the idea that you spoke from the data, and if you didn't have enough data, then you were wide, wide open, and you *got* it!"[40] The topics ranged widely. A typical semester's offerings: "The 1936 Nesting Study," "Symposium on Foods and Feeding," "The 1935 and 1936 Pheasant Census Drives," "Need of a Life History of Ragweed," "Game Management Objectives in Relation to Agronomy," "Literary Expression of Ecology," "Conservation in New Jersey."

Within the university at large, Leopold remained a little-known figure in an unproven field. "He was very thoroughly respected by a rather small, select group," Fran Hamerstrom recalled. "In general, he wasn't even noticed."[41] This low profile allowed him to avoid an overload of social obligations and academic committeeships, and enabled him to steer clear of infighting and campus politics.

Leopold apparently overworked himself in the latter months of 1937. Several times in his letters he referred to "difficulty with my eyes" and "a persistent bad spell with my eyes." The self-prescribed cure was a return trip to the Sierra Madre and the Rio Gavilan. On December 22, Aldo, his brother Carl, and Starker (who had moved on to wildlife studies at the University of California at Berkeley) flew into Casas Grandes on the Chihuahua Flyer—apparently Leopold's first experience in an airplane.

On Christmas Eve, the packtrain left for the inner recesses of the Rio Gavilan.[42] Hunting began in earnest the next day. Carl brought his rifle, while Aldo and Starker stayed with bows and arrows. The day ended without venison in camp, but "a cup of cherry bounce and a good plate of beans were ample Christmas celebration." The deer were as abundant as in 1936. During their sixteen days in the breaks of the Gavilan, they saw over 250 deer, and Carl took three deer with his rifle, two bucks and a doe. Although the archers would again leave empty-handed, Aldo enjoyed one of the most satisfying backcountry trips of his life. The days were warm, the company congenial, the country a perfect combination playground and laboratory. There was much loafing, roving, and slow stalking over the glades and open mesas. Every night, the "glee club" met and, inspired by the rounds of cherry bounce, sang "an infinite number of new Spanish songs" around the camp fire, dogs joining in.

After a week's stay on a high ridge, they moved down along the river to "a beautiful camp site with many oaks for scenery and good wood." The purl of the campside Gavilan would stay with Leopold, and become a metaphor for the almost palpable flow of life in the hills. Its sound was apparently gentler than its feel, however; after a swim in its icy waters, Starker recommended the Gavilan as "good drinking water but poor swimming—we were paralyzed for an hour." On their first day in the new camp they spied an otter gliding downstream, and then found fresh wolf tracks on the riverside trail. "We wish they would give us a concert some evening."

They worked the nearby mesas—Smoke, Blue, Perdita, Bear—for turkey and deer. Clarence Lunt displayed his method of calling turkeys by producing a chirp with a handful of macaroni. It worked. Aldo managed a number of close shots, missing his targets by inches, but his closest shot was one he never got off. "Dad was nearly run over by the granddad buck of the whole Gavilan. Clarence put him out, and he ran right into Carl who turned him down toward Dad with a well-placed charge of shot in the dirt. He arrived there really making knots and so took Dad by storm that he didn't even shoot. There should be traffic laws to prevent that sort of thing."

On January 9, they broke camp and left the Gavilan. After a lunch of enchiladas with the Lunts, they "waved adios to the Sierra Madres for this year. Once more the deer have evaded our arrows, and we took time as we rode along to try and analyze why we had failed and what to do next time. It's a great game."

Leopold was not destined to have a next time, at least not on the Gavilan. Although he still had many wild places yet to visit, this second trip to the Sierra Madre was in fact his last lengthy excursion into a great wilderness. The unique characteristics of the Gavilan prompted Leopold to initiate an effort to maintain it as an international research area. Later in 1938, Leopold tried to enlist the support of renowned geographer Carl O. Sauer, a professor of Starker's at Berkeley, but the plan was never pursued.[43]

The trip had its hoped-for therapeutic effect. "My eyes are at the moment giving me no trouble," Leopold wrote to a colleague after returning to Madison.[44] Moreover, the second visit to Mexico reinforced Leopold's deep sense of the land's ecological well-being. When he sat down several years later to write "Song of the Gavilan," he employed the musical metaphors that were beginning to appear more often in his writing.

This song of the waters is audible to every ear, but there is other music in these hills, by no means audible to all. To hear even a few notes of it you must first live here for a long time, and you must know the speech of hills and rivers. Then on a still night, when the campfire is low and the Pleiades have climbed over rimrocks, sit quietly and listen for a wolf to howl, and think hard of everything you have seen and tried to understand. Then you may hear it—a vast pulsing harmony—its score inscribed on a thousand hills, its notes the lives and deaths of plants and animals, its rhythms spanning the seconds and centuries.[45]

It was a harmony that Leopold not only heard, but in which he joined. He described one of his missed opportunities for a deer. "I overshot, my arrow splintering on the rocks the old Indian had laid. As the buck bounded down the mountain with a goodbye wave of his snowy flag, I realized that he and I were actors in an allegory. Dust to dust, stone age to stone age, but always the eternal chase!"[46]

ی

Leopold returned to work: a lecture on "Erosion and Game Cover" to graduates in the Soils Department; forty-eight students in the short course; two addresses at the Third North American Wildlife Conference ("The Need for Game Research" and "Spread of the Hungarian Partridge in Wisconsin"); a talk to the farmers at Riley on the history of the pheasant in America; an address at Platteville on prairie chicken research. Active as Leopold was, the future of his one-man Division of Game Management at the university was not assured. Its five-year trial period was coming to an end and the Wisconsin Alumni Research Foundation was in the process of reviewing its progress.

If the university entertained any doubts about Leopold's status, his graduate students certainly did not. In fact, they thought it high time the Professor be given more respectable working space. The basement of the Soils Building was simply inadequate. Leopold and his students had to work on their graphs, specimens, and field equipment in the gardener's adjacent potting shed. Leonard Wing recalled that "[Franklin Schmidt] had his office on a Superior seed drill and I had mine on a John Deere lime and fertilizer sower—boy how we could identify dried plants from those points of vantage. And was that dang fertilizer ever acrid!"[47]

One evening that spring, Aldo's students gathered and surreptitiously moved the Professor into new quarters. They had found some empty rooms in an old frame house along the railroad tracks—the one-time residence, in fact, of Dean Russell. In one long night, the students transferred the entire Division of Game Management—furniture, library, lab equipment, paintings, even the Professor's pipe and ashtray—over to 424 University Farm Place. Aldo arrived at the Soils Building the next morning only to find his office gone. After a grand tour of the new quarters, he tried to explain to the authorities what had happened. They told him that the rooms had already been assigned, and that he could not have them. He replied that, for better or worse, he already *did* have them. Aldo hung up the phone and looked bemusedly at his students. "At last Leopold settled back in his desk chair, reached for his pipe, and lit it slowly. He didn't need to say a word. He was smiling and so were we."[48]

Two weeks later, their faith in the Professor was rewarded, at least temporarily. Once again Dean Russell played the crucial role in promoting Leopold's work, and WARF came through with funds to support the game management program for one more year.

Squatter's rights prevailed at 424 University Farm Place. The old mid-Victorian house, weather-worn and railroad-shaken, became the permanent home quarters of Leopold and his gang of students. The students worked in their third-story offices, in a converted dark room, and in the kitchen-cum-laboratory. In time, "424" would come to acquire an unmistakable odor, which one student described as a combination of "books, pipe-tobacco, mothballs, secretaries' cologne, and, on a Monday morning, commercial cleaning fluids and floor wax."[49] Vivian Horn stood watch in the front room. Aldo's adjacent office was lined with wooden bookshelves and featured large bay windows—altogether luxurious compared to the Soils Building basement. This would remain Leopold's base of operations for the rest of his life.

Meanwhile, the shack opened up for the season, although, in fact, visits were no longer seasonal. A new chimney had finally sufficed to keep the place reasonably clear of smoke. On February 4, during a warm midwinter thunderstorm, the family made its first attempts to band birds—chickadees—and the notable bird #65290 was captured for the first time ("This bird very wild and active in trap," Leopold noted).[50] Bird-banding became a regular family activity during Wisconsin's dreary winter days, and chickadee #65290 was destined to return to their improvised traps more than any other single bird. In March 1938, Leopold recorded for the first time in his journal the spring "sky dance" of the woodcock. This event initiated an important development in his observations. From that point on, he began to pay much more attention to the sequence of events of the days and seasons: the blooming of maples and alders, the swelling of willow buds, the piping of the first frogs, the running of the northern pike. These detailed phenological notes began to fill up the pages of Leopold's journal.

When the ground thawed, planting resumed: a hundred aspens, hazels, dogwoods, sumacs. Most of the survivors from 1937 wintered without damage, but rabbits took their toll on white pines, especially near the old crop fields ("You can't put up brush shelters and plant WP at same time and place," Leopold observed). After putting in the new shrubs, Aldo declared "an anti-rabbit campaign from now on." On April 16, spring vacation and tree planting began: 100 white pines, 500 red pines, 500 jack pines, 500 red oaks, 50 tamaracks, 50 red cedars, 12 wahoo bushes, 40 red osier dogwoods, 30 hazel, 24 paper birch, and 12 hard maples. This year they gave the pines extra mulch, and fertilized with potash. A spring and summer of normal rains allowed most of the pines to finally take hold, stimulated some to second and third spurts of growth, and even revived a few of the stragglers from previous years. The birches and tamaracks, however, seemed to be more particular about their soil requirements, and had another poor showing.

The spring of 1938 saw a sudden outpouring of writing by Leopold on the cultural and esthetic aspects of conservation. In March, *Bird-Lore* published "Conservation Esthetic," Leopold's most extensive appraisal of outdoor recreation since his wilderness writings of the 1920s. Analyzing the diverse values that people seek in their contacts with nature, Leopold praised those activities that "create their own satisfaction with little or no attrition of land or life," and decried those which served only to dilute or destroy the resource on which they depended. He had no kind words for the ugly tourist. "He is the motorized ant who swarms the continents before learning to see his own back yard, who consumes but never creates outdoor satisfactions." Recreation, Leopold concluded, was threatened with "qualitative bankruptcy" by "the expansion of transport without a corresponding growth of perception. . . . Recreational development is a job, not of building roads into lovely country, but of building receptivity into the still unlovely human mind."[51]

On April 11, 1938, Leopold took his case directly into the lions' den, delivering a guest lecture for the College of Engineering entitled "Engineering and Conservation." The talk was a masterful piece of rhetoric, a gently worded but forceful plea for engineers to reexamine their attitude toward the natural world. "Every professional man must, within limits, execute the jobs people are willing to pay for. But every profession in the long run writes its own ticket. It does so through the emergence of leaders who can afford to be skeptical out loud and in public—professors, for example. What I decry here is not so much the prevalence of public error in the use of engineering tools as the scarcity of engineering criticism of such misuse." The engineer respects mechanical wisdom, Leopold suggested, because he creates it; he lacks respect for ecological wisdom not because he is contemptuous of it, but because he is unaware of it. "We end," Leopold concluded, "at what might be called the standard paradox of the twentieth century: our tools are better than we are, and grow better and faster than we do. They suffice to crack the atom, to command the tides. But they do not suffice for the oldest task in human history: to live on a piece of land without spoiling it."[52]

After the spring tree-planting vacation at the shack, Leopold traveled to Missouri to speak at the opening of a wildlife refuge in Boone County. On April 28, he delivered an address at the University of Missouri on "Natural History, the Forgotten Science." As in other expressions of his educational philosophy, Leopold criticized "the lop-sidedness and sterility of biological education as a means of building citizens." New to his critique, however, was an indictment of science that specialized in taking things apart, but neglected to explain how things hang together. He theorized a field trip with a typical Phi Beta Kappa student. "We can safely assume he knows how angiosperms and cats are put together, but let us test his comprehension of how Missouri is put together."

We are driving down a country road in northern Missouri. Here is a farmstead. Look at the trees in the yard and the soil in the field and tell us whether the original settler carved his farm out of prairie or woods. Did he eat prairie chickens or wild turkey for his Thanksgiving? What plants grew here originally which do not grow here now? Why did they disappear? What did the prairie plants have to do with creating the corn yielding capacity of this soil? Why does this soil erode now but not then?

Leopold held that any amateur ought to be able to speculate on such matters, "and have a lot of fun doing it." His point, though, was that science as taught in the classroom ignored this approach, and relegated natural history to the dusty backroom at a time when society needed it most. "Does the educated citizen," he asked, "know he is only a cog in an ecological mechanism? That if he will work with that mechanism his mental wealth and material wealth can expand indefinitely? But that if he refuses to work with that mechanism, it will ultimately grind him to dust? If education does not teach us these things, then what is education for?"[53]

Leopold was in the midst of a period of fermentation in his thought. On the intellectual frontiers where separate sciences overlapped, and where adventurous students in the sciences wandered, the unity of nature was presenting itself as a real and vital phenomenon, one which had to be confronted, and its consequences for conservation surmised. Leopold was moving incrementally, but steadily, in this direction, toward a convergence of ideas that was attracting not only him, but leaders throughout the natural sciences and the management professions. His mind was ideally suited to the task. Abstraction and fact played as the twin poles of Leopold's intellectual creativity. He was never content with mere theorizing, nor with mere application. Every field experience suggested a new philosophical adjustment; every new generalization demanded evidence from the field. Often serendipity altered the course of his movements, but just as often Leopold created his own opportunities. Even as he was cultivating these more abstract thoughts on conservation, he was putting them to the test, practicing them, implementing them on land as well as defining them on paper.

In his role as chairman of the Technical Committee of the American Wildlife Institute, Leopold was instrumental in the establishment of a new waterfowl research station on the marshy southern shore of Lake Manitoba near Winnipeg. Late in 1937, James Bell, a prominent businessman from Minneapolis, approached the AWI for funds to support a duck hatchery he had established on his own lands at Delta, Manitoba. Leopold at first discouraged the investment on both economic and strategic grounds. Speaking for his committee, he expressed his long-held doubts about the value of artificial propagation as a means of building up waterfowl populations. Then Miles D. Pirnie, a waterfowl expert and director of Michigan State's Kellogg Bird Sanctuary in Battle Creek, visited Delta and reported to Leopold that the set-up had great promise, due to its location alongside one of Canada's greatest wild marshes. Leopold encouraged Bell to resubmit his proposal along more general lines.

On May 6, Leopold met Bell in Minneapolis. Bell was enthusiastic about the new plan. The next day, Leopold submitted a report to the AWI explaining Delta's potential for research, emphasizing the opportunity for cooperation with Canadian wildlife agencies. To bolster the plan, Leopold enlisted Pirnie to serve as cosupervisor of research and offered to assign one of his own graduate students to the Delta station. At first, he thought Art Hawkins would be the appropriate man, but Hawkins was about to graduate and had already accepted a position with the Illinois Natural History Survey. Instead, he asked Albert Hochbaum to take the assignment. Hochbaum jumped at the chance.[54]

On June 6, the AWI approved the plan and forwarded nine hundred dollars to start up the work without delay. There was still enough time to get in a summer's worth of field observations. On June 9, Pirnie and Hochbaum left Madison for the marshes of Manitoba. The Delta Duck Station was destined to play a central role in the growth of waterfowl research. These were the great marshes, the bays, sloughs, channels, and prairie potholes that annually raised the ducks of the midcontinent, sent them south on the autumn winds, and drew them north again with the spring. The station itself was ideally situated on the Delta Marsh, a 75,000-acre expanse of phragmites, bulrush, and cattail separated from the main body of Lake Manitoba by a slender ridge of sand. Hochbaum would make the marsh and the station his life's work. He was then twenty-seven years old, a creative, original character, and a favorite of Leopold's. After a week at Delta, Hochbaum wrote to Leopold, "I can't begin to tell what a wonderful place this is. I would like to spend ten years here."[55]

In the midst of these plans to launch the Delta station, Leopold took on another consulting job. At the Third Midwest Wildlife Conference, held in Madison in November 1937, Leopold had met Dr. William P. Harris, a representative of the Huron Mountain Club. The club owned a 15,000-acre tract of virgin hardwood forest near Lake Superior. Harris asked Leopold to devise a land program for the club's holdings. For Leopold, it was a rare, important opportunity to experiment with his new approach to ecologically based land management.

The club's lands encompassed one of the last vestiges of the "big hardwoods" that Leopold had so eagerly explored as a boy at Les Cheneaux. The lands were not completely undisturbed. Some pines had been logged, artificial fish stocking had altered the stream life, and a number of large mammals had been exterminated: cougar, moose, wolverine, fisher, marten, lynx. Nevertheless, the Huron Club was still wild country, with few roads, a modest deer herd, a relatively intact native plant community, and even some wolves.

Leopold spent six days at the club in late May and early June of 1938, reading the landscape: white cedar and hemlock were not reproducing; all the striped maples were browsed, as were balsams along snow-plowed roads; a new logging railroad came within two miles of club lands; there was a logging camp a mile away; around the club headquarters, deer were being artificially fed with alfalfa; wolves were being driven out of the club's interior; a few mature pines remained; the fishermen were mad at the otters for eating fish; the groundskeeper had killed 119 blue herons since 1936 for the same reason.

To Leopold, the fate of the Huron Club's holdings was plain. Commercial logging operations were nearing its boundaries, a development likely to increase deer populations. Michigan's official wolf control policy added to the likelihood. The vegetation in the area was already beginning to show signs of damage by deer; the virgin hardwood forest did not support a high density of deer naturally, and could not except artificially. Facing a future of numerous deer and few wolves, the forest was potentially endangered. Further, the club's lands contained a number of rarities—Canada jays, otters, bald eagles, the timber wolves, undeveloped shoreline, old white pines —that were important for esthetic and scientific reasons.

Leopold returned to Madison and prepared a management plan for the area. He concluded that deer overpopulation constituted the greatest threat to the health of the forest as a whole. The aim of management, as at Rockford, was to maintain a safe margin between the land's carrying capacity and its deer population. Leopold recommended that a large portion of the club's interior be kept free from logging and preserved as a natural area. Around this core, a selectively logged buffer zone would ease deer pressure from outside the club, disperse the population within the club, encourage a number of other songbird and wildflower species, and even produce lumber for sale. "The smaller and more frequent the selective cuttings," Leopold advised, "the greater the benefit to wildlife." Leopold suggested that the campaign against predators be relaxed; "the wolves," he wrote, "make the Huron Mountain property more unique and valuable than deer possibly can."[56] Among other measures, Leopold also advocated that the club allow scientific studies to be carried out on its lands.

Leopold's plan was an elegant example of low-intensity land management, aimed at preserving and managing for long-term stability an island of biological integrity within the largely destabilized northwoods. Leopold submitted the report in June. Harris praised Leopold for "a splendid job," but Leopold himself was not satisfied. "It did not please me particularly," he replied, "because there are so many things I have in my mind that I could not get into it. As a rough picture of the kind of things to be considered, I think it will do."[57] Leopold was not being falsely modest; he did have a lot of things on his mind.

In August, Leopold returned to Michigan to present a slide show to the club members and summarize his recommendations. The club accepted his report and, in subsequent years, implemented most of the steps he advocated.

From the Huron Mountain Club, Leopold travelled directly to Delta to have a first look at the new set-up and to confer with Hochbaum and Pirnie on the early progress of their work. Leopold stayed at Delta for a week and helped Hochbaum organize what was obviously going to be a vastly larger undertaking than anyone had anticipated. But Hochbaum had made a good start over the summer, laying the foundation of his research— waterfowl inventories, botanical surveys, specimen collection, banding, and nesting observations. He had even put his artistic skills to work, preparing sketches of downy fledglings and paintings of the marsh landscape. Leo-

pold encouraged Hochbaum along these lines—he and Estella hosted show-
ings of Albert's work in their home several times during this period—and
advised him to "take enough time off to do additional paintings regardless
of any loss of technical output. How much, I will leave to you."[58]

∽

Ever since joining the university, Leopold had signed his letters "Professor of Game Management." In the fall of 1938, he began to refer to himself as "Professor of Wildlife Management."

The autumn was busy with hunts: a bow season at the shack, a duck
hunt with Tom Coleman in Trempealeau County, a dozen trips to Riley
with the family. When Art Hawkins left Madison to work for the Illinois
Natural History Survey, he bequeathed his German shorthair, Gus, to Aldo.
At first, Aldo was not intent on keeping the dog, but Gus grew on him
and before long was his loyal companion on every hunt and shack visit.
The animal population in the Leopold house was growing. Carl had taken
up falconry and kept his Cooper's hawk in the garage. Little Estella tamed
the first of her pet crows. The crow routinely roosted on the roof, woke
the neighbors bright and early, followed Estella to school, and disrupted
procedure by cawing outside her classroom window.

Charles Elton and his wife visited in September. Elton was visiting a
number of universities across Canada and the United States, and Leopold
immediately signed him up for a seminar. On a weekend trip to the shack,
the Eltons planted a handful of bur oak acorns to mark their visit.

Elton's visit came at an auspicious time. At the end of 1938, Leopold
was returning to a philosophical phase in his thinking. Elton was one of
several significant influences on whom Leopold would draw during the important months that followed. George Wehrwein was another. Just as Leopold turned to Elton as a greater authority on ecology than he, he turned
to Wehrwein as a greater authority on land economics. In the fall of 1938,
Leopold tried to promote university interest in a study that would bring
together the natural sciences and economics. In between the lack of private initiative in conservation and the wholesale substitution of governmental programs, Leopold saw a gap where economists and philosophers
feared to tread.

Economists have sought a profit motivation for conservation practice. There
are profits, but they usually *accrue to the community* rather than to the individual.
Hence men like Paul Sears, Stuart Chase, and Jay Darling are able to compile impressive lists of malpractices, i.e., practices obviously damaging to the community,
but no landowner lifts a finger to remedy them. The only action resulting from
these analyses is more governmental intervention. This may be good as far as it
goes, but . . . it cannot go far enough. . . . The system of land practice which

deserves the name "conservative" will be motivated by a mixture of economic, ethical, and esthetic considerations. Any one of these motives separated from the others produces actions which appear (to me) "unsound."[59]

Apparently, the only thing to come of Leopold's proposed study was his own enhanced interest in these questions. On November 23 he delivered a talk on "Economics, Philosophy, and Land": "We segregate esthetics so as to give farmers none and women's clubs a lot. In actual practice esthetics & utility are completely interwoven. To say we do a thing to land for either reason alone is prima facie evidence that we do not understand what we are doing, or are doing it wrong. Conclusion: there are virgin fields of inquiry where economics, philosophy, and land science meet."[60]

Leopold always returned to agriculture as the proving ground of any advance in conservation. All his life he had worked close to agriculture, of course, but owning his own land gave his words added authority and depth. That same month, he wrote the first in a long series of brief articles for the widely distributed *Wisconsin Agriculturalist and Farmer.* These articles, reminiscent of Leopold's earlier talks on WHA radio, provided farmers with basic information on wildlife conservation practices: "Success in attracting ordinary birds soon whets the appetite for extraordinary ones. A mountain ash in the yard may bring cedar waxwings, or even the rare Bohemian waxwing. A box elder tree may bring evening grosbeaks. Faithful feeding of suet may bring the uncommon red-breasted nuthatch. A south-facing hollow snag wired onto the top of a dense evergreen may add the screech owl to your list of guests."[61] Leopold would write over thirty of these pieces during the next four years. With illustrations provided by artist Byron Jorns, they became a favorite feature with the magazine's readers.

In February 1939, for the university's Farm and Home Week, Leopold delivered one of his most engaging and significant talks, a summary of his views on agriculture which he called "The Farmer as a Conservationist." "It is the individual farmer," Leopold said, "who must weave the greater part of the rug on which America stands. Shall he weave into it only the sober yarns which warm the feet, or also some of the colors which warm the eye and the heart?"[62] Leopold argued that an agricultural landscape shaped wholly to economic ends was not only de-planted and de-wildlifed, but dehumanized. For the first time in print, Leopold defined conservation as a state of "harmony between men and land"; "When land does well for its owner, and the owner does well by his land; when both end up better by reason of their partnership, we have conservation. When one or the other grows poorer, we do not." Leopold predicted that, once we have learned more of "the language" of the natural world, we will know that "there is . . . drama in every bush," and "when enough men know this, we need fear no indifference to the welfare of bushes, or birds, or soils, or trees.

We shall then have no need of the word conservation, for we shall have the thing itself."[63]

Leopold envisioned a future Wisconsin built in keeping with the farmer's own self-applied conservation standards:

The creek banks are wooded and ungrazed. In the woods, young straight timber-bearing trees predominate, but there is also a sprinkling of hollow-limbed veterans left for the owls and squirrels, and of down logs left for the coons and fur-bearers. On the edge of the woods are a few wide-spreading hickories and walnuts for nutting. Many things are expected of this creek and its woods: cordwood, posts, and sawlogs; flood-control, fishing, and swimming; nuts and wildflowers; fur and feather. Should it fail to yield an owl-hoot or a mess of quail on demand, or a bunch of sweet william or a coon-hunt in season, the matter will be cause for injured pride and family scrutiny, like a check marked "no funds."[64]

The same mixture of wild and tame attributes could be found in this imagined farm's fields and pastures, in its pond and on its roadfront, and in its "historic oaks, which are cherished with both pride and skill."

"The Farmer as a Conservationist" was among Leopold's most effective statements of conservation's aims. It dealt directly with the resource at issue, and it was written directly for farmers (it was later published in *American Forests*). Moreover, it exuded Leopold's love of land and his concern for the society built upon it. He referred to conservation as a "positive exercise of skill and insight, not merely a negative exercise of abstinence or caution." He spoke of the farm as "the owner's portrait of himself. Conservation implies self-expression in that landscape, rather than blind compliance with economic dogma."[65]

The last point was one on which Leopold was again focusing. In another manuscript he prepared at this time, Leopold lay the blame for faulty land use on "the current doctrine of private profit and public subsidy":

It expects subsidies to do more—and the private owner to do less—for the community than they are capable of doing. We rationalize these defects as individualism, but they imply no real respect for the landowner as an individual. They merely condone the ecological ignorance which contrasts so strongly with his precocity in mechanical things. But the final proof that it is bogus individualism lies in the fact that it leads us straight into government ownership. An orator could decry it as abject dependence upon government, tolerated by the owners of a free country. I do not decry it, but I hate to see us lean on it as a solution.[66]

Although Leopold expressed his devotion to individualism only on rare occasions, it was fundamental to his thinking. He was in many respects an enlightenment personality confronting the realities of the twentieth-century world, with the benefits of twentieth-century ecological science at hand. At one point in "The Farmer as a Conservationist," Leopold wrote a memorable paragraph that alluded to recent events in Europe:

Sometimes I think that ideas, like men, can become dictators. We Americans have so far escaped regimentation by our rulers, but have we escaped regimentation by our own ideas? I doubt if there exists today a more complete regimentation of the human mind than that accomplished by our self-imposed doctrine of ruthless utilitarianism. The saving grace of Democracy is that we fastened this yoke on our own necks, and we can cast if off when we want to, without severing the neck. Conservation is perhaps one of the many squirmings which foreshadow this act of self-liberation.[67]

Leopold challenged the status quo not by denying the rules of reason, but by playing by them so well and never to the exclusion of his other instinctive mental abilities, exploring the region where individual liberty met broader biological, social, and economic issues. In fact, he lived in that large territory most of his life, a fact that ironically may have prevented him from addressing the issue of individual freedom more directly. But always implicit in whatever he wrote was the idea that a lasting freedom must be predicated on an awareness of land. Natural rights had to begin with nature.

Like Thomas Jefferson, Leopold spoke to the issue of individualism and democracy most directly when discussing agriculture. Unlike Jefferson, however, Leopold could draw on the experience of American history and recent advances in science. His thoughts were rooted less in philosophy or political theory than in social and biological realities; his concerns were the quality, durability, and level of satisfaction of rural life. If Jefferson's dream of an agrarian democracy of yeoman farmers had been left in the wake of the industrial revolution, its premise, at least, was still sound. Ideas about land and liberty had changed, but they were still connected, and that connection still lay at the heart of the American experience. The challenge was now to reassert the democratic ideal while taking into account the historic development of conservation and the evolving agricultural landscape.

Leopold's characteristic mix of idealism and practicality was displayed to its best advantage on these points. His training as a conservationist impelled him to express his concerns and to propose alternatives, but his experience with farms and farmers, especially in the troubled 1930s, taught him not to let the vision get away from him. He was idealistic enough to define conservation as "a state of harmony between man and land," but practical enough to admit in the same breath that this harmony, "like harmony between neighbors, is an ideal — and one we shall never attain. Only glib and ignorant men, unable to feel the mighty currents of history, unable to see the incredible complexity of agriculture itself, can promise any early attainment of that ideal. But any man who respects himself and his land can try to."[68]

Leopold turned this line of thought on farming and freedom back to wildlife. During this same period, he wrote, "I expect, and hope for, a wide range of individualism in the ultimate development of the wildlife idea. There are, and should be, farmers not at all interested in shooting, but keen on forestry, or wildflowers, or birds in general. There are, and should be, farmers keen about none of these, but hipped on coons and coon dogs. I foresee, in short, a time when the wildlife on a farm will be the signature of a personality, just as the crops and stocks already are. The more varied the media of individual expression, the more the collective total will add to [the] satisfaction of farm life."[69] Quiet though Leopold's rhetoric was, he was issuing a powerful challenge to economic dogma, suggesting that when standard economics begins to limit options, and ceases to promote individual expression, then both conservation and individuality suffer, and it becomes time to reexamine means and ends.

By now, the science Leopold helped invent and the academic program he developed had both outgrown their original conceptions. In 1933 he had seen them both as culminations; in 1938 he knew that they were only first steps. That semester he began teaching a new course. He replaced Game Management 118 with Wildlife Ecology 118, a three-credit general course for beginning professionals and interested laymen alike. But the future of his chair was again uncertain. The funding from WARF was scheduled to run out in July; its future would then rest with the state legislature. On March 16, Leopold prepared a review of his six-year experiment. "It is clear by now," he began, "that *there is no short cut* to wildlife conservation."

Neither laws, nor appropriations, nor bureaus, nor the training of technical men, nor popular agitation on the subject is going to accomplish much until there exists:

(a) A critical judgment in the average citizen as to what wildlife conservation is, what methods are sound or unsound, what worthwhile or trivial.

(b) A personal enthusiasm for and enjoyment of wildlife in a high proportion of citizens, especially landowners.

(c) A much deeper knowledge of natural mechanisms, and a correspondingly sounder technique.

To bring these three things into existence is a job requiring generations rather than years. The function of a Chair of Wildlife Management is to build foundations for the eventual accomplishment of these objectives.[70]

ᔄ

On February 1, the family went to the shack only to find it in shambles. Vandals had broken in and destroyed most of the furniture. Pieces of shattered plates littered the clay floor. Estella's homemade honeys and jams were ruined, poured over with kerosene. The vandals—two local boys as it turned out—had taken an axe to the cedar fireplace mantel, and stolen a pair of tennis shoes (through which they were eventually traced).

"When we came in," Nina recalled, "[each of us] just went to a corner and began to cry. All, that is, but Dad. He just looked around, saw our state, and burst into a big smile. 'I didn't know how much this place meant to you,' he said. 'Let's get busy.'"[71]

Ever since the shack trips began, the family had maintained the place in a state of Thoreauvian simplicity: unpainted walls, straw mattresses, a few tools and books, cooking by Dutch oven. The vandals' work spurred some basic improvements. Estella had no philosophical attachment to clay floors. She finally persuaded Aldo and Carl to install a wooden floor, and to whitewash the shack's interior. Estella revelled in the shack as much as her husband and children, but to her thinking, simplicity did not preclude refinements.

It was a good spring for ducks. During the migrations, they came to the marshes and sloughs in abundance. One April evening, Aldo and the family stood by the backwater behind the shack and, as daylight dimmed, watched flock after flock of mallards, scaup, and teal come down from the sky. Hundreds of birds roiled the waters. Carl recorded it in the journal as "the most spectacular and extraordinary duck-show I've ever witnessed." On a nearby shore, a woodcock performed its aerial dance, peenting and rising and diving amid the incoming flocks.

After three years of work, the planting crew had perfected its technique. Aldo experimented with desodding around the trees ("The worst enemy of evergreens is grass. . . . Herbs or weeds, if not too rank, do no harm, and in the case of the shade tolerant evergreens may be beneficial"), and took careful note of site conditions, species interactions, and growth ("Tallest jacks up to Estella's collar"). Over spring vacation, 2300 more pines went into the ground, but yet another dry summer took its toll. On July 15, Leopold wrote that "Drouth is now killing tough weeds like ragweed, lamb's lettuce, goldenrod, and is getting 2-year-old trees as well as this year's plantings. Liatris is dying on the dryer ridges in the marsh. Much dewberry dried up. Planted aspen, dogwood, & hazel [are] dying in large numbers. Even the ragweed on the sandbars, subirrigated by high water only 2 weeks ago, is withered and dying."[72] Half of the year's plantings died by summer's end, but not without Aldo's careful attention to the place, timing, and cause of their demise. Even failures yielded information.

Meanwhile, a shocking reminder of events overseas arrived in the mail. Alfred Schottlaender, one of Leopold's hosts during his visit to Germany, wrote to Madison to appeal for assistance. Schottlaender was in Kenya, having barely escaped death at the hand of the Nazis. His wife (whom Leopold had described as "nice") betrayed him to the Gestapo, in hopes of gaining the family estate. Schottlaender wrote, "Each political remark I ever made to her I found by the Gestapo noted with date and hour I said it." Schottlaender told his tale:

It is for ages I'm afraid that you didn't hear anything about me but things were so awful and terrifying, that I was not able to write to anybody and it is quite a miracle that I am still alive. I am very happy that my good father died early enough not to live to see the atrocitys [sic] which the nazis did to our family and especially to me. Naturally they have stolen nearly all our property, from me alone about three and a half million marks. But not enough with that, they have sent me to their famous concentration camps at "Dachau" and "Buchenwald" and it is more than a miracle that I have escaped being killed there, like hundreds have been before my eyes![73]

In words of anguish, Schottlaender cursed the "Nazi-gangsters" and asked for Leopold's help in securing work for a brother who was still in Germany.

Over the next several months, Leopold took up the case, appealing to the State Department for immigration approval. When it turned out that the German immigration quotas were filled for several years to come, he wrote to Henry Smith, a Lawrenceville friend who had gone on to a successful business career in New York. Smith offered to find work for Schottlaender's brother, an electrical engineer, in his company's South African copper mines. Leopold never revealed an emotional response to the episode. The closest he came was in a letter to Smith when he told with somber restraint how the Schottlaender family "had been 'liquidated' in the manner now prevalent" because they were of "the ancestry now considered damaging."[74] "My dear friend Leopold," Schottlaender wrote back in July, after arrangements for his brother's move had progressed. "That I may call you like this, you have so deeply proved, and have given me back the faith of faithfulness, truth, and friendship still existing on earth, which I nearly had lost after having lived to see such terrible disappointments in my own country which I loved so much and served all my life."[75]

In the midst of this activity, Leopold wrote and delivered still another major address. "A Biotic View of Land" was given before an important joint meeting of the Society of American Foresters and the Ecological Society of America in Milwaukee on June 21, 1939. More than anything he had yet written, it directly concerned the relationship between the science of ecology and the practice of conservation. For four years he had grappled with the complexities of that relationship in his travels, his work, and his teaching. "A Biotic View of Land" was the summary of his findings. He told the audience that

The emergence of ecology has placed the economic biologist in a peculiar dilemma: with one hand he points out the accumulated findings of his search for utility, or lack of utility, in this or that species; with the other he lifts the veil from a biota so complex, so conditioned by interwoven cooperations and competitions, that no man can say where utility begins or ends. No species can be 'rated' without the tongue in the cheek; the old categories of 'useful' and 'harmful' have validity only as conditioned by time, place, and circumstance. The only sure conclusion is that the biota as a whole is useful, and biota includes not only plants and animals, but soils and waters as well.[76]

Leopold's purpose in this address was to provide his audience with a clear and generally applicable "mental image" of the functioning of the land community. He employed the "biotic pyramid" idea and explained at length the now familiar concepts of food chains, food webs, trophic layers, and energy flow, emphasizing the apparent relationship between "the complex structure of land and its smooth functioning as an energy circuit."[77]

Evolution, Leopold explained, had built up the biotic pyramid, adding new links to the food chain, lengthening the energy circuits, elaborating the species diversity. Evolutionary change, of course, was always occurring, but it was "usually slow and local." Technology, however, had enabled man to make changes "of unprecedented violence, rapidity, and scope." (Leopold apparently assumed a distinction between human and geological time scales.) Man incessantly rearranged nature's energy circuits, lopping off the large predators, shortening and simplifying food chains, altering the composition of floras and faunas, substituting domestic species for wild ones, overdrafting soils. This was a new thing under the sun, and to Leopold it raised two basic questions: "Can the land adjust itself to the new order? Can violence be reduced?"

In regard to the first question, Leopold noted that land differed in its ability to adjust to human-induced change according to geography and climate. History and ecology, however, supported one general deduction: "The less violent the man-made changes, the greater the probability of successful readjustment in the pyramid. Violence, in turn, would seem to vary with human population density; a dense population requires a more violent conversion of land."[78]

Can the "violence" (Leopold used the term a dozen times in the address) be reduced? Leopold thought so, and pointed out that the dissensions within conservation generally involved conflicts between radical and conservative means of manipulating the natural order. He provided examples of how conservation was "groping toward a nonviolent land use" in game and wildlife management, forestry, agriculture, and wilderness preservation. The real underlying conflict, Leopold suggested, was between "those who see utility and beauty in the biota as a whole, and those who see utility and beauty only in pheasants and trout."[79]

"A Biotic View of Land" was remarkable for the nonjudgmental stance that Leopold assumed in it. As its title implied, it was an attempt to view objectively the structure and function of land and to understand man's role in altering it. Leopold was speaking this time, not as a conservationist or a philosopher, but as a scientist. And yet, between its lines "A Biotic View" was a stronger statement than even "The Conservation Ethic." However convincing "The Conservation Ethic" was in stressing the moral aspect of conservation, it was still premature in terms of ecological understanding. By the end of the 1930s, that understanding had crystallized, not just for Leopold himself, but for the natural sciences in general. At the same time, Leopold's intuitive grasp of land as an entity comprised of interdependent parts, of "interwoven cooperations and competitions," had been forced forward by experience. In 1935, he had spoken of human society as "an organism which includes land." By 1939, he had inverted that logic. Land was the whole which included human society.

A "biotic view" of nature, however objective it tried to be, could not help but imply a deep criticism of trends in human history. It saw man as a creature among creatures, but eminently equipped to alter the diversity and stability of the life around him. It was characteristic of Leopold's style that, in criticizing the prevailing ways of his civilization, he did not condemn them. He never argued out of contempt, but instead simply stated the situation, explained it, and offered thoughts on what must be done to correct it. He did not begrudge humanity its technological prowess, nor its pioneering spirit. Those qualities had powered his own innovations in everything from game management to wilderness preservation. But from the late 1930s on, he would boldly affirm that, unless the complex processes of land health became duly recognized and appreciated, our tools would work to the ultimate impoverishment of both people and land. He was aware that this thinking "runs counter to pioneering philosophy, which assumes that because a small increase in density enriched human life, that an indefinite increase will enrich it indefinitely." For Leopold, neither reason, nor intuition, nor experience, supported that assumption.

For many, this new world view was difficult to appreciate. Joseph Grinnell, writing to Leopold in regard to Starker's interdisciplinary course of study at Berkeley, groused that "some of our potent professors do not grant the worthiness, or even the existence, of a field 'ecology.' You have probably heard of such in your neck of the woods! The combination of forestry, botany, and zoology looks to them like ecology, even though I myself took pains to avoid the word!"[80] Vivian Horn, who was steadfastly typing all of Leopold's writing, remembered that "I learned the word 'ecology' at this time. It was not a common word in those days. Even if I did not fully comprehend the significance of what I was typing, many others did not fully comprehend it either, judging by the belated recognition of his work."[81]

Although Leopold used the term "ecology" judiciously and defined it simply, even he had difficulty communicating its meaning to students. Robert McCabe, who would soon join Leopold as a graduate student and teaching assistant, recalled that, "If [Leopold] had a 'weak spot' in his teaching

procedure, it was that he often assumed that the students had more ecological understanding than they really did."[82] In the field, where he could
keep one foot in traditional natural history and the other in modern science, communication was always easier. It helped, of course, that he was
a superb hunter, fisherman, and woodsman. All these were means by which
Leopold allowed others to see the world as he saw it: as a naturalist.

Of all the realms of human genius, the naturalist's has always been
among the most difficult for society to appreciate, despite the fact that his
primary tools are common to all: eyes and ears, attention, sensation. The
naturalist offers society a view of itself from beyond, a more objective perspective on the health and development of a culture. To be sure, the view
gained can never be purely objective; the naturalist is still a human being,
still a product of society, and can distance but not detach himself. But by
stepping outside of the civilized and into the wild, the naturalist estab-
lishes continuity between them, and reminds us that the human view of
the earth is not the only view that has been granted.

ᔕ

The funding for Leopold's academic chair expired July 1, 1939. The
state legislature was in the midst of the budget deliberations that would
decide its fate. Leopold's friends and colleagues had done their best to
grease a path, but success was still not assured.

In the months before the legislature reconvened, Bill Schorger asked
Leopold's supporters to express their interest to university President Clarence Dykstra. Paul Errington wrote that Leopold's influence "more than
that of any other man . . . has accelerated and directed modern wildlife
conservation as practiced by the U.S. Biological Survey, the Soil Conservation Service, the National Park Service, and many of the more progressive state commissions." Owen Gromme commended Leopold's work and
expressed his hope "that nothing will be done that will endanger its continuance." Jay Darling was even more insistent. "Aldo Leopold," he wrote,
"is recognized in every circle of conservationists as the ranking authority
and leading voice in the country. His voluntary contributions to the conservation literature of the country are standards by which all lesser authorities are judged."[83]

By summer's end, the legislature had approved a new budget and Leopold became chairman of his own full-fledged, one-man Department of
Wildlife Management in the University of Wisconsin College of Agriculture.

18

Digging Deeper

(1939–1941)

ONE OF Leopold's closest friends and staunchest supporters in the Wisconsin Conservation Department was Ernie Swift. They had been friends for ten years, ever since Swift was a northwoods warden and Leopold was conducting his game surveys. Swift had since risen to become deputy director of the Conservation Department. Leopold admired his combination of woods sense and independent judgment. Swift, in turn, appreciated Leopold's innovative ideas and probing mind. "You would go out with him," Swift recalled, "and he'd stretch your brains until they were tired."[1]

Once he and Leopold were driving back to Madison after a field investigation upstate. They crested a high hill and on the drop-off to the right of the road was a prolific stand of second growth woods. In the middle, a great oak stood alone, overspreading the younger forest. Leopold suggested they stop and take a look. Then the questions poured forth. What happened here? What accounts for all this second growth? How did that lone tree happen to be there? "We must have sat there thirty minutes while he ruminated on whether the Indians had left it or whether the settlers left it. He chewed on that for an hour afterwards. That was the nature of the man. I think I had some natural curiosity. However, I honestly think that through my association with Aldo Leopold I became more curious. It rubbed off just being with that man. . . . [He] wasn't upstage about it. He'd say, 'Well now, what do you think about them? What happened here?' It wasn't a leading question. He wasn't trying to show any superiority. He'd say, 'I don't know, either' if he didn't know."[2]

Leopold's implacable curiosity and deep conviction prevented him from trimming back his workload at a time when he might reasonably have done so. He was fifty-two, and his status at the university secure. Active on the boards and committees of over a dozen local, national, and university organizations, he was also currently serving as president of the Wildlife Society. In only ten years he had helped bring a new profession into being. The landmark Pittman-Robertson Act, passed in 1937, was funding training for wildlife managers and researchers all across the country; *Game Management* was their standard text. It was not Leopold's nature, however, to rest on laurels; his commitments would continue to increase along with his stature.

As busy as Leopold's schedule was, and would continue to be, he and Estella kept almost every weekend free for shack visits. Her housekeeping routine relaxed now that the children were grown. Starker was now married and had moved to Missouri to begin a five-year study of wild turkeys in the Ozarks. Luna, studying under Kirk Bryan at Harvard, was beginning his own distinguished career as a hydrogeologist. Nina and Carl were enrolled at the University of Wisconsin, while Estella was a free-spirited twelve-year-old.

Nina, Carl, and Estella usually accompanied their parents on shack weekends. Aldo's journal grew steadily more detailed and voluminous: "River slightly up. Cool easterly breeze. Good dew. . . . Yellow foxtail has shed half its seed; green still intact heads. Picked grapes for jelly. Still a few blackberries and dewberries. Chokeberries ripe. . . . Squirrels beginning to work hickories near road cut. Nuts full size but shells still tight. . . . Birds seen: blue heron 1. Kingfisher 6. . . . Marsh hawk 1. . . . Solitary sandpiper on bar. Quail: 1 covey 12, several singles near shack. . . . Pheasants: 1 blackneck cock with 7 grown young, in rain on road near Lewis. . . . Put a cable around split elm. More lupine up. . . . Rabbits seem scarcer than a month ago. Gus got hot scent only in willow sandbar. . . . All hardwoods have now stopped growing, including watered maples and elms. Pines which started new buds with recent rains have quit."[3]

And so on. With each passing season, each additional year of work and play, each pine and puccoon that took root and survived, Leopold himself was growing more deeply attached to the sandy-soiled farm. It was now the focus of his curiosities. Such careful attention to the current affairs of plants and animals occasionally resulted in a less-than-current knowledge of other matters. On one trip back to Madison, Starker stopped in Sauk City for a pack of cigarettes while his father napped in the back seat. While Starker went into the drugstore, Aldo awoke and heard a football game on the radio. Starker returned and Aldo asked, "Starker, who are these Packers?" The Green Bay Packers had not yet attained football immortality, and such an oversight was not yet on the regional list of unpardonable sins. Still, Aldo did ask.

∽

At the end of August 1939, Leopold travelled north to Manitoba to check up on Albert Hochbaum's progress at the Delta Duck Station and to gather information for an official report to the American Wildlife Institute (one of Leopold's current interests was crow predation, so on the drive to Delta, he kept a running tally of crow sightings). His interest in the station's development was as much personal as it was professional. Hochbaum, recently married, was in his second field season there, and thoroughly engaged in the pioneering work. Lyle Sowls spent the summer there as well. Leopold was delighted with the progress they had already made. In his report to the AWI, he recommended that the Delta program be expanded and its funding extended, and that Hochbaum be employed as director on a year-round basis.[4]

Leopold returned to Madison for only a week before he was back on the road, this time through the western and southern states as a consultant for the Soil Conservation Service, reviewing wildlife conditions on a number of SCS projects, and paying particular attention to the status of rodent populations. Leopold's partner was Ernest Holt, his collaborator on the Coon Valley project earlier in the decade. Their tour lasted three weeks, and took them over a wide range of country, from Colorado Springs down to the Gila valley in Arizona, east to Las Cruces, across Texas, and ultimately to Georgia, where they inspected erosion-control projects and visited Herb Stoddard at his wildlife research area near Thomasville.

Stoddard's work, like Leopold's, had taken him well beyond the bounds of game management. He began by managing quail; by 1939, he was challenging basic forestry dogma. In the course of his studies, Stoddard discovered that the exclusion of fire from the pine woods of Georgia's coastal plains had resulted not only in poorer quail habitat, but in decreased longleaf pine reproduction and increased risk of large fires. Through the thirties, Stoddard experimented with controlled light-burning, achieving good results for quail, pines, and wildlife in general. This, of course, had not put Stoddard in the good graces of foresters, who were born, bred, and trained to extinguish all fires. Early experiments in burning on the university arboretum's prairies had yielded analogous results, and Leopold, a convert to the principle of controlled burning, rose to Stoddard's defense. "The common assumption," he wrote, "is that Stoddard *sacrifices* forestry and erosion control to game. It seems more likely that his opponents are sacrificing game, forest safety, and forest value to their desire to apply the usual rules to an unusual ecological set-up." He urged that Stoddard's techniques be "thoroughly examined by the SCS as a way to restore coastal plain lands for combined forest and wildlife crops."[5]

The more important aspect of Leopold's trip was his return to the western rangelands. He and Holt observed firsthand the problem of unstable rodent populations and of the government's efforts to bring them under control. The Biological Survey was practicing rodent control in 1939 as vehemently as it had practiced predator control in an earlier day. Across the West, the BBS was conducting expensive poisoning campaigns against prairie dogs, squirrels, and mice, without conducting even token research into rodent ecology (an interagency agreement prevented the SCS from conducting such research itself).

Leopold concluded that poisoning was "too expensive to fit the needs of low-value range lands. It is also too violent, i.e., it frequently kills many other animal species, and its results are often not durable." He suggested that "the SCS badly needs ecological techniques for rodent control, because they may be cheaper, less violent, and more durable than poisoning. . . . If it is possible to manage game upward, it is possible to manage rodents downward." Leopold saw the whole issue as one which offered promising opportunities for research. He drew up his own "incomplete list" of questions: How long does a poisoning last? How is its duration affected by predators and range recovery? Do rodents exhibit minimum population phenomena? What is the mechanism of reinfestation? Is there possibly a rodent succession corresponding to the plant succession? What rodent populations occur on unspoiled range? Can nets be used to capture prairie dogs? What is the ultimate effect of rodent burrows on soil fertility and absorptive capacity? What is the shape and length of burrows? What weed plants are destroyed by rodents?[6]

Before returning home, Leopold paid a visit to the Washington headquarters of the Biological Survey, where he pushed for federal research into ecological methods of rodent control. Although Leopold's ideas were coolly received, BBS Chief Ira Gabrielson later wrote to him that he was "very much interested in your point of view as it checks very closely with my own." Leopold's reply exemplified his concern for interagency cooperation on matters of common interest:

My principal anxiety is for you and the SCS to reach a better understanding of each other's viewpoints. I think I detect a tendency in the BBS to regard [the SCS] attitude as academic and impracticable, and conversely, I detect a tendency in the SCS to regard the BBS as unecological and unduly influenced by rodent control appropriations. Such a situation is potentially dangerous for both organizations and for conservation. I think this new approach might be made the means of bringing the two organizations together.[7]

Leopold did not let the issue go. He corresponded with scientists around the country, read up on the latest work in range management and rodent ecology, and submitted a refinement of his criticisms to the Biological Survey. The issue showed him at his objective best. On the one hand, he knew he was beyond his area of expertise. On the other hand, he felt he was on the right track. Meanwhile, both sides were pushing the issue. *Bird-Lore* was "on my heels asking for an article on poisoning. . . . I told them I would not write it until I knew more about it."⁸ Albert Day of the BBS respectfully suggested that Leopold's statements would be "misleading to people who are not fully informed." Leopold concurred. "I agree with you that my grasp of the recent work in rodent control is imperfect. I am distinctly in the attitude of wishing to learn. On the other hand, I detect a strong tendency toward 'thinking in grooves' on both sides of this question. I can see this already, even with my fragmentary background."⁹

In the end, the Biological Survey met Leopold's criticisms with an effective circling of wagons. Well aware of the weight his voice carried, Leopold assured Day that "you have convinced me that I do not know enough about the subject to 'pronounce' on it publicly, but you have also convinced me more strongly than ever that the [survey] is overlooking a bet in not attempting to unravel, by careful field experiments, some of the basic laws which underlie rodent populations. Why wait for somebody else to do it, and use it critically against you?"¹⁰ Leopold's tone was unfalteringly cordial. When he learned that Day was scheduled to visit Madison, Leopold invited him to speak with his students at a seminar.

Leopold returned to Madison on September 29. He had decided to limit the number of his graduate students to five in order to uphold the quality of his instruction. Two students signed on that fall. Harold Hanson was a newcomer to wildlife whose uncle was a chemical engineer at the university. Hanson eventually took over the ongoing quail research at Prairie du Sac, expanding on the study to include other wildlife of the area. Dan Thompson was a graduating senior at the university, feeling, in his own words, "strong inner stirrings about a career in wildlife ecology or management." Knowing that the draft might soon interrupt his plans, Thompson gathered the courage to visit Professor Leopold. He had read of Leopold and expected to find "John Muir in a dark business suit." Instead he found Leopold in tweeds. After facing the Professor's gentle but exhaustive interview, Thompson was accepted.¹¹

Robert McCabe was another new arrival that fall. A feisty product of the ethnic neighborhoods of south Milwaukee, McCabe had attended Carroll College in nearby Waukesha on an athletic scholarship, but his interests gradually shifted toward a career in game management. He ventured to Madison to see if there were a place for him. A zoology professor unceremoniously shunted him off to Leopold. McCabe had never heard of the Professor. Leopold tentatively accepted him, but explained that he had no funds to support an additional graduate student, and that a number of other students were in competition for a place. McCabe accepted the qualifications, found a subsistence job, and enrolled in the fall.

Having been out of town for a month, Leopold hurried back to work, readying fall plantings at the shack, visiting students at their study areas, catching up on his articles for the *Wisconsin Agriculturalist and Farmer* ("Birds Should Earn Their Keep," "Look for Bands," "Wild Foods on Farms").

In November, Leopold received word that Bob Marshall had died suddenly while riding the train between New York and Washington, victim of a mysterious heart problem. He was only thirty-eight. Leopold was deeply grieved and termed his passing "a loss to the Wilderness Society, not to mention the Forest Service and conservation in general."[12] The Wilderness Society had lost its main source of both moral fervor and financial backing. Fortunately, Marshall's will provided continuing funds for the society. Venerable Robert Sterling Yard, now seventy-eight, had always given coherence to the society. Now, with Marshall's death, he assumed an even greater portion of the day-to-day activities in the Washington headquarters.

In the months that followed, Yard often turned to Leopold for advice on matters both technical and administrative. As was the case during his SCS consulting job, Leopold was drawn close to the swirls and eddies of Washington conservation politics. Leopold apparently enjoyed what recognition he received from the Washington community, but his reputation there was mixed at best. Leopold was a "bad word" in some circles. He had no out-and-out enemies, but he was inevitably the object of some professional jealousy. Others saw him as an eccentric. In the rush-to-action days of the Roosevelt administration, agency officials regarded Leopold's calls for deeper research as wet blankets. When Hochbaum had first decided to go to Wisconsin, his father, a Department of Agriculture official based in Washington, was told by several associates in the Biological Survey not to "let Al go off to study with Leopold."[13]

By late 1939, Secretary of Interior Harold Ickes' incessant drive for political territory had reached a peak. Predictably, his moves disturbed Leopold. In an article criticizing Ickes' grand plan to build a federal Department of Conservation, Leopold wrote, "The real substance of conservation lies not in the physical projects of government, but in the mental processes of citizens. . . . All the acts of government, in short, are of slight importance to conservation except as they affect the acts and thoughts of citizens."[14] Leopold and Yard discussed the situation in their letters. At one point, Leopold commented, "As I watch the unfolding pageant of the Great War among conservation bureaus, I am struck by the deadly parallels with international politics. All or most of the bureaus have a power complex, but Interior seems to display the worst case, and the Park Service is rapidly assuming the Himmler ruthlessness. The conservation public is alternately wheedled, bribed, and kicked, like other 'small neighbors.' To dominate 'recreation' is the major strategy of all and sundry, and for this noble end any means is justified. . . . It makes one think again that there must be some cosmic infection of the human mind. 'It can't happen here?' It is happening here."[15] Later in 1940, Leopold used the same metaphor even more sharply. Yard reported an attempt by Ickes to gain park land from the Forest Service in the northern Cascades. Ickes won the support of mining interests for his scheme by offering to allow prospecting and mining in the planned park. Leopold responded to Yard:

I can see no difference between Secretary Ickes' tactics in interdepartmental conservation questions and Hitler's tactics internationally. By dropping all scruples (such as restriction on mining in parks) he is perfectly free to trade one bureau against another, and to trade all of them against local commercial interests (as in the Cascades), with the end result of dominating the entire landscape. Both are a reversion to unrestrained predation. The only difference is Mr. Ickes doesn't have an army—yet.[16]

Leopold's consciousness of power complexes in conservation kept his own ego anchored to the ground. As considerable as his reputation was, he had disciplined himself into modesty. During this period, Yard asked Leopold to prepare an article for *Living Wilderness* on the origins of the wilderness area idea in the Southwest. Leopold prepared a brief account of events leading up to the establishment of the Gila Wilderness, plainly calling attention away from himself. Yard wrote back to Leopold, asking him to change it to emphasize his own role more. Leopold refused. "I can't revamp my paper to tell 'I was the first to . . . ,'" Leopold wrote to Yard. "I see too much of this staking claims to glory; if it is to get done it will have to be done by somebody else."[17] Leopold's choice of phrasing was revealing: he appreciated recognition, but he would not seize it. His article appeared in its original form.

Leopold's tamped-down exterior belied a more complicated inner struggle to understand the implications that the newly defined "biotic view" held for conservation. The grip of original ideas and the constant mental effort of the previous few years was beginning to take its toll. If Leopold was seeing farther than most conservationists of his time, he was also internalizing his vision, which in turn forced him to recognize the distance that separated him from others. Eminently self-aware, he knew his position at the forefront of conservation, and he was quietly proud of it. Yet, in an intellectual sense, he was not content. As ecology suggested layers of understanding new to the natural sciences, Leopold could only dig still deeper for the nuggets of reason that would make sense of the rapidly changing world around him, and continue to search for words that would capture the thoughts.

The family began to notice an increasing contrast in his moods. At the shack on weekends, he was his usual relaxed, even playful self. In Madison, he was quieter, intense, unable to sleep. Always an early riser, he began to wake even earlier, long before dawn. The only other family member active at that hour was Estella's pet crow. When the crow awoke, it awoke with a vengeance, cawing and cackling for all the neighbors to hear (and curse). On many a morning Aldo went out to the garden in his bathrobe to quiet the cacophony. The crow flew to his feet to accept breakfast. Digging worms in the predawn, admonishing the crow to keep his peace, Aldo exercised the cowboy vocabulary that he kept in reserve for just such occasions. Into the mid-1940s, Leopold would put his insomnia to more satisfying use as he began to keep careful notes on the occurrence of various birdsongs (other than crows) as the basis for a phenological study.

In early 1940, Leopold began to elaborate the ideas he had laid out in "A Biotic View of Land." In February, he spoke to the members of Phi Sigma on "Biotic Theories and Conservation." At the same time, he worked on a manuscript he called "Biotic Land Use." In these and other statements, he began to define land health more precisely in terms of stability and diversity. "Land science," as he sometimes called it, was showing "that conservation, at bottom, is not to be accomplished by any mere mustering of technologies [including his own]. Conservation calls for something which the technologies, individually or collectively, now lack." Leopold suggested that two things were lacking. First, a unifying purpose: "stabilization of land as a whole." Second, a means of appraising such stabilization.

> Each technology has its own yardsticks, usually yields or profits. But only commercial land uses have any profit, and some of the most important land uses have only spiritual or aesthetic yields. The collective criterion must be something deeper and more important than either profit or yield.
>
> Among the ordinary yardsticks, I can think of but one which is obviously a common denominator of success in all technologies: soil fertility. That the maintenance of at least the original fertility is essential is now a truism, and needs no further discussion.
>
> What else? What, in the evolutionary history of this flowering earth, is most closely associated with stability? The answer, to my mind, is clear: diversity of fauna and flora.
>
> It seems improbable that science can ever analyze stability and write an exact formula for it. The best we can do, at least at present, is to recognize and cultivate the general conditions which seem to be conducive to it. Stability and diversity are associated. Both are the end-result of evolution to date. To what extent are they interdependent? Can we retain stability in used land without retaining diversity also?[18]

By going into more detail and drawing further conclusions than he had before, Leopold admitted that he was reaching "beyond the range of scientific evidence." Science was not yet framing these questions. The relationship between species diversity and stability in nature—in effect the relationship between structure and function of the biotic pyramid—would challenge the clearest thinkers in ecology for decades, and remains to this day a major point of discussion. The same issue challenged Leopold from the outset. "Would the deliberate retention of both fertility and diversity reduce instability? I think it would. But I admit in the same breath that I can't prove it, or disprove it. If the trouble is in the plant and animal pipelines, I think it would help to keep them more nearly intact. It is a probability based on evolution. It is the only probability in sight."[19]

More than ever, Leopold was using the word "land" as a catch-all term for the environment; it included "soils, water systems, and wild and tame plants and animals." Stability and diversity were the concepts that seemed best suited for a critical appraisal of land, be it a wilderness or a dust bowl. At the end of his "Biotic Land Use" manuscript, Leopold asked rhetorically, "Do we ourselves, as a group, believe what we cannot prove: that retaining the diversity of our fauna and flora is conducive to stable land? These are the questions now to be discussed."[20]

He discussed them with others. With Charles Elton, Norman Fassett, George Wehrwein, Bill Vogt, and his students. Vogt was an ornithologist and editor of *Bird-Lore*. He and Leopold had first met several years before, while Leopold was serving as a director of the Audubon Society. Vogt spoke at one of the departmental seminars in 1937, and had considered coming to Wisconsin to study under Leopold. "[Vogt] had an effervescent, sparkling mind," one of the students recalled. "His ideas were way ahead of their time. Vogt was concerned about soil erosion and poverty and water supply even then."[21]

Another influence at this time, though an indirect one, was Carl O. Sauer. Sauer's work at Berkeley was stretching the intellectual boundaries of geography, hitching it up with anthropology, ecology, economics, sociology. Although Leopold apparently never met Sauer, he read Sauer's books and articles with great interest, recommended him to others in letters, and talked over his ideas at length with Starker. He saw in Sauer another who was concerned with "putting the sciences together" in order to interpret landscapes, although Sauer's work was more oriented toward cultural factors than was Leopold's.

The most significant and direct influence on Leopold during these years was his old friend from the Michigan Department of Conservation, P. S. Lovejoy. They had first met during Leopold's game survey of Michigan, and had since served together on several committees while also maintaining a lively, lengthy, and utterly distinctive correspondence. They were both Forest Service products, and shared uncommon insight into the social and historical aspects of conservation, but their minds were completely different. Leopold was always orderly, deliberative, relaxed with a touch of formality. Lovejoy was excitable and joyously cantankerous.

Their letters captured both their differences and their affinities. Leopold wrote to Lovejoy more carefully than he wrote to most of his correspondents, informing him of recent research findings and asking policy questions raised by the data. Lovejoy responded in a peculiar, inimitable prose—"Lovejoyese," Leopold called it—that grew wittier (and more indecipherable to outsiders) over the years. In Lovejoy's lexicon, land-use experts were "terra-tinkers"; people were "Homo critters" or, more simply, "H-c"; "Homo critters" could be divided into "thinks" and "feels"; "Novos, Demos, and Buros" were researchers, politicians, and bureaucrats ("Novos nest in litters of old papers, from which, at intervals, they hatch out monographic young"). A good idea was a "sumpin," as in "Seems to me that you have been sorta fumbling with a very large & important Sumpin." To make reading more challenging, Lovejoy haphazardly tossed in abbreviations, compounds, and inventive punctuations. When Leopold left for Germany in 1935, Lovejoy wrote, "Damn iffen you aren't gettin professorish in your correspondence. And now Europe and so on. . . . well why not. Mebbe you can fetch back the low-down and USA significance of what they do over there. Can't get it from anything I ever saw to date. Go git 'em."[22]

Leopold always received a Lovejoy letter with a smile. Their correspondence was most intense in the early 1940s, right up until Lovejoy's death in 1942. In one letter after another, Lovejoy tried to refine a "formula" that explained the relationship of man to the environment, an effort that mostly gave him a chance to air his pent-up thoughts. Leopold enjoyed Lovejoy's communications, not only for their fanciful phraseology, but for the substance which lay within. Like Leopold, Lovejoy was able to talk both nuts-and-bolts conservation and abstract history with authority. Leopold once wrote to Lovejoy about cows, overgrazing, and the Rio Gavilan; Lovejoy wrote back about the war in Europe:

Might be a coming-up formula in what Churchhill (?) recently commented on (speaking of RAF) "Never before in all history so many people so indebted to so few". Well hell, iffen control of flying machines & men is control of all H-c affairs (as now seems to be), as that becomes clear we'll have a vastly potent new catylitic ? agent cutting in, won't we . . . & tending to make all other sorts of H-cs much-out-of-luck so as to force the query: What sorts do we *want,* when & where, how many etc.?

To replenish up th earth was the mandate until anticonception technic came along. What is the mandate now? There *isn't* any: ergo the current confusions — incl yours as to Cows, I take it. *My* query is as to whether the unsorted H-cs got savvy & guts enough to use cows (or anything) "in moderation" (for yet some Ms of years?). I figger they got to be pup-&-parlor-carpeted a long spell yet before they'll even start trying to be "consistently intelligent." It hurts & bothers too damn much (with the cortex arrangements what they currently are—or aren't).

There, you got a damn-nice dissertation on "cows in moderation."[23]

Leopold asked Lovejoy for comments on "A Biotic View of Land." Lovejoy, who never needed encouragement, wrote back at length on this "very large & important Sumpin." He concluded his letter with a clear insight into Leopold's development—and his own as well. "En route seems like as if you stray into various other slants & now & then into what is mostly (really?) poetry—i e more 'feeling' than 'thinking'. (Of course & why not? Me too. Could that be because both of us are mammal-critters but recently cephalized & functioning therein not too good & with the 'emotionals' often gumming up the 'rationals' as so often typical of Homo sap. behaviors? But anyway we 'like' and 'try' to use the cortex a la geometry, don't we? That's mebby sumpin—I hope."[24]

Lovejoy died on January 20, 1942. In an obituary that Leopold wrote for the *Journal of Wildlife Management,* he stated, "I believe that P.S. Lovejoy sired more ideas about men and land than any contemporary in the conservation field."[25] Many of those ideas ultimately reached the public through the pen of Aldo Leopold.

Even though Leopold was busily refining his philosophy, he did not bring it in its pure form into the classroom or the student conference. Seventy-nine enrolled in the farmers' course in February 1940. In March, forty signed up for Wildlife Ecology 118. He taught the courses as he always had. Bob McCabe remembers that Leopold "was not the type who revelled in having the unlearned sit at the feet of a sage who dropped pearls of wisdom. . . . Some of [his] students felt that he should have assumed the mantle of guru and discussed philosophy, especially the broad aspects of man's relationship to nature. But only rarely, and then only briefly, did he discuss philosophy as philosophy. . . . His students were to be trained as scientists, and if they succeeded, an appropriate philosophy would emerge and develop without his prompting."[26]

Leopold was indeed training scientists, but he realized that the times demanded new ideas about science, and some new definitions as well. While science and cultural values were converging in his own work, in the world at large they seemed to be growing apart. In March 1940, Leopold attended the Fifth North American Wildlife Conference, and the concurrently held annual meeting of the Wildlife Society. As president of the society, he delivered an address entitled "The State of the Profession." He stated openly, "We are not scientists. . . . A scientist in the old sense may have no loyalties except to abstractions, no affections except for his own kind." Not so in his own field. Even the most objective professional in wildlife had to admit an emotional attachment, of some sort, to wildlife and to the outdoors. And this led to respect. "The definitions of science written by, let us say, the National Academy, deal almost exclusively with the creation and exercise of power. But what about the creation and exercise of wonder, of respect for workmanship in nature?" That would require a renewed belief in the purposes of a humane science. "Our job," Leopold told his colleagues, "is to harmonize the increasing kit of scientific tools and the increasing recklessness in using them with the shrinking biotas to which they are applied. In the nature of things we are mediators and moderators, and unless we can help rewrite the objectives of science our job is predestined to failure."

"To change ideas about what land is for," Leopold said in conclusion, "is to change ideas about what anything is for."[27]

∽

The spring of 1940 came in on the wings of geese. In April, Leopold began to record, for the first time, the numbers of geese in the flocks he and his family observed. Spring also came in on the wings of herons, mallards, wood ducks, teal, ringnecks, cormorants, woodcock, red-tailed hawks, Cooper's hawks, mergansers, buffleheads, and sapsuckers. The spring planting trip was the family's fifth, and fifteen hundred more pines went into the ground. A pair of sandhill cranes trumpeted from hidden corners of the riverbottom. Aldo and Gus went out one daylight to investigate and found them in the neighbor's cornfield. "They flew out low, rattling the marsh with protest, and alighted in a brush marsh just west of Baxter's oak island."[28]

Through the summer and fall, the family visited the shack every weekend. Aldo was impatient to leave after his busy weeks at the office. It was Estella's responsibility to have the food and family ready to leave at the appointed hour. Sometimes, when dawdling delayed their departure, Aldo would simply bide his time in the car until the others were ready. During the growing season, he would trim the barberry hedge in front of the house ("When we saw Dad out trimming the hedge, we knew he was ready!").

Only two trips to Delta kept Leopold away from the shack that year. From June 24 to July 5, and again in mid-August, he went north to check in on Hochbaum and Sowls at the station. Leopold enjoyed his trips to the Manitoba marshlands as much as he enjoyed other, more classically "scenic" wildernesses he had known, and he always managed to put aside some time for exploration of the back bays and sloughs. The American Wildlife Institute that year approved Leopold's previous recommendation and funded Delta for three more years. Albert and his wife Joan took up permanent residence.

During his August visit to Delta, Leopold gave Hochbaum a draft copy of a new essay he had written, entitled "Escudilla." The essay was a recollection of his early days on the Apache National Forest, and of the demise of Old Bigfoot, the silver-tipped grizzly of Escudilla Mountain:

No one ever saw the old bear, but in the muddy springs about the base of the cliffs you saw his incredible tracks. Seeing them made the most hard-bitten cowboys aware of bear. Wherever they rode they saw the mountain, and when they saw the mountain they thought of bear. Campfire conversation ran to beef, *bailes,* and bear. Bigfoot claimed for his own only a cow a year, and a few square miles of useless rocks, but his personality pervaded the country.[29]

Prior to writing the essay, Leopold had cause to think about his early days in the Southwest on more than one occasion. His article on "Origins and Ideals of Wilderness Areas" had just been published in *Living Wilderness.* Earlier in the year he had received a letter from Gifford Pinchot, who was compiling his memoirs of the early Forest Service and asked for a contribution from Leopold. "Dear Chief," Leopold responded, "I applaud your proposal to write a history of the Service," adding, however, that "it is unlikely that any one book, even from your pen, will capture all the angles of the story, and perhaps a generation or two must elapse before its values can be truly weighed by anyone."[30] Then, in June 1940, Leopold received another letter, from John D. Guthrie via Fred Winn, asking for contributions toward a memorial in honor of Gustav Becker, a pioneer rancher on the Apache, a friend of the forest officers, and one who knew well Old Bigfoot and Escudilla. Leopold wrote the essay at about this time.

"Escudilla," like "Marshland Elegy," "The Thick-billed Parrot in Chihuahua," and the just-published "Song of the Gavilan," was writing of a different order than his technical, professional, and informational output. Leopold's lyrical voice had been present ever since he began writing, but until this point he had confined it largely to his journals, letters, and passages in more "purposeful" articles. Now he was going public. The response was favorable, even (and especially) from his scientific brethren. In reference to "Escudilla," Paul Errington wrote that "through these [writings] you make a contribution that I believe truly unique, that probably no other person could make."[31] Walter P. Taylor thought the essay "breathed the spirit of the true conservationist."[32]

Hochbaum was but one of several students with whom Leopold shared his preliminary drafts. He was unusually prolific in 1940, turning out two dozen articles, reviews, committee reports, and speeches. He did most of his work in his office in the quiet hours of the early morning, always writing in longhand, usually in pencil, on university-issue, blue-lined, yellow legal pads. His script had not changed much in thirty years; he still wrote in a small, neat, easily flowing hand. If the manuscript were not for immediate consumption, he slipped it into a portfolio in his Leopold desk (the "cooler") where it sat for weeks, months, sometimes even years before he removed it for further revisions. A painstaking editor of his own writing, he would erase and add, cut and paste, sometimes reworking a manuscript half a dozen times before slipping it back into the cooler or handing it over to Vivian Horn.

One day Leopold gave Horn a brief, six-paragraph essay entitled "Exit Orchis" to type. It told the story of a remnant prairie on the Faville Grove reserve that was about to be turned into pasture. Hawkins and McCabe had just spent the weekend transplanting some of the rare prairie plants to a safe haven. Leopold was struck by the fact that the Faville Grove land, "one of the largest and best remnants of unplowed, ungrazed prairie sod left in the state," might have been had for a twentieth of the cost it was taking to rebuild a small experimental prairie at the university arboretum. McCabe happened to be in the office while Horn was typing the essay. "Would you like to see," she asked, "what the boss wrote about your field trip?" He read it, and was surprised to find in his professor "a touch for literature; this was not the ordinary scribbling that a scientist would do. This comes from a mind that's quite different. Until now, he was just a major professor. This put a new light on the whole business."[33] McCabe took Leopold's rough draft out of the waste paper basket. Thinking that it might be worthwhile to save the originals, he asked Horn to keep them for him from then on.

The end of summer ushered in a new school year, beginning with a university-sponsored symposium on hydrobiology that brought together scientists from all corners of the campus, and from universities around the country. Leopold contributed a talk on "Lakes in Relation to Terrestrial Life Patterns." He might well have called it "A Biotic View of Land and Water," in that it extended the logic of his earlier synthesis: "Soil health and water health are not two problems, but one. . . . The recent history of biology is largely a disclosure of the importance of qualitative nutrition within plants and animals, and within land and water communities. Is it also important as between land and water? Does the wild goose, reconnoitering the farmer's cornfield, bring something more than wild music from the lake, take something more than waste corn from his field? Such questions are, for the moment, beyond the boundaries of precise knowledge, but not beyond the boundaries of intelligent speculation."[34]

The fall was rich in shack visits. Aldo and Carl had an autumnful of grouse and pheasant hunts, using the shack as basecamp for excursions into the tamarack swamps of Adams County. Clara Leopold (now eighty years old) and Aldo's sister Marie paid a visit in September. Carl and Dolores also came up from Burlington for a pheasant hunt. Gordon MacQuarrie, the *Milwaukee Journal*'s renowned outdoor reporter and a strong backer of Leopold, joined the family in October.

Winter was conference season for wildlife professionals. Leopold regularly attended two conferences: the Midwest Wildlife Conference, which usually met in December, and the North American Wildlife Conference, which met for the sixth time in February 1941. By now, Leopold was an elder statesmen in wildlife. His professional standing was unassailable, though some still considered him an impractical theorist (one joke in the Wisconsin Conservation Department offices involved the different ways of spelling this word "aesthetic" that Leopold used). Yet, for veterans and rookies alike, there was no better name to drop casually into postconference conversations. At the conferences, Leopold was not a jolly back-slapper. He enjoyed the meetings immensely, even though pressures grew on him year by year. In constant demand, often facing lines that literally formed to speak with him, he usually spent five or ten minutes with each individual, asking a few well-directed questions, offering suggestions, listening, always leaving his inquirer satisfied. When necessary, he could, as Frances Hamerstrom phrased it, "dismiss people painlessly." He always made an effort to introduce and include his own students in conversation with the notables, a tactic designed to accustom them to higher-level discussion.

Although Leopold was a deft reader of human nature, he had a definite blind spot when it came to the contrivances—almost always innocent— that some employed to gain his favor. Ernie Swift recalled that "people knew who Aldo Leopold was and they would try to make an effort to impress him. Something he might have an interest in, they would talk [about] with him, and some with complete sincerity. Lots of times they were trying to make an impression. Then afterwards, something would happen and he'd be terribly disappointed. It never even occurred to him that they were pulling his leg. . . . He couldn't understand human guile."[35]

∽

At the end of 1940, Leopold's student group underwent a turnover. Three of the students—Irven Buss, Lyle Sowls, and Bruce Stollberg, an undergraduate—took research positions in the Wisconsin Conservation Department, a sign of thawing in the department's previously frigid attitude toward the university and Leopold. Frederick and Fran Hamerstrom received their degrees in December and temporarily left Wisconsin to conduct research in Michigan. This left four students in the program: Hochbaum, Hanson, McCabe, and Thompson (several others worked with Leopold while pursuing majors in other departments). The question of the draft was beginning to affect inquiries and applications to the department. Before an uncertain future, potential wildlife students, like young people in all walks of life, were reluctant to make long-term commitments.

In December, Aldo and Estella went to Missouri to visit Starker and his wife Betty (who was pregnant with the family's first grandchild). Opportunities to see Starker and Luna came rarely now, once or twice a year at the most. Aldo conferred with Starker on the progress of his wild turkey field work. Starker and Betty returned to Madison for the holiday season, and joined the others on a foggy, thawing, after-Christmas weekend at the shack. Wisconsin's winters, far from deterring shack trips, only made for heightened drama, since winter sign was so plain to read. January 25: "Saw where a shrew killed a meadow-mouse near shack, ate his brain, and left him lie on the snow. Saw where a fox had dragged a rabbit down the creek to the mouth, where he entered a hole in the bank. Much rabbit hair and blood on drag."[36] On February 2, the family was banding birds when they caught, for the fourth consecutive year, chickadee #65287.

Leopold's involvement in the Wilderness Society intensified in early 1941. Robert Sterling Yard wrote to Leopold on February 6, trying to enlist Leopold's attendance at a joint meeting with the Izaak Walton League in Washington. Yard saw the meeting as a chance to solidify cooperation between the two organizations. "Another reason that appeals strongly to me is that you and I will get a chance to know each other a little better, and that you can see our office and meet some of our people."[37] Leopold's reply indicated his priorities. "I heartily approve of the idea, and still more so the opportunity for a visit with you. It is a question of time; that is, I have no alternate to turn my courses over to, and I insist on taking them seriously."[38]

A few days later, another issue arose. The latest edition of the *Saturday Evening Post* led off one of its articles with an account of Bob Marshall's communist connections. Marshall, anxious to keep the Wilderness Society free of implication, had maintained absolute silence about his politics in discussions with Yard and the others. Yard, one of the trustees of Marshall's will, was concerned about the effects of the *Post* disclosure. Marshall's brother George, identified in the article as "an orthodox Stalinist," still sat on the society's twelve-member council (along with Yard and Leopold). "I'm keeping my mouth shut," Yard wrote to Leopold. "But I need advice and shall be glad to know your thoughts, quite confidentially, if you should be moved to write me."[39]

Leopold's reply exemplified his refusal to bow, in any direction, to ideology:

I hadn't seen the *Post* article, nor did I ever have a political discussion with Bob Marshall. I had heard of his leaning, and his unlimited confidence in government ownership is visible in "The People's Forests." In my own dealing with Bob, he differed from others only in seeing, thinking, and speaking more clearly and sensibly than his fellows.

The fact that the *Post* calls George an "orthodox Stalinist" does not, of course, prove that he is, especially in the modern sense. I suspect both boys may have been Marxians rather than Stalinists—a very big distinction—and products of the "popular front" era when communism put on a respectable front to hide its more devious manipulations, and became outwardly indistinguishable from parlor socialism. (You doubtless know all this history, but if not, you will find it in "Out of the Night.")

Be that as it may, George's presence on the board need not hurt the Wilderness Trust; certainly my confidence would be unshaken as long as you and Olaus Murie are on the job. I wouldn't do anything; just see how George works out. If he devotes himself to the job and doesn't muddy the water, we needn't shy at political labels, especially those pinned on by the *Post*.[40]

Yard's next letter concerned more typical Wilderness Society matters. Lumber companies were taking advantage of prewar demands to go after virgin hardwood stands in Upper Michigan's Porcupine Mountains. Comprising some 140,000 acres, it was the last large area of hardwoods left in the Lake States. "If you have any ideas," Yard wrote to Leopold, "I will be glad to hear them."[41] Leopold responded a couple months later with a manuscript called "The Last Stand": "The sugar maple is as American as the rail fence or the Kentucky rifle. Generations have been rocked in maple cradles, clothed from maple spinning wheels, and fed with maple-sweetened cakes served on maple tables before maple fires. We still dance on maple floors. Yet the demise of the maple forest brings us less regret than the demise of an old tire. Like the shrew who burrows in maple woods, we take our environment for granted while it lasts."[42]

During these same weeks, Leopold summed up his ideas on the scientific value of wilderness in an article for *Living Wilderness* on "Wilderness as a Land Laboratory." Appearing twenty years after his first published article on wilderness preservation, it was a further measure of the distance he had traversed. Where in 1921, wilderness areas were needed for recreation, in 1941 recreation was "not their only or even their principal utility." First and foremost, wilderness was vital to "the science of land-health"; it offered "a base-datum of normality, a picture of how healthy land maintains itself as an organism."[43]

The science of ecology was beginning to yield insights into land health. Now, in the gloaming of war, Leopold turned to ecology for insights into the status of society as well. In March 1941, Wildlife Ecology 118 convened. Hitler's march through Europe had cast its shadow over the whole nation, bleakening in particular the college campuses. No one expected Hitler's expansionism to stop, and no one on campus, including the thirty-nine students and their professor in class that day, could avoid the fears at the back of their minds. Mindful of the atmosphere, Leopold walked into the lecture room, took his place at the rostrum, overlooked the new class, and launched into a prepared introductory lecture:

Ecology tries to understand the interactions between living things and their environment. Every living thing represents an equation of give and take. Man or mouse, oak or orchid, we take a livelihood from our land and our fellows, and give in return an endless succession of acts and thoughts, each of which changes us, our fellows, our land, and its capacity to yield us a further living. Ultimately we give ourselves.

That this collective account between the Earth and its creatures ultimately balances is implicit in the fact that both continue to live.

It does not follow, however, that each species continues to live. Paleontology is a book of obsequies for defunct species.

Man, for reasons sufficient to himself, would rather see than be one of the defunct.[44]

Leopold warmed to his topic. He defined war as "a disruption of the give and take equation. What, if anything, can ecology say about it? Not much, except by analogy with animals. Whether such analogies are valid is anybody's guess. I shall try to sketch the human enterprise, in its relation to war, as it now appears to me."[45] The students then heard a long, complex, fascinating discussion of what could only be termed "war ecology."

Leopold explained. Technology raises the land's carrying capacity for man; it increases man's "take," but it has so far ignored the "give," and further ignored the adjustments man forces onto other animals and plants. It has also assumed that man's "take" from the land, as well as human population, can be increased indefinitely. Technological innovation might very well continue to increase food supplies, but ecology teaches that food is not the only, or even the main, limitation on animal populations. Usually, some other limitation kicks in before food supplies are exhausted.

Not only had man's technological development suspended the "original" laws of carrying capacity; his ethical development had suspended the laws of predation. The two were interdependent. "Tools cannot be made or used without peace; peace cannot be sustained without tools, for men who are hungry, either for food or other necessities, automatically fight."[46]

To succeed in keeping the peace, ethics have to be mutually accepted. Sometimes this mutuality breaks down, resulting in a reversion to the "ancestral predatory order." The problem: each such reversion is more destructive than the last, due to advances in technology and social organization made during the interval.

The technologist seeks to bring peace through more technology, operating on the assumption that as the "take" is increased and standards of living are raised, ethics will rise accordingly. And should our neighbor lapse in his ethics, our accretions of technology in the meantime will help us in our defense against his predations.

Leopold doubted that this strategy would succeed in the long run. "Nations fight over *who shall take charge* of increasing the take and *to whom* the better life shall accrue. Even in peace-time the energies of mankind are directed not toward *creating* the better life, but toward *dividing* the materials supposedly necessary for it. From president to parlor-pink, from economist to stevedore, all are preoccupied with dividing the means rather than building the end. As for ethics, each seems to write his code to fit his material needs, rather than vice-versa."[47]

Declining to judge "this tragic dilemma," Leopold went straight to the root of the issue—the "soundness of the assumptions on which the whole modern structure is built. If science cannot lead us to wisdom as well as power, it is surely no science at all."[48] He granted the previous success of technology in raising carrying capacity and standards of living, but warned that "all ecology is replete with laws which begin to operate at a threshold, and cease operating at a ceiling. No one law holds good through the entire gamut of time and circumstances." Present world problems were a sign that man had exceeded, or approached too rapidly, a certain upper limit of population density. Continuing with the line of thought, Leopold traced its implications in regard to the course of science, the collapse of France, and the "illogical" calls by Hitler and Mussolini to their countrymen to increase their populations.

Leopold returned to his basic point: the assumption that better living made for higher ethics. He saw "much evidence against, as well as for, this universal thesis of technological culture. Perhaps ethics are too complex to follow automatically in the wake of newer Fords and shinier bathtubs."[49]

Leopold turned for hope to a further ecological principle. He cited the work of population geneticist Sewall Wright in support of the notion that the survival of a species depended, not on its day-to-day ups and downs, but on its ability to withstand infrequent catastrophes.[50] Species survive because certain individuals deviate from "normal" and are able to survive the unpredictable, abnormal catastrophic event. "I see in this," Leopold said, "an evolutionary mandate for individualism. Perhaps the deviations from physical and mental pattern which are tolerated in our social organization, but frowned upon or persecuted in more regimented societies, are an evolutionary 'safety device' which may one day determine our continuity."[51]

Half of the class must have wondered if they were in the right place. The other half were probably trying to make sense of their notes. All must have asked themselves what this had to do with bears, grouse, or rabbits. Leopold's detailed analysis was among his most ambitious flights of intellect, and in its argument one could see the influence of P. S. Lovejoy. In the end, the Professor did return to earth:

There can be no doubt that a society rooted in the soil is more stable than one rooted in pavements. Stability seems to vary inversely to the mental distance from fields and woods. The disruptive movements which now threaten the continuity of human culture are not born on the land where the take originates, but in the factories and offices where it is processed and distributed, and in the capitols where the rules of division are written. If courses like this one can decrease our mental distance from fields and woods, they are worth taking, and giving.[52]

After that, Leopold returned to his more usual teaching agenda. He and Estella became grandparents on April 13, when Betty Leopold gave birth to a son, Frederic Starker. The family spent their weekends at the shack. Nina came along less often now now that she was engaged to Bill Elder, a zoology student at the university. Spring planting proceeded at the end of April: seventeen hundred white, jack, and red pines. The woodcock began their peenting and sky dancing at 7:15 P.M. on April 23. The family transplanted more pasque flowers, and Dutchman's breeches, and blue phlox. In May Leopold noted, for the first time, the order of birdsong in the morning. It began with the wren and wood thrush at four o'clock, and ended with "about everything" half an hour later. The neighbor's tractor awoke, according to Leopold's notes, at five-thirty. The wildlife ecology class came up from Madison in May. To more easily explore the river's islands, sloughs, and far shore, Aldo acquired a boat. One morning in June, Aldo paddled upriver with Gus while the others slept, and noted two woodducks, one blue heron, one redtail, a kingfisher, and three muskrats. The next dawn, they went over to an island to survey pine reproduction. At the end of June, the weather was hot and sticky, the mosquitos were awful, the raspberry crop was the best ever, Nina and Estella found the first prothonotary warbler nest on the property, and young horned owls called from the woods at night.

～

Leopold flew to Manitoba on July 7, 1941, to confer with Miles Pirnie and William Rowan, the other members of the Delta Duck Station's Advisory Board. Under Hochbaum's leadership, the station in its three years of study had yielded important basic information on waterfowl breeding cycles, life histories, and population dynamics, and on prairie marsh ecology in general. Hochbaum and his crew, in fact, had *too much* new information; the board had hoped for a summary bulletin of research results, but there was so much to compile, and the marsh itself changed so quickly, that Hochbaum was not yet prepared to summarize his findings. Leopold wrote in his report to the AWI, "We know of no wildlife research venture which so far promises superior returns per unit of dollars, men, or years invested."[53]

For some time, Leopold and Hochbaum had spoken informally about working together on a book of essays, Aldo to provide the words, Albert the illustrations. Earlier in the year, Leopold thought that he might use the summer to get a start on it. He did produce one new essay, a hymn to the avian residents of Delta's Clandeboye Marsh: "Forester's terns, like troops of happy children, scream over the mudflats as if the first cold melt from the retreating ice sheet were shivering the spines of their minnowy prey. A file of sandhill cranes bugles defiance of whatever it is that cranes distrust and fear. A flotilla of swans rides the bay in quiet dignity, bemoaning the evanescence of swanly things."[54] By August 1941, plans for the collection of essays had become more definite and Hochbaum had agreed to do the drawings. They set no firm schedule; it was just something for both of them to keep in mind when their busy schedules provided a break.

After the Delta Station review, Leopold, as chairman of the American Wildlife Institute's Technical Committee, began a three-week swing through the West to inspect the progress of the Cooperative Wildlife Research Units in Utah and Oregon. On this trip, Leopold decided to keep a tally of hawk and owl sightings, thinking perhaps of the range-rodent situation he had investigated two years before. On July 19 he met his companions for the trip, Paul Miller of the AWI and Leo Couch of the U.S. Fish and Wildlife Service (which had recently taken over the work of the Biological Survey), in Kansas City.[55]

Their extensive itinerary took them across northern Colorado, in a wide loop around Utah as far south as the Kaibab Plateau, up to Logan, west across Nevada into northwest California, through southern Oregon and north to Portland. Beyond hawks and owls and research units, Leopold kept his eye on other western range phenomena. He lauded an effort to reintroduce beavers as a water-control technique at one refuge in eastern Utah. At the Modoc National Forest in Oregon he noted the invasion of the range by cheat grass, an exotic weed (after the trip he wrote an essay about it called "Cheat Takes Over").

What impressed Leopold most dramatically on the trip, however, was the deterioration of deer range in virtually every corner of the intermountain West. The bottom of Zion National Park's magnificent canyon was "badly chewed up by deer imprisoned within the canyon walls. Why not stock the canyon with a lion or two? The present efforts at trapping are expensive and feeble." At Fish Lake near Fillmore, Utah, the winter deer range was "as bad as the Kaibab in 1924." At Hart Mountain in Oregon, the aspen and mahogany showed the telltale high browsing line. At the Kaibab itself, Leopold got an on-site view of the aftermath of the 1920s' disaster. Although the range showed moderate signs of recovery, it was far from healthy, and current policy gave little indication that much had been learned from the past. "The trend of thought among administrators," Leopold reported, "is to regard the improved range conditions as good enough. The present objective is to *build up* the deer herd. I regard this trend as dangerous and unsound. That this actually is the present policy is proven by the fact that both lions and coyotes are now being officially controlled."[56] The old answer to the dilemma—that rifles would suffice to control deer numbers—was simply naive; Leopold recommended that the agencies deliberately maintain enough predators to stabilize big game herds.

The trip west brought home to Leopold the seriousness of the deer problem, which had been quietly worsening on ranges across the nation. Yet basic research on deer population ecology was only slightly more advanced than it had been when the Kaibab fiasco first came to light in 1924. In an effort to stimulate research, Leopold tried to arrange an interagency study of the deer "irruption" problem, but world events cut the effort short. The problem itself, however, remained. Within a year he would become deeply involved in it at home in Wisconsin.

Leopold returned to Madison on August 10. Over the summer, Vivian Horn, who for thirteen years had run Leopold's office, left Madison to find war-related work on the West Coast. Vivian, a woman of high principles, did not want to wait for war to break out before joining the effort. Her eventual replacement was Alice Harper, a cheery, outgoing young woman, who was as adept as Horn in running the office, but not quite so business-like. Although she had no background in biology, she soon became interested in wildlife, and possessed a remarkable understanding of Leopold and his work (unlike Vivian Horn, who displayed, to Leopold's utter bewilderment, "a perennial disinterest in natural history"). Taking to the job with enthusiasm, Alice worked more as an assistant than as a secretary, helping out in the classroom and assisting students with their writing. During her tenure with Leopold, Harper would in fact gain as thorough an education in wildlife as if she had signed on as a student herself.

On September 25, Nina Leopold married Bill Elder. It was one of the few instances in which Aldo consented to enter a church. Which was not to say that he was any more sympathetic toward the Church. Bill had to take the same vows Aldo had taken when he married Estella. As they discussed this at the dinner table one evening, Aldo let slip out one of his few open comments on the faith. He remarked that requiring the vow of noninterference from a man who was in love was "like selling a house to a drunk man."[57]

Meanwhile, the war loomed over the new academic year like a dark thunderhead. Just one new student arrived that fall. Joseph Hickey, a writer and ornithologist from New York City, came to Wisconsin to work with Leopold. Hickey was thirty-four years old; his 1-H draft classification meant that he would not be called up for immediate military duty. Hickey and Leopold knew one another through the Audubon Society, and although Hickey's specialty was ornithology, Leopold's only opening for funded research involved a soil conservation project in Wisconsin's driftless region. "I suspect we could sneak in some ecological research in the course of the travel which the position would entail," Leopold wrote to him.[58] Hickey began the work on November 1, the same day that Camp Madison, the Civilian Conservation Corps' base in the university arboretum, closed. The

CCCers were well-seasoned and ready for their change of environs; many went directly from the CCC camp to boot camp.

Leopold was busy with his pen that fall. Among his drafts were the first essays to draw directly on his family's experiences at the shack. One concerned the return of geese in spring: "Geese are a semi-annual reminder of the community of the Earth; if nations could share ideas as they share wind, sun, and geese, there would be less need of war, and a different concept of peace."[59] The other was a tribute to chickadee #65287: "That whimsical fellow called Evolution, having enlarged the dinosaur until he tripped over his own toes, tried shrinking the chickadee until he was just too big to be snapped up by flycatchers as an insect, and just too little to be pursued by hawks and owls as meat. Then he regarded his handiwork, and laughed. Everyone laughs at so small a bundle of large enthusiasms."[60] He sent these off to Hochbaum for review.

By the end of November, Leopold was beginning to think more seriously about some sort of book. The original idea took a new turn when Harold Strauss, an editor at Knopf, approached Leopold independently with an idea for "a good book on wild-life observation . . . a personal book recounting adventures in the field."[61] Leopold wrote back to endorse the idea, suggesting that it would best be handled by a team of wildlife professionals. "I doubt if there is any one person who could cover the territory I have in mind," Leopold wrote.[62] Strauss responded favorably. Leopold wrote back to say that he was willing to act as a leader for such a team, but that he had no time. He recommended Joe Hickey. Strauss replied that "with all due respects to Mr. Hickey, it would be an inestimable advantage to us to have your name on the published book."[63] Leopold wrote back again, bowing out of the project because he was "focusing my effort on a series of ecological essays, illustrated, as a Christmas book for next year. The M.S. is well along. Are you interested by any chance?"[64] Strauss replied that he was "emphatically interested . . . so much interested that I am not inclined to wait until the manuscript is altogether finished. Won't you send me whatever material is in shape?"[65]

One of the highlights of the Seventh Midwest Wildlife Conference that December was Leopold's address on "Wildlife in American Culture," an analysis of the values provided by wildlife and outdoor recreation. Leopold spoke of the "split-rail value" of outdoor experiences. There is value, he proposed, in any experience which "stimulates our awareness of American history. Such awareness is 'nationalism' in its best sense." There is value as well "in any experience which reminds us of our dependency on the soil-plant-animal-man food chain." In one of his most memorable sentences, Leopold noted, "We fancy that industry supports us, forgetting what supports industry." Third, outdoor experiences teach, in a way that economics never can, the value of using tools gently. The only way to avoid the destructive use of land, Leopold proposed, "is to extend our system of ethics from the man-man relation to the man-earth relation. . . . Any experience which stimulates this extension of ethics is culturally valuable."[66] Leopold then discussed at length the status of sport and sportsmanship in America, a topic much on his mind after several particularly irksome experiences with hunters at the shack during that fall's duck season.

At the end of his talk, Leopold added an extra section recalling his complicated class lecture of the previous spring. Wildlife population patterns, he suggested, offered insights into our own human social patterns. Human processes were, of course, quite different from those of lower animals, but it was conceivable that by observing animal populations we might find "analogues to our own problems. The ability to perceive these analogues, and to perceive them critically, is the woodcraft of the future." He cited the rabbit population cycle. The rabbit knows nothing of cycles, he explained, and studying individual rabbits reveals nothing of cycles. We know of cycles only through large-scale studies of rabbits through time. "This raises the disquieting question: do human populations have behavior patterns of which we are unaware, but which we help to execute? Are mobs and wars, unrests and revolutions, cut of such cloth?"[67]

History provided an answer of sorts. The day after the conference ended, the Japanese attacked Pearl Harbor.

Carl Leopold enlisted in the Marines the following day. He had just begun graduate studies in Missouri, and turned twenty-two later that month. Of the three sons, he was destined to become most deeply involved in the war.

In the weeks before Christmas, Aldo continued to write prolifically. He revised the conference address and wrote a new essay called "Odyssey," in which he described the structure of the biotic pyramid from the perspective of wandering atoms. He had to revise his essay on "65287"; on December 13, Aldo and Estella were at the shack with young Estella and a friend when they caught chickadee #65290. 65290 thus superseded 65287 as the chickadee with the longest tenure at the shack, the only one ever to survive into a fifth year after banding.

On December 23, Leopold arrived at the office at his usual early hour. The winter solstice was just past, so dawn was still some hours away. Sitting at his desk, he removed an essay from the cooler, a discussion of environmental perception that he called "Country." He worked on that one for a while, then turned over a new sheet of his blue-lined legal pad, and began writing a new essay:

Empires spread over the continents, destroying the soils, the floras and faunas, and each other. Yet the trees grow.

Philosophies spread over the empires, teaching the good life with tank and bomb. Machines crawl over the empires, hauling goods. Goods are plowed under, or burned. Goods are hawked over the ether, and along lanes where Whitman smelled locust blooms morning and evening. Quarrels over goods are planted thick as trees along all the rivers of America. The offal of goods floats down the rivers, settles in the swimming holes. Fish choked with goods float belly-up in the shallows. Dykes to grow goods dry up the waterfowl. Dams to make goods block the salmon runs, but not the barges carrying goods. Railroads carrying goods race the barges. Trucks carrying goods race the railroads. Cars carrying consumers of goods race the trucks. Yet the trees grow.

A folklore of goods fills the curricula. Farmers learn the farm is a factory. Chemists and physicists harness power, biology harnesses plants and animals, all for goods. Politics is the redistribution of goods. Literature and the arts portray the drama of the haves and have-nots. Research is not to decipher the universe, but to step up production. Yet the trees grow.

The rains which fall on the just and unjust wash silt from the factory-farms. The brooks that make the meadows green feed silt to the rivers. The vales, lying in pensive quietness between, feed silt to the brooks. The hills, rock-ribbed and ancient as the sun, feed silt to the vales. Yet the trees grow.[68]

Alice Harper typed up the essay, and Aldo put it back into the cooler to gather time.

Carl Leopold, with great horned owl, in Madison, about 1939 (Bradley Study Center Files)

Nina Leopold, prepared for a weekend at the shack, about 1937 (Bradley Study Center Files)

Estella Leopold playing in the Wisconsin River, about 1936. The "Parthenon" is in the background (Bradley Study Center Files)

Luna and Starker on a rabbit hunt, 1937 (Bradley Study Center Files)

Art Hawkins, Alice Harper, and Leopold in front of the University of Wisconsin Department of Wildlife Management offices at 424 University Farm Place in Madison, about 1942 (Courtesy A. Hawkins)

Leopold at his desk in "424," with Gus at his side (Photo by R. McCabe. Leopold Collection, UW Archives)

Bob McCabe, Flick, and Leopold after a woodcock hunt in 1946 (Leopold Collection, UW Archives)

Leopold and Albert Hochbaum, about 1942 (Bradley Study Center Files)

Leopold with Frederick (imitating the Professor's stance) and Frances Hamerstrom, 1939 (Courtesy Frances Hamerstrom)

Leopold in 1946 (Leopold Collection, UW Archives)

Leopold and students prepare a restored prairie for burning at the University of Wisconsin Arboretum, about 1945 (*left to right:* Pepper Jackson, Leopold, James Hale, Mary Ellen Helgren) (Bradley Study Center Files)

Leopold at the testimonial dinner for E. Sydney Stephens in St. Louis, in 1947, shortly before his surgery for tic douloureux. *Left to right:* Robert A. Brown, Leopold, Jay "Ding" Darling, Stephens, and Edward K. Love (Leopold Collection, UW Archives)

A meeting of Wilderness Society councillors in 1946 at Old Rag Mountain, Virginia. *Left to right:* Harvey Broome, Benton MacKaye, Leopold, Olaus Murie, Irving Clark, George Marshall, Laurette Collier, Howard Zahniser, Ernest Oberholtzer, Harold Anderson, Charles Woodbury, Robert Griggs, Ernest Griffith, and Bernard Frank (Courtesy the Wilderness Society)

Leopold with graduate students at the shack, early summer 1947. *Left to right:* Bruce S. Wright, Donald R. Thompson, Leopold, James R. Beer, Steven H. Richards, Clifford Bakkom (kneeling) (Photo by R. McCabe. Leopold Collection, UW Archives)

Leopold measuring red pines at the shack, 1946 (Photo by R. McCabe. Leopold Collection, UW Archives)

A family gathering at the shack, 1940. *Clockwise from top left:* Aldo, Estella, Luna, Starker, Gus, Estella Jr., Nina. Carl Leopold, missing from the photo, was the photographer (Bradley Study Center Files)

Leopold preparing journal notes at shack, 1946 (Bradley Study Center Files)

19

Land Use and Democracy
(1942–1945)

LEOPOLD acknowledged that, in wartime, conservation seemed like "a milk-and-water affair." Viewed from another angle, though, war defined the issue. "If America is here to stay," Leopold said at a seminar in 1942, "she must have healthy land to live on, for, and by. Hitler's taunt that no democracy uses its land decently, while true of our past, must be proven untrue in the years to come."[1]

Shortly after the United States entered the war, he wrote an article for *Audubon* magazine entitled "Land Use and Democracy," in which he again took up the theme of the individual's role in conservation. Leopold still doubted the effectiveness of government programs as a cure-all for land-use ills. He did note the "real and indispensable" functions of government in conservation: "Government is the tester of fact vs. fiction, the umpire of bogus vs. genuine, the sponsor of research, the guardian of technical standards, and, I hasten to add, the proper custodian of land which, for one reason or another, is not suited to private husbandry. These functions will become real and important as soon as conservation begins to grow from the bottom up, instead of from the top down, as is now the case."[2]

Leopold had a Jeffersonian faith in democracy: the only sure cure for democracy's ills was still more democracy. Simply put, if citizens wished to avoid the undue imposition of government, then they had to assume responsibility for conservation on an individual basis. Leopold's position was still determined, as it had always been, by a combination of practical necessity and his own stubborn brand of conservatism. Government actions, necessary though they were, no matter how good they were, could not stem the tide of land abuse. "One of the curious evidences that 'conservation programs' are losing their grip," Leopold wrote, "is that they have seldom resorted to self-government as a cure for land abuse. 'We who are about to die,' unless democracy can mend its land-use, have not tried democracy as a possible answer to our problem."³ To Leopold, "trying democracy" meant adopting "a simple formula by which we, and posterity, may act to make America a permanent institution instead of a trial balloon. The formula is: learn how to tell good land-use from bad. Use your own land accordingly, and refuse aid and comfort to those who do not. Isn't this more to the point than merely voting, petitioning, and writing checks for bigger and better bureaus, in order that our responsibilities may be laid in bigger and better laps?"⁴

Education and individual responsibility in land-use decisions remained the keys to good husbandry, and good husbandry was "the heart of conservation." Leopold also proposed a new tactic: consumer boycott. Discriminating consumers, he suggested, could actively seek out goods—milk, lumber, paper, wheat—that were produced by conscientious landowners. He had no illusions that "hitching conservation directly to the producer-consumer relation" would be easy, but it was important if for no other reason than that it allowed the city dweller and non-landowner to take direct action. Anxious to avoid political overtones, he explained that boycott as a conservation measure "may be radical in the sense of being new, but not in any other sense. Its political complexion is of a much paler hue than the now universal policy of laying all conservation problems in the lap of government."⁵

Leopold was self-critical enough to know that those who did not share his interests or experience were unlikely to adopt his own high standards of conservation. He made a positive point of this. His "formula" for effective conservation presented "an intellectual gradient suitable for all ages and all degrees of land-use education. No one person, young or old, need feel any obligation to act beyond his own personal range of vision."⁶

Leopold's personal range of vision was abnormally broad, and his sense of obligation proportionately strong. As a teacher, writer, landowner, and public official, Leopold would continue to work during the war years toward a wider public appreciation of land health and the issues it entailed. One particularly volatile issue—deer management—would embroil Leopold in a bitter debate that would make plain the difficulties involved in "trying democracy" as a solution to complex conservation problems.

"Culture is a state of awareness of the land's collective functioning," Leopold wrote at the end of "Land Use and Democracy." "A culture premised on the destructive dominance of a single species can have but short duration."⁷ That lesson from ecology spoke to the war effort as well as the conservation effort.

☙

Nowhere were the effects of war felt as pervasively as on the college campuses. Many of Leopold's present and former students entered the military immediately. Attendance in Wildlife Ecology 118 in the spring of 1942 was thirty-one, the third consecutive year of decline since a high of forty-five in 1939. In March, Leopold presented a special seminar on "German Ecology." The Oberlaender Trust, the group that had sponsored Leopold's 1935 trip to Germany, turned its attention to aiding displaced Jews and other German refugees. The secretary of the trust wrote to Leopold and the other forestry fellows to assure them that "we are following the same policies that were laid down in 1930–1931, long before this present situation arose."[8]

Leopold felt the effects as well in his personal life. After enlisting in the Marines, Carl came home to Madison in January to await his call. With his background as a geologist and civil engineer, Luna was offered commissions in the Navy and the Marines, but chose to enlist in the Army. After boot camp, he applied for training in the Army's meteorology division. Starker continued his graduate studies while awaiting his draft notice.

In the early months of 1942, Leopold devoted much of his time to editorial work on Albert Hochbaum's initial Delta Duck Station Bulletin. Headstrong and independent, Hochbaum had chosen an unconventional format for his report. Leopold expected a concise summary of the station's scientific accomplishments; Hochbaum envisioned a full, book-length portrayal of the marsh and its wildlife, illustrated with his own pen-and-ink drawings, focusing on the life history and ecology of the canvasback duck. He had already published two papers, including a classic report on sex and age determination of waterfowl, that he felt satisfied for the time being his obligations to the AWI. Now he turned to the canvasback project, intent on doing it his own way. In his defense, Hochbaum could quote Leopold's own original 1938 report to the AWI on the Delta project, which emphasized the "freedom of action" and "independence from pre-existing commitments" that the station enjoyed. Albert had taken that statement to heart when he accepted the Delta assignment, and he was prepared to stand up for it.

Leopold's stake in the project was great. Not only did he oversee Delta in an official capacity, but he had a deep attachment to the area and to Hochbaum himself. His determination to have Hochbaum produce a major publication would run head on into Hochbaum's determination to take the time to do it right. Leopold scrutinized the work with extra care. It was not an easy process for either of them. In one of the many letters that passed between them, Leopold admitted that "after a long and difficult session, my notes may show irritation, and I am afraid that after receiving the results you may feel hurt or otherwise frustrated. If we allow these little things to get the best of us, we might conceivably end up in an impasse. These little things are of absolutely no importance in comparison with our joint obligation to get the thing out."[9]

Leopold's passion for excellence in writing was easier to understand when discussed gently over his desk. By mail, with Hochbaum on the other end, the Professor's suggestions were not so clear. They jousted continually in their letters. Hochbaum: "Your comments leave me trying to say a thing as you would say it; the result is a hybrid organization that pleases neither one of us." Leopold: "I am considerably disturbed over the 'hybridizing' of styles. You may be entirely right, although I am unaware of it. . . . In such cases, I urge you to take the bit in your teeth and go your own way." Hochbaum: "I don't understand the downward trend [of your criticisms] of the paper from 'minor adjustments' of last January and 'microscopic revisions' of October, to large sections now entirely 'dead.'"[10] Overshadowing their bickering was the possibility that war might curtail the Delta research altogether. In March, the AWI provided continued funding for Delta, but on a reduced budget.

Delta's uncertain status was typical of wildlife research work during the war. Looking ahead to the North American Wildlife Conference in Toronto, Leopold wrote to AWI President Frederic Walcott on March 13, 1942, and explained his view of the war's effect on the profession:

Wildlife research in general is going to take an awful beating from the war. A severe shrinkage of programs is not only inevitable, but in my opinion desirable and proper. But there is a distinction between shrinkage and continuance. . . . Delta, I think, is a case in point. I, for one, would feel embarrassed to have Delta continue on the usual scale, but on the other hand, I would feel foolish to have Delta blow up, except under absolute pressure of compulsion. Looking now at the broader field, I think all research undertakings should shrink and shrink heavily, and it might even be good for them to do so provided the occasion be utilized for a vigorous weeding of ideas, personnel, and projects. On the other hand, the actual death of the Institute program would seem to me a very dubious brand of patriotism.[11]

That, in general, was the path that the AWI followed at Delta and at other research facilities around the country during the war.

At the Wildlife Conference, held April 8–10, Leopold spoke to the same point. His address, entitled "The Role of Wildlife in a Liberal Education," summarized the thoughts on education that he had been developing over the previous five years. The war, he emphasized, had not affected the need for education. "Wildlife teaching for laymen has the same war status as any other branch of science or of the arts," he proposed. "To suspend teaching is to suspend culture."[12]

The conference was sandwiched in between that spring's planting trips to the shack. A fire the previous November had singed many of the pines, but not fatally. (Leopold's sharp senses might have made him a good private eye; in his journal he noted that "the fire must have escaped from a rabbit or deer hunter. A bench had been moved and an iron nut was lying on the lawn, indicating somebody parked car in yard and probably ate lunch here.")[13] The planting crew that year consisted of Aldo, Estella, Carl, Estella Jr., the Colemans, and a Burlington contingent of three. They put in seventeen hundred more pines, junipers, and cedars. On April 12, a flock of five hundred Canada geese ("the largest I ever saw") flew upriver. The woodcock started peenting that night "at 8:01 pm war time."[14] Carl Leopold's call came in May. On June 1, he left Madison to begin officer training at the Marines' Quantico base.

The effect of wartime needs on wilderness soon became a crucial matter for conservationists. Robert Sterling Yard wrote to Leopold to gain his views. "I don't think we can protest the logging of special timber on wilderness areas," Leopold wrote back, "provided of course that the Forest Service certifies that the need is legitimate, and cannot be effectively met elsewhere. I think we well might, however, suggest that the roads thus opened be later destroyed or at least kept closed to public traffic."[15] If the nation's remaining wilderness had to be sacrificed, Leopold would argue, let it be as a last resort; if such wilderness was seen as fair game for exploitation now that a war was on, then it called into question, for Leopold at least, the very motivations behind the war. Yard informed Leopold of a federal plan to employ the interned Japanese-Americans in California to build a road through the Sierra Nevada. The civil rights issue notwithstanding, Leopold replied, "If we can think of nothing better to do with interned Japs than to ruin wilderness areas, then I think we are intellectually bankrupt. If this is really a serious proposal, you can count on me to do some tall fighting."[16]

The question came home back in the Midwest, where Leopold continued to speak out on behalf of the Porcupine Mountains in Michigan. His article "The Last Stand" appeared in the May 1942 edition of *Outdoor America*. He continued to write letters to the Michigan Department of Conservation to push for protection. He gathered support for bills before Congress to purchase the area. On June 25, he gave a public talk on the predicament. Roy Matson, one of Madison's prominent journalists, reported on Leopold's presentation in the *Wisconsin State Journal*:

> In this tragic era, anybody welcomes a few moments in which he figures he may lean back and listen to something far removed from death and destruction.
> You may figure to do that when Aldo Leopold, the man of the peaceful forest, the Professor of Wildlife Management at the University of Wisconsin, begins to speak. But instead, you hear, as I heard the other day:
> "I have come to report on an impending death, the end of an epoch, the fall of a great symbol."
> Then the lights go out and you see pictures as Mr. Leopold talks, pictures to break your heart, the picture of "The Last Stand."

Matson quoted Leopold as saying that Congress had hesitated to buy the imperiled forest, "fearing catcalls from patriotic constituents who assume that all internal problems can wait. Most of them doubtless can and should, but not this one. The war surely will outlast this remnant of forest." Matson quoted Leopold further. "A state law requires conservation education in Wisconsin, but how far will we get teaching democracy to youth if we [don't] have the remnants of [wilderness] with which to demonstrate? We need this sample of the unspoiled to keep alive the spirit of discontent in the minds of generations to come."[17]

Later that summer, the point was amply demonstrated during a canoe trip on the Flambeau River in northern Wisconsin. Ernie Swift had invited Leopold, Joe Hickey, and three others to join him on the trip. Swift was trying to rally support for state action to preserve a portion of the river in its wild state. The Flambeau forest was a magnificent remnant of the original northwoods. "Here," Leopold wrote in a subsequent essay, "the cream of the white pine grew on the same acres with the cream of the sugar maple, yellow birch, and hemlock." After dinner on the second day of their float, they met two college boys on the river who were plainly having the time of their lives. During a riverbank chat, they learned that the boys were slated for induction into the Army after their trip. "Now the *motif* was clear," Leopold wrote. "This trip was their first and last taste of freedom, an interlude between two regimentations: the campus and the barracks. The elemental simplicities of wilderness travel were thrills not only because of their novelty, but because they represented complete freedom to make mistakes. The wilderness gave them their first taste of those rewards and penalties for wise and foolish acts which every woodsman faces daily, but against which civilization has built a thousand buffers. These boys were 'on their own' in this particular sense. Perhaps every youth needs an occasional wilderness trip, in order to learn the meaning of this particular freedom."[18]

As Leopold's own students entered the war, they began a round robin letter to keep themselves informed of one another's activities during the war. The package of letters travelled around the country and out to sea several times during the three years of its existence. One of the first letters Leopold received came from Bruce Stollberg, who entered the Navy in early 1942. On board his ship, he kept a record of migrating birds that stopped for a rest. He wrote to the Professor, "I miss the land and wildlife study very much, and only now realize how much they meant to me. I don't worry too much about the future, however, since at times the odds are pretty good that I won't have one."[19]

 ᔕ

In the spring of 1942, the Wisconsin Conservation Department experienced a shake-up that angered many of the state's leading conservationists. At the same time, field observations were confirming what Leopold and others had long feared: that in the northern part of the state, deer were threatening to overpopulate their range, and in some areas already had. As events unfolded, these two developments, the biological and the political, merged. Aldo Leopold would find himself caught thoroughly in the crossfire.

Standard political chicanery had caused the problems in the Wisconsin Conservation Department.[20] Governor Julius P. Heil, no friend of conservation, was determined to remove WCD Director H. W. MacKenzie from his position. The 1927 law that established the WCD placed the power to appoint and remove the director in the hands of the six-man Conservation Commission. The intent of the provision was to prevent precisely such actions as Heil wanted to take, but the governor still had his way. He was able to appoint four new commissioners whose collective fitness for the job was dubious at best. On May 23, the newly constituted Conservation Commission "discharged" MacKenzie. Heil protested in public that he supported MacKenzie, but would abide by the decision of his commissioners.

The state's conservation organizations were outraged. The Wisconsin Conservation League, an association of local groups that came together in 1940 to replace the state's faltering chapter of the National Wildlife Federation, held a meeting in early June to take action. Many of the league's officers were veterans of the Izaak Walton League campaigns of the 1920s (Leopold served as a member-at-large of the executive committee). The WCL had privately cursed Heil from the outset of his term. When Heil's plans became plain, the WCL and its president, Lou Radke, came out in open opposition. MacKenzie's dismissal was the final straw. On June 7, the Conservation League met in Madison, called for Heil's ouster in the upcoming election, adopted a twelve-point reform program, and passed a resolution requesting that Wisconsin's three major political parties (Republican, Democrat, and Progressive) nominate MacKenzie for governor. Heil was a Republican, as were most of Wisconsin's conservation leaders. That, however, was about all they had in common. As the summer wore on, Heil found himself caught in his own trap, and subsequently lost his political and public support. The *Sheboygan Press* editorialized: "Conservation, once lost, cannot be restored in your time or mine. This is why the issue is greater than party. That is why the Governor finds himself alone with those who have no heart for conservation."[21]

Leopold was still ultrasensitive to the muddying of conservation by politics. He was certainly no admirer of Governor Heil. On the other hand, he shed no tears when MacKenzie left the Conservation Department. MacKenzie was a game man of the old school, and for years had stifled cooperation between the department and the university out of contempt for Leopold and his program. "Under MacKenzie's administration," Leopold wrote to a friend, "the policy toward the University had been one of rigid isolation."[22] In Leopold's view, MacKenzie's dismissal had taken place for all the wrong reasons—not for his stubborn resistance to new ideas or for his turbulent style of administration, but for his political stance. Furthermore, "the fact remains that he was let out without charges, which is a serious weakness in the anti-MacKenzie strategy." Even MacKenzie, apparently, had a right to a fair hearing.

If Leopold felt no sympathy for the two parties to the dispute, neither did he side with his fellow conservationists who stood on the sidelines. On June 10, Leopold resigned from his official position in the Wisconsin Conservation League. He wrote to Radke, "I cannot go along on the decision [to oppose Heil] because it seems to me to be injecting both personalities and politics into the League's program." Radke protested that "the conservationists of this state are sick and tired of petting the dog that constantly bites us," but he understood Leopold's position, and accepted the resignation.[23]

The fall election approached. The Democrats were actually considering running MacKenzie for governor, a ploy that Bill Aberg (himself a Conservation Commissioner since 1939) interpreted as "a thinly veiled effort to exploit conservation for political purposes."[24] The Republicans, meanwhile, had split into factions. In the end, it was a Progressive, Orland Loomis, who defeated Heil. Loomis, however, died prior to his inauguration and was succeeded by octogenarian Lieutenant Governor Walter Goodland, a Republican with close ties to Leopold's friend Tom Coleman. It was Goodland who later, in June 1943, appointed Leopold to the Wisconsin Conservation Commission.

As the political seas calmed, the Conservation Commission chose a new director for the department, Edward J. Vanderwall. Leopold's relationship with the Conservation Department was on the upswing. Aberg was chairman of the Conservation Commission. Ernie Swift was deputy director of the department. Another friend, Walter Scott, was supervisor of the Cooperative Game Management Section. And Vanderwall had to be better than MacKenzie, at least from Leopold's vantage point (in fact, their relationship would prove to be both smooth and productive).

Obscured by the storm in Madison were the objects of all this rancor— the state's forests, waters, soils, wildlife. By summer's end, interest had focussed on one topic in particular: white-tailed deer. Few public issues in the state were as explosive as deer policy. Especially in the northern part of the state, where the herd was then concentrated, deer were woven into the fabric of daily life. Deer were (and remain) a venerated totem, a symbol of the northwoods wildness, the most familiar expression of its rustic character. Everybody loved deer. The tourists wanted to see them, in abundance. The resort owners wanted them because they drew tourists, in abundance. The sportsman wanted to pursue them. The trophy hunter wanted the biggest and best of them. The only people who could possibly object to superabundant deer were gardeners, a handful of wildlife researchers, and foresters (deer, after all, had to eat). But foresters still knew very little about deer management. Game wardens, for that matter, knew little more. Understanding of deer in the early 1940s was about where understanding of waterfowl had been in the late 1920s: long on opinions and short on facts.

As Wisconsin's northern forestlands gradually recovered from the denudation of earlier decades, the deer herd rose proportionately. Aided by strict law enforcement, predator bounties, refuges, closed seasons, and fire protection, the deer thrived. By 1930, as Leopold was compiling his game surveys, the deer were gaining in population and expanding their range south into the central sand counties. As the forests continued to mature, the conditions under which the deer prospered shifted. Browse plants changed in abundance and distribution. The forest trees grew taller, and the canopy closed over. Important winter browse areas—especially the lowland white cedar "yards" where deer congregated during deep snow—came under greater pressure from both man and deer. Predators were conspicuous mainly by their absence. Lions were long gone. Coyotes had an indeterminate effect on deer. As for wolves, Leopold estimated that there were only a dozen left in the state by the late 1930s.

Reports of deer starvation and range damage had come in intermittently since 1930, but it was not until 1940 that serious study began on the deer situation.[25] MacKenzie's Conservation Department, ever reluctant to conduct basic habitat research, finally got into the act when threatened by a loss of Pittman-Robertson funds. The department authorized a deer research project, to be conducted under William Feeney, who until 1940 had worked as a biologist for the National Park Service and the CCC on the university arboretum. As such, he and Leopold had become good friends. Feeney immediately began surveying browse conditions in the northern winter deer yards. In the first season of the survey, the winter of 1940–1941, he and his six-man crew investigated eighty-one yards, and found substantial evidence of escalating deer populations: vegetation damage, starving deer, and high fawn mortality in the worst hit yards. A second winter of observation confirmed the findings.[26]

Convincing the public and the state officials that there was a real problem on the deer ranges would prove to be a long, frustrating task. The game wardens in the field distrusted Feeney and his men; they had a proprietary interest in the herd that they had worked so hard to build up and protect from harsh winters and poachers. They knew their territories and were not about to defer to experts from Madison who came north for a few weeks and told them about the condition of their range. Feeney's style did not help. He had his own way of performing his work and saw no need to enlist the support of the local wardens and rangers. Through the chaotic summer of 1942, as the MacKenzie row was blowing the top off the Conservation Department, discontent with Feeney's deer survey was filtering up from the field force below.

The Conservation Commission responded to Feeney's findings by appointing a nine-member Citizen's Deer Committee in September 1942. Leopold was named chairman (probably through Bill Aberg's influence). The committee was asked to conduct its own independent evaluation of the deer situation that winter, and to prepare a report by the following spring.

Shortly after Leopold's appointment, he was asked by his friend Bill Schorger to chair yet another committee. Schorger was currently serving a term as president of the Wisconsin Academy of Sciences, Arts, and Letters, and was eager to increase the academy's involvement in conservation. In this official capacity, he asked Leopold for suggestions. In his reply of October 2, Leopold wrote that "the most important single problem, and the one least likely to receive adequate attention, is the deterioration of the northern forests by excess deer. . . . The function of the Academy is probably not to write a remedial program, but to suggest the research on which it should be based."[27] On November 6, Schorger appointed Leopold chair of a new Committee on Natural Resources for the Wisconsin Academy, and named Norman Fassett and geologist Ernest Bean as the other members. The new committee met a few weeks later and formally decided to address the deer issue.

This left Leopold with the task, as chairman of both committees, of defining and dovetailing their separate chores. The situation called for current field information as well as general historical evidence, and Leopold had definite plans for collecting both. The academy committee, as he saw it, could not "and should not try to assess the Wisconsin situation in detail, for its knowledge of field conditions is second hand. The function of the Academy stops when it deduces from history the important *principles* to be used in arriving at a judgement."[28] The WCD Citizen's Deer Committee, on the other hand, was to address the Wisconsin situation specifically. Leopold arranged a January meeting of the latter committee and made plans with Feeney to conduct a late winter on-site tour of the northern deer yards. Leopold also concluded that both committees needed, "as a 'jumping-off place,' a history of excess deer problems in other states."[29] He proposed that the academy committee (meaning he personally) write such a history and offer it to the Conservation Department for use as they saw fit. "Unless there is objection," Leopold wrote, "I will proceed with a rough draft. This may take me several months. I am not visualizing a technical or lengthy document, but I do visualize one drawn with such care as to be unchallengeable as to facts."[30]

Leopold's determination was clear, and obviously came from a personal sense of obligation. He had learned the hard lessons of deer overpopulation, passed through the necessary preliminary stages of understanding, and encompassed the issue on a conceptual level; he was not going to allow Wisconsin's deer herd and forests to go the way of Pennsylvania, and the Kaibab, and Germany. The issue presented political problems, but he knew that it was a biological time bomb. He was committed to the task of turning around deer policy in Wisconsin.

Meanwhile, life was settling into its wartime circumstances. The fall of 1942 was the quietest the Leopold home had ever seen. Carl married Keena Rogers in October, before going into combat, leaving fifteen-year-old Estella the only child at home. Aldo took her on her first pheasant hunts that fall. Gas rationing cut the frequency of shack visits in half, beginning in October. The family's trips ceased altogether over the winter, as they conserved their gas coupons for more regular visits come spring.

The tire shortage forced cancellation of field studies at Riley and Faville Grove. For the time being, Leopold confined his personal research interests to the pheasant population at the arboretum and to the fifteen-year backlog of Prairie du Sac census data, which he and Paul Errington had planned to work into a paper. Joe Hickey finished his study of soil conservation in southwestern Wisconsin, and then left for the University of Chicago to work on chemical warfare research. Irv Buss briefly returned to the department to write his pheasant thesis, and then joined the Navy.

Bob McCabe completed his master's degree requirements that same fall. He had volunteered for the Army and the Navy, but they had turned him down for medical reasons. Usually, when a student completed his work, Leopold asked the student to come into his office for a discussion of employment possibilities. It was not a meeting McCabe looked forward to. He had grown fond of the Professor as a friend and mentor, and since he was unable to enter the military, he wanted to remain with Leopold at the university. They made some small talk until Leopold finally asked him what he wanted to do. McCabe replied, "I want to stay with you." Leopold had not considered such an option. After a long pause, he finally answered, "All right, I do need an assistant."[31] McCabe would remain with Leopold through the war and beyond, their personal and professional bond growing stronger with the years. By the fall of 1943, only one other graduate student, Cy Kabat, worked under Leopold, and in the summer of 1944 he left for the Army. For a time, Leopold, McCabe, and Alice Harper constituted the entire Department of Wildlife Management.

In Manitoba, Hochbaum was at work on his research bulletin, which he was now calling "Canvasback on a Prairie Marsh." Over the summer, Leopold had pressed him to set a completion date, but Hochbaum insisted that he needed time, at least another nine months, to complete the manuscript. Agreeing to this schedule, but anxious to keep the project rolling, Leopold wrote to him on October 10, "How are things going, both personally and officially? I haven't heard from you for some time, and have been worrying a little as to how things are coming along."[32] As a matter of fact, Hochbaum was sidelined by a combination of pneumonia and a ruptured appendix, and had not informed Leopold. The bulletin was stalled. "I have not been able to look at it for three or four weeks," Albert wrote back, "and when I left it I was still puzzling over some of your editorial comments."[33]

Leopold, in the meantime, had secured funds from the AWI to publish "Canvasback on a Prairie Marsh," and had informed the institute that the manuscript was near completion. It wasn't, and Hochbaum, still recovering, was not about to rush it. Leopold was working on Delta's 1943 budget when he wrote to him on November 19: "This forces me to ask you about your plans. Presumably all or most of the work on the Bulletin should be completed before the end of the year. If you anticipate military duty, I would be inclined to close up shop unless you can think of someone who could carry on in your absence. I have been unable to."[34]

Once again, Leopold and Hochbaum had crossed signals. Aldo had not only taken it for granted that the manuscript was finished, but had also assumed that Albert, like his other students, would shortly enter the military (Albert had volunteered for the armed services in both Canada and the United States, but had been rejected on both sides of the border). Albert, on his end, assumed that this was the Professor's gentle way of telling him that his services were no longer required. "I will make mistakes," Hochbaum concluded, "but if you have the same faith in me as a student as I have in you as a teacher, you won't let this weigh too much on your mind."[35]

The strain of their working relationship was at its peak. Hochbaum was prepared to resign from Delta. He did not, but a change was clearly needed in the Delta arrangement. Leopold wrote to Frederic Walcott and admitted that "stresses and strains . . . augmented by distance" had affected his association with Delta, and with Albert. "It so happens that Hochbaum is a valued personal friend. I therefore wish to be relieved of further official duties which might bring a recurrence or continuation of the situation which has unwittingly developed."[36] Walcott, who did not want to lose Hochbaum, readily agreed. He found it surprising that Leopold was not "conscious of the mess he was largely instrumental in creating. He may be getting irritable, possibly suffering from one or more of the innumerable complaints that are apt to accompany an accumulation of years."[37] Perhaps. More likely, the fault lay in Leopold's lifelong perfectionism, and in the fact that he had one too many irons in the fire this time.

Over the winter, all those involved with the Delta Station—Leopold, Hochbaum, Walcott, James Bell, Miles Pirnie, and William Rowan—exchanged letters on its status. At one point, Leopold was deeply despondent over the situation. "Hochbaum was my close personal friend," he wrote to Bell, "and naturally I feel pretty sick about the whole matter. [But] Hochbaum is now able to paddle his own [canoe]. There is no need for my further guidance."[38] In February, everyone met in Minneapolis to work out a plan whereby Delta would be set up as an independent research station with Hochbaum as director.

The episode was an emotional one for Leopold, but as it passed he and Hochbaum quickly acted to heal their friendship. Albert wrote a note of reconciliation. Aldo replied in kind. "I consider that we cleared everything up at Minneapolis. I have dismissed all those matters from my mind. Nevertheless, I appreciate your note."[39]

∽

As the Delta problems resolved themselves, Leopold turned his attentions to the Wisconsin deer situation.[40] The Citizen's Deer Committee held its first meeting on January 23. Leopold came prepared with an early version of his history of deer population problems. Illustrating his talk with slides, he described the fate of herds in Pennsylvania, Michigan, and the Kaibab, and touched on local conditions on the Flambeau, in Wisconsin's Door County, and in northern Michigan. He explained how ungulates differ from game birds in their effects on their food supplies, and briefly recounted what researchers had so far learned about the physiological effects of malnutrition in deer.

Leopold would give his argument greater detail and definition over the next several months, but his purpose was clear from the start. He was there to teach and to sell. He was teaching a lesson from his own experience of overpopulated deer ranges. He was selling the idea that if Wisconsin were to escape a similar fate, a substantial reduction in the deer herd was necessary. This inevitably meant instituting a doe season—the first in recent memory, and a move not likely to sit well with any segment of the public. Even hunters, accustomed to the traditional buck seasons, were bound to protest. It did not help, either, that Walt Disney's *Bambi* had just been released.

Other views were represented on the Deer Committee. Most of the members were northerners, and if not openly opposed to herd reduction, they were unfamiliar with the reasons for it. Leopold was not the only member who came to the meeting prepared. Joyce Larkin, editor of the *Vilas County News-Review* and an upstate leader in the cause of deer protection, brought along a carefully compiled collection of deer-hunting accounts and opinions from Vilas County. They told a different story, not of starvation, range damage, and a need for herd reduction, but of overhunting of bucks (especially by outsiders), abundant deer browse due to ongoing logging operations, and an ailing deer herd that needed more, not less, protection. Even resident hunters in Vilas County consistently opposed the liberalized seasons advocated downstate since the mid-1930s. This solid front of public opinion was to a great extent the work of Joyce Larkin herself, who for a decade had led the protection crusade. Her efforts in Vilas County paralleled almost exactly Leopold's own game protection work in New Mexico twenty-five years earlier, emphasizing the benefits to tourism and the need for proper enforcement of game laws.

The Deer Committee did not intend to reach a consensus at this first meeting, only to plan its investigation. Leopold tried to decentralize the work, challenging the local interests to assume responsibility, to look into their needs, and to express their views on policy. Leopold and Bill Feeney scheduled a tour of northern yards. The Conservation Department invited its field force and local conservation groups to take part, and contacted newspapers around the state. Gordon MacQuarrie was asked to go along, as was a Conservation Department film-maker.

For three days in March, the Citizen's Deer Committee and its entourage snowshoed through cedar swamps and cutover yards across northern Wisconsin. As fate would have it, the winter was a hard one, with deep snows and frigid cold. Deer starved in record numbers. All who were present saw ample evidence of a crisis in the making. Even Leopold was taken aback by the apparent magnitude of the problem. The committee examined eight deer yards. They found fawns dead or dying in seven, about a hundred individuals altogether. Many of the deer, fawns and adults alike, were so feeble that they could easily be caught by hand. Necropsies of the deer showed that their paunches were full of balsam fir and other inferior foods; their lungs were pneumonic, a frequent effect of malnutrition; their bone marrow, normally marbled with fat, was clear and red, proof that the deer had exhausted their fat reserves. All of the deer yards visited were severely overbrowsed. In every one, white cedar, the food of choice, was eaten up to a neat line indicating the height of the deer's reach. Downed trees were stripped of bark and gnawed to their cores. Of all the carcasses examined by the committee, few had been preyed upon; deer predators were apparently absent from the yards.[41]

The stark reality of deer dying "the hard way" (as MacQuarrie put it) convinced virtually everyone present that immediate steps had to be taken. Even Joyce Larkin recognized that there was trouble on the deer range, and returned to Vilas County to reassess conditions there.

Exposing a committee and a few interested individuals to the deer problem firsthand was a relatively simple task. Convincing the broader public was more difficult. At one point, during an inspection of a badly hit area on the Flagg River in Bayfield County, Leopold was talking with Mac-Quarrie. "The real problem," Leopold said, "is not how we shall handle the deer in this emergency. The real problem is one of human management. Wildlife management is comparatively easy; human management difficult." This, MacQuarrie commented in a subsequent article, was "the old, old truth in conservation management."[42]

The three-day tour sufficed to indicate that a problem existed, but not to indicate the exact extent of, nor the local exceptions to, the trend in the deer population. It could only be surmised, in the absence of hard numbers, that the herd as a whole was the largest in the state's history, and threatening to do in both itself and its range. The yards visited were chosen to illustrate, not the average nor even the threatened areas of the north, but those which were already suffering obvious damage. Citizens in other not-yet-affected areas complained that their healthy deer ranges had been overlooked. One of the Deer Committee members who missed the tour warned Leopold that "if the season is opened to kill antlerless deer next fall in Forest and Oconto Counties, without an investigation, merry hell will be to pay."[43] There was not time enough to inspect every locality, nor to educate calmly the public on the problem at hand. The committee faced a no-win situation, but one demanding action.

In the weeks following the tour, Leopold completed his academy paper on the history of deer irruptions. The Citizen's Deer Committee reached agreement on recommendations which Leopold reported to the Conservation Commission on May 12, 1943. He recommended an antlerless deer season for that fall, and asked for a complete closure on bucks in order to improve the sex ratio of the herd, prevent hunting accidents, and show to the public that the new policy was dictated solely by the status of the deer herd and not by a desire to provide more sport. Leopold also recommended that overbrowsed refuges be opened to hunting; that the bounty on wolves be lifted; that artificial feeding, which did not relieve overbrowsing, and possibly aggravated it, be curtailed; and that Bill Feeney's field data be used to decide which counties needed reduction the most. The committee report also advocated that "local interests . . . assume more and more responsibility for local policy," that in the wilder counties "a low population of timber wolves be deliberately maintained as insurance against undue congestion or excessive numbers of deer," and that the Conservation Department intensify its research and education programs. "There is no doubt in our minds," the report stated, "that the prevailing failure of most states to handle deer irruptions decisively and wisely is [due to the fact] that our educational system does not teach citizens how animals and plants live together in a competitive-cooperative system."[44]

One committee member remained unconvinced. Judge Asa K. Owen of Phillips published a minority report in the *Milwaukee Journal,* claiming that the scientists had not shown that barren does were disproportionately numerous, nor that any emergency existed beyond the winter deer yards. He argued against an antlerless season and for continued winter feeding. "The planned reduction amounts to an experiment," he wrote, "and why experiment? A lot of good men and women have worked to build up a conservation sentiment in this state. The people generally, who are now interested, are not going to like this sudden reversal of policy, whatever the excuse for it."[45] Owen's words neatly captured the difference of opinion: many in the state saw deer reduction as a reversal of conservation policy, while Leopold and his cohorts saw reduction as a necessary extension of conservation policy. Both, depending on experience and perspective, were correct.

The Conservation Commission agreed to release the report of the Deer Committee to the Wisconsin Conservation Congress, the state-wide elected body of sportsmen that met annually to discuss current conservation issues and advise the commission on proposed regulations. (The Congress was begun in the mid-1930s, after the commission gained authority over most hunting and fishing regulations, as a means of increasing democratic input into state conservation administration. The congress quickly assumed an influential role in the policy-making process in Wisconsin, pulling together and conveying the views of the state's active outdoor interests.) Meanwhile, political developments precipitated Leopold's appointment to the commission. According to the *Wisconsin State Journal,* Governor Goodland "tossed a dramatic bombshell into the Wisconsin senate" on the eve of a legislative recess. Goodland had been pushing for a wholesale reorganization of the commission set-up, but when the state senate rebuffed his plan and ignored his threats to reappoint the two most controversial commissioners, the governor did a swift about-face and nominated Leopold and John Moreland (a fellow member of the Citizen's Deer Committee) to the commission. On June 17, 1943, three days before the meeting of the congress, Leopold and Moreland were in short order nominated, considered, and confirmed overwhelmingly by the state senate.[46]

The Conservation Congress met at the Loraine Hotel in Madison on June 21–22. The responsibility for laying out the rationale for deer herd reduction fell primarily to Leopold and Ernie Swift, while leaders in the congress had engineered a formidable program of supporting speakers. They needed it. The delegates were not predisposed to support reduction.

The weekend was unusually hot and steamy. Leopold and Bob McCabe walked to the hotel from campus. Leopold, speaking in his shirt-sleeves, outlined the conclusions reached by the Citizen's Deer Committee. McCabe listened from the front row. The Professor spoke "without notes, and unlike other speakers who shouted into the microphone, he spoke in a normal tone. The attention to the talk was very good, but the response in commentary and questioning was unbelievably rude, and the biological and ecological understanding of the problem from the floor virtually nonexistent." The opposition dealt Leopold a sound verbal thrashing. He was prepared for the backlash, but McCabe was not. Bob came out of the meeting "mad as a hornet," and anxious to take the discussion into the alley. Leopold, a lifelong veteran of these disputes, never batted an eye.

"To hell with 'em," McCabe argued as they walked back to the office. "Why fight this thing? Let them go, let them be stuck with the results. It won't affect you, it won't affect me, it'll only affect the people who've been knocking your brains out up there! We should tell them to go to hell, and back away from the whole thing, let them do what they want!"

Leopold walked alongside and took in McCabe's bluster. "No, Bob," he said confidently. "They'll come around. Wait and see. We didn't lose today."

McCabe was not so sure. He thought the Professor had "slipped a cog this time."[47]

As it turned out, the congress came around sooner than expected. Representatives from the Forest Service and the Conservation Department spoke in favor of reduction. The delegates also watched *Starvation Stalks the Deer,* the film that came out of the March deer yard tour. This was not *Bambi.* The film depicted starving fawns, comatose adult deer, and necropsied carcasses. Ad nauseum. Even Leopold considered the film overemotional, and unbalanced in its neglect of deer biology and range quality considerations.[48] But it was effective. The delegates to the Conservation Congress voted by a fairly substantial margin to recommend to the Conservation Commission an antlerless season.

On June 23, two days after the congress adjourned, the new commissioners were sworn into office. Leopold was now a member of the commission that he had helped establish in 1927. His appointment came as a surprise, and not just to the state senators. The position had been so heavily politicized for so long that few thought Leopold would ever even be considered. Some of his friends, knowing that it meant sacrificing time and privacy, urged him to turn it down, but Leopold saw it as a personal duty and as an opportunity to educate the public on a broad scale. Among the state's conservationists, the news was greeted with elation. Wallace Grange was one of many who wrote to express congratulations:

I am still rubbing my eyes in disbelief over the state's inconceivably good fortune in having you on the Commission. I thought those things happened only in story books. I believe in destiny, and in the thesis that every troubled situation brings out a man capable of meeting it. You are the man. I congratulate you, but most of all I congratulate the State of Wisconsin. We so seldom get the best in the state

service. But here is your appointment to reaffirm one's faith in the state government. I am very glad. Thousands of others are glad with me.[49]

The *State Journal* published an editorial in support of the unexpected appointment:

Aldo Leopold may not be a popular commissioner with everyone. He, better
than any other man in Wisconsin and probably better than any other man in the
entire country, knows what real conservation is and how to achieve it. That will
involve stepping on toes, but, fortified by an informed love for nature and having
no political axes to grind, he will not be reluctant to step. . . . If the people of
Wisconsin allow men like Leopold to direct their conservation program, the generations to come will be blessed.[50]

᠎᠎᠎᠎᠎ഗ

Having saved gas coupons all winter, Aldo and Estella resumed regular
shack visits shortly after the March tour of the northern deer yards. In
April a depleted but still eager crew planted over two thousand more pines,
the family's eighth spring of planting. As might be expected, Leopold's
shack journal notes that year began to pay extra attention to the feeding
habits of deer. He also made one notably rewarding observation in regard
to the pines:

First Natural Pine Reproduction In the birch row, about half way down, found
a young jackpine 8" high, growing in a white pine scalp with a dead tree. I in-
fer the April 1942 fire opened some cones and a seed got started in the scalp.[51]

Almost a year and a half had passed since Leopold and Harold Strauss,
the editor at Knopf, last corresponded about the proposed book of essays.
In April 1943, Strauss went into the army. His successor informed Leopold
of the change, adding that he would be "very happy to hear from you
about your work whenever you have anything to say."[52]

Other friends had been encouraging Leopold to collect and publish his
essays, but his busy schedule in the early months of 1943 left little time.
He did manage to write one new essay in March, a short meditation on
draba, a tiny white flower of the sandy river bottom. "Draba plucks no
heartstrings. Its perfume, if there is any, is lost in the gusty winds. Its color
is plain white. Its leaves wear a sensible woolly coat. Nothing eats it, it
is too small. No poets sing of it. Some botanist once gave it a Latin name,
and then forgot it. Altogether it is of no importance — just a small creature
that does its job quickly and well."[53]

Leopold sent the essay to Hochbaum, and asked him about his "present leaning on the joint venture we planned sometime ago for an illus-

trated volume of literary essays?"[54] Less than two months had passed since the Delta problems were settled. Hochbaum replied that he would like to continue working on the drawings. Leopold was elated. "I would much rather work with you than anyone else," Leopold wrote to him, "but I did not want to assume that you were still enthusiastic about the venture. . . . Let's by all means reinstate the original plan and keep sending each other whatever materials we manage to bring together."[55]

Leopold planned to spend the summer writing. In addition to the collection of essays, he also wanted to begin work on another book, suitable for classroom use, that would "describe the workings of land by following the known history of a series of landscapes or communities"; in July he wrote an introductory chapter which he called "Land As a Circulatory System."[56] He had been thinking about such a book for several years, even before the idea for an essay collection arose, and he already had a title: "Conservation Ecology." By the end of the summer he decided "Land Ecology" would be more appropriate.[57]

Meanwhile, on July 13, Leopold attended his first Conservation Commission meeting. The major item up for consideration was the fall deer season. The Conservation Department, following the recommendations of the Citizen's Deer Committee and the Conservation Congress, had asked the commission to approve a nine-day antlerless season. After discussion, the commission broke precedent and decided instead to request of the department a new plan that would allow two seasons that fall, one on bucks and one on antlerless deer. The commission rarely countermanded the recommendations of the department and the congress, and had never done so before on such an important issue. The reasons behind their separate initiative were unclear, but apparently the commission felt uncomfortable switching to a straight antlerless season after so many years of buck seasons.[58] Leopold and Moreland, the new commissioners, kept quiet during the debate, probably because they were still standing members of the Citizen's Deer Committee. In any event, the commissioners asked the department to have the new plan ready in time for a final vote at their August meeting.

In August, Leopold came down with a sciatic leg. He was confined to bed for three weeks, put all writing projects on hold, and even canceled out on shack trips. On the one trip he and the family did make at this time, he noted apologetically in his journal that because of his illness "these observations are limited."[59] He proceeded to record a page and a half of detailed notes on woodcock behavior, deer fawn pelage, wildflower phenology, and morning birdsong, and speculated on the fate of a woodchuck who had met his end on the shack's lawn.

The state of Leopold's health kept him from attending the August meeting of the Conservation Commission. The deer debate, far from being resolved, had reached fever pitch, and it dominated the day's proceedings. No one wanted a split antlerless/buck season, apparently, except some members of the commission. The Conservation Department submitted a new plan as ordered, but only grudgingly; they still believed that a strictly antlerless season was best. So did the representatives of the Conservation Congress, who felt that if there were any alternative, it should be a traditional forked-buck season. Members of the congress from around the state had caught wind of the split-season plan, and many had written to the commissioners to state that they had changed their minds and opposed any antlerless season. Even the state assembly had entered the fray. One week before the meeting, a motion opposing the "slaughtering of deer" failed by just one vote on the assembly floor.[60]

By the time the August 10 commission meeting adjourned, the split-season plan had been approved by a vote of six to nothing. Leopold voted in absentia. He clearly would have preferred a straight antlerless season, but his top priority was a solid reduction of the deer herd, by whatever means. A buck-season alone would not have accomplished it.

The stage was set for an autumn hunt that would satisfy no one.

ᔆ

In August Starker and Betty Leopold and their two children arrived in Madison for a three-month stay. Starker had completed his study of wild turkeys and returned to Madison to write his dissertation. In September, Luna arrived home on furlough from the Army. Nina and her husband came up from Chicago. The family had two weekend reunions at the shack, taken up with duck hunting, fishing, river exploring, grape gathering, late night singing. Carl was somewhere in the islands of the south Pacific.

Early in the month, on September 8, Leopold penned an essay that would become one of his personal favorites. Until that fall, he had written very little about the shack and his family's experiences there: an essay on chickadees, one on geese, the draba piece. Lately, however, he had begun to draw on his shack journal for articles in the *Wisconsin Agriculturalist and Farmer* and the *Wisconsin Conservation Bulletin*. "Great Possessions" was unlike these; it was more reflective, more personal:

One hundred and twenty acres, according to the County Clerk, is the extent of my worldly domain. But the County Clerk is a sleepy fellow, who never looks as his record books before nine o'clock. What they would show at daybreak is the question here at issue.

Books or no books, it is a fact, patent both to my dog and myself, that at daybreak I am the sole owner of all the acres I can walk over. It is not the boundaries that disappear, but the thought of being bounded. Solitude, supposed no longer to exist in my county, extends on every hand as far as the dew can reach.

Leopold described the predawn coffee-pot-and-notebook ritual he practiced when recording birdsongs, and then took the reader through his daybreak inspection of the grounds with Gus: "We sally forth, the dog and I, at random. He has paid scant respect to all these vocal goings-on, for to him the evidence of tenantry is not song, but scent. Any inconsequential bundle of feathers can make a noise, he argues; now he is going to translate for me the olfactory poems which who-knows-what silent creatures have written in the summer night."[61] Leopold and Gus make the rounds, investigating the evidence of the nighttime creatures, and then, as the morning warms and the neighbors wake, they return to the shack for breakfast.

Alice Harper typed up the essay and sent it north to Hochbaum. "Of all your essays," he wrote to Leopold, "this is the gem. . . . I like it because of all you have written, this is the first I have read in which you give a picture of yourself. You did so unconsciously; but you, rather than your theme, are the strongest, and for this reason it will be particularly valued by the rest of us."[62]

The comments of Hochbaum and others who read the essay—Estella, Starker, Harper, McCabe—must have encouraged Leopold. That fall, a somber one on campus, he wrote voluminously. Much of his output was of the sort that he had always produced: book reviews, farm subjects, a feature article for *Audubon*. He drafted an introduction to Hochbaum's book, and worked as well on a number of scientific papers.

He and Paul Errington tried to make progress on the joint review of the Prairie du Sac quail data. The paper was an important one. The census numbers from Prairie du Sac constituted perhaps the most extensive record of wildlife population dynamics in the country. As work progressed, it became clear that Leopold and Errington had very different interpretations of the data. Errington could be a difficult man to work with (Estella, in fact, could hardly stand him; she thought that he took advantage of Aldo, and her temper flared brightly at the mention of his name). Aldo, every bit as strong-willed as Errington, recognized that the work was at an impasse. Rather than risk a fifteen-year-old personal and professional relationship—the near falling-out with Hochbaum was still a recent memory—he decided to withdraw from the collaboration. It was a bitter disappointment to Leopold, who had kept watch over the Prairie du Sac study for years, but the friendship was salvaged.

Another paper of that fall, coauthored with three colleagues, traced the fate of the arboretum's pheasant population. The paper, "Population Turnover on a Wisconsin Pheasant Refuge," was among Leopold's more creative scientific papers. Annual pheasant drives at the arboretum, along with the studies of several students, had yielded unique information on the fate of pheasants in the wild. Using human actuarial tables as a model,

Leopold was able to determine the average life span of a pheasant and establish the annual mortality rate in a given population. The results indicated that pheasants had a relatively brief life span in the wild, findings that had broad implications for pheasant management. Leopold's novel approach to the data would be utilized not only by game managers but by population ecologists as well.[63]

While Leopold was at work on these technical articles, he wrote several more of the lyrical, "Great-Possessions"-like essays. A series of sand county grouse hunts with Starker evoked a celebration of October in Wisconsin: "Lunch over, I regard a phalanx of young tamaracks, their golden lances thrusting skyward. Under each, the needles of yesterday fall to earth; at the tip of each the bud of tomorrow, preformed, poised, awaits the promise of another spring."[64] In another essay written that fall, Leopold recounted the benefits of early rising: "To arrive too early in the marsh is an adventure in pure listening." One passage particularly impressed Hochbaum. Leopold described the predawn arrival of migrating scaups on a marsh. "And when a flock of bluebills, pitching pondward, tears the dark silk of heaven in one long rending nose-dive, you catch your breath at the sound, but there is nothing to see except the milky way."[65] Hochbaum, who knew the scene well, thought the sentence "one of the most beautiful I have ever read. . . . I can't recall ever having seen this described, and you have done it perfectly."[66] A cohesive collection of essays was beginning to emerge as Leopold mined the wealth of his most personal outdoor experiences. The tone of his writing was becoming more detached, even as its subject matter was becoming more connected to the times and scenes he knew best—mornings at the shack, autumn hunts, walks with Gus. The poetic intensity fed on itself: as he made headway on the essays, he was encouraged not only to write more voluminously, but more deeply, to air his essentially private contemplations.

In November the deer season opened as planned. According to the final decision of the Conservation Commission, a four-day forked-buck season opened on November 18. Aldo passed it up. After a three-day respite, the antlerless season opened on November 25. Aldo, Estella, and little Estella went to the shack to take part.

The first day of the season was warm and heavily overcast. In the afternoon, Aldo and his daughter set out to pursue a deer. Inexplicably, Aldo allowed Gus to come along on the hunt. It was a violation of Wisconsin law to hunt deer with dogs. Leopold had to have been aware of the rule, but he made no mention of the blunder, even in his journal account of the subsequent events.

The woods were full of hunters. Aldo and Estella decided to find some solitude by paddling the boat out to an island in the river. It was a tough row; the Wisconsin was in fall flood stage. Aldo stood at the base of the island while Estella and Gus walked along the north shore, trying to drive any deer down. Just as they left, Aldo noticed the tracks and blood of a wounded deer that had also crossed the river to the island.

Upriver, Estella and Gus had found the cripple, a doe, shot in the shoulder. She was out on a submerged sandbar in the river. The wind carried the smell of fresh blood. Gus got the scent and broke into an instant, absolute frenzy. He leapt into the river in chase, yelping his "big-game" yelp. Aldo heard, and rushed to the scene.

Estella watched from the island shore as Gus caught up to the doe on the sand bar. The shocked doe raised up on her rear legs and came down on Gus' back with both forehooves. Estella, helpless on shore, watched in tears. The deer fled, bounding through the water to the northern bank of the river. Gus had always been a weak swimmer on account of his one crooked leg; the blow to the back apparently paralyzed his hind quarters, but, pulled on by the blood scent, he struggled through the water after the doe.

Aldo finally reached Estella. Without a word, he took his gun, boarded the boat, and launched out into the heavy current. The river swept Gus downstream and out of reach. After half an hour, Aldo finally reached the shore where Gus clung by his forelegs, half-submerged in the water. Exhausted and unable to move his rear legs, Gus moaned a soft howl as Aldo approached and carried him onto the bank. "Gus recognized me when I carried him up the bank," Aldo wrote later in his journal, "but he was soon seized by convulsions. I covered him with my coat, but could do nothing else for him. I had to tell him good-bye, and put him out of his misery."[67]

In his journal entry that evening, Leopold wrote, "No appetite for hunting today."[68]

Around the state, the antlerless season was fulfilling its purpose, at least in terms of herd reduction. Before the four days were over, 128,000 deer would be taken, almost three times as many as in any previous year. Sheer numbers, however, did not tell the full story. The kill was unevenly distributed, due in large part to deep snows up north. In some localities, the deer had hardly been touched. In others, they were "harvested" even beyond the hopes of the commission, or the fears of the opposition. The uneven results were all but inevitable given the situation. More disturbing were the reports of illegal kills, poor sportsmanship, trafficking in venison, and license abuses that filtered back to Madison. The confusion and lawlessness only ignited an already hostile public reaction to the killing of does and fawns. The season soon became branded the "crime of '43."[69]

Leopold did not have to wait for word from around the state. He estimated that in his own Sauk County, the herd was reduced by 90 percent, when 50 percent would have "sufficed."[70] In his journal, he noted that

"Hunters swarm in the woods. One hears many strings of 3-4 shots, a sure sign [that] someone is shooting a deer in the rear with buckshot. A few know enough to stand on passes. Warden Adamski says not many does were killed."[71]

The 1943 season would prove to be the last in which Leopold hunted deer.

∽

A Christmas trip to Burlington inspired a new essay. "Illinois Bus Ride" was written on New Year's Day, 1944. Several days later (on his fifty-seventh birthday), Leopold wrote an account of the canoe trip he and his brother had made on the delta of the Colorado twenty-two years before. His tone was unusually nostalgic, his memories of the trip golden, but his moral disturbing: "All this was far away and long ago," he wrote. "I am told the green lagoons now raise cantaloupes. If so, they should not lack flavor. . . . Man always kills the thing he loves, and so we the pioneers have killed our wilderness. Some say we had to. Be that as it may, I am glad I shall never be young without wild country to be young in. Of what avail are forty freedoms without a blank spot on the map?"[72]

Leopold sent "The Green Lagoons" to Hochbaum. Over the next six months, they would correspond extensively about the essays. Hochbaum was a direct, honest critic, and Leopold responded openly to his some-times quite personal suggestions. Their literary give-and-take would alter not only the flavor of Leopold's essays, but also the process of self-examination that went into them.

On January 22, Hochbaum gave Leopold his opinion of "The Green Lagoons." "I haven't a comment to offer," he wrote, "except that it is one of your best." Hochbaum did, however, comment on "the series as a whole."

In many of these [essays] you seem to follow one formula: you paint a beautiful picture of something that was — a bear, crane, or a parcel of wilderness — then in a word or an epilogue, you, sitting more or less aside as a sage, deplore the fact that brute man has spoiled the things you love. This is never tiresome, and it drives your point deep. Still, you never drop a hint that you yourself have once despoiled, or at least had a strong hand in it.

Hochbaum none too gently pointed out Leopold's role in the extermina-tion of the wolf in the Southwest.

In your writings of the day, you played a hand in influencing the policies, for your case against the wolf was as strong then as for the wilderness now. I just read they killed the last lobo in Montana last year. I think you'll have to admit you've got at least a drop of its blood on your hands.

You already sit in a circle which may never hold more than a dozen in the century. What you thought 20 years ago has small part in your influence. Still, I think your case for the wilderness is all the stronger if, in one of these pieces, you admit that you haven't always smoked the same tobacco.[73]

A few days later, Hochbaum sent four new illustrations to accompany the essays.

Leopold reacted cautiously to Hochbaum's suggestions. In principle, he agreed. "Your point is obviously well taken," he wrote on January 29, "and I think I can see several opportunities for admitting specifically that we all go through the wringer at one time or another, differing only in the date of emergence. Of course, the question is how to do this without spoiling literary effects, but I think there are several chances where the effect will not only be preserved, but perhaps improved."[74]

Hochbaum did not let the Professor off the hook; pleading "literary effect" was not sufficient. Albert's own artistic sensibility would not permit that. "If you really have something to say," he wrote back to Leopold on February 4, "you cannot afford to choose and discard the subject matter which builds the central theme on the basis of the ease or difficulty with which the technique can draw the picture." Then Hochbaum pressed hard:

> I can't exactly put my finger on your central theme, although I know what it is. What you write about is a state of mind, probably common to all men. For some, like yourself, it is found in the wilderness; but it isn't the wilderness. What you may feel in the heart of the Sawtooth Mountains may be found by another on lower Manhattan before sunrise, by another at the prow of a ship, or on a microscope slide, or in the melody of a song. As such this is indestructible as long as there is life on earth, although certain mediums, such as the wilderness, may be destroyed. You are aware of this of course; I just wanted to let you know that this thread is grasped by others.
>
> . . . Then I find no strong hint in your series that perhaps the greatest unspoiled wilderness is the search for the Truth and that he who would seek this wilderness will find the trail just as untraveled behind a white-footed mouse as behind a desert bighorn.[75]

Leopold could not refute Hochbaum's insights into the meaning of wilderness, so reminiscent were they of his own arguments in the 1920s. Hochbaum's opinion of Leopold's literary stance was no less direct:

> There is . . . a secondary chord which is probably more easily grasped: man's reaction to the American environment—yours and the Bureau Chief's, the college boy's and the CCC road builders'. And in this theme there is one false note—the reader cannot help but gather that you believe your reaction is always the proper one and that it has been always so. Don't get me wrong; the lesson you wish to put across is the lesson that must be taught—preservation of the natural. Yet it is not easily taught if you put yourself above other men. That is why I mentioned your earlier attitude towards the wolf. . . .

. . . I, for one, gather the impression from some of your pieces that man, particularly the poor brutes who work for the government, has spoiled the river deltas and the native fauna and the crane marshes in a dumb, stubborn, deliberate effort to always do the wrong thing. You almost chide him for not having the vision you didn't have 20 years ago. After all, many of the things we do, we do because we are men, the same as moles do what they do because they are moles. True, we have thought, but thought takes time and maturity. We are just getting to the point where mature thought is guiding the manipulation of land. This is a hope. If we regret what we have done, we must regret that we are men. It is only by accepting ourselves for what we are, the best of us and the worst of us, that we can hold any hope for the future.[76]

Only a character as strong as Leopold's own could have come back at him with criticisms that struck so close to home. Hochbaum, in turn, found his deep respect for Leopold laid bare. "If there is anyone in the land who should have more hope for the future than regret for past mistakes it is you, for you have played the strongest hand in building that hope. . . . Give your series some of this hope. . . . I only hope that you won't overlook the real thread of the series in your enthusiasm for 'literary effects.'"[77]

Leopold needed time to weigh Hochbaum's lengthy commentary. On February 11, he replied, "I wish I received more letters of the kind you have just written. It is probably the most valuable comment I have had so far on the essay series. . . . I particularly agree that they must have something more important than nostalgia. . . . I am not at all offended by your homily on 'literary effects.' There is much in what you say, but I think there is something in what I said. It is probably too tangled to thresh out by mail. I am entirely convinced that the essays collectively should make clear that everybody, including myself, goes through the points of view which are deplored in the essays."[78] Again the next day, Leopold wrote, "I have been thinking a great deal about your last comment on the essays. Please regard my reply as purely tentative, since I will think the whole thing through, and will have some more to say later."[79]

School was back in session. Only twelve students enrolled in the farmer's course; only eleven in Wildlife Ecology 118. Repercussions from the "crime of '43" began to come in. Of more personal concern, Aldo and Estella had not heard from Carl for several weeks. The family knew only that he was somewhere with the Marines in the south Pacific. Carl wrote home regularly, but his letters did not relate the full story of his war experiences. He was now a first lieutenant, and his company had taken part in the grievous island campaigns of 1943. In order to keep Estella calm, Carl kept the letters cheery. Then, early in 1944, military secrecy tightened and no mail at all was allowed through. Finally, in February, after a month of mystery, one letter made it to Madison. Carl was forbidden, for security reasons, to give his location, but he did describe the local bird life. Wildlife ecology did have its quite practical applications: with this scant information, Aldo was able to pinpoint Carl's location. He had a grand smile on his face as he excitedly told Estella, "I know where Carl is! I know where Carl is!"

Leopold wrote to Hochbaum again on March 1, after he had had time to ponder his comments. He was still not willing to concede Albert's point about the artistic approach in the essays:

Your comment on the essays has been turning over in my mind for a month now. I think you are partly right, but I am not persuaded that you are wholly right. Perhaps I can explain what is on my mind this way. When you paint a picture, it conveys a single idea, and not all of the ideas pertinent to the particular landscape or action. If you inserted all of your ideas in your picture, it would spoil it.

In order to arrive at an ethical judgement, however, about any question raised by the picture, you need to consider all pertinent ideas, including those which changed in time. It seems to me, therefore, that any artistic effort, whether a picture or an essay, must often contain less than is needed for an ethical judgement. This is approximately what I meant when I said I intended to revise the essays insofar as could be done without spoiling the literary effect.

Leopold was still arguing that aesthetic integrity and ethical argumentation were, by definition, mutually exclusive. He was now willing to admit, though, that Albert had a point: "I don't know whether you are right, but I do know that the essays can give a more accurate judgement, particularly in reference to my own changes of attitude in time, without hurting the literary effect."[80]

Hochbaum did not give an inch. On March 11, he came back at Leopold again, with a letter that Aldo labeled "important." Hochbaum focussed his criticism:

Perhaps more than anything else, the series is a self-portrait of yourself. Let me say this by way of pointing to the blanks. You have told a good deal more about yourself in this series than you probably realize. But it seems to me that, while you have covered your subject well, you have left obscure two of your strongest characteristics. One of these is your unbounded enthusiasm (at least as it has impressed me) for the future. . . . The second characteristic is that your way of thinking is not that of an inspired genius, but that of any other ordinary fellow trying to put two and two together. Because you have added up your sums better than most of [us], it is important that you let fall a hint that in the process of reaching the end result of your thinking you have sometimes followed trails like anyone else that lead you up the wrong alleys. That is why I suggested the wolf business.

. . . Please don't feel uneasy that I should call this a self-portrait. I doubt that you ever thought of it as such. I think it is very important that it should be. If you will put yourself in perspective you might realize that within your realm of influence, which is probably larger than you know, Aldo Leopold is considerably more than a person; in fact, he is probably less a person than he is a Standard.

I am probably not too clear on that point, but can't carry it any further. At any rate, this series of sketches brings the man himself into focus. . . . It tells not what is law and order in his chosen field, as most of his other writings have, but shows the process of his thinking. Just for fun, then, as you round out this collection, take a sidewise glance at this fellow and decide just how much of him you want to put on paper, and that I think is your best guide. . . .

. . . And about the wolf business, whatever you decide, I hope you will have at least one piece on wolves alone, for a collection with so much of the wilderness and yourself in it I think certainly would be incomplete without giving wolves a place all to themselves.[81]

Leopold accepted the criticisms gratefully, and with deep feelings of amity toward Hochbaum. He thought Albert's letter "one of the clearest analyses of our 'problem' that I could hope to get. It will not only help me to round off the collection of essays, but more importantly, it reconvinces me completely that you and I cannot afford to get ourselves into the kind of pickle we were in. We can understand each others' language, and that is saying a great deal." Leopold had also received his copy of Hochbaum's just-published *Canvasback on a Prairie Marsh*. He wrote, "I can't help but swell up with pride about the book."[82] There was a rewarding postscript to the *Canvasback* story. A year later, the book won Hochbaum the Brewster Medal of the American Ornithologists' Union, considered the highest honor in ornithology; it would also win the 1944 Literary Award of the Wildlife Society. The shared joy of this recognition rendered the earlier difficulties between Leopold and Hochbaum inconsequential. "'Congratulations' seems a mild term for my sentiments," Aldo wrote to Albert after the Brewster Medal announcement. "Naturally I am going to crow about this all that I can."[83]

Hochbaum's remarks were as timely as they were incisive. In the wake of the 1943 deer hunt, the question of predator "control," specifically wolf control, again presented itself. In 1943, the Wisconsin state legislature, following the recommendation of the Citizen's Deer Committee, curtailed the state bounty on predators. After the tumultuous deer season, the legislature responded to public demand by reinstating a bounty, but Governor Goodland vetoed the bill. Deer lovers around the state, certain that their deer were being massacred by predators, inundated the Conservation Commission with pleas for action.[84] In the early months of 1944, the issue was on Leopold's doorstep, and he addressed it as a commissioner, a wildlife biologist, and a writer.

As a commissioner, Leopold received numerous queries and complaints from interested citizens. Among the many who took him to task on the wolf question was Waldo Rinehard, an insurance agent from Shawano. He wrote to Leopold in March that "wolves must be eliminated to the vanishing point." Rinehard held that the wolf population had been increasing

457

for over a decade and that "if there is an excess of deer, the people of the state of Wisconsin and not the wolves of Wisconsin are entitled to those deer. The deer are living on my land. The wolves pay no taxes. The hunter demand for deer is not getting smaller."[85] Leopold replied that "No one seriously advocates more than a small sprinkling of wolves. When they reach a certain level they will certainly have to be held down to it. I voted for lifting the bounty because our field men said there were only a dozen or two left in the state."[86] Their correspondence continued for several months, and although they reached no common ground, their discussion remained cordial. Leopold's courtesy was never better exemplified than in the thoughtful replies he made to those with whom he differed.

In a manuscript on which Leopold was working at the end of March, he explained his current view of the wolf situation from a management standpoint.

It is probably no accident that the near-extirpation of the timber wolf and the cougar was followed, in most big-game states, by a plague of excess deer and elk and the threatened extirpation of their winter browse foods. . . . It is all very well, in theory, to say that guns will regulate the deer, but no state has ever succeeded in regulating its deer herd satisfactorily by guns alone. Open seasons are a crude instrument, and usually kill either too many deer or too few. The wolf is by comparison, a precision instrument; he regulates not only the number, but the distribution, of deer. In thickly settled counties we cannot have wolves, but in parts of the north we can and should.[87]

More facts were needed. Earlier that winter, the Conservation Commission had hired a veteran northwoodsman to conduct a survey of predators. In April, Leopold tried to gather support for a study, through the Wisconsin Academy, of "The Ecology of the Wolf in Wisconsin," to be headed up by Bill Feeney. "The idea is to bring together . . . all the pertinent information on the status of wolves and on their ecological function in the state. The study would be a companion piece to the report already published on the deer question."[88]

In the midst of these official deliberations, Leopold wrote one of his best-known essays. On April 1, 1944, he sat down, ready to respond to Hochbaum's proddings. The result was a poignantly worded mea culpa on the subject of wolves. In "Thinking Like a Mountain," Leopold told the story of the mother wolf he and his crewmates had shot from the Blue River rimrock, and of the "fierce green fire" that died in her eyes:

I realized then, and have known ever since, that there was something new to me in those eyes—something known only to her and to the mountain. I was young then, and full of trigger-itch; I thought that because fewer wolves meant more deer, that no wolves would mean hunters' paradise. But after seeing the green fire die, I sensed that neither the wolf nor the mountain agreed with such a view.

He described the results of wolf extirpation and deer overpopulation: bushes and seedlings browsed "first to anemic desuetude, and then to death"; trees "defoliated to the height of a saddlehorn"; the "starved bones of the hoped-for deer herd." He ended with one of his most memorable paragraphs:

> We all strive for safety, prosperity, comfort, long life, and dullness. The deer strives with his supple legs, the cowman with trap and poison, the statesman with pen, the most of us with machines, votes, and dollars, but it all comes to the same thing: peace in our time. A measure of success in this is all well enough, and perhaps is a requisite to objective thinking, but too much safety seems to yield only danger in the long run. Perhaps this is behind Thoreau's dictum: in wildness is the salvation of the world. Perhaps this is the hidden meaning in the howl of the wolf, long known among mountains, but seldom perceived among men.[89]

Leopold sent the essay to Hochbaum. "'Thinking Like a Mountain,'" Albert wrote back two weeks later, "fills the bill perfectly, and is, I think, a beautiful piece besides the meaning it carries."[90]

∽

At the shack, the spring planting took place as usual: 475 tamaracks, 500 red pines, 1000 white pines. Leopold observed a loon—or, rather, heard one wailing from the river—for the first time at the shack. A new dog, Flick, joined the family, and in his puppyhood developed a keen nose for dead mice. All spring, Flick laid mouse carcasses at the feet of his master. "Is this weather mortality or disease?" Aldo wondered. "I've never seen this before, but maybe because I've never had a pup with a taste for carrion."[91]

After the spring planting trip, Leopold attended the Ninth North American Wildlife Conference in Chicago, where a number of researchers from around the nation came together for an impromptu exchange of information on deer population problems. Led by Leopold, Walter P. Taylor, and Minnesotan Thomas Schroeder, the group prepared a summary of points concerning deer irruptions that may have been the first statement of national consensus on the topic.[92]

While attending the conference, Leopold also met the editor of outdoor books for the Macmillan Company. She expressed an interest in Leopold's essays and asked him to forward some material.

In June, after university business slackened, Leopold pulled the scattered essays together. He had thirteen. In the order that he placed them, they were: "Marshland Elegy," "Song of the Gavilan," "Guacamaja," "Escudilla," "Smoky Gold," "Odyssey," "Draba," "Great Possessions," "The Green Lagoons," "Illinois Bus Ride," "Pines above the Snow," "Thinking Like a Mountain," and "The Geese Return." Of these, eight had never been published. Hochbaum had provided drawings for three. Originally, Leopold had thought to call the collection "Marshland Elegy—And Other Essays." He dropped that doleful title after his recent exchange of letters with Hochbaum. Now he wanted to call it "Thinking Like a Mountain—And Other Essays."

On June 6, Leopold sent the essays and drawings to Macmillan; on June 8, he sent them to Knopf. "The first thing," he wrote to both, "is for you to say whether these materials have any appeal to you from the publisher's viewpoint. The object, which should need no elaboration if the essays are any good, is to convey an ecological view of land and conservation."[93] Hochbaum sent Leopold some additional drawings that month. "I know you will get news soon," Albert declared. "What if both houses want to publish!"[94] Aldo was delighted with the new drawings. "This is a personal venture," he wrote back to Hochbaum, "and I take special pride in its 'home-made' aspect."[95]

A month later, Leopold received initial responses to the essays. Wellmer Pessels, the editor at Macmillan, thought they were "beautiful," and sent them to her editor-in-chief. He thought that "many of them were exquisite," but Miss Pessels had to report back ("with real regret") that "we do not feel that we can make you a publishing offer for your volume of essays." She explained that essays always sold modestly, and that wartime paper allotments forced them to choose their new projects carefully. "I personally regret very much," she added, "that I shall not have the privilege of working on this book with you."[96] Leopold was not surprised by the response. He inquired as to the possibility of underwriting publishing costs himself, as he had for *Game Management.* She could give him no encouragement.

Clinton Simpson, Knopf's editor, wrote back on July 24 that "while we like your writing, [the essays] do not seem altogether suitable for book publication in their present form." The essays, he said, were too scattered in subject matter and too varied in length, writing style, and point of view. Simpson, however, offered more than a rejection. He made a number of significant criticisms and suggestions. "I wonder if you would consider making a book purely of nature observations," he wrote, "with less emphasis on the ecological ideas which you have incorporated into your present manuscript. It seems to us that these ecological theories are very difficult indeed to present successfully for the layman." Simpson suggested more narrative essays along the lines of "Great Possessions," and advised Leopold to give the collection more coherence by restricting its coverage to one geographical area. "Some sort of unifying theme or principle must be found for a book of this sort, we think, and perhaps it would hold together better if it were limited to a single part of the country." He also suggested that Leopold try to focus his message:

Sometimes it seems that you want more intelligent planning, but you point out that nature's balance was upset with the coming of civilization, and you certainly do not seem to like the ordinary brand of conservationists and government planners. I think the average reader would be left somewhat uncertain as to what you propose. Perhaps in a single essay, all these ideas could be related so that your basic theme would become clearer.

Simpson added that he and his colleagues were "impressed with your writing, with the freshness of observation which it reflects, and the skill of phrase. We believe that readers who like nature will enjoy such writing and hope that we can work out with you a successful plan for a volume."[97]

Leopold took the criticisms in stride. In fact, many of Simpson's comments confirmed points Hochbaum had made earlier in the year. Leopold sent both the Macmillan and Knopf letters to Delta, and asked Hochbaum for his interpretation. Albert considered the Macmillan letter a "flat rejection," but found the Knopf letter "definitely encouraging." He then offered Leopold some important advice:

You know that I know how you feel about changing the original plan of the book. It would be a tough job. Still, if you were so inclined, one way might be to take the sizable nucleus of essays that have been written with the Shack background — Great Possessions, the Chickadees, the Pines etc, and build the book wholly upon Shack backgrounds. I have no doubt that you can put everything you have to say in a Shack background; I believe the pieces you have written there are the best; all put something more than a word picture across. . . . The scene, of course, would be local, but the Shack setting need not keep you from thinking in continental terms.[98]

Simpson wrote again to Leopold in late August. He had turned the essays over to two reviewers, and both had reported favorably. Knopf considered it "likely that, with some changes, we will want to publish it."[99] Leopold was gratified by this reply, and considered it "a tentative but not a final agreement between us." Knopf wanted additional material, especially "a chapter which sums up the argument for the balance of the forces of nature and what you think can and should be done about it." Leopold had doubts about the feasibility of such a summary chapter. "Whether this can be done without getting 'heavy' is what I will have to prove by trial and error."[100]

Bolstered by Knopf's response, Leopold hoped to return to work on the book soon. But it was already late summer, a new academic year was beginning, and other projects had priority. He felt no need to rush the essays along; in fact, he knew he needed time to reconsider the structure of the collection. Later on, in November, Hochbaum wrote to Leopold about a new undertaking of his own, a book about the day-to-day changes in the Delta Marsh. Hochbaum was thinking of arranging his narrative in almanac form, a method whose effectiveness he had noticed in Donald Culross Peattie's *An Almanac for Moderns*. Leopold wrote to Hochbaum that the idea "sounds very good to me. I have been flirting with the Almanac idea myself as a means of giving 'unity' to my scattered essays."[101] This was the first reference to the almanac format that Leopold would ultimately follow in organizing the book. That, however, would not fall into place for another two and a half years.

As this private give-and-take over the essay collection unfolded in the spring and summer of 1944, round two of the public deer debate commenced. The emotional reactions to the 1943 season were still smoldering as the Conservation Commission prepared to set policy for the 1944 season. As bloody and chaotic as the 1943 hunt had been, Leopold saw it as only the first important step in reducing the herd to fit its carrying capacity and maintain healthy forest browse conditions.

In June, he took his case to the public. The *Wisconsin Conservation Bulletin* published his article "What Next in Deer Policy?" Leopold analyzed the figures from the 1943 kill and explained the implications for management strategy. He estimated the 1943 herd at 500,000 based on buck counts. He considered this, if anything, a conservative estimate, and admitted that it was a "pure guess" arrived at through imperfect methods, a choice of words he would later regret. He surmised that, under current conditions, Wisconsin's range could optimally support 200,000 deer. On the basis of the 1943 kill, five more years of herd reduction were needed to reach that level.[102] Leopold knew he was prescribing harsh medicine. "Herd reduction," he wrote "is like paying the national debt; nobody wants to do it now." But to delay further reductions would be truly to waste the deer kill of 1943.

Leopold took his case from the pages of the *Conservation Bulletin* to the floor of the Conservation Congress. On June 26, he made the same points in an illustrated talk to the congress which he called "Seven Prongs of the Deer Dilemma." Speaking as a commissioner, he said that he was "convinced that we must reduce further if we want to retain a permanent healthy herd in a natural forest." He pled for the delegates to act as advisors on local conditions. "The Commission needs the combined judgement of the technical deer men, the wardens, the rangers, the foresters, and the sportsmen on these difficult questions of local status."[103]

The congress had little interest in or patience for Leopold's arguments. The experience of 1943 had turned the delegates solidly against herd reduction. They voted for a return to a buck season and the staff of the Conservation Department concurred.

The Conservation Commission was scheduled to decide on the deer season at its July 6 meeting. Support for Leopold's position now seemed limited to Bill Feeney and his research crew, Ernie Swift and other management-minded members of the department, a few concerned foresters, and a minority of sympathetic citizens. The other five commissioners still agreed that reduction was required, but because they lacked statutory authority to distribute the kill through controlled hunting, they leaned toward a return to a buck season as the only alternative to another acrimonious season on antlerless deer. Leopold protested that "there is no argument for the proposed motion [for a buck season] except that the public prefers that particular action."[104] To no avail. The commission voted four to two for a buck season, Bill Aberg joining Leopold in dissent.

Then, in August, insult began to be heaped upon injury. That month, the first issue of *Save Wisconsin's Deer* appeared. *SWD* was the official newspaper of the Save Wisconsin's Deer Committee, a group of outraged deer protectors based in the northern counties. Its editor was Roy Jorgensen, publicity director of the Manitowish Waters Chamber of Commerce. The monthly paper quickly became the principal outlet of opposition to the policies of reduction advocated by Leopold. The Save Wisconsin's Deer Committee vehemently rejected Leopold's estimate of 500,000 deer in the 1943 herd, maintaining that 200,000 was a more realistic figure (which, if correct, meant that over half the state's deer had been killed the previous fall). Leopold's call for five more years of reduction seemed to them absurd, and they were determined to prevent the commission from "destroying" the herd. Their platform was strikingly akin to Leopold's own program of a quarter-century before: political reform, strict law enforcement, ironclad control of predators, augmented refuge plans. But there the similarities ended. The problem in Wisconsin, unlike that in New Mexico in 1918, was too many, not too few, deer. Explanations of wildlife management principles were lost on Jorgensen. He edited *Save Wisconsin's Deer* with open vindictiveness, ridiculing the "experts" in Madison and playing on the sentiments of nature lovers. Leopold, because of his high profile in the deer controversy, became and remained until the end of his life the principal target of Jorgensen's verbal abuse.

The smears began with the first issue. Its banner headline read: "Urges that Present Commission Be Abolished." The paper charged that "the infamous and bloody 1943 deer slaughter was sponsored by one of the commission members, Mr. Aldo Leopold, who admitted in writing that the figures he used were PURE GUESSWORK. The commission accepted his report on this basis. Imagine our fine deer herd shot to pieces by a man who rates himself a PROFESSOR and uses a GUESS instead of facts."[105]

That was only Jorgensen's opening comment. He would continue to snap at Leopold's heels on page after page of subsequent issues. *Save Wisconsin's Deer* made scant effort to reason through the issue. Jorgensen cast scorn on Leopold's biological and historical premises ("Well—pardon us while we yawn—they talk about the Kaibab area in Arizona. We're glad they did because we never heard about it except during the morning, noon, and night from our own Conservation Commission. . . . Really, it's getting like a scratched record.")[106] The first issue also featured the initial installment of "Bambi of Valhalla" for the children, "in order to help teach the principles of conservation at an early age." Bambi told her own story over the next sixteen issues. In the first episode, Bambi's mother taught her to walk ("Soon after she told me to stand up I did, but my little legs were ever so wobbly . . . so I just stood there.")[107] Leaving no propaganda tool unused, Jorgensen wrapped himself and his cause in the flag, painting Leopold and his backers as a threat not only to deer, but to the state that "our boys" were defending overseas ("IF, for trying to PRESERVE the wildlife and natural resources for our soldier boys TO COME HOME TO . . . IF FOR ALL THAT I AM A SENTIMENTALIST, I gladly accept the BRAND!")[108]

Leopold refused to answer Jorgensen's slander. He continued to argue from the facts such as they were, and pressed on in his conviction that the deer herd had to be reduced. As time went on, no response would prove to be the best response. Jorgensen, unable to draw him into a fight, grew increasingly annoyed, and his rhetoric increasingly malicious. He typically portrayed Leopold as an "armchair conservationist" who sat in his swivel chair in Madison, gleefully plotting the extermination of Wisconsin's deer. Leopold was not immune to the venom. Although he had been fighting on behalf of conservation principles most of his professional life, and often advised his students on the merits of thick skin, he was not so stoical as to be unaffected. The relentless public abuse exacted an emotional toll.

In a reverse manner, this deer controversy fed Leopold's growth as a conservation philosopher. In the fall of 1944, Leopold at several points revealed a subtle shift in emphasis and definition in his writing. One expression of this came in his work as part of a College of Agriculture committee examining postwar agricultural policy. In a draft essay that he called "Conservation: In Whole or in Part?" he defined "two kinds of conservationists and two systems of thought on the subject":

> One kind feels a primary interest in some one aspect of land (such as soil, forestry, game, or fish) with an incidental interest in the land as a whole.
> The other feels a primary interest in the land as a whole, with incidental interest in its component resources.
> The two approaches lead to quite different conclusions as to what constitutes conservative land-use, and how such use is to be achieved.[109]

Of course, Leopold had recognized this distinction years before, but the deer controversy brought it into sharp focus. His opponents were interested primarily in one aspect of land. He was interested foremost in land as a whole.

This brought him back, for the first time in several years, to the theme of "land health":

> Conservation is a state of health in the land.
>
> The land consists of soil, water, plants, and animals, but health is more than a sufficiency of these components. It is a state of vigorous self-renewal in each of them, and in all collectively. Such collective functioning of interdependent parts for the maintenance of the whole is characteristic of an organism. In this sense land is an organism, and conservation deals with its functional integrity, or health.[110]

This was a highly significant point; not a new one in his constellation of ideas, but a brighter one. Conservation, in the public's mind, still dealt mainly with the supply and demand of separate resources, not with the overall "functional integrity" of land. Wealth, not land health, was still conservation's bottom line. This view, Leopold held, was "inadequate, for a deficit in the supply in any given resource does not necessarily denote lack of health, while a failure of function always does, no matter how ample the supply." Conservation had to be premised, first and foremost, on the land's stability, diversity, and complexity:

> This leads to the "rule of thumb" which is the basic premise of ecological conservation: the land should retain as much of its original membership as is compatible with human land-use. The land must of course be modified, but it should be modified as gently and as little as possible.
>
> This difference between gentle and restrained as compared with violent and unrestrained, modification of the land is the difference between organic and mustard-plaster therapeutics in the field of land-health.[111]

The testimony of ecological science had long since permeated Leopold's teaching and his scientific work; now it was filtering more deeply into his philosophy. He did not avoid the rebuttal of conventional economics: "some components of land can be conserved profitably, but others not. All are profitable to the community in the long run. Unified conservation must therefore be motivated primarily as an obligation to the community, rather than an opportunity for profit."[112] Short-term profits may indeed accrue in conservation, Leopold noted, and ought to be emphasized when they do, but it was misleading and illusory to argue for conservation on economic grounds alone.

Although these were not new assertions, they were more precise, and more geared to current questions of public policy. As a commissioner, Leopold was trying to apply a philosophy that the public had not yet grown into, as had he. His friends had warned him that he was not really suited for work in a political vortex. Once there, he adamantly followed his conscience. The commission's legal responsibility was to promote the public's interest in a balanced conservation program. To Leopold, that meant maintaining the health of the environment in this functional sense, for his own and future generations. His fellow commissioners appreciated his position, but as lawyers and businessmen they were more attentive to public opinion than he. Leopold had a forester's time scale and a natural scientist's knowledge of the environment; he saw the public interest as a long-term matter that necessarily included the interests of future generations and the nonhuman world.

As these thoughts jelled through the fall of 1944, Leopold busied himself with a major paper on phenology, drawing on his shack journals. Although the political pressures around him were growing, he was mellowing in his outlook. The evidence was scattered. A letter to Ding Darling: "It should be brought out somewhere that the only thing to hate is too many, too few, or in the wrong place. Hate should never attach to species or classes."[113] His own husbandry of the shack property was affecting his view. Doug Wade, who of all Leopold's students had perhaps the most pronounced philosophical bent, wrote to the Professor on the interwoven subjects of conservation, government, freedom, and individual rights. "We need some philosophies to guide us," Wade implored. "So far, you are one of the few wildlife men who has attempted to give us some guideposts. We are in need of some more guideposts; or, at least, some thought that will disturb our complacency."[114] Leopold's reply gave a new, personal flavor to his conservation ethic. "Things that are done wholly by government," he wrote, "are really not done, because any decent land-use is worthwhile, not only for its effect on land, but for its effect on the owner. If the owner is an impersonal government, nobody is benefited except the government employee."[115] This idea, that conservation was not just an external process, nor just an internal process, but something that happened between the individual and his environment, would deepen in the remaining years of Leopold's life. For the time being, he considered it far too important to discuss by mail. He wrote to Wade, "Will you bring the matter up the next time we can have a beer together, or better still, two or three beers?"

Gas shortages that fall again reduced weekends at the shack by half. Aldo and Estella did get away for several grouse and pheasant hunts. On November 25, the opening day of the deer season, they stayed at the shack with young Estella, and Nina and Bill Elder, but Aldo did not hunt that year.

The passage of years, too, was mellowing Leopold. His old colleague Evan Kelly retired that fall. After learning the news, Aldo wrote to him in Montana to offer congratulations and to pay him tribute. Aldo's thoughts returned to New Mexico. "I was just playing with my job until you demonstrated how to heave with both shoulders, and especially how to steady the heaving process to make it more effective. For this personal instruction I shall be forever grateful. My career, such as it is, in the field of wildlife conservation might well be described as applying Evan Kelly's methods [to wildlife]."[116]

Kelly responded nostalgically, recalling their times together in the Southwest. "I always enjoyed my trips into that territory. I attributed a large part of the attitude of Region 3 to your influence, your absence of satisfaction with the what-is's of the time, and your restlessness of mind. Some of your statements rest with me still. I remember your remarking on one occasion that so-called radicalism was the promotive influence of progress, or words to that effect. How true that is, and how strong the opposing inertia. Well, it has all been a great experience, Aldo. I regret that the swing of time moves so rapidly, and only wish today that I had no more years upon my shoulders than I had when you and I spent that uncomfortably cold night up there on the Apache, under Bald Mountain."[117]

Aldo wrote back, "Your . . . letter makes me wish that we could have a visit sometime." Aldo had forgotten about the cold night on the mountainside.[118]

∽

Miraculously, none of the wildlife students had been claimed by the war, although two of Leopold's undergraduates were killed. Fred Greeley, who had planned graduate study with Leopold and who had spent one summer working at Delta, had his plane shot down over the Low Countries, but he was shuttled to safety by the Belgian underground. Carl Leopold was in Guam.

Starker had still not been called into military duty. While waiting for word, he went to work in Mexico as director of the Field Research Section of the Pan-American Union (working under Bill Vogt). He would remain there for the duration of the war, undertaking important early studies of Mexican wildlife. "The war has us all worried," Aldo wrote to Starker and his family on Christmas Day. "Not so good. Love to you all, AL."[119]

The war seemed at its darkest in the closing days of 1944. Leopold rarely talked about it outside of home, even with Bob McCabe, now his only full-time graduate student. Only fifteen students signed up for the farmer's short course in January 1945. Enrollment in the wildlife ecology course subsequently reached its all-time low of just eight.

The deer issue heated up once more in the early weeks of the new year. The results of the 1944 season had put Leopold in a difficult position. By all accounts, the herd was even smaller than could be accounted for by the big take of 1943: there seemed to be fewer fawns and yearlings; the proportion of bucks was up; coyotes and wolves had increased; the does seemed well-fed. Either Leopold had overstated his case from the outset, or herd reduction had yielded results faster than expected. There was a third explanation: wolves and coyotes had been on the upswing prior to 1943, and predation, combined with the starvation of 1942 and the hunt of 1943, had reduced deer numbers, at least in some places, more quickly than he had anticipated.

Nevertheless, it was no time for complacency. The superabundant herd of 1940–1942 had been trimmed down from crisis levels, but the public still viewed that abundance as normal (if not subnormal). The state had been fortunate to pass through the worst of the crisis; "as it is," Leopold wrote, "we have part of the herd left, and part of the original stock of food plants."[120] The great need now was for the commission to gain the legislative authority to distribute the kill through controlled hunts. Leopold wrote up a proposal to that effect, but it went nowhere in the legislature. The legislators, still reeling from the 1943 experience, would not seriously consider such a move for years.

The aspect of the controversy debated most heatedly in early 1945 was the predator bounty. The public clamor for a reenacted bounty was at a high pitch. The state legislature's antipathy toward the commission was likewise at its strongest. Leopold had argued himself into a corner. He had placed so much emphasis on predation as a controlling factor that, with deer numbers seemingly down to more moderate levels, he could no longer plead that wolves were needed to help control the herd. The deer protectors zeroed in. One sportsmen's club complained:

> The wolf is the Nazi of the forest. He takes the deer and some small fry. The fox is the sly Jap who takes the choice morsels of game and the song birds. Can Professor Leopold justify their existence because deer meant for human consumption should be fed to the Nazi because we must have that protection for the trees? Can he justify the Jap or Nazi because he eats a rabbit [or] a grouse which are meant for human food, or the song bird on its nest, which was meant by the Lord for our pleasure, because the hungry Jap must live to eat the rabbit to save the tree? . . . We must ask you a question—"Do you like the wolf better than the man?"[121]

At the January meeting of the Conservation Commission, Leopold voted in favor of a reenacted bounty on predators, even over the objections of his friend and fellow wolf-defender, Bill Feeney. Leopold tried to explain his position in an article in the *Wisconsin Conservation Bulletin*:

> Whatever the present status of the timber wolf, it is certain that a few years ago the species was on the verge of extermination. It was for this reason that I favored discontinuing the bounty a year ago.
>
> I now favor restoring the bounty because the increase in coyotes makes it necessary, there is a probability that timber wolves have increased, and it is impracticable to distinguish between the two species in paying bounties. I shall fight for again discontinuing the bounty whenever extermination again threatens. We have no right to exterminate any species of wildlife. I stand on this as a fundamental principle.

Leopold admitted in public what he had admitted privately in "Thinking Like a Mountain": "Many scoff at the idea that the wolf could be exterminated in Wisconsin. I can only reply that the wolf *has been* exterminated from fourteen states since 1915. I myself have cooperated in the extermination of the wolf from the greater part of two states, because I then believed it was a benefit. I do not propose to repeat my error." The aim of all wildlife conservation, Leopold stated, was to maintain "reasonable levels of all members of the native wildlife community. . . . It would be unreasonable for foresters to demand wiping out the deer herd because deer eat trees. It is equally unreasonable for deer hunters to demand wiping out wolves because they eat deer."[122]

In the course of his awkward self-explanation, Leopold stated that "those who assume that we would be better off without any wolves are assuming more knowledge of how nature works than I can claim to possess." Again, Leopold would regret his wording. Roy Jorgensen pounced on the remark, and dragged it into the headline of *Save Wisconsin's Deer:* "'Assume They Know More Than I Do'—Leopold." "The statement comes from none other than Professor Aldo Leopold, one of Wisconsin's conservation commissioners," Jorgensen sneered. "Read it again because it has that touch of 'Leopoldian egotism' and insinuates that he, the great Aldo, places his knowledge above that of any Wisconsin citizen."[123] Leopold still refused to respond, though he made occasional tongue-in-cheek references to his vocal opposition. At the conclusion of an extension talk on the deer problem, he presented his side of the argument and then concluded by admitting there was indeed another side. "Their position is plausible if (a) one loves deer, (b) knows nothing of what they eat, and (c) doesn't know one bush from another. . . . To the untrained eye, the woods were still full of 'brush.'"[124]

The legislature approved the reinstituted bounty and the Conservation Commission voted against any further reduction of deer through an antlerless season in 1945. The vote was again four to two, with Bill Aberg taking Leopold's side.

The family made only one trip to the shack that winter, on the first weekend in February. The snow was too deep to drive in, so they skied the three miles into the shack. Over the weekend, fourteen new inches buried them in the shack. They were just about to ski back out on Sunday afternoon when their neighbor, Mr. Lewis, came by with his team hitched to a sleigh. Lewis was worried about Mrs. Leopold. "I knew the mister could make it," he told her, "and the girl, but I didn't think you could manage in this deep fluffy snow!" She could manage quite fine, thank you, but she was not about to refuse a sleigh ride. She and Aldo happily accepted his offer.[125]

Through the war, Estella Sr. worked in Liberty Bond drives and volunteered her services at a local hospital. Returning to Madison after that snowy weekend, she and Aldo received the best kind of news. Carl was in Chicago on leave, and on his way home to Madison with Keena. Obviously relieved, she wrote to Starker, "Carl called us up this noon and sounded very natural and very happy of course, and it was wonderful to hear his voice! He will have a month's leave and then we do not know where his new assignment will be, but we won't worry about that yet. We are so *grateful* to have him home safe and sound."[126] A few days later, Carl and Keena took the train up to Madison. Aldo and Estella met them at the station, and Carl stepped off the train into his parents' arms. Carl had never before seen his father weep.

The war forced cancellation of the North American Wildlife Conference. In lieu of a proper meeting, the professionals from around the country prepared papers for publication. Leopold's contribution was a prognosis of agricultural conditions that he called "The Outlook for Farm Wildlife," a statement notable for several reasons. It was his first broad accounting of agriculture in several years; it showed the policy perspective that he had gained in the previous year; and it concluded with one of Leopold's strongest pleas for a conservation ethic in agriculture:

> In short, we face not only an unfavorable balance between loss and gain in habitat, but an accelerating disorganization of those unknown controls which stabilize the flora and fauna, and which, in conjunction with stable soil and a normal regimen of water, constitute land-health.
>
> Behind both of these trends in the physical status of the landscape lies an unresolved contest between two opposing philosophies of farm life. I suppose these have to be labelled for handy reference, although I distrust labels:
>
> 1. *The farm is a food factory,* and the criterion of its success is salable products.
>
> 2. *The farm is a place to live.* The criterion of success is a harmonious balance between plants, animals, and people; between the domestic and the wild; between utility and beauty.
>
> Wildlife has no place in the food-factory farm, except as the accidental relic of pioneer days. The trend of the landscape is toward a monotype, in which only the least exacting wildlife species can exist.
>
> On the other hand, wildlife is an integral part of the farm-as-a-place-to-live. While it must be subordinated to economic needs, there is a deliberate effort to keep as rich a flora and fauna as possible, because it is "nice to have around."
>
> It was inevitable and no doubt desirable that the tremendous momentum of industrialization should have spread to farm life. It is clear to me, however, that it has overshot the mark, in the sense that it is generating new insecurities, economic and ecological, in place of those it was meant to abolish. In its extreme form, it is humanly desolate and economically unstable. These extremes will some day die of their own too-much, not because they are bad for wildlife, but because they are bad for farmers.[127]

Leopold's view of the midwestern farmscape had not changed substantially since his game survey days of the late 1920s. The issue was the same:

the overall quality of rural life in a nation that was leaving the farm while simultaneously demanding more from it. What Leopold had gained by 1945 was a broad view of agriculture's social and biological context. Land-health, in his thinking, and in his public actions, looked to the "functional integrity" of land, though not to the exclusion of those who most closely lived and worked with land.

As the spring of 1945 came on, shack trips increased again. Five Leopolds planted sixteen hundred pines, tamaracks, and cedars.

၁

Robert Sterling Yard, president and secretary of the Wilderness Society, died at the age of eighty-four on May 17, 1945. Benton MacKaye used the sad occasion to point the Wilderness Society in a postwar direction. "Today is a turning point in a ripening mechanical age," he wrote. "A new way of life is in the making whereof the elements are many. Among these life elements is that of human environment—and a vital part of this is the wilderness environment. To preserve and develop this primal influence, as a healthful balance wheel in a mechanistic trend, constitutes, as I see it, the one particular role of our little organization."[128]

The immediacy and complexity of wilderness issues in postwar America soon impressed itself upon Leopold. A few days after Yard died, Leopold was asked to chair a National Research Council committee looking into the proper use of aircraft in and over wilderness areas.

In the following weeks, MacKaye acted as temporary head of the society, and through a series of six letters primed the society council on the tactical and philosophical repositioning of their group. MacKaye and society Treasurer Ernest Griffith arranged a July 14 caucus of the council in Washington. "This is probably the most important meeting the Society has ever held," Griffith wrote to Leopold.[129]

Leopold was preoccupied with Conservation Commission matters in Wisconsin, but managed to break away for the meeting. Benton MacKaye reaffirmed the Wilderness Society's decade-old commitment. "Now for a new start," he said in his opening statement. "What is our function in this the post-war period we are entering? Is it big or little? If 'little' we should liquidate. But I am assuming it is 'big'—if for no other reason than the condition of our average returning fighter from this war—his need for a place wherein serenity shall quell confusion."[130] The society emerged from its conclave with new leadership. Olaus Murie became director and Howard Zahniser executive secretary. Benton MacKaye was elected president and Aldo Leopold vice-president.

Leopold had planned to devote the summer to two major papers and the essay collection, but he found himself mired unexpectedly in just one of the projects, the phenology paper. He was working on it with Elizabeth Jones, a botany student, and thought it would be "a pushover," but they were turning up unforeseen complications. From the immense store of field observations at their disposal, they were finding some birds and plants which responded to the changing length of the days, and others that "jiggle all over the calendar" in response to weather. Reporting the evidence to Starker, Aldo confined his perplexity to a neat one-word question: "Meaning?"[131]

Trips to the shack became more frequent with summer. Aldo and Estella devoted much of their work that year to wildflower propagation and prairie seeding. Aldo's intensive work on bird song and wildflower blooming (as well as deer-feeding habits) kept him busy bookkeeping. His journal notes grew heavier than ever with the comings, goings, callings, feedings, leavings, and flowerings of more species than ever before. He added a new piece of equipment to his morning coffee-pot-and-notepad outfit: a light-intensity meter to correlate birdsongs and candlepower of sunlight.

The war came to its welcome, portentous conclusion in August. On August 11, Bruce Stollberg contributed the last word to the round robin letter that had given Leopold and his scattered students a common bond through the course of the war:

> The scene takes place on the forecastle of a destroyer, where rests, half sitting, half lying, a Wood Pee-wee, looking and doubtless feeling, as out of place as I on this cold and lifeless mass of steel. Its wings are drooping from a panic-stricken fight with the wind and sea, its eyes half closed as it tries to recover enough strength to once again pit its tiny fighting heart against the elements.
>
> A sailor comes lurching by, sees it, and casually tosses a block of wood, with a "Cheez, that sparrow must think he's home," thereby condemning one more harmless little soul to eternity, and proving the shallowness of his own.
>
> Well, enough of this idle raving.
>
> I am returning these letters to the Professor, should a possible reconvening of wayward Game Managers be in the offing.
>
> Smooth Sailing all—
Bruce[132]

Aldo and Estella went to the shack on August 9, and stayed for four days. That particular trip provided grist for a new essay, the only one of the summer, a meditation on the creative ways of the Wisconsin River and its sand bars:

> . . . Here and there a cardinal flower thrusts a red spear skyward. At the head of the bar, purple iron weeds and pale pink joepyes stand tall against the wall of willows. And if you have come quietly and humbly, as you should to any spot that can be beautiful only once, you may surprise a fox-red deer, standing knee high in the garden of his delight.

Do not return for a second view of the green pasture, for there is none. Either falling water had dried it out, or rising water has scoured the bar to its original austerity of clean sand. But in your mind you may hang up your picture, and also the hope that in some other summer, the mood to paint may come upon the river.[133]

Leopold left no apparent reaction to the manner in which World War II ended. If he discussed the atomic bomb with anyone, the conversations have been forgotten. The lesson, however, of this new technology, and of the war in general, was not lost on him. At one point, sometime after the war, he sat in his office and penned the beginning of a never-finished essay:

. . . we are now confronted by the fact, known at least to a few, that wars are no longer won; the concept of top dog is now a myth; all wars are lost by all who wage them; the only difference between participants is the degree and kind of losses they sustain. The reason for this change is obvious: science has so sharpened the fighter's sword that it is impossible for him to cut his enemy without cutting himself.[134]

Leopold had seen that tendency in his own science years before, and had moved to counteract it. In his own mind, there was now a clear connection between modern man's drive to conquer nature and the amoral application of the sciences. His personal response was to explore further a land ethic that might, on one level at least, bring about some reasonable reconciliation between humankind's science and its morality.

20

A Portent of a Different Future
(1945–1947)

T HE WEEKS following V-J Day brought forth what Leopold described as "the largest and best batch of graduate students I have ever seen." Returning soldiers wasted no time in beating a path to the doorstep of the Department of Wildlife Management. Leopold, McCabe, and Virginia Kiesel, the new department secretary, hustled to make their own peacetime transition a smooth one.[1] The scene repeated itself in universities and government agencies across the country. A distinctly new generation of wildlifers was coming into the profession. Many were simply resuming war-interrupted plans. Many others had picked up an interest in wildlife in the course of their global travels. Still others, war-weary and disillusioned, saw it as an alternative to the disoriented state of human affairs.

Leopold did his best to cope with the surge of applicants. He admitted half a dozen new students immediately; that was as many as he could effectively handle. In a search for assistants, he approached several of his former students—Art Hawkins, Irv Buss, Frederick Hamerstrom. They too were caught up in the postwar rush. The demand would not soon diminish: Leopold had nineteen students on line, with another twenty-five inquiring. Passage of the GI Bill ensured that the number of new applicants would remain high.

Leopold also tried to bring Albert Hochbaum back to the university, but Hochbaum had his hands full with the work at Delta. Over the summer, he had become embroiled in a dispute with Ducks Unlimited over the status of waterfowl populations. DU, the most influential private waterfowl conservation group in the country, was an outgrowth of the old More Game Birds group, with the important difference that it was more heavily committed to habitat acquisition and preservation than its precursor. Previously, the Delta station and DU had worked together on a number of projects (Leopold had strongly encouraged this cooperation), but after a summer tour of Manitoba's marshlands, including DU's field stations, Hochbaum became convinced that it was "primarily a money-making outfit and is fundamentally dishonest."[2] His quarrel was not with DU's membership or field men, but with its leadership and, above all, its publicity force. He accused them of dishonest motives, fraudulent reports, and, most damning, flagrant exaggeration of duck breeding and population figures. These misstatements, Hochbaum feared, were being used to convince American wildfowlers that there was a limitless supply of ducks on the wing. Hochbaum wrote one letter after another to Leopold substantiating his claims. Then, in September, Hochbaum lost his temper during a meeting with the head of Ducks Unlimited–Canada in Winnipeg.

Leopold had no official obligation to enter the fray, but his personal ties inevitably drew him into it. Far from the scene, he was unwilling to break with the DU leadership, and cautioned Hochbaum to show restraint —which only infuriated Albert. Their relationship, though, had grown beyond differences of opinion. Leopold wrote to him, "One of the premises of our friendship is that we are free to speak freely, and on past occasions you have done so . . . [and] in the long run I have thanked you for speaking your mind. Whether, in the present situation, I am right or wrong is beside the point. Very possibly I am wrong."[3] The dispute was a fundamental one, and it would admit of no quick or easy solution. In the meantime, horn-locking between Hochbaum and the Ducks Unlimited leadership would intensify as duck populations plummeted after the 1945 breeding season.

Students filtered back to Madison all autumn long. Lyle Sowls returned in October after four years in the Navy. "He is the same gentle humorous generous Lyle as before," Leopold wrote, "but of course a bit saddened by what he has seen, as any person of his sort must be."[4] Lyle was anxious to return to his wildlife work and to his studies of the Franklin's ground squirrel at Delta.

A few days after Sowls returned, on October 25, he and one of Leopold's new students, Bob Ellarson, took the Professor out on a pheasant hunt in the rolling ridges and draws of Green County. Each of them shot one cock pheasant. Aldo mistakenly shot a hen as well; hens were not legal game. A cock he had flushed sought cover in a field of standing corn. They raised a bird, but it was a hen that emerged instead. Before Bob and Lyle could shout "hen!" Aldo had hit it. He admitted in his journal account that "I got too quick on the trigger." Leopold, embarrassed by his faux pas, apologized to his students. "Lyle and I chuckled about the experience," Ellarson recalled. "Even a purist and veteran hunter can make a mistake in the field." "Well, we can't waste it, can we," Aldo decided. As they ate lunch on the roadside, the Professor weighed and measured the birds, recording the figures in his notebook. For the rest of the afternoon, Bob and Lyle shouted "hen!" quickly and loudly whenever they came upon one.[5]

That evening, Carl returned home from the Marines, and a week later he and his father went to Green County for another pheasant hunt. "His first hunt since war," Aldo noted in his journal. They enjoyed a pleasant day afield. The local countryside, with its interspersion of prairie remnants and mature creek-bottom hardwoods, impressed Aldo. They saw an abundance of red-tailed and rough-legged hawks, fifteen pheasant hens, but only one cock. They killed nothing. "Didn't fire a shot," Aldo wrote in his journal.[6]

Leopold's hunting habits were changing. In the last seasons of his life, he went into the field as enthusiastically (and with as sharp a shot) as ever, but a different quality characterized his hunts. His pursuit of woodcock exemplified this change. Ever since Aldo first tagged along with his father carrying an empty .22, the woodcock had been one of his favorite game birds. Years of charting the woodcock's spring dance grounds and studying its feeding and behavior patterns had sensitized him to its ways. The children had competed among themselves to see who could gain closest access to the peenting grounds and who could most accurately describe the ritual. Leopold credited the woodcock for introducing him to the study of light thresholds and the phenology of birdsong ("I remember feeling that I had wasted forty years in not sooner becoming aware [of] so entrancing a field for exploration and discovery.")[7] He continued to hunt woodcock, but with more appreciation, and less ammunition. "Woodcock are plenty and I am under pressure (from Tom Coleman, for ex.) to shoot them more heavily, but I just can't see any really heavy pressure against our 'pets.' I shot 2 limits last year, but only because there was nothing else for the dog before pheasants opened."[8] His hunting habits may have been changing, but not his sportsmanship. There was no gap, but a continuum, between his conscience as a hunter and his conscience as a wildlife ecologist. His ethics were not polarized. He found, to his own satisfaction, a pathway between the dual hazards of overweening sentimentality (as exemplified by the Save Wisconsin's Deer Committee) and desensitized ignorance (as exemplified by the indiscriminate gunners).

A development at the end of 1945 reflected this quiet shift in Leopold. Since 1917 he had recorded his hunting adventures in his hunting journals, which now amounted to three thick volumes. Since 1935 he had recorded his family's shack experiences in a separate set of journals, which now amounted to two volumes. After 1945, he combined them into a single, unlabeled journal.

Between the normal load of responsibilities, his new and returning students, and an active autumn in the field, Leopold had little time left for writing, and the essay collection was once again put on hold. His literary output was further slowed by an unforeseen health problem. Although still in good health generally, at some point that fall he began to suffer occasional spasms of pain in the left side of his face. At first these attacks came only intermittently, but when they did come, the pain was excruciating. In a letter to Joe Hickey, Leopold described the feeling as "equivalent to somebody rising suddenly from behind a bush and bashing you with a sledgehammer. The frequency and location of bushes is unpredictable."[9] He did not know the nature of the problem at the time, and simply ascribed it to "overexertion (of the armchair variety)."

Hickey was among the former students whom Aldo was trying to bring back to Madison as an assistant. This new health problem, Leopold explained to him, "coincides (phenology!) with a landslide of ex-military students. 9 on hand, 9 more 'promised' for February, all known and good. 6 more unknowns for February, 4 for Sept., 29 miscellaneous unknowns without dates. What to do? If you were through school, you would be getting an SOS from the Ag College. The few others I would want are obligated elsewhere."[10] Hickey finally decided to return to Madison and join Leopold and McCabe on the instructional staff, but he needed another year to clear away his responsibilities. Meanwhile, Leopold undertook a "long-overdue reorganization" of his time in an attempt to divest himself of extra commitments.

∽

A new frame of mind was emerging in conservation. Soldiers and civilians alike had grown accustomed to thinking internationally. The technological spoils of war — new chemistries, products, industries — began to filter into the peacetime marketplace. American industry, turbocharged by the demands of war, paused just long enough to shift direction without shifting gears. And all stood agape before the awful excitement of atomic power. In short, conservation was now a global issue, at least for a vanguard of those involved. Like many a fly-boy and buck private, it had lost its provincialism abroad. In the immediate aftermath of the war, everyone breathed a collective, six-month sigh of relief. Then, in the early months of 1946, they began to consider the path ahead.

Leopold participated in a number of these discussions. Among his many correspondents at this time, the most significant was Bill Vogt. Vogt had spent the war years in Latin America as chief of the Conservation Section of the twenty-one-nation Pan American Union. In that capacity he surveyed the natural resources and wartime social conditions across Latin America. What he saw — the cluster of unconscionable poverty, resource exploitation, burgeoning populations, unresponsive oligarchies, and an unyielding Roman Catholic stance on birth control—transformed him from an already brilliant ornithologist and writer to a conservationist with a mission. By early 1946, he was laying the groundwork for an "Inter-American Conservation Congress."

Vogt and Leopold had known one another for a decade, and for a time Vogt planned to study under Leopold at Wisconsin, but the plan fell through. At another point, Vogt tried to bring Leopold south on a lecture tour. "The importance of introducing ecology into the South American picture is so obvious that it needs no comment," Vogt wrote to him in 1942. "From what I know of Latin America, their problems, [and] you and your approach to such problems, I cannot help feeling that such a journey would result in extremely important accomplishments, both in the field of hemisphere science and its relations to strategic problems."[11] Aldo was never able to make such a trip. Starker Leopold, though, continued to work closely with Vogt in his studies of Mexican wildlife (in 1946, Starker completed his work with the Pan American Union and joined the staff of the Museum of Vertebrate Zoology at Berkeley).[12]

After the war, Vogt was determined to bring his dire message to the public. As envisioned, the Inter-American Conservation Congress was to be the first large-scale forum on Latin American environmental conditions, and would require several years to organize. In January 1946, Vogt sent to Leopold an early outline of the proposed conference. Leopold's response was gloomy:

The only thing you have left out is whether the philosophy of industrial culture is not, in its ultimate development, irreconcilable with ecological conservation. I think it is.

I hasten to add, however, that the term industrialism cannot be used as an absolute. Like "temperature" and "velocity" it is a question of degree. Throughout ecology, all truth is relative: a thing becomes good at one degree and ceases to be so at another.

Industrialism might theoretically be conservative if there were an ethic limiting its application to what does not impair (a) permanence and stability of the land (b) beauty of the land. But there is no such ethic, nor likely to be.

. . . Bill, your outline is excellent. That the situation is hopeless should not prevent us from doing our best.[13]

Even Vogt, who could hardly be classified an optimist, found Leopold's forecast "somewhat dismal but much appreciated." Vogt could not deny Leopold's main point. "You are, of course, correct in what you say about industrialism. I don't know how you would define ethic, but I am hopeful that horse sense may someday replace it as a limiting factor to preserve the permanence and stability of the land, even though there seems to be little hope for saving its beauty."[14] Leopold was no doubt sobered by the trend of world events, but, as in the past, he always resurfaced with his thoughts pointed toward the future. He wrote to Vogt a week later: "It is so impossible to write a letter about such a big question that I am afraid this alone depresses anyone trying to make an answer." He recommended that Vogt read Louis Bromfield's *Pleasant Valley* for "the optimistic side of the picture."[15]

In March, Vogt and Leopold met at the Eleventh North American Wildlife Conference in New York City. The theme of the conference was "The Place of Wildlife in a Changing World." The conference retained its base in local resource concerns and research findings, but the new international angle played prominently in the talks. Vogt spoke about Latin America: "The standard of living, the well-being, the political stability, the potentiality for industrialization, all things that are of very great interest to us here in the United States, are so influenced in Latin America by destruction or commercialization of natural resources that this whole problem is of serious concern to North Americans."[16] Fairfield Osborn, director of the New York Zoological Society, spoke in terms that could hardly have been imagined by those attending the first conference ten years before:

There are two major threats in the world today, either one of which would cause incalculable loss of human life, if not the breakdown of the entire structure of our civilization. The first is the misuse of atomic energy. Everybody everywhere knows about that now so presumably steps will be taken to ward off that perilous danger. The other is the continuing destruction of the natural living resources of this earth. This great conference of conservationists from all parts of North America is being held in order to help ward off this second incredible threat to everything that is alive on earth.[17]

Leopold did not present an address that year. His counsel, though, was more earnestly sought than ever. McCabe kept a close eye on his boss, discreetly interrupting the procession of interviewers to remind Leopold when it was time to retire for the evening. "Bob took excellent care of me," Aldo wrote home to Estella. "No one was ever more thoughtful."[18]

Leopold returned to Madison, and to revitalized class enrollments. Vogt came to town for a visit in March. There was a plan afoot to bring him to the university in an instructional capacity, although this never came to pass. During his stay, Vogt delivered several lectures on campus. If the controversy inherent in his message was not evident before then, it quickly became so. Vogt's tell-it-like-it-is account of problems in Central America brought forth passionate opposition from some of the university's Latin American students, but his evidence of resource degradation was as overwhelming as it was disturbing. Vogt would not be deterred. He was soon back in the tropics writing a book on his concerns. "There is a good deal of point in bringing out such a book as this as soon as possible," he wrote to Leopold, "because the problem of population and land use has been given only glancing consideration in the United Nations."[19]

The war and its aftermath had only underscored the importance of wilderness in the minds of the leaders of the Wilderness Society. As they prepared for their annual meeting, they planned to revise their by-laws and reconsider the role of wilderness in the nuclear age. Leopold wrote to Benton MacKaye on May 1, "I am thoroughly convinced of one basic point: that wilderness is merely one manifestation of a change of philosophy of land use, and that the Wilderness Society, while focussing on wilderness as such, cannot ignore the other implications and should declare itself on them, at least in general terms."[20] A few days later, MacKaye wrote to Leopold and the other councilors:

> Our ultimate job in the W.S. is the conservation of the earth as a fitting abode for humans; such abode is threatened by a certain recent, much publicized scientific discovery; a growing movement is underway toward the control of this discovery; the purpose of The Wilderness Society would be rendered void by the failure of such movement.
>
> What about it? What is this effort but a conservation movement? What is the situation cited but the "No. 1 conservation problem?" What else should be the focus of *all* conservation groups? . . . How about the W.S. taking a lead in this direction? Please ponder.[21]

Leopold and the others pondered. Clearly it was dangerous to extend the work of their group too far beyond its original commitment; but clearly there were some circumstances that demanded extension. The times called for a new sense of purpose, and even for a new sense of wilderness itself. Howard Zahniser brought up the point in a letter to Leopold, and Aldo concurred. "It is gratifying to me," he replied, "that you are convinced we must broaden our definition of wilderness."[22] At the end of the spring, Leopold and the other councilors met for three days at Old Rag Mountain in Virginia, discussing their thoughts, adopting the new by-laws, and setting a new agenda for the society (including "Cooperation in World Government").

There were other reflections of the broadening conservation movement in Leopold's life throughout 1946. He served that year as chairman of a new Committee on Foreign Relations within the Wildlife Society. In his first draft resolution to the committee members, he stated that "this Committee wishes to assert flatly its belief that provincialism is as dangerous in the wildlife field as in any other."[23] Leopold's conviction on this point was so strong that he even made another foray, though a modest one, into politics. Horace Fries, a member of the university's Department of Philosophy, asked him to write a brief conservation platform for a new, idealistically conceived national political party organizing under John Dewey and A. Philip Randolph. Leopold responded with a clear summary of his own personal philosophy:

We urge that two concepts, heretofore largely ignored, be built into the national program of conservation.

The first is that the average citizen, especially the landowner, has an obligation to manage land in the interest of the community, as well as in his own interest. . . .

The second concept is that the health of the land as a whole, rather than the supply of its constituent "resources," is what needs conserving. . . .

Conservation education does not, as yet, deal with these basic concepts of harmony between land-use and land-health. It must do so if we are to achieve a stable land-economy.[24]

The new party failed to take root, but its efforts impressed Leopold.

Other less promising changes were also coming to conservation. In the wake of the war, an engineering mania overtook more than one federal agency. The Soil Conservation Service, once the exemplar of conservation through agronomic means, came to be dominated by stream-straighteners and ditch-dredgers. The Army Corps of Engineers went to work on the nation's rivers. Word of the corps's plans for the Illinois River came to Leopold secondhand. The federal engineers had plans to build reservoirs at the headwaters of the Illinois's principal tributaries, and to channelize all the tributaries down to their mouths, all in the name of "flood control." Leopold received an appeal from his old friend Roberts Mann, the colorful superintendent of conservation for the Cook County Forest Preserve District, and one of Leopold's most ardent admirers:

I claim we do not want that kind of flood control. I claim that the best interests of the State of Illinois would be served by returning this flood plain to the river; that the wildlife and recreational values to be regained would considerably exceed the agricultural values to be preserved. In the U.S. engineers' report and proposal, the wildlife values have been minimized far below their real value, and the recreational values have been ignored. Agricultural values have been inflated. There is further intangible value to be gained from restoring the river to its original flood plain. No one can understand Illinois, nor grasp the processes by which it has attained its present state, unless he has travelled its rivers; unless he has looked upon the back doors that once were front doors. The Illinois River is the deep artery of Illinois, just as the Mississippi is the artery of the midwest—the whole the breadbasket of the nation. One cannot argue for intangibles. I merely state them in passing.[25]

Mann was a boisterous, jovial man, a superb field naturalist and seasoned veteran of Chicago politics, possessed of a booming voice and a wild shock of snow-white hair. He often came to Aldo as a sounding board, running up to Madison on short notice to confer, to ask perplexing natural history questions, or just to compare field notes. "If ever a colleague could be called a disciple of AL," McCabe recalled, "it was Roberts Mann."[26]

Leopold could do little more than listen sympathetically to Mann's plaint, but it evoked a revealing reply. "My own impression," Aldo wrote, "is that river 'development' is now going to such lengths as to leave people like myself virtually at odds with society. I can't ride in a car going in the opposite direction from my destination. I'd rather jump out."[27] Mann was not going to let Leopold get away with that attitude; he had endured too many scrapes himself to feel sympathy. "So you are virtually at odds with society," Mann responded. "Brother, I have been that way for twenty years! I think when my kids get through college I will find me a cave in the high Rockies. In order to deal with people and try to do a decent job in a metropolitan area like ours, you have to swallow an awful lot. I have wanted to quit many, many times. I wish I was a skunk."[28]

While they were exchanging these letters, Leopold delivered an address that conveyed his postwar thoughts in a more subtle manner. On April 6, he spoke to a meeting of the Wisconsin Society for Ornithology in Appleton on the subject of the extinct passenger pigeon and a proposed monument to commemorate its passing. The meeting room was dimly lit and the turnout poor, no more than thirty people. At least some of those present did sense a certain intensity in the room. "We had the feeling that there was something unusual happening," one recalled.[29] Leopold took his place at the rostrum, and in the poor light leaned closely to read his manuscript. The small audience was privy to one of his most moving speeches, containing some of his most inspired images:

There will always be pigeons in books and in museums, but these are effigies and images, dead to all hardships and to all delights. Book-pigeons cannot dive out of a cloud to make the deer run for cover, nor clap their wings in thunderous applause of mast-laden woods. Book-pigeons cannot breakfast on new-mown wheat in Minnesota, and dine on blueberries in Canada. They know no urge of seasons; they feel no kiss of sun, no lash of wind and weather. They live forever by not living at all.[30]

Leopold's delivery that day was not his best. He hesitated now and then in the middle of sentences. The delivery did not detract from the message, which one listener described as "overwhelming." "Long before he finished this tremendous poetic prose, he reached the hearts of the people who were present."[31] Leopold's original draft (it was later revised for the book of essays) contained a strong criticism of man's preoccupation with what he called "power-science" and of the "cosmic arrogance" which was charting the course of scientific endeavor. "Time was when the aim of science was to understand the world, and to learn how man may live in harmony with it. If I read Darwin right, he was more concerned with understanding than with power. But science, as now decanted for public consumption, is mainly a race for power. Science has no respect for the land as a community of organisms, no concept of man as a fellow passenger in the odyssey of evolution." Leopold did not deny outright the efficacy of "power-science," but decried our lethal addiction to it. "All our wars, external and internal, deal with little else," he stated.[32]

In his own mind, this was directly linked to the focus of his talk: extinction. "We have learned in politics that preoccupation with the nation, as distinguished from mankind, defeats its own end. We label this fallacy isolationism. Perhaps we have now to learn that preoccupation with mankind, as distinguished from the community of which man is a member, defeats its own ends. Perhaps this monument is not merely a symbol of a dead past, but also a portent of a different future. Perhaps we learn more from the dead than from the living."[33]

For Leopold, the proper study of man was not man alone, but man in his context: the earthly environment that provides both sustenance and meaning to the entire human enterprise. Attention to the natural world, rather than human society proper, had given Leopold a reverse view of his own species: he knew man because he knew what man was not. All recent evidence to the contrary, man was not a bloodthirsty killer out solely to save his own hide. Neither was he a passive recipient of cruel nature's blows. Nature knew no such animals. Man was a creature among fellow creatures, different from them as they were different from one another, endowed with special abilities and with a summons to some special enigmatic calling. The plants and animals had their own hidden aims. Man had his, among which was the striving for a more comprehensive and appreciative view of the life and the world around him.

The passenger pigeon, who "lived by the intensity of his desire for clustered grape and bursting beechnut, and by his contempt of miles and seasons," symbolized both the failure and the hope of this human adventure.

Into his address Leopold slipped a definition of man's place in nature's scheme, reminding his audience that, although we had inherited the privileges of self-awareness, noblesse oblige now compelled us to pay due respect to our biotic shipmates. He was never more eloquent:

For one species to mourn the death of another is a new thing under the sun. The Cro-Magnon who slew the last mammoth thought only of steaks. The sportsman who shot the last pigeon thought only of his prowess. The sailor who clubbed the last auk thought of nothing at all. But we, who have lost our pigeons, mourn the loss. Had the funeral been ours, the pigeons would hardly have mourned us. In this fact, rather than in Mr. Vannevar Bush's bombs, or Mr. DuPont's nylons, lies objective evidence of our superiority over the beasts.[34]

∽

Four days later, a tenth spring of tree planting at the shack commenced. Five Leopolds planted 935 more pines and tamaracks. Nina and Bill had begun a study of Canada goose flock formation that required careful tabulation of flock numbers. One evening the family counted 642 geese arriving in the marshes. "Flick nearly shivered himself into pieces watching them come in. . . . Many holes in the wings—souvenirs of Horseshoe Lake. All night there is a tremendous threshing of water by the assembly. I still haven't made out whether they beat the water with their wings or just rush about in courting antics. It's queer to watch the debate when they rise and disagree about whether to go to corn N. to Lewiston or S. to Baraboo Prairie. Looks like the U.N. debate."[35]

Ten years of time and attention had altered the shack landscape. Natural reproduction had increased the aspens, birches, cherries, red osiers, willows, and other marsh shrubs. The fringe of growth now hid the river and hemmed the sedge meadows. The experimental prairie in front of the shack had taken root—sandy though the soil was. A patchwork of odd-aged, variously successful tree plantations covered the alluvial flats and the sand hill. The line of elms still stood, but no longer alone. The family had planted upwards of thirty thousand trees and shrubs, and a lesser number of wildflowers, ferns, and prairie plants. Leopold noted with pride, "The trees are getting awkward to measure."[36]

Later in the spring, Aldo and Estella were called into baby-sitting service when Luna and his wife Carolyn dropped off Bruce, the second of three Leopold grandchildren, for two weeks. In town, Bruce was quite manageable. At the shack, he proved to be a ceaseless wanderer. Every time adult eyes turned, he was off to the pines. Aldo and Estella solved the problem when they discovered that, if Bruce's shoes were removed, he would confine himself to the vicinity of the shack. Thus, an early concept in grandchild management.

Except during the deep wintertime, Aldo and Estella went to the shack almost every weekend that year. They went by themselves more often now. Aldo's journal notes had reached a high plateau in terms of volume and detail. His entry for May 31 was typical:

Weather Warm, calm, hazy at daybreak, 58° at 3 AM. Changed suddenly to cold NE wind at 7 AM, with a long streak of cloud marking the NE front. 54° at 8 AM, cloudy. 41° 6 PM.

Daybreak Song A favorable morning for early song:

2:45	song sparrow
3:00	" "
3:05	field sparrow
3:07	Song sparrow
3:09	" ", field sparrow
3:11	field sparrow

3:15 Yellowthroat, field spar.
3:18 Crested Fly field spar. Indigo
 (after which all cut loose) (0.012)
3:26 meadowlark, towhee

The only difference between this and recent days is the scattered very early songs
 of the two very early species, song & field sparrow.

No clay-color heard this morning. Was our bird a migrant?

Robins Three sang for an overall total 330–345, 15 min. at 1. Orchard 2. Gate 3.
 Starker's point.

No Woodcock seen or heard last night or this morning.

Quail bobwhited 348, 400, 410, and off and on during morning, all from sandhill.
 Visiting cock?

Phenology Out: Birdfoot violet, Smilacina stellata, Jacob's ladder.

Last bloom: R. fascicularis, A. lyrata

Passing out: blue phlox, strawberry, geranium, yellow lady slipper

First bloom: wild rose, Lychnis alba, ox-eye daisy, Angelica, Ninebark, Potentilla
 arguta.

In bud: Walnut at Baraboo not yet in pollen. Green Dragon now full size. Pollen?

First Bloom (est 5/25) small "evening primrose"— Sundrops in park near Thomas land.

Woodcock Brood Just opposite Henika's gate Flick pointed and I flushed a feigning
 woodcock, dangling legs and trimmings. No young flew, so they must have
 been too young to fly. This brood (presumably) is 40 days later than that formed
 at pre-flying stage on April 21.

Deer Foods At Wahoo pond deer have been browsing an elm, and also many veroni-
 cas. These were 18″ high and were nipped back to about 12″ high.

Raspberries and Bees During the past week the red raspberries have been in bloom,
 and very heavily used both by honeybees and bumblebees. The near absence
 of petals makes the eagerness of the bees seem incongruous. They are so keen
 on the blossoms that they might sting on being disturbed.[37]

More than a year had passed since Leopold and Clinton Simpson, the
editor at Knopf, had last discussed the book of essays. In early April, Simpson wrote to Leopold and inquired about any progress he had made. Leopold's increased teaching load had precluded any actual writing, but he
had been giving the book much thought. He wanted to include several of
his philosophical essays, and he was now convinced that the collection
needed an introduction to provide coherence.

Leopold forwarded two of the philosophical essays. Simpson liked them,
and thought them of value, but advised Leopold that including them in
the same book with the descriptive essays would demand a "considerable
rearranging of material." He wrote to Leopold on April 29, "We certainly
have no objection to 'philosophical' writing, when it is as good as this,
but I wonder if the subjects of the other pieces are going to fit in with what
you have? Or do they group naturally together, so that the book might
be organized in two parts, one descriptive and the other philosophical?

I find whatever you write full of interest and vitality, and it seems to me our only problem is one of fitting together the pieces in a way that will not seem haphazard or annoying to the reader."[38]

It was the same old problem: how to tie the diverse essays together. Only now, by adding his philosophical articles, Leopold was making the collection even more varied. Previously, they had differed in style and geographical setting. Now they varied by level of abstraction. "I entirely agree with you," Leopold wrote back to Simpson. "I can see no easy way of getting unity between the philosophical essays and the descriptive essays. . . . Should I later evolve some scheme for achieving unification, I will send you a larger sample of the philosophical pieces."[39]

Leopold hoped to "hit this job hard" as soon as the university let out for the summer. In June, he did produce one new essay, in which he contrasted the economist's view of the sand counties with the ecologist's view. The essay was written after the visit of his rambling grandson.

Sometimes in June, when I see unearned dividends of dew hung on every lupine, I have doubts about the real poverty of the sands. On solvent farmlands, lupines do not even grow, much less collect a daily rainbow of jewels. If they did, the weed-control officer, who seldom sees a dewy dawn, would doubtless insist that they be cut. Do economists know about lupines?[40]

A week later, Leopold travelled east to the meeting of the Wilderness Society leaders at Old Rag Mountain. While stopping over in Washington, Aldo met briefly with Luna, who, after his discharge from the Army, had gone to work for the Soil Conservation Service in Washington. They talked about the book, discussing the problem of incongruity in the collection and the need for cooperation with the publisher and illustrator. They considered some possible titles. They also decided to engage a new illustrator. Hochbaum was simply too busy building up Delta and working on his own publications to devote time to illustrations. Another artist, an acquaintance of Luna's, rendered some drawings over the summer, but the arrangement did not work out, and once again Hochbaum was enlisted.[41]

Leopold's plans to set aside the summer for work on the essays never materialized. He managed to revise an essay or two, but beyond that he was too busy with his graduate students, research reports, changes in his department, and other writing obligations. Also, the Conservation Commission was about to enter its annual deer debate; as surely as the temperature rose, so did tempers around the state.

Then, too, the stabbing facial pains were persisting. Leopold knew by now that he had trigeminal neuralgia, commonly known as tic douloureux, an inflammation of the area around the main facial sensory and motor nerve. The causes of tic douloureux were (and remain) unclear, but apparently involve increased pressure on the trigeminal nerve from surrounding tissues and blood vessels. An attack may be brought on, unpredictably, by the slightest chance movements of the face. The pain is said to be as intense as any a person can suffer (many have described it as "like a toothache, only a hundred times worse").

Leopold began to have difficulty holding conversations. Often he would stop abruptly in midsentence, put his hand to his head, and close his eyes until the pain passed. The paroxysms usually lasted about thirty seconds. At home, Estella was supportive, but there was little she could do. At the office, Leopold tried not to let the tic affect his work, but he had no control over it. McCabe noticed that their meetings began to shorten. Since there was nothing wrong in their working relationship, he surmised that the Professor's health was to blame, although he was unaware of the exact nature of the problem. Aldo broke off one conference with a sudden, "Excuse me, I think I'll go home and have a rest." Leopold beat Bob to the office door, informed Virginia Kiesel that he was leaving, and set a brisk pace for home. Virginia looked at Bob. Bob just shrugged his shoulders.[42]

Leopold took the problem to a doctor, but there was little therapeutic treatment for the disease short of surgery, and even this was still in its experimental stage. Because the frequency and amplitude of the attacks fluctuated, Leopold and his doctor decided to hold off on this option. Aldo was advised to ease up on his schedule as much as possible over the summer.

ᑌᑎ

The deer argument took center stage at the July 9 meeting of the Conservation Commission. The sides were drawn along the same lines as in 1945. Despite evidence of changing opinion around the state, the Conservation Congress had voted for another buck season.[43] Ernie Swift and the Conservation Department recommended an any-deer season. Swift was uncompromising. "On the basis of our studies and in the view of the evidence collected over the years, the department regrets that it cannot go along with the recommendations of the Congress. We can conscientiously recommend only a season on any deer."[44] Leopold's fellow commissioners were primarily concerned with keeping the good will of the legislators, upon whom they depended for support for other items on their conservation agenda. Swift, hoping to forestall defeat, suggested that the public be given a chance to study the department's proposal. The commission deferred action for two weeks while discussions were held around the state. Before the morning's session ended, Leopold gave a capsule lesson on white pine reproduction as an example of the imperative need for deer herd reduction, his point being that decisions made in 1946 would affect the makeup of the entire forest a generation hence.

On July 24, the commissioners reconvened at the State Office Building

for a special meeting to decide on the deer season. The representatives of
the Conservation Congress reported on their state-wide sampling of opinion. Of seventy-one counties voting, forty-five opposed the department's
plan for an any-deer season. Opposition was most vehement in Roy Jorgensen's resort-area stronghold in the north.

Before the commissioners voted, Leopold pled his case. "To again postpone reduction of the deer herd will be, I think, the most important and
far-reaching error ever made by this Commission." The next hard winter,
he warned, would starve more deer than hunters would take in an antlerless season. "I want my exact words in the record," he stated. "The same
public which now insists that we postpone our reduction program will ask
us, after the starvation is over, why we did not foresee it." The majority,
he explained, was "in effect buying a few more years of easy deer hunting
at the expense of the future deer herd"; and in so doing they were allowing
the deer hunter to dominate forest policy. Every year's delay, Leopold argued, would compound the problem. To wait for the legislature to pass
a controlled-hunting law was futile. Fears of overreduction were unfounded,
and even local overreductions were preferable to a general overload of deer.
"To sum up," Leopold said,

this Commission was created, and was given regulatory powers, for the express
purpose of insulating it, to some degree, from the domination of fluctuating public
opinion. It was hoped that such a Commission might take the long view, rather
than the short view, of conservation problems. I cannot escape the conviction that
if we fail to reduce the deer herd now, we are taking the short view. . . . My plea
is that we vote on this issue, not as delegates representing a County, but as statesmen representing the long view of Wisconsin as a community.[45]

The vote went 5-1 against Leopold and for the usual forked-horn buck
season. This time, even Bill Aberg sided against his old colleague. Aberg
was "not willing to sacrifice the many important factors in conservation
for a deer season that was satisfactory only to the deer management men."[46]
Leopold and the other commissioners worked well together on the wide
variety of other issues before them, everything from warden pensions and
ice-fishing seasons to tractor purchases and state park concessions. On the
deer issue, though, Leopold voted as a land ecologist first and foremost,
thus drawing a thin but crucial line between himself and even as close a
friend and stalwart a conservationist as Aberg.

"I got beat on the deer issue again," he wrote to Starker.[47] Now it was
Leopold's turn to go public with a "Minority Report on Deer." The Au-
gust issue of the Conservation Department's *Bulletin* published it as "The
Deer Dilemma." "For once we agree with our conservation officials," Roy
Jorgensen intoned. "Dilemma is the right word for it! . . . In the case of
the people, they have but one alternative. That is to get rid of crackpot

conservation for all time. . . . Professor Leopold has never displayed an interest in conservation in general. He has but one hobby—get rid of deer!" Gordon MacQuarrie published Leopold's position in the *Milwaukee Journal* in September.[48]

The commission needed the controlled-hunt power. Only when they were able to distribute the hunt where it was most needed would the commissioners be able to make headway while kowtowing to both the legislature and the vocal opposition—as they seemed determined on the whole to do. But only the legislature could grant the commission that power, and they were not about to. The legislators, attentive to the wishes of the resort industry, were well content with traditional buck seasons and proper (and better yet, highly visible) winter feeding programs. They had shot down the last request from the commission for authority to hold a controlled hunt. The next legislature would not even have to fire; the commission, bowing as low as possible, did not even ask for the power, fearing that it would be construed as an imposition.

Facing this deadlock, Leopold tried a new tactic. Starting in September, he attempted to commit his fellow commissioners to a course of action in 1947 that would make them choose between "wishful-thinkers about deer and biological facts about deer." By proposing not just a special season, but an entirely new deer policy premised on herd reduction, Leopold hoped to call to account everyone involved—the commissioners, the legislature, the Conservation Congress, Roy Jorgensen's crowd. At best, the necessary reduction would take place. At worst, the cards would finally be out on the table and his critics could take on the responsibility for management strategy. "If the public will not tolerate intelligent deer management by its Commission," Leopold insisted, "then it does not need a commission. The old system of political conservation football would do just as well."[49] These attempts to force the issue were unsuccessful.[50] For the foreseeable future, the commissioners would muddle on and the welfare of the deer herd would be left to the devices of an irregular hunt, a near-extinct wolf population, a stop-gap feeding program, a gradually damaged forest, and the crucible of winter.

ᔕ

Leopold offered a new class in the fall of 1946. Advanced Game Management 179 was designed to give its twelve graduate students an intensive introduction to wildlife research. In the course, they covered a "check-list" of forty topics, from accidents, aggregations, and artificial propagation to water relations, weather, and weights and measurements. The material was essentially the same as in earlier years, but it had become necessary to teach it more systematically. The aim was the same: to develop the student's ability to think critically. One day the students watched the film *Starvation Stalks the Deer,* and picked out weaknesses in its presentation. At another point, halfway through the course, Leopold began a lecture on "The Critical Approach to Wildlife" by saying, "Modern science has saddled us with many vicious ideas; so many that it seems to me to have become a doubtful honor to be called a scientist. But science has also made one contribution to culture which seems to me permanent and good: the critical approach to questions of fact."[51]

Leopold's criticism of science in general did not prevent him from encouraging advancements in his own field. Under his guidance, these younger researchers were working new lines of study in wildlife behavior, physiology, endocrinology, nutrition, population ecology, refuge management, and endangered species. The scope of the science had broadened immensely.

At the shack that fall, Leopold paid particular attention to the timing of leaf color change and to pine weevil damage on some of the pines. Aldo and Estella were at the shack on the opening day of duck season, October 6. They saw only two ducks and heard only four shots the whole day. A few days later, Leopold and the other commissioners toured Horicon Marsh, the state's most important refuge, and saw a total of just three hundred ducks. All fall long, Leopold kept a tally of duck numbers. It was the third straight season of unusually low figures.

The figures seemed to substantiate the worst fears of Albert Hochbaum and other waterfowl experts. The continental duck population was down, and Ducks Unlimited's public relations department had plainly gone overboard in their optimistic assessments. Leopold had come near to resigning his membership the previous spring, but he held off. He and a number of his students and colleagues had met at the North American Wildlife Conference and drafted a critical memo to the directors of DU. It had no effect. That summer, Leopold had harshly reviewed S. Kip Farrington's book *The Ducks Came Back: The Story of Ducks Unlimited* in the *Journal of Wildlife Management.* Farrington painted a glowing picture of the duck situation, downplaying the effects of hunting and heaping praise on Ducks Unlimited. It was Leopold's opinion that the group had "a proud record, [which] should not be spoiled by claims of non-existent miracles. . . . Ducks Unlimited is too important an undertaking to fall victim to extravagant overclaims and outmoded exaggerations." He dismissed the book as "a charming fantasy."[52]

The issue was on the front burner all year. The hunting season turned up the heat. Leopold had the best firsthand information possible, not only from Hochbaum, but from Art Hawkins, who was back in Madison working for the U.S. Fish and Wildlife Service, and currently preparing an important Mississippi flyway report with a colleague, Robert Smith. Hawkins worked out of an upstairs office at 424, and as part of the arrangement, occasionally took over in class when Leopold was tied up with other business.

The duck season at Delta opened three weeks before Wisconsin's. The result was an American invasion of Manitoba. "In some areas," the Portage la Prairie paper reported, "[the hunters] were so closely spaced that members of one party would be sprayed by the shot of gunners in another blind. Probably it was the greatest concentration of shooters in the history of the marsh."[53] "It is heartbreaking," Hochbaum wrote to Leopold after interviewing many of the hunters and tallying their bags. "Most of these men belong to Ducks Unlimited—and most of them believe that their DU fees entitle them to do just about what they want with ducks; they actually believe they have paid for what they shoot and more."[54]

After receiving the Smith-Hawkins report, which exposed the false optimism in DU's picture, Leopold waited for a disclaimer from DU. It never came. Leopold felt it was time "to call a show-down." He wrote to the president of Ducks Unlimited asking for a reaction to the latest reports. "I do not expect DU to wear a halo," he concluded. "I have headed several organizations that had to find their own keep, and I know from experience that it is only human for such groups to distort the facts somewhat. It is a question of degree. DU is too important a venture to wreck its own credit by an unreasonable degree of distortion."[55]

Leopold was leaning over backward in his support of DU. In Hochbaum's opinion, he had already leaned too far. Before sending the letter, Leopold forwarded it to Hochbaum for review. Albert let fly.

. . . No. It is not a matter of degree. It is a matter of ethics.

Ducks Unlimited is made up of men who understand how strict codes of ethics must apply in their various professions—in medicine, law, university, press—ruling their behavior and guarding their professional welfare. But these very same men who hold to their own professional codes, are willing to wink at a degree of distortion in natural history. And that is exactly what is the matter with Ducks Unlimited.

Hochbaum had no patience when he perceived hypocrisy, especially when it affected Delta's ducks. He railed against the tone of Leopold's letter:

One does not have to wear a halo, as you say, to be honest. And if game management is willing to tolerate any degree of distortion—which is simply dishonesty by another name—then right here and now I no longer consider myself as belonging to that branch of your profession.

You may pass me off as an idealist. I am. I am for the same ideals in wildlife administration that other professions have won for themselves. And those ideals cannot brook such thoughts as you carry in your last paragraph.

Sometime wildlife administration will win its rightful place in the planning of the world. But it won't until we get squared around amongst ourselves and agree upon what is right and what is wrong.[56]

Leopold rewrote in stronger words his letter to Ducks Unlimited. "Are you able to assure your members that the [Smith-Hawkins] report gives DU a reasonably clean slate on the question of fact-distortion? If not, I for one shall expect some internal housecleaning. In fact, my confidence in DU will hinge on it. . . . By 'reform' I do not mean a rap on the knuckles. Either your personnel is worthy of the confidence of conservationists and should be supported in their work, or it is not, and should be replaced."[57]

The president of Ducks Unlimited, M. W. Smith, wrote back that "the matter of reorganization has been under consideration for some time." Leopold promised to "watch hopefully for the details as they are made public." Even Hochbaum was mollified, at least for the time being.[58]

On December 4–6 Leopold attended the Eighth Midwest Wildlife Conference at Des Moines. The conference had resumed after five years of wartime cancellations. Leopold took the opportunity to reflect on his role as an informed conservationist trying to effect change in public policy. He knew only too well the problems involved in changing policy when the public was not ready, not the least of which was the touchy title of "expert" that he had to bear. Obviously wearying of the constant involvement in professional battles, he nonetheless remained stalwart and candid. His presentation at the conference covered the history of the Wisconsin deer controversy, and was entitled "Adventures of a Conservation Commissioner."

After helping to set up several Commissions and serving on one, I have come to two conclusions.

The first is that a good Commission can prevent the conservation program from falling below the general level of popular ethics and intelligence.

The second is that no Commission can raise its program much above that level, except in matters to which the public is indifferent. Where the public has feelings, traditions, or prejudices, a Commission must drag its public along like a balky mule, but with this difference: the public, unlike the mule, kicks both fore and aft.

An issue may be so clear in outline, so inevitable in logic, so imperative in need, and so universal in importance as to command immediate support from any reasonable person. Yet that collective person, the public, may take a decade to see the argument, and another to acquiesce in an effective program.[59]

Leopold was no utopian, but he did hope that reasonable people, informed by facts, questioning myths, and guided by common concerns, could lay aside immediate differences in the interest of maintaining a healthy land community. When it became clear that people were not always so inclined, or that his own motives and efforts were misconstrued, then his faith wavered. The pressures on him were particularly high at the end of 1946. He was able to recharge his resolve by spending time with students, friends, and his family. On December 14, two of his students joined him on a trip to the shack. On the seventeenth, the Getaway Club, still going strong after twenty years, met for their monthly revelry. Five days later, Leopold and

Reuben Paulson hunted pheasants at Riley. Nina and Bill came to town for the holidays, and after Christmas the family spent two days at the shack.

ౌ

Leopold's professional standing was at its apex. As he turned sixty, he was elected an honorary vice-president of the American Forestry Association, and president of the Ecological Society of America. The former position was "bestowed in recognition of your constructive interest and leadership in the conservation of our nation's forests and land resources."[60] The latter took place even though Leopold did not usually attend the ESA's annual conference and was not even an active member. "I am astonished by my election," he wrote to a society colleague. "I feel deeply the responsibility implied in my being elected despite this failure on my part."[61] The ESA's choice of Leopold was testimony to the high regard in which he was held by the scientific community as well as the major conservation groups.

The Twelfth North American Wildlife Conference, held in San Antonio on February 3–5, 1947, was predestined to be a lively affair. The profession was fully on its feet again, coming out of the war larger and stronger than ever. Moreover, a number of provocative issues promised to keep the conference rooms abuzz.

The problem of excess deer was now recognized as national in scope. Leopold, with coauthors Lyle Sowls and David Spencer, had just put the finishing touches on a joint paper, "A Survey of Over-Populated Deer Ranges in the United States," the first attempt to coordinate the scattered reports of deer irruptions from across the country. At the conference, the ad hoc group of deer researchers that had first met in 1944 was formalized into an official committee, and was directed to prepare a book-length study of deer management in the United States.

During the meetings, the waterfowl controversy exploded. Albert Hochbaum and Harrison Lewis pressed the case. Laying out his evidence, Hochbaum decried the trend toward overshooting, and made a blunt prediction. "In terms of history," he said, "this can't last long. The days of lush shooting on the prairies are numbered. If duck hunting, particularly of the diving ducks, continues along the present plan, regardless of what we do to maintain land and marsh, breeding stocks will continue to decline."[62] No one denied the fact that ducks were down, nor that overshooting was the main reason. The U.S. Fish and Wildlife Service, heretofore staying in the background, instituted changes in its policy to defend the ducks and geese. Ducks Unlimited found its back to the wall. "I have attended this Conference for twenty years," Leopold said, "but this is the first session that ever was unanimous on waterfowl. Misfortune is a great leveler."[63]

A new issue on the minds of those at the conference was the plan being perpetrated by business interests to wrest control of federal lands in Arizona, Utah, New Mexico, Nevada, and Idaho. Hoping to take advantage of the postwar atmosphere, a group of western livestock, lumber, oil, and mining interests was endeavoring to have the federal holdings of the West transferred to the states for easier pickings. Bernard DeVoto had just broken the story of the land grab in *Harper's,* and his exposé had the conference electrified.[64] Although the topic was not on the formal program, it was discussed in the halls and backrooms. Leopold, who was asked to summarize the conference, brought the issue to the main rostrum:

I have this to say:
1) It is perhaps the biggest conservation battle since the Ballinger Controversy.
2) Let no man think that the issue is a western affair, of no consequence to other states. The defeat of public land conservation in the west would be felt by every state.
3) Let no man think that this is a grazing district fight. Disrupt the public domain, and the National Forests will follow; disrupt the National Forests and the National Parks will follow.
4) It is pure evasion to say that the states, or private owners, could practice conservation on these lands. Neither, by and large, have demonstrated either the capacity or the wish to do so. To organize the practice of conservation on large areas takes decades of hard work.
5) Now is the time for a critical self-examination by all federal land bureaus.[65]

There was no stronger advocate of private conservation efforts than Leopold, but neither was there anyone more willing to defend the public lands against the short-sighted efforts of private interests. Federal regulation may not have been the preferred route to conservation, but under circumstances such as these, where the motives of the perpetrators were clear, it was the only route.

By now, many of the younger participants in the conference looked up to Leopold in particular as one of the founding fathers of the conservation professions, and as one whose stalwart emphasis on basic research kept progress on track. Leopold kept his usual tight conference schedule of meetings and private counseling, and McCabe kept his usual close eye on the Professor. Hochbaum and Leopold had breakfast together one morning. Albert was shocked to see how Aldo had aged since their last encounter. His face was grey and deeply lined, showing the effects of the tic. Albert asked to be let off the hook concerning illustrations for Aldo's essays. "We were both relieved," Albert recalled. "He knew I had my hands full, and I had a hunch he could find another artist.[66]

After the conference, Leopold and eleven other wildlifers were guests at the King Ranch at Kingsville, Texas. For two days, they toured the ranch, an extensive, diverse range of live-oak ridges, mesquite flats, and seacoast prairies. Leopold called it "the highlight of my year," and considered it "one of the best jobs of wildlife restoration on the continent, [with] unparalleled opportunities for both management and research. Still more important: it is a gem among natural areas, and must be kept intact."[67] All was not to his liking, however. Leopold and Ira Gabrielson toured the ranch with its president, who "killed 1 coyote and chased another over the coastal prairie in the car, shooting several times with a six-shooter, but failing to score. He also shot at every hawk and owl that offered a fair chance, but happily something was askew in his telescopic sight so none were hit."[68] Leopold diplomatically suggested adjustments in the ranch's predator extermination work ("I cannot speak too loudly on this," Leopold wrote at one point, "for I myself got high-pressured into assenting to a wolf-bounty in Wisconsin.")[69] A few weeks later, the ranch president instructed his men to leave the remnant population of mountain lions alone.

Among those Leopold conferred with in San Antonio was George Brewer, a staff member of the New York Zoological Society. Brewer and his colleagues at the society, under the leadership of President Fairfield Osborn, were currently planning a new conservation organization that would operate on a worldwide basis. Brewer sought to enlist Leopold's support and solicit his advice. On March 7–10, Leopold went to New York to discuss the plan with Osborn, Bill Vogt, and the staff of the Society. Leopold came away impressed. "The outfit is a good one," he wrote to Starker. "I was pleasantly surprised at their ability to absorb advice that must have sounded pretty stiff. Bill [Vogt] and I found ourselves giving identical views, even tho we had hardly seen each other for years."[70]

The Conservation Foundation incorporated shortly thereafter. Leopold served on the advisory council with such notables as Vogt, Charles Elton, Alexander Wetmore of the Smithsonian Institution, and G. Evelyn Hutchinson of Yale. Its express purpose was "to advance, for the benefit of mankind throughout the world, knowledge and understanding of the earth's natural and living resources and their essential relation to each other and to the sustenance and enrichment of life on earth."[71] The foundation saw as its main function the funding of research and educational activities at key areas around the world, working if possible through indigenous institutions.[72]

The formation of the Conservation Foundation was one more expression of conservation's expanded perspective. Leopold was too occupied with other business to devote much time to the foundation's program, but he was able to offer advice via mail. Significantly, the three central figures at the March 1947 meeting—Leopold, Vogt, and Osborn—were simultaneously working on major books which would appear within two years and become landmarks in conservation history.

Back in Madison, sixty-six were enrolled in the wildlife ecology course.

This increase in volume inevitably forced a change in Leopold's classroom manner. He was still a highly effective instructor, but some of the spontaneity was lost from earlier years. Leopold's forte had always been his ability to solicit conflicting or uncertain viewpoints from his students and carefully work them together in a satisfactory synthesis. Class size made that approach less practical.[73]

By now, though, the course was honed down to its essentials. He began with general discussions of plants, animals, soils, and land use, shifted to wildlife population characteristics, focussed on species occurring in Wisconsin, expanded on these to discuss ecological communities, and expanded further to discuss the landscapes of other regions. He still refrained from direct transfusions of conservation philosophy. At one point in the course, though, he did confess to "an ulterior motive" in his teaching:

I am interested in the thing called "conservation." For this I have two reasons: (1) without it, our economy will ultimately fall apart; (2) without it many plants, animals, and places of entrancing interest to me as an explorer will cease to exist. I do not like to think of economic bankruptcy, nor do I see much object in continuing the human enterprise in a habitat stripped of what interests me most.[74]

Leopold then gave one of his most pointed expressions of his approach to teaching. He suggested that conservation suffered from the fallacy, "clearly borrowed from modern science, that the human relation to land is only economic. It is, or should be esthetic as well. In this respect our current culture, and especially our science, is false, ignoble, and self-destructive."

If the individual has a warm personal understanding of land, he will perceive of his own accord that it is something more than a breadbasket. He will see land as a community of which he is only a member, albeit now the dominant one. He will see the beauty, as well as the utility, of the whole, and know the two cannot be separated. We love (and make intelligent use of) what we have learned to understand.

Hence this course. I am trying to teach you that this alphabet of "natural objects" (soils and rivers, birds and beasts) spells out a story, which he who runs may read — if he knows how. Once you learn to read the land, I have no fear of what you will do to it, or with it. And I know many pleasant things it will do to you.[75]

Few students could resist an appeal like that.

When the pain from Leopold's tic douloureux grew worse in March and April, he tried to take time away from his workload. One Sunday, he and Flick visited the shack by themselves. The spring planting trip proceeded on schedule in April, but was cut short by an emergency meeting of the Conservation Commission. (The latest altercation involved the proposed development of a power dam on the Flambeau River. The commission was leaning toward approval of the dam. Leopold took the position that "if each occasion of a proposed dam is satisfied in the light that uncertain economic values of that dam exceed the recreational values, the state would end up with no free-running rivers." The commission voted to withdraw its opposition to the dam.)[76]

By early May, Leopold could no longer bear up under the recurring tic pains. Although there were only two weeks remaining in the college semester, he decided to seek immediate relief. Early in May, he received an "alcohol block," the only available nonsurgical treatment for tic dou-loureux. Alcohol was injected into his trigeminal nerve in order to deaden the critical neurons. The method was uncertain at best, both in its preci-sion and its duration.

The block seemed to work. The doctor again ordered him to rest over the summer, commencing immediately. Leopold was forced to cancel a much-anticipated consulting trip to Isle Royale National Park at the end of May. After exams, he and Estella vacationed for a week at the shack. The doctor's firm orders left him with no alternative but to spend the sum-mer working on the essay collection. In early June, he began to revise two essays, his first work on the book in six months. In the meantime, the alcohol block was showing mixed results. On June 4, he wrote to Victor Cahalane of the National Park Service, who was to have arranged Leopold's inspection of Isle Royale, that he could not set another date because he was experiencing "a slight recurrence of my face trouble."[77]

∽

With their children all away from home (twenty-year-old Estella had gone to Delta to spend the summer as an assistant), Aldo and Estella would have the time to themselves. First, Aldo had several obligations to fulfill. The council of the Wilderness Society was scheduled to meet in northern Minnesota the third week in June. While Leopold waited on a train plat-form in Watertown, Wisconsin, he did some phenologizing: wild rose and marsh blueflag in first bloom, wild grape and thornapple in full bloom, black locust in last bloom, a bobolink still singing, a coal-sooted upland plover on a power line pole. The councilors met on an island in Rainy Lake for four days, reviewing a number of local wilderness issues and launching a campaign "to extend throughout the continent a system of wilderness areas for permanent preservation."[78] This system, more ambitious than any previously conceived, aimed to secure representative samples of eleven primary natural communities across North America. During the meetings, Leopold was reelected vice-president.

On June 27 in Minneapolis he delivered one of the most forcefully worded addresses of his career. His audience was the Conservation Com-mittee at the annual meeting of the Garden Club of America, and he chose the occasion to give a speech that had been a long, long time in the building. In "The Ecological Conscience," Leopold finally came clear. He decided to speak his mind, without reservation.

"Everyone ought to be dissatisfied with the slow spread of conservation to the land," he began. "Our progress still consists largely of letterhead pieties and convention oratory. The only progress that counts is that on the actual landscape of the back forty, and here we are still slipping two steps backward for each forward stride."[79] The theme was a familiar one from Leopold's quiver: the lack of real accountability to the needs of land. His tone this time, however, was much more direct, even desperate:

> The basic defect is this: we have not asked the citizen to assume any real responsibility. We have told him that if he will vote right, obey the law, join some organizations, and practice what conservation is profitable on his own land, that everything will be lovely; the government will do the rest.
>
> This formula is too easy to accomplish anything worthwhile. It calls for no effort or sacrifice; no change in our philosophy of values. It entails little that any decent and intelligent person would not have done, of his own accord, under the late but not lamented Babbittian code.
>
> No important change in human conduct is ever accomplished without an internal change in our intellectual emphases, our loyalties, our affections, and our convictions. In our attempt to make conservation easy, we have dodged its spiritual implications. The proof of this error lies in the fact that philosophy, ethics, and religion have not yet heard of it.[80]

What conservation lacked, he suggested, was a sense of personal responsibility in our relationship with land—an "ecological conscience."

He turned on his slide projector and related four case histories that showed "the futility of trying to improve the face of the land without improving ourselves." He first described the soil conservation problem in southwestern Wisconsin, where too many farmers, after fifteen years of prodding, "continued only those practices that yielded an immediate and visible economic gain for themselves. . . . No one has ever told farmers that in land-use the good of the community may entail obligations over and above those dictated by self-interest." The second example involved Wisconsin's deer. Leopold berated those who, "for the sake of maintaining an abnormal and unnatural deer herd for a few more years, are willing to sacrifice the future forest, and also the ultimate welfare of the herd itself." It was Leopold's most pointed reply to his persistent critics:

To understand the deer problem requires some knowledge of what deer eat, of what they do not eat, and of how a forest grows. The average deer hunter or resort keeper is sadly lacking in such knowledge, and when anyone tries to explain the matter, he is branded forthwith as a long-haired theorist. This anger-reaction against new and unpleasant facts is of course a standard psychiatric indicator of the closed mind.

We speak glibly of conservation education, but what do we mean by it? If we mean indoctrination, then let us be reminded that it is just as easy to indoctrinate with fallacies as with facts. If we mean to teach the capacity for independent judgement, then I am appalled by the magnitude of the task. The task is large mainly because of this refusal of adults to learn anything new.

The ecological conscience, then, is an affair of the mind as well as the heart. It implies a capacity to study and learn, as well as to emote about the problems of conservation.

The third case history involved a Sauk County neighbor of Leopold's who had taken advantage of wartime prices to gut a remnant grove of old white pines. The fourth recounted the commission's decision to allow a dam on the Flambeau.[81] Leopold's choice of cases was almost symbolic. They represented the concerns of a lifetime: soil, wildlife, forests, waters, and, implicitly, people.

Leopold concluded that a new motive had to guide land-use (or even land-nonuse) decisions. "The practice of conservation must spring from a conviction of what is ethically and esthetically right as well as what is economically expedient. A thing is right only when it tends to preserve the integrity, stability, and beauty of the community, and the community includes the soil, waters, fauna, and flora, as well as people."[82]

Leopold's philosophy had come to a sharp point. Still squeezed between a stubborn reluctance to hand responsibility over to government and the reality of public indifference to that responsibility, he chose the only other alternative: a forthright assertion of individual responsibility for land health. It took a postwar world and a personal sense of urgency to draw that assertion out of him with such vehemence. He spoke in undiluted terms: "economic provocation is no longer a satisfactory excuse for unsocial land-use. Or, to use somewhat stronger words, for ecological atrocities. This, however, is a negative statement. I would rather assert positively that decent land-use should be accorded social rewards proportionate to its social importance."[83]

He knew he was entering new territory. There was precedence for the idea he was propounding, not only in his own past writings, but in all those that had influenced him, from the Bible to P. S. Lovejoy. But it was, for him, a new kind of statement, and as in any kind of groundbreaking, physical or philosophical, he was acutely aware of both its opportunities and its practical limitations. "I have no illusions about the speed or accuracy with which an ecological conscience can become functional. It has required 19 centuries to define decent man-to-man conduct and the process is only half done; it may take as long to evolve a code of decency for man-to-land conduct. In such matters we should not worry too much about anything except the direction in which we travel."[84] That direction was clear: "the first step is to throw your weight around on matters of right and wrong in land-use. Cease being intimidated by the argument that a right action is impossible because it does not yield maximum profits, or that wrong action is to be condoned because it pays. That philosophy is dead in human relations, and its funeral in land-relations is overdue.[85]

"The Ecological Conscience" garnered a greater reaction than Leopold anticipated. Several periodicals published it, and Leopold's own reprint supply was quickly depleted. Among the many letters he received was one from Max Otto, of the university Department of Philosophy. "I like the combination of frankness and restraint which you achieve. These are praiseworthy qualities as I see things, and to come upon them always gives me new confidence. Still, I value even more a quality in your paper which I can only call *spiritual*. You have a *philosophy of wildlife management* which is itself part of a philosophy of life. . . . I'm sure that your argument is sound, and I wish religious people — *church* people, I mean — could see it to be part of religion to enlist in your cause. I'm afraid most of them do not see life in these terms." Leopold replied that he was "deeply pleased that the essay should have struck you as having value," adding that "this reminds me of something I have thought of for years; that I have wasted many opportunities for real discussions with you."[86]

On July 1, Leopold was back in Madison for the Conservation Commission's annual midsummer deer season decision. The battlelines had not budged and the results did not change: the Conservation Department requested an any-deer season, the Conservation Congress recommended another buck season, and the majority of the Conservation Commission yielded to fears of legislative reprisal. Leopold's motion for approval of the department's plan was not even seconded. Once more he was obliged to record his dissent in a minority report.[87]

Another controversy came to a head that week. Albert Hochbaum passed along the latest evidence of duplicity on the part of Ducks Unlimited's public relations department. "I wouldn't bother you with this if I didn't think it was important," Albert wrote. The deception was too blatant for Leopold to ignore. On July 8, he wrote to M. W. Smith, "The present waterfowl crisis is so close to my heart that I cannot support any organization that withholds the truth about it. This, then, is the withdrawal of my membership in and my moral support of Ducks Unlimited."[88] Leopold still had many good friends in DU and voiced support for its overall goals, but until he and his informants were proven wrong, he refused to renew his membership. They never were, and he never did.

With a measure of tranquility restored to his life and his other obligations fulfilled, Leopold finally returned to the essays. The last three weeks of July proved to be critical to the development of the manuscript. He revised seven of the essays. More important, he decided to overhaul the entire structure of the collection. He divided it into three parts, the first consisting of essays about the shack, arranged month by month, under the subtitle "A Sauk County Almanac"; the second, "Sketches Here and There," pulled together fifteen essays about other parts of Wisconsin, the Midwest, the West, Mexico, and Canada; the third, "The Upshot," included several of his philosophical essays. For the collection as a whole, he chose the title "Great Possessions."

At some point, probably in late July, Leopold composed what would become his best known essay. He had already decided to use two older essays in the "Upshot" section—"Conservation Esthetic" from 1938, and "Wildlife in American Culture" from 1941. He planned to summarize in a third essay his thoughts on wilderness. He needed one additional essay that would integrate the various components of his argument for an ecological understanding of land and land-use.

Evidently he had tried before to write such an essay, but these attempts never made it beyond his "cooler." The assignment was a challenging one. The essay had to draw on history, science, and philosophy without getting befogged in abstractions. It had to convey both the social and biological aspects of conservation, and to advance the cause of conservation by being simultaneously critical and supportive. It had to throw down its gauntlet as compellingly and tactfully as possible. In short, Leopold had to reduce forty years of experience and reflection to one coherent essay.

His solution was ingenious. Instead of writing a wholly new essay, he decided to update and splice together three of his most significant previous statements. Out of his reprint file he took "The Conservation Ethic" from 1933, "A Biotic View of Land" from 1939, and the recent "The Ecological Conscience." These three provided the basis for a new essay, which he called "The Land Ethic."[89]

Over a period of several days, Leopold excised pieces of the older texts, painstakingly revised them, and fitted them together. He borrowed the opening discussions of the "ethical sequence" and the ecological interpretation of history from "The Conservation Ethic." From "The Ecological Conscience" came a subsection of the essay bearing the same name. The explanation of the "land pyramid" in "A Biotic View of Land" became the scientific backbone of the new essay. Leopold bonded these older passages together with a substantial amount of newly written material, amounting to about half the essay. The result was a distillation of thought, a condensed account of Leopold's philosophical development, infused with his most current thinking.

Leopold's careful revisions of the older essays revealed not only a poet's craftsmanship, but an elder statesman's circumspection. Many of the changes were purely stylistic—deletions, rephrasings, changes in punctuation. Others reflected Leopold's uncanny attention to clarity and completeness, as well as his increased sophistication as an observer of nature. In their subtlety, they also reflected changes in Leopold's emphases. An original passage explaining food chains read:

> The lines of dependency for food and other services are called food chains. Each species, including ourselves, is a link in many chains. Thus the bobwhite quail eats a thousand kinds of plants and animals, i.e., he is a link in a thousand chains. The pyramid is a tangle of chains so complex as to seem disorderly, but when carefully examined the tangle is seen to be a highly organized structure.[90]

The revision read:

> The lines of dependency for food and other services are called food chains. Thus soil-oak-deer-Indian is a chain that has been largely converted to soil-corn-cow-farmer. Each species, including ourselves, is a link in many chains. The deer eats a hundred plants other than oak, and the cow a hundred plants other than corn. . . . The pyramid is a tangle of chains so complex as to seem disorderly, yet the stability of the system proves it to be a highly organized structure.[91]

With these few simple changes, Leopold was able to incorporate an example — deer and corn — familiar to a broader range of readers, show that ecological principles did not pertain only to wildlife, and emphasize stability as the measure of a system's order. His choice of deer as an example was, consciously or not, indicative of his concentration on the deer issue.

In dozens of other passages of "The Land Ethic," Leopold made similar changes. Taken in sum, they revealed an obvious shift in his tone. Even as his argument was gaining strength in the synthesis, his voice became more measured, self-assured, and less severe. In 1939, he asked "Can violence be reduced?"; in 1947, he wrote, "Can the desired alterations be accomplished with less violence?" An early draft of "The Ecological Conscience" read, "Land-use ethics and esthetics are still governed by ruthless competitive economic self-interest, just as social ethics were in 1875."[92] By the time the sentence appeared in "The Land Ethic," it read, "Land-use ethics are still governed wholly by economic self-interest, just as social ethics were a century ago."

These rhetorical shifts were evident in the key passage from "The Ecological Conscience." The earliest extant version read:

> The practice of conservation must spring from a conviction of what is ethically right, as well as what is economically expedient. A thing is right only when it tends to preserve the integrity and stability of the community, and the community includes the soil, waters, fauna, and flora, as well as people.[93]

By the time it appeared in "The Land Ethic," Leopold had edited it twice. Now it read:

> The 'key-log' which must be moved to release the evolutionary process for an ethic is simply this: quit thinking about decent land-use as solely an economic

problem. Examine each question in terms of what is ethically and esthetically right, as well as what is economically expedient. A thing is right when it tends to preserve the integrity, stability, and beauty of the biotic community. It is wrong when it tends otherwise.[94]

This would become one of Leopold's most oft-quoted and carefully criticized remarks. Ironically, it was somewhat out of character. He was wary of the liabilities in so grand a pronouncement, but came forward with it in the exasperated context of "The Ecological Conscience." When he chose to include it in "The Land Ethic," he eased up, broadened his focus, and turned it from a proclamation to a firm appeal for self-inquiry.

These older manuscripts gave Leopold only half an essay. His new material gave them coherence. Only in these new passages did he employ the term "land ethic." The same quality of calm but profound concern was evident: "In short, a land ethic changes the role of *Homo sapiens* from conqueror of the land-community to plain member and citizen of it. It implies respect for his fellow-members, and also respect for the community as such."[95] On this point he referred to world history for a moral:

In human history, we have learned (I hope) that the conqueror role is eventually self-defeating. Why? Because it is implicit in such a role that the conqueror knows, *ex cathedra,* just what makes the community clock tick, and just what and who is valuable, and what and who is worthless, in community life. It always turns out that he knows neither, and this is why his conquests eventually defeat themselves.[96]

At the end of the essay, he tried to strike a balance between the reality of economic necessity and the truth that standard economic definitions of "necessity" did not suffice in conservation:

It of course goes without saying that economic feasibility limits the tether of what can or cannot be done for land. It always has and always will. The fallacy the economic determinists have tied around our collective neck, and which we now need to cast off, is the belief that economics determines *all* land-use. This is simply not true.[97]

In conservation matters, a profit motive was not enough. Nor, for that matter, was a sentimental motive. With a sidelong glance toward his vocal detractors, he warned that "conservation is paved with good intentions which prove to be futile, or even dangerous, because they are devoid of critical understanding of the land, or of economic land-use." The ethic Leopold envisioned had to combine the practical and the emotional with the intellectual. It had to fuse wise use and beauty in human occupation of land, and to underlie this with a fundamental respect for the integrity of the natural world.

"The Land Ethic" was, and remains, an extraordinary statement, the homing point of Leopold's geographical and intellectual travels. He was trying to frame a large idea, and very possibly a great one. Yet, he realized that "nothing so important as an ethic is ever 'written.'" An ethic could only evolve "in the minds of a thinking community," and any written expression of one—even his own—would by its very nature be tentative, since evolution never stops. And at any given time, there were limits as well on an ethic's effectiveness, or at least on the style in which one might apply it. "Breakfast comes before ethics" he once told his daughter Nina. But for continued sustenance, the opportunity to enjoy it, and the freedom to thrive on it, an adjustment of human attitudes toward nature was necessary and proper. This was the sum and substance of Leopold's credo. Only if individuals were responsible to the needs and possibilities of land could modern civilization and wild nature endure and coexist, in health and in perpetuity.

By the end of July, the manuscript was coming together and he had completed a foreword that explained at length the contexts of the forty or so essays in the "Great Possessions" collection. It was a rare autobiographical expression. "These essays," he wrote, "are one man's striving to live by and with, rather than on, the American land. I do not imply that this philosophy of land was always clear to me. It is rather the end-result of a life-journey, in the course of which I have felt sorrow, anger, puzzlement, or confusion over the inability of conservation to halt the juggernaut of land abuse. These essays describe particular episodes en route."[98]

Leopold continued to work on the essays through August. He retrieved several articles from the *Wisconsin Agriculturalist and Farmer* series to fill in gaps in the almanac structure. In a process akin to that which he followed in writing "The Land Ethic," he summarized his views on wilderness in a new essay simply entitled "Wilderness." It would be his last major statement on the topic. His final word carried echoes of Ralph Waldo Emerson's "American Scholar":

> Ability to see the cultural value of wilderness boils down, in the last analysis, to a question of intellectual humility. The shallow-minded modern who has lost his rootage in the land assumes that he has already discovered what is important; it is such who prate of empires, political or economic, that will last a thousand years. It is only the scholar who appreciates that all history consists of successive excursions from a single starting-point, to which man returns again and again to organize yet another search for a durable scale of values. It is only the scholar who understands why the raw wilderness gives definition and meaning to the human enterprise.[99]

It was an intriguing point on which to conclude thirty years of writing about wilderness. In 1917, when Leopold and his friends in New Mexico talked of the wilderness, they saw it as a place to hunt, fish, and camp.

In 1947, it was an almost cerebral entity, an alternative to which civilization could turn to assess not only its ecological health, but even its social and psychological well-being.

Another year had passed since Leopold's last contact with Clinton Simpson, the editor of Knopf. On September 5, he wrote to Simpson that he had a "new manuscript" ready for review, not yet finished, but sufficient to give "an overall view of the job." Simpson was still "very much interested" in the manuscript and anxious to see it. Leopold sent the essays off to New York on September 11.[100]

21

Finale
(1947–1948)

THE ALCOHOL block that Leopold received in May 1947 wore off over the summer. The tic spasms returned and finally became painful beyond the point of tolerance. On August 19, Leopold matter-of-factly wrote to the Mayo Clinic to arrange a date for surgery. Dr. Alfred Adson, a neurosurgeon at the clinic, scheduled an appointment for a month later. In the interval Leopold was confined to bed. Dan Thompson, one of his graduate assistants, had to begin the Advanced Game Management course without him.

Leopold took advantage of the wait to draw together the loose ends of "Great Possessions." Young Estella, home from her Delta summer, took advantage of her father's incapacity in her own way. Here was a rare opportunity to speak with him heart to heart. Normally, he was too active or too reticent to pin down in deep conversation. The mood, however, was appropriate. To Estella, he seemed bored and depressed lying in his bed, and eager to talk. She cheered him up by recounting the highlights of her summer at Delta, presenting an enthusiastic travelogue of the canoe trip that she and Nina had taken to Clandeboye Bay.

As they talked, Estella saw her chance finally to find out what was going on inside her father's mind. She veered the conversation toward religion, a subject about which he still never spoke. Estella asked him point blank whether he believed in God. "He replied that he believed there was a mystical supreme power that guided the Universe," Estella recalled. "But to him this power was not a personalized God. It was more akin to the laws of nature. He thought organized religion was all right for many people, but he did not partake of it himself, having left that behind him a long time ago. His religion came from nature, he said." Luna gave a similar assessment of his father's spiritual beliefs. "I think he, like many of the rest of us, was kind of pantheistic. The organization of the universe was enough to take the place of God, if you like. He certainly didn't believe in a personal God, as far as I can tell. But the wonders of nature were, of course, objects of admiration and satisfaction to him."[1]

Prior to the operation, Leopold travelled to St. Louis to speak at a testimonial dinner for E. Sydney Stephens, a friend since his game survey days and the preeminent figure in Missouri's enterprising conservation program. While there, Leopold met with Charlie Schwartz, an illustrator working for the Missouri Conservation Commission. Over the years, Schwartz had become acquainted with three of the Leopold children—Starker, Luna, and Nina. Earlier in the year, Luna had suggested that Schwartz would be a good choice as illustrator for "Great Possessions." Luna approached Schwartz with the idea, and Charlie agreed to give it a try. Aldo sent along a copy of the essays in anticipation of their meeting. They spent a day together discussing the manuscript. Aldo was impressed with Schwartz's ideas ("he really knows what it is all about") and agreed to provide additional articles and photographs for him to work with.

Leopold returned briefly to Madison, and attended the monthly meeting of the Conservation Commission.[2] He did not inform anyone at the office of his planned surgery, but simply left for Rochester without even leaving instructions on what to do in his absence.

He was admitted to St. Mary's Hospital in Rochester on September 19. Estella joined her husband on the twenty-fifth. Dr. Adson performed the delicate surgery two days later. An opening was cut into Leopold's skull near his left ear. The hole had to be large enough to allow the use of surgical instruments within the skull cavity. The brain was then lifted to expose the trigeminal nerve. The afflicted portion of the nerve was severed, rendering the receptors in the brain insensible. The skull fragment was replaced and the hole sutured shut.[3] Two days after the operation, Leopold felt well enough to dictate a long letter of instructions to Bob McCabe, and reported that he was "coming out of my operation fine." Although he was weakened, and the left side of his face now registered no feeling, his convalescence at the hospital took only one week, during which time he made a number of new friends. He discussed books with his nurse and invited one of his doctors to pay a visit to the shack.

Leopold was discharged and returned to Madison on October 3. Ever the attentive observer, he recorded his sensations during his recovery and prepared a "Memo for Dr. A. W. Adson on Post-operative stage of Aldo Leopold." His entry for the second week read:

Felt much better, but strong constriction of face and jaw muscles, almost but not quite painful, after every exertion. This constriction disappeared on lying down.

An attempt to write a paper disclosed poor ability to organize ideas, and severe loss of memory for detail such as names of people, names of plants, etc. This perhaps after-effect of ether?[4]

By October 10, he was well enough to take a weekend trip to the shack, although not yet to hunt. The next day he gave a previously scheduled talk to the Wisconsin Press Association in Madison, entitled "Conserving Wisconsin." Returning to the office the following Monday, he kept a very light schedule, working only an hour or two before returning home. McCabe and Pat Murrish, the newest department secretary, thought that even this was excessive and were surprised that he came to work at all. At first, Leopold confined himself to catching up on his mail. There were letters from well-wishers to answer, as well as the usual quota of complaints from Roy Jorgensen's minions. Albert Hochbaum wrote to remind him that ten years had passed since their first meeting. Aldo's reply began, "I was deeply touched by your remembering the start of our doings ten years ago. I can say without reservation that despite the mistakes each of us has made in dealing with the other, that our intellectual partnership is one of the anchors of my ship. Without it I would be adrift."[5]

In another letter, to his son-in-law Bill Elder, Leopold complained that "the worst mistake I have made this year was to put off my operation until so close to hunting season. I missed opening day on woodcocks, but do not intend to miss opening day on pheasants next Saturday."[6] That Saturday, he was at the shack with Estella, daughter Estella, Bob McCabe, and Fred Greeley, another student, and they hunted pheasants. On Sunday, they went for woodcock. "My 'hunting,'" Leopold wrote to Starker, "consisted of sitting in a chair hoping for a pass, but it was nevertheless good to get out."[7] A few days later, McCabe and Greeley stole the Professor away for another woodcock hunt in Adams County. While Flick led the hunt through the lowland alders, Leopold sat in a folding chair on an adjacent hillside.

By the third week of his recovery, Leopold was putting in half days at the office. "Feel still better," he noted for Dr. Adson, "but facial constrictions continue, and now include constrictions of half of tongue." As expected, the operation had resulted in a temporary loss of memory and paralysis of the left side of Leopold's face. The memory loss was most apparent in meetings with his graduate students. McCabe sat in on these meetings and assisted Leopold by prompting him with clues on the student's work. Leopold's inability to retain information was particularly evident at one of these meetings. During the course of a half-hour discussion, McCabe purposefully mentioned the student's name several times. Afterward, though, Leopold asked, "Who was that student and what is his research program?"[8]

His memory improved day-to-day, but his general health seemed to lag. He was weaker, and the paralysis caused his facial muscles to droop. The numbness in particular annoyed him. The tear duct in his left eye could not respond to stimuli, necessitating regular administration of eyedrops. In addition, Leopold had begun to lecture again and he worried that he was slurring his speech. His students said they did not notice, but he suspected they were simply showing consideration. At home he asked Estella, "Can you tell me, am I mumbling? I can't tell and it feels to me as though I'm mumbling. How does it sound to you, dear?" Estella assured him that he was not mumbling, but he continued to ask, almost every day.[9]

Four weeks after his surgery, Leopold reported a little optimistically that he was "practically back to normal." "Felt still better," he wrote in his notes. "Facial constrictions milder, constriction of tongue also milder. . . . Occasional shooting pain, sudden but mild (no resemblance to tic pain) in lips and head. . . . Did first full day's work. Went hunting and walked around several miles without after-effect. Still notice loss of names."[10]

He managed to keep up with some light reading. His most recent raves were for Sally Carrigher's books, Ronald M. Lockley's *Shearwaters,* and A. B. Guthrie's *The Big Sky* (". . . without doubt one of the finest pieces of description I have ever read").[11] He wrote one new essay during his recovery. A morning recital of quail song at the shack, issuing unexpectedly from some nearby pines, inspired "The Choral Copse": "We felt honored by this daybreak hymn sung almost at our doorstep. Somehow the blue autumnal needles on those pines became thenceforth bluer, and the red carpet of dewberry under the pines became even redder."[12] Leopold originally entitled the essay "Ave Maria." He had taken a liking at the time to Estella's phonograph record of the hymn.

რ

On November 5, Simpson wrote to Leopold in regard to the "Great Possessions" manuscript. After three readings and lengthy discussions, the publishers had concluded that it was "far from being satisfactorily organized as a book":

> What we like best is the nature observations, and the more objective narratives and essays. We like less the subjective parts—that is, the philosophical reflections, which are less fresh, and which one reader finds sometimes "fatuous." The ecological argument everyone finds unconvincing; and as in previous drafts, it is not tied up with the rest of the book.
>
> In short, the book seems unlikely to win approval from readers or to be a successful publication as it now stands, and a more fundamental kind of revision is needed than the detailed, page-by-page comments you asked [for] would suggest.

Simpson suggested that, rather than addressing "abstract subjects" and trying to cover so much territory, Leopold overhaul the book to make it a simple narrative of the family's activities at the shack. This would give it "a natural continuity that the present book lacks."[13]

Leopold was upset and disappointed with the rejection, and especially with the reasons given. He was incensed that they could have failed to appreciate the time he put into the essays; to suggest that he sit down and completely rewrite it was incredible. After recovering from the letdown, he wrote back to Knopf. "Of course I am disappointed, but I thank you for your taking the pains to analyze the reasons why. . . . I still think that [the essays] have a unity as they are, but I have evidently failed to make clear how and why such is the case."[14]

He was unsure where to go now. He was still angry when he talked to Luna, hinting that he might just give up on other publishers and bring the book out himself. Luna was not yet ready to go that route, and had another idea. "Dad," he told his father, "you're just too soft-hearted to deal with these people. Put the publication in my hands." "Fine," Aldo answered. "I'd love it. Get me off the hook."[15] Luna was in the process of moving to Hawaii to begin a new job, but took over the book negotiations from that point on.

The first order of business was to retain Charlie Schwartz. Aldo wrote to Schwartz to inform him of Knopf's turn-down, but also of his hope that they could continue collaborating. Schwartz replied that his "enthusiasm hasn't dwindled a bit," and that he would be able to devote more time to the illustrations after the end of the year.[16]

Leopold's own enthusiasm rebounded after the initial disappointment. At the end of November he wrote "Axe-in-Hand," a delightful bit on the choices confronting the axe-wielding owner of a woodland. The essay contained a deceptively simple definition of conservation: "It is a matter of what a man thinks about while chopping, or while deciding what to chop. A conservationist is one who is humbly aware that with each stroke he is writing his signature on the face of the land." He went on to examine his own prejudices and predilections in matters arboreal, admitting a personal bias in favor of pines. "The only conclusion I have ever reached is that I love all trees, but I am in love with pines."[17]

He decided that the lengthy foreword he had written in July had to be rewritten, "the better to orient the reader on why or how the essays add up to a single idea."[18] On December 5, he composed a new, two-page foreword, pared of the original's autobiographical sidelights, and more pointed in its message. "Until we love and respect the land," he wrote, "there is no chance for it to survive the impact of mechanized land-use, nor for us to reap from it the esthetic harvest it is capable, under science, of contributing to culture. These essays attempt to illumine this concept."[19]

Luna, in the meantime, had talked over the manuscript with Philip Vaudrin, trade editor at Oxford University Press. Vaudrin wrote to Leopold that he was "very much interested in reading your manuscript with a view toward making you an offer of publication."[20] At the same time, Bill Vogt was putting the final touches on his book, and mentioned to his publisher, William Sloane Associates of New York, that Leopold's work was available. Sloane, a new house looking for worthy titles, asked Leopold to submit the essays. On December 19, Leopold sent copies of the essays, with the new foreword, to both Oxford and Sloane. He was still not satisfied that the manuscript in its present form was ready for publication, and cautioned that it might still contain "phrases or sentences that are trite or pretentious. I hope to get these out if I can get my critics to spot them for me."[21] Despite such nagging doubts, he felt the material was sound enough for them to make a decision.

Toward the end of the fall, Leopold began to experience complications with his eyes. His left eye, still unable to lubricate itself, became irritated and bloodshot, and Leopold's vision became intermittently blurred. He was not sure whether this blurring was real or just a secondary symptom of the "false sensations" that still afflicted the operated left side of his face. He wore a bandage over the eye for a week, but without effect. Then his right eye, acting in sympathy with the left, also began to go dry, so that drops had to be applied to both.

These health problems did not keep him away from class or Conservation Commission meetings, but the physical and psychological effects were obvious to those close to him. In early December he went to Lafayette, Indiana, to attend the Midwest Wildlife Conference, for which he had been asked to deliver the main banquet address. He stayed for only one day. Unable to give the talk, he asked Hochbaum to speak in his place. Albert extemporized while Aldo listened at the head table. After the dinner, he and Albert chatted, and then walked downtown to the hotel with Bill Elder and several others. This was the first time Aldo had met his old colleagues since the operation, and when they reached the hotel, Aldo suggested, "Let's all go in and have a nightcap." The others were somewhat confused. It was too early for a nightcap, but they agreed. Over drinks, they discussed Albert's earlier talk. Albert was not very proud of it; he had never before given that kind of address. At one point in the conversation, Aldo looked about the group and said in an offhand way, "This is great getting together like this. You know, we're not around here forever."[22]

After the conference, Hochbaum stopped briefly in Madison on his way back to Manitoba. Later, Albert wrote what to Leopold must have been a satisfying letter about the Lafayette meetings. "For a long time the crowd has been more or less following (and sometimes objecting to) *rules* for wildlife management which you have prescribed. Now they are beginning to follow your *philosophies,* by and large without realizing whence they came. That is progress!"[23]

In a reminiscent state of mind, Leopold uncharacteristically sent Christmas notes to a number of old acquaintances that year. Carl and Nina came to Madison with their families for the holiday. His eye still bandaged,

Leopold showed the strain of the recent months, but the reunion was no less festive for the fact. The family did not manage a trip to the shack, but after the Christmas morning merry-making subsided, Aldo, Nina, and Bill did make a leisurely inspection of the university arboretum. An inch of snow was on the ground, so tracking was good. They walked through the 1934 red and white pine plantations, the first at the arboretum. "Many trees now bear cones," Leopold wrote of the reds, "some of which must be opening at this time, for seeds were seen on the snow."[24]

After the holiday, Leopold along with many of his present and former students travelled to Chicago for the annual meeting of the Ecological Society of America. His only official duty was to chair a session on bird and mammal population mechanisms, but as current president of the ESA he was kept busy throughout the three-day conference. Halfway through the third day he was "pretty well 'bushed'" and decided to take an early train back to Madison.[25]

∽

Leopold turned sixty-one on January 11. His eye problems failed to clear up, forcing a brief return to the Mayo Clinic, where he was fitted with an antiseptic cotton pad to exclude air from the inflamed eye.

These complications were more bothersome than disabling. They did prevent Leopold from reading and from going to the shack, but not from working. The mid-winter break in the school year gave him a chance to loosen his logjam of delayed chores. Letters of praise for "The Ecological Conscience" were coming in, and he gratefully answered them all. Charlie Schwartz forwarded his first batch of six illustrations for "Great Possessions." Leopold was full of admiration. "The more I study them the more I like them," he wrote to Schwartz. "In addition to their over-all merit, I like the accuracy of your details even down to the species of grasses suitable for each."[26] Aldo wrote another new essay. "Good Oak" chronicled the past drama of Wisconsin's landscape by interpreting the "chips of history" that he and Estella, his "chief sawyer," sawed out of an eighty-year-old, lightning-killed black oak: "In March 1922, the 'Big Sleet' tore the neighboring elms limb from limb, but there is no sign of damage to our tree. What is a ton of ice, more or less, to a good oak? Rest! cries the chief sawyer, and we pause for breath."[27] There had been no word from either of the prospective publishers.

The Wisconsin Conservation Commission held its monthly meeting on January 19. Once again, as for several months past, a major item of discussion was the siting of hydroelectric power projects. Three proposed dams, on the Menominee, Chippewa, and Wisconsin Rivers, were up for review. The commission was generally wary of being stampeded into decisions, and in December had voted against the dam on the scenic Menominee. At the January meeting, Leopold was firm. "The building of a power dam is an act of violence on nature and it is up to somebody to prove a dam will make the river more valuable than it is without it."[28] Leopold and four of the other five commissioners voted to delay their decisions on dam sites until the state's rivers could be surveyed and classified according to their suitability for power development. Leopold hastened to point out that "the standards of recreational values change constantly and if a classification of rivers is made, it will be necessary to look into the future rather than assume they will be the same as today."[29]

The postwar boom had paid little heed to either the tangible or intangible values of wilderness. In a time of economic expansion, wilderness was of very little account. Leopold never let down his guard. The day of the commission meeting, he wrote a letter to Carl Russell, superintendent of Yosemite National Park, opposing construction of the new highway through Tioga Pass. "I think the Park Service has already acquiesced in far too much motorization, and that the time to call a halt on that process is now, while there are still some wilderness values left to conserve."[30]

Closer to home, Wallace Grange wrote to Leopold to state his concern about the Conservation Commission's latest dam decisions. "I believe that one thing you should consider very seriously is the probable status of Wisconsin and American industrial development at the time of the apparently inevitable fighting war with communism. In order to save 'wilderness areas' and in fact our whole way of life, we may need (and in my opinion will need) every source of power we can muster. . . . I question whether you have the right to decide such issues on the basis of a single narrow viewpoint, namely the love of wilderness."[31] Leopold was unconvinced by this appeal from his old colleague. "You are mistaken," he replied, "in supposing that the Commission is going to oppose everything and anything, simply because it is a power dam. . . . I disagree with you that we should make any blank sacrifices of wilderness values simply on the chance that we might need them in another war. If we lose our wilderness, we have nothing left in my opinion, worth fighting for; or to be more exact, a completely industrialized United States is of no consequence to me."[32]

Leopold was as stubborn as ever in his refusal to accept pat answers to complex issues, even when he agreed with the general aim. He declined an invitation to join the recently established Arctic Institute of North America because of a single sentence in its prospectus that mentioned its hope of combining "pure science with very practical considerations as to the future development of the Arctic." Leopold replied in early February that "I think the governments involved, including my own, should demonstrate their capacity to conserve the polar fauna before development is encouraged to proceed."[33] At about the same time, Leopold was asked to sign his name to a vaguely conceived "Conservation Credo of an American," to be submitted to Congress. The credo backed federal water power rights and called for "the comprehensive development of our river basins." Although Leopold sympathized with many of the provisions of the statement, he declined this invitation as well. When asked to provide an explanation of his dissent, Leopold sent back a reprint of "The Ecological Conscience." "I do not here imply," he wrote, "that I have a completely logical philosophy all thought out, in fact on the contrary, I am deeply disturbed and do not myself know the answer to the conflicting needs with which we are faced."[34] He did know that the answer did not lie in poorly thought-out credos.

The first week in February, Leopold underwent another minor operation to mend the problem with his eye, and had to wear an eyepatch for the rest of the month. Wildlife Ecology 118 started up; a total of ninety-seven students attended, thirty more than in any of the fourteen previous years that Leopold had taught the course or its variants. "I am not sure at all that I am any good at mass production in students," he admitted in a letter to Hochbaum.[35] He did have help, though. Joe Hickey had returned to Madison to join the department, and he and Dan Thompson assisted Leopold in teaching.

On the morning that the class was to open, Leopold walked to his office. It was a cold day, the temperature two below, and Leopold was surprised to hear (at 7:26) a cardinal sing. He looked up and saw two males fighting as a female watched. Leopold concluded that this was a territorial battle. He further concluded that the spring endocrine change was on in cardinals, enough so as to override the depressive cold when stimulated by trespassing rivals. Leopold turned the incident and the observation into his introductory class remarks:

> In the classroom, the sciences are assumed to be separate. This is convenient for professors, who have a hard enough time explaining even one science, but it doesn't help much in the field, where you invariably have to put sciences together to explain even the simplest event. . . .
>
> Here I have put together physiology, meteorology, and ornithology in the form of an hypothesis. To formulate hypotheses about wildlife, and to test them for conformity to observed facts, is wildlife ecology. A person is an ecologist if he is skillful in seeing facts, ingenious in formulating hypotheses, and ruthless in discarding them when they don't fit.[36]

Hickey then took over and gave a lecture on the effects of climate on wildlife.

∽

At the end of February, Leopold was asked by Secretary of the Interior Julius Krug to serve as one of forty or so advisors on American participation in the International Scientific Conference on the Conservation and Utilization of Resources. The conference, sponsored by the Economic and Social Council of the United Nations, was due to be held in the United States in 1949 or 1950. "This consulting group," Krug wrote in his letter to Leopold, "can make a tremendous contribution in assuring that the conference will be comprehensive and that it will contribute to the world's knowledge of conservation, development, and utilization practices."[37] The appointment came as the climax to Leopold's career in conservation.

Leopold's eyepatch came off on March 1. For the first time in several months, he enjoyed unimpaired vision in both eyes. It was an inestimable relief to him. His eyes were, after all, the primary tools of his trade. Understandably protective afterward, he decided to skip the North American Wildlife Conference in St. Louis in order to avoid unnecessary pressure. "I am so pleased to have both eyes back," he wrote to Hochbaum, "that I am inclined to be cagey as to extra strains."[38] He had prepared a paper for the conference, but when he decided not to attend, he asked McCabe to present it for him. Later that week, on March 4, he revised two of the older essays and the foreword to "Great Possessions."

Although Leopold himself did not attend the conference, his influence there was strong. Starker, Nina, and Estella were all astute speakers in their own right, and more than held their ground in their father's absence. At the end of a day of serious formal meetings — the conference was threatening to become unusually grave — they enlivened the after-sessions with their voices and guitars. "Being a non-technician," one of Leopold's colleagues wrote to him, "I am in no position to judge Starker's technical attainments, but I am a damn good listener to rough and ready music, and I have never in my life heard music that I enjoyed as much as I did theirs."[39] The morning after the festivities, Starker presented a polished paper on his studies of wild turkey in the Ozarks.

Aldo's mark was apparent, more formally, in his paper, entitled "How and Why Research?" Through McCabe, Leopold spoke out against the recent trend in federal wildlife research policy, which was away from long-term studies and toward those which yielded short-term "practical" results. Funding for one of his own quail projects had recently been withdrawn "because it had delivered no practical results and repeated the same work year after year." These were exactly the qualities, Leopold held, that made it worthwhile. Twenty years of wildlife research, he explained, had exhausted the "easy pickings." "The thing for us to do now is what science always does in the same predicament — start over and dig deeper." That meant paying more, not less, attention to wildlife banding and censusing, age and sex studies, and physiological investigations, regardless of short-term returns. In the long run, such studies would prove to be both informative and practical. In other words, Leopold was still bearing the standard for fundamental research.[40]

The paper was designed to draw fire, and it did. McCabe's presentation was flawless. He had no sooner finished when Clarence Cottam, chief of the U.S. Fish and Wildlife Service, rose to defend his agency. He disputed Leopold's points, suggested that Leopold was pleading sour grapes, and implied that support for Leopold's quail project had been granted previously only because of his reputation. McCabe was forced to defend his boss. In the end, Cottam was the only one in the audience who challenged Leopold's point. He had attacked so fiercely that the sympathies of the audience all flowed toward Leopold.

After the conference, Starker paid a week's visit to Madison. Aldo was now well enough to resume full-time teaching duties and weekend trips to the shack. The combination of a hard winter and health problems had discouraged Leopold's field activities ever since November. On March 12, the family went to the shack together, where Starker made a point of building up his old grape tangles to encourage grouse and quail. Aldo was pleased to see that Starker, who by now had his own strong professional reputation, still "retained his appetite for that sort of thing."[41]

Leopold began to resume his normal schedule, attending the monthly meeting of the Conservation Commission on March 19 and an arboretum research meeting three days later, leading his class on a field trip on the twenty-sixth, and going to the shack with Estella the last two weekends in March. Outwardly, he seemed to be regaining his general good health. His eyes were fully back to normal, and his strength was returning, but he remained apprehensive about lingering problems with his facial nerves. On April 7, he reported on his progress in a letter to Dr. Adson at the Mayo Clinic: "Everything has gone perfectly except for the 'adventitious sensations' in my face. These were not bad for the first month or two, but have since become progressively more annoying and extending over a greater part of the day. They are worse evenings, and of course intensify with fatigue."[42]

The sensations were bothersome enough to prevent him from attending the annual spring dinner with the students and farmers at Faville Grove, normally one of the highlights of the season. The doctor had advised him to avoid evening engagements, so he and Estella went to the shack instead. They fixed the leg on the outdoor table, cut down an elm, and hauled down from their neighbor Lewis' place the old canoe that Aldo had bargained for the previous fall. They counted a few geese, saw dozens of gulls at sunset, and watched hundreds of migrating juncos go to roost in the pines. The next day, their daughter Estella came up with a friend. The geese began to arrive more numerously, but ducks that spring were extra scarce.

The following Wednesday, April 14, Leopold went into the office at his usual early hour, intent on catching up on some correspondence. He wrote one letter to Ernie Swift, who was now director of the Wisconsin Conservation Department (to Roy Jorgensen's everlasting dismay). Aldo had been talking to his friend Andrew Weaver, a professor in the speech department, about a project both of them, and others in the state, had often considered: "the acquisition of at least one of the two boyhood farms of John Muir as a state park." The original Muir farmstead was near Portage, not far from Leopold's shack. Muir's *The Story of My Boyhood and Youth* had long been on Leopold's recommended reading list due to its evocative descriptions of frontier Wisconsin. Ironically, this in part was why Leopold had not acted on the park idea before:

> One reason I have hesitated to recommend this project in the past has been that the Muir farm is undoubtedly badly depleted floristically and otherwise, and hence any possible restoration at this time might be a pretty drab affair compared to the original farm described in Muir's book. It now occurs to me, however, that this area might fall half way between a state park in the ordinary sense and a "natural area," the objective being to restore the flora to something approaching the original.[43]

Leopold suggested that "such a state park should be something more than a mere stopping place for tourists lacking something to do. It might be made a public educational institution in the ecological and intellectual history of Wisconsin." Leopold sent copies of the letter to Swift, Weaver, Norman Fassett, and to his fellow commissioners.

Later that morning, Phillip Vaudrin called Leopold from New York and informed him that Oxford wished to publish his book. Assuming Leopold would be able to spend the summer making final revisions, they would have the book ready for the fall 1949 publishing season. In a follow-up letter, Vaudrin wrote that "we are all extremely pleased by the prospect of publishing this book for you."[44]

Leopold was overjoyed, obviously gratified, and he accepted the offer. He wrote to the other prospective publisher, William Sloane Associates, to thank them for their interest. Sloane replied "Well, it's our own fault; I think we've lost a good book, but fortunately to a good publisher."[45] Estella was absolutely delighted by the news, and they talked about it excitedly after that. To his daughter Estella, Leopold seemed "a little more at ease, feeling better about life."[46] The next day, Aldo wired the good news to Charlie Schwartz, who, it was now agreed, would definitely provide the illustrations. Leopold and Vaudrin spoke again, and closed the deal.

The next morning, a Friday, Leopold went to the office to tie up some loose ends. Lecture days were Tuesday and Thursday, so he only had to dictate a few more letters. He wrote to Schwartz to explain some book details, to the chairman of the Wisconsin Izaak Walton League's Pollution

Committee to express his approval of a list of recommendations they had prepared and sent to the governor, and to Bill Vogt in Washington. Vogt was busy completing the agenda for the two-week Inter-American Conference on Conservation that was to be held that September in Denver. Vogt, as representative of the Pan American Union, was collaborating with the U.S. State Department in planning the ambitious program. Leopold was assigned to lead one of the discussion sessions and to assist Vogt as head of a subcommittee on conservation education.[47]

Leopold also wrote to Luna, informing him of the news about "Great Possessions" and thanking him for his efforts on the book's behalf. He walked home for lunch, and then he and Estella loaded up the car. They left for the shack in the afternoon with Estella Jr., eager to get an early start on the spring planting.

∽

Before getting down to serious planting, they enjoyed a leisurely weekend of goose-counting, birdsong-noting, and pine-tending.[48] The woodcock peented on schedule. On Saturday, Aldo made a short trip over to Portage to address the Tri-County Conservation Club. ("Back 10:30 — saw 2 rabbits on road"). The next day Jim Ragan, a neighbor farmer, came by and plowed the garden plot.

Monday morning Aldo awoke before his wife and daughter and counted geese at the marsh. He heard three gunshots in the distance. Later, the three drove into town to pick up the year's order of trees — two hundred white pines and two hundred reds. They did not need as many trees as in years past, nor did they have as many hands available. Back at the shack, Aldo led his wife and daughter to some blooming pasque flowers and showed off some hepaticas. He also had a "surprise": a lone toothwort on the clayhill. That evening, after some drinks on the lawn, they went over to an aspen hummock in the marsh to watch and count the incoming geese. The geese were coming in low, and in abundance. They were able to count about four hundred and fifty; more than that came in. Estella was struck by her father's enthusiasm as he watched the performance. He remarked at one point that the incoming flocks constituted one of the last great displays of wildlife still available, that "a man can't find any but remnants of wildlife nowadays." The tone of his voice was not exactly regretful, just realistic. After the sun was down and the geese had all settled in, the Leopolds returned to the shack. Aldo wrote up his journal. Estella knitted while Estella Jr. sat on the doorstep and accompanied herself on a guitar.

The next morning, Aldo was up at five o'clock drinking coffee, listening to birdsongs, and watching and counting the geese as they winged their way north. A hundred more pines went into the ground that morning. In the afternoon, Aldo and Estella took a canoe ride by themselves through the river sloughs. That evening, Aldo retired early. Estella remarked to her daughter that he seemed unusually tired, despite his high spirits.

Wednesday, April 21, dawned clear and calm, the temperature just a little above freezing. Aldo was up, as usual, before daybreak. A magnificent goose flight was on. He counted eight hundred and seventy-one, the most he ever recorded in his notes. He wrote the figures into the journal, and ended his entry with two phenological items:

Eur. white birch, almost in pollen 4/19, is spent today.
Bloodroot in Shower Bed Closed 6 AM

After breakfast, the family prepared for the day's work. Aldo was again in a lighthearted mood, and they laughed and teased one another. They decided to fix up all the broken tools at the shack; Aldo called the tools "a disgrace to the outfit." A wind had risen, and was coming out of the east at about ten-thirty, when they spotted smoke in the direction of Jim Ragan's house. Initially, Leopold was not concerned, and figured it was just a farmer burning his hay meadow. Soon his forester's instincts told him that something was wrong. A trash fire at Ragan's had spread to dried grass and leaves in his farmyard. One flank of the fire, approaching Ragan's barn and milk pens, had been halted. The other west flank was moving downhill toward the marsh, and toward the Leopolds' pines.

As soon as he sensed the threat, Leopold became excited and rushed into action, directing his wife and daughter. All three grabbed equipment —gloves, coats, buckets, a sprinkling can, a water pump, a broom, a shovel—and jumped into the car. They drove slowly down toward Ragan's. When they arrived near the blaze, they could see that it was gaining speed. Aldo warned the others to stay away from the front of the fire. He stationed his wife on the road with a broom and a gunnysack, told her to watch that the fire did not cross north across the road, and instructed her to dip the gunnysack and the broom in the marsh water to wet down any places that might catch sparks. He ordered her to get in the car and move off if the fire came too close. Then Aldo and his daughter crossed in front of the fire to size up the situation.

A dozen neighbors had gathered to fight the blaze. The flames had spread into some alders and were moving fast over the dry marsh border. Aldo looked over the burned area and the meadows and hurriedly gave his daughter directions, telling her to go to a nearby farmhouse and call up the local fire department for help. If that did not work, she was to call the Wisconsin Conservation Department station at Wisconsin Dells and tell them to send their fire-fighting equipment as soon as possible. He shouted the instructions to her. "Use my name and tell them the Leopold plantations are endangered!" After making her father promise to be careful, she left to make the call. To Estella, her father seemed overexcited, but not particularly tired. He was not fighting the fire directly, just using the fire pump strapped on his back to wet down the back edges of the flames.

Estella returned to the car and drove down the road to make the calls. The first call brought no response at all. Estella made the second call, but they paid no attention to her plea, even when she gave her father's name. They told her that it was too far away and too small an area.

She drove back down the road to meet her mother, who was doing her best to stamp out ashes with the wet broom. The flames had jumped a small ditch to the main body of the marsh. The local fire department finally did send one truck. When it came down the road, Estella appealed to them to spray down a vital stretch of the marsh, but instead they went down the road to the farmhouse. Estella waded into the marsh. As her mother kept watch on the road, she soaked a lane of sedges by depressing the stalks into the water. They were watching for Aldo, but so many people had gathered by then that they could not locate him.

There were no witnesses to Leopold's final moments. After Estella went to make the calls, Aldo crossed to the north side of the flames with his pump, evidently planning to wet the unburned grass along the road. As he walked, he was seized by a heart attack. He apparently set down the full pump, lay down on his back, rested his head on a clump of grass, and folded his hands across his chest. The attack did not subside. The fire, still alive but weakened in intensity, swept lightly over his body.

Estella continued to dampen the marsh lane, and then waded across the pond to help douse the last flames. It was about noon, and neither she nor her mother had seen Aldo for an hour and a half. She grew afraid and kept her eye on the slope below Ragan's house, where she thought her father was. Baxter, a local farmer, came down the hill toward the marsh, toward her. Estella sensed, when she first saw him, what he was going to say. "Your Dad's sick," Baxter told her. His voice told more. "No," she answered, "tell me the truth." Finally, she got out of him that her father was dead. She ran off to find her mother.

The neighbors had wisely brought Estella over to the farmhouse, to keep her away from her husband. Her daughter drove her back down to the shack, and the neighbors tried to comfort her, but she was in shock. Someone had called Tom Coleman in Madison and told him the news. Coleman and the Schorgers quickly drove up to the shack, made immediate arrangements, and escorted Mrs. Leopold back to Madison.

Epilogue

A LDO LEOPOLD's odyssey ended where it began, in the limestone bluffs above the Mississippi River at Burlington, Iowa. He was buried in the Starker-Leopold family plot at Aspen Grove Cemetery, on a small knoll between two white pines and two white oaks. The funeral was held with little ceremony. Leopold's grave was marked with a simple stone. Out of respect for Estella's religious beliefs, his body was not cremated, as others in the family had been, but interred in the grounds that his grandfather Starker had planned, beneath the trees that Starker himself might well have planted.

Two of the children, Starker and Carl, were able to travel to Burlington. Luna and Carolyn in Hawaii, and Nina and Bill Elder in Missouri, were expecting at any moment the arrival of new babies (Carl and Keena were also about to become parents; within days, the family would gain three grandchildren). Young Estella stayed in Madison.

The moments at the cemetery were difficult. Estella was emotionally spent, but pulled through the worst times with the help of her close friends and family. The same was not true of Clara Leopold. She was eighty-eight and already infirm. Everyone present noticed the debility that overcame her with the news of Aldo's death. After that, she seemed to lose the will to live. She never did regain her characteristic verve, and died a few weeks later.

The mourners dispersed to carry on. Estella went to Missouri to stay with Nina and Bill through the birth of their child. When Ninita arrived, Estella was able to channel her sorrow into care. Her grief would pass very slowly, but for the immediate interval, a new grandchild was the best thing that could have come along.

As word of Leopold's death fanned out across the continent, those who had worked with him over the years were shocked into the realization that they had known a remarkable man. They knew it while he was alive, of course, but Leopold had exerted his influence in the conservation movement so skillfully that many had taken his guiding presence for granted. Consolatory letters and telegrams poured in to Madison. Ward Shepard wrote from Virginia, "I feel sure that Aldo was just reaching the height of his powers and his wisdom, at the peak of his rich and creative life, so that the blow comes doubly hard for all of us who loved and admired him."[1] "The cause of conservation has lost its best friend," Harry Russell wrote. "No one had the charm of expression and the depth of feeling to equal his."[2] Charles Bradley, a close family friend, wrote that "the things which Aldo gave to us are as deathless as the Human Race."[3] Dozens upon dozens of letters repeated the sentiments. Beneath the expressions of grief, there ran an undertone of gratitude for having been fortunate enough to know Leopold, to work, go afield, and share a conversation with him. Norman Fassett wrote, "I know that my spirit has been strengthened and I have been made more nearly the man I would like to be by years of association with Aldo Leopold. In spite of the grief and sense of loss so many of us feel, there is that, which cannot be taken from me."[4]

Leopold's students felt a special sense of loss. For wildlife researchers, the first full days of spring were always busy with field work, so the news reached many of them only gradually. Bob McCabe, Fred Greeley, and the Hamerstroms were observing the spring courtship of the prairie chickens on Clyde Terrell's farm in Waushara County. McCabe did not learn of Leopold's death until he came into the office and one of the graduate students told him. Thinking it to be a bad joke, McCabe chastised the student. The weight fell only after Bob looked around at the others in the room.[5] McCabe passed the word along to the Hamerstroms, who decided not to attend the funeral. The Professor, they reasoned, would have wanted them to continue with the field work.

Dan Thompson heard the news over his car radio, driving home from a wolf study trip in northern Wisconsin. He and his partner, dumfounded, drove on in silence. Thompson's thoughts returned to the previous night, when he was awakened by the distant whistle of a locomotive pulling out of Ashland. In response to the train, a wolf lifted its howl above the forest.[6]

Art Hawkins, Lyle Sowls, and Albert Hochbaum were working together at Delta at the time. Hochbaum surmised bad news when he saw Archie MacDonald walking toward the station. MacDonald was a storekeeper in Delta, and kept the only telegraph office in town. He brought a telegram from Aldo's brother Frederic: "Aldo died today fighting a grass fire at the shack."[7]

The next day, Hochbaum wrote a eulogy to his mentor that spoke for many of those who had felt firsthand Leopold's influence:

Yesterday, as on all days since he touched our lives, we had some reason to think of Aldo Leopold, once or a dozen times. In my own case I saw a small flock of Sandhill Cranes in Brown's Slough about noon, the first I had ever seen there; and at once there came to mind the time at the shack when he showed me my first cranes, and the half-dozen times since when we had seen cranes together. Yesterday, Aldo left our world.

Grief is so very deep at the moment that we think little beyond our loss; and yet there is no end to the goodness that lives after him. We who knew him closely are living lives patterned by his kindness, his wisdom, and his everlasting courage. The land he loved will be forever a better land because of him. We now know what history will record: Aldo Leopold was a Great American. Few men loved the land so deeply as he loved America; few who have loved the land have examined it so carefully; and few who have examined the land have been so articulate in detailing their discoveries. Aldo Leopold's discoveries and his philosophies are just as important to America as Benjamin Franklin's.

. . . In sorrow let us not forget the hope he has given us. In years to come we must never forget the lesson he taught. And in bad times let us always remember how hard he worked to give us what we now have.

Few men in any walk of life at any time in history have lived so closely to what must have been God's pattern for mankind.[8]

∽

Leopold was indeed at the height of his powers at the time of his death. In his teaching, he was leading his students down the latest avenues of research, and promulgating the global relevance of conservation. In his own studies, he was as curious as ever; like the seasons themselves, his insights as a naturalist only built on themselves with time. In his writing, he was still exploring the possibilities of his voice, and of his evolving philosophy.

He had planned to work full-time at the university only for a few more years. He and Estella had talked about building a home on the shack property, and had a site chosen on the sandhill by the river. At the time of his death there were three main projects on his agenda: he meant to spend the summer making final revisions of the "Great Possessions" manuscript; he also wanted to revise *Game Management,* which he considered "sadly out of date";[9] and, finally, he hoped to write the book of ecological case histories that he had first envisioned in the early 1940s.

Leopold's death not only cut short these plans, but called into question the publication of "Great Possessions." Phil Vaudrin wrote to Joe Hickey on April 22, "I don't know now what happens about the book. He was going to spend the summer working it over and getting it into final shape —a job which he alone would have been able to manage, I should have thought."[10]

Just after confirming the deal with Oxford, Leopold had written out a note asking a number of trusted readers—Vogt, the Hamerstroms, Hickey, McCabe, and several others — if they would be willing to review the essays.

"What I need, of course, is the most critical attitude you are able to muster. Which are weak ones? What is ambiguous, obscure, repetitious, inaccurate, fatuous, highbrow?"[11]

Leopold never did send the note. In the immediate aftermath of his death, Hickey and McCabe discussed the book. Since Hickey knew the publishing business, he took the lead. He wrote a confidential letter to the family and to those on the list of readers, stating that "we must close our ranks and get this book into print."[12] He also wrote to Vaudrin to assure him that Leopold had done some additional work on the manuscript, that it was already in substantially publishable form, and that the machinery was in place to get a final version in Oxford's hands within six months. Over the next month and a half, Hickey and the others mobilized. Hickey acted as go-between for Oxford, the family, and the panel of readers, and took over contract arrangements. Luna became chief editor, with final say over the text and layout. Vogt met with Vaudrin in New York to shore up Oxford's confidence. Charlie Schwartz went to work on the illustrations.

Estella, Luna, and the others reviewed the essays and suggested a number of minor changes in the text: changes in punctuation, some clarification of facts, deletions of dated references, spelling corrections. Reluctant as the readers were to alter Leopold's own words, only a few of their suggestions involved major rephrasing. "This is a beautiful thing," the Hamerstroms commented. "Better to leave in a few things that might perhaps have been said differently than to risk taking liberties (no matter how well intended) with Aldo's own way of expressing things."[13]

In the end, Luna made very few major changes in the manuscript. He retitled two essays, shifted a couple others, added another. "The Land Ethic" was moved to the end of Part III, "The Upshot." The title of Part I was changed from "A Sauk County Almanac" to "A Sand Country Almanac," and ultimately to "A Sand County Almanac."

In July, Vaudrin wrote to Luna suggesting that an alternate title be chosen for the collection as a whole. "Great Possessions," Vaudrin thought, would not communicate the substance of the book to the general public. It sounded too much like Dickens' *Great Expectations*. Vaudrin had in mind a title similar to that of Vogt's new book, *Road to Survival*, or Fairfield Osborn's *Our Plundered Planet*. Searching for a title that would convey a similar sense of urgency, he offered a number of possibilities: "Our Mounting Loss," "This We Lose," "Fast Losing Ground," etc.[14] None of these, in Luna's opinion, came close to the flavor of his father's work. The committee of readers came up with some suggestions of their own, but none seemed quite as appropriate as the original. After discussing the matter with Oxford, Luna reluctantly agreed to the title *A Sand County Almanac*.

~.

The book appeared in the fall of 1949, under the full title *A Sand County Almanac and Sketches Here and There*. With its publication, Aldo Leopold and his ideas became known to a broader public, and the conservation movement gained one of its preeminent works.

The book garnered critical praise from the outset. This was nature writing of a different sort, highly personal, rich in humor and irony, imbued with a sense of respect and wonder, and profoundly comprehensive. It was free of mawkishness, its flavor as tart and wild as a hickory nut. The *Green Bay Gazette* reviewer wrote of Leopold that "philosophers of his breed have double sight or at least some senses that are not common to the rest of humanity."[15] Joseph Wood Krutch, writing in *The Nation,* praised Leopold's "original sensibility" and his "special humorous awareness of the paradoxes of conservation."[16] Lewis Gannett reviewed *A Sand County Almanac* for the *New York Herald Tribune.* "To read it is a deeply satisfying adventure. This was a man who wrote sparsely, out of intense feeling and experience."[17]

The critical acclaim was matched by the public response. The book not only hit an appropriate note; it fulfilled a positive need. Vogt's and Osborn's books had opened people's eyes. Leopold's *Almanac* did not sell nearly so widely as these at first, but for conservationists looking for a respite from unleavened gloom, it came along at just the right time, reminding them that a love of nature was still the impulse behind their work, even when facing the most difficult contemporary issues. Out of this triumvirate of premonitory postwar books, *A Sand County Almanac* would, for whatever reasons, emerge as the one with the broadest influence. By the early 1950s, a new wave of active conservationists was coming on, most of them with dog-eared copies of the *Almanac* in hand. Vogt himself predicted that it would be read "for decades, and probably centuries, to come."[18]

In 1953, Luna edited and Oxford published *Round River,* a collection of excerpts from Leopold's hunting journals and essays from his "cooler." *Round River,* despite favorable reviews, did not achieve the same success as *A Sand County Almanac.* For one thing, the unrelenting procession of hunting tales did not sit well with nonhunting conservationists. This aspect of Leopold's life had also bothered some readers of the *Almanac,* but the balance and fullness of that book had made it easier to overlook. *Round River* painted Leopold mainly as a hunter, and even Estella was disturbed by this overemphasis. (No less a figure than Rachel Carson took Leopold to task, proving if nothing else that conservation still had its internal divisions. In this case, fate prevented any meeting of minds.)

By the late 1950s and early 1960s, Leopold was firmly established as a major figure in conservation history, philosophy, and practice, often mentioned in the same breath with Henry David Thoreau and John Muir. Then in 1970, Oxford arranged with Ballantine Books to reissue *A Sand County Almanac* in a paperback volume that included several of the essays from *Round River.* Until that point, the *Almanac* had sold modestly, perhaps 20,000 copies. Leopold was renowned within the conservation movement, but remained little known beyond it. The paperback edition changed all that. Again, the timing was fortuitous. Rachel Carson had rocked the nation with *Silent Spring.* In 1964, Congress passed the landmark Wilderness Act. Nuclear power and nuclear proliferation became public issues where before they had been only technological trends. As the conservation movement metamorphosed into the environmental movement, and ecology became a catchword, Leopold's modest book of essays became both stimulus and beneficiary of a broad social awakening. Sales of *A Sand County Almanac* skyrocketed as a new generation of readers, eager to learn about and understand their natural surroundings, seized upon Leopold's words. As Vogt had predicted, those words had staying power.

There was, almost inexorably, a measure of excess in all this. The urge to canonize was difficult to resist. In books and articles, Leopold became the "priest" and "prophet" of the environmental movement; *A Sand County Almanac* became the movement's "bible" or its "scripture." In the irony of ironies, Leopold, who had rebelled all his life against dogma, orthodoxy, and "thinking in grooves," became lodged by many of his own readers in a considerable groove, ignoring his own first rules of critical thinking. All of this was probably a necessary phase in the emergence of the nation's environmental consciousness, reflecting as much on society's needs as on Leopold himself, but Leopold required no exaggeration of his accomplishments.

Life, for all that lives, is a process of give and take. Leopold took much from life; he gave back much more. His influence on conservation in America remains pervasive. As a forester, he gave to the profession a standard of wise stewardship, a balance of the visionary and the pragmatic, that still stands. As a defender of wild lands, he framed his concern in terms that struck to the roots of the nation's historical and philosophical development; he helped make respect for wilderness a matter of national priority, and national pride. The science of wildlife ecology and the practice of wildlife management would have developed without him, but not with the same degree of integrity or sense of direction. As a teacher, he inspired hundreds of students to see and understand land, to study it rigorously, and to care for it. As a thinker, he gave the conservation movement philosophical definition. As a poet, he enriched the nation's bookshelf of nature writing.

Historical figures are ahead of their times only in the rhetorical sense. Leopold was a man *of* his times whose sensitivity, insight, and dogged belief in his own ideas allowed him to see into his environment with unusual depth. He was born at the end of the nineteenth century and lived to experience and confront the complexities of the twentieth. His reaction to the changes he witnessed was not a nostalgic thirst for the past, nor a blanket condemnation or celebration of the present, nor an uncritical acceptance of some predestined future. It was an exquisitely reasoned, broad-range view of mankind and his natural environment that tried to reconcile the short-term and long-term benefits that human progress—not merely economic, but cultural progress—provided.

It seems paradoxically appropriate that the physical monuments to Leopold are few. One early tribute was given on the occasion of the thirtieth anniversary of the Gila Wilderness Area. In September 1954, Senator Clinton Anderson of New Mexico (who years before had ridden the mountains with Leopold on a number of occasions), officials of the Forest Service, and the leaders of the Wilderness Society gathered together on a remote highway outside of Glenwood, New Mexico, in the outliers of the Mogollon Mountains and the Gila Wilderness, to dedicate a bronze plaque honoring Leopold. A storm threatened to disrupt the proceedings as the caravan of cars arrived at the appointed time and place. A great wind blew down out of the Blue Range to the west. Rains pelted the rangeland. The guests gamely tried to begin the ceremony, but the ugly clouds thickened, the wind blew faster, and the rain fell harder. It was a complete wash-out. The assembled dignitaries scurried back to the safety of their cars, and back to town.[19]

∽

All of the Leopold children became accomplished naturalists and dedicated conservationists in their own right. Starker's career most closely paralleled his father's. He taught at the University of California at Berkeley for thirty-two years, and was, until his death in 1983, one of the nation's premier wildlife ecologists. Luna spent most of his career with the U.S. Geological Survey, where his fundamental work in the hydrology of river systems established him as a leading figure in that field. After many years as chief hydrologist of the survey, he joined his brother as an instructor at Berkeley. Nina did not pursue a graduate degree, but worked for years assisting her first husband Bill Elder in wildlife studies ranging from waterfowl in Illinois to waterbuck in Africa. With her second husband, geologist Charles Bradley, she returned to the Leopold family property to found and maintain a research center for the continuing study of what is now the Leopold Reserve. Carl's interests led him into plant physiology and work on world agricultural problems, and eventually to a leading research position at Cornell University's Boyce Thompson Institute for Plant Research. Estella also spent many years with the U.S. Geological Survey, achieving recognition as a paleobotanist; in 1976 she became head of the Quaternary Research Center at the University of Washington. Three of the siblings—Starker, Luna, and Estella—became members of the National Academy of Sciences, a unique record in the annals of American science.[20]

Estella Leopold outlived her husband by thirty years. The earliest years were for her the most trying. She had devoted herself for so long to her family and, above all, to her Aldo, that when he died, the center of her life was gone. For several years she was lost in mourning, but as time passed, she emerged to begin a second life. She became socially active again, well known around Madison for her graciousness and hospitality. "Mother began to grow into her own person," Nina recalls. "She started being herself, rather than just Dad's wife. She became very strong in her political convictions, a very definite personality."[21] Estella reserved some of her strongest opinions for conservation issues, and worked on behalf of a number of environmental causes. Enjoying the role of matriarch, she made yearly trips to the homes of each of her children, wherever they were (promising to stay only a few days at a time; she did not believe in lengthy visits). She also became the "adopted grandmother" for a number of students and neighbors in Madison.

In an interview conducted a few years before her death in 1975, Estella reflected on her husband's life. The years had given her a more objective view of their relationship, but her pride in Aldo remained undiminished— simply phrased, but unmistakably strong. "He always brought out the best in everybody," she remembered. "His kindness and his leadership made everybody respect him, and made people feel kindly not only toward him, but toward the world." When asked what she thought Aldo's outlook for the future was, she replied, "I think he was just hopeful that people would become aware of things."[22]

The shack remained one of Estella's principal joys until the end of her life, and she continued to bring family and friends with her on her regular visits. She enjoyed telling a favorite story—she had learned it from Aldo— to her guests. It concerned the white pines that once grew in the vicinity of the shack. In the late 1820s, Jefferson Davis was a young army officer stationed at Fort Winnebago, the point of portage between the Fox and Wisconsin Rivers. Legend had it that he needed lumber for the fort, and led a contingent of soldiers to the nearest pines, which were growing on islands in the Wisconsin River near to where the shack would later stand. In Leopold's day the islands had few pines. Aldo figured that all the pine had been taken for lumber.

One spring, several years after Aldo died, Estella announced that she had ordered some pine seedlings, and that there was going to be a planting trip that year. "Okay, mother," her daughter Estella said with some surprise, "but where are you going to put them?"

"Well," she replied, "we're going to put them on the island. Dad never planted any on the island, and I bet he wanted to. They should be on the island."[23]

So that spring, they went out to the island and planted pines.

Abbreviations

Notes

Bibliography

Index

Abbreviations Used in Notes
and Bibliography

ACL	A. Carl Leopold (son)
ACR	Arthur C. Ringland
AESB	*Agricultural Experiment Station Bulletin* (University of Wisconsin)
AGPA	American Game Protective Association
AL	Aldo Leopold
ASL	A. Starker Leopold (son)
AWI	American Wildlife Institute
BBS	Bureau of Biological Survey
BV	Bill Vogt
CAL	Carl A. Leopold (father)
ClL	Clara Leopold (mother)
CSL	Carl S. Leopold (brother)
EBL	Estella Bergere Leopold (wife)
EEL	Estella E. Leopold (daughter)
FL	Frederic Leopold (brother)
FWP	Fred Winn Papers
GM	*Game Management*
GPO	Government Printing Office
HAH	Hans Albert Hochbaum
JF	*Journal of Forestry*
JJH	Joseph J. Hickey
JND	Jay Norwood Darling
JWM	*Journal of Wildlife Management*
LBL	Luna B. Leopold (son)
LP	Aldo Leopold Papers
ML	Marie Leopold (sister)
NAWC	North American Wildlife Conference
NLB	Nina Leopold Bradley (daughter)
NMGPA	New Mexico Game Protective Association
OFPR	Official Federal Personnel Record

RGSNCS	*Report on a Game Survey of the North Central States*
RR	*Round River*
RSY	Robert Sterling Yard
SCA	*A Sand County Almanac and Sketches Here and There* (1949)
SCA/RR	*A Sand County Almanac with essays on Conservation from Round River* (1966)
SHSW	State Historical Society of Wisconsin
TNFF	Tonto National Forest Files
USDA	United States Department of Agriculture
USDI	United States Department of Interior
USFS	United States Forest Service
USFWS	United States Fish and Wildlife Service
USFPL	United States Forest Products Laboratory
UW	University of Wisconsin–Madison
WAF	*Wisconsin Agriculturalist and Farmer*
WARF	Wisconsin Alumni Research Foundation
WASAL	*Transactions of the Wisconsin Academy of Sciences, Arts, and Letters*
WCB	*Wisconsin Conservation Bulletin*
WCC	Wisconsin Conservation Commission
WCD	Wisconsin Conservation Department
WMI	Wildlife Management Institute

Notes

CHAPTER 1. SOURCES

1 FL, interview with author; FL, "Leopold Family Anecdotes," (MS, 1982),
   7–8; "Carl A. Leopold," in *Portrait and Biographical Album of Des Moines
   County, Iowa* (Chicago: Acme Publishing Co., 1888), 202.
2 Details of this early attempt to drive the sheep to California are sketchy. The
   flow of settlers along the Oregon Trail was still only beginning; according
   to historical sources, about a thousand emigrants used the trail in 1843. This
   account is based on overlapping stories from the sources cited in n. 1.
3 Two colorful accounts of logging and rafting on the upper Mississippi which
   were helpful in this and subsequent chapters are Walter A. Blair, *A Raft Pilot's
   Log: A History of the Great Rafting Industry on the Upper Mississippi* (Cleveland: Arthur H. Clark Co., 1930) and Charles E. Russell, *A-Rafting on the
   Mississip'* (New York: The Century Co., 1928).
4 Charles Starker's life and career are recalled in: Steven Brower, "Charles
   Starker: A German Immigrant Contributes to Burlington's Development"
   (report prepared for Aldo Leopold Community Tribute, Burlington, Iowa,
   April 15, 1980); S. Brower, "Starker-Leopold Historic District Application
   Form," (report prepared for National Historic District Nomination, 1981);
   "Charles H. W. Starker," in *The United States Biographical Dictionary and
   Portrait Gallery of Eminent and Self-Made Men,* Iowa Volume (Chicago and
   New York: American Biography Publishing Co., 1878), 557–58; "Charles
   Starker," in *Portrait and Biographical Album of Des Moines County, Iowa,*
   221–22; "Charles Starker," in *The Financier's Album of Prominent Bankers
   of America* (New York: The Financier's Co., 1899), 539; FL, "Leopold Fami-
   ly Anecdotes," 1–7; FL, interview with author; FL, transcript of interview,
   Des Moines County Historical Society. Various documents in the Leopold
   Papers also were helpful, as were several long interviews with Steven Brower
   of Burlington, Iowa.
5 The history of Burlington, Iowa, is recounted in Augustine Antrobus, *History of Des Moines County and Its People* (Chicago: S. J. Clarke Publishing
   Company, 1915); Phillip D. Jordan, *Catfish Bend: River Town and County
   Seat* (Burlington: Craftsman Press, 1975); Helen Turner McKim and Helen

Parsons, eds., *Burlington On The Mississippi, 1883–1983* (Burlington: Doran and Ward Lithographing Co., 1983). For a complete history of the Chicago, Burlington, and Quincy Railroad, See Richard C. Overton, *Burlington Route: A History of the Burlington Lines* (New York: Alfred A. Knopf, 1965).

6 FL, "Leopold Family Anecdotes," 8–13. For further information on Carl A. Leopold, see nn. 1, 4; see also George Stanley, "A Visit with Frederic Leopold," *Ducks Unlimited* 49:5 (September–October 1985), 35–36, 96–103; Sharon Kaufman, "Built on Honor to Endure: Evolution of the Leopold Family Philosophy" (master's thesis, University of Iowa, 1985); S. Kaufman and F. Leopold, "Built on Honor to Endure," *Iowa Natural Heritage* (Winter 1985), 1.

7 "Isham Gilbert," in *Biographical Review of Des Moines County, Iowa* (Chicago: Hobart Publishing Company, 1905), 1070. Gilbert's career was a saga in itself. In 1846, at the age of twenty-two, he rafted the first timber off Wisconsin's Black River down to Nauvoo, Illinois, to build the new Mormon Temple there. His father Samuel was among the first pioneering lumbermen in Wisconsin. The family stayed in the business, and the Gilbert and Hedge Company of Burlington became one of the region's primary lumber concerns. During the Civil War, Gilbert commanded the Second Brigade of the Second Division in the Sixteenth Army Corps of the Union Army. He and his faithful war-horse Dandy led his troops into ten major battles, most in the last bloody year of the war, and played a crucial role in the Union victory in the Battle of Nashville. Gilbert came home to Burlington in 1865, joined the family business, and built himself the house on Prospect Hill. But Gilbert, too, was an adventuresome sort, and not yet ready to retire to his elegant home on the bluff. He renewed an old friendship with "Diamond Joe" Reynolds, a onetime business partner who achieved fame as one of the giants of the steamboat industry on the Mississippi. Gilbert turned his attentions west and persuaded Reynolds to join him in a mining enterprise in Colorado. In 1877 he moved west to prospect in the hills behind Denver. His career as a prospector was not successful. After wandering around Colorado for several years, he ended up in Topeka, where in 1884 "paralysis of the heart" claimed "one of the most distinguished and gallant soldiers of the Civil War."

8 Burlington *Hawkeye*, undated clipping in Leopold family files, c. June 1894. Quoted in Brower, "Starker-Leopold Historic District Application Form," item 8, 4.

9 CAL to Anna Leopold, 4 August 1878, LP 10–8, 4.

CHAPTER 2. PROSPECT HILL

1 Mark Twain, *Life on the Mississippi* (London: Oxford University Press, 1962), 374–75, 29.

2 Frederick Jackson Turner, "The Significance of the Frontier in American History," in *The Frontier in American History* (New York: Henry, Holt, and Co., 1920), 1.

3 Ibid., 37.

4 Twain, *Life On The Mississippi,* 379–80.
5 FL, interview with author; ML, Voegeli-Leopold Collection, SHSW; FL, "Leopold Family Anecdotes," 5–7, 13–15; and various letters in LP.
6 "Birds," in Composition Book, c. 1898, LP 10–12, 3.
7 Historical records of the Leopold Desk Company are located at the University of Iowa in Iowa City. See also references in chap. 1, n. 6.
8 For general discussions of market hunting in the United States, see James B. Trefethen, *An American Crusade for Wildlife* (New York: Winchester Press and the Boone and Crockett Club, 1975), 55–65; David and Jim Kimball, *The Market Hunter* (Minneapolis: Dillon Press, 1969).
9 It is difficult to date the shift in Carl Leopold's hunting habits. He is recorded as having shot on a single day in March 1890 seventeen ducks and four geese — high by today's standards, but hardly extraordinary for its day (see Jordan, *Catfish Bend,* 318). In any case, by the end of the decade Carl no longer brought home such bags, and had stopped spring shooting.
10 FL, "Leopold Family Anecdotes," 19–22; FL, interview with author.
11 FL, "Recollections of an Old Member," (MS, 1977), 7–13. See also *SCA,* 120–22; *SCA/RR,* 127–29.
12 Edwin Hunger, untitled memoir, 8, Aldo Leopold Files, SHSW Archives.
13 FL, "Leopold Family Anecdotes," 21.
14 Ibid., 59–60.
15 AL to CSL, 26 February 1905, LP 10–8, 4.
16 For a discussion of the history and design of Crapo Park, see Steven Brower, "Research Report: Crapo Park Master Plan," (report, December 1979, Burlington, Iowa).
17 "The Record of Charles Starker," *Burlington Democrat-Journal,* 10 February 1900.
18 FL, "Aldo's Middle School Years," 6.
19 Material from Leopold's school years in Burlington is not voluminous, but reveals a solid, broad background in biology, history, literature, geography, composition, and beginning Latin. Burlington's schools benefitted from the German influence in town, and are said to have been among the best in the region. See materials in LP 10-12, 3.
20 FL, interview with author.
21 E. Hunger, untitled memoir, 1.
22 Ibid., 5–6.
23 AL to CAL and ClL, 13 March 1903, LP 10-8, 4.
24 "Journal 1903," LP 10-7, 1.
25 AL, *RR,* 171; *SCA/RR,* 230–31.
26 AL to ClL, 12 September 1903, LP 10-8, 4.
27 CAL to ClL, 19 September 1903, LP 10-8, 4.
28 FL, "Leopold Family Anecdotes," 11.

CHAPTER 3. LAWRENCEVILLE

1 ClL to AL, 5 January 1904, LP 10-8, 4.
2 Ibid.

3 CAL to AL, 7 January 1904, LP 10-8, 4.
4 AL to ClL, 6 January 1904, LP 10-8, 4.
5 For historical background on the Lawrenceville School, see Samuel R. Slaymaker II, *Five Miles Away: The Story of the Lawrenceville School* (Princeton: Princeton University Press, 1985).
6 AL to CAL, 29 January 1904, LP 10-8, 4.
7 AL to ClL, 6 February 1904, LP 10-8, 4.
8 AL to ClL, 10 February 1904, LP 10-8, 4.
9 AL to ClL, 11 February 1904, LP 10-8, 4.
10 AL to ClL, 9 January 1904, LP 10-8, 4.
11 AL to CAL, 20 March 1904, LP 10-8, 4.
12 AL to ML, 6 May 1904, LP 10-8, 4.
13 AL to ClL, 18 May 1904, LP 10-8, 4.
14 AL to ClL, 2 April 1904, LP 10-8, 4.
15 AL to ClL, 16 March 1904, LP 10-8, 4.
16 CAL to AL, 2 March 1904, LP 10-8, 4.
17 AL to ClL, 12 March 1904, LP 10-8, 4.
18 AL to CAL, 25 May 1904, LP 10-8, 4.
19 AL to ClL, 21 March 1904, LP 10-8, 4.
20 CAL to AL, 8 October 1904, LP 10-8, 4.
21 ClL to AL, 7 October 1904, LP 10-8, 4.
22 AL to ClL, 22 January 1905, LP 10-8, 4.
23 AL to ML, 25 January 1905, LP 10-8, 4.
24 AL to ClL, 15 February 1905, LP 10-8, 4.
25 CAL to AL, 5 March 1905, LP 10-8, 4.
26 CAL to AL, 12 March 1905, LP 10-8, 4.
27 AL to ClL, 2 April 1905, LP 10-8, 4.
28 AL to CAL, 31 May 1905, LP 10-8, 4.
29 AL to ClL, 9 April 1905; AL to CAL, 24 April 1905, LP 10-8, 4.
30 AL to ClL, 5 March 1905, LP 10-8, 4.
31 AL to CAL, 30 March 1905, LP 10-8, 4.
32 AL to ClL, 9 April 1905, LP 10-8, 4.
33 AL to ClL, 19 April 1905, LP 10-8, 4.
34 AL to ClL, 3 May 1905, LP 10-8, 4.
35 AL to ClL, 1 May 1905, LP 10-8, 4.
36 AL to CAL, 24 April 1905, LP 10-8, 4.
37 AL to CAL, 30 March 1905, LP 10-8, 4.
38 AL to CAL, 6 May 1905, LP 10-8, 4.
39 AL to ML, 12 April 1905, LP 10-8, 4. *Hepatica triloba,* the scientific name for the Round-lobed Hepatica, was later changed to *Hepatica americana.*
40 AL to ClL, 21 May 1905, LP 10-8, 4.
41 AL to ClL, 20 April 1905, LP 10-8, 4.
42 ClL to AL, 11 March 1905, LP 10-8, 4.
43 AL to ClL, 11 April 1905, LP 10-8, 4.
44 S. McPherson to CAL, 30 June 1905, LP 10-8, 4.
45 AL to CAL, 29 June 1905, LP 10-8, 4.

CHAPTER 4. NEW HAVEN

1 "Wherefore Wildlife Ecology?" undated, LP 10-6, 16.
2 AL to CAL, 27 September 1905, LP 10-8, 5.
3 AL to ClL, 9 December 1905, LP 10-8, 5.
4 ClL to AL, 24 September 1905; CAL to AL, 28 September 1905, LP 10-8, 5.
5 AL to CAL, 15 October 1905, LP 10-8, 5.
6 AL to ClL, 7 December 1905, LP 10-8, 5.
7 AL to ClL, 11 October 1905, LP 10-8, 5.
8 AL to ClL, 5 November 1905, LP 10-8, 5.
9 Ibid.
10 AL to ClL, 5 October 1905, LP 10-8, 5.
11 AL to CAL, 28 October 1905, LP 10-8, 5.
12 ClL to AL, 3 December 1905, LP 10-8, 5.
13 AL to ClL, 7 December 1905, LP 10-8, 5.
14 H. Drummond to AL, 5 January 1906, LP 10-8, 5.
15 H. Drummond to AL, 15 January 1906, LP 10-8, 5.
16 AL to ClL, 9 January 1906, LP 10-8, 5.
17 AL to ClL, 28 March 1906, LP 10-8, 5.
18 AL to ClL, 1 February 1906, LP 10-8, 5.
19 L. Peasley to AL, 29 January 1906, LP 10-8, 5.
20 AL to ClL, 5 May 1906, LP 10-8, 5.
21 AL to ClL, 15 April 1906, LP 10-8, 5.
22 CAL to AL, 15 January 1906, LP 10-8, 5.
23 AL to ClL, 11 February 1906, LP 10-8, 5.
24 ClL to AL, 23 February 1906, LP 10-8, 5.
25 Ibid.
26 CAL to AL, 21 February 1906, LP 10-8, 5.
27 CAL to AL, 27 March 1906, LP 10-8, 5.
28 ClL to AL, 15 May 1906, LP 10-8, 5.
29 AL to ClL, 19 May 1906, LP 10-8, 5.
30 AL to ClL, 1 February 1906, LP 10-8, 5.
31 ClL to AL, 15 May 1906, LP 10-8, 5.
32 AL to ClL, 1 June 1906, LP 10-8, 5.
33 B. Jacobosky to AL, 4 May 1906, LP 10-8, 5.
34 AL to CAL, 10 June 1906, LP 10-8, 5.
35 ClL to AL, 31 March 1906, LP 10-8, 5.
36 AL to FL, 25 March 1906, LP 10-8, 5.

CHAPTER 5. FOREST SCHOOL

1 AL to CAL, 16 September 1906, LP 10-8, 5.
2 AL to ClL, 23 September 1906, LP 10-8, 5.
3 AL to ClL, 9 September 1906, LP 10-8, 5.
4 ClL to AL, 6 November 1906, LP 10-8, 5.
5 ClL to AL, 2 December 1906, LP 10-8, 5.

6 AL to CAL, 30 November 1906, LP 10-8, 5.

7 ClL to AL, 14 December 1906, LP 10-8, 5.

8 AL to ClL, 17 December 1906, LP 10-8, 5.

9 AL to CAL, 23 January 1907, LP 10-8, 5.

10 AL to CAL, 29 January 1907, LP 10-8, 5.

11 AL to ClL, 20 January 1907; AL to CAL, 29 January 1907; AL to ClL, 7 February 1907, 23 January 1907, LP 10-8, 5.

12 AL to CAL, 29 January 1907, LP 10-8, 5.

13 CAL to AL, 5 February 1907, LP 10-8, 5.

14 AL to ClL, 19 February 1907, LP 10-8, 5

15 AL to ClL, 18 March 1907, LP 10-8, 5.

16 AL to ClL, 27 March 1907, LP 10-8, 5.

17 AL to ClL, 7 April 1907, LP 10-8, 6.

18 CAL to AL, 1 April 1907, LP 10-8, 6.

19 AL to CAL, 13 April 1907, LP 10-8, 6.

20 AL to ClL, 26 April 1907, LP 10-8, 6.

21 AL to ClL, 7 May 1907, LP 10-8, 6.

22 CAL to AL, 9 May 1907, LP 10-8, 6.

23 AL to CAL, 13 May 1907, LP 10-8, 6.

24 ClL to AL, 15 May 1907, LP 10-8, 6.

25 AL to ClL, 18 May 1907, LP 10-8, 6.

26 Ibid.

27 H. Drummond to AL, 31 May 1907, LP 10-8, 6.

28 CAL to ClL, 23 June 1907, LP 10-8, 6.

29 AL to ClL, 23 June 1907, LP 10-8, 6.

30 CAL to ClL, 23 June 1907, LP 10-8, 6.

31 AL to ClL, 26 June 1907, LP 10-8, 6.

32 AL to CAL, 15 July 1907, LP 10-8, 6.

33 AL to ClL, 8 July 1907, LP 10-8, 6.

34 AL to ClL, 11 August 1907, LP 10-8, 6.

35 AL to ClL, 11 July 1907, LP 10-8, 6.

36 AL to ClL, 26 August 1907, LP 10-8, 6.

37 G. Miller to AL, 1 October 1907, LP 10-8, 6.

38 CAL to AL, 9 October 1907, LP 10-8, 6.

39 AL to CAL, 11 October 1907, LP 10-8, 6.

40 AL to ClL, 2 November 1907, LP 10-8, 6.

41 ClL to AL, 19 October 1907, LP 10-8, 6.

42 ClL to AL, 2 December 1907, LP 10-8, 6.

43 CAL to AL, 11 January 1908, LP 10-8, 6.

44 ClL to AL, 18 February 1908, LP 10-8, 6.

45 AL to ClL, 25 April 1908, LP 10-8, 6.

46 AL to ClL, 3 May 1908, LP 10-8, 6.

47 AL to ClL, 22 April 1908, LP 10-8, 6.

48 CAL to AL, 31 January 1908, LP 10-8, 6.

49 See "Class History of 1908 Sheffield Scientific School," *Yale University Yearbook* (New Haven: Yale University, 1908), 174.

50 This discussion of the origins of the Forest Service is based on accounts in Michael Frome, *The Forest Service* (New York: Praeger Library, 1971); Gifford Pinchot, *Breaking New Ground* (New York: Harcourt, Brace and Co., 1947); Darrell H. Smith, *The Forest Service: Its History, Organizations, and Activities* (Washington, D.C.: Brookings Institution, 1947); Harold K. Steen, *The U.S. Forest Service: A History* (Seattle: University of Washington Press, 1976). For background on the Yale Forest School, see Pinchot, *Breaking New Ground*, 152–53; *Biographical Record of the Graduates and Former Students of the Yale Forest School, with Introductory Papers on Yale in the Forestry Movement and the History of the Yale Forest School* (New Haven: Yale Forest School, 1913); Henry Solon Graves, "Beginnings of Education in Forestry," *Proceedings of the Society of American Foresters*, 16–18 December 1948, Boston, Massachusetts (Washington, D.C.: SAF, 1949), 329–33; Samuel N. Spring, ed., *The First Half-Century of the Yale School of Forestry* (New Haven: Yale School of Forestry, 1950).

51 USDA, USFS, *The Use of the National Forest Reserves: Regulations and Instructions*, 1 July 1905, 7. See also Pinchot, *Breaking New Ground*, 264–68; Steen, *The U.S. Forest Service: A History*, 78–80.

52 Pinchot, *Breaking New Ground*, 252. Before Roosevelt left office in 1909, Congress would authorize an additional 44 million acres of National Forest land, bringing the total to 195 million acres.

53 "The Fable of the Forest Ranger Examination," FWP, Box 5.

54 Steen, *The U.S. Forest Service: A History*, 83.

55 John Muir's life has been the subject of several historical and biographical studies in recent years. Throughout the course of this present study, the most helpful source—not only for its biographical insight but for its overview of the American conservation movement—has been Stephen Fox, *John Muir and His Legacy: The American Conservation Movement* (Boston and Toronto: Little, Brown & Co., 1981; reprinted as *The American Conservation Movement* [Madison: University of Wisconsin Press, 1986]).

56 AL to CIL, 2 October 1908, LP 10-8, 6.

57 See "Silvical Characters of American Conifers and Yews," in LP 10-6, 14.

58 AL to CIL, 29 October 1908, LP 10-8, 6.

59 AL to CIL, 5 January 1909, LP 10-8, 6.

60 AL to CIL, 21 February 1909, LP 10-8, 6.

61 AL to CIL, 20 January 1909, LP 10-8, Box 6. "Either there," Leopold wrote in his letter, "or to the Sierras in California (District 5)."

62 AL to CIL, 21 February 1909, LP 10-8, 6.

63 AL to CAL, 1 February 1909, 11 February 1909, LP 10-8, 6.

64 AL to CIL, 7 March 1909, LP 10-8, 6.

65 Ibid.

66 Ibid.

67 AL to CIL, 19 March 1909, LP 10-8, 6.

68 AL to CIL, 4 May 1909, LP 10-8, 6.

69 AL to CIL, 25 April 1909, LP 10-8, 6.

70 AL to CIL, 28 May 1909, LP 10-8, 6.

CHAPTER 6. APACHE

1 In the early years of the Forest Service, personnel were required to keep logs of their daily activities. Leopold's official diaries provided much of the basic factual information on which this and the next three chapters are based. Extant diaries are in LP 10-7, 1, and cover the periods 14 April–31 July 1909; August 1909; December 1909; 1 January–31 December 1910; 1 January–1 September 1911; 1 November 1912–27 April 1913; 14 September 1914–2 December 1915.

2 Official Diary, 20 July 1909, LP 10-7, 1.

3 "Clifton Addition to the the Black Mesa Forest Reserve, Arizona," c. 1905, 1, National Archives, Record Group 95, Records of the Forest Service, Research Compilation File, Description and Resources–1, Apache National Forest, 1905–1910. This report was prepared by W. H. B. ("Whiskey Highball") Kent, the boundary man who surveyed the area.

4 Leopold's papers provided most of the information on southwestern wildlife. Other helpful sources were: Florence Merriam Bailey, *Birds of New Mexico* (Santa Fe: New Mexico Department of Game and Fish, 1928); Vernon Bailey, *Mammals of New Mexico* (USDA, BBS, North American Fauna 53: 1–412); E. L. Cockrum, *The Recent Mammals of Arizona* (Tucson: University of Arizona Press, 1960); J. S. Findlay et al., *Mammals of New Mexico* (Albuquerque: University of New Mexico Press, 1975); Raymond Hall, *Mammals of Nevada* (Berkeley: University of California Press, 1946); A. S. Leopold, *Wildlife of Mexico* (Berkeley: University of California Press, 1959); J. Stokely Ligon, *Wild Life of New Mexico* (Santa Fe: New Mexico Department of Fish and Game, 1927); Edgar Alexander Mearns, *Mammals of the Mexican Boundary of the United States* (Washington, D.C.: GPO, 1907).

5 For background on early forest reconnaissance, see William Lawson Pinknew, *The Log of a Timber Cruiser* (New York: Duffield and Company, 1915); Raymond E. Marsh, "Timber Cruising in the Early Days," *American Forests* 74, 2 (February 1968): 28–31, 43–44; R. E. Marsh, "Timber Cruising on National Forests of the Southwest," *Journal of Forest History* 13, 3 (October 1969): 22–32

6 AL, *SCA, 134, SCA/RR, 142.*

7 AL to CAL, 25 September 1909, LP 10-8, 7.

8 AL to ML, 4 October 1909, LP 10-8, 7. The two "expert lumbermen" to whom Leopold referred were probably Daniel W. Adams and District 3 engineer E. H. Jones. The road from Clifton to Springerville, known as the "Coronado Trail," was the first federally funded highway project authorized under the Federal Road Act of July 11, 1916. Its story is told in Robert W. Bates, "The Coronado Trail: First Federal Aid Highway," Cultural Resources Report No. 26, (Albuquerque: USDA–USFS, Southwestern Region, December 1978), 12–33. John D. Guthrie's dedication address is recorded in Edwin Tucker, *The Forest Service in the Southwest,* unpublished MS (Albuquerque: USDA, USFS, Southwestern Region, undated), 548–52. Tucker's work provided substantial background information on the people and events described in this and the following five chapters. A condensed version of

his work may be found in Edwin Tucker and George Fitzpatrick, *Men Who Matched the Mountains* (Washington, D.C.: GPO, 1972).

9 Ibid.

10 The evidence for this date is circumstantial. The only extant documentary evidence of the incident is in Leopold's own later essay, "Thinking Like a Mountain," (*SCA,* 129–33; *SCA/RR,* 137–41). His letters, diaries, notes, and reports fail to mention it. The only other reference to it in Leopold's writings comes in a 1919 article, "A Turkey Hunt on the Datil National Forest": ". . . I once knocked down three big [turkeys] with steel bullets and two of them got up and flew half a mile. I never saw them again. The same season, while turkey-hunting, I knocked down three big lobo wolves and two of them got away."

By process of elimination, the 1909 reconnaissance seems to be the only period in which the incident could have taken place. There is no note of it in his hunting journals, which he began keeping in the summer of 1917 and in which he recorded virtually all of his outdoor activities; it is highly unlikely that Leopold would have failed to record an event as significant as the killing of a wolf. Likewise, the shooting could not have taken place during Leopold's period of illness and recuperation, when he was not hunting at all. Leopold's USFS diaries give a nearly complete record of his field activities (again with no mention of the incident) during his years on the Apache and the Carson. Two periods are not covered in these diaries: September–November 1909 (the diaries for these months were requisitioned during the subsequent investigation of Leopold's conduct during the 1909 reconnaissance, and apparently were never returned) and September 1911–October 1912 (see n. 1 above). Of these two periods, the former seems the most likely possibility as a date for the incident. Elliot Barker has confirmed this interpretation in an interview with the author.

For a detailed review of the wolf control effort in the Southwest during this period, see David E. Brown, ed., *The Wolf in the Southwest: The Making of an Endangered Species* (Tucson: University of Arizona Press, 1983), 41–71.

11 AL to ClL, 7 October 1909, LP 10-8, 7.

12 AL, *SCA,* 135; *SCA/RR,* 143.

13 AL to ClL, 7 October 1909, LP 10-8, 7.

14 AL to ClL, 17 November 1909, LP 10-8, 7.

15 AL to ACR, 26 November 1909, LP 10-8, 7.

16 AL to ClL, 26 November 1909, LP 10-8, 7.

17 AL to ClL, 30 November 1909, LP 10-8, 7.

18 AL to ClL, 10 February 1910, LP 10-8, 7.

19 AL to ClL, 1 February 1910, LP 10-8, 7.

20 AL to ClL, 14 February 1910, LP 10-8, 7.

21 AL to ClL, 18 April 1910, LP 10-8, 7.

22 AL to ClL, 9 May 1910, LP 10-8, 7.

23 Ibid.

24 AL to CAL, 11 June 1910, 18 May 1910, LP 10-8, 7.

25 R. Moak to T. S. Woolsey, 28 May 1910; D. Adams to ACR, 26 May 1910;

T. Longwell, 3 June 1910; S. Smith to ACR, 26 May 1910; R. King to T. S. Woolsey, 25 May 1910, OFPR. Leopold's official record contains employment papers from 1909–1939 and official correspondence from 1909–1929. The original file was apparently housed in the U.S. Federal Records Center at St. Louis. This file was microfilmed and placed in LP 10-11, Microfilm 1.

26 C. Heller, 25 May 1910, OFPR.

27 AL to ACR, 14 May 1910, OFPR.

28 AL to ClL, 19 June 1910, LP, 10-8, 7.

29 AL to CAL, 27 June 1910, LP 10-8, 7.

30 AL, *SCA,* 135; *SCA/RR,* 143.

31 The demise of the grizzly in the Southwest is recounted in David E. Brown, *The Grizzly in the Southwest: Documentary of an Extinction* (Norman: University of Oklahoma Press, 1985), 108–19.

32 AL to ML, 5 July 1910, LP 10-8, 7.

33 AL to ClL, 21 April 1910, LP 10-8, 7.

34 J. H. Allison to ACR, 17 July 1910, OFPR.

35 J. H. Allison to ACR, 29 July 1910, OFPR.

36 AL to ML, 14 July 1910, LP 10-8, 7.

37 AL to ClL, 2 September 1910, LP 10-8, 7.

38 AL, *SCA,* 126; *SCA/RR,* 134.

39 "Minutes of the Apache Ranger Meeting," 8–14 September 1910, 13, LP 10-11, 2.

40 Marsh, "Timber Cruising on National Forests of the Southwest," 27.

41 AL to CAL, 18 September 1910, LP 10-8, 7. Maps of lands surveyed by Leopold's 1909–1910 reconnaissance crews may be found in the Sharlot Hall collection of Forest Service documents and artifacts, Box 34, FS 472, at Prescott, Arizona.

42 AL to ClL, 17 November 1910, LP 10-8, 7.

43 AL to ClL, 11 September 1910, LP 10-8, 7.

44 AL to ClL, 13 January 1911, 19 February 1911, LP 10-8, 7.

45 AL to CAL, 21 February 1911, LP 10-8, 7.

46 For an account of this period in Forest Service history, see Steen, *The U.S. Forest Service: A History,* 103–44.

47 E. H. Clapp, Memo for O[perations], 7 December 1910, OFPR.

48 AL to ML, 27 March 1911, LP 10-8, 7.

49 Ibid.

50 The Roosevelt Dam, located within the Tonto National Forest, was the first federally funded water reclamation project in the West. The dam was dedicated on March 18, 1911.

51 AL to ML, 5 April 1911, LP 10-8, 7.

52 ACR to the Bergere sisters, 30 April 1911, LP 10-8, 7.

CHAPTER 7. CARSON

1 AL to ML, 8 May 1911, LP 10-8, 7.

2 AL to ClL, 7 June 1911, LP 10-8, 7.

3 AL to ClL, 12 May 1911, LP 10-8, 7.

4 E. R. Smith, "History of Grazing Industry and Range Conservation Developments in the Rio Grande Basin," *Journal of Range Management* 6, 6 (November 1953): 407. For a general history of the regional environment, see William deBuys, *Enchantment and Exploitation: The Life and Hard Times of a New Mexico Mountain Range* (Albuquerque: University of New Mexico Press, 1985).

5 AL to EBL, 13 May 1911, LP 10-8, 7.

6 AL to ClL, 3 June 1911, LP 10-8, 7.

7 AL to CAL, 20 May 1911, LP 10-8, 7.

8 AL to CAL, 17 May 1911, LP 10-8, 7.

9 *Carson Pine Cone,* June 1911. A collection of *Pine Cones,* consisting of Leopold's own copies and later acquisitions, is in LP 10-11, 1, and includes twenty-eight issues from June 1911 to March 1914.

10 AL to CAL, 17 June 1911, LP 10-8, 7.

11 AL to ClL, 14 July 1911, LP 10-8, 7.

12 AL to ClL, 7 July 1911, LP 10-8, 7.

13 AL to EBL, 8 July 1911, LP 10-8, 7.

14 Jack J. Kenney of Santa Fe, New Mexico, provided much of the background information for this family history, and shared his mimeographed collection of family records, "La Reunion de La Familia de Eloisa Luna de Otero de Bergere." Luna Leopold and Nina Leopold Bradley were also generous in sharing their recollections and records. See also Lucretia Pitman, "Solomon Luna, Sheepmaster and Politician of New Mexico, 1858–1910," (master's thesis, St. Louis University, 1944).

15 AL to CAL, 9 July 1911, LP 10-8, 7.

16 AL to ClL, 14 July 1911, LP 10-8, 7.

17 AL to EBL, 14 July 1911, LP 10-8, 7.

18 AL to ClL, 6 August 1911, LP 10-8, 7.

19 AL to EBL, 7 August 1911, LP 10-8, 7.

20 AL to ClL, 16 August 1911, LP 10-8, 7.

21 Ibid.

22 AL to CAL, 11 August 1911, LP 10-8, 7.

23 *Carson Pine Cone,* August 1911. The note was slipped in by Supervisor Hall.

24 AL to ClL, 21 August 1911, LP 10-8, 7.

25 AL to EBL, 22 August 1911, LP 10-8, 7.

26 AL to ClL, 12 May 1911, LP 10-8, 7.

27 AL to EBL, 4 September 1911, LP 10-8, 7.

28 AL to ClL, 20 October 1911, LP 10-8, 7.

29 AL to EBL, 25 September 1911, LP 10-8, 7.

30 AL to EBL, 14 September 1911, LP 10-8, 7.

31 AL to EBL, 7 September 1911, LP 10-8, 7.

32 AL to ClL, 3 October 1911, LP 10-8, 7.

33 AL to ClL, 20 October 1911, LP 10-8, 7.

34 AL to ClL, 1 November 1911, LP 10-8, 7.

35 Unfortunately, few of Estella's replies to Aldo are extant. This interpretation is based on those in the Leopold Papers, on Leopold's own letters, and on interviews with family members.

36 AL to ClL, 18 November 1911, LP 10-8, 7.
37 Ibid.
38 CAL to EBL, 26 November 1911, LP 10-8, 7.
39 CAL to ClL, 25 December 1911, LP 10-8, 7.
40 AL to ClL, 25 November 1911, LP 10-8, 7.
41 For historical background on USFS grazing policy, and on the southwestern range in particular, see Will C. Barnes, "Winning the Forest Range," *American Forests and Forest Life* 36, 7 (July 1930): 398–400, 466; William M. Raines and Will C. Barnes, *Cattle, Cowboys, and Rangers* (New York: Grosset and Dunlap, 1930); Pinchot, *Breaking New Ground*, 177–82, 268–72; Harold K. Steen, "Grazing and the Environment: A History of Forest Service Stock-Reduction Policy," *Agricultural History* 49, 1 (January 1975), 238–42; Steen, *The U.S. Forest Service: A History*, 162–67; Paul H. Roberts, *Hoof Prints on Forest Ranges: The Early Years of National Forest Range Administration* (San Antonio: The Naylor Company, 1963); Paul H. Roberts, *Them Were the Days,* (San Antonio: The Naylor Company, 1965); William D. Rowley, *U.S. Forest Service Grazing and Rangeland: A History* (College Station: Texas A&M University Press, 1985); and Tucker, *The Forest Service in the Southwest.*
42 AL to EBL, 12 February 1912, LP 10-8, 8.
43 AL to ClL, 12 February 1912, LP 10-8, 8.
44 LBL, interview with author. See also Tucker, *The Forest Service in the Southwest,* 349–54.
45 *Carson Pine Cone,* March 1912.
46 AL to EBL, 29 April 1912, LP 10-8, 8.
47 AL to ClL, 29 April 1912, LP 10-8, 8.
48 AL to EBL, 2 February 1912, LP 10-8, 8.
49 AL to EBL, 6 March 1912, LP 10-8, 8.
50 AL to EBL, 21 May 1912, LP 10-8, 8.
51 AL to EBL, 24 August 1912, LP 10-8, 8.
52 AL to ClL, 8 September 1912, LP 10-8, 8.
53 AL to ClL, 31 October 1912, LP 10-8, 8.
54 Official Diary, 18 April 1912, LP, 10-7, 1.
55 R. E. Marsh to E. P. Cliff, August 1967, quoted in Tucker, *Men Who Matched the Mountains,* 39.
56 AL to CAL, 23 April 1913, LP 10-8, 8.

CHAPTER 8. ON TOP

1 Dr. Avery Harrington of the Department of Nephrology at the University of Wisconsin Hospital and Clinics provided helpful information on the nature of nephritis and the history of its treatment.
2 AL to ACR, 26 April 1913, OFPR.
3 ACR to T. S. Woolsey, 3 May 1913, OFPR.
4 AL to CAL, 26 April 1913, LP 10-8, 8.
5 AL to ACR, 3 June 1913, OFPR.
6 AL, "To the Forest Officers of the Carson," 15 July 1913, *Carson Pine Cone,* July 1913.

7 Ibid.

8 Ibid.

9 AL to ACR, c. August 1913, OFPR.

10 Al to ACR, 2 September 1913, OFPR.

11 AL, "To the Boys on the Job," 14 November 1913, *Carson Pine Cone,* December 1913.

12 At the time, Barnes was assistant forester under Gifford Pinchot, and a principal formulator of USFS Grazing Policy. Previous to his appointment he had operated cattle ranches in New Mexico and Arizona, and in his later years would take up writing full time.

13 Leopold inscribed the book before giving it to his father. After his father died the following year, Leopold received the book. Starker Leopold later inherited it from his father. It is now held in the Leopold Library at the University of California–Berkeley's Department of Forestry and Resource Management.

14 A. M. Bergere to EBL, 23 October 1913, LP 10-8, 8.

15 AL to H. H. Chapman, 25 October 1913, LP 10-1, 1.

16 For a personal glimpse of this era see Barker's books *Ramblings in the Field of Conservation* (Santa Fe: Sunshine Press, 1976), *Beatty's Cabin: Adventures in the Pecos High Country* (Albuquerque: University of New Mexico Press, 1953), and *Western Life and Adventures in the Great Southwest* (Kansas City, Mo.: Lowell Press, 1974).

17 AL, "To the Officers of the Carson," 16 January 1914, *Carson Pine Cone,* January 1914.

18 The *Pine Cone* item referred to USFS Circular No. 82-G-19, which indicated "that the protection of migratory and insectivorous birds will be made an active matter." "Co-operation — Biological Survey," *Carson Pine Cone,* January 1914.

19 AL, "Resolutions of a Ranger," 1 January 1914, *Carson Pine Cone,* January 1914.

20 AL, "To the Officers of the Carson," 15 February 1914, *Carson Pine Cone,* March 1914.

21 CAL to FL, 19 March 1914, LP 10-8, 8.

22 AL to ACR, 22 July 1914, OFPR.

23 AL to ClL, 1 May 1914, LP 10-8, 8.

24 AL to ACR, 22 July 1914, OFPR.

25 AL to CAL, 1 October 1914, LP 10-8, 8.

26 See Leopold's "Personal Notebook," LP 10-8, 2. This notebook contains quotations that Leopold gleaned from books, articles, the Bible, and other sources. Many of the passages eventually found their way into his own essays and speeches. Leopold seems to have used the notebook most regularly in the 1910s and early 1920s, though he continued to add to and draw from it into the 1930s. The authors cited give some indication of the breadth of Leopold's reading: Johnson, Walpole, Cervantes, Muir, Benjamin Franklin, William James, Robert Louis Stevenson, Victor Hugo, Carlyle, Rousseau, Seton, Edgar Lee Masters, Jefferson, John Stuart Mill, Samuel Butler, Thoreau, Kipling, Schopenhauer, Milton, Turgenev, Washington, Ouspensky, Ariosto, Voltaire, Lao-tzu, Roosevelt, Cicero, Epicurus, Aristotle, Xenophon, Tactitus, Hero-

dotus, Julian Huxley, Edward Gibbon, John Burroughs, Bertrand Russell, Carl Sandburg, Rupert Brooke, Stephen Vincent Benet, Shakespeare, Vachel Lindsay, Oscar Wilde, Keats, Machiavelli, Plutarch, Jean Henri Fabre, Liberty Hyde Bailey, Izaak Walton, etc.

27 AL to ClL, 25 October 1914, LP 10-8, 8.

28 AL to CAL, 27 November 1914, LP 10-8, 8.

29 AL to CAL, 8 December 1914, LP 10-8, 8.

30 AL to CAL, 19 December 1914, LP 10-8, 8.

31 Official Diary, 9 January 1915, LP 10-7, 1.

32 Background information on the history of wildlife management in the Forest Service was drawn from documents in the Leopold Papers and the Fred Winn Papers. See especially "Wildlife Management in the Early Days of the Forest Service," FWP, Box 2.

33 L. Kneipp to ACR, "Memorandum for District Forester," 6 February 1915, National Archives, Record Group 95, Records of the Forest Service, Records of the Division of Operations: Operations File, 1910–1923. See LP 10-11, Microfilm 2.

34 See Henry Graves, "The National Forests and Wild Life," *Recreation* (May 1915): 236–39.

35 Official Diary, 19 March 1915, LP 10-7, 1.

36 AL to ClL, 9 June 1915, LP 10-8, 8.

37 AL to ClL, 20 May 1915, LP 10-8, 8.

38 ACR to H. Graves, 11 June 1915, OFPR.

39 AL to ClL, 9 June 1915, LP 10-8, 8.

CHAPTER 9. "TO PROMOTE THE PROTECTION AND ENJOYMENT OF WILD THINGS. . ."

1 Official Diary, 16–20 June 1915, LP 10-7, 1. This brief diary account is the only extant record of Leopold's initial visit to the Grand Canyon. His entries contain no personal impressions of the Canyon. Copies of the Grand Canyon Working Plan may be found in LP 10-11, Folio 1, and in the archives of Grand Canyon National Park. For additional information on the administration of the Canyon within District 3, see Arthur Ringland with Fern Ingersoll, "Pioneering in Southwest Forestry," *Journal of Forest History* 17, 1 (April 1973): 9–11.

2 In Paul Schullery, *The Grand Canyon: Early Impressions* (Boulder: Colorado Associated University Press, 1981), 102.

3 AL, *USFS Game and Fish Handbook,* USDA, USFS, D-3, December 1915, 9.

4 Ibid., 10.

5 Ibid, 106. The white-tailed ptarmigan still occurs in the alpine regions of New Mexico, which is the southern extent of its range.

6 ACR to H. Graves, 25 September 1915, OFPR.

7 For background on wildlife conservation prior to 1915, see James Trefethen, *An American Crusade For Wildlife,* 117–94; Fox, *John Muir and His Legacy,* 148–59; John F. Reiger, *American Sportsmen and the Origins of Conservation* (New York: Winchester Press, 1975), 50–72, 114–51.

8 Trefethen, *An American Crusade for Wildlife,* 177.

9 William T. Hornaday, *Our Vanishing Wild Life* (New York: New York Zoo-logical Society 1913), x.

10 "In speaking of conditions in New Mexico," the *Albuquerque Morning Journal* reported the next day, "the speaker said he deemed that the conditions were serious here, not so much from the lack of proper laws for the preservation of game, but from indifference on the part of citizens at large to assist the game wardens by reporting violations of the existing laws." "Hornaday Tells Good Crowd All About Wild Life," *Albuquerque Morning Journal,* 14 October 1915.

11 Hornaday inscribed the book: "To Mr. Aldo Leopold, On the firing line in New Mexico and Arizona. With the kind regards of the author. W. T. Hornaday." Leopold Library, University of California–Berkeley.

12 Official Diary, 12-17 November 1915, LP 10-7, 1.

13 "Our Aim," *The Pine Cone,* Christmas 1915, 1. *The Pine Cone* was issued as a regular quarterly from 1915 to 1920, with an occasional extra (or missing) issue. Leopold also put out a special issue in early 1924. Authorship of articles in *The Pine Cone* was almost never given, but Leopold evidently wrote most of the copy himself until Ward Shepard joined him in 1916. A nearly complete set of *The Pine Cone* may be found in LP 10-6, Folio 1.

14 "The Varmint Question," *The Pine Cone,* Christmas 1915, 1–2.

15 AL to ClL, 2 December 1915, LP 10-8, 8.

16 "Memorandum," AL to D. D. Bronson, 11 December 1915, OFPR. It is indicative of the trust that Ringland placed in Leopold that he apparently asked Leopold to write this response, and then signed his own name to it. See virtually identical memo, ACR to D. D. Bronson, 18 December 1915, OFPR.

17 "Miles W. Burford: Father of Game Conservation in New Mexico," *The Pine Cone,* January 1918, 2.

18 "Fine Lecture on Game Protection," *Silver City Independent,* 1 February 1916.

19 AL to ClL, 20 January 1916, LP 10-8, 8.

20 AL to ACR, 14 February 1916, OFPR.

21 Ibid.

22 Ibid.

23 AL, "Putting the 'AM' in Game Warden," *Sportsman's Review* 54, 9 (31 August 1918): 173.

24 "Game Situation Critical," NMGPA press release, 23 October 1916, LP 10-8, 8.

25 AL, "Putting the 'AM' in Game Warden," 173.

26 Susan L. Flader, *Thinking Like a Mountain: Aldo Leopold and the Evolution of an Ecological Attitude toward Deer, Wolves, and Forests* (Columbia: University of Missouri Press, 1974), 61.

27 "NMGPA Resolution No. 4: Predatory Animals," *The Pine Cone,* April 1916, 6.

28 "Famous Grizzly Brought to Bag," *The Pine Cone,* October 1916, 4.

29 AL to ClL, 20 March 1916, LP 10-8, 8.

30 Ibid.

31 Grand Canyon Working Plan, 1–3. The section of the plan dealing with fish and game, presumably written by Leopold, stated that "the value of the game in [the Grand Canyon refuge] is so great as to merit a special effort on the

part of the officer in charge to prevent all hunting." The refuge had "so far been a refuge principally in name." Among other suggestions, Leopold recommended that the feral burro population be monitored, and if found bothersome to tourists and a threat to the food supply of mountain sheep, exterminated. The job had to be "handled carefully, but it is nevertheless advisable."

32 "The Crisis," *The Pine Cone,* July 1916, 2.

33 AL, "Putting the 'AM' in Game Warden," 173.

34 Ibid.

35 T. Roosevelt to AL, 18 January 1917, copy in LP 10-8, 2.

36 The history of the Tenth and Twentieth Engineers is recalled in Henry S. Graves, "The Forest Engineers," *American Forestry* 25, 306 (June 1919): 1109; William B. Greeley, "The American Lumberjack in France," *American Forestry* 25, 306 (June 1919): 1093–108; John D. Guthrie et al., '*The Carpathians,*' *Tenth Engineers (Forestry), A.E.F., 1917–1919: Roster and Historical Sketch* (Washington, D.C.: The Carpathians, 1940).

37 "Beef and Ideals," *Arizona Star,* 20 May 1917.

38 AL to ClL, 11 May 1917, LP 10-8, 8.

39 AL to ClL, 3 May 1917, LP 10-8, 8.

40 AL to ClL, 11 May 1917, LP 10-8, 8. Those taking part in this field trip into the Grand Canyon included: Leopold; Frank C. W. Pooler; Assistant Chief Forester Edward A. Sherman, whom Leopold described as "a second Abraham Lincoln"; Frank Waugh; "Miss Colter," an architect and landscaper for the Santa Fe Railroad; Walter Hubbell, "head of the Harvey Transportation Department"; and a Mr. and Mrs. Wylder. For Waugh's assessment of the Grand Canyon recreation strategy, see Frank Waugh, "A Plan for the Development of the Village of Grand Canyon," USDA, USFS (Washington, D.C.: GPO, 1918).

41 Ibid.

42 Ibid.

43 "Address before the Albuquerque Rotary Club on Presentation of the Gold Medal of the Permanent Wild Life Protection Fund," c. July 1917, LP 10-8, 8.

44 In Tucker, *The Forest Service in the Southwest,* 324–25.

45 "Recommendation to the Secretary," 1 July 1917, OFPR.

46 New Mexico Journal 1917–1924, 16 August 1917, LP 10-7, 2.

47 AL to ClL, 22 October 1917, LP 10-8, 8.

48 "Potting Ducks: A Little Talk on the Ethics of Sportsmanship," *The Pine Cone,* January 1918, 3.

49 "On Killing the Limit," *The Pine Cone,* July 1917, 2.

50 "The Drag Net Makes Another Haul," *The Pine Cone,* October 1917, 1.

51 The quote is from "The Undergraduate Background," an article by Henry Seidel Canby which appeared in *Harper's* in February 1915. See Leopold's "Personal Notebook."

52 "GPA and Jicarilla Club Go To the Mat," *The Pine Cone,* January 1918, 1.

53 The poem, "A Lost Land—To Germany," appeared in *The Literary Digest* of October 20, 1917. Included in letter, AL to ClL, 30 October 1917, LP 10-8, 8.

54 AL, "The Civic Life of Albuquerque," 5, 27 September 1918, LP 10-8, 9.

55 Ibid., 5, 1, 3.
56 Ibid., 5–6.
57 Ibid., 8–9.
58 AL, "What About Drainage?" *Bernalillo County Farm Bureau News* 1, 1 (June 1918): 2.
59 According to the list of publications in the Leopold Papers, Leopold's first non-Forest Service article was "Game Conservation: A Warning, also an Opportunity," *Arizona* 7, 12 (December 1916): 6.
60 At one point during this period, Leopold even laid grandiose plans for a "United Council of Wild Life Conservationists," to include representatives from all the major national groups and government agencies. It was, in retrospect, a naive undertaking. The unified support that Leopold experienced in New Mexico was rare, and he had little inside understanding of the eastern wildlife establishment, or of the divisions within it. Apparently, Leopold did not take the idea past the planning stage. See "Proposed Circular" in AL to ClL, 26 September 1917, LP 10-8, 8.
61 AL, "The Popular Wilderness Fallacy: An Idea That Is Fast Exploding." *Outers' Book–Recreation* 58, 1 (January 1918): 43, 46.
62 AL, "Forestry and Game Conservation," *JF* 16, 4 (April 1918): 406.
63 Ibid., 410.
64 In "Wild Lifers vs Game Farmers: A Plea For Democracy in Sport," *Bulletin AGPA* 8, 2 (April 1919), we do gain an early hint of Leopold's interest in nongame wildlife. Interestingly, it came as a consequence of his criticism of game farmers. The tension between game farming and game management forced the point: "the game farmer seeks to produce merely something to shoot, while the Wild Lifer seeks to perpetuate, at least, a sample of all wild life, game and non-game." Leopold concluded that, in comparison to game farmers, "the Wild Lifer enjoys the advantage of an ethical as well as of an utilitarian objective."
65 John Muir, *Our National Parks* (Boston: Houghton Mifflin Co., 1901), 57. Leopold recorded the quote in his "Personal Notebook."
66 AL, "Wild Lifers vs. Game Farmers," 6.
67 Ibid.
68 AL, "A Plea for State-Owned Ducking Grounds," *Wild Life* (October 1919), 9.
69 *The Pine Cone,* January 1914, 4; see also "Boomerangs," *The Pine Cone,* April 1918, 3.
70 "Cuidado! The Elk," *The Pine Cone,* April 1918, 2.
71 "Discovered," *The Pine Cone,* April 1918, 4.
72 FL, "Leopold Family Anecdotes," 80–81.
73 AL to ClL, 29 December 1918, LP 10-8, 9.
74 "Why Governor Larazzolo Should Re-appoint Rouault," *The Pine Cone,* January 1919, 1.
75 Ibid.
76 Elliot Barker, interview with author.
77 "GPA Loses; Gable Wins," *The Pine Cone,* February 1919, 1.
78 "A Word to Our Critics," *The Pine Cone,* July 1919, 2.
79 "Memorandum," 20 May 1919, OFPR. In January 1919, John Burnham, presi-

dent of the American Game Protective Association and a central figure in eastern wildlife circles, offered Leopold a prominent position in his group. The fact that Leopold declined indicates both that Leopold wanted to stay in the Southwest and that he placed priority on rejoining the Forest Service. The chief of operations position opened when Don P. Johnston, Leopold's former colleague on the Grand Canyon Working Plan, was transferred out of the district.

80 AL to ClL, 13 June 1919, LP 10-8, 9.

81 AL to ClL, 4 July 1919, LP 10-8, 9.

82 Untitled, *The Pine Cone,* July 1919, 4. The style of this essay suggests that it was probably one of Ward Shepard's contributions.

CHAPTER 10. CHIEF OF OPERATIONS

1 Gifford Pinchot outlined the duties of inspection in Service Order No. 125, "Inspection," 16 February 1907. The order directed inspectors "1) To assist, advise, and encourage Forest Officers in their work. 2) To examine conditions on the ground, and report what they find. 3) To recommend changes for the better." Inspectors were encouraged to "use every opportunity to imbue forest officers with a spirit of pride in their duties, and in their contact with the public they should endeavor to increase understanding of the work and aims of the Forest Service."

2 "Inspection Memorandum for District Forester," 13 October 1919. This inspection report, and most of the others referred to in this and the following chapter, are held in the files of the Tonto National Forest Headquarters (TNFF) in Phoenix, Arizona. I am indebted to USFS archaeologist Martin McAllister for bringing these crucial reports to my attention.

3 For background on Carhart and events leading up to his meeting with Leopold, see Donald Baldwin, *The Quiet Revolution: The Grass Roots of Today's Wilderness Preservation Movement* (Boulder: Pruett Publishing Company, 1972), 11–30; Roderick Nash, *Wilderness and the American Mind,* 3d ed. (New Haven: Yale University Press, 1982), 185–86. Baldwin's assertion that Carhart, not Leopold, deserves credit for the first implementation of the wilderness idea in the National Forests sparked a brief academic brushfire; see Flader, review of *The Quiet Revolution, Journal of Forest History* 18, 1–2 (April 1974): 36; Lawrence Rakestraw, "News, Comments, and Letters," *Journal of Forest History* 19, 1 (January 1975): 41; Nash, "Arthur Carhart: Wildland Advocate," *Living Wilderness* 44, 151 (December 1980): 32–34; see also Flader, "Aldo Leopold and the Wilderness Idea," *Living Wilderness* 43, 147 (December 1979).

4 Elliot Barker has indicated that Leopold had raised the idea of wilderness preservation in New Mexico by 1913; see Dennis Roth, "The National Forests and the Campaign for Wilderness Legislation," *Journal of Forest History* 28, 3 (July 1984): 113. Fred Winn mentions 1918 as the year in which plans to set aside the Gila were first discussed; see Harvey Broome, "Our Basis of Understanding," *Living Wilderness* 19, 51 (Winter 1954–55): 47. See also Flader, *Thinking Like a Mountain,* 79.

5 See especially AL to RSY, 23 May 1940, LP 10-2, 9.

6 "Memorandum for Mr. Leopold, District 3," 10 December 1919; original on file in Arthur Carhart Papers; copy in LP 10-11, 2. See Baldwin, *The Quiet Revolution,* 31–35.

7 AL, *SCA,* 96; *SCA/RR,* 102.

8 F. C. W. Pooler to H. Graves, 18 December 1919, OFPR.

9 Ibid.

10 See E. W. Nelson to AL, 27 December 1919; AL to E. W. Nelson, 5 January 1920; OFPR.

11 New Mexico Journal 1917–1924, 26–31 December 1919.

12 Over a dozen of these brief reports appeared in the pages of *The Condor* between 1918 and 1924. See references in the bibliography of Leopold's writings which follows.

13 "Here Is the Program of Game Management for New Mexico," *The Pine Cone,* March 1920, 1.

14 Leopold's refuge ideas at this time are explained in detail in Flader, *Thinking Like a Mountain,* 61–65. A refuge, Leopold reasoned, if too large, would simply forbid hunting over one large area and concentrate it on another. If a refuge were too small, it would not support a viable breeding stock. A well-planned refuge (which, at the time, would have been aimed primarily toward increasing deer, waterfowl, and turkey populations) would be large enough to harbor breeding populations and small enough to produce a constant "overflow" for hunting in adjacent areas. "In short," Leopold wrote with his gift for metaphor, "it puts the spigot in the side instead of the bottom of the barrel."

     During this period, Leopold was concerned foremost with improving deer populations, both in terms of quantity and quality. In addition to an overall shortage of deer, the Southwest suffered from a shortage of bucks. The shooting of does was forbidden, with the result that hunters would sometimes see dozens of does for every buck. There was a danger that immature males breeding with females could lead to physical deterioration of the herd. The refuge system would theoretically solve this dilemma and improve hunting prospects simultaneously. Deer are polygamous, with the dominant bucks appropriating the greater number of does. According to the refuge plan, smaller non-breeding males would be forced, as excess, beyond the refuge boundaries, while a strong and stabilized population would be sustained within the boundaries. With "natural" conditions restored, natural breeding patterns would resume.

     The Nelson Bill, Leopold wrote, "entirely meets the requirements of game refuges. . . . Moreover, it removes the only possible local objections to such refuges (by) making their creation dependent on the approval of the governor, and by guaranteeing that the refuges will not be locked up against the utilization of the range by livestock or their other resources" ("Extermination or Reform," *The Pine Cone,* March 1920, 1).

15 Leopold took the lead on this issue as well. The February 1920 issue of the *Journal of Forestry* carried his article "Determining the Kill Factor for Blacktail Deer in the Southwest." "The first step," he wrote, "toward efficient management of big game on the National Forests must consist of a quantitative

regulation of the annual kill. In other words, the kill must be limited to the productive capacity of the herd." Game managers needed a mathematical formula that would indicate how many animals could be culled without harming the productivity of the herd (or, when applied in reverse, would indicate the size of the herd that had been successfully culled). Leopold borrowed from cattlegrowers an analogous formula for determining beef production, plugged in rough deer census numbers that he had gathered from District 3 rangers, and had at least a working "kill factor" to apply. The result was to be tested, with the help of the Otero ranchmen, in the mountains near Magdalena.

16 AL to ClL, 27 April 1920, LP 10-8, 9. A draft of the bill appeared in the July 1920 *Pine Cone.*

17 See Brown, *The Wolf in The Southwest,* 61–64.

18 AL, "The Game Situation in the Southwest," *Bulletin AGPA* 9, 2 (April 1920): 5.

19 LBL, interview with author.

20 AL, "A Man's Leisure Time," 15 October 1920, LP 10-8, 9. A substantially revised version of this essay appears in *RR,* 3–8, and in *SCA/RR,* 181–88.

21 AL, "Forestry of the Prophets," *JF* 18, 4 (April 1920): 412–13, 416.

22 Ibid., 415.

23 Ibid.; the quote, which Leopold employed several times in his writings, is from Ezekiel 34:18.

24 For background on the history of ecology, see especially Robert P. McIntosh, *The Background of Ecology: Concept and Theory* (Cambridge: Cambridge University Press, 1985); Donald Worster, *Nature's Economy,* (Cambridge: Cambridge University Press, 1985); and F. N. Egerton, "History of Ecology: Achievements and Opportunities, Part I," *Journal of History of Biology* 16, 2 (Summer 1983): 259–310; Egerton, "History of Ecology: Achievements and Opportunities, Part II," *Journal of History of Biology* 18, 1 (Spring 1985): 103–43. Worster presents an intellectual and cultural history of ecology, while McIntosh and Egerton trace more closely the development of the science of ecology. All have been extremely helpful in this study.

25 AL to ClL, 5 April 1920, LP 10-8, 9.

26 AL to ClL, 27 April 1920, LP 10-8, 9.

27 "Tajique District Report," 22 April 1920, 10–11, TNFF.

28 AL to ClL, 6 May 1920, LP 10-8, 9.

29 AL to ClL, 15 May 1920, LP 10-8, 9.

30 "Memo, Supervision-Prescott, Erosion," 15 May 1920, TNFF.

31 "Memo, Jemez Division, Grazing & Erosion," 7 June 1920, TNFF.

32 AL to ASL, B. Leopold, 18 April 1945, LP 10-1, 2.

33 F. C. W. Pooler to AL, 24 December 1920, OFPR.

34 Especially helpful interpretations of the southwestern landscape were Ron Cooke and Richard Reeves, *Arroyos and Environmental Change in the American Southwest* (New York: Oxford University Press, 1976); James R. Hastings and Raymond M. Turner, *The Changing Mile: An Ecological Study of Vegetation Change with Time in the Lower Mile of an Arid and Semiarid Region* (Tucson: University of Arizona Press, 1965); C. F. Cooper, "Changes in Vegetation Structure and Growth of Southwestern Pine Forests since White Settle-

ment," *Ecological Monographs* 30, 2 (April 1960): 129–64; Harold Weaver, "Fires as an Ecological Factor in the Southwestern Ponderosa Pine Forests," *JF* 49, 2 (February 1951): 93–98.

35 AL, "Charles Knesal Cooperrider, 1889–1944," *JWM* 12, 3 (July 1948): 337.

36 AL, "Erosion and Prosperity," 18 January 1921, 1, LP 10-8, Box 9.

37 Ibid., 4–5.

38 AL, "A Plea for Recognition of Artificial Works in Forest Erosion Control Policy," *JF* 19, 3 (March 1921): 267.

39 Ibid., 269, 273.

40 See chap. 6, n. 8.

41 AL, "A Plea for Recognition of Artificial Works," 270–71.

42 "Memo for Mr. Pooler," 13 June 1921, OFPR.

43 E. Kelley to R. Headley, 13 June 1921, 14 June 1921, National Archives, Records of the Forest Service, Record Group 95, Records of the Division of Operations, Operations File, 1910–1923. See LP 10-11, Microfilm 2. Leopold and Kelley crossed paths again later in 1921, when they attended a conference of Forest Service brass at Mather Field in California, a landmark meeting in the development of USFS fire-fighting policy. It is probably no coincidence that Leopold paid particular attention to both fire ecology and fire-fighting strategy on the Gila and Prescott Forests during his subsequent 1922 inspections. For a discussion of the Mather Field conference, see Stephen Pyne, *Fire in America: A Cultural History of Wildlife and Rural Fire* (Princeton: Princeton University Press, 1982), 268–72.

44 "General Inspection Report, Apache National Forest, May & June, 1921," 29–30, TNFF.

45 "Blue River," 11 June 1922, LP 10-6, Box 16. Published in *RR*, 108–9. Leopold wrote this brief essay during his 1922 inspection of the Gila National Forest, but it was unpublished during his lifetime.

46 HAH, letter to author, 28 June 1986.

47 New Mexico Journal 1917–1924, 25 December 1921–3 January 1922.

48 By mid-1921, Leopold and Winn had probably discussed some actual on-the-ground move to maintain wilderness conditions somewhere in the district, and perhaps had even considered such an area on the Gila National Forest, of which Winn was now supervisor. Ward Shepard was also an important source of input at this time, and apparently District Forester Frank Pooler had expressed support.

49 The "good roads movement" was sparked by the passage of the Federal Aid Road Act of July 11, 1916 (39 Stat. 355, 358). The act provided appropriations of $11 million annually over the next ten years for road construction, in co-operation with local governments, in the National Forests (the Coronado Trail was the first to be authorized under the act). Congress made additional grants of $3 million per year in 1919, 1920, and 1921. The road construction budget of the Park Service was likewise rising, and would continue to expand throughout the 1920s.

50 See Nash, *Wilderness and the American Mind*, 198.

51 AL, "The Wilderness and Its Place in Forest Recreation Policy," *JF* 19, 7 (November 1921): 719, 718.

52 Ibid., 721, 718.
53 Ibid., 719.
54 Ibid., 720.
55 Leopold used the quotation, which he attributed to Yale University president Arthur Twining Hadley, several times in speeches and articles. See "The Civic Life of Albuquerque," LP 10-8, 9; "Some Fundamentals of Conservation in the Southwest," LP 10-6, 16; circular bulletin on wilderness, FWP, Box 5.
56 A. Carey to AL, 5 March 1922, LP 10-4, 8. For perhaps the earliest published reference to Leopold's proposal, see G. A. Pearson, "Preservation of Natural Areas in the National Forests," *Ecology* 3, 4 (October 1922), 284–87. Pearson's article argued for preservation of natural areas for scientific reasons, but approvingly cited Leopold's article and pointed out the scientific fringe benefit of recreational wilderness areas.
57 R. Headley, "Notes on Leopold," 21 January 1922, OFPR.
58 F. Winn, USFS Official Diary, 21 May 1922, FWP.
59 Ibid., 2 June 1922. Leopold's Gila Inspection Report, TNFF, also contains an account of the Gila fire-fighting activities.
60 *Silver City Enterprise,* 23 June 1922.
61 See "Assistant District Forester a Visitor," *Silver City Independent,* 27 June 1922. Leopold is quoted at length on the local erosion and watershed problems. "It used to be supposed," he said, "that erosion of bottom lands was caused only by overgrazing or forest fires on the watershed. But it is occurring every year in dozens of watersheds that have not been overgrazed, and where fires have not burned for a long time. . . . If we intend to live in and develop these mountains, the ways and means must be found. . . . We cannot build with one hand and tear down with another. We must face and solve the problem of erosion before we can speak honestly about conservation or development in the Southwest."
62 "General Inspection Report of the Gila National Forest, May 21–June 27, 1922," 12–13, TNFF.
63 Ibid., 13–14.
64 F. C. W. Pooler to AL, 4 August 1922, OFPR.
65 "Skill in Forestry," c. July 1922, 5, 2, LP 10-6, 16.
66 Comments on "Skill in Forestry" were attached to the manuscript. See LP 10-6, 16.
67 "Report of General Inspection of Prescott National Forest, July 31–September 1, 1922," 1, TNFF.
68 Ibid., 26.
69 Ibid., 27.
70 "Standards of Conservation," c. August 1922, 1, LP 10-6, 16.
71 Ibid., 3, 4.
72 "Report on Proposed Wilderness Area," 2 October 1922, LP 10-4, 8. While Fred Winn backed Leopold's proposal, A. H. Douglas, supervisor of the Datil, was cautious. On September 5, he wrote to Pooler to state that he agreed with the idea in principle, but that it ought not "stand in the way of development of a country in which we have a great deal of timber which is ready

for sale." Leopold read Douglas' comments and sent a note to Pooler: "Do you care to have me complete the proposal for your consideration? AL." Pooler replied: "AL—Yes Pls. FCWP 9/18" (see Baldwin, *The Quiet Revolution*, 157–58).

Interestingly, in his proposal Leopold emphasized the hunting aspect of the recommendation more so than he had in the Gila inspection report, suggesting that the lands be designated "The Gila Wilderness Area or Gila National Hunting Ground." Leopold spelled out the need for such a place. Since 1917, three similiar areas in D-3, suitable for the pack trips he envisioned, had been opened to automobile travel: the Blue Range on the Apache, the Jemez Division of the Santa Fe, and the breaks of the Tonto Basin in Arizona. Three areas remained: the Kaibab plateau on the north rim of the Grand Canyon, the breaks of the Verde north of Phoenix, and the Gila. Of these, the Gila was the most attractive and the least suited for development. Only the timber had much value, and Leopold asked, "Is it not possible that an untouched reserve of stumpage for a possible National emergency might be a good thing?"

73 "Thoughts on a Map of Liberia," undated, LP 10-6, 16.

74 "The River of the Mother of God," undated, 2, LP 10-6, 16.

75 Ibid., 4.

76 Ibid., 5–8.

77 This account of the trip through the Colorado Delta is based on Leopold's entries in his New Mexico Journal 1917–1924, 25 October–14 November 1922; published in *RR*, 10–30.

78 AL, *SCA*, 147; *SCA/RR*, 156. Cachinilla and arrow-weed are common names for *Tessaria sericea* (Nutt.) Shinners, known also as *Pluchea sericea* (Nutt.) Coville.

79 Ibid. The shrub was probably *Sesbania macrocarpa* Muhl., or Colorado River hemp.

80 Calabasilla is the common name for *Cucurbita foetidissima*, a foul-smelling, lowland member of the gourd family.

81 AL, *SCA*, 146; *SCA/RR*, 155.

82 New Mexico Journal 1917–1924, 14 November 1922; *RR*, 29–30.

83 This address was not published at the time of its delivery. In 1946, Dana Parkinson of the Forest Service sent a copy to Herman H. Chapman, a former professor and good friend of Leopold's at the Yale School of Forestry. Chapman asked Leopold for permission to update and publish the article in the *Journal of Forestry*. In his editorial comments, Chapman called the address "a landmark . . . the first statement by a member of the profession of forestry, so far as known, which called attention to the magnitude and seriousness of soil erosion in the restricted areas of fertile valleys in the arid Southwest." See AL, "Erosion as a Menace of the Social and Economic Future of the Southwest," *JF* 44, 9 (September 1946), 627–33.

84 AL, "Erosion as a Menace," 628, 627.

85 Ibid., 631.

86 Ibid.

87 Ibid., 629.

CHAPTER 11. PIONEERS AND GULLIES

1 AL to EBL, 9 March 1923, LP 10-8, 9.

2 AL, "Some Fundamentals of Conservation in the Southwest," undated, c. March 1923, 5–13, LP 10-6, 16. This essay, unpublished during Leopold's lifetime, appeared in *Environmental Ethics* 1, 2 (Summer 1979), 131–41. See also Susan Flader, "'Some Fundamentals of Conservation': A Commentary" in the same issue, 143–48.

3 Ibid., 14.

4 Ibid., 16.

5 Pyotr Ouspensky, *Tertium Organum* (New York: Alfred A. Knopf, 1925), 199. For a survey of Ouspensky's life and thought, see J. H. Reyner, *Ouspensky: The Unsung Genius* (London: George Allen and Unwin, 1981).

6 Ibid., 201.

7 "Some Fundamentals," 15–16.

8 Ibid., 16.

9 Ibid., 18–19.

10 F. Waugh to AL, 26 May 1923; M. Cheney to AL, 17 April 1923, LP 10-6, 16. See also Flader, "Leopold's 'Some Fundamentals of Conservation': A Commentary," 145–48.

11 R. Headley to F. C. W. Pooler, 9 January 1923; see "General Inspection Report, Manzano National Forest," TNFF.

12 In Tucker, *The Forest Service in the Southwest,* 702.

13 Ibid., 372. Lee Kirby was a ranger on the Tonto at the time of Leopold's inspection. He recalled, "you could ride in a day and see hundreds of dead animals, victims of starvation. In those days, there was no trucking of animals; they had to be driven from wherever their range was, in to the market place. Sometimes they got so weak that they couldn't be handled at all. I've seen times in the Upper Salt River Valley when many of the cowboys carried axes to cut down cottonwood trees so the animals could eat the leaves. . . . Others carried regular plumber blowtorches, gasoline blowtorches, that would burn the spines off those prickly pear cactus so the stock could eat those things."

14 "General Inspection Report, Tonto National Forest, 6–31 August 1923," 36, TNFF.

15 "General Appraisal of Tonto Forest," undated, included with "General Inspection Report," TNFF.

16 AL, "'Piute Forestry' vs. Forest Fire Prevention," *Southwestern Magazine* 2, 3 (March 1920): 12.

17 AL, "Wild Followers of the Forest: The Effect of Forest Fires on Game and Fish—The Relation of Forest to Game Conservation," *American Forestry* 29, 357 (September 1923): 515, 568.

18 "General Inspection Report, Tonto National Forest," 1, 3.

19 New Mexico Journal 1917–1924, 6 September 1923. Leopold's entry gave no indication of Starker's success.

20 Ibid., 13 October 1923.

21 Ibid., 28 October 1923.

22 Ibid., 23–24 November 1923.

23 Ibid., 1 January 1924.
24 AL, *Watershed Handbook,* USFS, USDA, D-3, December 1923. See LP 10-11, 1. The title page explained: "This is the first section of the proposed 'Lands Handbook' which will extend and supercede the present 'Uses handbook.'" Leopold revised the handbook after his 1933 tour of duty with the CCC camps in the Southwest.
25 Ibid., 25.
26 "A Criticism of the Booster Spirit," 6 November 1923, 1, LP 10-6, 16.
27 Ibid., 4–5, 6a.
28 Ibid., 6b–6c.
29 Ibid., 8. Leopold borrowed the quote from Charlotte Brontë.
30 Ibid., 10.
31 AL, "Grass, Brush, Timber, and Fire in Southern Arizona," *JF* 22, 6 (October 1924): 2–3.
32 Ibid., 6–7.
33 Ibid., 7.
34 Despite Leopold's emphasis on the important role of fire as a disturbing factor in the Arizona brushfields, this article shows that at this point Leopold clearly saw plant succession in a Clementsian light. Leopold wrote, "In brief, the climax type is and always has been woodland. The thick grass and thin brush of pre-settlement days represented a temporary type. The substitution of grazing for fire brought on a transition of thin grass and thick brush." He added, in an interesting turn of phrase, "This transition type is now reverting to the climax type—woodland." The influence of Frederic Clements at this point in the development of plant ecology was pervasive, and Leopold inevitably adopted the Clementsian framework; yet, in his early appreciation of the role of fire (if not its full significance), Leopold had at least taken notice of the cracks in that framework.

 Perhaps the most significant omission in Leopold's analysis was the effect of the Apache Indians, who used fire regularly to concentrate game, to send smoke signals, to fight their enemies, and to clear (and cover) trails. Stephen Pyne writes in *Fire In America,* ". . . after the tribe's centuries of migration the range of the Apache came to be identical to the range of that great lightning fire regime that nature had shaped over the millennia" (519).
35 "Keep One Wilderness Hunting Ground," *The Pine Cone,* March 1924, 3.
36 "Keep the Upper Gila as Last Wilderness Home of Big Game," *Silver City Enterprise,* 23 May 1924.
37 See Baldwin, *The Quiet Revolution,* 161–64. The figure for the original acreage of the area is derived from "Memo, Gila Wilderness Boundary History, USDA-USFS, R-3," 30 June 1977, in files of the Gila National Forest, Silver City, New Mexico. See also "Gila N.F. Recreational Working Plan" in the Gila files.
38 *The Pine Cone,* March 1924, 4, 2.
39 W. B. Greeley to F. C. W. Pooler, 18 March 1924, OFPR.
40 AL to C. P. Winslow, 9 May 1924, OFPR.
41 F. C. W. Pooler to AL, 30 April 1924, OFPR.
42 "Jed" to AL, 2 May 1924, LP 10-8, 1.
43 F. Winn to AL, 2 May 1924, LP 10-8, 1.

CHAPTER 12. A FISH OUT OF WATER

1 AL to EBL, 5, 6 June 1924, LP 10-8, 9.
2 Wisconsin Journal 1924–1935, 14 June 1924, LP 10-7, 2. Leopold's journal account of this trip was published in *RR,* 34–56.
3 Ibid., 20 June 1924.
4 Ibid., 15 June 1924.
5 Ibid., 25 June 1924.
6 Ray A. Billington, *Frederick Jackson Turner: Historian, Scholar, Teacher* (New York: Oxford University Press, 1973), 393–96.
7 Charles A. Nelson, *History of the U.S. Forest Products Laboratory, (1910–1963)* (Ph.D. diss., University of Wisconsin, 1963; published by USFPL, 1971), 54, 67, 82.
8 L. J. Markwardt, interview with author.
9 AL to EBL, 9 September 1924, LP 10-8, 9.
10 Ibid.
11 AL to EBL, 13 September 1924, LP 10-8, 9.
12 Ibid.
13 AL, "Forests and Recreation in the Lake States" (MS, USFPL, 29 October 1924), 4.
14 Information on the early conservation movement in Wisconsin came from the collected issues of *The Wisconsin Conservationist,* published by the old State Conservation Commission prior to 1927; Dennis East, "Water Power and Forestry in Wisconsin: Issues of Conservation, 1890–1919" (Ph.D. diss., University of Wisconsin, 1971); and various items in LP and SHSW collections. See n. 16 below.
15 AL, "Forests and Recreation in the Lake States," 8.
16 A number of Wisconsin's early conservation leaders were interviewed as part of the Natural Resources History Project conducted jointly by the State Historical Society of Wisconsin and the Wisconsin Conservation Department. Transcripts of these interviews are available in the Archives of the SHSW in Madison. Particularly helpful in this section, and throughout this chapter, were interviews conducted with Frank Graass, William J. P. Aberg, and Ernest Swift, as well as documents in the Izaak Walton League of Wisconsin Papers, the Haskell Noyes Papers, the William J. P. Aberg Papers, and the Ernest Swift Papers.
17 Fox, *John Muir and His Legacy,* 162. In Fox's words, "By design, a typical chapter of the league resembled not one of the older conservation groups, but rather a Rotary Club that liked to go fishing."
18 AL, "Forestry in Wisconsin," 25 October 1925, 1, LP 10-2, 4.
19 AL, "Ten New Developments in American Game Management," address at American Game Conference, New York City, 8–9 December 1924, 1, LP 10-6, 16. A published version of this address appeared in *American Game* 14, 3 (July 1925): 7–8, 20.
20 See Worster, *Nature's Economy,* 256–90; Thomas R. Dunlap, "Values for Varmints: Predator Control and Environmental Ideas, 1920–1939," *Pacific Historical Review* 53 (May 1984): 141–61; John P. Russo, *The Kaibab North Deer*

Herd: Its History, Problems, and Management," Arizona Game and Fish Department, Wildlife Bulletin No. 7 (Phoenix, 1964). An important corrective to the historical interpretation of the Kaibab situation may be found in Graeme Caughley, "Eruption of Ungulate Populations, with Emphasis on Himalayan Thar in New England," *Ecology* 51, 1 (Winter 1970): 53–72. For a discussion of Leopold's use of the term "irruption," see Graeme Caughley, James M. Peek, and Susan Flader, "Comments on 'Irruption,'" *Wildlife Society Bulletin* 9, 3 (Fall 1981): 232–38.

21 Dunlap, "Values for Varmints," 147–58.

22 "Memorandum for District Forester Kelly," 22 November 1925, LP 10-3, 9.

23 Wisconsin Journal 1924–1935, 15 August 1925.

24 AL, "The Last Stand of the Wilderness," *American Forests and Forest Life* 31, 382 (October 1925): 600, 602.

25 AL, "Wilderness as a Form of Land Use," *Journal of Land and Public Utility Economics* 1, 4 (October 1925): 398.

26 Ibid., 403–4.

27 Ibid., 401.

28 Ibid., 404.

29 *Proceedings of the National Conference on Outdoor Recreation,* 20–21 January 1926, Senate Document no. 117 (Washington, D.C.: GPO, 1926), 63, 62.

30 AL, "Pig in the Parlor," *USFS Bulletin* 9:23 (Washington, D.C.: USFS, 8 June 1925): 1–2.

31 Howard R. Flint, "Wasted Wilderness," *American Forests and Forest Life* 32, 391 (July 1926): 410.

32 AL, "Comment," *American Forests and Forest Life* 32, 391 (July 1926): 411.

33 AL, "Conserving the Covered Wagon," *Sunset Magazine* 54, 3 (March 1925): 21.

34 AL, "Wilderness as a Form of Land Use," 400.

35 AL, "Conserving the Covered Wagon," 21.

36 AL, "Comment," 411.

37 See R. Newall Searle, *Saving Quetico–Superior: A Land Set Apart* (St. Paul: Minnesota Historical Society Press, 1977). See also Searle, "Autos or Canoes: Wilderness Controversy in the Superior National Forest," *Journal of Forest History* 22, 2 (April 1978): 68–77.

38 Quoted in Searle, "Autos or Canoes," 76–77.

39 B. MacKaye to AL, 24 February 1930, LP 10-3, 4. MacKaye was quoting from his own 1928 book, *The New Exploration.*

40 R. Marshall to AL, 21 February 1930, LP 10-3, 4.

41 Frank A. Waugh, "Wilderness to Keep," *Review of Reviews* 81 (1939): 146. See Nash, *Wilderness and the American Mind,* 191.

42 AL to N. C. Brown, 24 November 1926, LP 10-8, 1.

43 NLB, interview with author.

44 Ibid.

45 EEL, interview with author.

46 Interviews with Frank Graass and William J. P. Aberg, SHSW Archives.

47 Pinchot addressed the Wisconsin State Assembly on March 24, 1927. See text

and related correspondence in Aberg Papers, Box 4, SHSW. I am indebted to Tom Huffman of the University of Wisconsin Department of History for bringing these documents to my attention.

48 See interview with William J. P. Aberg; AL, "Organizing Conservation in Wisconsin" and "Rough Outline of an Organic Act for Conservation in Wisconsin" MSS, AL files, SHSW Archives; documents in Izaak Walton League file, LP 10-2, 4.

49 Interview with Frank Graass, SHSW Archives.

50 AL to EBL, 7 August 1927, LP 10-8, 9.

51 Ibid.

52 "By Their Works Shall Ye Know Them," *Wisconsin State Journal,* 29 September 1927.

53 "Preface," "Southwestern Game Fields," 4–5, LP 10-6, 10.

54 "Southwestern Game Fields," 17, 24.

55 Wisconsin Journal 1924–35, 13 November 1927.

56 Ibid., 14 November 1927.

57 Ibid., 15 November 1927.

58 J. Stokely Ligon, "Preliminary Report — Gila Deer Situation," in letter to AL, 10 September 1927, LP 10-3, 8.

59 See W. C. Barnes to AL, 24 January 1927, LP 10-4, 1.

60 "Science and Game Conservation," 8, LP 10-6, 16. The convention was held in Omaha on April 19–21, 1928.

61 AL to R. Y. Stuart, 18 April 1928, OFPR.

62 J. D. Guthrie to AL, 8 July 1928, LP 10-3, 9.

63 AL, "Mr. Thompson's Wilderness," *USFS Bulletin* 12:26 (Washington, D.C.: USFS, 25 June 1928): 2.

64 "Foreword," 31 July 1947, 6, LP 10-6, 16.

CHAPTER 13. "GAME METHODS: THE AMERICAN WAY"

1 The account that follows is drawn primarily from Fox, *John Muir and His Legacy,* 163–67; Trefethen, *An American Crusade For Wildlife,* 174–94; and from letters and documents in the Leopold Papers.

2 See especially AL, "The Way of the Waterfowl," *American Forests and Forest Life* 32, 389 (May 1926): 287–91.

3 "Game Survey, Report No. 1, Covering Preliminary Trip, June 4–5, 1928," LP 10-6, 11. Leopold's trip took him to the offices of the individuals and organizations most crucial to his assignment: Carlos Avery, new head of the AGPA; the National Lumberman's Association; E. W. Nelson, Stanley P. Young, Vernon Bailey, and W. L. McAtee, the collective brain trust of the U.S. Biological Survey; headquarters of the Forest Service, where he met with Robert Y. Stuart, Earle Clapp, and Evan Kelley; Arthur Ringland; Seth Gordon of the Izaak Walton League. All pledged cooperation and offered to spread word to their colleagues around the country.

4 Ibid.

5 AL to EBL, 7 August 1928, LP 10-8, 9.

6 AL, *Report on a Game Survey of the North Central States* (Madison: Demo-

crat Printing Company for the Sporting Arms and Ammunitions Manufacturer's Institute, 1931), 23.

7 "Report on Game Survey of Michigan," 20 July 1928; "Report on Game Survey of Minnesota," 1 September 1928; "Report on Game Survey of Iowa,"
25 August 1928, 5, LP 10-6, 11.

8 V. Horn, Voegeli-Leopold Collection, SHSW.

9 See Herbert L. Stoddard, *The Bobwhite Quail, Its Habits, Preservation, and
Increase* (New York: Charles Scribner's Sons, 1931).

10 Herbert L. Stoddard, *Memoirs Of A Naturalist* (Norman: University of Oklahoma Press, 1969), 218.

11 Ibid., 225, 218.

12 "Report on Game Survey of Ohio," 27 November 1928, 7, LP 10-6, 11.

13 Other members of the committee were George Lawyer, A. Willis Robertson,
J. B. Royall, Sam F. Rathbun, I. Zellerbach, and, in 1930, William J. Tucker,
J. W. Titcomb, and H. C. Bryant.

14 "Report on Game Survey of Mississippi," 1 February 1929, 10, LP 10-6, 11.

15 AL to E. Conkling, 24 January 1929, LP 10-3, 7.

16 Among those present: Bill Aberg, the John Mains, the Tom Colemans, Ray
Roark, Cap Winslow, Howard Weiss, Bill Schorger, Frank Graass, L. J.
Markwardt, Raphael Zon; Dean Harry Russell of the College of Agriculture, Noble Clark of the Agricultural Experiment Station, Wallace Grange,
head of the Game Division of the Wisconsin Conservation Department; three
state assemblymen, a variety of natural scientists and sportsmen, as well as
Estella, Starker, and Luna Leopold. Forty registered for the series of five lectures, and nearly one hundred and fifty attended at least one, some driving
several hours to and from Madison. See "Attendance at Lectures on Game
Management," College of Agriculture, Office of the Dean and Director, General Subject Files, UW Archives, Series 9/1/1/5-3, Box 37.

17 J. Dixon to AL, 12 March 1929, LP 10-3, 3.

18 "Report on a Game Survey of Illinois," 1 May 1929, 8-9; Report on a Game
Survey of Indiana, 15 June 1929, 7, LP 10-6, 11.

19 "Report on a Game Survey of Wisconsin," 1 October 1929, 144, LP 10-6,
11.

20 AL to R. Fred Pettit, 19 October 1929, LP 10-3, 8.

21 Flader, *Thinking Like a Mountain*, 71–72.

22 F. C. W. Pooler to AL, 15 March 1929, LP 10-3, 8.

23 AL to F. C. W. Pooler, 21 March 1929, LP 10-3, 8.

24 In this, Leopold echoed the interpretation of his friend Stokely Ligon, who
believed that the accumulation of "barren" does was at least in part ascrib-
able to coyote predation on fawns. The does, it followed, were not barren
at all, but losing their fawns to the tenacious coyotes. A shortage of fawns,
whether due to predation, physiological problems in the does, or other factors, meant lower deer populations, and this was enough to justify coyote
control. See Flader, *Thinking Like a Mountain*, 92–102.

25 Wisconsin Journal 1924–1935, 18 November 1929.

26 Ibid., undated.

27 AL, "Report of the Committee on American Wild Life Policy," *Transactions*

of the Sixteenth American Game Conference, New York, 2–3 December 1929 (Washington, D.C.: American Game Association, 1930), 196.

28 Ibid., 199.

29 Ibid., 200–201.

30 AL to Committee on Wild Life Conservation Policy, 15 February 1930, LP 10-2, 1.

31 AL to EBL, 9 January 1930, LP 10-8, 9.

32 "Report on a Game Survey of Missouri," 1 March 1930, 5, 137, LP 10-6, 11.

33 Paul Errington, "In Appreciation of Aldo Leopold," *JWM* 12, 4 (October 1948): 342.

34 AL to H. C. Bryant, 24 July 1930, LP 10-2, 1.

35 AL to J. P. Knapp, 18 September 1930, LP 10-2, 5.

36 "'More Game Birds in America': A Foundation," in letter to O. Butler, 30 September 1930, LP 10-2, 1.

37 AL, "Game Methods: The American Way," *American Game* 20, 2 (March–April 1931), 31.

38 AL, "Report to the American Game Conference on an American Game Policy," *Transactions of the Seventeenth American Game Conference,* New York, 1–2 December 1930 (Washington, D.C.: American Game Association, 1931), 285, 287–88.

39 Ibid., 285.

40 Ibid., 143–44, 146.

41 "An American Game Policy," *American Forests* 37, 1 (January 1931): 41. See "Game Conference," *Time* 16, 24 (15 December 1930): 29–30.

42 See Durward Allen et al., "Report of the Committee on North American Wildlife Policy," *Transactions of the Thirty-Eighth North American Wildlife and Natural Resources Conference,* 18–21 March 1973, Washington, D.C. (Washington, D.C.: WMI, 1973), 152–81.

43 W. A. Riley to AL, 11 May 1931, LP 10-5, 6.

44 P. S. Lovejoy to AL, 9 May 1931, LP 10-5, 6.

45 J. Grinnell to AL, 9 May 1931, LP 10-5, 6.

46 W. T. Hornaday to AL, 5 May 1931, LP 10-5, 6.

47 W. Van Name to AL, 26 June 1931, LP 10-5, 6.

48 AL to R. F. Pettit, 19 October 1929, LP 10-3, 8.

49 AL to S. Gordon, 8 May 1931, LP 10-6, 3.

50 AL to S. Gordon, 30 March 1931, LP 10-6, 12.

51 AL to C. S. Comeaux, 22 May 1930, Records of the WMI, Washington, D.C.

52 AL, "History of the Riley Game Cooperative, 1931–1939," *JWM* 4, 3 (July 1940): 291.

53 LBL, interview with author.

54 AL, *RGSNCS,* 134. A historical sidelight: in October 1930, Leopold exchanged letters with ecologist Frederic Clements, who had written an article on the cycle phenomenon for the latest issue of *Outdoor America.* This is the only record of communication between them in the Leopold Papers, although the tone of the correspondence suggests earlier contacts. See AL to F. E. Clements, 2 October 1930; F. E. Clements to AL, 12 October 1930, LP 10-4, 6.

55 J. M. Olin to AL, 7 May 1931, LP 10-2, 5.

56 "Science Finds Everything Goes Up and Goes Down Once Every 10 Years." *American Weekly*, 1 November 1931, 5.

57 Leopold may have learned of Elton through Frederic Clements (see n. 54 above). Clements's letter of 12 October 1930 provides the first mention of Elton in the Leopold Papers. By 6 January 1931, Leopold, in a letter to Werner Nagel of Missouri (LP 10-3, 7), speaks of ecology as "the rock bottom of game management." This connection, however, is circumstantial. Leopold's first direct references to Elton occur in regard to the Matamek Conference.

58 Flader, *Thinking Like a Mountain*, 25.

59 Charles Elton, *Animal Ecology* (New York: Macmillan Company, 1937), 1.

60 For discussions of the influence of Elton's *Animal Ecology*, see McIntosh, *The Background of Ecology*, 88–93; Worster, *Nature's Economy*, 294–301.

61 AL to H. L. Stoddard, 7 August 1931, LP 10-1, 3.

62 AL to R. M. Anderson, 28 September 1931, LP 10-3, 5.

63 AL, "Report of the Iowa Game Survey: Chapter One, the Fall of the Iowa Game Range," *Outdoor America* 11, 1 (August–September 1932): 7. This was the first of nine chapters of the Iowa Game Survey that were to have appeared in *Outdoor America*. Only four chapters—"The Fall of the Iowa Game Range," "Iowa Quail," "Iowa Pheasants," and "The Hungarian Partridge in Iowa"—appeared before the magazine suspended publication in mid-1933.

64 AL to J. M. Olin, 25 October 1931, LP 10-3, 5.

65 AL to S. Walpole, 16 November 1931, LP 10-6, 4.

66 W. F. Brown to AL, 17 November 1931, LP 10-6, 4.

67 O. Murie to AL, 30 October 1931, LP 10-3, 10.

68 AL to O. Murie, 11 November 1931, LP 10-3, 10.

69 E. A. Goldman to AL, 16 November 1931, LP 10-6, 4.

70 W. L. McAtee to AL, 16 January 1932, LP 10-2, 8.

71 AL to F. Walcott, 10 January 1932, LP 10-2, 1.

72 AL, *Game Management* (New York: Charles Scribner's Sons, 1933), 247. Historian Thomas Dunlap writes: "Other research on small game species confirmed the broad outline of Errington's ideas, particularly that predation was not normally a major check on prey populations. Animals did not seem, as the common view held it, to live in terror, nor did they breed in a frantic race to keep ahead of relentless thinning by flesh-eaters. Errington had not, as he pointed out, found a key to explain predation. He had, though, shown that old ideas needed to be tested and should not be accepted casually." ("Values for Varmints," 159–60). Lately, Errington's ideas on predation and small game have undergone extensive criticism and refinement.

73 AL, *GM*, 252.

74 T. T. McCabe, "More Game Birds in America, Inc.," *Condor* 33, 6 (November–December 1931): 260.

75 AL, "Game and Wild Life Conservation," *Condor* 34, 2 (March–April 1932): 103–4.

76 Ibid.

CHAPTER 14. CONSULTING FORESTER

1 Errington, "In Appreciation of Aldo Leopold," 348.
2 Quoted in Luther Carter, "The Leopolds: A Family of Naturalists," *Science* 207, 4453 (March 7, 1980): 1052.
3 LBL, interview with author.
4 AL, *GM*, 3.
5 Ibid., 392.
6 Ibid., 21.
7 AL to W. O. Nagel, 6 January 1931, LP 10-3, 7.
8 S. P. Baldwin to AL, 11 April 1932, LP 10-3, 9.
9 AL, "Report of the Iowa Game Survey: Chapter One," 7.
10 "Social Consequences of Conservation," undated MS, 1, LP 10-6, 16. The details of the Audubon Society's internal disputes are presented in Fox, *John Muir and His Legacy*, 173–82. Leopold stayed on the sidelines of this controversy, but see correspondence with R. Edge, LP 10-3, 8, and AL to S. P. Baldwin, 27 October 1932, LP 10-3, 9.
11 "Social Consequences" material, LP 10-6, 16.
12 Ibid.
13 "Social Consequences of Conservation," 4–6.
14 "Social Consequences" material.
15 Untitled fragment, LP 10-6, 16.
16 AL, *GM*, 422–23.
17 Albert Hochbaum recalls that Leopold originally hoped to have A. L. Ripley provide drawings for *Game Management*, but Ripley's price was too high. Leopold, however, was highly pleased with Brooks's work, and later adopted the *GM* frontispiece drawing of a ruffed grouse for his library label.
18 AL to W. G. Low, 28 July 1932, LP 10-6, 4.
19 AL to C. Elton, 1 August 1932, LP 10-3, 10.
20 See transcript of interview with Paul Roberts, Regional Oral History Project, 19, Bancroft Library, University of California–Berkeley.
21 "The American Game Policy on Predators," statement for the game policy symposium at the Nineteenth American Game Conference, LP 10-6, 16.
22 "Proposed Chair of Conservation, University of Wisconsin," 23 January 1933, University of Wisconsin Arboretum Papers, General Files, J. W. Jackson, 1928–1934, UW Archives, Series 39/3/2, Box 1.
23 AL to W. T. Hornaday, 1 March 1933, LP 10-6, 4. In his letter, Leopold mistakenly gave the year of Hornaday's visit to Albuquerque as 1916.
24 AL, *GM*, 19.
25 AL to W. T. Hornaday, 1 March 1933.
26 Starker Leopold's copy of *Game Management*, presented to him by his father, is in the Leopold Library, University of California–Berkeley.
27 AL, "The Conservation Ethic," *JF* 31, 6 (October 1933): 634.
28 Ibid., 635.
29 Ibid.
30 Ibid., 637.
31 Ibid., 639.

32 Ibid., 639–40.

33 Ibid., 641–42.

34 Ibid., 643.

35 AL, "Conservation Economics," *JF* 32, 5 (May 1934): 340. While in the Southwest, Leopold worked with University of Arizona botanist Franklin J. Crider to establish at the Boyce Thompson Southwestern Arboretum a nursery for the propagation of native plants suitable for erosion control. The nursery, apparently the first of its kind, proved so successful that it became a model for later efforts, while Crider moved on to government service in soil conservation. See Frank S. Crosswhite, "Editorial," *Desert Plants* 8, 2 (April 1987): 50, 95.

Leopold's return to the Southwest also resulted in a refinement of his theory of the process of erosion. At the end of 1935, he summarized his thoughts in a lecture that he called "An Erosion Theory for the Southwest" (LP 10-2, 8). By now he was well acquainted with Kirk Bryan's work, which showed that the process of gullying was not new to the Southwest, but had occurred prior to heavy grazing by Europeans. This implied an overriding climatic influence. Leopold admitted the validity of Bryan's evidence, but suggested that gullying was still a local, not regional, effect, and therefore a random result of local watershed characteristics. He tried at the end of his lecture to reconcile the theories: "The grazing theory, all by itself, is not coherent. Bryan's theory, all by itself, seems insufficient. Pieced together, with the additional postulate of random timing [of erosion and sedimentation cycles], they seem to hold water." It is no wonder that Luna Leopold was drawn to study this subject, and made his own landmark contribution in "The Erosion Problem of the Southwestern United States," (Ph.D. diss., Harvard University, 1950).

36 W. T. Hornaday to AL, 17 August 1933, LP 10-8, 9.

CHAPTER 15. THE PROFESSOR

1 "Building a Wisconsin Game Crop," radio address, 8 September 1933, LP 10-6, 14.

2 Merle Curti and Vernon Carstensen, *The University of Wisconsin: A History, 1848–1923*, vol. 1 (Madison: University of Wisconsin Press, 1949), 287.

3 Ibid., vol. 2, 422–24.

4 AL, "Necessity for Game Research," *Transactions of the Twentieth American Game Conference*, New York, 22–24 January 1934 (Washington, D.C.: American Game Association, 1934), 93.

5 AL, "Game Cropping in Southern Wisconsin," *Our Native Landscape* (December 1933). In LP 10-6, 1.

6 J. Dixon to AL, 8 November 1933, LP 10-3, 3.

7 J. C. Phillips to AL, 1 December 1933, LP 10-3, 4.

8 H. Jones to AL, 15 January 1934, LP 10-8, 1.

9 B. Jacobs to AL, 20 January 1934; AL to B. Jacobs, 1 February 1934, LP 10-3, 3.

10 AL to ClL, 31 January 1934, LP 10-8, 9.

11 A. S. Hawkins, letter to author, 3 April 1986. See Robert McCabe, "The

Stoughton Faville Prairie Preserve: Some Historical Aspects," *WASAL* 66 (1978): 25–49.
12 AL, "Coon Valley: An Adventure in Cooperative Conservation," *American Forests* 41, 5 (May 1935): 206–7.
13 Ibid., 205.
14 Ibid., 208.
15 AL to C. L. Horn, 26 December 1933, LP 10-3, 6.
16 JND to C. Cottam, 25 June 1959, quoted in David Lendt, *Ding: The Life of Jay Norwood Darling* (Des Moines: Jay N. Darling Conservation Foundation, 1984), 65.
17 Thomas Beck, "What President's Committee Intends to Do," *Transactions of the Twentieth American Game Conference,* 84.
18 AL, "Necessity for Game Research," 92.
19 LBL, interview with author.
20 Lendt, *Ding,* 64. See also 63–68.
21 AL to JND, 29 January 1934, LP 10-2, 7.
22 AL to T. H. Beck, 13 February 1934; T. H. Beck to AL, 16 February 1934, LP 10-2, 7.
23 Lendt, *Ding,* 67–68.
24 AL to F. W. Luening, 26 February 1934, LP 10-1, 2. Leuning was an editor with the *Milwaukee Journal,* and corresponded with Leopold from time to time.
25 Lendt, *Ding,* 69.
26 AL, "Conservation Economics," 537.
27 Ibid., 539.
28 Undated fragment, LP 10-6, 16.
29 AL, "Helping Ourselves," *Field and Stream* 39, 4 (August 1934): 32.
30 AL, "Conservation Economics," 540.
31 Ibid., 542.
32 H. L. Stoddard to AL, 26 July 1934, LP 10-1, 3.
33 JND to AL, 22 September 1934, LP 10-1, 1.
34 EEL, interview with author.
35 A. Mitchell to NLB, 26 November 1979, Bradley Study Center Files, Baraboo, Wisconsin.
36 Frances Hamerstrom, interview with author.
37 AL, "Franklin J.W. Schmidt," *Wilson Bulletin* 48, 3 (September 1936): 181.
38 Frances and Frederick Hamerstrom, interview with author.
39 I. F. Lewis to F. Payne, 16 August 1934, LP 10-2, 6.
40 Lendt, *Ding,* 75.
41 JND to AL, 16 May 1934, LP 10-8, 1.
42 J. C. Merriam to AL, 21 May 1934, LP 10-8, 1.
43 A. W. Schorger to AL, 14 May 1934, LP 10-8, 1.
44 NLB, "Salary?" *Wisconsin Academy Review* 26, 1 (December 1979): 7.
45 JND to AL, undated, LP 10-8, 1.
46 JND to AL, 27 May 1934, LP 10-8, 1.
47 AL to JND, 29 May 1934, LP 10-8, 1.

48 AL, "What Is the University of Wisconsin Arboretum, Wild Life Refuge, and Forest Experiment Preserve?" University of Wisconsin Arboretum Papers, General Files, UW Archives, Series 38/3/1, Box 1.

49 Ibid.

50 Nancy Sachse, *A Thousand Ages: The University of Wisconsin Arboretum,* (Madison: Regents of the University of Wisconsin, 1965), 28.

51 Ibid., 33.

52 For an account of the 1934 drought in central Wisconsin, see Michael Goc, "The Great Dust Bowl: It First Came to Wisconsin," *Wisconsin Trails* 25, 4 (July–August 1984): 20–24.

53 Wisconsin Journal 1924–1935, 20 July 1934.

54 Ibid., 29 September 1934.

55 AL, *SCA,* 96; *SCA/RR,* 102–3.

CHAPTER 16. THE VALUE OF WILDERNESS

1 "Look Out Mr. Buck!" *The Capital Times,* 21 November 1934.

2 Wisconsin Journal 1924–1935, 24–28 November 1934. See AL to R. Case, 11 November 1935, LP 10-7, 3.

3 Accounts of the first visits to the Sauk County farm vary. This account is based on interviews with the family and on Leopold's own recollection in the Leopold Shack Journal 1935–1942, "Journal for 1935," LP 10-7, 3.

4 LBL, interview with author.

5 Leopold Shack Journal 1935–1942, 27–29 April 1935.

6 Ibid., 5–6 July 1935.

7 Quoted in note, RSY to AL, undated, LP 10-2, 9.

8 See Stephen Fox, "We Want No Straddlers," *Wilderness* 48, 167 (Winter 1984): 5–19.

9 R. Marshall to AL, 25 October 1934; "Invitation to Help Organize a Group to Preserve the American Wilderness," 19 October 1934, LP 10-2, 9. Marshall's life is recounted in Nash, *Wilderness and the American Mind,* 200–208; John G. Mitchell, "In Wildness Was the Preservation of a Smile," *Wilderness* 48, 169 (Summer 1985): 10–21; James Glover, "Bob Marshall: A Natural," *American Forests* 92, 9 (September 1986): 24–26, 54–55; James and Regina Glover, "Robert Marshall: Portrait of a Liberal Forester," *Journal of Forest History* 30, 3 (July 1986): 112–19.

10 AL to R. Marshall, 29 October 1934, LP 10-2, 9.

11 R. Marshall to AL, 14 March 1935, LP 10-2, 9.

12 AL to R. Marshall, 25 March, 3 April, 27 March 1935, LP 10-2, 9.

13 RSY to AL, 23 June 1935, LP 10-2, 9.

14 AL, "Why the Wilderness Society?" *Living Wilderness* 1, 1 (September 1935): 6.

15 Ibid.

16 Ibid.

17 AL, "Whither 1935? A Review of the American Game Policy," *Transactions of the Twenty-First American Game Conference,* New York City, 21–23 January 1935 (Washington, D.C.: American Game Association, 1935), 51.

18 Ibid., 52.
19 A. Hawkins in Robert A. McCabe, "Aldo Leopold: The Professor" (MS, 1986), 290–91.
20 "Dear Judge Botts," undated, LP 10-6, 16. Botts was a friend of Leopold's from New Mexico.
21 Donald Worster, *Dust Bowl: The Southern Plains in the 1930s* (New York: Oxford University Press, 1979), 213.
22 Ibid., 17.
23 Ibid., 220–22.
24 P. Roberts to Al, 21 March 1935, LP 10-4, 3.
25 "Land Pathology," 15 April 1935, 1, LP 10-6, 16.
26 Ibid., 4.
27 Ibid. 4–5.
28 Ibid., 7–8.
29 W. K. Thomas to AL, 21 June 1935, LP 10-2, 7. See also press release from The Oberlaender Trust, 5 August 1935, in the Leon Kniepp Papers, Arizona Historical Society, Tucson, Arizona.
30 AL to EBL, 31 July 1935, LP 10-8, 9.
31 AL to EBL, 2 August 1935, LP 10-8, 9.
32 AL to ClL, 7 August 1935, LP 10-8, 9.
33 AL to EBL, 15 August 1935, LP 10-8, 9.
34 Ibid.
35 AL, "Deer and Dauerwald in Germany, Part I: History," *JF* 34, 4 (April 1936): 374.
36 Ibid.
37 AL, "Deer and Dauerwald in Germany, Part II: Ecology and Policy," *JF* 34, 5 (May 1936): 463.
38 See Fox, *John Muir and His Legacy,* 345–51.
39 *Game Research News Letter* 6 (16 September 1935), 2, UW Department of Wildlife Ecology Library.
40 "School Forest at Tharandt," in German Notes, LP 10-6, 14.
41 AL to EBL, 1 September 1935, LP 10-8, 9.
42 "Partridge Hunt at Rothenhaus," 10 September 1935, in German Notes.
43 AL to EBL, 1 September 1935, LP 10-8, 9.
44 *Game Research News Letter* 6, 3.
45 AL to EBL, 25 August 1935, LP 10-8, 9.
46 AL, "Franklin J. W. Schmidt," 182, 185-186.
47 "Partridge Hunt at Rothenhaus."
48 AL to EBL, 30 September 1935, LP 10-8, 9.
49 AL to EBL, 22 October, 1935, LP 10-8, 9.
50 AL to EBL, 26 September 1935, LP 10-8, 9.
51 AL to EBL, 22 October 1935, LP 10-8, 9.
52 AL, "Naturschutz in Germany," *Bird-Lore* 38, 2 (March–April 1936): 111.
53 "Wilderness," undated, LP 10-6, 16.
54 AL, "Naturschutz in Germany," 102.
55 "Wilderness," undated, LP 10-6, 16. The note is presented here as it appears in full. Leopold pencilled in many revisions; this version follows his latest

corrections. Leopold, of course, never meant to publish this fragment, which was one of several attempts he made to write an essay on the theme of wilderness out of his German experience (see n. 53 above). Both these manuscripts remained in Leopold's "cooler."

56 LBL, interview with author.
57 "Lecture on Deer & Forestry in Germany," 19 December 1935, LP 10-6, 14.
58 AL to K. T. Frederick, 20 December 1935, LP 10-2, 5.
59 AL to H. A. Smith, 20 December 1935, LP 10-2, 9.

CHAPTER 17. TOWARD A BIOTIC VIEW OF LAND

1 Leopold hoped to secure one of the Cooperative Wildlife Research Units for Wisconsin, but those hopes were abruptly dashed by the Wisconsin Conservation Commission and by Conservation Department Director H. W. Mac-Kenzie. MacKenzie, a game man of the old school, saw no value in conducting "impractical" research. MacKenzie responded to Leopold's proposal for state cooperation in the CWRU program by informing him that "research is considered distinctly a function of the University of Wisconsin and the United States Biological Survey." See H. W. MacKenzie to AL, 9 May 1935, LP 10-2, 8.
2 "Suggestions for American Wildlife Conference," in letter, AL to S. Gordon, 27 October 1935, LP 10-2, 8.
3 JND to AL, 20 November 1935, LP 10-2, 8.
4 AL, "Wildlife Conference," *JF* 34, 4 (April 1936): 430.
5 Leopold Shack Journal 1935–1942, 17–21 May 1936.
6 AL, "Threatened Species," *American Forests* 42, 3 (March 1936): 116, 117.
7 "Second Report of Game Policy Committee," 15 August 1936, LP 10-2, 8.
8 AL to K. Beechel, 26 March 1936, LP 10-3, 2.
9 "Means and Ends in Wild Life Management," 5 May 1936, LP 10-6, 16.
10 "Report to WARF on the Chair of Game Management, 1934–1936," 25 September 1936, 3, Department of Wildlife Ecology Papers, UW Archives, Series 9/25/3, Box 1.
11 AL, "Conservationist in Mexico," *American Forests* 43, 3 (March 1937): 119.
12 AL, "The Thick-Billed Parrot in Chihuahua." *Condor* 39, 1 (January–February 1937): 9. Reprinted in *SCA,* 137–41; *SCA/RR,* 146–49.
13 "Foreword," 6.
14 AL, "Conservationist in Mexico," 120.
15 "Report to Mr. Howard D. Colman on Rockford Deer Area," 15 October 1936, LP 10-2, 7.
16 Leopold's colleague at Rockford was Paul Riis, a landscape architect whom he first met during the Quetico-Superior controversies of the 1920s. On October 1, 1936, Leopold wrote to Riis that recent events had given the deer overbrowsing problem "not only a local, but also a national prominence. A regular epidemic of overbrowsed spots has come to light, extending all the way from Pennsylvania to California, and such organizations as the Forest Service are getting extremely worried about the matter." AL to P. Riis, 1 October 1936, LP 10-2, 7.

17 Leopold Shack Journal 1935–1942, 26–29 December 1936.
18 AL, review of A. E. Parkins and J. R. Whitaker, *Our Natural Resources and Their Conservation, Bird-Lore* 39, 1 (January–February 1937): 74.
19 AL, "Teaching Wildlife Conservation in Public Schools," *WASAL* 30 (1937): 80.
20 AL, review of *Our Natural Resources,* 75.
21 AL, "The Research Program," *Transactions of the Second NAWC,* St. Louis, 1–4 March 1937 (Washington D.C.: AWI, 1937), 106.
22 Ibid., 105.
23 Ibid., 106.
24 AL et al., "The University and Conservation of Wisconsin Wildlife," February 1937, University of Wisconsin, Serial No. 2211, 27.
25 AL, "Teaching Wildlife Conservation in Public Schools," 81. "Paradox," Leopold wrote, "is the earmark of valid truth, and to the extent that any textbook fails to point this out, it fails of attaining university status."
26 Ibid., 82.
27 AL, *SCA,* 224; *SCA/RR,* 262.
28 AL, "The Farmer as a Conservationist," *American Forests* 45, 6 (June 1939), 296–97.
29 EEL, interview with author.
30 "Lecture 4: Teaching Conservation," c. 1937; "Lecture 2: The Mechanisms of the Plant-Animal Community, 5/14/36," LP 10-6, 15.
31 A. Hawkins in McCabe, "Aldo Leopold: The Professor" 297.
32 "Report of the Chair of Game Management to WARF," 15 June 1937, 1, 6, Department of Wildlife Ecology Papers, Series 9/25/3, Box 1.
33 V. Horn, Voegeli-Leopold Collection.
34 EEL, interview with author.
35 Leopold's impatience with dogma did not stop at politics or religion. At the North American Wildlife Conference in 1938, he turned the light on his own professional followers: "The privilege of pulling the curtain strings on the unknown always engenders priestcraft. We who divine the future for snipe and woodchuck mystify our congregations by the same devices as those who propound the law for sect and synagogue. It is an amusing coincidence that both enhance the stage effects by generous use of Latin. Is there danger in the scientific struttings and boomings? I think not, as long as we have the grace to laugh when some wag sticks a cockle burr in our professional robes and vestments." See "Wildlife Research — Is It a Practical and Necessary Basis for Management?" *Transactions of the Third NAWC,* Baltimore, 14–17 February 1938 (Washington, D.C.: AWI, 1938), 45.
36 Leopold Shack Journal 1935–1942, 30 July 1937.
37 Mrs. L. Wing, Voegeli-Leopold Collection.
38 His favorite actresses were Deborah Kerr and Ingrid Bergman. Albert Hochbaum remembers that "he found some of his best ideas came to him while he was at the movies — and thus went often. He cited this as an example of how the subconscious works for the writer." HAH, letter to author, 28 June 1986.
39 O. Gromme to AL, 21 December 1937, LP 10-4, 4.

40 Frances and Frederick Hamerstrom, interview with author.

41 Ibid.

42 See Starker Leopold's record of the trip in *RR*, 130–41.

43 See AL to C. O. Sauer, 29 December 1938, LP 10-3, 3.

44 AL to P. Riis, 18 January 1938, LP 10-2, 7.

45 AL, "Song of the Gavilan," *JWM* 4, 3 (July 1940): 329. Reprinted in *SCA*, 149–54; *SCA/RR*, 158–63.

46 Ibid., 329–30.

47 L. Wing, 19 July 1945, LP 10-1, 3.

48 This account is based on interviews with the students and on Frances Hamerstrom's written account in *Strictly for the Chickens* (Ames: Iowa State University Press, 1980), 26–28.

49 McCabe, "Aldo Leopold: The Professor," 26.

50 Leopold Shack Journal 1935–1942, 4–6 February 1938.

51 AL, "Conservation Esthetic," *Bird-Lore* 40, 2 (March–April 1938): 108, 109.

52 "Engineering and Conservation," 11 April 1938, LP 10-6, 16.

53 "Natural History: The Forgotten Science," 26 April 1938, LP 10-6, 16. A revised version of this essay was published in *RR*, 57–64, and in *SCA/RR*, 202–10.

54 HAH, letter to author, 28 June 1986.

55 HAH to AL, 18 June 1938, LP 10-2, 3.

56 "Report on Huron Mountain Club," 3, 8, LP 10-6, 1. Leopold's information on selective cutting in northern mixed hardwood-conifer forests came directly from his friend Rafael Zon, who was developing the technique at the Lakes States Forest Experiment Station. See F. H. Eyre to AL, 4 May 1938, LP 10-2, 4. Francis Eyre and John Neetzel of the USFS had published their findings in the April 1937 issue of the *Journal of Forestry*.

57 W. P. Harris to AL, 16 June 1938; AL to W. P. Harris, 17 June 1938, LP 10-2, 4.

58 AL to HAH, 1 September 1938, LP 10-2, 3.

59 "Proposed Conservation Economics Study," 7 November 1938, LP 10-6, 12.

60 "Economics, Philosophy, and Land," 23 November 1938, LP 10-6, 16.

61 AL, "Feed the Song Birds," *WAF* 65, 25 (3 December 1938): 5.

62 AL, "The Farmer as a Conservationist," 298.

63 Ibid., 295, 299, 316.

64 Ibid., 316.

65 Ibid.

66 "The Farm Wildlife Program: A Self-Scrutiny," undated, LP 10-6, 16. This manuscript was prepared for presentation before the university's Taylor-Hibbard Economics Club, and never published.

67 AL, "The Farmer as a Conservationist," 298.

68 "The Farmer as a Conservationist," original MS, Stencil Circular 210, February 1939, Extension Service, College of Agriculture, University of Wisconsin, LP 10-6, 1. This passage was stricken in the published version, but a similar passage occurs at the conclusion of the essay "Country" in *RR* and *SCA/RR*.

69 "The Farm Wildlife Program: A Self-Scrutiny."

70 "Chair of Wildlife Management. University of Wisconsin," 16 March 1939, Department of Wildlife Ecology Papers, Series 9/25/3, Box 1.

71 Quoted in Boyd Gibbons, "Aldo Leopold: A Durable Scale of Values," *National Geographic* 160, 5 (November 1981): 703.

72 Leopold Shack Journal 1935–1942, 15–16 July 1939.

73 A. H. Schottlaender to AL, 18 April 1939, LP 10-1, 3.

74 AL to H. D. Smith, 9 May 1939, LP 10-1, 3.

75 A. H. Schottlaender to AL, 1 July 1939, LP 10-1, 3.

76 AL, "A Biotic View of Land," *JF* 37, 9 (September 1939): 727.

77 Ibid., 728. For historical overviews of the "biotic pyramid" idea, see McIntosh, *The Background of Ecology,* 72–76, 91–92; Worster, *Nature's Economy,* 296–98.

78 Ibid., 728–29.

79 Ibid., 729.

80 J. Grinnell to AL, 22 May 1939, LP 10-8, 1.

81 V. Horn, Leopold-Voegeli Collection.

82 McCabe, "Aldo Leopold: The Professor," 65.

83 P. L. Errington to C. A. Dykstra, 19 October 1938; O. Gromme to C. A. Dykstra. 21 October 1938; JND to C. A. Dykstra, 26 October 1938; A. L. Schorger Papers, UW Archives, Series 9/25/10-13, Box 1.

CHAPTER 18. DIGGING DEEPER

1 "Reminiscences of Ernest Swift," SHSW Archives.

2 Ibid.

3 Leopold Shack Journal 1935–1942, 19–20 August 1939.

4 "Report on Delta Duck Station, 1939," 1 September 1939, LP 10-2, 3.

5 AL to E. Holt, 2 October 1939, LP 10-2, 8.

6 Ibid.

7 I. N. Gabrielson to AL, 20 October 1939; AL to I. N. Gabrielson, 1 November 1939, LP 10-4, 8.

8 AL to J. M. Linsdale, 4 January 1940, LP 10-4, 8.

9 A. M. Day to AL, 14 December 1939, LP 10-4, 8.

10 AL to A. M. Day, 17 February 1940, LP 10-4, 8.

11 D. Thompson, in McCabe, "Aldo Leopold: The Professor," 392.

12 AL to RSY, 18 November 1939, LP 10-2, 9.

13 HAH, interview with author.

14 AL, "Conservation Blueprints," *American Forests* 43, 12 (December 1937): 596.

15 AL to RSY, 29 April 1940, LP 10-2, 9.

16 AL to RSY, 13 September 1940, LP 10-2, 9.

17 AL to RSY, 8 May 1940, LP 10-2, 9.

18 "Biotic Land Use," undated, 4–5, LP 10-6, 16.

19 Ibid., 8.

20 Ibid., 9.

21 Frances and Frederick Hamerstrom, interview with author.

22 P. S. Lovejoy to AL, 12 July 1935, UW Department of Wildlife Ecology Library.

23 P. S. Lovejoy to AL, 22 September 1940, UW Department of Wildlife Ecology Library.

24 P. S. Lovejoy to AL, 12 July 1939, UW Department of Wildlife Ecology Library.

25 AL, "P. S. Lovejoy," *JWM* 7, 1 (January 1943): 125.

26 McCabe, "Aldo Leopold: The Professor," 66.

27 AL, "The State of the Profession," *JWM* 4, 3 (July 1940): 343–44, 346.

28 Leopold Shack Journal 1935–1942, 15 April 1940.

29 AL, "Escudilla," *American Forests* 46, 12 (December 1940): 540. Reprinted in *SCA*, 133–37; *SCA/RR*, 141–45.

30 AL to G. Pinchot, 4 January 1940, LP 10-3, 9.

31 P. Errington to AL, 9 January 1941, LP 10-8, 1.

32 W. P. Taylor to AL, 13 January 1941, LP 10-8, 1.

33 R. McCabe, interview with author.

34 AL, "Lakes in Relation to Terrestrial Life Patterns," in James Needham et al., *A Symposium on Hydrobiology* (Madison: University of Wisconsin Press, 1941), 22.

35 "Reminiscences of Ernest Swift."

36 Leopold Shack Journal 1935–1942, 25–26 January 1941.

37 RSY to AL, 6 February 1941, LP 10-2, 9.

38 AL to RSY, 11 February 1941, LP 10-2, 9.

39 RSY to AL, 14 February 1941, LP 10-2, 9.

40 AL to RSY, 26 February 1941, LP 10-2, 9.

41 RSY to AL, 7 March 1941, LP 10-2, 9.

42 AL, "The Last Stand," *Outdoor America* 7, 7 (May–June 1942): 8.

43 AL, "Wilderness as a Land Laboratory," *Living Wilderness* 6 (July 1941): 3. Leopold included this as part of the larger essay "Wilderness" in *SCA*, 188–201.

44 "Ecology and Politics," undated, 1, LP 10-6, 16.

45 Ibid., 2.

46 Ibid., 3.

47 Ibid., 4.

48 Ibid.

49 Ibid., 6.

50 Wright was then at the University of Chicago, already renowned for his pioneering work in explaining the phenomenon of "genetic drift" in populations.

51 "Ecology and Politics," 6–7.

52 Ibid., 7.

53 "Report of the Advisory Board, Delta Duck Station, 1940–1941," 13 July 1941, LP 10-2, 3.

54 AL, *SCA*, 159; *SCA/RR*, 169.

55 The Bureau of Biological Survey was transferred to the Department of Interior in 1939. In 1940, the BBS was merged with the Bureau of Fisheries to create the Fish and Wildlife Service.

56 "Report to the American Wildlife Institute on the Utah and Oregon Wildlife Units," 10 August 1941, LP 10-2, 1.

57 NLB, interview with author.

58 AL to JJH, 1 November 1941, LP 10-1, 1.
59 "The Geese Return," 8 September 1941, LP 10-6, 18. This essay was based on one of Leopold's pieces for the *Wisconsin Agriculturalist and Farmer* series. See "When the Geese Return Spring Is Here," *WAF* 67, 7 (April 6, 1940): 15.
60 "65287," undated, LP 10-6, 18. See final version of this essay, "65290" in *SCA,* 87–92; *SCA/RR,* 93–98.
61 H. Strauss to AL, 26 November 1941, LP 10-6, 5.
62 AL to H. Strauss, 3 December 1941, LP 10-6, 5.
63 H. Strauss to AL, 18 December 1941, LP 10-6, 5.
64 AL to H. Strauss, 29 December 1941, LP 10-6, 5.
65 H. Strauss to AL, 9 January 1942, LP 10-6, 5.
66 "Wildlife in American Culture," 4 December 1941, LP 10-6, 18. This passage was included in the essay as first published in the *Journal of Wildlife Management* of January 1943, but deleted from the version ultimately published in *A Sand County Almanac.*
67 Ibid.
68 "Yet Come June," 23 December 1941, LP 10-6, 16. Leopold's manuscript of this unpublished essay shows extensive revision. This version follows as closely as possible Leopold's last editorial remarks.

CHAPTER 19. LAND USE AND DEMOCRACY

1 "Armament for Conservation," 23 November 1942, 9, LP 10-6, 16.
2 AL, "Land-Use and Democracy," *Audubon Magazine* 44, 3 (September–October 1942): 265.
3 Ibid., 264.
4 Ibid., 260.
5 "Armament for Conservation," 23 November 1942, 7, LP 10-6, 16. This was a seminar presentation of the same ideas that Leopold had written up in "Land-Use and Democracy."
6 "Land-Use and Democracy," 260.
7 Ibid., 265.
8 W. K. Thomas to AL, 8 January 1942, LP 10-2, 7.
9 AL to HAH, 20 January 1942, LP 10-2, 3.
10 HAH to AL, 15 January 1942; AL to HAH, 22 January 1942; HAH to AL, 27 January 1942, LP 10-2, 3.
11 AL to F. C. Walcott, 13 March 1942, LP 10-2, 3.
12 AL, "The Role of Wildlife in a Liberal Education," *Transactions of the Seventh NAWC,* 8–10 April 1942, Toronto (Washington, D.C.: AWI, 1942), 485.
13 Leopold Shack Journal 1935–1942, 29–30 November 1941.
14 Leopold Shack Journal 1935–1942, 12–13 April 1942.
15 AL to RSY, 4 April 1942, LP 10-2, 9.
16 AL to RSY, 23 April 1942, LP 10-2, 9.
17 "This World of Ours," *Wisconsin State Journal,* 6 July 1942.
18 AL, *SCA,* 114, 113; *SCA/RR,* 121, 120. See also E. Swift to AL, 16 September 1942, 2 October 1942; AL to E. Swift, 23 September 1942, LP 10-6, 9.
19 B. P. Stollberg to AL, 29 January 1942, LP 10-8, 1. This letter predates the

beginning of the round robin in late 1942. The round robin letters may be found in LP 10-1, 3.

20 This account has been pieced together from various documents in LP 10-2, 10, files of the Wisconsin Conservation League and the Wisconsin Conservation Commission.

21 "Twelve-Point Program," *Sheboygan Press,* 22 August 1942.

22 AL to H. D. Ruhl, 24 July 1942, LP 10-2, 10. See also chap. 17, n. 1.

23 AL to L. Radke, 10 June 1942; L. Radke to AL, 11 June 1942, LP 10-2, 10.

24 W. J. P. Aberg to F. Leuning, 12 June 1942, LP 10-2, 10. Aberg and Leopold undoubtedly saw eye to eye on the proper role of politics in conservation administration. "Individuals may come and go," Aberg wrote to Leuning, editor of the *Milwaukee Journal,* "but the conservation program, with such deviations as time, experience, and learning may necessitate, must go on without interruption. . . . Conservation cannot afford to enter the political arena as a candidate or partisan. We may support an individual because of his sincerity in the conservation cause, regardless of his political affiliations, but when a conservationist becomes a politician and a partisan politician, which he must become in order to be elected on any ticket, his conservation proclivities are merged into the more comprehensive classification of Democrat, Republican, or Progressive, and when conservationists propose such a move, they have for themselves removed their best and strongest weapon, because they are no longer non-political."

25 As early as 1930, Ernie Swift and other game wardens in the north reported isolated instances of overbrowsing and deer starvation to headquarters in Madison. Their reports were ignored. In 1935, the Forest Service used the CCCs to conduct a census of the Chequamegon National Forest and found an average of one deer for each eighteen acres of range, a dangerous ratio. In the winter deer yards, cedars showed "little or no foliage and a great many heavily browsed tree boles and defoliated reproduction." The Forest Service requested permission to reduce the herd, but the Conservation Commission denied the request and instituted a winter feeding program, decisions which were widely applauded by the public. See R. E. Trippensee, "Deer Problem in the National Forests in Wisconsin," 4 December 1935, LP 10-4, 1. See also Flader, *Thinking Like a Mountain,* 144–45, 180–83.

26 Dan Thompson, one of Leopold's graduate students, joined Feeney's crew that second winter while waiting to be called into military service. He remembers that Feeney "instilled both drama and athletic zeal in his survey crews. Three months of vigorous surveying was needed to complete the 1941–42 survey. . . . The results of our field reports were not yet tallied, but my mental pictures from snowshoeing through about 220 miles of overbrowsed winter deer range gave no doubt about the need for more flexible and liberal hunting regulations." In McCabe, "Aldo Leopold: The Professor," 396–97.

27 AL to A. W. Schorger, 2 October 1942, LP 10-2, 10.

28 AL to A. W. Schorger et al., 14 December 1942, LP 10-2, 10.

29 Ibid.

30 Ibid.

31 McCabe, "Aldo Leopold: The Professor," 55–56.

32 AL to HAH, 10 October 1942, LP 10-2, 3.
33 HAH to AL, 22 October 1942, LP 10-2, 3.
34 AL to HAH, 19 November 1942, LP 10-2, 3.
35 HAH to AL, 29 November 1942, LP 10-2, 3.
36 AL to F. C. Walcott, 14 December 1942, LP 10-2, 3.
37 F. C. Walcott to J. Bell, 21 January 1943, LP 10-2, 3.
38 AL to J. Bell, 16 January 1943, LP 10-2, 3.
39 AL to HAH, 15 March 1943, LP 10-2, 3.
40 For a general discussion of this phase of the deer controversy, see Flader, *Thinking Like a Mountain*, 183–93.
41 "Majority Report of the Citizen's Deer Committee to the Wisconsin Conservation Commission," 1-2, LP 10-2, 10. Published in *WCB* 8, 8 (August 1943): 19–22.
42 "Prejudice or Science: That Is the Issue," *Milwaukee Journal*, 4 April 1943.
43 E. G. Ovitz to AL, 30 March 1943, WCD Files, SHSW. See Flader, *Thinking Like a Mountain*, 188–89.
44 "Majority Report of the Citizens' Deer Committee," 3–5.
45 Asa K. Owen, "Necessity of Antlerless Deer Season Denied by Citizens' Committeeman," *Milwaukee Journal*, 30 May 1943.
46 See "Catlin, Adams Lose Their Jobs," *Wisconsin State Journal*, 18 June 1943.
47 McCabe, "Aldo Leopold: The Professor," 148; R. McCabe, interview with author.
48 See AL to V. L. Dickenson, 16 October 1946, LP 10-2, 10.
49 W. Grange to AL, 7 July 1943, LP 10-8, 1.
50 "For Generations To Come," *Wisconsin State Journal*, 22 June 1943.
51 Leopold Shack Journal 1942–1945, 25 July 1943, LP 10-7, 3.
52 J. R. de la Torre Bueno to AL, 5 April 1943, LP 10-6, 5.
53 AL, *SCA*, 26; *SCA/RR*, 28. The original opening line of the essay, deleted during a later revision, was more topical: "During this the longest winter, in this the longest war, in this the month of the big tax, it is salutary to think upon Draba, the smallest flower that blooms." The species under consideration was *Draba reptans* (Lam.) Fernald.
54 AL to HAH, 15 April 1943, LP 10-2, 3.
55 AL to HAH, 7 May 1943, LP 10-2, 3.
56 "Land as a Circulatory System," 12 July 1943, LP 10-6, 16.
57 See AL to HAH, 23 September 1943, LP 10-2, 3.
58 See Flader, *Thinking Like a Mountain*, 197–98.
59 Leopold Shack Journal 1942–1945, 21–22 August 1943.
60 Flader, *Thinking Like a Mountain*, 197–98.
61 "Great Possessions," 9 September 1943, LP 10-6, 18. Revised and published in *SCA*, 41–44; *SCA/RR*, 44–47.
62 HAH to AL, 11 October 1943, LP 10-2, 3.
63 AL, "Population Turnover on a Wisconsin Pheasant Refuge," *JWM* 7, 4 (October 1943), 383–94.
64 "Smoky Gold," 27 October 1943, LP 10-6, 8. Revised and published in *SCA*, 54–58; *SCA/RR*, 58–62.

65 "Too Early," 20 November 1943, LP 10-6, 8. Revised and published in *SCA*, 59–62; *SCA/RR*, 62–66.

66 HAH to AL, 27 November 1943, LP 10-2, 3.

67 "Gus' Last Hunt," in Leopold Shack Journal 1942–1945, 25–27 November 1943. Published in *RR*, 106–7. EEL, interview with author.

68 Leopold Shack Journal 1942–1945, 25–27 November 1943.

69 See Flader, *Thinking Like a Mountain*, 198–99.

70 AL to A. K. Owen, 31 August 1944, LP 10-2, 10.

71 Leopold Shack Journal 1942–1945, 25–27 November 1943.

72 AL, *SCA*, 148–49; *SCA/RR*, 157–58.

73 HAH to AL, 22 January 1944, LP 10-6, 5.

74 AL to HAH, 29 January 1944, LP 10-6, 5.

75 HAH to AL, 4 February 1944, LP 10-6, 5.

76 Ibid.

77 Ibid.

78 AL to HAH, 11 February 1944, LP 10-2, 3.

79 AL to HAH, 12 February 1944, LP 10-2, 3.

80 AL to HAH, 1 March 1944, LP 10-2, 3.

81 HAH to AL, 11 March 1944, LP 10-6, 5.

82 AL to HAH, 21 March 1944, LP 10-2, 3. In a letter to J. Paul Miller of the American Wildlife Institute, Leopold wrote, "I take pride in the fact that the new chapters which I had never seen are written just as clearly and simply as those I edited, and I detect no dilution of Albert's personal style anywhere in the volume. Also notice the extent to which the work has been tied in to the modern literature. This more than justifies what at times probably appeared to be undue delays in finishing the MS." AL to J. P. Miller, 27 March 1944, LP 10-2, 3.

83 AL to HAH, 2 November 1945, LP 10-2, 3.

84 See Flader, *Thinking Like a Mountain*, 209–10.

85 W. W. Rinehard to AL, 17 March 1944, LP 10-2, 10.

86 AL to W. W. Rinehard, 24 March 1944, LP 10-2, 10.

87 "The 1944 Game Situation," 24 March 1944, LP 10-6, 18.

88 Memo to E. Bean, N. Fassett, H. Schuette, 17 April 1944, LP 10-2, 10.

89 "Thinking Like a Mountain," 1 April 1944, LP 10-6, 18. Revised and published in *SCA*, 129–33; *SCA/RR*, 137–41.

90 HAH to AL, 15 April 1944, LP 10-6, 5.

91 Leopold Shack Journal 1942–1945, 21 April 1944.

92 This committee also served to lay the foundation for Taylor's later classic *The Deer of North America* (Harrisburg, Pa.: The Stackpole Co. and WMI, 1956). See file in LP 10-2, 5.

93 AL to W. Pessels, 6 June 1944; AL to C. Simpson, 8 June 1944, LP 10-6, 5.

94 HAH to AL, 30 June 1944, LP 10-6, 5.

95 AL to HAH, 18 June 1944, LP 10-2, 3.

96 W. Pessels to AL, 20 July 1944, LP 10-6, 5.

97 C. Simpson to AL, 24 July 1944, LP 10-6, 5.

98 HAH to AL, 31 July 1944, LP 10-6, 5.

99 C. Simpson to AL, 24 August 1944, LP 10-6, 5. One of the readers that Knopf asked to read the essays was William Beebe, Director of the New York Zoological Society. Beebe wrote to Leopold on 5 August 1944 that he had given the essays "the highest praise possible to my limited vocabulary. I like them from the ground up and hope the volume will soon appear. We so need writing which does in natural history and science the things which the prose of Kipling, and Dunsany, does in other fields." W. Beebe to AL, 5 August 1944, LP 10-6, 5.

100 AL to C. Simpson, 31 August 1944, LP 10-6, 5.

101 HAH to AL, 12 November 1944; AL to HAH, 20 November 1944, LP 10-2, 3.

102 AL, "What Next in Deer Policy?" *WCB* 9, 6 (June 1944): 3–4. See Flader, *Thinking Like a Mountain,* 201–2. Leopold figured (and hoped) that Wisconsin, by virtue of its early start in doe removal, could get by with a 60 percent reduction from peak herd numbers. By comparison, the Kaibab population was down to an estimated 10 percent of its mid-1920s high, and Pennsylvania was said to need a 70 percent reduction. Leopold feared that further delays would lower the ultimate level at which a balance might be reached, both in terms of deer numbers and range quality. He admitted that conditions in the state were not uniform. "Nevertheless," he concluded, "the average northern county seems to be just started on the route to a normal healthy herd and a normal healthy forest."

103 "Seven Prongs of the Deer Dilemma," 22 June 1944, LP 10-6, 14.

104 WCC Minutes, 6 July 1944, WCD Files, SHSW. See Flader, *Thinking Like a Mountain,* 218.

105 "An Open Letter to the Governor, State Senators, and Assemblymen," *Save Wisconsin's Deer* 1, 1 (August 1944): 8. A complete collection of *Save Wisconsin's Deer* is available on microfilm at the SHSW.

106 "Tsh! Tsh! It's the Conservation Bulletin Again," *Save Wisconsin's Deer* 1, 5 (December 1944): 6.

107 "Bambi of Valhalla," *Save Wisconsin's Deer* 1, 1 (August 1944): 5.

108 "Browsing Around with the Editor," *Save Wisconsin's Deer* 1, 2 (September 1944): 4.

109 "Conservation: In Whole Or In Part," 1 November 1944, 1, LP 10-6, 16.

110 Ibid., 1.

111 Ibid., 2, 8–9.

112 Ibid., 14.

113 AL to JND, 31 October 1944, LP 10-1, 2.

114 D. Wade to AL, 30 September 1944, LP 10-8, 1.

115 AL to D. Wade, 23 October 1944, LP 10-8, 1.

116 AL to E. Kelly, 13 October 1944, LP 10-8, 1.

117 E. Kelly to AL, 13 November 1944, LP 10-8, 1.

118 AL to E. Kelly, 22 November 1944, LP 10-8, 1.

119 AL to ASL, B. Leopold, 25 December 1944, LP 10-1, Box 2.

120 AL, "Deer, Wolves, Foxes, and Pheasants," *WCB* 10, 4 (April 1945): 3. H. R. Siegler, a former student assistant and a biologist for the New Hampshire Fish and Game Department wrote to Leopold at this time asking for advice on his state's deer situation. New Hampshire's herd was healthy and stable;

its ratio of bucks to does was normal and had varied only slightly over the years; for twenty-five years hunters had taken a constant number of both bucks and does. Leopold must have read the figures enviously. But, Siegler reported, there was growing sentiment among some New Hampshire sportsmen to close hunting on does, in an attempt to increase the population. Siegler asked for Leopold's views. Leopold replied that the population could indeed be raised, but the important point to consider was whether the browse could withstand an increase. "Believe me, after my recent experiences, I would rather have too few deer than too many. Your sportsmen probably haven't the faintest comprehension of what they are getting into if they allow an over-browsed situation to develop." AL to H. R. Siegler, 10 January 1945, LP 10-2, 10.

121 Statement of the Trego Rod and Gun Club, "The Fox, Wolf, and Deer," c. January 1945, LP 10-2, 10.

122 AL, "Deer, Wolves, Foxes, and Pheasants," 3–5.

123 "'Assume They Know More Than I Do'—Leopold," *Save Wisconsin's Deer* 1, 11 (June 1945): 1.

124 "The Deer Problem of Northern Wisconsin," 8 March 1945, LP 10-6, 14.

125 EBL to ASL, 12 February 1945, LP 10-1, 2.

126 Ibid.

127 AL, "The Outlook for Farm Wildlife," *Transactions of the Tenth NAWC* (Washington, D.C.: AWI, 1945), 168.

128 B. MacKaye to fellow councilors, 22 May 1945, LP 10-2, 9.

129 E. S. Griffith to AL, 2 July 1945, LP 10-2, 9.

130 "Council Meeting of the Wilderness Society," 14 July 1945, LP 10-2, 9.

131 AL to ASL, 22 August 1945, LP 10-1, 2.

132 B. Stollberg, 11 August 1945, LP 10-1, 3.

133 "The Green Pasture," 15 August 1945, LP 10-6, 5. Revised and published in *SCA,* 51–52, *SCA/RR,* 54–56.

134 "The Biotic War," undated, LP 10-6, 16.

CHAPTER 20. A PORTENT OF A DIFFERENT FUTURE

1 Alice Harper left the Department in 1945 to marry Allen Stokes, a graduate student who began work under Leopold toward the end of the war. Other students who joined the department after the war were Antoon de Vos, Robert S. Ellarson, Frederick Greeley, James B. Hale, Richard D. Taber, and Donald R. Thompson. For profiles of all Leopold's secretaries, see McCabe "Aldo Leopold: The Professor," 31–40.

2 HAH to AL, 18 August 1945, LP 10-2, 3.

3 AL to HAH, 25 October 1945, LP 10-2, 3.

4 Ibid.

5 See Wisconsin Journal 1936–1945, 28 October 1945, LP 10-7, 2; R. Ellarson in McCabe, "Aldo Leopold: The Professor," 252; L. Sowls in McCabe, "Aldo Leopold: The Professor," 361–62.

6 Wisconsin Journal 1936–1945, 2 November 1945

7 "Birdsong Phenology in Southern Wisconsin," c. October 1944, LP 10-6, 18.

8   AL to ASL, 22 August 1945, LP 10-1, 2.
9   AL to JJH, 24 November 1945, LP 10-1, 1.
10 Ibid.
11 BV to AL, 8 August 1942, LP 10-1, 3.
12 Starker's two years of fieldwork in Mexico ultimately resulted in the publication of *Wildlife of Mexico: The Game Birds and Mammals* (Berkeley: University of California Press, 1959), an important early survey of that nation's wildlife.
13 AL to BV, 21 January 1946, LP 10-2, 4.
14 BV to AL, 28 January 1946, LP 10-2, 4.
15 AL to BV, 8 February 1946, LP 10-1, 3.
16 BV, "Pan-American Conservation," *Transactions of the Eleventh NAWC*, 11–13 March 1946, New York City (Washington, D.C.: AWI, 1946), 10.
17 Fairfield Osborn, "Urgency of Conservation Education," *Transactions of the Eleventh NAWC*, 74.
18 AL to EBL, 13 March 1946, LP 10-8, 9.
19 BV to AL, 27 September 1946, 10-1, 3.
20 AL to B. MacKaye, 1 May 1946, LP 10-2, 9.
21 B. MacKaye to councilors of the Wilderness Society, 6 May 1946, LP 10-2, 9.
22 AL to H. Zahniser, 5 June 1946, LP 10-2, 9.
23 "Report of the Committee on Foreign Relations of the Wildlife Society," 1 August 1946, LP 10-2, 9.
24 "Conservation," in letter, H. Fries to AL, 8 August 1946, LP 10-1, 1.
25 R. Mann to AL, 16 April 1946, LP 10-1, Box 2.
26 McCabe, "Aldo Leopold: The Professor," 132–33.
27 AL to R. Mann, 20 April 1946, LP 10-1, 2.
28 R. Mann to AL, 29 April 1946, LP 10-1, 2.
29 George Becker, Voegeli-Leopold Collection. Becker had encountered Leopold as an undergraduate at the University of Wisconsin, and went on to a distinguished career in fisheries management and teaching at the University of Wisconsin at Stevens Point.
30 "On a Monument to the Pigeon," 25 August 1946, 1, LP 10-6, 9. Revised and published in *SCA*, 108–12; *SCA/RR*, 116–19.
31 G. Becker, Leopold-Voegeli Collection.
32 "On a Monument to the Pigeon," 3.
33 Ibid., 4.
34 Ibid., 2.
35 AL to ASL, B. Leopold, 22 April 1946, LP 10-1, 2.
36 AL to D. B. Cook, 4 September 1946, LP 10-6, 12. David B. Cook was Supervising Forester of the New York State Conservation Department. His interest in the seasonal growth of conifers coincided with Leopold's. After Cook published a paper on the subject in *Ecology* in 1942, Leopold wrote to him suggesting that they compare notes. In subsequent years they exchanged data on pine growth. Leopold's most detailed observations of pine phenology and ecology date from this period.
37 Untitled Journal, 31 May 1946, LP 10-7, 3. Leopold did not emboss this volume with a title. Since this was the last of his bound journals, he was prob-

ably waiting until an end date to give it a title (as he had the others). Leopold inadvertently dated this entry "3/31."

38 C. Simpson to AL, 29 April 1946, LP 10-6, 5.

39 AL to C. Simpson, 10 May 1946, LP 10-6, 5.

40 AL, *SCA*, 102; *SCA/RR*, 109.

41 See AL to H. J. Sanborn, 27 May 1946, 28 June 1946, 29 August 1946; H. J. Sanborn to AL, 23 June 1946, 5 July 1946, 15 August 1946, 8 September 1946, LP 10-6, 5.

42 McCabe, "Aldo Leopold: The Professor," 194.

43 The WCD had just published Ernie Swift's ninety-six-page "History of Wisconsin Deer," detailing the history and status of the herd and its range. Roy Jorgensen lambasted the department for "wasting" taxpayers' dollars on "anti-deer propaganda." Despite Jorgensen's work, public opinion across the state was beginning to shift. The effort of the WCD to include its field force in the winter deer surveys was paying early dividends. One representative of the Conservation Congress sitting in on the July commission meeting was willing to go along with the department despite his district's vote. Another admitted that the congress' vote "was not biologically sound, nevertheless, it did represent the sentiment of the congress members and the people of the counties."

44 WCC Minutes, 9 July 1946, 18, SHSW; see LP 10-2, 10.

45 "The Crisis in Deer Policy," 24 July 1946, in letter to ASL, 2 August 1946, LP 10-1, 2. See also WCC Minutes, 24 July 1946, SHSW; LP 10-2, 10.

46 WCC Minutes, 24 July 1946, 14, SHSW; LP 10-2, 10.

47 AL to ASL, 2 August 1946, LP 10-1, 2.

48 See AL, "The Deer Dilemma," *WCB* 11, 8–9 (August–September 1946): 3–5; "Leopold Explains Opposition to Deer Hunting Restrictions," *Milwaukee Journal*, 1 September 1946; "Spiked Bucks," *The Badger Sportsman* 3, 5 (December 1946): 1. *Save Wisconsin's Deer* changed its name to *The Badger Sportsman* in October 1945. It is still published under that name, and has long since abandoned its initial position on deer management in Wisconsin.

49 AL, "The Deer Dilemma," 4.

50 See Flader, *Thinking Like a Mountain*, 222–29.

51 "The Critical Approach to Wildlife," 5 November 1946, in lecture notes for Advanced Game Management 179, LP 10-6, 15.

52 AL, review of *The Ducks Came Back* by S. Kip Farrington, *JWM* 10, 3 (July 1946): 283.

53 "Many Ducks Crippled Due to High Winds," *The Daily Graphic,* 17 September 1946.

54 HAH to AL, 16 October 1946, LP 10-2, 2.

55 AL to M. W. Smith, undated, LP 10-2, 2.

56 HAH to AL, 28 October 1946, LP 10-2, 2.

57 AL to M. W. Smith, 5 November 1946, LP 10-2, 2.

58 M. W. Smith to AL, 6 November 1946; AL to M. W. Smith, 12 November 1946, LP 10-2, 2; HAH to AL, 18 November 1946, LP 10-2, 3.

59 "Adventures of a Conservation Commissioner," 1 December 1946, 1, LP 10-6, 16.

60 O. Butler to AL, 8 January 1947, LP 10-2, 1.

61 AL to W. A. Dreyer, 11 January 1947, LP 10-2, 2.

62 H. Albert Hochbaum, "The Effect of Concentrated Hunting Pressure on Water-fowl Breeding Stock," *Transactions of the Twelfth NAWC*, 3–5 February 1947, San Antonio (Washington, D.C.: WMI, 1947), 58.

63 AL, "Summarization of the Twelfth North American Wildlife Conference," *Transactions of the Twelfth NAWC*, 531.

64 Bernard DeVoto's bombshell article, "The West Against Itself," appeared in the January 1947 issue of *Harper's*. The story of DeVoto's career as a conservationist is recounted in Wallace Stegner, *The Uneasy Chair* (Garden City, N.Y.: Doubleday and Company, 1974), 287–322.

65 AL, "Summarization," 529–30.

66 HAH, letter to author, 9 July 1986.

67 AL to V. W. Lehmann, 12 March 1947, LP 10-3, 10.

68 Untitled Journal, 6–7 February 1947, LP 10-7, 3.

69 AL to V. W. Lehmann, 12 March 1947, LP 10-3, 10.

70 AL to ASL, undated, LP 10-1, 2.

71 "Memorandum re: Certificate of Incorporation," undated, LP 10-2, 2.

72 Ibid. See also AL to ASL, undated, LP 10-1, 2; "The Conservation Foundation: A Statement of Purpose and the Proposed Program for 1948," November 1947, LP 10-2, 2.

73 D. Thompson, in McCabe, "Aldo Leopold: The Professor," 401.

74 "Wherefore Wildlife Ecology?" undated, LP 10-6, 16.

75 Ibid.

76 WCC Minutes, 8 April 1947, 25–26, SHSW; see LP 10-2, 10.

77 AL to V. H. Cahalane, 4 June 1947, LP 10-2, 4.

78 "Continental Wilderness System Advocated," 26 June 1947, LP 10-2, 9.

79 "The Ecological Conscience," 27 June 1947, 1, LP 10-2, 16.

80 Ibid.

81 Ibid., 2–7.

82 Ibid., 7.

83 Ibid., 8.

84 Ibid.

85 Ibid., 9.

86 M. C. Otto to AL, 2 March 1948; AL to M. C. Otto, 8 March 1948, LP 10-8, 1.

87 See WCC Minutes, 1 July 1947, SHSW; LP 10-2, 10. The vote, as recorded in the minutes, was 4-1 against Leopold. His dissent was published under the title "Mortgaging the Future Deer Herd," *WCB* 12, 9 (September 1947): 3.

88 HAH to AL, 25 June 1947; AL to M. W. Smith, 8 July 1947, LP 10-2, 2.

89 The discussion that follows is based on the author's "Building 'The Land Ethic': A History of Aldo Leopold's Most Important Essay," (master's thesis, University of Wisconsin–Madison, 1983).

90 AL, "A Biotic View of Land," 728.

91 AL, *SCA,* 215; *SCA/RR,* 252.

92 "The Ecological Conscience," original MS, 2, LP 10-6, 16.

93 Ibid., 7.
94 AL, *SCA,* 224–25; *SCA/RR,* 262.
95 Ibid., 204; *SCA/RR,* 240.
96 Ibid.
97 Ibid., 225; *SCA/RR,* 262–63.
98 "Foreword," 2.
99 AL, *SCA,* 200–201; *SCA/RR,* 279.
100 AL to C. Simpson, 5 September 1947; C. Simpson to AL, 9 September 1947; AL to C. Simpson, 11 September 1947, LP 10-6, 5.

CHAPTER 21. FINALE

1 EEL, letter to author, 30 March 1986; LBL, interview with author.
2 Another chapter in Leopold's ongoing troubles in the WCC unfolded while he was in Madison. On September 17, the WCC held an open hearing on the question of when to open the duck season that fall. The U.S. Fish and Wildlife Service had given the WCC a choice of two dates, October 7 or 21. The WCC had originally chosen the latter date in the interest of giving local breeding ducks a chance. Leopold estimated that, with the recent waterfowl shortages, five years of late openings would be needed to rebuild the local stock to satisfactory levels. A vociferous segment of the state's duck hunter's disagreed. A group of self-proclaimed "representative hunters" submitted a petition asking for a switch to the earlier date, asserting the age-old claim that if local shooters did not get the state's ducks, hunters down south would. Their petition ended with a tug at the heartstrings, appealing to the commission to preserve the special sentimental experiences of duck-hunting. Leopold, who would have preferred if possible a compromise date of October 15, explained the need for a late season. "The conservation of our locals is a responsibility of this Commission." After rancorous debate, the commission reversed its original stand. See AL, "What Date for Duck Shooting?" 6 September 1947, LP 10-6, 16.
3 Dr. Jeff Brown of the University of Wisconsin Hospitals and Clinics provided information and advice for this explanation of trigeminal neuralgia and its treatment.
4 "Memo for Dr. A.W. Adson on Post-operative stage of Aldo Leopold," undated, LP 10-8, 1.
5 AL to HAH, 17 October 1947, LP 10-2, 3.
6 AL to W. Elder, 16 October 1947, LP 10-1, 1.
7 AL to ASL, undated, LP 10-1, 2.
8 McCabe, "Aldo Leopold: The Professor," 195–96.
9 EEL, interview with author. See also "Memo for Dr. Adson."
10 "Memo for Dr. Adson."
11 AL to BV, 24 October 1947, LP 10-1, 3.
12 AL, *SCA,* 54, *SCA/RR,* 58.
13 C. Simpson to AL, 5 November 1947, LP 10-6, 5.
14 AL to C. Simpson, 18 November 1947, LP 10-6, 5.

15 LBL, interview with author.
16 AL to C. Schwartz, 11 November 1947; C. Schwartz to AL, 17 November 1947, LP 10-6, 5.
17 AL, *SCA,* 68, 70; *SCA/RR,* 73, 74.
18 AL to P. Vaudrin, 2 December 1947, LP 10-6, 5.
19 "Foreword," 5 December 1947, LP 10-6, 9. Leopold revised this foreword on March 4, 1948. This later revision was finally published in *A Sand County Almanac.* A comparison of texts reveals only a few alterations, most significantly in the final subsection. The original draft of this subsection contained only two paragraphs. Leopold's March 4 revision broke these down into five paragraphs, and emphasized more strongly the unity he saw in the whole collection.
20 P. Vaudrin to AL, 28 November 1947, LP 10-6, 5.
21 AL to W. Sloane, 19 December 1947; AL to P. Vaudrin, 19 December 1947, LP 10-6, 5.
22 HAH, letter to author, 28 June 1986.
23 HAH to AL, 26 December 1947, LP 10-2, 3.
24 Untitled Journal, 25 December 1947; NLB, interview with author.
25 AL to W. A. Dreyer, 2 January 1948, LP 10-2, 2.
26 AL to C. Schwartz, 28 January 1948, LP 10-6, 5.
27 AL, *SCA,* 10; *SCA/RR,* 11.
28 WCC Minutes, 19 January 1948, 14, SHSW; LP 10-2, 10.
29 Ibid., 15.
30 AL to C. Russell, 19 January 1948, LP 10-2, 5.
31 W. Grange to AL, 19 December 1947, LP 10-1, 1.
32 AL to W. Grange, 3 January 1948, LP 10-1, 1. At the end of this letter, Leopold stated that he planned to discuss his views in greater detail in his presidential address to the Ecological Society of America for 1948. Unfortunately, he was not able to devote time to this prior to his death. On the same broad topic, it should be noted that Joseph McCarthy had been elected Wisconsin's senator in 1946. Leopold's papers include several letters to McCarthy, but these involved only current conservation legislation in Washington.
33 AL to W. A. Wood, 9 February 1948, LP 10-2, 1.
34 AL to M. L. Cooke, 17 March 1948, LP 10-1, 1.
35 AL to HAH, 2 March 1948, LP 10-2, 3.
36 "Putting the Sciences Together," in letter to ASL, undated, LP 10-1, 2.
37 J. A. Krug to AL, 27 February 1948, LP 10-2, 8.
38 AL to HAH, 2 March 1948, LP 10-2, 3.
39 R. A. Brown to AL, 12 March 1948, LP 10-8, 1.
40 See AL, "How and Why Research?" *Transactions of the Thirteenth NAWC,* 8–10 March 1948, St. Louis (Washington, D.C.: WMI, 1948), 44–48.
41 AL to ACL, 31 March 1948, LP 10-8, 9.
42 AL to A. W. Adson, 7 April 1948, LP 10-8, 1.
43 AL to E. Swift, 14 April 1948, LP 10-2, 10. Leopold evidently saw the Muir homestead as a possible addition to the Conservation Department's fledgling Natural Areas Program. Leopold, as a conservation commissioner, was instrumental in initiating the program in 1945, though Norman Fassett seems

to have been the driving force behind the plan. Leopold, Fassett, and Albert M. Fuller of the Milwaukee Museum of Natural History served on the Natural Areas Committee of the WCD, which was charged with identifying and evaluating sites of special geological and ecological significance for protection. See "Natural Areas Committee" file in LP 10-2, 10.

44 P. Vaudrin to AL, 14 April 1948, LP 10-6, 5.

45 W. Sloane to AL, 19 April 1948, LP 10-6, 5.

46 EEL, interview with author.

47 See file "Inter-American Conference on Conservation of Renewable Natural Resources," LP 10-2, 4.

48 This account of Leopold's death is drawn from the following sources: EEL to NLE, 26 April 1948, LP 10-8, 9; interviews with family members; untitled journal, 18-21 April 1948; EEL, letter to author, 18 August 1986.

EPILOGUE

1 W. Shepard to EBL, 22 April 1948, LP 10-8, 3.

2 H. L. Russell to EBL, 27 April 1948, LP 10-8, 3.

3 C. Bradley to EBL, 28 April 1948, LP 10-8, 3.

4 N. Fassett to EBL, 28 April 1948, LP 10-8, 3.

5 McCabe, "Aldo Leopold: The Professor," 198.

6 Dan Thompson, in McCabe, "Aldo Leopold: The Professor," 402.

7 HAH, letter to author, 28 June 1986.

8 HAH, untitled, 22 April 1948, LP 10-2, 3.

9 AL to W. Rowan, 4 March 1947, LP 10-1, 2.

10 P. Vaudrin to JJH, 22 April 1948, LP 10-6, 5.

11 AL to "reading committee," undated, LP 10-6, 5.

12 JJH to LBL et al., 24 April 1948, LP 10-6, 5. In the months following Leopold's death, there was much speculation about who would succeed Leopold as chairman of the university Department of Wildlife Management. A number of prominent biologists from around the country submitted applications, but that summer Dean Ira Baldwin called Joe Hickey and Bob McCabe into his office and informed them that the administration had decided not to hire any of the applicants. Hickey and McCabe would guide the department for the next three and a half decades. In the mid-1960s, the name of the department was changed to the Department of Wildlife Ecology.

13 See "Great Possessions" MS, LP 10-6, 5; Dennis Ribbens, "The Making of *A Sand County Almanac*," *WASAL* 70 (1982): 3–12.

14 LBL to JJH, 19 July 1948, LP 10-6, 5. See LBL, "Notes on the History of the Publication of Aldo Leopold's Sand County Almanac," 20 September 1984, Knox College Library, Galesburg, Illinois. Luna's edited manuscript of *A Sand County Almanac* is on deposit in the Knox College Library.

15 "A Wisconsin Philosopher," *Green Bay Gazette,* 3 November 1949.

16 Joseph Wood Krutch, "Wild Geese — or Television," *The Nation* 169, 26 (24 December 1949): 628.

17 Lewis Gannett, "Books and Things," *New York Herald Tribune,* 27 October 1949.

18 BV, untitled review, LP 10-5, 6.

19 See "Aldo Leopold Memorial"; Clinton B. Anderson, "The Wilderness of Aldo Leopold"; Harvey Broome, "Our Basis of Understanding," all in *Living Wilderness* 19, 51 (Winter 1954–55): 43–49. Documents in the files of the Gila National Forest indicate that the ceremony was even less successful than journalistic accounts suggested.

20 For a review of the careers of the Leopold children, see Luther J. Carter, "The Leopolds: A Family of Naturalists."

21 NLB, interview with author.

22 EBL, Voegeli-Leopold Collection.

23 EEL, interview with author.

Bibliography

A. BOOKS

Antrobus, Augustine. *History of Des Moines County and Its People.* Chicago: S. J. Clarke Publishing Company, 1915.

Bailey, Florence Merriam. *Birds of New Mexico.* Santa Fe: New Mexico Department of Game and Fish, 1928.

Bailey, Vernon. *Mammals of New Mexico.* USDA, BBS, North American Fauna 53: 1–412.

Baldwin, Donald. *The Quiet Revolution: Grass Roots of Today's Wilderness Preservation Movement.* Boulder: Pruett Publishing Company, 1972.

Barker, Elliot. *Beatty's Cabin: Adventures in the Pecos High Country.* Albuquerque: University of New Mexico Press, 1953.

Barker, Elliot. *Ramblings in the Field of Conservation.* Santa Fe: Sunshine Press, 1976.

Barker, Elliot. *Western Life and Adventures in the Great Southwest.* Kansas City, Mo.: Lowell Press, 1974.

Beardsley, Edward H. *Harry L. Russell and Agricultural Science in Wisconsin.* Madison: University of Wisconsin Press, 1969.

Billington, Ray A. *Frederick Jackson Turner: Historian, Scholar, Teacher.* New York: Oxford University Press, 1973.

Biographical Record of the Graduates and Former Students of the Yale Forest School. New Haven: Yale Forest School, 1913.

Biographical Review of Des Moines County, Iowa. Chicago: Hobart Publishing Co., 1905.

Blair, Walter A. *A Raft Pilot's Log: A History of the Great Rafting Industry on the Upper Mississippi, 1840–1915.* Cleveland: Arthur H. Clark Co., 1930.

Brink, Wellington. *Big Hugh: The Father of Soil Conservation.* New York: Macmillan Co., 1951.

Brown, David E. *The Grizzly in the Southwest: Documentary Of An Extinction.* Norman: University of Oklahoma Press, 1985.

Brown, David E., ed. *The Wolf in the Southwest: The Making of an Endangered Species.* Tucson: University of Arizona Press, 1983.

Callicott, J. Baird, ed. *Companion to* A Sand County Almanac. Madison: University of Wisconsin Press, 1987.

Clepper, Henry. *Professional Forestry in the United States.* Washington, D.C.: Resources for the Future, 1971.

Cockrum, E. L. *The Recent Mammals of Arizona.* Tucson: University of Arizona Press, 1960.

Connett, Eugene V. *Wildfowling in the Mississippi Flyway.* New York: Van Nostrand Co., Inc., 1949.

Cooke, Ron, and Richard Reeves. *Arroyos and Environmental Change in the American Southwest.* New York: Oxford University Press, 1976.

Correll, Donovan S., and Helen B. Correll. *Aquatic And Wetland Plants of Southwestern United States.* Stanford: Stanford University Press, 1975.

Curti, Merle, and Vernon Carstensen. *The University of Wisconsin: A History.* 2 vols. Madison: University of Wisconsin Press, 1949.

Curtis, John T. *The Vegetation Of Wisconsin: An Ordination of Plant Communities.* Madison: University of Wisconsin Press, 1959.

Dana, Samuel Trask. *Forest and Range Policy: Its Development in the United States.* New York: McGraw-Hill, 1956.

Davis, Richard C., ed. *Encyclopedia Of American Forest And Conservation History.* 2 vols. New York: Macmillan Co., 1983.

deBuys, William. *Enchantment and Exploitation: The Life and Hard Times of a New Mexico Mountain Range.* Albuquerque: University of New Mexico Press, 1985.

Elton, Charles. *Animal Ecology.* New York: Macmillan Co., 1927.

Errington, Paul L. *Of Predation and Life.* Ames: Iowa State University Press, 1967.

Fassett, Norman. *Spring Flora of Wisconsin.* 4th ed., revised and enlarged by Olive S. Thompson. Madison: University of Wisconsin Press, 1976.

Faul, Ronald J. *North American Forest and Conservation History: A Bibliography.* Forest History Society, 1977.

The Financier's Album of Prominent Bankers of America. New York: The Financier's Co., 1989.

Findley, J. S., A. H. Harris, D. E. Wilson, C. Jones. *Mammals Of New Mexico.* Albuquerque: University of New Mexico Press, 1975.

Flader, Susan, with Charles Steinhacker. *The Sand Country Of Aldo Leopold.* San Francisco: Sierra Club Books, 1973.

Flader, Susan. *Thinking Like a Mountain: Aldo Leopold and the Evolution of an Ecological Attitude toward Deer, Wolves, and Forests.* Columbia: University of Missouri Press, 1974.

Fox, Stephen. *John Muir and His Legacy: The American Conservation Movement.* Boston: Little, Brown and Co., 1981. Reprint: *The American Conservation Movement: John Muir and His Legacy.* Madison: University of Wisconsin Press, 1986.

Frome, Michael. *The Forest Service.* New York: Praeger Library, 1971.

Graves, Henry Solon. "Beginnings of Education in Forestry." In *Proceedings of the Society of American Foresters, 16–18 December 1948, Boston.* Washington, D.C.: Society of American Foresters, 1949.

Guthrie, John D. *The Forest Ranger And Other Verse.* Boston: Gorham Press, 1919.

Guthrie, John D., James A. White, Henry B. Steer, and Harry T. Whitlock, "*The*

Carpathians," *Tenth Engineers (Forestry), A.E.F., 1917–1919: Roster and Historical Sketch.* Washington, D.C.: The Carpathians, 1919.

Hall, Raymond. *Mammals Of Nevada.* Berkeley: University of California Press, 1946.

Hamerstrom, Frances. *Strictly for the Chickens.* Ames: Iowa State University Press, 1980.

Hastings, James R., and Raymond M. Turner. *The Changing Mile: An Ecological Study of Vegetation Change with Time in the Lower Mile of an Arid and Semi-arid Region.* Tucson: Universtiy of Arizona Press, 1965.

Hays, Samuel P. *Conservation and the Gospel of Efficiency.* Cambridge: Harvard University Press, 1959.

Hochbaum, Albert. *Canvasback on a Prairie Marsh.* Washington, D.C.: American Wildlife Institute, 1944.

Hornaday, William Temple. *Our Vanishing Wild Life.* New York: New York Zoological Society, 1913.

Hornaday, William Temple. *Thirty Years War for Wild Life.* Stamford: Permanent Wild Life Protection Fund, 1931.

Hornaday, William Temple. *Wild Life Conservation in Theory and Practice.* New Haven: Yale University Press, 1914.

Jordon, Philip D. *Catfish Bend: River Town and County Seat.* Burlington, Iowa: Craftsman Press, Inc., 1975.

Kimball, David, and Jim Kimball. *The Market Hunter.* Minneapolis: Dillon Press, 1969.

Larsen, James Arthur. *Wisconsin's Renewable Resources.* Madison: University of Wisconsin Press, 1957.

Lawson, William Pinknew. *The Log of a Timber Cruiser.* New York: Duffield And Company, 1915.

Lendt, David L. *Ding: The Life Of Jay Norwood Darling.* Des Moines, Iowa: Jay N. Darling Conservation Foundation, 1984.

Leopold, A. Starker. *Wildlife of Mexico.* Berkeley: University of California Press, 1959.

Ligon, J. Stokely. *Wild Life of New Mexico.* Santa Fe: New Mexico Department of Game and Fish, 1927.

McIntosh, Robert P. *The Background of Ecology: Concept and Theory.* Cambridge: Cambridge University Press, 1985.

McKim, Helen Turner, and Helen Parsons, eds. *Burlington on the Mississippi, 1883–1983.* Burlington, Iowa: Doran and Ward Lithographing Co., 1983.

Mearns, Edgar Alexander. *Mammals of the Mexican Boundary of the United States.* Smithsonian Institution, Bulletin 56. Washington, D.C.: GPO, 1907.

Muir, John. *Our National Parks.* Boston: Houghton Mifflin Co., 1901.

Nash, Roderick. *Wilderness and the American Mind.* 3d ed. New Haven: Yale University Press, 1982.

Nesbit, Robert C. *Wisconsin: A History.* Madison: University of Wisconsin Press, 1973.

Nixon, Edgar B., ed. *Franklin D. Roosevelt and Conservation, 1911–1945.* 2 vols. Washington, D.C.: GPO, 1957.

Osborn, Fairfield. *Our Plundered Planet.* Boston: Little, Brown and Co., 1948.

Ouspensky, Pyotr. *Tertium Organum.* New York: Alfred A. Knopf, 1925.

Overton, Richard C. *Burlington Route: A History of the Burlington Lines.* New York: Alfred A. Knopf, 1965.

Pinchot, Gifford. *Breaking New Ground.* New York: Harcourt, Brace and Company, 1947.

Portrait and Biographical Album of Des Moines County, Iowa. Chicago: Acme Publishing Co., 1888.

Pyne, Stephen. *Fire in America: A Cultural History of Wildland and Rural Fire.* Princeton: Princeton University Press, 1982.

Raines, William McLeod, and W. C. Barnes. *Cattle, Cowboys, and Rangers.* New York: Grosset and Dunlap, 1930.

Reiger, John F. *American Sportsmen and the Origins of Conservation.* New York: Winchester Press, 1975.

Reyner, J. H. *Ouspensky: The Unsung Genius.* London: George Allen and Unwin, 1981.

Robbins, William G. *American Forestry: A History of National, State, and Private Cooperation.* Lincoln: University of Nebraska Press, 1985.

Roberts, Paul H. *Hoof Prints on Forest Ranges.* San Antonio: The Naylor Company, 1963.

Roberts, Paul H. *Them Were the Days.* San Antonio: The Naylor Company, 1965.

Rowley, William D. *U.S. Forest Service Grazing and Rangelands: A History.* College Station: Texas A&M University Press, 1985.

Russell, Charles Edwin. *A-Rafting on The Mississipp'.* New York: The Century Company, 1928.

Russo, John P. *The Kaibab North Deer Herd: Its History, Problems, and Management."* Phoenix: Arizona Game and Fish Department, Wildlife Bulletin No. 7, 1964.

Sachse, Nancy D. *A Thousand Ages: The University of Wisconsin Arboretum.* Madison: Regents of the University of Wisconsin, 1965.

Salmund, John A. *The Civilian Conservation Corps, 1933–1942: A New Deal Case Study.* Durham, N.C.: Duke University Press, 1967.

Schullery, Paul, ed. *The Grand Canyon: Early Impressions.* Boulder: Colorado Associated University Press, 1981.

Searle, R. Newell, *Saving Quetico-Superior: A Land Set Apart.* St. Paul: Minnesota Historical Society Press, 1977.

Simms, D. Harper, *The Soil Conservation Service.* New York: Praeger Publishers, 1970.

Slaymaker, Samuel R., II. *Five Miles Away: The Story of the Lawrenceville School.* Princeton: Princeton University Press, 1985.

Smith, Darrell Hevenor. *The Forest Service: Its History, Organizations, and Activities.* Washington, D.C.: The Brookings Institution, 1930.

Solberg, Erling D. *New Laws for New Forests: Wisconsin's Forest Fire, Tax, Zoning, and County Forest Laws in Operation.* Madison: University of Wisconsin Press, 1961.

Spring, Samuel N., ed. *The First Half Century of the Yale School of Forestry.* New Haven: Yale University, 1950.

Steen, Harold K. *The United States Forest Service: A History.* Seattle: University of Washington Press, 1976.

Stegner, Wallace. *The Uneasy Chair: A Biography of Bernard DeVoto.* Garden City, N.Y.: Doubleday and Company, 1974.

Stegner, Wallace. *Beyond the Hundredth Meridian: John Wesley Powell and the Second Opening of the West.* Boston: Houghton Mifflin, 1954.

Stoddard, Herbert L. *The Bobwhite Quail: Its Habits, Preservation, and Increase.* New York: Charles Scribner's Sons, 1931.

Stoddard, Herbert L. *Memoirs of a Naturalist.* Norman: University of Oklahoma Press, 1969.

Tanner, Thomas, ed. *Aldo Leopold: The Man and His Legacy.* Ankeny, Iowa: Soil Conservation Society of America, 1987.

Taylor, Walter P. *The Deer of North America.* Harrisburg, Pa.: The Stackpole Co. and WMI, 1956.

Tennyson, Jon R. *A Singleness of Purpose: The Story of Ducks Unlimited.* Chicago: Ducks Unlimited, Inc., 1977.

Trefethen, James B. *An American Crusade for Wildlife.* New York: Winchester Press and the Boone and Crockett Club, 1975.

Trefethen, James B. *Crusade for Wildlife.* Harrisburg, Pennsylvania: Stackpole Co., 1961.

Turner, Frederick Jackson. *The Frontier in American History.* New York: Henry, Holt, and Company, 1920.

Twain, Mark. *The Adventures Of Huckleberry Finn.* Pocket Books. New York. 1973.

Twain, Mark. *Life on the Mississippi.* London: Oxford University Press, 1962.

The United States Biographical Dictionary and Portrait Gallery of Eminent and Self-Made Men. Iowa Volume. Chicago and New York: American Biography Publishing Co., 1878.

Vogt, William. *Road to Survival.* New York: William Sloane Associates, 1948.

Wadland, John Henry. *Ernest Thompson Seton: Man and Nature in the Progressive Era, 1880–1915.* New York: Arno Press, 1978.

Wild, Peter. *Pioneer Conservationists of Western America.* Missoula, Mont.: Mountain Press Publishing Co., 1979.

Worster, Donald. *Dust Bowl: The Southern Plains in the 1930s.* New York: Oxford University Press, 1979.

Worster, Donald. *Nature's Economy: A History of Ecological Ideas.* Cambridge: Cambridge University Press, 1985.

Yale University Yearbook, 1908. New Haven: Yale University Press, 1908.

B. ARTICLES

Allen, Durward. "These Fifty Years: The Conservation Record of North American Wildlife and Natural Resources Conferences." In *Transactions Of The Fiftieth North American Wildlife And Natural Resources Conference.* Washington, D.C.: WMI, 1985. Pp. 11–67.

Allen, Durward, et al. "Report of the Committee on North American Wildlife Policy." In *Transactions of the Thirty-Eighth North American Wildlife and Natural Resources Conference.* Washington, D.C.: WMI, 1973. Pp. 152–81.

Anderson, Clinton. "The Wilderness of Aldo Leopold." *Living Wilderness* 19, 51 (Winter 1954–55): 44–46.

Barnes, Will C. "Winning The Forest Range." *American Forests* 36, 7 (July 1930): 398–400, 466.

Beck, Thomas. "What President's Committee Intends to Do." In *Proceedings of the Twentieth American Game Conference.* Washington, D.C.: American Game Association, 1930. Pp. 82–91.

Blewett, Thomas J., and Grant Cottam. "History Of The University Of Wisconsin Arboretum Prairies." *WASAL* 72 (1984): 130–44.

Bradley, Nina Leopold, et al. "Great Possessions." *Wisconsin Academy Review.* 26, 1 (December 1979): 3–9.

Bradley, Harold C. "Aldo Leopold: Champion Of The Wilderness." *Sierra Club Bulletin* 36, 5 (May 1951): 14–18.

Broome, Harvey. "Our Basis of Understanding." *Living Wilderness* 19, 51 (Winter 1954–55): 47.

Callicott, J. Baird. "Aldo Leopold on Education, as Educator, and His Land Ethic in the Context of Environmental Education." *Journal of Environmental Education* 14 (1982): 34–41.

Callicott, J. Baird. "Animal Liberation: A Triangular Affair." *Environmental Ethics* 2, 4 (Winter 1980): 311–38.

Callicott, J. Baird. "Hume's Is/Ought Dichotomy and the Relation of Ecology to Leopold's Land Ethic." *Environmental Ethics* 4, 2 (Summer 1982): 163–74.

Callicott, J. Baird. "The Land Aesthetic." *Environmental Review* 7 (Winter 1983): 345–58.

Callicott, J. Baird. "Leopold's Land Aesthetic." *Journal of Soil and Water Conservation* 38, 4 (July–August 1983): 329–32.

Cart, Theodore W. "'New Deal' for Wildlife: A Perspective on Federal Conservation Policy, 1933–1940." *Pacific Northwest Quarterly* 63 (July 1922): 113–20.

Carter, Luther F. "The Leopolds: A Family Of Naturalists." *Science* 207, 4453 (7 March 1980): 1051–55.

Caughley, Graeme. "Eruption of Ungulate Populations, with Emphasis on Himalayan Thar in New Zealand." *Ecology* 51, 1 (Winter 1970): 53–72.

Caughley, Graeme, James T. Peek, and Susan Flader. "Comments on 'Irruption.'" *Wildlife Society Bulletin* 9, 3 (Fall 1981): 232–38.

Clements, Kendrick. "Herbert Hoover and Conservation, 1921–1933." *American Historical Review* 89 (February 1984): 67–88.

Cooper, C. F. "Changes in Vegetation Structure and Growth of Southwestern Pine Forests since White Settlement." *Ecological Monographs* 30, 2 (April 1960): 129–64.

Davis, Tom. "Aldo Leopold, 1887–1987, Part I: Aldo Leopold's Forgotten Book." *Wisconsin Sportsman* 16, 1 (January–February 1987): 25–28.

Denevan, William. "Livestock Numbers in Nineteenth-Century New Mexico and the Problem of Gullying in the Southwest." *Annals of the Association of American Geographers* 57 (1967): 691–703.

DeVoto, Bernard. "The West Against Itself," *Harper's* 194 (January 1947): 1–13.

Dolph, James A. "A Dedication to the Memory of William Temple Hornaday, 1854–1937." *Arizona and the West* 25, 3 (Autumn 1983): 209–12.

Dunlap, Thomas R. "Values for Varmints: Predator Control and Environmental Ideas, 1920–1939." *Pacific Historical Review* 53 (May 1984), 141–61.

Editorial. "Adventures In Cooperative Conservation." *American Forests* 63, 10 (October 1957): 15.

Editorial. "An American Game Policy." *American Forests* 37, 1 (January 1931): 41.

Editorial. "Preservation of the Rincon Mountains and Creation of Saguaro National Monument as Little-Known Consequences of the Establishment of the Boyce Thompson Southwestern Arboretum. *Desert Plants* 8, 2 (1987): 50, 95.

Egerton, F. N. "History of Ecology: Achievements and Opportunities, Part I." *Journal Of History Of Biology* 16, 2 (Summer 1983): 259–310.

Egerton, F. N. "History of Ecology: Achievements and Opportunities, Part II." *Journal of History of Biology* 18, 1 (Spring 1985): 103–43.

Elder, John. "Hunting in Sand County." *Orion Nature Quarterly* 5, 4 (Autumn 1986): 46–53.

Errington, Paul. "In Appreciation Of Aldo Leopold." *JWM* 12, 4 (October 1948): 341–50.

Etter, Alfred. "A Day with Aldo Leopold." *The Land* 7, 3 (Fall 1948).

Flader, Susan. "Aldo Leopold, AFA, And The Southwest." *American Forests* 87, 10 (October 1981), 38–41, 55–57.

Flader, Susan. "Aldo Leopold and the Wilderness Idea." *Living Wilderness* 43, 147 (December 1979): 4–8.

Flader, Susan. "Aldo Leopold's Challenge to Educators." In *Transactions of the Forty-Eighth North American Wildlife and Natural Resources Conference*. Washington, D.C.: WMI, 1983.

Flader, Susan. "Leopold's 'Some Fundamentals of Conservation': A Commentary." *Environmental Ethics* 1, 2 (Spring 1979): 143–48.

Flader, Susan. "Review Of *The Quiet Revolution*." *Journal of Forest History* 18, 1–2 (April 1974): 36.

Fleming, Donald. "Roots of the New Conservation Movement." *Perspectives in American History* 6 (1972): 7–91.

Flint, Howard R. "Wasted Wilderness." *American Forests and Forest Life* 32, 391 (July 1926): 407–10.

Fox, Stephen. "Liberty Hyde Bailey: The Earth as Whole, The Earth as Holy." *Orion Nature Quarterly* 2, 4 (Autumn 1983): 12–19.

Fox, Stephen. "We Want No Straddlers." *Wilderness* 48, 167 (Winter 1984), 5–19.

French, Lewis G. "Coon Valley Saga." *American Forests* 63, 10 (October 1957): 20–23, 50–60.

Frey, David G. "Wisconsin: The Birge-Juday Era." In *Limnology in North America*, David G. Frey, ed. Madison: University of Wisconsin Press, 1963. Pp. 3–54.

Fritzell, Peter A. "Aldo Leopold's *A Sand County Almanac* and the Conflicts of Ecological Conscience." *WASAL* 64 (1976): 22–46.

Gibbons, Boyd. "A Durable Scale Of Values." *National Geographic* 160, 5 (November 1981): 682–708.

Glover, James, and Regina Glover. "Bob Marshall: A Natural." *American Forests* 92, 9 (September 1986): 24–26, 54–55.

Glover, James, and Regina Glover. "Robert Marshall: Portrait of a Liberal Forester." *Journal of Forest History* 30, 3 (July 1986): 112–19.

Goc, Michael. "The Great Dustbowl: It First Came to Wisconsin." *Wisconsin Trails* 25, 4 (July–August 1984): 20–24.

Graves, Henry S. "The Forest Engineers." *American Forestry* 25, 306 (June 1919): 1109.

Graves, Henry S. "The National Forests and Wild Life." *Recreation* (May 1915): 236–39.

Graves, Henry S. "When Forestry Education Began." *American Forests* 55, 2 (February 1949): 18–19, 37, 40.

Greeley, William B. "The American Lumberjack in France." *American Forestry* 25, 306 (June 1919): 1093–108.

Haugen, Arnold O. "History of the Iowa Cooperative Wildlife Research Unit." *Iowa Academy of Science* 73 (1966): 136–45.

Hays, Samuel P. "Gifford Pinchot and the Conservation Movement." *Living Wilderness* 44, 149 (June 1980): 4–9.

Heald, Weldon F. "The Aldo Leopold Memorial Plaque." *American Forests.* 60, 12 (December 1954): 23, 47–49.

Heffernan, James. "The Land Ethic: A Critical Appraisal." *Environmental Ethics* 4, 4 (Winter 1982): 235–47.

Helms, Douglas. "The CCC: Demonstrating the Value of Soil Conservation." *Journal of Soil and Water Conservation* 40, 2 (March–April 1985): 184–88.

Hochbaum, Albert. "The Effect of Concentrated Hunting Pressure on Waterfowl Breeding Stock." In *Transactions of the Twelfth NAWC.* Washington, D.C.: AWI, 1947. Pp. 53–64.

Huey, Ben M. "Evan W. Kelley." *JF* 48, 7 (July 1950): 499–500.

Kaufman, Sharon, and Frederic Leopold. "Built on Honor to Endure." *Iowa Natural Heritage* (Winter 1985): 1.

Krog, Carl E. "Organizing the Production of Leisure: Herbert Hoover and the Conservation Movement in the 1920's." *Wisconsin Magazine of History* (Spring 1984): 199–218.

Krutch, Joseph Wood. "Wild Geese — or Television." *The Nation* 169, 26 (24 December 1949): 628.

Leopold, Luna B. "Vegetation of Southwestern Watersheds in the Nineteenth Century." *Geographical Review* 41 (1951): 295–316.

Little, Charles E. "Aldo Leopold's Legacy." *American Land Forum* 6, 3 (Summer 1986): 21–22.

Little, Charles E. "In a Landscape of Hope." *Wilderness* 48, 168 (Spring 1985): 21–30.

Malin, James. "Ecology and History." *Scientific Monthly* 70 (May 1950): 295–98.

Mann, Roberts. "Aldo Leopold: Priest and Prophet." *American Forests* 60, 8 (August 1954): 23, 42–43.

Marsh, Raymond E. "Timber Cruising in the Early Days." *American Forests* 74, 2 (February 1968): 28–31.

Marsh, Raymond E. "Timber Cruising on National Forests of the Southwest." *Journal of Forest History* 13, 3 (October 1969): 22–32.

McCabe, Robert A. "The Stoughton-Faville Prairie Preserve: Some Historical Aspects." *WASAL* 66 (1978): 25–49.

McCabe, T. T. "More Game Birds in America, Inc." *Condor* 33, 6 (November–December 1931): 259–60.

Bibliography

Mitchell, John G. "In Wilderness Was the Preservation of a Smile." *Wilderness* 48, 169 (Summer 1985): 10–21.

Mortensen, Daniel R. "The Deterioration of Forest Grazing Land: A Wider Context for the Effects of World War I." *Journal of Forest History* 22 (October 1978): 224–25.

Mulhern, Rick. "Seventy-five Years of Wisconsin Forestry." *Wisconsin Natural Resources* 11, 2 (March–April 1987): 19–31.

Nash, Roderick. "Arthur Carhart: Wildland Advocate." *Living Wilderness* 44, 151 (December 1980): 32–34.

Nash, Roderick. "Path to Preservation." *Wilderness* 48, 165 (Summer 1984): 5–11.

Noland, Lowell. "Some Wisconsin Biologists of the Past and the Significance of Their Work." *WASAL* 54 (1965): 95–106.

Osborn, Fairfield. "Urgency of Conservation Education." In *Transactions of the Eleventh NAWC*. Washington, D.C.: AWI, 1946. Pp. 74–75.

Pager, John. "The CCC Program with Emphasis on Wisconsin." *Proceedings of the Forest History Association of Wisconsin*. Appleton, September 16–17, 1983. Pp. 11–15, 1933–45.

Pearson, G. A. "Preservation of Natural Areas in the National Forests." *Ecology* 3, 4 (October 1922): 284–87.

Rakestraw, Lawrence. "Conservation Historiography: An Assessment." *Pacific Northwest Quarterly* 51 (August 1972): 271–88.

Rakestraw, Lawrence. "News, Comments, and Letters." *Journal of Forest History* 19, 1 (January 1975): 41.

Ribbens, Dennis. "The Making of *A Sand County Almanac*." *WASAL* 70 (1982): 3–12.

Ribbens, Dennis. "Making of a Title: *A Sand County Almanac*." *Wisconsin Academy Review* (September 1982): 8–10.

Ringland, Arthur, with Fern Ingersoll. "Pioneering in Southwest Forestry." *Journal of Forest History* 17, 1 (April 1973): 4–11.

Roth, Dennis. "The National Forests and the Campaign for Wilderness Legislation." *Journal of Forest History* 28, 3 (July 1984): 112–25.

Sachse, Nancy D. "Madison's Public Wilderness: The University Of Wisconsin Arboretum." *Wisconsin Magazine of History* 44, 2 (Winter 1960–61): 117–31.

Sartz, Richard S. "Soil Erosion in the Lake States Driftless Area – A Historical Perspective." *WASAL* 65 (1977): 5–15.

Schmaltz, Norman J. "P.S. Lovejoy: Michigan's Cantankerous Conservationist." *Journal of Forest History* 17, 2 (April 1975): 72.

Schoenfeld, Clay. "Aldo Leopold Remembered." *Audubon* 80 (May 1978): 28–37.

Schorger, A. W. "Aldo Leopold." *WCB* 39 (January–February 1974): 16.

Searle, R. Newall. "Autos or Canoes: Wilderness Controversy in the Superior National Forest." *Journal of Forest History* 22, 2 (April 1978): 68–77.

Smith, E. R. "History of Grazing Industry and Range Conservation Development in the Rio Grande Basin." *Journal of Range Management* 6, 6 (November 1953): 405–9.

Sorenson, Douglas. "Coon Creek Watershed: Cradle of Conservation." *Journal of Soil and Water Conservation* 38, 5 (September–October 1983): 393–95.

Stanley, George. "A Visit with Frederick Leopold." *Ducks Unlimited.* 49, 5 (September–October 1985): 35–36, 96–103.

Steen, Harold K. "Grazing and the Environment: A History of the Forest Service Stock-Reduction Policy." *Agricultural History* 49, 1 (January 1975): 238–42.

Stegner, Wallace. "Living on Our Principal." *Wilderness* 48, 168 (Spring 1985): 5–21.

Swanson, Gustav A. "Creation and Early History." *Wildlife Society Bulletin* 15, 1 (Spring 1987): 9–14.

Swift, Ernest. "Aldo Leopold: Wisconsin's Conservation Prophet." *Wisconsin Tales And Trails* 2, 3 (Fall 1961): 2–5.

Swift, Ernest. "They Laughed at Us." *American Forests* 67, 5 (May 1961): 20–22, 54–56.

Thomsen, John W. "Norman C. Fassett." *Taxon* 4, 3 (May 1955): 49–51.

Turnage, William. "A Land Ethic for the 1980's." *Living Wilderness* (December 1979): 33–35.

Vogt, William, and Hoyes Lloyd. "Pan-American Conservation." In *Transactions of the Eleventh NAWC.* Washington, D.C.: AWI, 1946. Pp. 5–10.

Watkins, T. H. "The Terrible-Tempered Mr. Ickes." *Audubon* 86 (March 1984): 94–111.

Waugh, Frank A. "Wilderness to Keep." *Review of Reviews* 81 (1939): 146.

Weaver, Harold. "Fire as an Ecological Factor in the Southwestern Ponderosa Pine Forests." *JF* 49, 2 (February 1951): 93–98.

Wegner, Rob. "The Deer Hunting Adventures Of Aldo Leopold." *Deer And Deer Hunting* 4, 3 (January–February 1981): 17–24.

Wehrwein, George S. "The Economist's Approach to Ecology." *JF* 37, 9 (September 1939): 731–34.

Wehrwein, George S. "A Social and Economic Program for the Sub-Marginal Areas of the Lake States." *JF* 29, 10 (October 1931): 915–24.

White, Richard. "American Environmental History: The Development of a New Historical Field." *Pacific Historical Review* 54, 3 (August 1985): 297–335.

Wolfe, Michael. "The History of German Game Administration." *Journal of Forest History* 14, 3 (October 1970): 6–16.

Yates, Norris. "The Inadequate Politics of Aldo Leopold." *Proceedings of the Fifth Midwest Prairie Conference.* Ames: Iowa State University, 1978. Pp. 219–21.

C. NEWSPAPERS

American Weekly
Arizona Star
The Badger Sportsman (Wisconsin)
Burlington (Iowa) *Democrat-Journal.*
The (Burlington, Iowa) *Hawkeye*
Albuquerque Morning Journal.
The Capital Times (Madison, Wisconsin)
The Daily Graphic (Portage la Prairie, Manitoba)
Green Bay Gazette
Milwaukee Journal
The Nation

Bibliography

New York Herald Tribune
Save Wisconsin's Deer (Wisconsin)
The Sheboygan (Wisconsin) *Press*
Silver City (New Mexico) *Enterprise.*
Silver City (New Mexico) *Independent.*
Wisconsin State Journal (Madison)

D. GOVERNMENT PUBLICATIONS

Bates, Robert W. "The Coronado Trail: First Federal Aid Highway." *Cultural Resources Report No. 26.* Albuquerque: USDA, USFS, Southwestern Region, December 1978, 12–33.
Brokaw, H. P., ed. *Wildlife in America: Contributions to an Understanding of American Wildlife and its Conservation.* Washington, D.C.: Council on Environmental Quality, GPO, 1978.
Hawkins, A. S., R. C. Hanson, H. K. Nelson, H. M. Reeves. *Flyways: Pioneering Waterfowl Management in North America.* USDI, USFWS. Washington, D.C.: GPO, 1984.
Hendee, J. C., G. H. Stankey, R. C. Lucas. *Wilderness Management.* USDA, USFS, Misc. Publ. No. 1365. Washington, D.C.: GPO, October 1978.
Kallman, Harmon, ed. *Restoring America's Wildlife: 1937–1987.* USDI, USFWS. Washington, D.C.: GPO, 1987.
Minutes of the Wisconsin Conservation Commission. Wisconsin Conservation Department. SHSW.
Nelson, Charles A. *History of the U.S. Forest Products Laboratory (1910–1963).* USDA, USFS, USFPL, 1971.
Proceedings of the National Conference on Outdoor Recreation, 20–21 January 1926. Senate Document No. 117. Washington, D.C.: GPO, 1926.
Scott, Walter E. "Conservation's First Century in Wisconsin: Landmark Dates and People." Conservation Centennial Symposium, May 1967. Madison: WCD, 1967.
Swift, Ernest. "A History of Wisconsin Deer." WCD Bulletin, Publ. 323. Madison: WCD, 1946.
Tucker, Edwin, and George Fitzpatrick. *Men Who Matched the Mountains.* Washington, D.C.: GPO, 1972.
The Use of the National Forest Reserves: Regulations and Instructions. USDA, USFS, 1 July 1905.
USFS Bulletin. Washington, D.C.: USDA, USFS.

E. UNPUBLISHED MANUSCRIPTS

Boles, Donald E. "Administrative Rule Making in Wisconsin Conservation." Ph.D. diss., University of Wisconsin, 1956.
Brower, Stephen. "Charles Starker: A German Immigrant Contributes to Burlington's Development." Prepared for Aldo Leopold Community Tribute, Burlington, Iowa. 15 April 1980.
Brower, Stephen. "Research Report: Crapo Park Master Plan." Burlington, Iowa. December 1979.

Brower, Stephen. Starker-Leopold Historic District Application Form. Burlington, Iowa. December 1981.

East, Dennis. "Walter Power and Forestry in Wisconsin: Issues in Conservation, 1890–1915." Ph.D. diss., University of Wisconsin, 1971.

Flader, Susan. "Aldo Leopold: A Historical and Philosophical Perspective." Des Moines County (Iowa) Historical Society. 1980.

Flader, Susan. "Ecological Science and the Expansion of Our Forest Heritage." Society of American Foresters National Convention. Washington, D.C. 20 September 1975.

Gilligan, James P. "The Development of Policy and Administration of Forest Service Primitive and Wilderness Areas in the Western United States." Ph.D. diss., University of Michigan, 1953.

Hunger, Edwin. Untitled memoir. SHSW Archives. Undated.

Kaufman, Sharon. "'Built on Honor to Endure': Evolution Of The Leopold Family Philosophy." Master's thesis. University of Iowa. 1985.

"La Reunion de La Familia de Eloisa Luna de Otero de Bergere." Prepared by Jack J. Kenney. Santa Fe, New Mexico. 1980.

Leopold, Aldo. "Organizing Conservation in Wisconsin/Rough Outline of an Organic Act for Conservation in Wisconsin." SHSW Archives. 18 October 1926.

Leopold, Frederic. "Aldo's Middle School Years—Summer Vacation." Undated.

Leopold, Frederic. "Leopold Family Anecdotes." 1982.

Leopold, Frederic. "Recollections of an Old Member." 1977.

Leopold, Luna B. "Notes on the History of the Publication of Aldo Leopold's *A Sand County Almanac*." Knox College Library. Galesburg, Illinois. 20 September 1984.

McCabe, Robert. "Aldo Leopold: The Professor." 1986.

Main, Jackson Turner. "History of the Conservation of Wild Life in Wisconsin." Masters thesis, University of Wisconsin, 1940.

Meine, Curt. "Building 'The Land Ethic': A History of Aldo Leopold's Most Important Essay." Master's thesis. University of Wisconsin–Madison. 1983.

Pitman, Lucretia. "Solomon Luna, Sheepmaster and Politician of New Mexico, 1848–1910." Master's thesis. St. Louis University, 1944.

Reisch, Anna Lou. "Conservation under Franklin Delano Roosevelt." Ph.D. diss., University of Wisconsin, 1952.

Scott, Walter E. "Biographical Notes on W. J. P. Aberg." SHSW Archives. Madison, Wisconsin. 12 March 1952.

Scott, Walter E. "Chronology of the Public's Part in Wisconsin Conservation History." SHSW Archives. 25 May 1948.

Tucker, Edwin. "The Forest Service in the Southwest." USDA, USFS, Southwestern Region, Regional Headquarters. Albuquerque, New Mexico. Undated.

F. PAPERS

William J. P. Aberg Papers. SHSW Archives. Madison, Wisconsin.

Clinton B. Anderson Papers. Library of Congress. Washington, D.C.

A. M. Bergere Family Papers. New Mexico State Records Center and Archives. Santa Fe, New Mexico.

Bibliography

Bradley Study Center Files. Baraboo, Wisconsin.

Arthur Carhart Papers. Division of State Archives and Published Records. Denver, Colorado.

Arthur Carhart Papers. State Historical Society of Iowa. Ames, Iowa.

Carson National Forest Files. Carson National Forest Headquarters. Taos, New Mexico.

Herman H. Chapman Papers. Yale University Archives. New Haven, Connecticut.

Cosmos Club Records. Washington, D.C.

John T. Curtis Papers. UW Archives. Madison, Wisconsin.

Jay N. Darling Papers. University of Iowa Library. Iowa City, Iowa.

Paul Errington Papers. Iowa State University Library. Ames, Iowa.

Norman Fassett Files. Department of Botany. Madison, Wisconsin.

Gila National Forest Files. Gila National Forest Headquarters. Silver City, New Mexico.

Grand Canyon National Park Records. Grand Canyon, Arizona.

Henry Solon Graves Papers. Yale University Archives. New Haven, Connecticut.

John D. Guthrie Papers. Yale University Archives. New Haven, Connecticut.

C. L. Harrington Papers. SHSW Archives. Madison, Wisconsin.

Izaak Walton League of Wisconsin Papers. SHSW Archives. Madison, Wisconsin.

Knox College Archives. Galesburg, Illinois.

Leon Kneipp Papers. Arizona Historical Society. Tucson, Arizona.

Leopold Desk Company Records. University of Iowa Library. Iowa City, Iowa.

Aldo Leopold Documents. USFPL Library. Madison, Wisconsin.

Aldo Leopold Files. SHSW Archives. Madison, Wisconsin.

Aldo Leopold File. The Lawrenceville School. Lawrenceville, New Jersey.

Leopold Library. University of California–Berkeley, Department of Forestry and Resource Management. Berkeley, California.

Aldo Leopold Papers. UW Archives. Madison, Wisconsin.

Gordon MacQuarrie Papers. SHSW Archives. Madison, Wisconsin.

Haskell Noyes Papers. SHSW Archives. Madison, Wisconsin.

Harry L. Russell Papers. UW Archives. Madison, Wisconsin.

A. W. Schorger Papers. UW Archives. Madison, Wisconsin.

Walter E. Scott Papers. SHSW Archives. Madison, Wisconsin.

Paul B. Sears Papers. Yale University Archives. New Haven, Connecticut.

Ward Shepard Papers. Yale University Archives. New Haven, Connecticut.

Ernest Swift Papers. SHSW Archives. Madison, Wisconsin.

Tonto National Forest Files. Tonto National Forest Headquarters. Phoenix, Arizona.

UW Arboretum Papers. UW Archives. Madison, Wisconsin.

UW College of Agriculture Records. UW Archives. Madison, Wisconsin.

UW Department of Wildlife Ecology Records. UW Archives. Madison, Wisconsin.

UW Department of Wildlife Ecology Library. Madison, Wisconsin.

US Forest Products Laboratory Library. Madison, Wisconsin.

USFS History Section. USDA Headquarters. Washington, D.C.

USFS Records. Archives of the United States. Record Group no. 95. Washington, D.C.

USFS, Southwestern Region Records. Sharlot Hall Museum. Prescott, Arizona.

USFS, Southwestern Region Records. Southwestern Region Headquarters. Albuquerque, New Mexico.

George S. Wehrwein Papers. UW Archives. Madison, Wisconsin.

WCD Files. SHSW Archives. Madison, Wisconsin.

Wilderness Society Records. Washington, D.C.

Wildlife Management Institute Records. Washington, D.C.

Fred Winn Papers. Arizona Historical Society. Tucson, Arizona.

G. INTERVIEWS

1. INTERVIEWS WITH AUTHOR

Elliot Barker. 1 April 1985.

Charles and Nina Leopold Bradley. 1–2 November 1984.

William Elder. 11 July 1985.

Francis and Frederick Hamerstrom. 30 July 1985.

Arthur Hasler. 21 November 1986.

Arthur Hawkins. 7 June 1986.

Joseph J. Hickey. 22 May 1984.

Hans Albert Hochbaum. 5 February 1986.

Jack Kenney, Bergere Kenney. 3 April 1985.

A. Carl Leopold. 4–5 September 1985.

Estella E. Leopold. 22–24 January 1985.

Frederic Leopold. 7–9 March 1984. 18–21 June 1984.

Luna B. Leopold. 15–17 January 1985.

L. J. Markwardt. 30 September 1985.

Robert McCabe. 9–12 April 1984.

Clarence Shoenfeld. 5 March 1986.

Lyle Sowls. 25 March 1985.

Douglas Wade. 31 March 1986.

2. JIM VOEGELI/ALDO LEOPOLD COLLECTION

SHSW Archives. This collection of taped interviews with Aldo Leopold's family, friends, and colleagues was prepared by Jim Voegeli, a student in the Department of Communication Arts in the early 1970s, for use in the production of a radio documentary, "Remembering Aldo Leopold." Used with the permission of Mr. Voegeli.

George Becker. 1 September 1973.

Nina Leopold Bradley. 10 August 1973.

Robert Ellarson. 9 August 1973.

John and Virginia Emlen. 17 November 1973.

Seth Gordon. Undated.

James Hale. 5 April 1974.

Francis and Frederick Hamerstrom. 31 August 1973, 5 April 1974.

Arthur Hawkins, Laurence Jahn, Dave Tillotson. 23 November 1973.

Ruth Hine. 5 April 1974.

Vivian Horn. 20 April 1974.

A. Carl Leopold. 18 October 1973.
Frederic Leopold. 12 January 1974, 9 March 1974.
Marie Leopold Lord. 12 January 1974.
Robert McCabe. 22 January 1974, 5 April 1974.
Patricia Schleicher. 21 September 1973.
Lyle Sowls. Undated.
Alice Harper Stokes. 11 January 1974.
Dr. H. Kent Tenney. 20 August 1973.
Douglas Wade. 23–24 November 1973.
Anne (Mrs. Leonard) Wing. 3 April 1974.

3. *MISCELLANEOUS INTERVIEWS* *(transcripts)*

William J. P. Aberg. SHSW Archives. 25 May 1961.
Frank Graass. SHSW Archives. 28 January 1965.
Frederic Leopold. Des Moines County Historical Society. Burlington, Iowa. 28 April 1981.
Marvin Schweers. SHSW Archives. 29 August 1960.
Ernest Swift. SHSW Archives. 11 November 1964.
Arthur C. Ringland. Regional Oral History Project. Bancroft Library, University of California–Berkeley. Berkeley, California. 1965, 1966.
Paul Roberts. Regional Oral History Project. Berkeley, California. 1964, 1965.
Raymond Marsh. Regional Oral History Project. Berkeley, California. 14 February 1966.

H. LETTERS

Owen J. Gromme to author, 18 August 1985.
Arthur S. Hawkins to author, 3 April 1986, 18 April 1986, 18 May 1986.
JJH to author, 9 May 1985.
HAH to author, 28 June 1986, 9 July 1986.
Elizabeth (Mrs. A. Starker) Leopold to author, 1 May 1986, 5 July 1986.
EEL to author, 30 March 1986, 17 August 1985, 11 December 1986.
Douglas Wade to author, 12 August 1985, 26 June 1986, 18 July 1986.

I. PUBLISHED WRITINGS OF ALDO LEOPOLD

This list of the published writings of Aldo Leopold is adapted from that in the index of the Leopold Papers in the University of Wisconsin Archives. An early version of this list was prepared by Joseph Hickey in the aftermath of Leopold's death. A more extensive bibliography was prepared for the University of Wisconsin Archives by Susan Flader in the 1970s. This listing follows that of Flader, who deserves principal credit for its compilation.

EARLY PUBLICATIONS

The Carson Pine Cone. Newsletter of the Carson National Forest. 1911–1914. Tres Piedras, New Mexico. Various contributions.

Bibliography

Game and Fish Handbook. Albuquerque: USFS, USDA, D-3, 5 September 1915.
The Pine Cone. Albuquerque: NMGPA, nineteen issues, December 1915–July 1931.
(Edited, many articles written by AL.)

1916

Letter signed by AL et al. "Protectionists Take Issue with George Willets." *The Evening Herald* (Albuquerque, 1 March 1916), 8.
"Game Conservation; A Warning, Also an Opportunity." *Arizona* 7: 1–2 (Oct.–Nov.–Dec. 1916): 6.

1917

"Progressive Cattle Range Management." *The Breeder's Gazette* 71, 18 (3 May 1917): 919.
"Unique Punishment for Slayers of Song Birds." *Bulletin* AGPA 6, 4 (October 1917): 22.

1918

"The Popular Wilderness Fallacy: An Idea That Is Fast Exploding." *Outers' Book –Recreation* 58, 1 (January 1918): 43–46.
"Do Purple Martins Inhabit Bird Boxes in the West?" *Condor* 20:2 (March–April 1918): 93.
"Forestry and Game Conservation." *JF* 16, 4 (April 1918): 404–11.
"Make Stinking Lake a Game Refuge." *Outers' Book – Recreation* 58, 4 (April 1918): 291. Also in *Bulletin* AGPA, 7, 1 (January 1918): 16.
"Are Red-headed Woodpeckers Moving West?" *Condor* 20, 3 (May–June 1918): 122.
"Restocking the National Forests with Elk: Where and How It May Be Done." *Outers' Book – Recreation* 58, 5 (May 1918): 412–15.
"What About Drainage?" *Bernalillo County Farm Bureau News* 1, 1 (June 1918), 2.
"Putting the "AM" in Game Warden: The Story of How the New Mexico Game Protective Association Substituted *Push for Politics* in Their State Game Department." *Sportsmen's Review* 54, 9 (31 August 1918), 173–74.

1919

"Notes on Red-headed Woodpecker and Jack Snipe in New Mexico." *Condor* 21, 1 (January–February 1919): 40.
"The National Forests: The Last Free Hunting Grounds of the Nation." *JF* 17, 2 (February 1919): 150–53.
"Notes on the Behavior of Pintail Ducks in a Hailstorm." *Condor* 21, 2 (March–April 1919): 87.
"Forest Service Salaries and the Future of the National Forests." *JF* 17, 4 (April 1919): 398–401.
"Wild Lifers vs. Game Farmers: A Plea for Democracy in Sport." *Bulletin* AGPA 8, 2 (April 1919): 6–7.

"Relative Abundance of Ducks in the Rio Grande Valley." *Condor* 21, 3 (May–June 1919): 122.

"Notes on the Weights and Plumages of Ducks in New Mexico." *Condor* 21, 3 (May–June 1919): 128–29.

"A Breeding Record for the Red-headed Woodpecker in New Mexico." *Condor* 21, 4 (July–August 1919): 173–74.

"City Tree Planting." *American Forestry* 25, 308 (August 1919): 1295.

"Differential Sex Migration of Mallards in New Mexico." *Condor* 21, 5 (September–October 1919): 182–83.

"A Plea for State-owned Ducking Grounds." *Wild Life* (October 1919): 9.

"A Turkey Hunt in the Datil National Forest." *Wild Life* (December 1919): 4–5, 16.

"The Mystery," "Resolutions of a Ranger," "Spare Time," "The Tourist and the Ranger," "The Busy Season." In John D. Guthrie, ed., *The Forest Ranger and Other Verse,* 45–46, 53–54, 66–67, 80–81, 116.

"Destroying Female Trees." *American Forestry* 25, 311 (November 1919): 1479.

1920

"Wanted – National Forest Game Refuges." *Bulletin AGPA* 9, 1 (January 1920): 8–10, 22.

"Determining the Kill Factor for Black-tail Deer in the Southwest." *JF* 18, 2 (February 1920): 131–34.

"'Piute Forestry' vs. Forest Fire Prevention." *Southwestern Magazine* 2, 3 (March 1920): 12–13.

"The Game Situation in the Southwest." *Bulletin AGPA* 9, 2 (April 1920): 3–5.

"The Forestry of the Prophets." *JF* 18, 4 (April 1920): 412–19.

"Range of the Magpie in New Mexico." *Condor* 22, 3 (May–June 1920): 112.

"Further Notes on Differential Sex Migration." *Condor* 22, 4 (July–August 1920): 156–57.

"Mallard Decoys." *Forest and Stream* (November 1920).

"What Is a Refuge?" *All Outdoors* 8, 2 (November 1920): 46–47. Condensed as "The Essentials of the Game Refuge." *The Literary Digest* 68, 3 (15 January 1920): 54.

"A Complaint." *The Game Breeder* (24): 288–89.

1921

"A Hunter's Notes on Doves in the Rio Grande Valley." *Condor* 23, 1 (January–February 1921): 19–21.

"A Plea for Recognition of Artificial Works in Forest Erosion Control Policy." *JF* 19, 3 (March 1921): 267–73.

"Weights and Plumage of Ducks in the Rio Grande Valley." *Condor* 23, 3 (May–June 1921): 85–86.

"The Wilderness and Its Place in Forest Recreational Policy." *JF* 19, 7 (November 1921): 718–21.

1922

"The Posting Problem." *Outdoor Life* 49, 3 (March 1922): 186–88.

"Road-runner Caught in the Act." *Condor* 24, 5 (September–October 1922): 183.

1923

"Wild Followers of the Forest: The Effect of Forest Fires on Game and Fish—The Relation of Forests to Game Conservation." *American Forestry* 29, 357 (September 1923): 515–19, 568.

"The 'Following' Habit in Hawks and Owls." *Condor* 25, 5 (September–October 1923): 180.

Watershed Handbook. Albuquerque: USFS, USDA, D-3, December 1923. Revised and reissued October 1934.

1924

"Pioneers and Gullies." *Sunset Magazine* 52, 5 (May 1924): 15–16, 91–95.

"Grass, Brush, Timber, and Fire in Southern Arizona." *JF* 22, 6 (October 1924): 1–10.

"Quail Production—A Remedy for the 'Song Bird List.'" *Outdoor America* 3, 4 (November 1924): 42–43.

"Coot Caught by Turtle." *Condor* 26, 6 (November–December 1924): 226.

1925

"The Utilization Conference." *JF* 23, 1 (January 1925): 98–100.

"A Seven-year Duck Census of the Middle Rio Grande Valley." *Condor* 27, 1 (January–February 1925): 8–11.

"Recent Developments in Game Management." *USFS Bulletin* 9, 9 (2 March 1925): 1–2.

"Conserving the Covered Wagon." *Sunset Magazine* 54, 3 (March 1925): 21, 56.

"Natural Reproduction of Forests." *Parks and Recreation* 9, 2 (April 1925): 366–72.

"The Pig in the Parlor." *USFS Bulletin* 9, 23 (8 June 1925): 1–2.

"Ten New Developments in Game Management." *American Game* 14, 3 (July 1925): 7–8, 20.

"The Last Stand of the Wilderness." *American Forests and Forest Life* 31, 382 (October 1925): 599–604. Abstracted as "The Vanishing Wilderness" in *The Literary Digest* 90, 6 (7 August 1925): 54, 56–57; excerpted in "Recreation Resources of Federal Lands," *Proceedings of the National Conference on Outdoor Recreation* (Washington, D.C.: 1928), 86–88, 91.

"Wilderness as a Form of Land Use." *The Journal of Land & Public Utility Economics* 1, 4 (October 1925): 398–404.

"Forestry in Wisconsin." *Report of 3rd Annual Convention of the Wisconsin Division of IWLA,* 14–15 October 1925, Green Bay, Wisconsin.

"A Plea for Wilderness Hunting Grounds." *Outdoor Life* 56, 5 (November 1925): 348–50.

"Wastes in Forest Utilization—What Can Be Done to Prevent Them." *Empire State Forest Products Association Bulletin* 22 (December 1925): 6–9; *Proceedings of the State-wide Wood Utilization Conference,* Syracuse, N.Y., 12 November 1925; abstracted as "Wastes in Utilization" in *Southern Lumberman* 121, 1574 (28 November 1925): 39–40.

"Forestry and Game Management." *Colorado Forester* (Ft. Collins: Colorado Agriculture College, 1925), 29–30.

Bibliography

1926

Untitled address on wilderness conservation. *Proceedings of the Second National Conference on Outdoor Recreation, 20–21* January 1926 (Senate Document no. 117, Washington, D.C., 1926), 61–65.

"Wood Preservation and Forestry." *Proceedings of the Twenty-second Annual Meeting of the American Wood-Preservers' Association,* 26–28 January 1926, 30–35. Reprinted in *Railway Engineering and Maintenance* 22, 2 (February 1926): 60–61); *Railway Age* 80, 5 (30 January 1926): 346.

"On the Reputations of Forests." *The Forest Worker* 2, 3 (May 1926): 17–18.

"The Way of the Waterfowl: How the Anthony Bill Will Help Ducks and Duck Hunting; An Example of New Mexico's Refuge System in Actual Operation." *American Forests and Forest Life* 32, 389 (May 1926): 287–91.

"Comment [on Howard R. Flint, 'Wasted Wilderness.']" *American Forests and Forest Life* 32, 391 (July 1926): 410–11.

"Fires and Game." *JF* 24, 6 (October 1926): 726–28.

"The Next Move: A Size-up of the Migratory Bird Situation." *Outdoor Life* 58, 5 (November 1926): 363.

"Short Lengths for Farm Buildings." *USFPL Report.*

1927

"The Whistling Note of the Wilson Snipe." *Condor* 29, 1 (January–February 1927): 79–80.

"Forest Products Research and Profitable Forestry." *JF* 25, 5 (May 1927): 542–48.

"Game Cropping in Southern Wisconsin." *Our Native Landscape.* (October 1927).

1928

"Pineries and Deer on the Gila." *New Mexico Conservationist* 1, 3 (March 1928): 3.

"The Home Builder Conserves." *American Forests and Forest Life* 34, 413 (May 1928): 276–78, 297.

"Mr. Thompson's Wilderness." *USFS Bulletin* 12, 26 (25 June 1928): 1–2.

"The Game Survey and Its Work." *Transactions of the Fifteenth National Game Conference* (3–4 December 1928), 128–32. Reprinted in *American Game* 18 (April–May 1929): 45–57.

1929

"Glues for Wood in Archery." *USFPL Technical Note,* no. 226 (May 1929): 4.

"Some Thoughts on Forest Genetics." *JF* 27, 6 (October 1929): 708–13.

"Progress of the Game Survey." *Transactions of the Sixteenth American Game Conference* (2–3 December 1929), 64–71.

"Report of the Committee on American Wild Life Policy." *Transactions of the Sixteenth American Game Conference,* 196–210.

"Environmental Controls: The Forester's Contribution to Game Conservation." *The Ames Forester* 17 (1929): 25–26.

"How the Country Boy or Girl Can Grow Quail." *Wisconsin Arbor and Bird Day Annual* (10 May 1929): 51–53.

"Mesa de Los Angeles," "Ho! Compadres piñoneros!" In John D. Guthrie, ed., *Forest and Fire and Other Verse* (Portland, Oregon: Dunham Printing Co., 1929), 18, 152.

1930

"Wild Game a Farm Crop." *The Game Breeder* 34, 2 (February 1930): 39.

"Environmental Controls for Game through Modified Silviculture." *JF* 28, 3 (March 1930): 321–26.

"Game Management in the National Forests." *American Forests* 36, 7 (July 1939): 412–14.

"The Decline of the Jacksnipe in Southern Wisconsin." *Wilson Bulletin* 2, 3 (September 1930): 183–90.

"Game as a Side-line for Foresters." *Yale Forest School News* 18, 4 (October 1930): 71.

"Game Survey Bulletin." SAAMI. October 1930–November 1931. Issued monthly by Leopold to inform SAAMI members and cooperators of the progress of the game survey.

"Discussion on the American Game Policy." *Transactions of the Seventeenth American Game Conference* (1–2 December 1930), 143, 146–47.

"The American Game Policy in a Nutshell." *Transactions of the Seventeenth American Game Conference,* 281–83. Reprinted with "Report to the National Game Conference on an American Game Policy" by the American Game Association. Reprinted as "Game Policy in a Nutshell" in *American Game* 19 (November–December 1930): 8.

With thirteen other members of the American Game Policy Committee of the American Game Conference. "Report to the American Game Conference on an American Game Policy." *Transactions of the Seventeenth American Game Conference,* 284–309.

"Game Conditions in the North Central States." *Proceedings of the Eighth Annual Convention of the Izaak Walton League of America,* 56–165.

1931

"The Forester's Role in Game Management." *JF* 29, 1 (January 1931): 25–31.

"Game Methods: The American Way." *American Game* 20, 2 (March–April 1931): 20, 29–31.

"Game Restoration by Cooperation on Wisconsin Farms." *WAF* 59, 16 (18 April 1931): 5, 16.

With John N. Ball. "The Quail Shortage of 1930." *Outdoor America* 9, 9 (April 1931): 14–15, 67.

"A History of Ideas in Game Management." *Outdoor America* 9, 11 (June 1931): 22–24, 38–39, 47. Excerpted from Leopold's *Game Management.*

"The Role of Universities in Game Conservation." *DuPont Magazine* 25, 6 (June 1931): 8–9, 24. Reprinted as "Universities in Game Conservation," *Outdoor Life* 68, 3 (September 1931): 33–34; reprinted in *Louisiana Conservation Review* 2, 11 (October 1932): 15–16.

With John Ball. "Grouse in England." *American Game* 20, 4 (July–August 1931): 57–58, 63.

"Science Attacks the Game Cycle." *Outdoor America* 10, 2 (September 1931): 25.

With John Ball. "British and American Grouse Management." *American Game* 20, 5 (September–October 1931): 70, 78–79.

With John Ball. "British and American Grouse Cycles." *The Canadian Field-Naturalist* 45, 7 (October 1931): 162–67.

"Game Range." *JF* 29, 6 (October 1931): 932–38.

"Rebuilding the Quail Crop." *Outdoor America* 10, 4 (November 1931): 38.

"Report of the American Game Policy Committee." *American Game* 20, 6 (November–December 1931): 86.

"The Prairie Chicken: A Lost Hope, or an Opportunity?" *American Field* 116, 50 (12 December 1931): 1.

"Game Food and Cover in the Cornbelt." *Proceedings of the Ninth Annual Conference of the IWLA.*

Report on a Game Survey of the North Central States. Madison: The Democrat Press for the Sporting Arms and Ammunition Manufacturers' Institute, 1931.

1932

"Game System Deplored as 'Melting Pot.'" *JF* 30, 2 (February 1932): 226–27.

"Game and Wild Life Conservation." *Condor* 34, 2 (March–April 1932): 103–6.

"The Alder Fork: A Fishing Idyll." *Outdoor America* 10, 10 (May 1932): 11. Reprinted in *SCA*.

"A Flight of Franklin's Gulls in Northwestern Iowa." *Wilson Bulletin* 44, 2 (June 1932): 116.

"Report of the Iowa Game Survey, Chapter One: The Fall of the Iowa Game Range." *Outdoor America* 11, 1 (August–September 1932): 7–9.

"Report of the Iowa Game Survey, Chapter Two: Iowa Quail." *Outdoor America* 11, 2 (October–November 1932): 11–13, 30–31.

"Results from the American Game Policy." *Transactions of the Nineteenth American Game Conference* (28–30 November 1932): 62–66.

Comment on Address by L. W. T. Waller, Jr., "The Need for Educated Man Power." *Transactions of the Nineteenth American Game Conference,* 88–89.

"Management of Upland Game Birds in Iowa: A Handbook for Farmers, Sportsmen, Conservationists and Game Wardens." Des Moines: Iowa State Fish and Game Commission, 1932. Mostly prepared by AL, with contributions by William Schuenke, 16–17, and Wallace Grange, 27–29.

1933

"Report of the Iowa Game Survey, Chapter Three: Iowa Pheasants." *Outdoor America* 11, 3 (December–January 1933): 10–12, 31.

"Weatherproofing Conservation." *American Forests* 39, 1 (January 1933): 10–11, 48.

"How Research and Game Surveys Help the Sportsman and Farmer." *Proceedings of the New England Game Conference,* 11 February 1933 (Cambridge: Samuel Marcus Press for the Massachusetts Fish and Game Association), 51–56.

"Report of the Iowa Game Survey, Chapter Four: The Hungarian Partridge in Iowa." *Outdoor America* 11, 4 (February–March 1933): 6–8, 21.

"Turkish Bows of the New Mexico Indians." *Ye Sylvan Archer* 7, 1 (May 1933): 4–6.

"The Mockingbird in Wisconsin." *Wilson Bulletin* 45, 3 (September 1933): 143.

"Game as a Land Crop in the Central States." *Central States Forestry Congress, Proceedings of Fourth Annual Conference* (21–23 September 1933), 137–41.

"ABC's of Winter Feeding Birds." *American Game* 22, 5 (September–October 1933): 70, 77–79.

"The Conservation Ethic." *JF* 31, 6 (October 1933): 634–43. Reprinted as "Racial Wisdom and Conservation" in *The Journal of Heredity* 37, 9 (September 1946): 275–79; reprinted by Ministerio de agricultura y cría, Venezuela, as "La Etica de la Conservación," *Boletín del Departamento de conservación de Suelos* 1 (July 1948): 9–10.

Game Management. New York: Charles Scribner's Sons, 1933.

1934

"Necessity of Game Research," *Transactions of the Twentieth American Game Conference* (22–24 January 1934), 92–95.

"Ecology of Jackrabbits." Review of C. T. Vorhies and W. P. Taylor, *The Life History and Ecology of Jackrabbits in Relation to Grazing in Arizona. Ecology* 15, 1 (January 1934): 63–64.

Game Research Newsletter 10 March 1934–1 May 1939. Title changed to *Wildlife Research Newsletter* 25 October 1939–13 November 1947. This newsletter was issued several times a year by Leopold's department "for the personal information of the field workers and financial cooperators of the Chair of Game Management, and of faculty members and state and federal officials concerned with wild life research in Wisconsin."

Review of N. A. Orde-Powlett, *Forestry and Sport. JF* 32, 4 (April 1934): 497.

"Conservation Economics." *JF* 32, 5 (May 1934): 537–44. Reprinted in *American Game* 23, 4 (July–August 1934): 56, 63; and 23, 5 (September–October 1934): 71, 77–78.

Review of M. T. Townsend and M. W. Smith, *White-tailed Deer of the Adirondacks. Journal of Mammalogy* (May 1934): 163–64.

With Reuben Paulson. "Helping Ourselves: Being the Adventures of a Farmer and a Sportsman Who Produced Their Own Shooting Ground." *Field and Stream* 39, 4 (August 1934): 32–33, 56.

"The Wisconsin River Marshes." *National Waltonian* 2, 3 (September 1934): 4–5, 11.

"The Arboretum and the University." *Parks and Recreation* 18, 2 (October 1934): 59–60.

Review of Ward Shepard, "Notes on German Game Management, Chiefly in Bavaria and Baden." *JF* 32, 7 (October 1934): 774–75.

"The Game Cycle—A Challenge to Science." *Outdoor Nebraska* 9, 4 (Autumn 1934), 4, 14. Also in *Minnesota Conservationist* 19 (December 1934): 2–3, 14.

"An Outline Plan for Game Management in Wisconsin," In *A Study Of Wisconsin: Its Resources, Its Physical, Social and Economic Background.* First Annual Report, Wisconsin Regional Planning Committee, December 1934, 243–55.

"Some Thoughts on Recreational Planning." *Parks and Recreation* 18, 4 (December 1934): 136–37.

With T. H. Beck and J. N. Darling. "Report of the President's Committee on Wildlife Restoration." Washington, D.C., 1934.

1935

"Whither 1935?—A Review of the American Game Policy." *Transactions of the Twenty-First American Game Conference* (21–23 January 1935), 49–55.
"Wildlife Research Rapidly Growing." *American Game* 24, 1 (January–February 1935): 5, 13.
"'Game Conference Not Accidental,' says Aldo Leopold." *American Game* 24, 1 (January–February 1935): 9.
"Gun and Glass Hunters." *American Forests* 41, 2 (February 1935): 71.
Review of Joseph S. Dixon, "A Study of the Life History and Food Habits of Mule Deer in California. *Journal of Mammalogy* 16, 1 (February 1935): 74–75.
"Preliminary Report on Forestry and Game Management." *JF* 33, 3 (March 1935): 273–75.
"Coon Valley: An Adventure in Cooperative Conservation." *American Forests* 41, 5 (May 1935): 205–8.
Review of S. Charles Kendeigh, "The Role of Environment in the Life of Birds." *Wilson Bulletin* 47, 2 (June 1935): 166–67.
"Why the Wilderness Society?" *Living Wilderness* 1, 1 (September 1935): 6.
Review of Charles Elton, *Exploring the Animal World. Bird-Lore* 37, 5 (September–October 1935): 364.
"Sporting Poetry," review of Edward S. Parker, *One More Bend. American Wildlife* 24, 6 (November–December 1935), 90.
Review of D. Nolte, *Zur Biologie des Rophuhns. Wilson Bulletin* 47, 4 (December 1935): 300–303.
"Forerunners of Game Management." *Colorado Forester* (Ft. Collins: Colorado State College, 1935), 12.
With W. H. Twenhofel, Nobel Clark, and G. S. Wehrwein. "The University and the Erosion Problem." *Bulletin of the University of Wisconsin,* Series 2097, General Series No. 1881, Science Inquiry, undated, 46.
"Wild Life Research in Wisconsin." *WASAL* 29 (1935): 203–8.

1936

"Remarks" *Proceedings of the NAWC,* 3–7 February 1936 (Senate Committee Print, 74th Congress, 2d session, Washington, D.C., 1936), 156–58.
"Farmer-sportsman Set-ups in the North Central Region." *Proceedings of the NAWC,* 279–85.
"Study Influence of the Sun on Wildlife Cycles." Game Management section in "To-day's Science For Tomorrow's Farming." *AESB* 435 (March 1936): 29–30.
"Threatened Species: A Proposal to the Wildlife Conference for an Inventory of the Needs of Near-extinct Birds and Animals." *American Forests* 42, 3 (March 1936): 116–19.
"Wildlife Management on Private and State Lands." *American Forests* 42, 3 (March 1936): 120–21, 147.

"Naturschutz in Germany." *Bird-Lore* 3, 2 (March–April 1936): 102–11.

"Wildlife Conference." *JF* 34, 4 (April 1936): 430–31.

"Deer and Dauerwald in Germany: I. History." *JF* 34, 4 (April 1936): 366–75.

"Deer and Dauerwald in Germany: II. Ecology and Policy." *JF* 34, 5 (May 1936): 460–66.

Review of Horace Mitchell, *Raising Game Birds. American Wildlife* 25, 3 (May–June 1936): 40.

Review of Walter P. Taylor, "Ecology and Life History of the Porcupine (*Erethizon epixanthum*) as Related to the Forests of Arizona and the Southwestern United States." *JF* 34, 6 (June 1936): 632–33.

Review of Robert H. Connery, "Governmental Problems in Wild Life Conservation." *JF* 34, 6 (June 1936): 635–36.

"Franklin J.W. Schmidt." *Wilson Bulletin* 48, 3 (September 1936): 181–86.

"Farm Game Management in Silesia." *American Wildlife* 25, 5 (September–October 1936): 67–68, 74–76.

"The Conservation Quandary." Review of Thomas Barbour and Margaret Dewar Porter, *Notes on South African Wild Life Conservation Parks and Reserves. Geographical Review* 26, 4 (October 1936): 694–95.

"Quail Population Studies in Iowa and Wisconsin." Review of Paul L. Errington and F. N. Hamerstrom, Jr., "The Northern Bob-White's Winter Territory." *Ecology* 17, 4 (October 1936), 680–81.

"Notes on Game Administration in Germany." *American Wildlife* 25, 6 (November–December 1936): 85, 92–93.

Review of "Upland Game Restoration." *Outdoor America* 2, 2 (December 1936): 11.

With Gardiner Bump, George C. Embody, Carl L. Hubbs, and Herbert L. Stoddard. "Wildlife Crops: Finding Out How to Grow Them." (Washington, D.C.: AWI, 1936), 23.

1937

"How to Build a Game Crop? The University Sets Out to Find the Answer." *Wisconsin Sportsman* 1, 5 (December–January 1937): 2–3.

Review of A. Freiherr von Vietinghoff-Reisch, *Naturschutz — Eine national politische Kulturaufgabe. JF* 35, 1 (January 1937): 87–88.

"The Thick-billed Parrot in Chihuahua." *Condor* 39, 1 (January–February 1937), 9–10. Reprinted in *SCA.*

Review of A. E. Parkins and J. R. Whitaker, *Our Natural Resources and Their Conservation. Bird-Lore* 39, 1 (January–February 1937): 74–75.

"Killing Technique of the Weasel." *Journal of Mammalogy* 18, 1 (February 1937): 98–99.

"Second Report of Game Policy Committee." *JF* 35, 2 (February 1937): 228–32.

With L. J. Cole, N. C. Fassett, C. A. Herrick, C. Juday, and G. Wagner. "The University and Conservation of Wisconsin Wildlife." *Bulletin of the University of Wisconsin,* Serial No. 2211, General Series No. 1995, Science Inquiry Publication 3, February 1937, 39.

"The Research Program." *Transactions of the Second NAWC,* 104–7. Reprinted in *American Wildlife* 26, 2 (March–April 1937): 22, 28.

"Conservationist in Mexico." *American Forests* 43, 3 (March 1937): 118–20, 146.

"Farm Game Population Increased in Trials at Riley; Study Response of Prairie Chickens and Sharptail Grouse to Fall and Winter Feeding." Poultry and game birds section of "Findings in Farm Science." *AESB* 438 (March 1937): 61–64.

"White-winged Scoter in Missouri." *Wilson Bulletin* 49, 1 (March 1937): 49–50.

"Conservation in the World of Tomorrow." *Milwaukee Journal.* 4 April 1937.

"Conservation of Wildlife," 52–54; Bibliography, 56–57; Appendix A: Biography of a Covey, 58–61; Appendix E: Chronology of Wisconsin Wildlife conservation, 69–71. In Wisconsin Department of Public Instruction, "Teaching of Conservation in Wisconsin Schools," Curriculum Bulletin 1, 1 (May 1937).

"The Effect of the Winter of 1935–36 on Wisconsin Quail." *American Midland Naturalist* 18, 3 (May 1937): 408–16.

"1936 Pheasant Nesting Study." *Wilson Bulletin* 49, 2 (June 1937): 91–95.

"The Wildlife Program of the University." *Wisconsin Sportsman* 1, 10 (June 1937): 8.

Review of A. Vietinghoff-Reisch, *Forstlicher Naturschutz und Naturschutz im nationalen Lebensraume Deutschlands. JF* 35, 8 (August 1937): 794–95.

"Marshland Elegy." *American Forests* 43, 10 (October 1937): 472–74. Reprinted in *SCA.*

Review of Margaret Morse Nice, "Studies in the Life History of the Song Sparrow." *The Canadian Field-Naturalist* 51, 8 (November 1937): 126.

Review of Rudolf Bennitt and Werner O. Nagel, "A Survey of the Resident Game and Furbearers of Missouri." *Journal of Mammalogy* 18, 4 (November 1937): 520–21.

"Conservation Blueprints." *American Forests* 43, 12 (December 1937): 596, 608.

"Compare Value of Grains for Winter Game Feeding; Game Cover May Be Provided Cheaply; Marked Birds Tell the Story of Their Movements." *AESB* 439 (December 1937): 49–52.

"The Chase Journal: An Early Record of Wisconsin Wildlife." *WASAL* 30 (1937): 69–76.

"Teaching Wildlife Conservation in Public Schools." *WASAL,* 77–86.

1938

"Chukaremia." *Outdoor America* 3, 3 (January 1938): 3.

With Orville S. Lee and Harry G. Anderson. "Wisconsin Pheasant Movement Study, 1936–37." *JWM* 2, 1 (January 1938): 3–12.

"Wildlife Research—Is It a Practical and Necessary Basis for Management?" *Transactions of the Third NAWC,* 42–45, 55.

With Harry G. Anderson. "The 1936 Cotton-tail Scarcity in Wisconsin." *Journal of Mammalogy* 19, 1 (February 1938): 110–11.

"Haymowers, Fires and WPA Men Called More Perilous Than Crows." *Wisconsin State Journal.* 10 March 1928.

"Conservation Esthetic." *Bird-Lore* 40, 2 (March–April 1938): 101–9. Condensed in *Conservation* 4, 3 (May–June 1938): 18–21. Reprinted in *SCA.*

With F. B. Trenk, S. A. Wilde, A. J. Riker, Noble Clark, and G. S. Wehrwein. "The University and Wisconsin Forestry." *Bulletin of the University of Wisconsin,* Serial No. 2334, General Series No. 2118, Science Inquiry Publication 7, June 1938, p. 56.

"Whither Missouri?" *The Missouri Conservationist* 1, 1 (July 1938): 6.

"Wildlife Conservation on the Farm." *WAF* 65, 23 (5 November 1938): 5.

"Wildlife Conservation on the Farm." *WAF* 65, 24 (19 November 1938): 8.

"Ups and Downs of Quail Furnish Clues to Best Management"; "Why Do Game Birds Nest in Hayfields"; "Mature, Well-Developed Pheasants Survive Best." *AESB* 442 (November 1938): 48–51.

"Feed the Song Birds." *WAF* 65, 25 (3 December 1938): 5.

"Woodlot Wildlife Aids." *WAF* 65, 27 (31 December 1938): 4.

"Report on Huron Mountain Club." Printed by Huron Mountain Club, Michigan, 1938, 18 pp. Reprinted in *Report of Huron Mountain Wildlife Foundation, 1955–1966* (January 1967), 40–57.

1939

With Ellwood B. Moore and Lyle K. Sowls. "Wildlife Food Patches in Southern Wisconsin." *JWM* 3, 1 (January 1939): 60–69.

"The Farm Pond Attracts Game." *WAF* 66, 3 (11 February 1939): 7.

"Farmer-sportsman, a partnership for wildlife restoration." *Transactions of the Fourth NAWC,* 145–49, 167–68; *Bird-Lore* 41, 2 (March–April 1939): 94–97.

"Burned Marsh Means a Loss." *WAF* 66, 8 (22 April 1939): 22.

With Rudolf Bennitt, chairman, and seven others. "Report of the Committee on Professional Standards [of the Wildlife Society]." *JWM* 3, 2 (April 1939): 153–55.

"Academic and Professional Training in Wildlife Work." *JWM* 3, 2 (April 1939): 156–61.

"Dane County Management Areas." *The Passenger Pigeon* 1, 4 (April 1939): 49–50. Reprinted in *Wisconsin Wildlife* 1, 6 (May 1939): 7.

"Game Areas of Wisconsin [map]." *The Passenger Pigeon* 1, 4 (April 1939): 55. Reprinted in *The Passenger Pigeon* 2, 9 (September 1940): 105.

"Plant Evergreens for Bird Shelter." *WAF* 66, 9 (6 May 1939): 5.

"The Farmer as a Conservationist." Stencil Circular 210 (February 1939), Extension Service, College of Agriculture, University of Wisconsin. Published in *American Forests* 45, 6 (June 1939): 294–98, 299, 316.

With John T. Curtis. "Wild Flower Corners." *WAF* 66, 12 (17 June 1939): 16.

"A Biotic View of Land." *JF* 37, 9 (September 1939): 727–30. Condensed in *The Council Ring* (National Park Service monthly mimeographed publication) 1, 12 (November 1939): 4. Reprinted as a pamphlet by Forest and Bird Protection Society of New Zealand.

"Wild Feed on Farms." *WAF* 66, 23 (18 November 1939): 19.

"The Hungarian Partridge Pioneers"; "Can Prairie Chickens Winter on Buds?"; "What Is the Yield of Wild Food Crops?"; "Rabbits Range at Least a Mile." *AESB* 446 (November 1939): 21–23.

"Look for Bird Bands." *WAF* 66, 24 (2 December 1939): 19.

Bibliography

1940

"New Year's Inventory Checks Missing Game." *WAF* 67, 3 (27 January 1940): 10.

Obituary of Royal M. Chapman. *JWM* 4, 1 (January 1940): 104.

Review of A. F. Gustafson et al., *Conservation in the United States, Ecology* 21, 1 (January 1940): 92–93.

"Windbreaks Aid Wildlife." *WAF* 67, 5 (9 March 1940): 15.

"When Geese Return Spring Is Here." *WAF* 67, 7 (6 April 1940): 18.

With Victor H. Cahalane, chairman, William L. Finley, and Clarence Cottam. "Report of the [A.O..U.] Committee on Bird Protection, 1939." *The Auk* 57, 2 (April 1940): 279–91.

Letter to Dr. Schmitz regarding "fox squirrel dens." *JF* 38, 4 (April 1940): 375.

"Farm Arboretum Adds to Home Beauty." *WAF* 67, 10 (18 May 1940): 4.

"History of the Riley Game Cooperative, 1931–1939." *JWM* 4, 3 (July 1940): 291–302. Excerpted by Russ Pyre in *Wisconsin State Journal*, 3 November 1940.

"Origin and Ideals of Wilderness Areas." *Living Wilderness* 5 (July 1940): 7.

With Rudolf Bennitt, chairman, and eight others. "Report of the Committee on Professional Standards [of the Wildlife Society]." *JWM* 4, 3 (July 1940): 338–41.

"Song of the Gavilan." *JWM* 4, 3 (July 1940): 329–32.

"The State of the Profession." *JWM* 4, 3 (July 1940): 343–46.

"Pheasant Damage Checked." *WAF* 67, 17 (24 August 1940): 14.

"Exit Orchis: A Little Action Now Would Save Our Fast Disappearing Wildlife." *Wisconsin Wildlife* 2, 2 (August 1940): 17. Reprinted in *American Wildlife* 29, 5 (September–October 1940): 207. Reprinted in *Wisconsin Academy Review* 9, 1 (Winter 1962): 26–27. Revised and updated as "Faville prairie preserve," *Wild Flower* 18, 4 (October 1941): 67–68.

Review of Milton B. Trautman, "The Birds of Buckeye Lake, Ohio." *Wilson Bulletin* 52, 3 (September 1940): 217–18.

Review of "The Status of Wildlife in the United States: Report of the Special [Senate] Committee on the Conservation of Wildlife Resources." *JF* 38, 10 (October 1940): 823.

"Birds Earn Their Keep on Wisconsin Farms." *WAF* 67, 24 (30 November 1940): 18.

"Half a Duck Apiece." *American Forests* 46, 11 (November 1940): 509.

"Wisconsin Wildlife Chronology." *WCB* 5, 11 (November 1940): 8–20. Reprinted as WCD Publication 301. Summarized in the *Milwaukee Journal*, 19 January 1941.

"Cover Plantings Need Winter Protection." *WAF* 67, 26 (28 December 1940): 11.

"Escudilla." *American Forests* 46, 12 (December 1940): 539–40. Reprinted in *Maryland Conservationist* 18, 1 (Winter 1941): 20–21. Reprinted in *SCA*.

With Robert A. McCabe. "Snow-filled Bobwhite Covey." *Wilson Bulletin* 52, 4 (December 1940): 281.

"Spread of the Hungarian Partridge in Wisconsin." *WASAL* 32 (1940): 5–28.

1941

"Pheasant Planting Requires Skill." *WAF* 68, 2 (25 January 1941): 19.

Review of E. G. Cheyney and T. Shantz-Hansen, *This Is Our Land: The Story of Conservation in the United States. JF* 39, 1 (January 1941): 72.

"Houses for Birds Make Friends." *WAF* 68, 5 (8 March 1941): 28.

With F. N. Hamerstrom, Jr. "John S. Main." *Wilson Bulletin* 53, 1 (March 1941): 31–32.

With Robert McCabe. "Other Records of Snow-killed Bob-white Coveys." *Wilson Bulletin* 53, 1 (March 1941): 44.

"Bur Oak Is Badge of Wisconsin." *WAF* 68, 7 (5 April 1941): 10. Revised and reprinted in *SCA* as "Bur Oak."

"Bluebirds Welcome." *WAF* 68, 8 (19 April 1941): 16.

With V. H. Cahalane, Wm. L. Finley, and C. Cottam. "Report of the [A.O.U.] Committee on Bird Protection, 1940." *The Auk* 58, 2 (April 1941): 292–98.

"Pest-hunts." *The Passenger Pigeon* 3, 5 (May 1941): 42–43.

Wildlife Likes Water." *WAF* 68, 13 (28 June 1941): 10.

"Bob White Numbers Can Be Increased." *WAF* 68, 15 (26 July 1941): 19.

"Wilderness as a Land Laboratory." *Living Wilderness* 6 (July 1941): 3. Reprinted in *Outdoor America* 7, 2 (December 1941): 7. Condensed in *Forest and Bird* (New Zealand) 65 (August 1942): 2.

"Fifth Column of the Fence Row." *WAF* 68, 17 (23 August 1941): 11.

"Wildlife Conservation on the Farm." Booklet of reprints from the *WAF* series, published by the *Wisconsin Agriculturalist and Farmer,* c. September 1941.

"Feed the Birds Early." *WAF* 68, 24 (29 November 1941), 10.

"Fur Crop in Danger." *WAF* 68, 25 (13 December 1941): 19.

"Cheat Takes Over." *The Land* 1, 4 (Autumn 1941): 310–13. Reprinted in *Conservation* 8, 3 (May–June 1942), 27–30. Revised and reprinted in *SCA*.

"Farmers and Rabbits." *WAF* 68, 26 (27 December 1941): 19.

"Riley Game Cooperative Proves a Success"; "History of Faville Grove Shows Wildlife Changes." *AESB 453* (December 1941): 58–60.

"Lake in Relation to Terrestrial Life Patterns." In James G. Needham et al., *A Symposium on Hydrobiology,* 17–22. Madison: University of Wisconsin Press, 1941.

"Wilderness Values." *1941 Yearbook, Park and Recreation Progress* (National Park Service, 1941), 27–29. Reprinted in *Living Wilderness* 7 (March 1942): 24–25.

1942

"Farming in Color." *WAF* 69, 2 (24 January 1942): 4.

"A Raptor Tally in the Northwest." *Condor* 44, 1 (January–February 1942): 37–38.

"Wild Ducks Need More Pond-room." *WAF* 69, 7 (4 April 1942): 25.

"The Role of Wildlife in a Liberal Education." *Transactions of the Seventh NAWC,* 485–89. Reprinted in *Michigan Conservation* 12, 1 (January 1943), 8.

"The Grizzly—A Problem in Land Planning." *Outdoor America* 7, 6 (April 1942): 11–12.

With V. H. Cahalane, Wm. L. Finley, and C. Cottam. "Report of the [A.O.U.] Committee on Bird Protection, 1941." *The Auk* 59, 2 (April 1943): 286–99.

With Wm. L. Finley. "Substitute Statement on Pole-trapping of Raptors." *The Auk* 59, 2 (April 1942): 300.

"The Plover Is Back from Argentine." *WAF* 69, 10 (16 May 1942): 10. Reprinted in *SCA*.

"The Last Stand." *Outdoor America* 7, 7 (May–June 1942), 8–9. Reprinted in *Living Wilderness* 8 (December 1942): 25–26. Reprinted in *WCB* 9, 2 (February 1944): 3–5.

Bibliography

"Odyssey." *Audubon Magazine* 44, 3 (May–June 1942): 133–35. Reprinted in *SCA*.

"Packratting." *Wildlife News* 2, 1 (20 June 1942): 11.

"Half-Excellent." Review of George T. Renner, *Conservation of Natural Resources*. *The Land* 2, 2 (July 1942): 111–12.

"Wildlife Conservation." *Wisconsin State Journal*, 23 August 1942.

"'Control' of the Golden Eagle in Texas." *Wilson Bulletin* 54, 3 (September 1942): 218.

"Land-use and Democracy." *Audubon Magazine* 44, 5 (September–October 1942): 259–65.

Introduction to Francis H. Kortright, *The Ducks, Geese and Swans of North America*. Washington D.C.: AWI, 1942.

1943

"Flambeau: The Story of a Wild River." *American Forests* 49, 1 (January 1943): 12–14, 47. Reprinted as "The Flambeau" in *WCB* 8, 3 (March 1943): 13–17. Revised and reprinted in *SCA*.

"Wildlife in American Culture." *JWM* 7, 1 (January 1943): 1–6. Previously mimeographed in *Proceedings of the Seventh Midwest Wildlife Conference,* 19–25. Reprinted in *Pacific Discovery* 2 (July–August 1949): 12–15. Reprinted in *SCA*.

"Obituary: P.S. Lovejoy." *JWM* 7, 1 (January 1943): 125–28. Reprinted as "Lovejoyiana" in *Michigan Conservation* 12, 4 (May 1943): 10–11.

"A Lesson from the Woodlands." *WCB* 8, 2 (February 1943): 25–27. Reprinted as "A Mighty Fortress" in *SCA*.

"Pines above the Snow." *WCB* 8, 3 (March 1943): 27–29. Reprinted in *SCA*.

Review of Sherman Strong Hayden, "The International Protection of Wild Life." *The Geographical Review* 33, 2 (April 1943): 340–41.

Review of Norman F. Smith, "A Study of the Spread of Forest Cover into Wildland Openings." *JF* 41, 5 (May 1943): 381–82.

"The Excess Deer Problem." *Audubon Magazine* 45, 3 (May–June 1943): 156–57.

Review of Ira N. Gabrielson, *Wildlife Refuges*. *JF* 41, 7 (July 1943): 529–31.

"Deer Irruptions." *WCB* 8, 8 (August 1943): 1–11.

With J. R. Jacobson, Henry C. Kuehn, Joyce Larkin, John O. Moreland, Dr. E.G. Ovitz, Howard Quirt, and Mrs. Harry E. Thomas. "Majority Report of the Citizens' Deer Committee to Wisconsin Conservation Commission." *WCB* 8, 8 (August 1943): 19–22. Reprinted in "Wisconsin's Deer Problem," WCD Publication 321, 20–23.

"Home Range." *WCB* 8, 9 (September 1943): 23–24. Reprinted in *SCA*.

With Theodore M. Sperry, William S. Feeney, and John A. Catenhusen. "Population Turnover on a Wisconsin Pheasant Refuge." *JWM* 7, 4 (October 1943): 383–94. Also issued with arboretum cover as Journal Paper no. 4 of the University of Wisconsin Arboretum.

Review of Helen W. Martin, ed., *They Need Not Vanish*. *JF* 41, 12 (December 1943): 924.

Review of William R. Van Dersal, *The American Land*. *JF* 41, 12 (December 1943): 928.

"Facts on Pheasants Appear from Arboretum Study." *AESB 461* (December 1943): 13–15. Reprinted in *WCB* 9, 5 (May 1944): 11–13.

"Deer Irruptions." *WASAL* 35 (1943): 351–66. Previously published with permission in *WCB* 8, 8 (August 1943): 1–11. Reprinted in "Wisconsin's Deer Problem," WCD Publication 321, 3–11.

1944

Review of H. M. Bell and E. J. Duksterhuis, "Fighting the Mesquite and Cedar Invasion on Texas Ranges." *JF* 42, 1 (January 1944): 63.
"Post-war Prospects." *Audubon Magazine* 46, 1 (January–February 1944): 27–29.
"The Present Winter and Our Native Game Birds." *WCB* 9, 2 (February 1944): 25–26.
"Does Inbreeding Cause the Cycle in Game Animals?" *WCB* 9, 2 (February 1944): 9.
Review of Montague Stevens, *Meet Mr. Grizzly*. *JF* 42, 3 (March 1944): 222.
With Irven Buss. "Cliff Swallows to Order." *WCB* 9, 4 (April 1944): 21–22.
With W. F. Grimmer. "The Crow." *WCB* 9, 5 (May 1944): 10.
"What Next in Deer Policy?" *WCB* 9, 6 (June 1944): 3–4, 18–19.
Review of Edward H. Graham, *Natural Principles of Land Use. Soil Conservation* 10, 2 (August 1944): 38–39.
With sixteen others. "Six Points of Deer Policy." *WCB* 9, 11 (November 1944): 10.
With Miles D. Pirnie and William Rowan. Introduction to HAH, *Canvasback on a Prairie Marsh*, xi–xii. Washington, D.C.: AWI: 1944.

1945

Review of Stanley P. Young and Edward H. Goldman, *The Wolves of North America*. *JF* 43, 1 (January 1945): 928–29.
"The Outlook for Farm Wildlife." *Transactions of the Tenth NAWC*, 165–68.
With Hans Peter Thomsen. "War Status of Predators in Norway." *Journal of Mammalogy* 26, 1 (February 1945): 88–89.
"Deer, Wolves, Foxes and Pheasants." *WCB* 10, 4 (April 1945): 3–5.
Review of Sally Carrighar, *One Day on Beetle Rock*. *JF* 43, 4 (April 1945): 301–2.
Review of Durward L. Allen, "Michigan Fox Squirrel Management." *JF* 43, 6 (June 1945): 462.
"Wildlife Explorations at Prairie du Sac." *WCB* 10: 7–8 (July–August 1945): 305.
"The Green Lagoons." *American Forests* 51, 8 (August 1945): 376–77, 414. Reprinted in *SCA*.

1946

Review of A. G. Tansley, *Our Heritage of Wild Nature. JF* 44, 3 (March 1946): 215–16.
With Robert A. McCabe. Review of W. L. McAtee, ed., *The Ring-Necked Pheasant and Its Management in North America. Wilson Bulletin* 58, 2 (June 1946): 126–27.
Review of S. Kip Farrington, Jr., *The Ducks Came Back: The Story of Ducks Unlimited. JWM* 10, 3 (July 1946): 281–83.
"The Deer Dilemma." *WCB* 11, 8–9 (August–September 1946): 3–5.
"Leopold Explains Opposition to Deer Hunting Restrictions." *Milwaukee Journal*. 1 September 1946.
"Erosion as a Menace to the Social and Economic Future of the Southwest." *JF* 44, 9 (September 1946): 627–33. With an introduction by H. H. Chapman.

Bibliography

Originally read by Leopold at the meeting of the New Mexico Association for Science in 1922.

With W. F. Grimmer. "The History and Future of the Pheasant in Wisconsin," 15–25. In Irven O. Buss, "Wisconsin Pheasant Populations." WCD Pub. 326, A-46.

1947

With Sara Elizabeth Jones. "A Phenological Record for Sauk and Dane Counties, Wisconsin, 1935–1945." *Ecological Monographs* 17, 1 (January 1947): 81–122. Also issued with arboretum cover as Journal Paper no. 8 of the University of Wisconsin Arboretum.

"Summarization of the Twelfth North American Wildlife Conference." *Transactions of the Twelfth NAWC*, 529–36. Reprinted in *The Pennsylvania Game News* 17, 12 (March 1947): 14–15, 30–31. Condensed in *National Parks Magazine* 21, 89 (April–June 1947): 26–28.

"The Distribution of Wisconsin Hares." *WASAL* 37 (1945; issued 10 April 1947): 1–14.

With Lyle K. Sowls and David L. Spencer. "A Survey of Over-populated Deer Ranges in the United States." *JWM* 11, 2 (April 1947): 162–77. Summary reprinted as "National Deer Survey" in *WCB* 12, 5 (May 1947): 27–30.

Review of E. M. Queeny, *Prairie Wings: Pen and Camera Flight Studies*. *JWM* 11, 2 (April 1947): 190–91.

"On a Monument to the Passenger Pigeon." In *Silent Wings*, 3–5. Wisconsin Society for Ornithology, Madison, 11 May 1947. Revised and reprinted in *SCA*.

"The Ecological Conscience." *Bulletin of the Garden Club of America* (September 1947): 45–53. Reprinted in *WCB* 12, 12 (December 1947): 4–7. and WCD Pub. 343, 4. Condensed in *Plants and Gardens* 3, 4 (Winter 1947): 210–11. Reprinted in *Journal of Soil and Water Conservation* 3, 3 (July 1948): 109–12. Excerpted in *The Missouri Conservationist* 9, 6 (6 June 1948): 2.

"Mortgaging the Future Deer Herd." *WCB* 12, 9 (September 1947): 3.

With Irven O. Buss. Review of Frank C. Edminister, *The Ruffed Grouse: Its Life Story, Ecology, and Management.*" *Condor* 49, 6 (November–December 1947): 246–47.

With Olaus J. Murie et al. "Wilderness and Aircraft." *Living Wilderness* 12, 22 (Autumn 1947): 1–6.

"Game Management." In *Encyclopaedia Britannica* (1947).

1948

"One Test Tells Age of Cottontails"; "Check Pheasant Hens' Egg Records, Chicks' Ages"; "Pheasants Winter in Same Spot Each Year"; "Prairie du Sac Quail Numbers Drop"; "Young Muskrats Identified by Pelts." *AESB 474* (January 1948): 46–49.

"Why and How Research?" *Transactions of the Thirteenth NAWC*, 44–48.

"Charles Knesal Cooperrider, 1889–1944." *JWM* 12, 3 (July 1948): 337–39.

1949f

A Sand County Almanac and Sketches Here and There. New York: Oxford University Press, 1949. Reissued as *A Sand County Almanac with Essays on Conser-*

vation from Round River (New York: Ballantine Books, 1966); *A Sand County Almanac with Other Essays from Round River* (New York: Oxford University Press, 1968).

Luna B. Leopold, ed. *Round River: From the Journals of Aldo Leopold.* New York: Oxford University Press, 1953.

With Alfred E. Eynon. "Avian Daybreak and Evening Song in Relation to Time and Light Intensity." *Condor* 63, 4 (July–August 1961), 269–93.

"Some Fundamentals of Conservation in the Southwest." *Environmental Ethics* 1, 2 (Summer 1979): 131–41. Originally written c. March 1923.

Index

Index